TRANSPORTATION AND LOGISTICS

Transportation and Logistics

Marvin L. Fair, Ph.D.
Professor of Transportation Emeritus
Formerly Director
Transportation and Logistics Program
The American University

Ernest W. Williams, Jr., Ph.D.
Graduate School of Business
Columbia University

1981 Revised Edition

BUSINESS PUBLICATIONS, INC. Plano, Texas 75075
Irwin-Dorsey Limited Georgetown, Ontario L7G 4B3

JM

Previous edition of this book was published under the title
Economics of Transportation and Logistics.

© BUSINESS PUBLICATIONS, INC., 1975 and 1981

ISBN 0-256-02308-5
Library of Congress Catalog Card No. 80-69962
Printed in the United States of America

1 2 3 4 5 6 7 8 9 0 MP 8 7 6 5 4 3 2 1

Preface

When the first edition of this book was written, the theory and practice of business logistics had been undergoing rapid development for several decades. The increase in course offerings in logistics suggested the desirability of change in the basic transportation course. The principles of transportation as conventionally taught appeared to require a tie with the principles of logistics. Thus the first course could establish a background for both fields and explore the relationships between them. The resulting treatment relates transportation cost and service to the economics of total flow in the conduct of commerce. It also provides a more adequate frame of reference for the study of business and community logistics. The plan adopted in the first edition is continued here.

Among social scientists there is a rising tide of interest in the economics of regional development and the importance of spatial relations in determining not only the extent of markets and scale of production, but also the social and political relationships in metropolitan areas, regions, and nations. This book is designed to explore these relationships more effectively. Not only does it expand the treatment of transport in relation to economic development, but it adds urban transport to the range of subject matter surveyed.

Interest in materials management and physical distribution, both of which can be encompassed within the term *business logistics*, has mounted in the business world. Indeed, logistics may be regarded as the latest revolution in scientific management, comparable to the earlier ones in production and merchandising. Control of total cost and time in the physical flow of orders and deliveries has given us a new business profession. Schools of business increasingly recognize logistics as a prime business function along with production, finance, and marketing. Accordingly, the literature of the subject has expanded rapidly.

Transportation will remain the primary function and major source of cost in physical distribution. Unlike most other aspects of logistics, much of it will remain outside the direct control of the distribution manager and deeply entwined with public policy. Hence an adequate understanding of the economics of transportation, including both rates and services, is most essential for management training in this area. It is of equal importance for those preparing for the expanding and changing field of carrier management. Once the student is fully embarked upon the methodology of distribution systems management the complexities of transport procurement and policy tend to move into the background. A solid beginning with transportation, therefore, helps to establish a firm foundation for advanced work in logistics principles.

This book preserves the across-the-board treatment of the several transport modes with respect to the economics of rates and service which has tended to replace separate modal analysis. It well-nigh eliminates the historical approach to transport. It encapsulates the development and substance of regulation in a single chapter. Most important, it endeavors to describe the functions of business logistics and the way logistics managers relate them to transportation realities in decision making. The effects upon carriers that flow from the changed emphasis which the logistics discipline has brought to the carriers' customers appear in the examination of carrier performance.

The present edition has been greatly affected by the changes in the plan of economic regulation which have occurred in the past five years. The reduction in regulatory control over rates and the emphasis that is placed upon the competitive making of rates today has made discussion of rate structures and the regulation of intercarrier competition mostly of historic interest. Hence the chapters that dealt with these topics have been deleted. The treatment of the structure and substance of regulation has been brought up to date to include the motor and rail acts passed this year and early steps for their implementation.

MARVIN L. FAIR
ERNEST W. WILLIAMS, JR.

Contents

The Transport System of the United States:
Its Importance, the Saga of
Its Development, Its Competition

IMPORTANCE OF MOVEMENT CAPABILITY

The economic, political, and social progress of any group, whether nation, region, or community, depends upon reduction of the inconvenience and cost of overcoming space. All of Man's activities are involved. Accordingly, movement capability has always occupied center stage in human experience whether for prehistoric or modern Man. Transportation and logistics are the institutions designed to provide movement capability.

The raft, the canoe, the sledge, and the wheel were prehistoric Man's greatest inventions. Historical Man has continued to give major emphasis to improved transportation. Yet today our advanced western society finds itself deeply concerned with the advancement of movement capability without harmful ecological effects, the relief of congested airports and streets, and the development of coordinated transportation service and logistics systems that deliver what is needed for defense or business at the right time and at lowest practical cost. For the transportation of people we add convenience and comfort to time and cost. To minimize time and cost, transportation routes between points tend to be in a straight line unless natural barriers including mountains, swamps, bodies of water, congestion, and unfavorable winds interfere. Therefore, time and cost are the true dimensions for overcoming space, and the actual distance may be incidental.

In economics, transportation is considered a part of production because it creates place utility. Goods must be brought from where nature provides them or people produce them to where they are consumed. The larger the country and the more advanced its economy, the more extensive its transport system must be. Our nation is among the largest and has by far the most extensive economy in terms of both production and consumption. To provide the necessary movement capability, the United States requires a transport industry that dwarfs that of any other nation and directly and indirectly exacts $400 billion a year or 20 percent of the Gross National Product in pay for services performed. This relationship has held true for more than 20 years.

THE AMERICAN TRANSPORTATION SAGA

The history of the United States is a study in the conquest of spatial relations. Settlers came to a vast continental area which became the United States with 3,000 miles across and 1,500 miles north and south. They were confronted on both the east and the west with mountain ranges that paralleled the coast lines. Only the St. Lawrence and the Mississippi river systems provided access to the vast interior free of mountain barriers. For that reason, penetration of settlers inland from the Atlantic and Pacific coasts was for many years limited to the rather short river courses between the mountains and the oceans. In the meantime settlements by the French via the St. Lawrence and Mississippi were made along the Great Lakes and the midcontinent area.

The Beginnings

Until the 19th century, reliance for transportation was on sailing boats along the coast; rafts, dugouts, and keel boats on the rivers; and on land either carts or wagons on dirt roads and pack horses and mule trains for cross-mountain transportation. For two and one-half centuries the colonists struggled with primitive transportation facilities. The only relatively economic services were those of coastal sailboats and downstream rafts; but in the last decade of the 18th century, turnpikes and canals made their appearance. The next chapter of the saga was that of intense activity in surfacing main highways to permit year-round availability and to reduce wagon and stagecoach costs and the building of canals to circumvent rapids and to connect navigable rivers. Later longer canals were built to parallel rivers and tributaries. In contrast to flowing rivers, canals provided two-way economic water transportation. Beginning in the mid-1790s, short canals were built to circumvent rapids and to connect navigable rivers in New England, New Jersey, Pennsylvania, and South Carolina. Longer canals to parallel rivers and tributaries followed after 1825 in both the eastern and middle western states. Four of these extended canals were projected to cross the Appalachian mountain range to connect the developing seaboard with Ohio River valley and Great Lakes settlements. These were in order of completion: the Erie Canal, 1825; the Pennsylvania Public Works, 1834; the Chesapeake and Ohio Canal to Cumberland, Maryland, 1850; and the James River Canal completed to Buchanan, Virginia in 1856.

The Erie Canal was one of the two which was completed as projected and was by far the most successful. Favorably situated between the chain of Great Lakes and the extensive tidewater Hudson, it provided a new level of economic transportation between the developing Great Lakes region and the growing metropolis and seaport of New York. The success of the Erie was enhanced by a number of lateral canals constituting an extensive statewide system. The Pennsylvania Public Works was completed from Philadelphia to Pittsburgh, but it involved railroad operation to Columbia on the Susquehanna, canal to Hollidaysburg, portage railroad over the mountain to Johnstown, and canal down the Conemaugh and Allegheny rivers to Pittsburgh.

The Chesapeake and Ohio and the James River canals stopped at the foot of the Appalachian Mountain barrier because locomotive-powered railroads by midcentury had shown their superiority to the portage railroads that had been projected to surmount the mountains. The Chesapeake and Ohio Canal system was planned to go to Pittsburgh via a canal along the Monongahela, and the James River Canal was to reach the Ohio River via a canal along the Kanawha River. That over 40,000 miles of canals were built before 1850 in relatively elevated topography shows the determination and initiative of a people anxious to make of this a great country and convinced that transport was the first essential.

The need to improve principal roads for better wagon and stagecoach operation was apparent because passenger and mail service largely relied on the stagecoach. Canals were slower and did not give direct service between many commercial centers. So beginning in the 1790s, between Lancaster and Philadelphia, Pennsylvania, many post roads were surfaced with macadam, including the Cumberland Road from Cumberland, Maryland, to Vandalia, Illinois, started in 1811 and completed in 1836. While the individual states largely financed the canals and the shorter turnpikes were private enterprises, the Cumberland Road was a federal enterprise. Not until almost a century later was the federal government again to become a major factor in highway construction because reliance was placed on steam railroad development prior to the age of automotive transportation.

Steam-Powered Transportation (Railroads and Steamboats)

It remained for the railroad to provide the facilities to open up the productive and commercial potential of this vast country, although steamboat transportation stimulated some areas before the railroads developed. The first practical use of the steam engine in transportation was in watercraft. Beginning in the first decade of the 19th century, use of the steamboat rapidly spread in the second decade to the eastern tidewater rivers, the Mississippi system, and the Great Lakes. Its early development was contemporaneous with the early turnpike and canal development but in no way interfered as a competing transport service. In fact it further stimulated canal building which would connect the larger navigable rivers with the Great Lakes. Steam packets providing economic two-way transportation greatly stimulated commercial development along the water routes they served. New Orleans, as the chief outlet for the commerce of the Mississippi River system's midcontinent area, quickly became the principal city on the Gulf Coast. The decade of the 50s was the peak period for river steamboat transportation. Over 3,500 steamboats arrived in New Orleans in 1850.[1] The limited size and slow movement of packets on circuitous rivers caused them gradually to give way after 1850 to rail competition. On the Great Lakes, however, the opening up of the St. Mary's Channel to Lake Superior and the discovery of the Mesabi iron ore resources to feed the expanding steel industry started a whole new era of large steamship transportation on the Great Lakes in midcentury.

Steam railroad transportation was begun in 1830 by the Baltimore and Ohio Railroad between Baltimore and Ellicott City, Maryland, a distance of 12 miles. A crude little vertical-boiler engine known as the "Tom Thumb" began the great age of railroads in the United States. Railroad construction elsewhere followed quickly: in 1831 between Charleston and Hamburg, South Carolina; and in 1832 between Albany and Schenectady, New York; between New Orleans and Lake Pontchartrain, Louisiana; and between Philadelphia and Columbia, Pennsylvania. New Jersey's Camden and Amboy connecting the New York and Philadelphia areas and several short railroads in Ohio were built in the early part of the same decade. The railroad fever spread rapidly from state to state. It was not until the decade of the 50s that improved technology of the new mode of transportation, and the extension and combining of early short lines, enabled the railroad to demonstrate its clear superiority over the canal boat and the steam packet for freight, and over the stagecoach for passengers as well. It is interesting to note that the decade between 1840 and 1850 was the decade of great canal building in spite of the fact that an ultimately superior mode had been discovered in 1830.

The saga of the expanding railroad system and its interaction with a growing national economy perhaps has not had a parallel in modern

---

[1] F. H. Dixon, *Traffic History of the Mississippi River* (Washington, D.C.: U.S. Government Printing Office, 1915), p. 5.

history. The 9,000 miles built between 1830 and 1850 were extended to 30,000 miles in 1860. The acceleration of railroad building prewar in the north gave the Union side a great advantage in military logistics which in time proved decisive. Aided by federal land grants, homesteading, and significant development in railroad technology, the postwar period experienced a railroad expansion that has remained unequaled. From 53,000 miles in 1876, the network expanded to 163,000 in 1890. In the meantime track gauges had been standardized and connected for through service. Steel replaced iron rails and the airbrake replaced the hand brake, permitting heavier and faster trains.

Railroad construction was paralleled and fed by a comparable expansion of industry, commerce, and population. In the words of a leading historian of the period: "In four great provinces bound together by ever-constricting ties of federation—manufacturing, extractive industries, transportation, and finance—the leaders of business enterprises . . . marched from victory to victory in the decades that followed the triumph of Grant at Appomattox."[2] Almost all the trunk lines were established by 1890, but network expansion continued until the early 1920s when the mileage reached a peak of over 250,000.

Because of growing competition of other modes, railroad mileage has declined since and is presently about 190,000 miles. The once extensive intercity passenger traffic has been very largely lost to air transport and the bus and motorcar. Break-bulk less-than-carload traffic has all but disappeared. Although strengthened by dieselization of its motive power and aided by consolidation, the industry is facing a precarious future; yet it remains the largest carrier of freight in terms of ton-miles.

The 20th-Century Competitors

After 75 years of dominance and 50 of actual monopoly, the railroad industry in the second quarter of the 20th century was confronted with the beginnings of four new major modes of transportation. Two were new versions of earlier forms (highway and inland water). Another, the pipeline, resulted from the technological transformation of a hitherto rather primitive mode, while air transport belongs entirely to the 20th century. Collectively they were to have an enormous impact upon the railroad system, on the mobility of people, and on the locational structure of the economy. They were to give rise to problems of public policy altogether more complex than those which had ruled the railroad era. Each, moreover, was to be developed separately from

---

[2] Charles A. Beard and Mary R. Beard, *The Rise of American Civilization*, vol. 2 (New York: Macmillan Co., 1941), p. 176.

the others so that more nearly a structure than a system of transport emerged.

By the late 20s highway development had proceeded sufficiently and the technological development of motor vehicles had imparted enough carrying capability and efficiency to enable motor transport to assume importance in local and short-distance transport, both passenger and freight. By the late 30s the truck and bus had become strong competitors over longer distances and the stage was set for a nationwide network of high-quality motor transport.

Although steamboat transportation on the rivers had succumbed to rail competition, barge operations developed in bulk commodities on portions of the river system, notably in the movement of coal on the Monongahela and Upper Ohio rivers. Revived attention to waterways improvement in the 20s enabled such operations to extend over the whole of the improved inland and protected coastal waterways system. American operators pioneered the shoved tow, applied the diesel engine to towboats of large horsepower, and built a capability for moving tows which, today, sometimes reach 40,000 tons at costs well below those achieved by railroads in the movement of bulk commodities. At several periods since 1950 barge transport has been our fastest growing mode.

The Tidewater Pipe Line had been built in 1879 to pump crude oil from western Pennsylvania fields to Philadelphia. Long-distance pipelining of crude developed slowly, however, and only gradually ousted the tank car from the business. Not until the 1920s was the technology of moving refined products in pipelines worked out. Pipe diameters were gradually increased, the 12-inch lines which were large in the 30s being supplemented since 1950 by lines ranging up to 48-inches in diameter. Steam gave way to diesel as power in pumping stations; then the remotely controlled electrically propelled centrifugal pump commenced to take over. Not only were the railroads displaced from the movement of crude and refined petroleum but even the coastwise tanker gave way in part to long-distance pipelining of products.

In the present century no form of transport has captivated the public as has air transportation. Commercial operations began in the late 20s. After 1950 air transport rapidly replaced the railroad in the long-distance movement of passengers and, with the advent of jets, quickly moved into position of the nation's major commercial passenger carrier. While still a small factor in the freight market, air cargo is also rapidly growing and the speed of air transport has opened up new opportunities for the marketing of perishable and high-value goods.

Deepwater Shipping

Unlike the steam packet on the rivers, the larger steamships on the Great Lakes and in deep-sea coastal service proved able to compete with the evergrowing efficiency and availability of railroad operations. The large, especially designed Great Lakes steamships bringing ore and grain down from the upper lakes area and returning with coal from Lake Erie and Lake Michigan provided a service for which railroads were not competitive. Now much ore movement comes to Lake Erie ports destined to Ohio and Pennsylvania steel mills from Labrador through the St. Lawrence Seaway. Also, large passenger and general cargo steamship operations thrived between Buffalo in the east and Detroit and Chicago in the west until the late 30s and early 40s. But it was highway rather than railroad developments that hastened the end of these magnificent ships. Similarly, coastwise and intercoastal passenger and general cargo shipping withstood railroad competition but succumbed to the added competition on the highway in the late 30s and early 40s and to the growing labor costs of break-bulk cargo operations. Since World War II there has been some revival of general cargo shipping both coastwise and intercoastal in containerships. Intercoastal and coastwise bulk cargo shipping has continued to grow, providing a lower cost service than railroads can supply.

MODAL SYSTEMS AND ROUTE PATTERNS

To understand the functioning of the transportation system of the continental United States, it is necessary to examine briefly the patterns of the several modes and their principal routes. They provide the framework for the logistics of industry categories and even of individual business enterprises.

The continental United States constitutes a vast territory possessing far-flung resources often remote from the concentrations of population and industry that must consume them. The principal physiographic disadvantages of the area are the location of the eastern, westcoast, and Rocky Mountain ranges which run counter to the west-to-east flow of resources to the populous areas. The chain of Great Lakes fortunately does not conflict and the Mississippi system well serves the north and south flows incident to the productive midcontinent area.

In spite of important regional industrial developments along the west and Gulf coasts and in the south, the major concentration of industry and population nurtured by early water and, more recently, railroad transportation, remains east of the Mississippi River and north of the Ohio River. This area is largely dependent on the agricultural products and raw materials which come from the west and southwest. Accordingly, the main long-distance routes for these materials are west to east and southwest to northeast. Maps showing the network of all the modes reflect the dominance of these routes.

The continental railroad network shown in Figure 1-1 is not unlike those of air and highway transportation, because these later modes

FIGURE 1-1
The Railway System of the United States

Courtesy Association of American Railroads

developed to serve the concentration of industry and population created by the railroads. Their main routes, indeed, paralleled, for the most part, those of the railroads. Because of mountain barriers railroad main routes are more definitive. The so-called transcontinental trunk lines must utilize the few usable western mountain passes of the north, central, and southern areas, so we have the northern, central, and southern transcontinental railroads respectively. But they are not truly transcontinental because they terminate at the Mississippi River or Chicago since our railroads developed independently within the northeast, southeast, and west. The points of interchanges became the classification and rate breaking points. The north-south main routes follow the two seaboards and the Mississippi basin. Only the latter early became interregional.

Over these great west-east and southeast-northeast routes, both by rail and highway, move the agricultural and basic industrial production of the west and southwest, including forest products, grain, coal, mineral products, livestock, meats, petroleum products, and fruits and vegetables. One significant exception to the pattern is the export movement of grain which has grown sharply in recent years and moves predominantly through the Gulf ports reached by rail and by barge via the Mississippi.

The southwest and south central areas have been the principal sources of petroleum, although the western plains and Rocky Mountain areas are becoming more prominent. Only iron and coal have come largely from the eastern half of the nation although the western states, particularly Montana, Wyoming, and Colorado, are becoming important sources. The southeast region has been a principal source of cotton and cotton products, fertilizer, paper and paper products, lumber, and citrus fruit. The rail trunk routes in this region have run either northeastward to the Washington-Norfolk areas or northwestward to the Ohio valley and Chicago, and the highway routes duplicate them closely.

The main water routes are defined by nature and benefited by channel and harbor improvements. They are the Great Lakes, the Atlantic-Gulf seaboard including the protected intracoastal waterways, and the Mississippi River system. In the west the Columbia River has seen significant traffic growth.

The development of the steel industry, centered as it has been in the Pittsburgh and Great Lakes areas, illustrates the result of a happy combination of raw material location and low-cost water transport routes. Pittsburgh, the first great center, was established by the proximity of ore mined in Pennsylvania and coal mined along the Monongahela River. High grade coking coal went directly from river-front mines into barges on the river and thence to blast furnaces at Pittsburgh. When a shift to Minnesota ores became necessary, the Great Lakes chain made possible low-cost delivery. The Mesabi iron range lies but 170–190 miles from the Lake Superior waterfront, hence specialized rail facilities could bring the ore cheaply to the docks for loading. Lake vessels designed particularly for this traffic provided very low ton-mile cost to the Lake Erie and Lake Michigan ports that served established steel mills. How the Great Lakes and St. Lawrence River serve the logistics of the steel industry is shown in Chapter 12, Figure 12-2.

The principal routes for petroleum are from the production centers of Texas, Oklahoma, and Louisiana to the midwest Great Lakes area and the northeast. Large-diameter pipelines have generally replaced railroads to refining areas, while tankers are depended upon to take much of the petroleum from the Gulf of Mexico area to the eastern seaboard refineries. There is also now the tanker movement from the Alaskan pipeline to California and, via the Panama Canal, to the Gulf refining areas. Figure 1-2 shows the network of petroleum pipelines. California has long had its own petroleum industry and pipeline system. Similar developments can be expected in areas of newer discovery, such as Mississippi, Colorado, and Wyoming.

The pattern of major routes to serve a basic industry grows out of the interrelation of national resources location, topography, and the

FIGURE 1–2
Refined Petroleum Products Movement by Pipeline, 1974

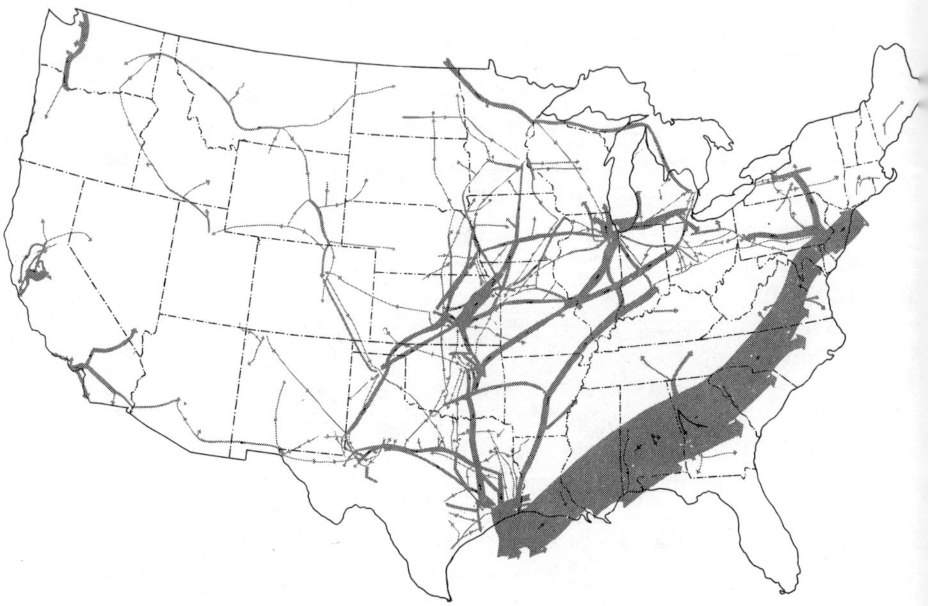

population centers. Thus, the stage is set for the logistics of all production-oriented businesses. The location of the initial processing centers may be largely influenced by the weight-losing characteristics of the basic materials as it is for lumber, iron ore, and meat packing. Availability of adequate water for processing as well as low-cost fuel supplies by water may influence the location of alumina and steel plants and electric power generators. Accordingly, the Ohio River offers a preferred location for some of these plants.

The movement of passengers and consumer-goods traffic is largely between the major urban areas. This is most pronounced in respect to the air-route network and is reflected in the design of the Interstate System of highways. The air and highway routes between major urban areas provide the stage for the logistics systems of distribution-oriented businesses discussed in Chapter 13. The pattern of movement strongly reflects the relative population concentrations, their proximity to one another, and the interrelationships among their business and financial interests.

THE MODERN TRANSPORTATION SYSTEM OF THE UNITED STATES

To provide the movement capability for the vast territory and highly developed economy of the United States requires what is by far the world's greatest system of transportation. Millions of vehicles move daily intercity over a million and a half miles of routes.[3] See Table 1-1.

Over the highways move (in round numbers) 114 million motorcars, 30 million motortrucks, 145,000 school and other noncommercial buses, and 98,000 commercial buses. Over the rail system move 1.67 million freight cars, 5,700 passenger cars, and 30,000 locomotives. On the air routes 178,000 aircraft are employed; while the waterways employ 33,000 barges and towboats, and on deepwater routes 540 U.S. flag ships are in service.

TABLE 1-1
Intercity Route Mileage in Continental United States, 1977

Transport Mode	Route Mileage	Comment
Highways	686,329	Paved, primary, and secondary roads, but excludes over 2 million miles of rural roads
Airways	327,822	
Pipelines	228,243	
Railroads	191,205	Includes over 300,000 miles of track
Waterways	25,543	Rivers and canals only, does not include Great Lakes

Investment in U.S. Transportation

No industry in this or any other nation represents a comparable investment. In most countries public investment in transport dominates. In the United States, there is extensive private and public investment. Investment in railroad and pipeline transportation is almost exclusively private; but in other modes public investment provides the way facilities, while private investment provides vehicles, offices, and certain terminal facilities. The net investment in privately owned transport equipment and facilities alone exceeds $263 billion. This does not include publicly owned noncommercial buses, trucks, or other transportation facilities. Above all it does not include the many billions of dollars in way facilities spent by the federal and state governments. The net investment in privately owned equipment and facilities by mode of transportation is shown in Table 1-2.

With respect to public investment in way facilities for the carrier industries, it is difficult to estimate the net investment because so much of the highway capital expenditures are for replacement. The annual expenditures of federal, state, and local governments in 1977 are shown in Table 1-3.

The total annual expenditure has climbed steadily from $3.2 billion

---

[3] Transportation Association of America, *Transportation Facts and Trends* (Washington, D.C., July 1979), p. 31.

TABLE 1-2

Net Investment in Privately Owned Transport Equipment and Facilities in 1977 ($ billions, rounded)

Highway (automobiles, trucks, and buses)	$193.9*
Railroads	34.7
Air carriers	15.7
Oil pipelines	12.9
Water carriers (inland, Great Lakes, ocean)	4.9
	$262.1

* Excludes dealers, service stations, repair, garages, and so on.
Source: Estimate, Transportation Association of America, *Transportation Facts and Trends* (Washington, D.C., July 1979), p. 28. Equipment manufactures and transit facilities excluded.

in 1947 to the $33 billion of 1977. While no determination of exact net public investment is possible, it is safe to say that the net public investment in way facilities probably exceeds the $262 billion in equipment and facilities which are privately owned. This gives us a probable net transport investment of well over $500 billion.

The amount paid by the shipping public for transportation service involves rates paid to private carriers and other costs incurred by shippers in handling the management of transportation service. In spite of the large subsidy inherent in public expenditures, the freight bill estimated in 1977 amounted to over $172 billion, or 9.12 percent of the nation's gross national product.

TABLE 1-3

Federal, State, and Local Expenditures for Transport Facilities, 1977 ($ millions, rounded)

Highways	$28,095	Federal ($7,589)—state and local ($20,506)
Air—total....................	3,432	Federal ($2,105)—state and local ($1,327)
Airways $1,715		
Airports $1,717		
Water (rivers and harbors)	1,448	Federal ($680)
Total	$32,975	$32,975

Source: Estimate, Transportation Association of America, *Transportation Facts and Trends* (Washington, D.C., July 1979), p. 26.

ECONOMIC ADVANTAGES AND DISADVANTAGES OF PUBLIC ENTERPRISE IN TRANSPORTATION

The principal aspects of public enterprise in transportation involve investment in way facilities, direct subsidy to private carrier operation, and free services to carriers of certain modes. Investment is involved in construction of highways, waterways, airways, and airports. Direct subsidies are paid to ocean shipping lines under the U.S. flag. Government service includes operation of dams, waterways, and traffic control centers; and airports, airport towers, and weather service for air transport. There are also such ancillary aids as loans, tax relief for construction reserves, and accelerated depreciation. In recent years federal research in transportation has greatly expanded.

The principal advantage of public enterprise is a more rapid development of transportation than would be possible if left entirely to private initiative. Basic facilities are provided earlier, and development of the technology of the mode aided is accelerated. The entire economy may be stimulated and national defense may be strengthened by a rapid development of facilities and service that could not have been otherwise available, or by the establishment and maintenance of capacity in excess of normal commercial needs.

Private investment requires a prospect of profit, and therefore comes after or with the development of traffic. The Cumberland Road in all likelihood would not have been built by private capital; and canal building, in the absence of action by the several states, would have been minimal. Our modern highway system has developed much more rapidly than could have been possible through dependence on private toll-road companies. The same is true of improved waterways. Our national airway system would be impossible except as a federally sponsored enterprise, and we would not retain a maritime fleet in the foreign trade in the absence of direct and indirect subsidies to U.S. flag shipping.

Although the economic and social benefits of public enterprise in transportation have been great, such enterprise has not been undertaken without causing waste and burden on the taxpayers, and inequity in the competition between the modes. Economic waste in government construction arises, as we shall see in Chapter 3, from general, social, and political considerations including defense in the selection of the place and kind of facilities provided and from the fact that overexpansion far beyond traffic needs and prospects takes place. Uneconomic and politically inspired waterway appropriations of Congress have long been designated as "pork barrel" legislation. Highway construction has been greatly influenced by general social and political considerations, some of which may have justification in general economic benefits obtained.

Economists are concerned with the uneconomic allocation of transportation resources which public aid has caused because it has been focused on water, air, and highway transportation independently. Problems of inequity arise from the fact that railroad and pipeline carriers must provide their own facilities and yet must compete with the highway, water, and air carriers that use publicly provided facilities. User taxes to cover public costs have been urged to restore the necessary equity. Federal and state gasoline, tire, and license taxes, while less than adequate, cover much of the public highway costs. Gasoline, shipment, and passenger taxes, and landing fees are being applied to air carriers, but they are not fully adequate. Inland water carriers, hitherto free of user taxes, became subject to fuel taxes October 1, 1980. Finally aid to some competitors and not to others makes regulation of intermodal competition very complicated and difficult.

TRAFFIC DISTRIBUTION AMONG MODES

The growth of new modes during the present century has had striking effects upon rail transportation participation in the nation's business, both passenger and freight. Each of the new modes, moreover, has distinctive characteristics which tend to define its participation as compared with the general-purpose capability of the railroad. Motor transport is, by all odds, the most flexible and thus the most pervasive of the newer modes. The pipeline is the most constricted; yet the vast growth in use of petroleum fuels has insured a rapid increase in the share of freight volume for this mode.

The comparison in Table 1-4 reveals the substantial decline in relative importance of railroads and the contemporaneous increase in importance of oil pipelines, motortruck, and air operations. As of 1977, the freight revenue of regulated intercity motor carriers was first—$31 billion compared to $19.6 billion for the second-place railroads. In passenger traffic the private motorcar dominates the passenger-miles, performing an estimated 84.6 percent of all passenger-miles in 1977. Table 1-5 shows the trend in the distribution in passenger traffic of commercial carriers.

The expansion of air passenger traffic and decline of rail passenger traffic stand out. Although bus traffic expanded some up to 1974 and far exceeds rail traffic, its position has declined relative to both air traffic and the total passenger-miles of commercial carriers.

TABLE 1-4
Freight Market Share by Mode (percent of freight ton-miles including mail and express)

	1940	1950	1970	1978
Railroads	63.2	56.2	39.7	35.8
Oil pipelines	9.1	12.1	22.3	23.3
Motor trucks	9.5	16.3	21.3	24.7
Water (inland and Great Lakes)	18.2	15.4	16.6	15.9
Air	—	0.03	0.18	0.21
Total	100.0	100.0	100.0	100.0

Source: Estimate, Transportation Association of America, *Transportation Facts and Trends* (Washington, D.C., July 1979), p. 81.

TABLE 1-5
Commercial Passenger Market Share by Mode (percent of passenger-miles)

	1940	1950	1970	1978
Air...	2.7	14.15	73.0	84.0
Bus...	30.0	34.53	16.9	11.3
Rail..	63.9	49.46	7.8	4.7
Water......................................	3.4	1.86	3.3	—
Total................................	100.0	100.00	100.0	100.0

Source: Estimate, Transportation Association of America, *Transportation Facts and Trends* (Washington, D.C., July 1979), p. 18.

DEVELOPMENTS AND PORTENTS IN TRANSPORTATION TECHNOLOGY

Developments

New and improved technology can affect the range of capability, quality of service, and cost of any mode of transport and can, thus, alter its prospective role in the nation's transport system. The post–World War II period has been marked by unprecedented technologic development in all of the major forms of transport and by considerable augmentation of research and development activities. To the latter trend the Department of Transportation has contributed significantly since 1968 by widening government concerns to include rail transport as well as the modes that have traditionally been recipients of government investment.

It is hardly too much to say that railroads were preserved from economic disaster in the period after World War II by the shift from steam to diesel power, the rapid mechanization of maintenance of way work, and the growth of trailer-on-flatcar service. That the hardware for these developments was generated outside the industry indicates the longstanding reliance upon supply industries for rail technical progress. Rail research has been considerably expanded in recent years, however, especially in such fundamentals as track design and vehicle performance.

The shift to diesel power has been important, too, for the economy of bus and truck transportation. Refinements in vehicle design have also played a part, together with heavy investment in motor-carrier terminals improved both in layout and in materials-handling systems. Developments external to the private carrier industries, however, have been of more far-reaching significance. The Interstate Highway System has been of enormous importance in reducing distance, time, and cost. Liberalization and increasing uniformity of size and weight restrictions have given widened scope to vehicle design. Extension from a few western states to more than 30 states of the right to use double bottoms (tractor, semitrailer, and full trailer comprising a rig) has improved the flexibility of motor-carrier operations as well as enhancing tractor loading.

Technological development on the inland waters has already been briefly noticed. On the oceans dry-bulk-cargo ships of 100,000 tons deadweight and upward are replacing the much less economic pre-war ships of 10,000–15,000 tons. Tankers have moved even more rapidly in size, the largest now approaching 500,000 tons. With the increase in size, crew complements have held steady or shrunk in consequence of engine room automation. Containerships are rapidly replacing conventional general cargo vessels in the major liner trades. The cellular containership which holds hundreds of truck trailer bodies is one of the great transportation innovations of the century. Both in the bulk trades and in general cargo, shipping is rapidly becoming a capital-intensive industry; and the whole pace of operations has been speeded accordingly.

While the conversion of air transport from reliance on propeller aircraft powered by reciprocating gasoline engines to jet aircraft has been noticed for its effect upon the speed and comfort of air travel, the economic consequences have also been noteworthy. Break-even factors have been greatly reduced and reliability much improved. The current generation of wide-bodied jets spawned an undigestible increase in capacity at a time of retarded traffic growth in 1973–74; hence financial problems of unprecedented magnitude. In the longer run, however, they pointed the way to further growth in both cargo and passenger volumes and assisted in alleviating congestion on heavily traveled routes.

Portents

Research and experimentation have been directed to the development of wholly new concepts of transportation as well as to the improvement of existing systems. Two hybrid forms have received attention—the hydrofoil boat and the ground effects machine (air cushion vehicle). The former, capable of high speeds in relatively calm waters, has found considerable use in Europe and the Soviet Union but is classed as experimental in the United States. The ground effects machine is capable of operating over either land or water with airplane type propulsion. When operating on a fixed glide path (single rail), it can also use the linear induction motor as a means of propulsion and magnetic levitation in lieu of the air cushion. In the guided form very high speeds have been attained and promise is seen for airport feeder service and in short-distance corridor passenger operations. An older concept, the elevated monorail, has had several commercial applications but thus far fails to show promise in competition with conventional two-rail transit.[4]

The gas turbine had a brief application in freight service, principally on the Union Pacific, but has been retired from that role. This form of power is performing successfully in passenger service, however, both in North America and abroad. Gas turbines have also been employed on some oceangoing ships and experimentally in automotive vehicles. Promise is held out especially for their application to trucks and buses. While these units emit lower levels of hydrocarbons than reciprocating engines, their fuel economy is as yet inferior.

The pipeline, with its extraordinary economy, has served almost exclusively in the transport of petroleum and products, anhydrous ammonia, and natural gas. In the 50s, however, a 12-inch line successfully moved pulverized coal in slurry form from Cadiz, Ohio, to Cleveland. At present a larger line moves coal slurry from the Black Mesa, New Mexico, mines to power stations in southeastern Nevada operating over a route where no railroad exists. A wider range of slurries seems likely to be accommodated by pipelines in the future, and some general cargo may well take to pipelines encased in capsules which can be borne by the liquid stream.

The nuclear ship *Savannah* made her trial run in 1962 amidst much optimism about atomic power for merchant ships. A decade of operation did not lead to further application of nuclear power in merchant ships, for while the safety of the system seems to have been demonstrated, its economic viability was not. The prospective range of usefulness has been narrowed down to very large intensively used craft. The idea of employing nuclear plants on locomotives was quickly dropped, but railroad electrification is again a very active subject, and nuclear power may, of course, be the source of current, at least in part. Enormous progress has been made in the design of electric locomotives for rail use, using solid state systems and commercial frequencies. Two short railroads built to haul utility coal employ such power and, in addition, are automated. The promise of automation is far greater in transit than conventional rail operations, however; and the first thoroughly new rail transit system with computer control of operations came into partial service in 1972.

Among the interesting technological questions looking to the near future are:

1. Can the hydrofoil principle be applied to large vessels which can negotiate with safety under conditions of substantial wave action?
2. Can the air cushion vehicle become entirely dependable and be

---

[4] Edward Hungerford in *The Modern Railroad* (Chicago: A. C. McLurg & Co., 1911) devoted several pages to the monorail, already operative in a public park, and predicted a great future for it.

successfully integrated with an urban transit system in serving outlying communities and airports?

3. Because jumbo-sized jet aircraft represent huge investments, a rapid turnaround at airports is necessary. How long will it be until the major airports that serve them will be free of congestion and have the mechanized facilities to realize their economic potential? Will short landing and takeoff aircraft find a place in intermediate distance transport?

4. Will advance in the technology of gas turbines in time make fuel consumption comparable to that of the internal combustion engine and possibly replace diesel power for locomotives, trucks, and buses?

5. Will solution of the switching and other technical problems in time make the monorail a viable mode of urban or local commercial transportation?

6. Will determination of best size and shape of capsules, efficient loading and unloading facilities, and propellants make transportation of packages in pipelines possible?

7. Will reduction in investment and operating costs together with adequate safety equipment bring nuclear powered ships into general use? Will the increased cost of bunker oil lead to a revival of the sailing ships in some services or a return to coal, perhaps by the fluidized bed method of consumption?

8. Can supersonic aircraft become either financially profitable or, because of settlement of environmental issues, socially acceptable?

9. Will automation of transit operations alter the economics of mass transit sufficiently to permit frequent 24-hour schedules, attractive levels of fares, and ability to cover operating costs from the fare box?

10. Will "people movers," now experimental, permit banning the automobile from central cities while providing convenient circulation therein?

11. Will new techniques for tunnel boring make it possible to place high-speed systems below ground?

12. Will relatively higher fuel costs and a continuing necessity to conserve permanently alter modal relationships in favor of the fuel-efficient forms?

QUESTIONS FOR THE FUTURE

As we look to the future there are two questions that stand out. First as our population and GNP expand in the future, will the expansion of transport facilities in quantity and kind among the modes be that which will be most effective in advancing the economy?[5] All modes are presently expanding except the railroads. Their loss of passenger, less-than-carload, perishable, and petroleum traffic with their huge investment threatens their ability to survive as privately owned carriers. Assuming that an expanded national economy will require a substantial increase in volume freight movement over long distances, can the rail plant be preserved and improved to meet this eventuality as no other mode can?[6] Will greater energy economy of the rails as compared with the highways produce a shift in growth rates toward the rail mode?

The other question relates to how to mold these several modes into a more efficient national system, an objective which is increasingly regarded as a desirable one. Separate promotional expenditures for three modes by different government agencies without well-conceived and enforced common criteria, together with the absence of adequate user charges applied to carriers using tax supported facilities, militate against equitable competition among the modes and prevent a rational integration of all modes into an optimum coordinated and balanced system. Efficiency of transport suffers—in consequence the economic system as a whole falls short of the achievement of which it is capable. Much of the study of transport economics necessarily turns on the means available to improve this condition.

SELECTED REFERENCES

Anderson, Romala. *The Sailing Ship: Six Thousand Years of History.* London: G. G. Harrup, 1947.

Baldwin, Leland Dewitt. *The Keelboat Age on Western Waters.* Pittsburgh: University of Pittsburgh Press, 1941.

Beard, Charles A., and Beard, Mary R. *The Rise of American Civilization.* New York: Macmillan Co., 1941.

Brooks, Peter. *The Modern Airliner: Its Origins and Development.* London: Putnam, 1961.

Davies, R. E. G. *Airlines of the United States since 1914.* London: Putnam, 1972.

Fair, Marvin L., and Williams, Ernest W., Jr. *Economics of Transportation,* chaps. 4–8. Rev. ed. New York: Harper & Row Publishers, 1959.

---

[5] In its 1979 report the National Transportation Policy Study Commission forecast capital needs for all transport of some $4 trillion by the year 2000.

[6] The remaining intercity rail passenger services are now operated by Amtrak, a semipublic corporation which is discussed in Chapter 7. At present a heavy subsidy is required. In the Northeast, where six major bankrupt railroads were incorporated into Conrail, public funds continue to be necessary to support the system. There is financial weakness on the part of some companies elsewhere in the country.

Goodrich, Carter, et al. *Canals and American Economic Development.* New York: Columbia University Press, 1961.

Harlow, Alvin Fay. *Old Towpaths: The Story of the American Canal Era.* New York: Appleton-Century-Crofts, 1926.

Hay, William Walter. *An Introduction to Transportation Engineering.* New York: John Wiley & Sons, Inc., 1961.

Hennes, Robert Graham. *Fundamentals of Transportation Engineering.* New York: McGraw-Hill Book Co., 1961.

Hunter, Louis C. *Steamboats on the Western Rivers.* Cambridge: Harvard University Press, 1949.

Kalla-Bishop, P. M. *Future Railways and Guided Transport.* London: ITC Transport Press, Ltd., 1972.

Locklin, D. Philip. *Economics of Transportation,* chaps. 5, 6, 26, 28, 30, and 33. 7th ed. Homewood, Ill.: Richard D. Irwin, Inc., 1972.

Margary, Ivan Donald. *Roman Roads in Britain.* London: Phoenix House, 1955.

Meyer, Balthasar Henry, ed. *History of Transportation in the United States before 1860.* Washington, D.C.: Carnegie Institution, 1917.

Savage, Christopher Ivor. *An Economic History of Transport.* London: Hutchinson, 1959.

Stover, John F. *American Railroads.* Chicago: University of Chicago Press, 1961.

Transportation Association of America. *Transportation Facts and Trends.* Washington, D.C.: see last annual edition.

————. *Transport Technological Trends.* Washington, D.C., 1969.

Williamson, Jeffrey G. *Late Nineteenth-Century American Development: A General Equilibrium History,* chap. 9. New York: Cambridge University Press, 1974.

2

Transport and Economic Development

The years since World War II have generated increased concern about the principles of economic development. As American national policy shifted its emphasis from the economic reconstruction of Western Europe to the problems of the less developed areas of the world, critical questions arose as to where to place the emphasis in technical and financial assistance in order to induce economic growth. Since they were extremely short of capital, the question of investment priorities was even more urgent in the developing countries themselves.

The industrial revolution in western Europe, coinciding rougly in time with the first application of mechanical power to transport and the opening up of the North American continent to settlement, had both been studied by economists and economic historians alike. That extended and improved transport had played an important role was generally agreed. But it had not been necessary to define that role precisely nor to draw conclusions for application on a major scale elsewhere.

Can the provision of transport facilities generate economic development? Can it do so under some circumstances and not others? How must transport investment be related in time to other types of investment in order that maximum development be induced? What proportion of limited investment capabilities ought to be placed in the transport sector? These were hard questions, and firm answers were not readily forthcoming. It became increasingly clear that European and American experience was in many respects unique—that it could not safely be relied upon as a guide to policy in other environments and cultures. Moreover both those experiences lay within the railroad era when little choice presented itself as to the technology of transport that ought to be fostered. Today not only the amount of investment and the routes over which service is to be provided must be decided but also the type of transport to be employed—whether air, highway, rail, improved water, or some combination of them.

TRANSFORMATION TO A MARKET ECONOMY

The development of an exchange or market economy, one in which goods are transferred from points of production to points of sale and consumption, depends upon the ability to move goods, that is, on the availability of transportation service. Where transportation is of a primitive sort, populations are consigned to a subsistence form of economic existence. They depend upon the area immediately around them for food, clothing, and other bare essentials of existence. They do not produce goods to be exchanged for other types of goods that can only be produced in some other area, except to a most limited degree.

Most of the world depended upon subsistence agriculture or grazing in the period prior to the application of mechanical power to transport. Exceptions were principally in the northern hemisphere in those areas bordering on the sea where natural harbors were abundant and naturally navigable streams gave limited access to the interior. Progress in the seafaring arts had much to do with the more rapid economic development of some nations so circumstanced than of others.

Today large areas, especially in the Asian, African, and South American continents, remain remote from improved transport routes. Their populations subsist on local resources that are often limited in quantity as well as variety and are precariously dependent on the vagaries of weather. Standards of living are abysmally low. Economic progress which can raise those levels depends upon the utilization of localized resources and the development of manufacturing enterprises. These in turn require the development of exchange relationships for which efficient transport is a prerequisite.

TRANSPORT IN THE INFRASTRUCTURE

Economic progress requires the development of commercial agriculture capable of supplying urban populations and export markets, the exploitation of mineral and forest resources as supply sources for industry, and the development of manufacturing enterprises. All of these require transport facilities to enable the goods to reach their markets, communications, power and other utilities, and effective governmental and commercial institutions. Moreover the transformation toward an industrial economy cannot be accomplished without extensive provision for education and public health. All of these must, in some degree, precede industrialization. Hence these broad public services which are not specific to particular industrial projects have come to be called the *infrastructure* or *social overhead* in the literature of economic development. They require substantial capital investment in advance of rapid growth in productivity. Thus it may be said that capital accumulation is the core of economic development.[1]

As Rostow has pointed out, not only are social overheads of large quantitative importance but they have three characteristics that distinguish them from investment in general: (1) long periods of gestation and payoff, (2) lumpiness, and (3) often a return to the community as a whole rather than directly to investors.[2] All three of these characteristics are readily discernable in railway development and are found, although in somewhat lesser degree, in all other forms of transport.

Transport systems require the development of agriculture, industry, and commerce along their routes to generate the traffic that will sustain them. This may take many years. There is a minimum lump of investment that will lay down a railway between two points. Without the minimum, no rail service can be conducted: yet the minimum capacity which the nature of the technology requires to be installed may be well above any foreseeable traffic requirements.[3] For this reason a choice of highway rather than rail development may be made. Finally, while the provision of a transportation facility may make industrial development possible with accompanying improvement in standards of living, there may be no return to investors from earnings for extended periods of time. Indeed substantial losses have characterized much transport construction in various parts of the world. As Grodinsky points out, investments made by all parties in American transcontinental railroads in the decade of the 1870s were largely lost.[4] More recently the heavy post–World War II investment in the Chilean

---

[1] See Benjamin Higgins, *Economic Development: Problems, Principles, and Policies* (New York: W. W. Norton & Co., Inc., 1959), chap. 8, for a summary of general theories of development.

[2] W. W. Rostow, *The Stages of Economic Growth* (New York: Cambridge University Press, 1960), pp. 24–25.

[3] Reduced productivity of inputs in Soviet transportation in recent years is suggestive. See N. M. Kaplan, "Growth in Soviet Transport and Communications," *American Economic Review* vol. 57, no. 1154 (1967).

[4] Julius Grodinsky, *Transcontinental Railway Strategy: 1869–1893* (Philadelphia: University of Pennsylvania Press, 1962), p. 421.

Railways has generated mounting losses while the St. Lawrence Seaway, two decades after its opening, has yet to generate revenues sufficient to cover charges.

Despite the necessity for infrastructure, including transport, if economic development is to be fostered there are serious questions of what, how much, and where. Capital scarcity, especially in the earlier phases of industrialization, insures that capital devoted to transport development will be unavailable for other purposes. Hence development may be slowed by the unwise expenditure of funds for social overhead. A nice question of balance is presented. As Gerschenkron points out in the Russian case: "One does not have to conjure up the dramatic and pathetic vision of a huge boiler being dragged by teams of oxen through the mud of the Ukranian steppes on its way to the construction site of the first blast furnace in the Donbas in order to understand that some railroad building had to antedate the period of rapid industrialization."[5] But he goes on to point out that rapid industrialization does not materialize merely because an institutional barrier has been removed. Simultaneous progress is necessary in many directions.

Yet it is clear that in the face of limited capital accumulation and limited assistance from more advanced areas, concentration of resources must be accomplished in the sorts of investment that are deemed to be strategic, that is, most likely to induce the desired result of economic growth however measured. In this context transport is almost certain to play a major role. As Galbraith puts it, in illustrating the sense of strategy which characterizes an effective plan for economic development, "a highly efficient transportation system and an economic and reliable source of power are indispensable. With these available something is certain to happen; without them, one can be less sure."[6] For it is these industries that provide the external economies for others and make it possible for them to exist.

It is not surprising, therefore, that transport has accounted for a large share of actual and planned investment in countries where efforts are underway to induce economic development. The proportion of total public investment allotted to transport is often in the range of 25-30 percent, and in some countries in recent time periods it has exceeded 40 percent.[7] Yet in large parts of the world the provision of comprehensive transport networks such as have long characterized Europe and North America has been barely begun.

[5] Alexander Gerschenkron, *Economic Backwardness in Historical Perspective* (Cambridge: Harvard University Press, 1962), pp. 24-25.

[6] John Kenneth Galbraith, *Economic Development* (Cambridge: Harvard University Press, 1964), p. 73.

[7] Wilfred Owen, *Strategy for Mobility* (Washington, D.C.: The Brookings Institution, 1964), p. 64.

TRANSPORT AS A GENERATOR OF ECONOMIC DEVELOPMENT

Despite Galbraith's optimism that with efficient transport and power sources provided, something is bound to happen, it is far from clear how and to what extent development will in fact be stimulated. The opening of North America by the western extension of the railway system is often cited as a shining example of the efficacy of a policy directed toward stimulating the development of a transport system. The case was, however, in many respects unique. Sparsely populated virgin lands were being opened to settlement, including enormous areas of good soils, favorable topography, and excellent climate for agricultural purposes. This was being done in an economic and political climate devoted to individual initiative and material progress. And the settlement was accomplished by the more vigorous and venturesome elements of populations already accustomed to exercise initiative in a commercial system.

Sight should not be lost, either, of the aggressive efforts of railroads and communities to secure as settlers people already experienced in commercial agriculture, preferably under environmental circumstances not grossly different from those to be encountered in the West, and possessed of sufficient capital to tide them over the first crop year.[8] The movement, too, was aided by events in Europe which tended to precipitate large-scale emigration. And the happy concurrent development of the steel plow, the harvester, barbed wire, and the implements essential to an extensive grain culture played its part. These conditions have rarely been duplicated elsewhere, though they are seen on a much smaller scale in the opening of the Argentine pampa, the South African veld, and the Ukranian steppe—all in the temperate zone and in two of the three cases; free of major topographical hindrance.

More basically the problem of developing nations today is of a quite different order of difficulty. Hence, while we recognize the essential place of transport plant in the infrastructure, we should be very hesitant to predict results by extrapolating historic experience. As George D. Woods, former president of the World Bank, put it in comparing 19th-century development with the present:

> The pioneer nations were trebly fortunate. On the whole, their trends of population growth, urbanization and mechanization helped and reinforced each other.

---

[8] On this effort, see Paul Wallace Gates, *The Illinois Central Railroad and Its Colonization Work* (Cambridge: Harvard University Press, 1934); and James B. Hedges, *The Federal Railway Land Subsidy Policy of Canada* (Cambridge: Harvard University Press, 1934).

For present-day developers the opposite is the case. All the various elements—population, patterns of technology, urban expansion—contradict and impede the others. . . . The spurt of population is taking place *ahead* of the means of feeding and absorbing it—at a time when farming is still insufficiently modernized to provide food at a comparable rate for the whole population and at a time when the trend in industry is to need fewer but more highly skilled workers.[9]

Single-minded concentration upon the fostering of transport improvements will not suffice in the underdeveloped nations today. Balanced programs of development must be sought in which transport investment is linked closely to other forms of investment. Hence the transport specialist is obliged to fit his work into some form of comprehensive plan which responds to stated goals for national development.

POPULATION MOVEMENT AND REGIONAL DISTRIBUTION

Each of the three continental land masses in which the majority of the world's underdeveloped areas are to be found possesses sectors where population presses severely on the land; while other areas, though they enjoy large latent potentials for productivity, are well-nigh empty in consequence of the barriers of distance and topography. Populations are immobile; and in the absence of transport development which can open up frontier areas, the pressures upon the land will increase. At the same time present areas of dense population rely heavily upon their regional produce. Crop failures attributable to weather are difficult, sometimes impossible, to relieve by the importation of foodstuffs—and when possible, a heavy burden of cost, characteristically including a high percentage of shrinkage, is encountered in consequence of primitive or inadequate transport and storage facilities.

A good example of the type of situation referred to is the wet eastern slopes of the Bolivian-Peruvian Andes and the adjacent Llanos. These incredibly remote areas may serve as a new frontier for the countries concerned; yet the provision of transport is rendered difficult by topography and by the fact that heavy rainfall will require paved roads. Preliminary colonization efforts are underway, but more is involved than extension of the road system. The suitability of particular crops for the soil and climatic conditions must be determined, highland peoples

---

[9] "Development—The Need for New Directions," address to the Swedish Bankers Association, Stockholm, October 27, 1967.

must be encouraged to migrate, and public services must be provided.[10]

Important as may be the increase of the area open to cultivation, there is little attraction in developing countries for the mere extension of subsistence agriculture. Efficient transport, hence, is a key not only to the redistribution of population but the augmentation of supply crops for the sustenance of the areas of older and dense settlement and for the moderation of the effects of drought and other sources of regional crop failure. Finally, a growing agricultural base provided with the means for wide distribution of output may well be an essential prerequisite to industrial growth.

CHOICE AND LOCATION OF TRANSPORT SYSTEMS

The several forms of transport that have general-purpose capability, that is, are capable of handling passengers as well as freight of nearly all types, differ in the investment cost required per route-mile operated and in the operating cost per ton-mile of carrying capacity generated. They differ, also, in the density of traffic per route-mile at which their lowest unit operating costs are achieved. In general, air transport operating costs per ton-mile are higher than those of any other form of transport; but since investment in surface facilities may be confined to airports, the investment cost per route-mile will customarily be lower than for other forms. Highway transport may lie between air and rail both in investment and in operating costs if what we have in mind is a two-lane highway of minimum all-weather standards versus a single-track railway of modest carrying capacity. The carrying capacity in any time period will be lowest for air and highest for the railway.

In the developing countries still other features of the transport modes will need to be considered. Air transport is flexible, can surmount topographical features of all kinds, can utilize water bodies in lieu of landing fields as in the Canadian bush, and can operate by flying in and out of small fields with appropriate aircraft. These factors suggest that for the movement of passengers, the mails, and modest quantities of goods this means may permit the fastest progress in tying areas together. Indeed air transport may well be the first step toward pro-

---

[10] See Robert T. Brown, *Transport and the Economic Integration of South America* (Washington, D.C.: The Brookings Institution, 1966), pp. 22–23; and Barbara R. Bargmann, "The Cochabamba–Santa Cruz Highway in Boliva," in George W. Wilson et al., *The Impact of Highway Investment on Development* (Washington, D.C.: The Brookings Institution, 1966), chap. 2. For a bold scheme to open up South American frontiers, see Tom Alexander, "A Wild Plan for South America's Wilds," *Fortune*, December 1967, pp. 148 ff.

viding a transport net. And this is the way in which it performs today in areas as widely separated as Ethiopia, the Canadian Northwest Territories, and the still-frontier area surrounding Brasilia.[11]

As freight transport volumes develop, however, and as relatively low-value bulk and staple commodities must be moved, surface transportation of some type becomes essential. Where naturally navigable waterways penetrate the areas concerned, they are customarily employed for this purpose since carrying costs by water are low. Unfortunately only limited access by water is to be had in the African and South American continents, since the great river systems are either impeded by rapids or penetrate areas which have limited prospect for early development, for example, the rain forest of the Amazon Basin. Rivers, moreover, tend to be highly circuitous in their courses and require inland transportation in a feeder and distribution role if their influence is to be widely felt.

The most critical choice, commonly, is whether to devote limited investment funds upon highway or upon railway construction. Many countries which have inadequate transport systems nevertheless have some railway mileage which it may be feasible to incorporate into an expanded transportation system. In some instances a considerable rail network, more or less comprehensive in coverage, is available. When by 1921 the ravages of the revolution had been overcome, the Soviet Union had some 69,000 kilometers of railway in operation. Motor transport at the time was in a very early stage of development, and the expansion of inland water transport presented many difficulties. A policy of reliance upon railway development was adopted and persisted until quite recent times when pipeline construction reached significant proportions and investment in road transport began to expand. The present rail system of 130,000 kilometers carries more freight traffic than the much larger system of North America. High selectivity in choice of new route construction and intensive use of capital have characterized the Soviet approach.[12]

The railways of India constitute a system of some 59,000 kilometers which serve principal routes throughout the subcontinent. Unfortunately the principal mileage is divided almost equally between broad and meter gauges, while nearly 5,000 kilometers are divided between two different narrow gauges.[13] Nevertheless, a network of main routes

[11] On this last and the role of air transport, see John Gunther, *Inside South America* (New York: Harper & Row Publishers, 1967), pp. 77–80.

[12] The principles applied are instructive. See Holland Hunter, *Soviet Transportation Policy* (Cambridge: Harvard University Press, 1957), esp. chaps. 2–4; and Ernest W. Williams, Jr., *Freight Transportation in the Soviet Union* (Princeton: Princeton University Press, 1962).

[13] Diversity of track gauges afflicts a number of other areas, Australia being the best known example.

of considerable capacity provides a nucleus upon which extensions of the system can be grafted while a policy of intensive development of existing lines is followed. By contrast, the Argentine, with a comparatively dense network coursing the Pampas, faces not only obsolescence of its railway plant but redundancy. This condition is not dissimilar from that of the Granger Territory (principally Wisconsin, Illinois, Iowa, South Dakota, and Nebraska) in the United States, in consequence of the paralleling of much of the system by highways and the attempted continuance of a value of service rate structure. Rail tonnage in 1963 was actually less than half that of 1945, and the railway deficits constitute a serious continuing drain upon the Argentine economy.[14] Highway development which principally parallels existing rail routes may dissipate limited capital resources without making a major contribution to economic development.[15] Major railway modernization and improvement, as undertaken in Chile after World War II and in the Argentine in the 70s may not redress the competitive imbalance. Indeed, experience suggests increased rather than reduced rail deficits.

Where new country is to be opened up by extension of existing transport facilities, there is much to be said for highway development. Highways can be of moderate capacity by comparison with railroads; they can be built largely with indigenous materials and with steeper grades and sharper curvature where the terrain is inhospitable. Beyond that they touch the population more intimately all along the route and open up opportunities for small-scale enterprise which can contribute more to a rise in the level of aspiration than other forms. Air transport routes make no impact on the country below. Rail transport tends to concentrate its effects at a few main points along the routes. But a highway can be used by individual vehicles entering anywhere on the route and can stimulate numerous small truck and bus enterprises capable of being started upon a small investment. Finally many of the developing countries which enter upon motor-vehicle assembly and manufacture could not support a railway equipment industry. Hence railway development often imposes larger import commitments with consequent drain upon foreign exchange.

The principal circumstances in which railway construction is indispensable are those which involve movement of minerals in large tonnages to ports or to processing plants. New railway construction, frequently done by mining companies themselves and unconnected with other existing rail lines, has been required in recent years to open up

---

[14] Brown, *South America*, pp. 177–86.

[15] For an example of an essentially parallel highway, see Martin S. Klein, "The Atlantic Highway in Guatemala," in Wilson, et al., *Impact of Highway Investment*, chap. 3.

ore bodies to export channels in Northwest Australia, Liberia, Venezuela, and other countries. Along with the railway construction must go port development, often at new locations. The improvement and expansion of ports for general cargo is also of importance in many developing countries whose trade is often more heavily oriented to the more developed areas of the world which are necessarily reached by sea.[16] Moreover where the inland transport net is inadequately developed and serious natural obstacles impede the linkage of countries by inland routes, ocean transport may remain a principal means for the conduct of regional commerce. This is notably the case in both South America and Africa.

It is well to emphasize, in concluding this brief account of the available transport modes, the importance of careful choice of available technologies in the light of the prospective movement requirements in any area under development. Each instance requires separate study. The art of traffic forecasting is poorly developed; and much can often be said for holding commitment to fixed investment, accepting higher operating costs in the short run, and increasing investment only after traffic development has confirmed the forecast.[17]

TRANSPORT AND INDUSTRIAL CONCENTRATION AND URBANIZATION

The development of large-scale industry and of urban centers is dependent upon supporting transportation systems. Cities cannot function without hinterlands with which they are connected. The size of such hinterlands is determined principally by the kind of transport available and the costs and speed of movement associated with it. The city must be fed and supplied, its industries must be provided with materials they are to process, and distribution must be available into market areas adequate to support whatever scale of operations is achieved. The larger the city, the larger must be its supporting hinterlands. Governmental cities, such as national capitals, afford a partial exception since they may be devoid of nonservice industries and heavily supported by tax revenues.[18] A Brasilia or an Addis Ababa can grow to moderate size as a governmental center with indifferent surface transportation relying upon air transport both of passengers

---

[16] See Walter P. Hedden, *Mission: Port Development* (Washington, D.C.: American Association of Port Authorities, 1967).

[17] See Richard M. Soberman, *Transport Technology for Developing Regions* (Cambridge: M.I.T. Press, 1966), chaps. 4 and 5.

[18] On the growth of Paris as a tax-supported city in the time of Philip IV, see Harlan W. Gilmore, *Transportation and the Growth of Cities* (Glencoe: The Free Press, 1953), pp. 37–39.

and of perishable and valuable goods. An industrial center, however, must have economical surface linkages with its raw material sources and markets.

The tendency for cities to develop upon navigable waters in earlier times reflected the fact that only water transportation was sufficiently economical, prior to the development of the railroad, to permit goods movement in quantity over substantial distances. There are strong agglomerative forces in industrial communities which lead to the location of specialized, tool making, and service industries in close juxtaposition with primary manufacturing industries and which bring about the concentration of a work force of highly varied skills. The size of enterprises in particular types of manufacturing will tend to be determined by the economies of scale inherent in the technology of the industry in relation to the costs of reaching a market of the territorial size required to absorb the output. With heavy manufacturing industry, such as steel or automobiles, this scale is frequently very large. Hence economical transport over long distances is essential to its attainment of optimum size in particular urban locations.

The increase of affluence in a nation, however, along with technological development at an increasing rate, brings into the distribution system a much enlarged variety of goods for direct consumption. These goods are often of considerable bulk in relation to weight, of high unit value, and of numerous styles and models. Economies of scale in their manufacture may be much less noteworthy than in heavy industry. The time element in distribution may be of great importance. Hence, whereas the railroad exerted a considerable influence in favor of the concentration of heavy and staple industry because of the low cost of movement it was able to provide, decentralization in relatively small establishments is likely to characterize many of the newer industries which manufacture consumer products. Truck transportation permits rapid distribution in comparatively small lots and frees these manufacturing establishments from conformity to the locational pattern imposed by the railway system. While they may locate in the larger urban areas because of the concentrated markets available there and because such urban areas are hubs for highway distribution, they are not bound to the older centers of industrial concentration but may move quite freely into the less congested peripheral areas.

TRANSPORT AND THE ECONOMY: RECIPROCAL RELATIONS

The relation of transportation to general economic growth was always in a sense reciprocal. Neither could precede the other for any length of time because of the closeness of their mutual dependence. "The rapid growth of the population, the great areas over which it is spread, and the character of its activities have led to a great development of freight (and passenger) transportation. This development has, in turn, made possible the growth of industry and commerce not even remotely approached in any other country."[19] The closeness of the relationships is witnessed by the operation of American businesspeople in carrying forward the enterprises which put our resources to use. Through transportation improvements, the rich agricultural areas of the Middle West, Far West, and Deep South found adequate and profitable markets in the populous Northeast and in the export trades. Abundant ore and petroleum deposits, whatever their location, were made available to American industry at reasonable cost; and large-scale manufacturing was fostered by low transportation cost of supplies and efficient transportation service to all sectors of a national market. This is how "we, as a nation, marched from victory to victory."

The growth process is one of interaction of economic forces. Improvement in transportation stimulates advances in the technology of industry at large, and improvement in industry in turn stimulates advances in transportation facilities and service. The relation between advances in transportation and communication is particularly close. The invention of the telegraph in the 1840s greatly hastened the progress of railroad transportation. It provided a control in the dispatching and movement of trains that was impossible before. Telegraph, telephone, and teletype together provide the nervous system of a modern railroad, keeping all parts functioning smoothly. Radiotelegraph and radiotelephone have enhanced both the safety and the operating efficiency of ocean and Great Lakes transportation. Airlines find the radio indispensable in maintaining contact between the plane and the airport, supplying weather data to the pilot, and navigating under instrument conditions. Conversely, the development of any mode of transportation creates a demand for the extension and improvement of one or more modes of communication. Microwave transmission, the use of communication satellites, and the direct connection of computer installations all found early demand in the transport enterprises.

Every important invention in manufacturing, agriculture, or mining increases the demand for transportation. It was the joint invasion of the railroad and the twine binder that brought about the rapid conquest of the Granger states after the Civil War. The binder multiplied the acreage of grain which could be produced. Migration to the grain-producing states increased very rapidly. The resulting increase in production stimulated rapid expansion of railroads in Illinois, Iowa, Minnesota, and Wisconsin. Similarly, the invention of the Bessemer

---

[19] L. F. Loree, *Railroad Freight Transportation* (New York: D. Appleton & Co., 1922), pp. xiv, xv.

steelmaking process laid the basis of the growth of steel-producing centers with extensive demands for transportation service. The forces of technical advance are freely and vigorously interactive.

Transportation agencies in a large nation become important industries themselves. The construction and maintenance of ways and the manufacture and maintenance of vehicles give rise to many supporting industries. Since the early 1870s much of the iron and steel manufactured has gone into railroad rails, bridges, locomotives, and cars. Since 1920 the motorcar industry has become the largest consumer of metal manufactured in the United States. It was estimated in 1947 that automotive manufacturing generated business for a half-million concerns.[20] Air transport is a leading user of aluminum and lightweight alloys. Therefore, as a consumer, too, transportation does much to influence the growth of industry as a whole.

The importance of transport and communication in providing the facilities for political and social intercourse has made its development vital in shaping the political history of the United States. The improvement in transportation made possible the extension of the frontier and the binding together of the country. Only because of the enhanced means of intercourse was political organization feasible on so vast a scale. Recognition of the national character of trade featured the compromises reached in framing the Constitution, placing the powers to regulate interstate and foreign commerce with the federal government rather than with the several states and thus remedying one of the crowning defects of the weak government under the Articles of Confederation. Internal improvements became a matter of great concern under the new government—it being recognized from the start that the western country could only be developed and retained as a part of the Union by the improvement of communications. The great economic development consequent upon the growth of the railway net was the basis of ever-increasing political prestige. To this may be credited the high position of the United States among the nations of the world in the 19th century and which increased in the 20th century.

The same economic growth gave rise, moreover, to new problems which necessitated a considerable expansion in the scope and importance of government activity. Forced into the regulation of business enterprise, first in the transportation field in 1887, the federal government has proceeded along everwidening paths in the direction and regulation of economic activity. In the process, state and local authority have been more and more curbed as they came into conflict with the national interest, government activity has been centralized and strengthened, and the manifold and expanding activities of government have come to affect intimately the lives of the entire population.

---

[20] *Statistical Abstract of the United States (1958)*, p. 716.

34

The development of the national economic, political, and cultural life has taken a new turn since the advent of the new types of transportation—automotive and air—and the coincident widespread adoption of telephone, radio, and television. Distances have shrunk as never before, both in time and cost; contacts have become closer and more frequent. The automobile has helped ease the isolation of the farmer and given to the people at large a mobility hitherto undreamed of, contributing strongly to the development of greater nationwide homogeneity in thought and experience and breaking down most of the last remnants of narrow local interests. At the same time these new modes of transport have created vast new industries and reshaped the general patterns of our economy.

SELECTED REFERENCES

Barger, Harold. *The Transportation Industries, 1889–1946.* New York: National Bureau of Economic Research, 1946.

Billington, Ray Allen. *Westward Expansion: A History of the American Frontier.* New York: Macmillan Co., 1949.

Brown, Robert T. *Transport and the Economic Integration of South America.* Washington, D.C.: The Brookings Institution, 1966.

Fishlow, Albert. *American Railroads and the Transformation of the Ante-Bellum Economy.* Cambridge: Harvard University Press, 1971.

Fogel, Robert William. *Railroads and American Economic Growth.* Baltimore: The Johns Hopkins University Press, 1964.

Fromm, Gary, ed. *Transport Investment and Economic Development.* Washington, D.C.: The Brookings Institution, 1965.

Gephart, William F. *Transportation and Industrial Development in the Middle West.* New York: Columbia University, 1909.

Gilmore, Harlan W. *Transportation and the Growth of Cities.* Glencoe: The Free Press, 1953.

Hedden, Walter P. *Mission: Port Development.* Washington, D.C.: American Association of Port Authorities, 1967.

Hultgren, Thor. *American Transportation in Prosperity and Depression.* New York: National Bureau of Economic Research, 1948.

Kresge, David T., and Roberts, Paul O. *Systems Analysis and Simulation Models.* Washington, D.C.: The Brookings Institution, 1971.

Lansing, John B. *Transportation and Economic Policy.* New York: The Free Press, 1966.

Owens, Wilfred. *Strategy for Mobility.* Washington, D.C.: The Brookings Institution, 1964.

———. *Distance and Development: Transport and Communications in India.* Washington, D.C.: The Brookings Institution, 1968.

Prest, A. R. *Transport Economics in Developing Countries.* New York: Frederick A. Praeger, Inc., 1969.

Rostow, W. W. *The Stages of Economic Growth*. New York: Cambridge University Press, 1960.

Williamson, Jeffrey G. *Late Nineteenth-Century American Development: A General Equilibrium History*, chap. 9. New York: Cambridge University Press, 1974.

Wilson, George W., et al. *The Impact of Highway Investment on Development*. Washington, D.C.: The Brookings Institution, 1966.

3

Transport and Sociopolitical Development

TRANSPORTATION AND SOCIAL INSTITUTIONS

Cultural institutions including literature, the arts, education, science, and political structures are dependent on improved transport conditions. Civilization has ever appeared where the people were freed from isolation. Transportation, it has been said, is in many ways the "heartbeat of civilization." All social institutions are nourished by exchange of goods and ideas which depend on the free movement of persons. Where these conditions were present, civilization appeared whether along the Yangtze River of China, in the Tigris-Euphrates valley of Babylon, along the Nile with its access to the Mediterranean Sea, in water accessible Greece, or along the Roman Tiber in Italy. Before the age of mechanically powered transportation, waterways provided the best facilities for movement capability. Interior areas of continents away from navigable rivers did not figure in the development of early civilization. We are indebted to water-oriented culture for the foundations of modern law, the cement that holds our society together. Transportation is a central factor in the formation and progress of social organizations, including the size and power attained by nations and independent states.

The preceding chapter analyzed the importance of transportation in economic development and suggested that political development may go hand in hand. Economic aid programs since World War II to less developed countries have been handicapped where social and legal institutions are inadequate and control economic development. Improved transportation over time is required for these institutional developments.

TRANSPORTATION AND DEVELOPMENT OF POLITICAL ORGANIZATION AND POWER

Prior to the development of mechanized transportation in the 19th century, rugged mountainous terrain could dictate a multiplicity of small nations such as those which evolved in the Balkan states and in Central America. Improvements in transportation may result in absorption of smaller states into larger units or lead to conquest and expansion in less developed areas. It is said that improved transportation was a major factor in the breakup of the Greek city states. It made obsolete the small state founded upon the single city and its environs. At the same time it created the conditions favoring larger and more effective political units.[1] A similar fate was faced by the Italian city states in the 13th and 14th centuries and the German city states in the 18th and 19th centuries.

Large and powerful nations whether of ancient or modern times have recognized the need for the development and nurture of transportation for defense, expansion, and control. Power attained by conquest, as Alexander the Great and others learned, when not supported by a system of communications and movement by military and administrative personnel, does not last. Great nations must see that both systems are provided. The classic examples are, in ancient times, Rome and, in modern times, Great Britain and the United States.

Rome not only provided a system of military and administrative communications and control through its magnificent system of roads to all parts of its empire but also developed an adequate commerce to sustain the conquered countries and the home nation. Boats were used to ply the Nile, Rhine, and other rivers, feeding the larger seagoing sailing ships on the Mediterranean and Atlantic. Navigation during the winter and during the six weeks of the etesian winds was practically out of the question. Having no compass, vessles kept within a few miles of the shore, and only on clear nights would a ship attempt to navigate across the Mediterranean by observation of the stars. Nevertheless, the commerce of the empire was such that the West became the great storehouse of raw materials. Lead came from Spain. Gold, silver, and copper came from possessions in western Europe. Tin came from Britain. Clocks, blankets, rugs, tapestries, carpets, pottery, glass vessels, cosmetics, perfumes, ornaments, spices, gums, cotton,

---

[1] R. M. McIver, *The Web of Government* (New York: Macmillan Co., 1947), pp. 164–65.

and Indian steel came from the East.[2] Alexandria was the great manufacturing center. Caravans of camels brought the commerce from
India and other eastern countries through Arabia to Alexandria and
other points of transshipment. Canals were built at the mouth of the
Nile and in the lowlands of northwestern Europe. Even lighthouses
were constructed to aid in the navigation of the Mediterranean.[3]

The breakup of the Roman Empire in the fifth century was followed
by a general disruption of trade and commerce. The great transportation lanes of the Mediterranean were abandoned. Piracy again became widespread. The network of Roman roads was neglected and in
time virtually abandoned. Europe was plunged into a period known as
the Dark Ages which extended for centuries and during which no great
civilization or commercial empire appeared. In the tenth century,
Venice, a city-state, extended its trade to all parts of the Mediterranean
and the west coast of Europe. Venice became the cultural center of
early medieval Europe.

The exploration and extensive trade resulting from the use of the
compass by the 14th century brought a new political and commercial
era. The 19th century saw the advent of mechanical power in transportation greatly increase its economy, adequacy, and speed. New
economic, political, and social forces were thereby set in motion; and a
new order was ushered in. Economic progress and the formation of
vast political states were made possible as a result of this great advance in transportation and of the industrial development which it in
turn made possible. The conditions requisite to the formation and maintenance of a great nation-state or a world empire came into being.

The world empire of Great Britain and the lesser empires of France,
Holland, and other European states were welded together out of territory commanded by the sea power of these nations. Britain's predominance on the sea assured for her greater success in holding together
her farflung possessions. With the world's largest merchant marine at
her command, she established the channels of trade and communication which tied the new areas economically and politically to the British
Isles. Without these vital contacts these areas would have fallen away
from the otherwise tenuous ties of empire. Instead, while seeking
greater independence in home affairs, culminating in dominion status
for most of them, they became thoroughly tied to the mother country as
parts of a social, economic, and political system which was without
parallel in world history. Despite the weakening of political ties in later
years, close commercial relationships persist. Ocean transport, now
supplemented by air transport, surmounts the great water distances

---

[2] M. P. Charlesworth, *Trade Routes and Commerce of the Roman Empire* (Cambridge, Mass.: The University Press, 1924), pp. 230–34.

[3] Ibid., pp. 237–38.

which separate the component countries and channels their trade and other connections through the home islands.

The progress of transportation made possible the rapid political expansion of the continental United States and has been from the start an important factor in the preservation of unity. The National Road was pushed over the Appalachian Mountains to insure the political solidarity of the newly formed states of Ohio and Kentucky with the original 13 states. The advent of rail service across the Alleghenies to the banks of the Ohio was hailed as having great political importance. As one writer puts it: "Already they were talking about the probable exit of the steamboat, and fears of national disintegration were vanishing, the West having at last been bound to the East by a tie that was thought to be permanent and effective."[4] When our union and solidarity were seriously threatened between 1861 and 1865 by the Civil War, the advantage of the North in railroad transportation proved a decisive factor in their preservation. Similarly, the necessity of a satisfactory land connection across the continent to the Pacific seaboard was long recognized as a political as well as a military necessity. The long vessel route around Cape Horn and the tortuous route across the Isthmus of Panama were both too feeble to form effective ties. The danger of the peoples of the Pacific slope seeking political independence, as well as that of foreign intrusion by Great Britain or Russia, was obvious. First the telegraph and then the railways to the Pacific, fostered by liberal government aid, were thrown into the struggle to preserve the continental United States as a political unit.

Events of the same sort, though even more clearly recognized, were afoot in Canada. There the Intercolonial Railway was undertaken as a government enterprise to tie in the Maritime Provinces with Upper and Lower Canada, the economic heart of the present nation. Serious physical and ethnic barriers divided them from one another, and a marked tendency to separatism developed. The railroad was brought into being to establish unity.[5] Back of the British North America Act (1867) was a similar effort to include the western provinces within the Dominion established by that organic act. To preserve British Columbia as a part of the united Canada, and particularly to prevent its absorption into the United States, it was agreed that the Dominion government would undertake to construct a transcontinental railroad.[6] Thus the Canadian Pacific was born.

Today the large colonial empires have disappeared. The giants in

[4] C. H. Ambler, A History of Transportation in the Ohio Valley (Glendale, Calif.: Arthur H. Clark Co., 1932), p. 185.

[5] See Sanford Fleming, The Intercolonial—A Historical Sketch (Montreal: Dawson Brothers, 1876), chaps. 1–5.

[6] Harold A. Innis, A History of the Canadian Pacific Railway (London: P. S. King & Son, Ltd., 1923), pp. 68–90.

world political power are the United States and the Soviet Union. They exercise substantial control beyond their borders. Naval strength, air power, electronic communications systems, and space navigation are all brought into play in the maintenance of their respective spheres of influence and control. In terms of commerce, fleet development, international air facilities and communications, the United States dwarfs those of its only rival. Thousands of overseas bases are served constantly by the military air and sea commands. Not even Rome or Great Britain ever attempted to sustain such far-flung commitments. Yet, on the oceans, the growing naval and merchant fleets of the USSR are increasingly viewed as threats while the dependence of the United States on imported oil and other essential materials for its industrial and transport requirements constitutes an unprecedented weakness.

GOVERNMENT AND TRANSPORTATION

Because of the vital role of transportation in the economic, political, and social life of a country, governments, national and local, have participated vigorously in the planning, programming, and support of transportation. Rarely is transportation left entirely to private enterprise in a free competitive market. Ancient Carthage, in addition to its natural harbor in the Lake of Tunis, had two landlocked basins which the city-state had constructed. One of these, rectangular in shape, was used for commerce; and an inner and second one, circular in shape, was used to accommodate naval craft. A small island in the center of this circle was dominated by a town in which was stationed the admiral who controlled operations of the entire basin area.[7] To this day government aid to ocean shipping has been an almost universal practice. The federal government of the United States dredges and maintains deep water channels, provides navigation aids, subsidizes ship construction and operation, extends tax relief and loan benefits, and grants cargo preference to American flag shipping. A few nations own whole or part of their steamship lines.

Except for the United States and part of the Canadian system, government ownership of railroads has prevailed. We have resorted to elaborate regulation in lieu of ownership of railroads to protect the public interest. Highways are normally provided by national and local governments. In air transportation, government aid, national and local, is significant in all countries in the building of airways, airports, and in the control of operations. Government ownership of overseas, intercontinental airlines prevails except in the United States.

---

[7] Reginald Bosworth Smith, *Carthage and the Carthaginians* (New York: Longmans, Green & Co., 1913), pp. 353–55.

The purposes of government aid to transportation are reflected in the laws of the United States which provide for subsidies and aid to water, highway, and air transportation to promote commerce, the postal service, and national defense. Transportation even in capitalistic countries is a mixture of private and public enterprise. A later chapter analyzes public aid to transportation and its impact in the United States.

TRANSPORTATION AND THE SOCIOECONOMIC PATTERN

In the location of cities and towns and in the general distribution of population, transportation is of major importance. Some cities of ancient and medieval origin owe their location to the fact that they were or are religious centers. Others were first forts which were strategically located for the defense of the ancient feudal state. Economic factors, however, are always present and are usually dominant. Population in general tends to concentrate in those regions of the world which have rich and accessible natural resources. Cities and towns spring up along the valleys and other favorable natural commercial routes. When valuable resource areas are separated by mountain barriers, passes are sought out for travel and trade routes. The mountain passes of central Asia have always exercised a controlling influence on inland commerce. Likewise the general pattern of commercial routes in Europe and the United States has been determined by the location of the more important mountain passes and river valleys.

Cities and towns appear and develop at points convenient for manufacturing and trade. Natural harbors along the seaboard have been favored locations, since navigable streams and valleys afford access to the interior and commerce can be conducted readily by ship up and down the coast and with foreign lands. Inland cities may be located at inland river or lake ports or at other points which are convenient centers of land transportation.

Commercial centers spring up where transfer of goods is required. The transfer at ports, for example, is between land and air carriers and inland watercraft, on one hand, and ocean, lake, or other watercraft, on the other. To realize the economy of large, modern facilities of transportation, goods or persons must be assembled at a convenient point by means of smaller and in some instances cruder forms of transportation. The bulk movement then takes place between the main commercial centers, which are called primary markets, and the tendency of transportation is to connect these centers directly insofar as topography of the region will permit. From these main centers the routes radiate to subcenters and from them to sub-subcenters. A study of the transport routes in this country will show that our transportation follows the plan only in general outline. There are many deviations from direct routes because of the necessity of using river valleys and mountain passes and because a newer form of transport finds it profitable to establish routes to serve the cities and towns developed by an older form which were themselves influenced in turn by these same physical features.

It is evident that the distribution of resources, topography, and the development of commerce and transportation are interdependent and complementary in explaining the distribution of population. Each of the 13 American colonies began as a settlement on a natural harbor on the seaboard or at the head of tidewater navigation. Following river courses, commercial, agricultural, forest, and mining activities were carried inland and population spread. Via the few passes through the Appalachian Mountains, settlers established themselves along Lakes Ontario and Erie and on the Ohio River and its important tributaries because they were then dependent on water transport. The changing picture of population distribution in this country during the entire period of settlement and commercial expansion reflects the great importance of transportation in determining the direction and speed of population shifts.[8] With the passing of the frontier the nation entered a period of industrialization and urbanization. Urbanization of modern industrial society grows out of the economic division of labor and specialization which transportation improvement makes possible. The development of the railroads and water carriers served in this way to influence the location of great industrial centers.

TRANSPORTATION AND THE COMMUNITY PATTERN

Transportation not only largely influences the national economic pattern but it also influences the physical growth pattern of the local community which evolves in order to conduct its economic and social functions.

The relative economic importance of cities may change as new modes of transport develop. Before the days of the railroad, Charleston, South Carolina, and not Atlanta was the leading commercial city of the South Atlantic states. Atlanta, located just south of the higher Appalachian range, later became the great railroad center of the Southeast and the leading commercial center in the whole area. The

---

[8] The controlling influence of transportation is apparent also in the local sense. The direction and speed of city growth depend on improvements and extensions of local transport facilities. The improvements of rapid-transit and motor-highway transportation have made this shift to suburban and country districts possible. Since 1940 the census shows a decline in population in many of our large cities but an increase in the population of the county or counties surrounding the city.

family automobile and good roads have caused local towns to lose economic and social functions to the larger town or city in the area. The location of towns is not solely controlled by the intersection or transfer point of major transport routes. There must be adequate sources of supply of food, fuel, and building materials in such proximity as can be made available by existing transportation. The city in turn is required to provide the services for the area which supplies the necessities.[9] How large a city will grow depends on the availability of supplies which can be economically transported to the city and on the economic surplus which can be produced and transported to market. These principles apply whether the economic sphere of a city is local, national, or worldwide. The extent of a city and its market will depend upon the technical state of both production and transportation invention.[10] Rapid advance in both explains why the potential dimensions of cities have grown rapidly during the industrial age.

The development of urban transportation has changed both the size and pattern of the typical urban centers of America. The city pattern, according to Ogburn, has shifted from a congested globular or clam shape to a spokes-of-a-wheel design and then to a more recent starfish pattern, as shown in Figure 3-1.[11] Before streetcars, towns were compact with multiple-story buildings built adjacent to narrow streets. This was for the convenience of workers and shoppers, most of whom walked to work or shop. Early historic Philadelphia before the streetcars (horse or electric) was a compact, globular-shaped town some 20 blocks in either direction between the Schuylkill and Delaware rivers.

Intensive streetcar transit development allowed the congested area to be multiplied and to take on a fan-shaped design as shown in the shaded area of Figure 3-2A. However, the degree of congestion was reduced as the city extended. Some workers could live in the nearby suburbs because as shown in Figure 3-2A local railroads developed commuter service and the electric streetcar lines extended beyond the city proper to the satellite towns. As population and business developed along these rail lines, the "spokes-of-a-wheel" population distribution came into being, as shown in Figure 3-2B. The clusters about the main transportation routes, railroad suburban transit and highways, resulted in the starfish pattern illustrated by Figures 3-2A and 3-2B. Then came the automobile. The typical metropolitan pattern today (located on a main highway route) shows the growth of important

---

[9] Walter Cristaller, *Die Zeutrahen Orte in Suddenlschland* (1935), referred to in P. K. Hatt and A. J. Rees, Jr., *Reader in Urban Sociology* (Glencoe: The Free Press, 1951), pp. 124–25.

[10] Harlan W. Gilmore, *Transportation and the Growth of Cities* (Glencoe: The Free Press, 1953), p. 3.

[11] W. F. Ogburn, "Development of Local Transportation and the Pattern of Cities," in Hatt and Rees, *Reader in Urban Sociology*, pp. 239–67.

FIGURE 3-1
Illustration of Ogburn's City Patterns

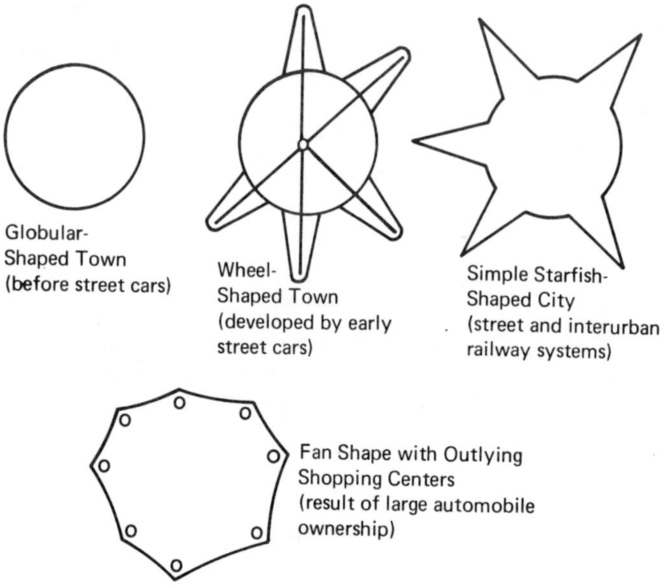

Globular-
Shaped Town
(before street cars)

Wheel-
Shaped Town
(developed by early
street cars)

Simple Starfish-
Shaped City
(street and interurban
railway systems)

Fan Shape with Outlying
Shopping Centers
(result of large automobile
ownership)

business subcenters equipped with supermarkets, department stores, and many professional services. The starfish design in this last phase has a large "eye" in each of its radial areas (see Figure 3-1). The segments of the star become ever wider, the whole approximating a fan shape because motor transport has made it possible to fill in the intervening areas.

The economic and social pattern of a city is affected by where the basic functions are performed. The economic areas are the downtown commercial center, the wholesaling and transport terminal areas, the industrial areas, and the residential areas. Offices for business services and professional specialists tend to be in the downtown commercial area as are the large hotels, theaters, and nightclubs. Schools, local movie theaters, churches, food stores, and family doctors tend to be widely distributed among residential areas.

Improved local transportation by rail and later by automobile made possible large cities in which the dominance of downtown city areas in merchandising, finance, professional services, and entertainment was established. However, in recent years car ownership has become so extensive that the reverse trend of decentralization has set in. The problem of street traffic in downtown areas has become increasingly serious. Hence, shopping centers with supermarkets have developed in outlying areas of suburbs and cities to serve the widespread population of metropolitan areas. As we shall note later in this chapter, a regional metropolis of interconnected urban clusters may be the design target of the future.

In spite of extensive construction of freeways and outlying shopping centers, the problem of urban transportation is increasingly serious. The logistics of a city requires efficient unobstructed flow of goods and persons if its economic and social life are to remain healthy. The problem of urban logistics faced by cities is analyzed in Chapter 7.

TRANSPORTATION IN MODERN SOCIETY

Continental United States is a vast area but it is a closely knit political and social unit. Transport facilities aid the administration of justice and the preservation of law and order in city, county, state, and nation. The automobile and, recently, hijacked aircraft, unfortunately, have often been used by criminals to escape justice. Nevertheless, all the functions of government including the maintenance of our defense are in many ways furthered by our modern transportation facilities. Candidates can readily contact voters, legislators can devote more time at the state or national capitol and less time going back and forth to their constituencies, and administrators are able to be more efficient. Police are aided by modern transportation and communication in the apprehension of criminals, and military forces can be dispatched more effectively to quell riots or to meet enemy forces.

Our religious, educational, and social life have greatly benefited from transportation improvement. People on farms are no longer isolated. On improved highways they have ready access not only to nearby towns but also to distant cities. The one-room rural school has given way to the consolidated graded school which provides superior educational and social advantages to rural youth. Busing has often been the means by which racial integration has been promoted in school systems. Standards of housing, clothing, and food are improved by cheaper and faster transport service. Recreational and cultural opportunities are multiplied; rural and city dwellers come to have much in common. Modern highways and motorcars enable those living in rural areas frequently to enjoy the benefits of the commercial, cultural, and entertainment life of the city and similarly make it easy for those living in the city regularly to enjoy mountains, beaches, and rural life in general. The whole scope and tempo of life of the community is increased by every significant advance in transportation.

TRANSPORTATION AND MODERN SOCIAL PROBLEMS

Prior to the last three or four decades the effect of advancing transportation technology on our social life appeared to be entirely positive.

46

FIGURE 3-2
Population Pattern of Metropolitan Philadelphia Compared with Pattern of Transportation
Lines (maps prepared by Philadelphia City Planning Commission)

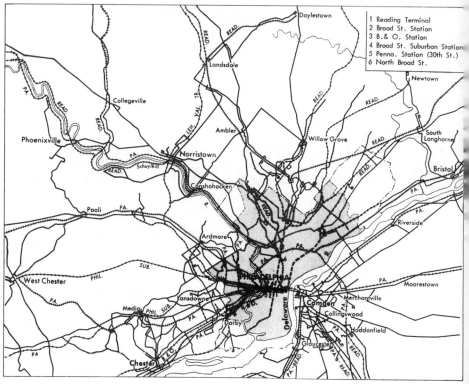

A. Transportation Lines

However, in recent years the problems of the small remote crossroad communities and of the metropolitan areas have increased.

Small local industries and merchants are less able to compete and survive. Branch-line railroad passenger and freight service has largely disappeared, and bus and truck lines with their modern large equipment are increasingly reluctant to leave the throughways and major highways to serve a very small crossroads community located on an out-of-the-way secondary road. So these communities are not as well served as they once were. The rural resident still has his local church and consolidated school not far away, but he must go to the city for much of his material needs.

It is in the urban areas, especially in the larger cities, that the interaction of transportation and social problems is most acute. In the words of Wilfred Owen, "urbanization and motorization have become increasingly incompatible."[12] Here the increase in population, growth

---

[12] Wilfred Owen, The Accessible City (Washington, D.C.: The Brookings Institution, 1972), p. 1.

GURE 3-2 *(continued)*

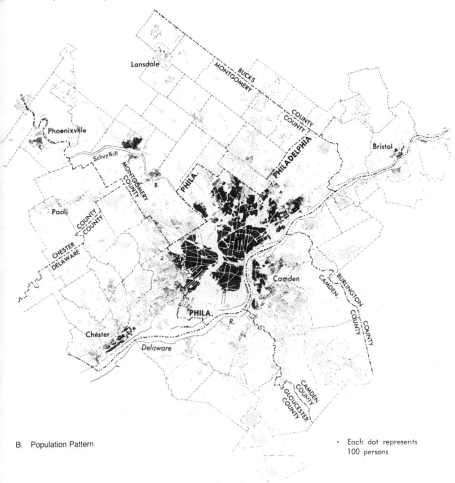

B. Population Pattern

· Each dot represents
100 persons

of motor transportation, and inadequate design of urban structure
have combined to bring about congestion and pollution, creating a
threat to the preservation of the midcity's functions. Historically, the
proximity provided by concentration in cities was designed to facilitate
economic and social interaction between separated social and commercial elements. The motor vehicle for two or three decades appeared to provide a new level of interaction and mobility, but now in
all major cities it has become a constraint and a threat to the safety,
health, convenience, and well-being of their inhabitants. Street congestion, especially at peak traffic hours, has reduced mobility to a
fraction of what it was. This has brought a revolution in the distribution
of urban population and employment. Aided by freeways, the
well-to-do white population has largely moved out of the city to the

suburbs and industries have moved out to new locations away from the midcity area. Merchandising institutions have shifted to new outlying shopping centers. The result has been the creation of midcity ghettos, where conditions of health, education, recreation areas, and transportation to and from work have gone from bad to worse.

City and urban transport planners hope to bring about revamped transportation conditions to alleviate the situation. Aided by the federal government, modern rapid-transit systems are being promoted and planned in metropolitan areas. Throughways that permit through traffic to pass over congested areas have helped. However, many freeways have not been an unmixed blessing. They encourage more automobiles to enter the midcity areas. Again they seem to become a new area of congestion in a few short years after completion. Worst of all they destroy homesites of midcity dwellers and often isolate them from schools, churches, and markets. Many dead-end streets make for decreased access of all public services, including fire equipment. They have not contributed toward the solution of the major problem of the midcity ghetto worker in getting to 'and from the new locations of employment opportunities. Beltways have been useful in slowing down radial extension of employment centers, but they are far from the present ghetto areas.

After an analysis of the problem, Wilfred Owen offered these conclusions among others: First, transportation can be effective in the solution of the urban problem if it is an integral part of overall city planning. Second, there will in many instances have to be a redesigning of the downtown street areas allowing for open space and balanced land use. Third, metropolitan areas could be designed on a regional basis with interconnected urban clusters surrounded by low-density areas. Regional systems of transit, sewerage treatment, waterworks, and electric service would be required in place of the present systems administered by smaller political units.

TRANSPORTATION: IMPROVEMENT AND INTERNATIONAL AFFAIRS

As improved transportation overcomes distance and physical barriers between nations, trade and cultural contacts increase. In time, New York is closer to Tokyo and much closer to Moscow than it was to Philadelphia when there were 13 states in the United States. This shrinking of the world, hastened by recent developments of commercial and military aviation, increases the opportunity and the necessity of cooperation among nations in commercial, political, and cultural matters. Unfortunately national governments frequently impose discriminatory restrictions on international transportation growing out of a desire to aid their nations in the competition of national air and ship lines or out of a desire to use it as a means of trade protection. These restrictions may relate to entry of foreign flag airlines or to transfer and entrance dues against foreign-flag steamship lines. Reciprocal bilateral arrangements prevail in respect to entry of foreign flag airlines and in some nations to cargo preference in steamship service. More serious is the closing of efficient trade routes because of international political and military conflicts. World trade has several times suffered from the closing of the Suez Canal since it adds over 5,000 miles to the shipping routes between Europe and most of Asia. It is to be hoped that the result of greater proximity will be a more united world neighborhood and not a divided one with two or three rival economic and political systems. The problem of peaceful relations which today confronts the United Nations Organization is an example of how man's genius in technical matters may run ahead of his genius in social accommodation through institutional adjustment.

SELECTED REFERENCES

Ambler, C. H. *A History of Transportation in the Ohio Valley.* Glendale, Calif.: Arthur H. Clark Co., 1932.

Bonavia, M. R. *The Economics of Transport,* chap. 1. London: Nisbet & Co., Ltd., 1942.

Catanese, Anthony James. *Structural and Socio-Economic Factors in Communities.* Athens: Georgia Institute of Technology, 1970.

Charles River Associates, Inc. *Evaluation of Transit Service.* Cambridge, Mass.: 1968.

Charlesworth, M. P. *Trade Routes and Commerce of the Roman Empire.* Cambridge: The University Press, 1924.

Cooley, C. H. *The Theory of Transportation from the Standpoint of Sociological Theory and Research.* Baltimore: American Economic Association, 1894.

Cornehls, James V., and Taebel, Delbert A. *The Political Economy of Urban Transportation,* chap. 2. Port Washington, N.Y.: Kennikat Press, 1977.

Dodson, E. *Employment Accessibility for Special Urban Groups.* Washington, D.C., 1970. Prepared for Housing and Urban Development Department.

Fleming, Sanford. *The Intercolonial–A Historical Sketch,* chaps. 1–5. Montreal: Dawson Brothers, 1876.

Gilmore, Harlan W. *Transportation and the Growth of Cities.* Glencoe: The Free Press, 1953.

Herring, Frank. *Components of Urban Travel.* New York: Port of New York Authority, 1967.

Owen, Wilfred. *The Accessible City.* Washington, D.C.: The Brookings Institution, 1972.

————. *The Transportation Dilemma of Greater Metropolitan Areas.* Washington, D.C.: The Brookings Institution, 1962.

Riley, J. Philip. "Effect of Expressways on Urban Neighborhoods," In the Ohio State University, *Transportation Problems in Urban Areas*, pp. 57–64. Columbus, Ohio; 1959.

U.S. Department of Transportation. *Economic and Social Effects of Highways.* Washington, D.C.: Federal Housing Administration, 1972.

4

Systems of Goods Movement: Economics of Business Logistics

Transportation is not an economic function that stands apart from others. Instead it is a connective among the several steps which result in the conversion of resources into useful goods in the name of the ultimate consumer. Traditionally these steps involved separate companies for production, storage, transportation, wholesaling, and retail sale. Production or manufacturing plants required the assembly of materials, components, and supplies, with or without storage; processing and materials handling within the plant; and plant inventory. Warehousing services between plant and marketing outlets involved separate companies as did transportation. Merchandising establishments completed the chain with delivery to the consumer. The manufacturer limited himself to the production of goods, leaving marketing and distribution to other firms. It is the planning of all these functions and subfunctions into a system of goods movement in order to minimize cost and maximize service to the customers that constitutes the concept of business logistics. The system, once put in place, must be effectively managed.

The principal developments in management preceding this recognition of logistics as a distinct function were: (1) improvement of production-management efficiency by synchronizing the functions of purchasing, processing, and inventory systems for purposes of quantity and quality control and (2) integration of the manufacturer toward the market by assuming functions hitherto performed by the wholesaler and jobber. The first is the essence of scientific management which flowered by the second decade of the 20th century. The second reflected the growing proliferation of product lines and the diversification of manufacturing firms which got underway soon after, generated increased complexity in the marketing function, and required a degree of control not available with earlier methods of distribution.[1]

In consequence of these developments the functions of the shipping clerk became transformed into those of the traffic manager. As markets expanded, transportation alternatives multiplied and transport regulation became more complex and comprehensive; the need for specialists to plan and buy transportation services was recognized. In many instances the operation of private trucks or watercraft was added to the roster of traffic-management functions.

Nevertheless, many multiplant firms like General Foods, General Mills, and the large appliance manufacturers found that expert buying of transportation alone could not assure optimum product delivery to customers. Integration with other operations, especially the warehousing of inventory, was required. Distribution management was seen as the road to lower delivery costs and improved service. Hence order processing, transportation, warehousing, inventory control, and delivery scheduling were integrated into a distribution system.

We are indebted to the military for the definition and application of the logistics concept. It was developed notably in World War II. Packaging, materials handling, and storage along with transportation were synchronized into a control system to assure and expedite final delivery. In business logistics we are similarly concerned with control of both total time and cost in respect to all goods movement or flow. Therefore logistics applies to all handling and movement applicable to procurement and production as well as to distribution of finished product. Design of an optimum logistics system involves consideration of the location of processing plants, of warehouses, and of market outlets as well as the methods of operation to be employed. Such complex systems design has been made possible by recent developments in data processing capability and in the techniques of systems analysis. Logistics has taken its place as a major function of business along with finance, production, and marketing.

OBJECTIVES OF A LOGISTICS SYSTEM

The end product of a logistics system is availability of the items contained in a firm's product line at the point of sale for the firm (retail or dealer outlet, or wholesaler carrying stocks). This availability is not

---

[1] On these developments see Alfred D. Chandler, Jr., *The Visible Hand: The Managerial Revolution in American Business* (Cambridge: Harvard University Press, 1977), chaps. 7 and 9.

absolute in the sense of ability to make instant delivery of any item in the product line, for that is impossible to attain. Indeed the level of service to be accorded at the delivery end of a logistics system is a parameter to be supplied by management in the light of competitive circumstances and market objectives. The higher the standard in respect to speed and reliability of delivery to customers, the more costly the distribution phase of the system will become.[2] Hence the advantages of improved service must be weighed against the accompanying increase of cost with a view to determine whether profit will increase as a result.

Given a service standard, the objective in planning and managing the logistics system is to meet that standard at the lowest total cost or, to put it more positively, at maximum profit to the firm. This is not accomplished simply by minimizing the costs encountered in the logistics function itself for, as will be shown, there are important interrelations among production, logistics, and marketing that affect total cost delivered to the customer. An increase of production cost may be offset by a greater reduction in logistics cost. Or profit improvement may follow from an increase of sales at margins which exceed the added logistics costs incurred. Effective physical distribution, indeed, is a competitive tool which can be employed to enlarge market areas and to improve market share.

Figure 4-1 shows distribution channels as employed in a marketing plan. These are the chains of enterprises used in reaching the ultimate customer. They may not typify the actual flow of goods. Figure 4-2 traces actual goods flows in a logistics system.

The logistics function must be managed in conjunction with the other functions of the business in a way calculated to increase profit. Unless the various tasks involved in goods handling are conceived as a system, they cannot be managed in that way. Cost minimizing standards applied to particular goods handling tasks may as readily reduce as increase profit. Our concern in this chapter will be with the elements of distribution systems and their interrelationships. The management of such systems will be discussed in Chapter 18. Many of the functions embraced within logistics systems are highly complex, including especially the transportation function which requires selection among the many modes of transport as well as cognizance of the impact of government regulation. The management of distribution is better understood, accordingly, after some of these complexities have been reviewed.

---

[2] Such a standard might call for ability to deliver to any customer within 72 hours from receipt of the order with 95 percent reliability and, in addition, with stock-outs occurring in not more than 5 percent of the instances.

54

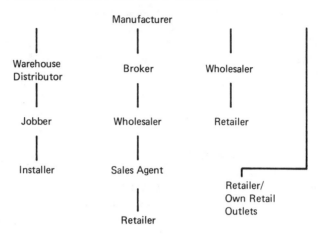

Typical Distribution Channels (marketing)

ELEMENTS OF A MOVEMENT AND DISTRIBUTION SYSTEM

Line-haul transportation from one load center to another achieves
economy by the assembly of goods volumes into large-scale units for
concentrated movement. The technology of the form of transport employed and the characteristics of the route over which the movement is
to take place determine the size of unit which is most economical for the
line-haul. It is often true that these most economical units of movement
are not realized in practice because adequate volume cannot be concentrated within allowable time limits. Motor and air transport have
the smallest units of line-haul movement—the rig (tractor and semitrailer or double bottom) and the aircraft. Rail movements are by the
trainload, and water movements by the vessel load or tow of barges.
Both trains and barge tows of 40,000 tons and more have been operated, although the usual units are considerably smaller. Although the
pipeline has a steady flow, minimum tenders (the minimum quantity
which must be tendered as a single batch, e.g. 10,000 barrels) are
necessary where different products are to be batched through the line
in order to avoid such intermixture of products as would alter their
specifications.

Concentration into economical line-haul units can be performed
either by the shipper or by the carrier. Commonly each performs a part
of the process. The division of the work of concentration between the
two will affect the incidence of the costs which fall upon each and the
level of the charges which the shipper pays and the carrier collects.

The railroad affords a good example of the division of concentration
functions between shipper and carrier. Since railroads have virtually
abandoned the handling of less-than-carload business except through

FIGURE 4-2
A Simple Logistics System

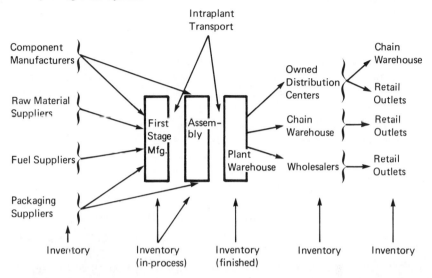

piggyback services, the shipper must usually tender goods in carload quantities. The railroad then switches the car to a yard where it can be incorporated, along with others gathered from many shippers, into a train of perhaps 100 or more cars for the line-haul movement. To an increasing extent railroads offer reduced rates for multiple-car shipments or even full trainloads tendered by shippers within a single 24-hour period. Such rates are useful particularly in the movement of bulk and staple commodities which at least some shippers can assemble in the requisite quantities.

In using rail carload or multiple-car services, shippers singly, or through shippers' cooperative associations, hold goods long enough to forward the required quantities, assemble and load the goods, and unload at the other end of the haul. They may use truckload services in similar fashion, but quite frequently face a lower truckload minimum weight than the published carload minimum weights and a higher freight rate. Straight carloads or truckloads composed of a single commodity for which the rate can be precisely tailored mark a great deal of the movement from producers' premises to break-bulk points from which goods can be channeled to customers in the market area. For in the trade in finished consumers' goods it is rare for retailers, or even wholesalers and chains, to be prepared to accept goods in straight carloads. Hence the manufacturer who utilizes low-cost line-haul transportation as the first step in movement toward a customer must be prepared to disperse these units of movement at a point that is central to a market area.

For this purpose owned or leased warehouse facilities are used, or the services of public warehouses are secured, at strategic points where customers can be quickly reached with smaller units of product. These are often known as distribution centers (see Figure 4–3). One of their major purposes is to stand along the channel of movement toward customers where they can receive goods in quantities that permit economical line-haul movement and manipulate the goods into consignments of the size and mix that customers are prepared to buy and receive. In performing this process they will hold inventory, since the sale of a straight carload of a single product in a given market may take many days. In addition there may be short-period fluctuations in buying that are not easily taken care of through adjusting the inbound flow of goods, since this is governed by relatively large indivisible minimum quantities. Hence stock will be held to enable a fluctuating demand to be satisfied in the face of a relatively constant inbound movement.

To complete the process of distribution by actually placing goods on the customers' receiving docks, outbound transportation will be employed that is adjusted to the individual customer's desires and practices. Chain-store warehouses, large dealers, and some few large retailers may be prepared to accept mixed carloads or truckloads of a company's products, thus avoiding the higher costs of smaller shipments. This presupposes a broad product line on the part of the manufacturer, all of which is stocked in his distribution centers, and some storage capacity at the customers' premises.

More often, distribution to customers is made in lots smaller than the unit of transportation, characteristically in less-than-truckload lots. This

FIGURE 4–3
Multiple-Plant Distribution

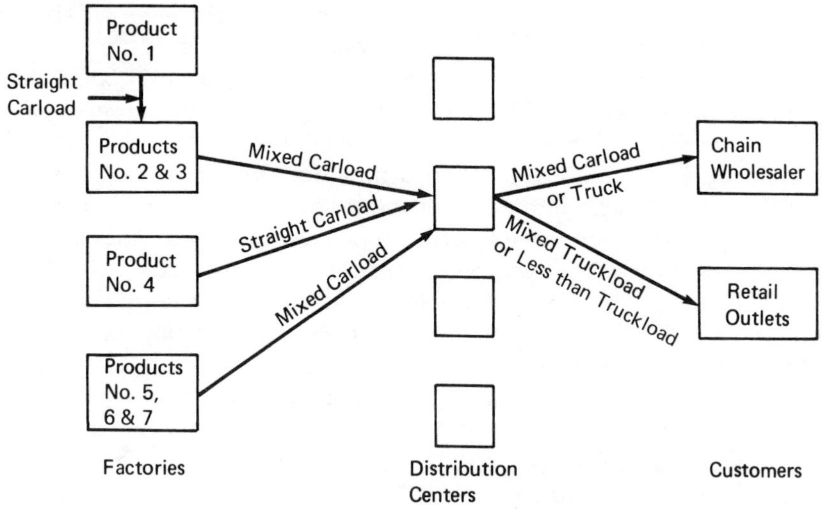

is relatively expensive transportation and becomes the more so the smaller the orders. Motor carriers commonly provide lower rates at certain weight breaks—say at 6,000 pounds, 10,000 pounds, 12,000 pounds, and so on—and assess minimum charges on very small shipments which may make the per-pound cost very high indeed. Manifestly the numbers and location of distribution centers must be determined not only with a view to being close enough to customers to meet delivery-time standards but also with consideration of the costs for transport which develop if small shipments must be moved over long distances.

In many lines of trade, private truck transportation owned or controlled by the shipper is a virtual necessity out of distribution centers. This will sometimes occur because the available common carrier less-than-truckload services are not sufficiently reliable. But it is also a feature of distribution of those products where the manufacturer takes on responsibility for maintaining the shelf stock in retail outlets. In such circumstances the truck driver or another person accompanying the vehicle will check the stock and make replacements.

TRADE-OFFS IN DISTRIBUTION SYSTEMS

The processes just briefly reviewed involve a number of cost-generating elements; namely: (1) stock at the end of the production line as straight carloads or truckloads of individual products are being accumulated, (2) stock in transit while line-haul service is being generated by the rail or motor carriers, (3) line-haul transportation charges, (4) vehicle loading-and-unloading costs, (5) materials handling costs between inbound cars or trucks and stock locations in the distribution center, (6) order processing costs, (7) order picking costs as products are pulled out of stock to fill customers' orders, (8) inventory carrying costs on warehouse stock, (9) outbound vehicle loading costs, and (10) transport costs from warehouse to customer. These costs are closely related to one another in the sense that a reduction of one may well generate increases in others. Hence it is necessary to look at the whole series of functions and to seek the lowest total distribution cost that will provide the standard of service to customers that has been determined to be necessary.

The principal trade-off is between the cost of carrying inventory and the cost of transportation. For example, nationwide distribution from a single manufacturing location with acceptable standards of customer service is no longer an impossibility. But in most situations it will require movement from the factory to the majority of customers in less than vehicle-load quantities. Thus less-than-truckload rates will have to be paid on distances up to about 1,000 miles. Beyond that distance it will be necessary to use the services of air cargo in order to accomplish sufficiently speedy delivery to meet competitive marketing require-ments. With few exceptions the air cargo rates are, at present, mate-rially higher than less-than-truckload rates. The added transport cost resulting from a sacrifice of the ability to move in carload or truckload service and from the necessity to use "premium" transport service on the longer hauls is, however, at least partially offset by the reduction or elimination of other elements of distribution cost.

The aggregate volume of standing inventory required is generally reduced as the number of points at which inventory is held diminishes. Minimum inventory is required where, as here, it is concentrated at a single location—the factory. Inventory carrying costs are, accordingly, at a minimum by comparison with any other possible system. Since field warehouses are entirely eliminated, so also are the costs of put-ting stock into warehouses and moving it out again. Under some cir-cumstances, at present limited to high unit-value manufactured goods, the warehouse and inventory carrying-cost savings may offset the high transportation costs. There are, however, numerous possible ar-rangements for warehouse distribution, one of which might generate lower total distribution costs in a given situation.

In a very real sense the art of devising an efficient distribution sys-tem that will come close to achieving minimum total distribution costs over its life-span is the art of determining the number, size, and loca-tion of distribution centers to be employed. It thus turns on the question of whether and in what quantities inventories are to be held. These aspects of the problem will be touched upon in Chapter 14. Once the system of distribution points is determined, the careful control of in-ventory level and composition of each is essential to the efficient oper-ation of the system. Market conditions will, of course, change. Sales in some territories will grow faster than sales in others. Some market areas may experience an actual decline in sales. These developments over a period of time equivalent to the life of distribution center facilities cannot be forecast with a desirable degree of accuracy; hence flexibility in the system is of great advantage. In general, the fewer the distribution centers and the larger the territory each can effectively serve, the less the risk that a center will be made obsolete by changes in the territorial pattern of sales.

The characteristic approach to the market of manufacturers of con-sumers goods is the provision of a broad product line. This means a larger number, perhaps thousands, of different items to be transported and held in inventory. The problem is further complicated by dif-ferences in consumer package size (for example, soap powders and detergents) and by differences in size, design, and color (for example, refrigerators). In any time period some items in the line will move in large volume while others sell at a slower pace. To be unable to de-liver fast-moving items to customers promptly will generally be more fatal to sales volume and market position in relation to competitors than a similar inability in respect to slow-moving items. Yet the significance of an out-of-stock situation for any item at the distribution center will depend a great deal on what kind of service customers can expect from competitors.

Inventory control systems are designed to insure the maintenance of stock levels and composition at all points in the system that will insure the quality of service to customers that has been determined to be desirable. They must cope with fluctuating demand for each item stocked, with varying unit values of items held in stock, with different levels of inbound transportation cost depending upon the type of transport and the size of the order placed with the factory, and with variations in transit time between the factory and the warehouse. The object is a system that will provide the standard of customer service desired at lowest total cost. Inward transportation in large lots on a slow and unreliable basis will necessitate higher inventory levels because reorders from the factory will be relatively infrequent and the stock level will need to be adequate not only to protect against unanticipated fluctuations of demand but also against unpredictable arrival of shipments.

DISTRIBUTION AND PRODUCTION SCHEDULING

Although for some products and in some industries production is on a job-shop basis with the output produced in response to orders on hand, the more characteristic situation is production for stock against predicted or hoped-for sales at multiple outlets accessible to customers. While some products can be manufactured endlessly against continuing demand, in the more usual situation production lines will manufacture one product, size, style, or model until a desired stock level has been generated and will then be shifted to production of another item in the line. Downtime is inevitable while the machinery is being adjusted for the next product that is to come off the line. But downtime is expensive as it involves idle machinery and, perchance, idle labor as well. The adjustment itself generates setup costs. Further adjustment may be required after the line is started on the new item, and full production efficiency may not be obtained immediately.

Manifestly unit manufacturing costs increase the more often the line is changed to shift from one product to another. Production management, therefore, prefers long production runs on each product and the smallest possible number of products in the line. Thus manufacturing unit cost is minimized; and this is a ready measure by which the efficiency of production management may be judged—indeed, often is judged.

By contrast, sales and marketing personnel recognize that sales volume and competitive market position may be strengthened by enlarging the product line, multiplying models, styles, and other variations. They may insist upon variety well beyond the point at which increased sales volume can cover the added cost of manufacture. Distribution personnel, like production people, find multiplicity of products expensive in respect to inventory levels and cost of carrying them, assembly of customers' orders, and transport costs. On the other hand they know that long production runs of particular products will necessitate large inventories that will require much time to work off. The problem of handling, storing, protecting, and accounting for inventory beyond the manufacturing plant in the chain of distribution falls upon them, not upon the production or marketing people. Finally they know that the risk of product obsolescence grows with the length of time inventory must be held in order to work off stock against demand. Hence logistics management will seek a product policy different both from that of the production manager and that of the marketing manager.

Such differences among major departments obviously require policy determination at the corporate general management level. Yet the major departments will not receive adequate direction if each department is judged by standards confined to its own function and the relationships are not perceived and subjected to comprehensive analysis. The route of maximum profit will almost certainly compromise these views, incorporating some shortening of the product line as well as of production runs. The trade-offs must be recognized—increased downtime and setup cost in return for reduced inventory costs (including product obsolescence) and the sacrifice of some sales volume in order to preserve margins by holding manufacturing and distribution costs in check. This is a difficult process requiring change of attitudes, reform of information systems, and often changes in organization as well. It is a process that has gone farther in some industries and firms than in others. Some of the management aspects will be noticed in Chapter 18.

A properly engineered distribution system will, thus, be closely coordinated with production scheduling. The demand for production is generated by forecast sales, rate of disappearance from stock, and stock levels. Changes in sales volume and sales expectation must be translated quickly into changes in production schedules lest inventories become excessive or, in the case of expanding sales, too small to protect against stock-outs. Especially in the face of falling sales, the cost of holding higher inventory levels must be assessed against the increased production costs that would follow from reducing production runs in accordance with the decline of sales volumes. Clearly the decision will be affected by the length of time during which the lag of sales is expected to persist—a matter upon which opinions may easily differ.

MATERIALS CONCENTRATION

At the input end of the production line, materials, components, and subassemblies must be brought together in required quantities and at the appropriate time to permit uninterrupted production in accordance with schedule. In addition, fuel, maintenance materials, and packaging materials must be supplied. The procurement function searches out sources of the necessary materials which must then be purchased, transported, and stored in advance of use. Many of the same principles apply to materials concentration as have been observed in connection with distribution. But firms may exercise more complete control over their purchasing operations than over their distribution activities since the former are keyed to the production schedule and, thus, are less exposed to the vagaries of consumer demand which are encountered in the distribution of finished products.

Materials must be procured from that combination of sources that will generate lowest delivered costs at the manufacturing plant, quality specifications always being met. Price concession for large-scale or regular purchases and reduced volume transportation rates must be weighed against the costs and risks of stocking materials and components at the plants. Receiving and storage facilities must be generated at plant sites in accord with the quantities to be received, the type of transport to be employed, and the maximum stock levels to be held. Materials handling costs between stock locations and production departments can be held in check by appropriate attention to plant layout.

Where multiple-plant operations are conducted, manufacturing costs may differ among the plants and the behavior of costs may also differ at various levels of operation, for example, unit manufacturing costs may fall more rapidly as output increases toward capacity at one plant than at others. Whenever the system is working at less than capacity, therefore, it may be important to analyze the appropriate operating rates for each plant so that total cost may be minimized. Note that what is to be minimized, however, is not manufacturing cost but the sum of procurement, manufacturing, and distribution costs. The location of a high-cost plant may counsel its continued operation even at low levels of business if its closeness to materials sources and to important market areas results in differentially lower inbound transport costs and outbound distribution costs of sufficient magnitude to offset the manufacturing cost differential.

Continuous production and, thus, ability to satisfy the market for finished product depends upon continuous availability of raw materials, components, and subassemblies. Hence steps may be warranted to insure that availability. This is a major reason for backward integration in a number of industries, for example, the metals, petroleum, chemicals, fertilizer, paper. It leads the automotive companies to seek dual sources for components so that strike, fire, or other incident disabling a single supplier need not shut down the assembly lines. Alternate sources may be developed by assisting a supplier with opening out a new mineral deposit or other raw material supply, by assisting a component supplier with tooling, or simply by contracting for a sufficient term and quantity to make investment by a supplier seem worthwhile. Rate negotiations with carriers may open up a more distant source of supply at a cost competitive with present sources. Under systems of f.o.b. mill pricing, however, manufacturers may be tied to a single source of material for any one plant if minimum delivered cost is sought. Whether and to what extent insurance is to be bought by utilizing more costly sources is a question of policy.

Manufacturers increasingly endeavor to hold down or altogether eliminate stocks at the beginning of the production line. If a reliability of transport service can be secured, whether from commercial carriers or by private transportation, which permits inbound transport in effect to be incorporated into the production line (so that goods flow direct from transport equipment into process) at no added cost compared with a less reliable service, it is plain that the elimination of materials inventory is clear gain. This result is approximated in regional automobile assembly plants where the inbound flow of parts is meshed with the assembly-line schedule. See Figure 4-4. Though rail or truck transport reliability can attain a high standard of perfection, it is always subject to occasional interruption or delay. Hence, when assembly plants work without stock, the manufacturer's traffic department must be prepared to make emergency shipments, often by air, in order to avoid costly shutdowns of assembly. Continuous information about the progress of shipments in transit is essential to permit such moves to be made in time. Accordingly, the information systems operated by rail and motor carriers for the advice of shippers are continually being improved.

ADJUSTMENT OF PRODUCTION TO DEMAND THROUGH INVENTORY

We have noted the role of inventory as a buffer between various functions and the cost of inventory carrying as the source of important potential trade-offs. Among the roles for inventory already identified are: (1) enabling purchase and receipt of discrete volume lots to support a relatively constant use in manufacture, (2) protecting against irregularities of performance in transport, and (3) adjusting a relatively constant rate of production to irregularities in the disappearance of goods into sales channels. These uses for inventory are likely to be found in most production situations. There are, however, circum-

FIGURE 4–4
Supply of Automotive Assembly Plant

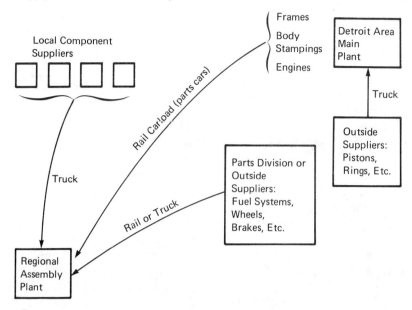

stances in particular types of industry that necessitate a larger role for inventories.

Virtually all of agricultural production is seasonal in character. In those areas of the world where climatic conditions compel single cropping, the entire year's output comes to harvest in a short period of time—often being brought out of the fields in a few weeks. Demand, on the other hand, is spread over the year and may occur, particularly in staple items, at a fairly constant rate throughout all seasons. Inventory, accordingly, will reach a peak as the harvest is completed and will flow out gradually over the ensuing 12 months with greater or less carry-over to insure against a shortfall in the subsequent crop. Canning of fresh fruits and vegetables similarly generates large inventories.

Seasonal market demands are another cause for heavy inventory buildup in some industries. Production plants adequate to meet such demands when they occur would stand idle the larger part of the year; hence manufacturing is begun well in advance and stocks built in anticipation of demand, thus enabling considerably smaller plants to meet the seasonal requirement. Buildup of stocks of coal, oil fuels, and natural gas to meet winter heating requirements is an annual phenomenon as is some buildup of gasoline against heavy summer demand.

Other seasonal stocking occurs in consequence of seasonal interruption of movement. Iron ore and taconite pellets from upper lakes and from Canadian sources via the St. Lawrence Seaway move into lower lake ports during the navigation season which generally closes about December 15th to reopen in late March. Ore must accordingly be stocked at mills and at lower lake ports to enable continued steel production during the closed season. In this situation the cost of stocking ore is judged to be less than that of an all-rail movement of ore through the winter. Other principal commodities which utilize the lakes during the navigation season, however, often seek alternate rail routes during winter.

Increased unit values for many materials and especially for manufactured products, as well as the high opportunity cost of capital tied up in inventory, have led to increased sensitivity on the part of business management to inventory accumulations. In addition, inventory buildup during the expanding phase of an economic cycle and subsequent liquidation are now better understood as factors contributing to the amplitude of business fluctuations and the vulnerability of firms during the downward phase of cycles. Cyclical turning points continue to resist accurate forecast, however; and expectations seem often to lag behind events. Hence the control of aggregate inventories in relation to the level of economic activity in general continues to be unsatisfactory. Inventory liquidation can, and often does, exaggerate the effect of a business downturn upon the carrier industries and contribute to a lag in the recovery of those industries.

SELECTED REFERENCES

Ackoff, R. L., ed. *Progress in Operations Research.* New York: John Wiley & Sons, Inc., 1961.

Arbury, James N., et al. *A New Approach to Physical Distribution.* New York: American Management Association, Inc., 1967.

Ballou, Ronald H. *Business Logistics Management.* Englewood Cliffs, N.J.: Prentice-Hall, Inc., 1973.

Bowersox, Donald J.; Smykay, Edward W.; and La Londe, Bernard J. *Physical Distribution Management: Logistics Problems of the Firm.* New York: Macmillan Co., 1968.

Brown, R. G. *Statistical Forecasting for Inventory Control.* New York: McGraw-Hill Book Co., 1959.

Constantin, James A. *Principles of Logistics Management.* New York: Appleton-Century-Crofts, 1966.

Fetter, R. B., and Dalleck, W. C. *Decision Models for Inventory Management.* Homewood, Ill.: Richard D. Irwin, Inc., 1961.

Fox, J. *An Analysis of Inventory Management.* New York: Sperry Rand Corp., 1957.

Heskett, J. L.; Ivie, R. M.; and Glaskowsky, N. A., Jr. *Business Logistics: Physical Distribution and Materials Management*. 2d ed. New York: The Ronald Press Co., 1964.

Magee, John F. *Industrial Logistics: Analysis and Management of Physical Supply and Distribution Systems*. New York: McGraw-Hill Book Co., 1968.

Marlow, W. H. *Modern Trends in Logistics Research*, Cambridge: M.I.T. Press, 1976.

Mossman, Frank H., and Morton, Newton. *Logistics of Distribution Systems*. Boston: Allyn & Bacon, Inc., 1965.

Smykay, Edward W.; Bowersox, Donald J.; and Mossman, Frank H. *Physical Distribution Management*. New York: Macmillan Co., 1961.

Starr, Martin K. *Production Management: Systems and Synthesis*. Englewood Cliffs, N.J.: Prentice-Hall, Inc., 1964.

———, and Miller, D. W. *Inventory Control: Theory and Practice*. Englewood Cliffs, N.J.: Prentice-Hall, Inc., 1962.

Taff, Charles A. *Management of Physical Distribution and Transportation*. 6th ed. Homewood, Ill.: Richard D. Irwin, Inc., 1978.

Williams, Ernest W., Jr. *Physical Distribution*. Part 10 of A. R. Oxenfeldt et al., *Executive Action in Marketing*. Belmont, Calif.: Wadsworth Publishing Co., Inc., 1966.

5

Goods Movement and the Location of Economic Enterprise

Chapter 4 has suggested the importance of locational considerations in the siting of warehouses or distribution centers in logistics systems. Superior access to the transport net and nearness to the center of gravity of the market area to be served showed up as strategic factors. A wider range of consideration bears upon the location of production facilities which is often of even greater consequence to profitable operation and efficient logistics. In recent decades important contributions have been made to location theory and there is a growing body of empiric study. Increasing attention has been devoted to industrial location by business firms, especially by the large multiplant corporations, and by carriers and public bodies interested in attracting industries to particular areas. Consulting firms have turned to this area of practice, some developing a high degree of specialization. Just as the growing ability to process great quantities of data and to subject it to analysis has made possible control of physical distribution as a system of related functions, so also the analysis of alternative location possibilities has gained from the capabilities.

Transfer costs—transportation costs plus other costs involved in the transfer of goods from one location to another—are central to location theory. If goods movement were both instantaneous and costless, we would have no need for location theory even with a highly uneven distribution of resources. Transfer costs tend to follow a pattern governed in largest part by distance. There are many departures, of course, since cost and distance are not synonymous and since transportation charges frequently depart from cost relationships. Nevertheless approximations can be secured from distance relationships and a preliminary choice of the more eligible locations made as a basis for more detailed comparisons. The number of possible locations is frequently very great when it is considered that (1) many production processes require the assembly of numerous materials from various discrete sources, (2) alternate sources are not infrequently available, and (3) the market sought to be served may cover a rather wide area that has a quite uneven distribution of buying potential. As Walter Isard has pointed out, "location theory seeks principles to narrow down, and greatly narrow down, the number of points to be considered as potential locations for the production of any given commodity."[1]

Ordinarily transportation cost is the largest element in transfer costs. Transportation rates are prices; and they form one portion of the price structure which, in a market economy, governs the flow of goods and services between producers and consumers. Transportation is a substitute for other elements in the production process. Thus the transportation of a high-grade raw material from a distance may be substituted for the use of an inferior raw material close at hand. Or the transportation of a product from a point of low-cost production to a market may be substituted for the consumption of a similar product produced locally but at greater cost. When the scale of manufacturing is increased by concentrating a larger volume of production at a single point, increased transport cost is accepted in exchange for the lower manufacturing costs which are achieved. If transportation prices fall in comparison with other prices; the opportunities for such substitutions grow; if transportation prices increase in relation to other prices, these opportunities diminish.

SCALE OF MANUFACTURE VERSUS COSTS OF ASSEMBLY AND DISTRIBUTION

Adam Smith opened Chapter 3 of his *Wealth of Nations* with the proposition that "as it is the power of exchanging that gives occasion to the division of labour, so the extent of this division must always be limited by the extent of that power, or, in other words, the extent of the market." Since he wrote in a period before mechanical power had been applied either to manufacture or transportation, he saw the market as sharply constrained by the cost of overland transport and as having an extent that could support a high degree of division of labor (i.e., specialization of function) only where water transport was available.

---

[1] Walter Isard, *Location and Space Economy* (Cambridge: M.I.T. Press, 1956), pp. 167–68, n. 52.

Much of the subsequent history of transport in respect of its economic importance concerns the successive widening of markets by reduction of the cost of transport and increase of its speed and carrying capacity.

Little has been done to date in the theory of location to cope with economies of scale. Isard holds out the belief that the use of a spatial transformation function will facilitate the fusing of production theory and location theory.[2] In a wide variety of manufacturing industries as well as in several of the extractive industries, economies of scale develop with technological advance until they reach to very high levels of output for individual installations. Plants of various sizes can be built, but larger ones generate lower unit production costs at equivalent rates of capacity use until the limits of present technology are reached.

Plant scale is, of course, to be distinguished from enterprise scale and both from capacity phenomena. In an electric utility, for example, a generating station of 1 million kilowatts capacity may be substituted for two of 500,000 kilowatts capacity and, given the same load factor for the new plant, the cost of generation per kilowatt-hour will be reduced. An economy of plant scale has been realized. The cost per kilowatt-hour in both instances will, however, vary with the rate of utilization. If demand falls and load factor worsens, utilization will fall and kilowatt-hour costs will increase. If with an increase of demand the plant is forced to the limits of its designed capacity, another area of increasing unit costs may be disclosed. These economies and diseconomies are the result of fluctuating rates of utilization of a given plant, that is, capacity phenomena. Our generating station may be but one of many in a large power system. As that system grows, economies associated with the size of the enterprise, as distinct from the size of the individual generating stations which are linked in the system, may be realized. These may be found in the distribution grid when peak loads of one area can be met by underused capacity elsewhere and by the ability to spread management skills over broader areas of responsibility.[3]

It is plant scale that is of particular interest in explaining the relation of transport to location. Increased plant scale requires an expansion of the market area which can be served if its output is to be absorbed. Not infrequently the supply area from which materials, components, and subassemblies are drawn must also be increased. In short, average distances over which product is shipped and from which supplies are drawn must increase. In some instances, added supply distances will affect subcontractors or sellers to the primary firm—component producers which, under the principle of agglomeration, are located close

---

[2] Ibid., p. 286.

[3] Diseconomies in enterprise scale are commonly traced to inefficiencies in the management of very large enterprises.

to the primary firm but whose own increased scale of operation implies an increased drawing area. Increased prices for components may result.

Now it is apparent that advantage can be taken of plant economies of scale in manufacture only so long as the reduction of unit cost of manufacture exceeds the increase of unit cost for logistics. The latter includes not only increased transport cost attributable to longer average hauls but also increased costs for warehousing as the number of warehouses must be increased in order to adequately serve the expanding market and increased costs of inventory associated with longer lines of supply and distribution—inventory in transit and inventory to stock the numerous warehouses. A larger inventory in transit could be obviated in large part if increased speed of transport offset greater average haul. Likewise improvement in the regularity of transport service could mitigate the increase of stocks necessitated by more numerous warehouses. Both cost and quality of transportation service, therefore, are reflected in the unit logistics *costs* which are to be weighed against declining unit manufacturing costs.

One might argue that when the marginal logistics cost associated with supply and market expansion is less than the decline of marginal manufacturing cost, a firm will add to the scale of its operation. Such a formulation is, however, more appropriate to determination of the operating rate of an existing plant. Economies of scale are to be had from plant expansion or new plant installation; and these come in discrete units of considerable magnitude, representing blocks of new investment in manufacturing capacity. Hence a more appropriate comparison with existing costs at present plant scale is of aggregate manufacturing cost at the proposed level of output, including amortization of plant investment, added to aggregate logistics cost at that same level of output, including amortization of investment in goods handling and warehouse facilities. Manufacturing capacity should be expanded until minimum total unit cost is achieved, that is, until it is no longer profitable to substitute outlays on logistics for outlays on production. This approach is illustrated in Figure 5-1.

Logistics costs, then, may place a limit upon the degree to which it is profitable to carry economies of scale in a single plant which, necessarily, is at a single location. Where the enterprise serves a market too wide for a single plant, one or more additional plants will be built or acquired at other locations, and a division of the market will be made among them.

WEIGHT LOSS AND WEIGHT GAIN

When the "pull" of the raw material or of the market is spoken of as a locating factor, its significance arises from the reduction of transfer

70

FIGURE 5–1
Production Scale versus Distribution Cost

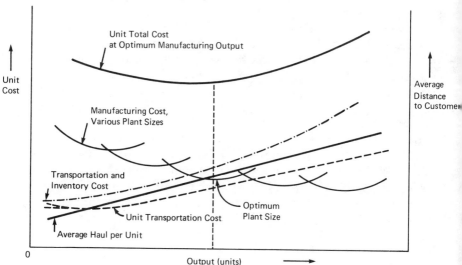

costs which will be achieved by location near the source of materials or the market as the case may be. Cost in this context includes not merely the necessary money outlay to accomplish the transfer of the goods but also the loss of time and losses resulting from perishability which are important in some instances.

Location is affected by other factors, often significantly. Differentials in labor costs in various areas, often quite persistent; differential availability of capital; the accumulation of skills in particular locations; the ties of one industry to another; the availability of sites, water supplies, and other items; the general sociological environment; and numerous institutional factors such as tariff barriers, zoning restrictions, and the aids extended by communities to attract industry all have their effect. Moreover, much existing location is primarily the result of historical accident—of establishment without adequate analysis of the economic position. Locations which are relatively unsound nevertheless persist over long periods of time, contributing an important element of inertia to the development of locational shifts. An industrial plant once built often represents substantially a sunk cost, and a decision to relocate may not be made until the plant becomes worn out or obsolescent.

All approaches to the theory of location recognize that some industries and plants tend to be oriented toward raw materials, others toward markets, while still others seek locations between their materials and their markets. The aggregate cost of transfer of materials to the plant and of products from the plant to the market is the determining factor. Other things being equal, an industry will, therefore, tend to locate at a point where it will have the least total cost of transportation to and from the plant. This is known as the principle of *aggregate transportation costs*.

Alfred Weber, the father of location theory, recognized[4] several classes of materials which might enter into a manufacturing process and exert locational pulls according to their nature: (1) pure materials which are included in the manufactured article without loss of weight; (2) weight-losing materials, only a part of whose weight is represented in the weight of the finished article (coal used as fuel is an example of a material which experiences complete weight loss), and (3) ubiquities, or materials found everywhere, hence lacking in locational influence. The Weber analysis proceeds on the unrealistic assumption that transport costs are uniform per ton-mile. An industry using a single pure material thus might locate with indifference at the source of the material, at the market, or at any point between. Where a weight-losing material was employed, however, location would be at the source of the material for it would cost less to transport the lighter product to the market than to transport the material itself. If a ubiquity were the material used, production would be at the market, since the material would presumably be available there as elsewhere.

The more difficult circumstances arise when several materials are used, some of which may be pure and others weight-losing. An intermediate point which minimizes total transport costs will be chosen and will tend to be closer to the source of the material used in heaviest quantity and involving the largest weight loss, since other materials and the market will exercise less locational influence. The Weber approach is suggestive of the forces which must be taken into account in actual situations where existing rates can be substituted for the assumptions of the theory.[5]

Producers are customarily material oriented when large weight loss is involved, that is where the process is accompanied by heavy fuel consumption, large amounts of waste in the material, or the production of unmarketable by-products or scrap. Thus low-quality mineral ores are usually smelted or concentrated near the mine since they contain much waste. Similarly, the manufacture of various materials requiring heavy use of fuel, such as cement, glass, and numerous chemicals, is customarily material oriented with reference to the source of fuel.[6]

---

[4] *Ueber den Standort der Industrien*, Tubingen, 1909, trans. by C. J. Friedrich, as *Alfred Weber's Theory of the Location of Industries* (Chicago: University of Chicago Press, 1928). See the excellent brief summary in Stuart Daggett, *Principles of Inland Transportation*, 4th ed. (New York: Harper & Bros., 1955), pp. 430–48.

[5] Greater realism was introduced in a later work: Tord Palander, *Beitrage zut Standortstheorie*, Uppsala, 1935.

[6] See Edgar M. Hoover, *The Location of Economic Activity* (New York: McGraw-Hill Book Co., 1948), pp. 31–35; also D. Philip Locklin, *Report on Interterritorial Freight Rates* (Washington, D.C.: U.S. Board of Investigation and Research, 1943), pp. 240–41.

Location close to power, as in the reduction of alumina, is essentially an orientation to materials where the large consumption of electric power necessitates closeness to sources of cheap generation.[7] But power transmission is a form of transportation, and technical improvements will presumably permit economical transmission over greater distances in the future than at present.

Market orientation may occur where there is a weight gain encountered in the processing, as may result from the use of a ubiquity (such as water in the manufacture of beverages). Or again, transfer costs per ton-mile may be higher on the product than on the material without sufficient offset from weight loss or other factors. This occurs particularly in the late stages of manufacturing when consumers' goods are complete for the market, for the outgoing product, such as furniture, may exceed in bulk and value, if not in weight, the incoming materials and fuel.[8]

Some other industries, especially those manufacturing style goods, may have a close affinity for the market by reason of the necessity to be in close touch with the changing whims of demand. But even in a clothing industry some emancipation from market location is coming as a result of faster transport. Thus at least one New York clothing manufacturer has transferred its operations to the Southeast, relying on fast air express to bring its style goods quickly to New York showrooms. Quality of transportation service, therefore, may also influence location. Finally various types of goods, especially in foods, enjoy only a short shelf-life. This is notable in the case of crackers and other baked goods where necessity to achieve freshness compels a market orientation of production as well as, in the majority of cases, private transport channels to the stores. Distribution practices will differentiate between such products and others of longer shelf-life which can sustain more centralized production and longer (in both distance and time) distribution channels.

MARKET SCOPE AND STRUCTURE

The market side of location theory presents more difficulty than does the analysis of least cost locations in relation to production inputs. Early theory treated the market as a point. Later approaches sought to define market areas but upon highly simplified assumptions with respect to population distribution and transport costs and availability.[9]

---

[7] D. Philip Locklin, *Report on Interterritorial Freight Rates* (Washington, D.C.: U.S. Board of Investigation and Research, 1943), p. 245.

[8] See Hoover, *Location of Economic Activity*, pp. 35–38.

[9] August Lösch, *The Economics of Location*, trans. from 2d rev. ed. by William H. Woglem with the assistance of Wolfgang F. Stolper (New Haven: Yale University Press, 1954).

When the attempt is made to merge production cost and demand factors affecting location, it becomes plain that command of customers plays an important role in location and that least cost is to be sought in relation to a market area. Moreover locational choice by new firms entering imperfectly competitive markets depends heavily upon assumptions as to the behavior of existing producers. Where price competition is not anticipated, maximum returns may result from locating at the same point as existing producers. Where price competition is expected, the protection of distance may be sought by a location remote from existing producers which can command a submarket of its own.

As Greenhut puts it, "Each firm entering the competitive scene will seek that site from which its sales to a given number of buyers (whose purchases are required for the greatest possible profit) can be served at the lowest total cost."[10] The pull of the consumer, indeed, has been of large importance in the gradual shift of industry in the United States to the south and west. As the potential of these markets grew to the point where they would support manufacturing facilities of economic scale, it was plain that reductions in distribution cost could be achieved as compared with serving them from older and more remote producing centers. Finally, mere proximity to customers is in some industries judged to have an expansionary effect upon demand.[11]

The adjustment of location to demand factors can be conceived as ultimately generating a locational equilibrium involving such a pattern of plants that the relocation of any one would occasion losses.[12] Changes in demand conditions will, then, upset such an equilibrium and occasion changes in location. Changes in cost and speed of transport must be counted among the possible causes, for these have an impact upon the necessary proximity of plants to customers and hence will alter demand factors. Pricing systems may, however, dilute the effect of transportation cost changes. Systems of uniform delivered prices or of zoned prices related by arbitraries to one or more base prices often determine the price offering of producers in the market. Changes in the level or structure of freight rates may not, then, be reflected in prices charged customers, hence cannot influence demand. Carriers seeking, in these situations, to enhance their traffic volume by rate reductions may find their efforts frustrated by industry pricing practices.

Divergence of price from cost including freight at varying locations where goods are sold occurs particularly in connection with nationally advertised products sold at uniform prices over wide areas and in

[10] Melvin L. Greenhut, *Plant Location in Theory and in Practice* (Chapel Hill: University of North Carolina Press, 1956), p. 285.

[11] Glenn E. McLaughlin and Stephen Robock, *Why Industry Moves South* (National Planning Association Committee of the South, 1949).

[12] Greenhut, *Plant Location*, p. 285.

connection with basing point systems of pricing. Thus many a consumers' good produced in the New York area will sell in Buffalo at the same price as in New York City, and even in Chicago and St. Louis. On some items produced in the East a higher price is charged west of the Mississippi, but on many the price is uniform the country over. In this type of pricing, the price is fixed on the basis of the producer's average shipping cost in lieu of pricing on rates to individual locations.[13] Thus the prices in the markets near the point of production cover more than their share of transport costs, whereas the prices at distant markets reflect less than their actual contribution to the firm's marketing costs.

More interesting phenomena occur in connection with basing point pricing where freight absorption is a rather widespread practice. With multiple basing points at which standard prices are quoted (as in the steel and cement industries for long years before abandonment of the system in favor of f.o.b. mill prices in 1948), prices to points away from the basing point are calculated as the base price plus freight to destination. (Usually rail rates are employed even though some other mode of transportation may actually be used in effecting delivery.)[14] Destination prices therefore increase as they fan out in every direction from each basing point. But two basing point mills, say, 100 miles apart, with base prices at one mill slightly higher than at the other, might be selling at equal delivered prices at a point 40 miles from the high-cost mill and 60 miles from the low-cost mill. One mill, or both, might be unwilling to limit its market to this distance from its mill and would begin to sell within the other mill's "natural territory," reducing its delivered price as it secured customers closer to the competing mill in order to meet the price of its competitors, notwithstanding the continual increase of freight rates for the longer hauls. Thus the mill "absorbs" a portion of the freight charge.[15] See Figure 5–2. But in the long run its revenues must cover all of its costs. Hence its base price must be set high enough to cover these freight absorptions. Crosshauling of the same product may result from this practice, and the consumer in the long run must bear a greater burden of freight than if products were

---

[13] As an example, this situation was discussed in connection with rates on tea. See W. T. Jackman, *Economic Principles of Transportation* (Toronto: University of Toronto Press, 1935), p. 577.

[14] The best known systems of this type were abandoned responsive to the decision of the Supreme Court in the cement basing-point case.

[15] On basing-point practices, see Arthur R. Burns, *The Decline of Competition* (New York: McGraw-Hill Book Co., 1936), pp. 290–371; Temporary National Economic Committee, *Hearings, Iron and Steel Industry* (1940), part 26, pp. 13794–847; C. R. Daugherty, M. G. deChazeau, and S. S. Stratton, *Economics of the Iron and Steel Industry* (New York: McGraw-Hill Book Co., 1937), vol. 1, pp. 533–44; Fritz Machlup, *The Basing Point System* (Philadelphia: Blakiston, 1949); and J. M. Clark, "Law and Economics of Basing Points," *American Economic Review*, vol. 39 (1949), p. 430.

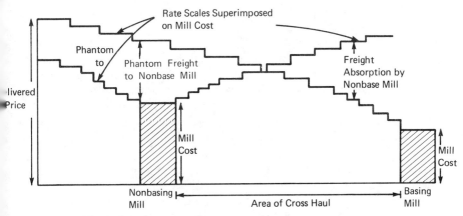

sold only within the "natural territory" of each mill where it has a freight rate advantage as compared with other mills.[16]

RATE POLICIES WHICH AFFECT LOCATION AND MARKET STRUCTURE

Effect of Rates upon the Development of Resources

The industrial economy of the United States has been closely tied to its fuel resources, particularly coal. Aside from the relative quality of coals and mining costs in the various production areas, transportation rates are the principal determinants in the marketing of coal. The pattern of canal and railway development opened first the anthracite fields of eastern Pennsylvania and subsequently the bituminous fields of central and western Pennsylvania. In order to build traffic and open resources tributary to their lines, the railroads early made rates sufficiently low to move these coals into the important seaboard cities where the growth of industry stimulated consumption. Likewise, at Baltimore and Philadelphia, large quantities were transshipped for cheap water movement to New York and New England. The rapidly growing industry of New England, founded originally upon abundant water power, shifted quickly to the use of cheap waterborne coal. Tidewater rates to Atlantic ports were differentially lower than rates for local delivery in the same ports and tended to encourage the water movement.

---

[16] This latter practice ·vould, of course, eliminate a measure of competition which might well be considered of some value by the consumer.

The importance of railroad rates on coal to the economic welfare of producing areas began to be forcefully demonstrated when the great Pocahontas and southern fields were opened up. The construction of the Norfolk and Western and Chesapeake and Ohio railways had by 1880 opened the more easterly of these fields for shipment to tidewater. Exceptionally favorable rates permitted the mines along these roads to ship into New York and New England considerable quantities of coal in competition with Pennsylvania mines.[17] It was not until the Pocahontas roads developed satisfactory connections to the West and arranged a favorable rate structure that West Virginia coal began to be marketed extensively north and west of the Ohio River. The interested carriers established a rate structure for southeastern Ohio, Pennsylvania, West Virginia, and Kentucky fields which attempted to put the various producing areas into such a relationship as to enable them all to share in the large markets north of the Ohio River.

The rapid development of the southern coal fields, fostered by the expansion of the Pocahontas railroads and their network of branches brought about a significant growth of coal production in that area. As a result, the old established Pennsylvania producers came into conflict with the economic interests of the newly opened fields. Until about 1912 Ohio and Pennsylvania fields were shipping some 70 percent of the lake-cargo coal, but after 1914 the proportion of West Virginia coal increased to the detriment of the northern fields. There began a series of rate maneuvers on the part of the interested railroads and a long series of cases before the Interstate Commerce Commission.

The economic interests of two important sections of the country were vitally affected. The proportion which the freight rate represents of the consumer's price of coal is sufficient so that modest adjustments in the freight rate have far-reaching effects upon the output and sale of coal from particular fields. Likewise, since coal represents so large a proportion of the traffic of railroads serving the more important fields, such rate relationships are of vital significance to the prosperity of the carriers. The lake-cargo coal rate structure as it stands today minimizes the factor of distance between the Pittsburgh and West Virginia fields in favor of the latter and enables the West Virginia coals to reach northern markets on an extremely favorable basis.[18]

In recent years environmental regulation has forced a shift from coal to oil and gas on the part of a substantial portion of the electrical utility industry. Generating plants which continue to burn coal have sought

---

[17] See Joseph T. Lambie, *From Mine to Market* (New York: New York University Press, 1954), esp. chaps. 8 and 9.

[18] For a detailed account of the lake cargo adjustments, see H. C. Mansfield, *The Lake Cargo Coal Rate Controversy* (New York: Columbia University Press, 1932). A more concise discussion is contained in Kent T. Healy, *The Economics of Transportation in America* (New York: The Ronald Press Co., 1940), pp. 473-76.

to meet emissions standards by shifting to low-sulfur coals which are primarily available in the west. Hence the capacity of the Pocahontas fields is underutilized, coal volumes on the eastern roads are down and mining expansion is centered in Wyoming, Utah, and Colorado. Very long hauls are involved to southwestern and midwestern utilities. Yet new generating plants, when not nuclear powered, are forced to turn to coal. Rates from Wyoming to the southwest on coal moved in unit trains frequently exceed the price at the mine. Undoubtedly a shift back toward eastern coals will occur as the technology for removal of sulfur at the generating station improves and freight rates again begin to exert their traditional role of territorial allocation of coal purchase.

Transportation costs have a large effect upon the opening of agricultural land and upon the type of farming engaged in the various agricultural areas. These costs include not only the freight rate but also the cost of protective services for perishables, the cost of packing, and the loss and deterioration in transit. As a general principle, agricultural commodities which, because of bulkiness or perishability cannot afford transportation over long distances, will tend to be produced close to markets.[19] This principle is obviously substantially modified by the peculiar requirements of certain crops as to soils and climate and with respect to off-season supply of northern markets from areas of longer growing seasons.

The areas around large concentrations of urban population are largely devoted to the growing of truck crops for the city market. These crops will stand little transportation. In the off season, however, they move in some volume at premium prices from more southerly producing areas. Beyond the truck belt, farms are usually devoted primarily to dairying, whole milk being produced nearest the city, followed by cream, butter, and cheese at the more remote farms. These latter products are of reduced bulk and higher unit value, hence support a heavier transportation charge. Moreover, they are less perishable and can better stand the longer haul. The growing of grains has been pushed farther and farther from the large cities by high land values and the need for large acreage. Its movement is therefore greatly influenced by transportation charges. Fortunately, bulk grain can be moved very economically by rail and boat, and a delicately adjusted grain rate structure has been built up which permits all important producing areas to serve major markets. Bulky farm produce grown far from consuming areas is often converted into livestock, poultry, or dairy products by feeding, thus producing a product of high value per unit of weight which can afford the transportation rate to markets.

---

[19] D. Philip Locklin, *Economics of Transportation*, rev. ed. (Chicago: Business Publications, Inc., 1938), p. 136. This principle is recognized in some of the earliest writing upon the theory of location, notably by Johann F. Von Thunen, *Der Isolierte Staat* (Berlin: Schumacher-Zarchlin, 1875).

Change in relative freight rates and in rate structures may have important effects upon the prosperity of producers in the affected locations. Horizontal rate increases or decreases, made as a percentage of existing rates, upset many differentials and relationships and may adversely affect certain areas to the benefit of others. The sharp increase in rates after World War I, for example, benefited potato producers in New York, although they were disadvantageous to growers in Idaho and Michigan.[20] The latter producers, more remote from major markets, found their farm prices sharply reduced and their share of the market declining. The traffic in citrus fruit and the relative prosperity of the three major producing areas have been sharply influenced by rate structures. The western railroads sought to build up the California industry in competition with the Florida product. In order to effect this, California citrus was moved into eastern markets on very low rates, and eventually a broad rate blanket was developed under which rates of California citrus to all points Denver and east were the same regardless of length of haul. This blanket persisted until very recently. When citrus growing began to develop in Texas, similar favorable treatment was accorded by the interested railroads to enable this area to secure a portion of the market.

With an accelerating pace, the movement of perishable agricultural products, livestock, and dressed meats shifted from rail to truck after World War II. The process was speeded by the development of western feed lots and the westward movement of the packing-house industry out of Chicago and other traditional packing centers. Rates, though fluctuating with supply of and demand for exempt trucks, necessarily came to reflect distance more directly since motor carrier costs are closely related to length of haul. Both the level of rail rates and the deficiencies of rail service rendered the growth of motor carriage inexorable. But the circumstances today are very different from those prevailing when the rails were seeking to extend the cultivated area and place new producing territories in competition with those of earlier development. The agricultural frontier is effectively closed and demand customarily absorbs output even at differential delivery costs.

Since it is cheap and bulky, lumber is a commodity which is very sensitive to transportation conditions and rates. Relatively small variations in the rate structure may determine the boundaries of the market which any lumbering area can serve.[21] The forests of the Pacific Northwest were opened up originally to supply large midwestern lumber markets. Since the northern transcontinental railroads were interested in securing an eastbound backhaul from the Far West, they

---

[20] H. S. Gabriel, *Index Numbers of Freight Rates and Their Relation to Agricultural Prices and Production*, Bulletin No. 446, Cornell University Agricultural Experiment Station (1925), pp. 31–34.

[21] Daggett, *Principles of Inland Transportation*, pp. 215–16.

were willing to make exceptionally low rates.[22] The effect of this action was to accelerate the growth of logging operations in the western forests. The advent of water competition via the Panama Canal further reduced the cost of movement into major northeastern and middle-western markets. As a result, southern lumber producers were placed at a disadvantage in this territory and lost proportionately in the trade. This situation was not redressed until truck transportation captured the shorter hauls.

Freight Rates and Industrial Location

Although local skills and the accident of development from personal interests play a part, the major factors affecting industrial location are availability of raw materials, availability of power, and accessibility to markets. In a very large degree all three of these factors are functions of transport costs. Nearness of markets is usually a matter of the cost of reaching markets; only in rare cases is physical identity of point of production and market desirable for reasons other than cost. Likewise, fuel and raw materials need be near only in terms of cost, that is, the sum of production and transportation costs.

The influence of transport rates will be of greater or less significance depending upon the proportion of final delivered costs which is represented by transportation charges. Semifinished steel prices reflect a very large sum of transport charges, including the cost of assembling raw materials and fuel and the cost of delivering steel from the plant to the customer. Assembly costs may exceed 30 percent of the total cost of manufacturing pig iron, the basic raw material of steel manufacture. Delivery of the finished steel involves freight costs averaging more than 10 percent of its base price.

In many manufactured items, however, total transportation charges represent a small portion of the price of the finished article. The shift in cotton textile production from New England to southern mills has been attributed in part to the reduced transport cost resulting from nearness to the sources of raw cotton. Analysis of the relation of transport charges to total manufacturing costs, however, indicates that the saving was relatively insignificant and that the shift was due primarily to lower labor costs in the South.

Although there is a tendency for manufacturing to locate close to raw materials, there are many industries which have concentrated some distance from their raw materials and which have apparently been attracted by other factors. Which of these results will come about is due largely to the relation between the rates on raw materials and

---

[22] See James J. Hill, *Highways of Progress* (New York: Doubleday, Page & Co., 1910), pp. 159–64.

those on the finished goods and the weight loss incurred in manufacturing. The steel industry is a notable example of an industry in which substantial weight loss is involved, but in this case the large quantity of fuel required often results in a greater attraction toward coal supplies than toward ore and flux, since the coal employed occasions a nearly complete weight loss of the particular input. Scrap, moreover, is a major input, and its availability tends to coincide with the market. The typical solution is a compromise which seeks to minimize total assembly costs. Sawmills often locate in the woods or close to them, except where sluicing or rafting by river is readily possible at low cost. The rough-sawed lumber may, however, be transported great distances before further processing occurs. Cotton ginning and beet sugar refining likewise tend to locate close to the sources of raw materials.[23]

Where substantial weight loss is not involved in processing, the relative rates upon raw materials and finished goods will largely govern whether manufacturing is located near material sources, near the markets, or at some intermediate point. It is a general practice, though not a universal one, to charge rates which progress with the stage of fabrication. This is in part a reflection of the value principle of rate making and in part a result of cost factors. Some manufactured items, for example, are very bulky in proportion to weight, hence costly to handle. Consider the bulk of automobiles, agricultural machinery, and furniture in relation to the bulk of the materials used to manufacture them. Some manufactured items are not only bulky but subject to damage in transit. Tin cans, for example, take great space in comparison with weight and require careful handling to avoid crushing. The production of such items naturally concentrates close to markets to minimize the cost of distributing the finished product.

The relationships between rates on raw materials and semifinished and finished manufactured goods have been the subject for many a controversy. In the late decades of the 19th century it was alleged that manufacturing development in the intermountain area, and particularly in Colorado, was prevented by the fact that the finished goods could be brought in more cheaply from the East than the materials and components for manufacture, since the rates on materials were at a higher level than those on finished goods.[24] More recently it was argued that manufacturing development in the South had been deterred by unfavorable rate adjustments which tended to drain raw materials out of the South at low rates, admit northern manufactures at low

---

[23] Edward S. Lynch, "The Influence of Transportation on the Location of Economic Activities," in U.S. National Resources Planning Board, *Transportation and National Policy* (Washington, D.C., 1942), p. 72.

[24] John B. Phillips, *Freight Rates and Manufacturers in Colorado* (Boulder: University of Colorado Studies, 1909).

rates, and prevent the movement of southern manufactures into northern markets by an unreasonably high rate level.[25] Although the contention was too broad to be entirely true, there were nevertheless instances in which such results appeared to be indicated by the experiences of southern manufacturers. It was established that the northbound class-rate basis was less favorable than the southbound,[26] and the Interstate Commerce Commission ordered corrective action.[27]

There has been a tendency in recent years to locate steam power plants for the generation of electricity at or close to a mine mouth. This is a result of the decreasing cost of long-distance power transmission as compared with the cost of transporting coal by rail or water. A lower adjustement of coal rates might retard or stop this tendency. The manufacture of glass, on the other hand, which has always tended to locate close to supplies of natural gas because of its large fuel requirements, may be somewhat freed from such a tie-up by the increasing efficiency of long-distance pipeline transport of gas. Here, as in a number of other instances, the effects of fuel scarcity and higher prices are yet to be observed.

For many types of industrial output the accessible market from any given center of production has grown to enormous scope because of the improvements in transportation which have so greatly reduced the cost and increased the speed of movement. Many products are sold all over the nation and even exported in considerable quantities. Yet the influence of markets is still felt on the location of producers of these goods, and there is a great variety of manufactures the unit value of which is low enough so that transport cost is still a significant proportion of delivered price. Location near markets is decidedly important to producers of such products. There are, indeed, some industries that cannot successfully exist far from the immediate vicinity of their markets. The manufacture of bakery products, the bottling of milk, and job and specialty printing are of this sort and may be termed local industries. Their distribution agrees quite closely with the distribution of population, and little transportation is involved in marketing.

We have already noted the tendency for manufactures which carry a high freight rate as compared with the raw materials going into them to locate close to markets. Many manufactures tend, however, to be sold over broad areas. Such items as cement, brick, and fertilizer are commonly produced close to supplies of fuel and raw material. Yet the influence of the market is also important in plant location and closely

---

[25] See Tennessee Valley Authority, *The Interterritorial Freight Rate Problem of the United States*, 75th Cong., 1st sess., House Doc. 264 (1937).

[26] Locklin, *Report on Interterritorial Freight Rates*, pp. 90–91.

[27] *Class Rate Investigation, 1939*, 262, ICC 447 (1945). While the proceeding was fought over rail rates, similar adjustments were made in motor-carrier class rates.

governs the size to which individual plants may grow. Such items cannot be marketed profitably over wide distances; and their manufacture, therefore, is inclined to become regionalized, choosing points within market regions where the necessary fuel and materials are available. The relatively high cost of transporting finished automobiles has brought about a similar regionalization of automobile assembly plants, to which the parts are shipped from the highly centralized industry of the Detroit area.

Cement and assembled automobiles, however, afford two important examples of the way in which marketing patterns and, ultimately, location may be changed by technological developments in transport. A new entrant in the cement business erected a plant on navigable waters from which it began to ship in barge-load lots in bulk to coastal distribution points on the eastern seaboard. Established regional manufacturers, finding new competition in their backyards and faced with underutilized capacity, commenced to establish bulk distribution points in more remote markets, servicing them by rail bulk movement in covered hopper cars. The differential pressure car which came along at this time, permitting discharge of the cement into bulk trucks by air pressure, facilitated this move. Cement marketing became more competitive, hauls longer, distribution costs greater, and manufacturers' margins even slimmer than before.

In the case of assembled automobiles, regional assembly plants distributed to dealers by truck. Railroads thus lost most of the assembled automobile traffic, although they retained much of the automobile parts movement to assembly points. The development in the late 50s of bi-level and tri-level auto racks mounted on long piggyback flatcars enabled railroads to provide economical movement of assembled automobiles over long distances. Centralized assembly was rendered competitive with regionally dispersed assembly, and the railroads by 1967 had recaptured about 50 percent of the movement of assembled automobiles. In the 60s the viability of regional assembly plants was restored by the development of specialized high-cube auto parts cars, generally of 60-foot length compared with the usual 40-foot and 50-foot boxcars, and equipped with special racks and wide doors for economical loading of parts. Thus both centralized and decentralized assembly can compete on relatively equal terms.

The center of population of the United States has been moving steadily westward. As a result the shoe, clothing, and publishing industries, as well as many other types of consumers' goods manufacturing, have been moving westward as they follow the market. On the other hand, the relatively light population of the Far West has handicapped the cities of the intermountain area in their aspirations to become industrial centers. The local market is not sufficiently large to support manufacturing industries of economical size. In shipping eastward to more populous areas, such industries come against stiff competition.

World War II brought rapid industrialization to the Gulf Coast as well as significant industrial development to California. Rapid population growth in these areas since the war has generated markets of a size sufficient to support many types of industry. Hence an important postwar decision for many firms which market nationwide has been whether and when to develop manufacturing facilities in the Southwest and on the West Coast. The development of containerized intercoastal steamship services by Sea-Land and the growth of airfreight capability along with reduced air-cargo rates has presented alternatives which, in some instances, may delay or render unnecessary a west-coast manufacturing location. But the development of a west-coast plant by one firm in an industry is likely to impel others to follow suit for competitive reasons.

Environmental Factors

Two decades ago the type of industry and its possible effect upon the quality of the environment rarely entered into locational decisions. Communities held growth to be desirable and actively sought new candidates for location with little regard to possible effects upon air, water, and other environmental circumstances. Esthetic considerations entered the picture somewhat earlier and affected plant design, landscaping, and specific site selection. Today, environmental effects must be considered; certain types of industry are unwelcome in particular areas or communities, and, if acceptable, the steps to be taken to reduce environmental impact are often critical. Thus a new factor has been introduced into location practice which limits choice and may offset all other locational considerations. Because of the morass of administrative agencies which require satisfaction, it may also seriously delay locational decision.

The effect of environmental issues on transport will be noticed at various places in this book. Carriers and communities are being affected by the abandonment of older plants which cannot economically be cleaned up. Location decisions are being forced which compel higher transport costs because of greater remoteness from fuel or material sources, greater distance from market, or both. Such locations can sometimes be made economically viable only by changes in transport arrangements, construction of new transport facilities or improvement of old, and the negotiation of unusual rate and service arrangements.

COMPETITIVE RATE TACTICS AND LOCATION

Transit Privileges

Rates for short distances are commonly at a higher ton-mile basis than those for longer distances because the rate must absorb two terminal charges regardless of the length of haul. Consequently, a combination of two or more local rates between two points is usually higher than the single through rate between the same two points. Under such a rate structure, industries would tend to locate either at the raw material source or at the market, rather than at some point between, where the combination of the in and out rates would exceed the through rate. This situation is modified, however, by the railroads practice of granting transit privileges. The first such privilege on record seems to have been offered in 1870 at Nashville, Tennessee.[28]

In 1908–9 the Wheeling and Lake Erie Railroad, to increase its share of the steel traffic, published rates granting the privilege to stop steel in transit at Canton and Toledo for fabrication.[29] Structural steel moved to the point of fabrication on the applicable local rate, but when it was reshipped to destination after fabrication, charges were reassessed on the basis of the through rate from the point of origin of the structural steel to the final destination of the fabricated steel. See Figure 5–3. Fabricators in Toledo and Canton were thus able to compete with those in Pittsburgh. Other railroads quickly met this competition with similar arrangements, and the system spread rapidly to other fabricating points and to many other commodities. Milling-in-transit for grain, compressing-in-transit for cotton, planing-in-transit for lumber, creosoting-in-transit, mixing-in-transit, fabrication-in-transit, and other transit privileges have become common.[30]

The milling-in-transit privilege on grain originated primarily to enable eastern flour mills to compete with the newer mills of the Middle West located closer to the expanding sources of grain. The latter were able to ship flour to the Atlantic seaboard at through rates which were considerably below the local inbound rates on grain to eastern mills plus the local outbound rates on flour to destination.[31] The milling-in-transit privilege tended to equalize the rate burden and permit eastern mills to compete. Subsequently the privilege was extended to western

---

[28] 35 ICC 477, 482 (1916).

[29] H. B. Vanderblue and K. F. Burgess, *Railroads: Rates, Service, Management* (New York: Macmillan Co., 1924), pp. 136–37.

[30] For an account of the development of transit privileges, see Reginald V. Hobbah, "Railroad Transit Privileges," *Journal of Business of the University of Chicago*, vol. 17, pt. 2 (July 1944).

[31] E. R. Johnson, G. G. Huebner, and G. L. Wilson, *Transportation: Economic Principles and Practices* (New York: D. Appleton-Century Co., 1940), pp. 83–84.

FIGURE 5–3
Effect of Transit on Freight Charges

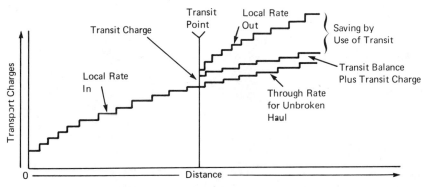

mills, the later to still newer milling centers in the Southwest, contributing significantly to their growth. As such arrangements receive wide application, the special advantage of the few locations at which they were originally applied disappears. Lacking transit privileges, milling would tend to concentrate at primary grain markets, whence the through rate on flour would apply, or at markets where grain would be received on through rates. One additional alternative would be to locate at rate-break points over which through rates are made as combinations.

The growth of nonrail transport has led to increased competition in iron and steel, grain, and other commodities to which transit privileges have extended. While grain transit was for a time effective in retaining traffic for the railroads against the efforts of barge lines operating out of Missouri, Mississippi, and Illinois River markets, the growth of trucking into these points from the growing areas gradually eroded rail business. Moreover the grain rate structure was not cost based but involved extensive grouping and equalization of markets, milling centers, and ports. Where rates were high in relation to cost, traffic tended to be diverted by trucks until much of the remaining traffic was unprofitable. In the face of these circumstances railroads have moved to introduce cost-based mileage rates on grain without the transit privilege, multiple-car and unit-train rates, and other devices. Milling centers founded upon transit naturally oppose these changes, and relocations are a likely long-run effect.

Rate Groups

The practice of carriers in grouping various origins and destinations on the same rate basis may have significant effects upon the location of manufacturing (and wholesaling) as between particular cities in close proximity to one another. Railroads have frequently made rates between "key" points and developed groups around these points extending along the line in each direction. Such groups have often been quite large.[32] Motor carriers have resorted on occasion to the same practice, and intercoastal water carriers have grouped all North Atlantic and North Pacific ports at the same rates. The groups may not, however, coincide on traffic to and from the several directions of movement, with the result that the "key" point itself enjoys an advantage as compared with other points grouped with it. Where rate groups meet, points in the nearer group enjoy an advantage, and it is frequently the practice to extend the group to just take in a large competitive point, leaving the towns beyond on a higher rate basis. This tends to concentrate industry at the larger competitive point so favored.

Broad grouping has long been applied to points in New England. On business to and from points west of Pittsburgh and Buffalo, rates were made equal to virtually all cities and towns in New England. The result has been a surprising decentralization of industry, with much of it carried out in the small towns.[33] The development of ubiquitous motor transportation tends to support this condition. Similar results were secured by the old rate system in Texas, under which all the principal towns of the state were treated as common points for both in and out rates; that is to say, they were given the same rates to and from points in the North, East, and Middle West.[34] The southern basing-point system, on the other hand, favored selected locations at which water or vigorous railroad competition was present, with the result that industry and commerce tended to be strongly centralized.[35] From these examples it may be concluded that the peculiarities of rate structures may have sharp effects upon the specific location of industries within a region and may govern the extent to which industry becomes centralized or dispersed.

Grouping practices developed by the railroads in neutralizing their own competition or in meeting water competition are tending to break down under the more pervasive competition present today. The trend toward cost-based rates is strong, but new incentive rates tied to heavy loading and high utilization of equipment tend to be superimposed upon the existing rate structure so that the older basis of rates may continue to be available. Nevertheless, it is becoming increasingly difficult to maintain artificial advantages of location attributable to peculiarities of rate structure in the face of the present intensity of

[32] Even where rate structures were most orderly; see *Eastern Class Rate Investigation*, 164 ICC 364 (1930).

[33] Eliot Jones, *Principles of Railway Transportation* (New York: Macmillan Co., 1924),

[34] E. R. Johnson and G. G. Huebner, *Railroad Traffic and Rates* (New York: Key Publishing Co., 1914), vol. 1, pp. 436–38.

[35] See 8 ICR 409 (1900); and *Alabama Midland Case*, 168 U.S. 144 (1897).

intermodal competition and the ability of the shipper to use private truck or water transport when common-carrier rates exceed the costs of specific hauls.

Developing and Maintaining Competition

Carriers, with their power to initiate rates, can exert considerable influence on location by means of specific rate policies. They can assist in perpetuating existing but badly located industries and can often hamper the development of similar industries in more favorable locations.[36] Most carriers, and particularly railroad companies, take an active interest in promoting industrial development along their lines. It is the common practice, as far as permitted by regulatory authority, not only to fix rates to enable all rival producing and marketing areas to compete but also to make such concessions as may be necessary to foster new industrial developments on the lines of a particular carrier. Each carrier seeks to develop and retain a volume of traffic which will yield the maximum net return.

Modern industrial location practice does not take the rates existing in the tariffs for granted. Large industrial concerns, in particular, when seeking new locations for expansion of their productive plant will determine what rates are necessary to make a proposed location viable and undertake negotiations with carriers with a view to secure such rates. If the necessary rates are above probable carrier costs for conducting the service and if they are not so far out of line with existing rate structures as to suggest widespread disruption, they may be capable of being put into effect. Hundreds of rate and service negotiations may precede a final location decision.

FACILITIES AND SERVICE

Though transportation cost often rates high as a locating factor, specific site location is much influenced by service availability. Sites adjacent to navigable waters are often chosen for heavy industry whether or not there is expectation that water transport will be needed or used. The potential confers bargaining power in securing the needed supply of service from land carriers and may exert a downward influence on rates charged by such carriers for traffic that is susceptible of water movement. Many industries, particularly those in high technology areas and in light manufacturing, have no need for rail transportation. But they will seek locations which have good ac-

---

[36] See J. M. Clark, *Standards of Reasonableness in Local Freight Discriminations* (New York: Columbia University Studies in the Social Sciences, 1910), vol. 97, pp. 68–69.

cess to the highway system and which can attract the service of numerous competitive motor carriers which reach broad destination territories. Thus adequate supply of equipment may be secured and attention to delivery schedules invited. Where large volume shipments over long distances must be made, direct access to the rail system will also be sought. Service by more than one railroad is frequently specified, since competitive service improves the likelihood of adequate car supply and confers bargaining power. It is no accident, therefore, that state and local governments which seek to attract industry place considerable emphasis on their transport endowment.[37]

Both abandonment of routes and service and those mergers which may eliminate competition within a mode are likely to be resisted by established industry. Rail mergers which result in service being provided by a single company at a given location eliminate the bargaining power of shippers dependent on rail service. Few operating rail lines, no matter how light their traffic and unremunerative their results to the railroad, are without some connected industry built in reliance on the continued availability of rail service. Truck transport is always procurable, but for low-grade or bulk traffic its use is likely to occasion higher costs than are imposed by existing rail rates. Abandonment of the rail line could mean demise of the industry at its present location. It could mean, also, the economic decline of the community which depends on that industry for its livelihood.

We will note later that railroad abandonment has become an important issue because of the burden which losses on light-traffic lines impose upon the industry. At the moment the proposed reorganization of the failed Milwaukee road calls for the abandonment of some 6,000 miles of line, while Conrail is seeking to drop several thousand miles whose closing was expected at the time the system was established. These proposals incite sharp resistance by rail labor and by affected industries and communities. The wisdom of extensive abandonment is also challenged on grounds that railroads produce less environmental impact than highways and that railroads are more efficient users of fuel.[38] Despite the uncertainties, the railroads of the Northeast have continued to bid successfully for new industrial locations on their principal lines which, it is plain, must be preserved in the regional and national interest.

---

[37] Mere provision of added transport capabilities may prove insufficient to induce industrial location, for the site selection process compares advantages. Thus the Appalachian Highway program appears to have had a minimal effect upon improving the economic base of the region.

[38] This last can be shown on average, but it is far from clear that a diesel locomotive consumes less fuel trundling a few cars down a branch line than would trucks moving the same volume of freight.

SELECTED REFERENCES

Daggett, Stuart. *Principles of Inland Transportation*, chap. 22, 4th ed. New York: Harper & Bros., 1955.

Florence, P. Sargent. *The Logic of British and American Industry*. London: Routledge and Kegan Paul, Ltd., 1953.

————. *Economics and Sociology of Industry: A Realistic Analysis of Development*. Rev. ed. Baltimore: The Johns Hopkins Press, 1969.

Greenhut, Melvin L. *Plant Location in Theory and in Practice*. Chapel Hill: University of North Carolina Press, 1956.

Holmes, W. G. *Plant Location*. New York: McGraw-Hill Book Co., 1930.

Hoover, Edgar M. *The Location of Economic Activity*. New York: McGraw-Hill Book Co., 1948.

Isard, Walter. *Location and Space Economy*. Cambridge: M.I.T. Press, 1956.

Locklin, D. Philip. *Economics of Transportation*, chap. 4. 7th ed. Homewood, Ill.: Richard D. Irwin, Inc., 1972.

————. *Report on Interterritorial Freight Rates*. Washington, D.C.: U.S. Board of Investigation and Research, 1943.

Lösch, August. *The Economics of Location*. Trans. from 2d rev. ed. by William H. Woglem with the assistance of Wolfgang F. Stolper. New Haven: Yale University Press, 1954.

Lynch, Edward S. "The Influence of Transportation on the Location of Economic Activities." In U.S. National Resources Planning Board, *Transportation and National Policy*. Washington, D.C., 1942.

McLaughlin, Glenn E., and Robock, Stephen. *Why Industry Moves South*. National Planning Association Committee of the South, 1949.

Richards, Hoy A. "Transportation Costs and Plant Location: A Review of Principal Theories." In Hale C. Bartlett, ed., *Readings in Physical Distribution*, 3d ed., 1972, pp. 124–31.

Weber, Alfred. *Theory of the Location of Industries*. English edition with introduction by Carl Joachim Friedrich. Chicago: University of Chicago Press, 1929.

6

Principles of Transportation—Restated

Writers and practitioners in the field have long used the term *principles* without giving themselves, much less the beginning student, the benefit of a clear statement of what transportation principles really are. The principles should relate to the controlling essentials for the efficient performance of the economic function that is transportation. They should identify the conditions of efficient performance on the part of every carrier whether modal or intermodal. These conditions for optimum efficiency are as follows:

1. Continuous flow: minimization of backhaul handling, transfer, and delay.
2. Optimum unit of cargo.
3. Maximum vehicle unit.
4. Adaptation of vehicle unit to volume and nature of traffic: multiple versus single vehicle units.
5. Standardization: vehicles, terminals, and procedures.
6. Compatibility of standard unit loads and equipment.
7. Minimum ratio of deadweight to total weight of unit of movement.
8. Optimum utilization of capital, equipment, and personnel.

In any situation a carrier should recognize these principles and seek to find the most workable balance at a given time. Likewise these principles should be applied in planning and programming changes in plant, facilities, and operation. We shall examine them in turn.

CONTINUOUS FLOW

The function of transportation is to convey goods and persons from point of origin to desired destination. The principle of continuous movement is that the objectives of minimum cost and time require the avoidance of reverse or out-of-line movement and a minimization of handling, interchange of equipment, and transfer of goods and persons. Continuous flow is the desired objective. This potential provides the economic advantage of pipeline transportation—so much so that with continued advance in pipeline technology and with application to it of the other principles discussed below, this mode is in time likely to be the most economic mode for all kinds of traffic that it can be adapted to carry. Both suspension of dry bulk commodities in a liquid (usually water) to form a slurry and the movement of goods in capsules floated in the pipeline stream are making rapid advance.

The end-to-end merging of railroads has been characteristic of railroad development in the United States because it promoted the application of this principle. So long as there were six or more interchanges and transfers of lading by the six railroads between New York City and Buffalo, the Erie Canal route, because it provided the capability of continuous flow, was able to compete. But when those lines were merged into the New York Central Railroad, the advantage for much traffic went quickly to the railroad with its superior speed, capacity, and dependability. Intercity bus transportation between many cities has attained new levels of efficiency because of superhighways bypassing intermediate communities and providing controlled access and egress with no traffic lights. Fast through service now competes favorably with the speed of rail service at a lower cost to the passenger. Motor transport of freight has similarly been greatly improved in efficiency by these same highway developments.

Transfers and interchange generate loss of time and raise costs, both of which should be reduced to a minimum. This accounts for the recent and prospective rapid development of containerization for interchange and transfer operations, the preblocking of freight trains to avoid reclassification at interchange points, and the introduction of long-distance interline freight-train schedules which bypass customary interchange procedures and often utilize pooled locomotives and cabooses so that the entire consist may run through. It accounts, also, for increased interchange of loaded trailers between connecting motor carriers. While containerization of air cargo is essential to the rapid turnaround of valuable aircraft, it also affords a means for rapid interchange between connecting airlines and with off-airport assembly points.

OPTIMUM UNIT OF CARGO

Within the capabilities of standard vehicles and cargo-handling accommodations and equipment, the cost of handling cargo tends to vary inversely with the size of the unit of shipment. Very large units, such as large structural materials and assembled units including, but not limited to, missiles, generators, and large vehicles, often exceed the dimensions of standard trucks, cars, and platforms and the weight capacity of vehicles and cranes and other standard handling equipment. They therefore require special equipment in both vehicles and terminal facilities. Because this means added cost and time for transfer in addition to large investment, transport costs tend to be high. However, within the limits of standard facilities, the larger the unit of shipment, the lower the cost per ton-mile, as illustrated in Table 6–1 for a particular type of railroad equipment. The reason for this lower cost of transporting a larger unit is that the time required to handle it to and from terminals, to and from transportation vehicles, and to move it within terminals is as little as for smaller units; hence there is no added cost of movement. Furthermore, the clerical cost incident to documentation and recordkeeping is approximately the same regardless of the size of the shipment. The optimum-sized unit of cargo is that which a lift truck, conveyor, or crane can handle at terminals and warehouses properly designed for their use. For example, the larger the draft of cargo going into or coming out of an ocean vessel, the lower the cost per ton of loading or unloading.

TABLE 6–1
Costs in Cents per 100 Pounds for
500-Mile Haul (southern territory,
covered hopper cars)

Revenue Load (tons)	Variable Cost	Fixed Cost	Total Cost
50	27.1	33.2	60.3
60	23.6	29.7	53.3
70	21.2	27.3	48.5
80	19.3	25.4	44.7
90	17.9	24.0	41.9
100	16.7	22.8	39.5

Source: Interstate Commerce Commission, *Rail Carload Cost Scales by Territories for the Year 1969* (1971), p. 66.

MAXIMUM VEHICLE UNIT

This principle corresponds to the previous one and has much the same logic behind it. The normal trend in the development of technology of any type of transportation is to go from smaller units to larger units of vehicle movement. The individual vehicle unit tends to get ever larger; and where, as with rail and barge transport, multiples of freight-carrying vehicles are assembled into trains or tows for line-haul movement, the size of these aggregate units tends to increase. There are two principal reasons for this development: first, the operating costs of the vehicle unit do not increase proportionately to its size; second, the cost of handling, dispatching, and documentation tend to be the same regardless of size. The ratio of payload to the gross weight of the loaded vehicle tends to increase with increasing size. The ratio of labor cost to ton-miles performed tends to decline as the size of the vehicle unit increases. The one or two drivers required in intercity motortruck operation are the same regardless of the capacity of the vehicle. In larger aircraft the size of the officer crew tends to increase, but not proportionately. Even the number of flight attendants may not increase in proportion to the size of the aircraft. In the ocean cargo vessel not only is the crew size of a very large ship often no greater than that of a much smaller one, but construction costs per ton of capacity decline with increase of size, and water resistance per ton is less with larger hulls so that horsepower and fuel consumption per ton are reduced for any given speed.

Extending the principle of the single-vehicle unit is the multiple-vehicle movement that is characteristic of railroad and barge operation. The assembly of a number of these vehicle units to form a large tow or train accounts for the great economy and low cost of these two modes of transportation. Prior to World War II a tow on the Mississippi or Ohio River of 10 to 15 barges was considered a large tow. Not only are the barges larger but tows are now assembled which include from 30 to 40 barges. Similarly, trains of slightly over 100 cars were considered very large trains in prewar times, but today trains may exceed 200 cars. In both barge and rail transportation, these larger size multiple units have been made possible by the development of power units to accommodate them. The power unit for a modern tow may reach 9,500 horsepower. The diesel engine has made it possible to increase the amount of power indefinitely in train operation without increasing the number of crews to operate locomotive units, since diesel units operate together under control of a single engineman. Remote control permits slave units to be spotted in a midtrain position, thus improving power distribution and minimizing slack action.

In pipeline transportation, the optimum vehicle unit and multiple vehicle unit concepts are merged. Prior to the beginning of World War II, a ten-inch pipeline was common. During the war, the Little Big Inch (20-inch diameter) and the Big Inch (24-inch diameter) were put into operation. They extended from the Texas-Louisiana producing areas to the northeastern markets. Postwar several companies cooperated to build the Colonial Pipe Line from Houston to New York, with a diameter of 36 inches. Recent pipelines in the Middle East and in western Europe range up to 48 inches in diameter as does the Alaska Pipeline. The limit has certainly not yet been achieved. Assuming good utilization, the larger the pipe the lower the cost of transport. At any given rate of flow, power requirements tend to be governed largely by the friction encountered along the pipe wall, hence capacity increases as the square of the diameter of the pipes. These giant pipelines, like the large multiple-vehicle units of barge and rail transport, were made possible by development of power units, in this case pumps.

Multiple trailers for highway tractors have come into use in some parts of the country. The so-called double bottom operation is common in the West and Middle West and on some of the toll roads of the East. Further improvement in the efficiency of truck transportation depends heavily on the liberalization of size and weight limitations and the extension of the area in which double bottoms are permitted. There has been speculation in regard to multiple-unit aircraft operation, but to date there has been no successful demonstration of this.

ADAPTATION OF VEHICLE UNIT TO VOLUME AND NATURE OF TRAFFIC

The flow of traffic of any carrier tends to vary not only over an extended period of time but often during days of the week and hours of the day. The adaptation of the amount of equipment to the traffic to be carried in a given time must be effectively accomplished if efficiency is to be obtained. This presents a serious problem to single-vehicle units which prevail in deep-sea shipping and air and motor-highway transportation. The vehicle is kept on schedule in both directions regardless of the volume of traffic which may be available at a given time. The multiple-unit carriers, that is, the barge lines and railroads, have a distinct advantage in adapting the size of the unit of movement to the volume of traffic. This is another explanation of the economy to be found in these two modes of transport. The diesel locomotive has enabled the railroads to apply this principle to a degree that was impossible in the era of steam locomotives. To handle a train which in size and weight exceeded the capacity of a single steam locomotive, it was necessary for the railroad to double the amount of power for the few added cars which were involved and to have two engine crews instead of one. In addition, helper locomotives were commonly used on steep, but short, grades. The diesel-electric locomotives tend to come in smaller power units which may be multiplied as necessary to provide the right amount of power for the size and weight of the trains, considering the grades with which they will have to contend.

Adaptation of equipment to the nature of the traffic may make for heavier loads and quicker loading and unloading and, in fact, make possible the very existence of the traffic. Perishable traffic could not become important for the railroads or trucks until refrigerator equipment had been made available. Hopper cars of high weight and cubic capacity have much to do with the low cost of rail transport for coal, fertilizer, and other bulk commodities. Recently we have seen railroads go further in specialized equipment. Two classic examples are the rack cars for handling automobiles and the covered-hopper cars for grain, both of which have substantially reduced the cost of transport of these commodities. We tend to think of motor carriers as essentially merchandise carriers; but because of the ease of developing and using specialized equipment, they are extensive haulers of livestock, grain, perishables, chemicals, and plastics over substantial distances and lumber, pulpwood, petroleum products, coal, and even sand and gravel over relatively short distances.

Perhaps one of the oldest classic examples of adaptation for special service is the development of the ore/coal boats on the Great Lakes, which for so many years provided the lowest cost transport to be found in the United States. These vessels are very large, with considerable width and limited draft providing throughout most of their length a series of open hatches to facilitate delivery of ore by numerous spouts at the docks in Lake Superior and to permit the use of grab buckets in all parts of the hold at the Lake Erie and Lake Michigan ports of unloading. Ten thousand tons of ore can be loaded in two to four hours and unloaded in eight to ten hours. As in the case of ocean-going vessels, the size of lake bulk ships has been greatly increased. The most recent such craft accommodate up to 58,000 tons of ore. The trend today is toward self-unloading vessels with discharge rates up to 10,000 tons per hour.

It follows from this example that the adaptation of the transport vehicle for bulk commodities usually requires development of specialized terminal facilities like car dumpers, ore docks, and mechanical unloading devices. These along with the low ton-mile costs of the loaded specialized vehicle account for the economy of the bulk-freight operations. But the size of ship that it is economical to employ depends upon the length of haul and the rate of loading and unloading—the longer the haul, the faster the rate, the larger the ship that may be used. See Figure 6-1. Bulk freight generally lends itself to specialization of both carrying equipment and terminal facilities. For manufactured goods and merchandise, specialized equipment reduces or eliminates packing costs. Typewriter trucks, for example, are equipped with numerous little compartments appropriately lined and padded. Automobile parts cars have racks designed to secure the particular parts intended to be loaded.

STANDARDIZATION

This principle of transportation efficiency in theory is contrary to the principle of adaptation as applied to equipment to handle specific

FIGURE 6-1

Unit Cost of Iron Ore Transport by Size of Ship and Capacity of Shore Equipment

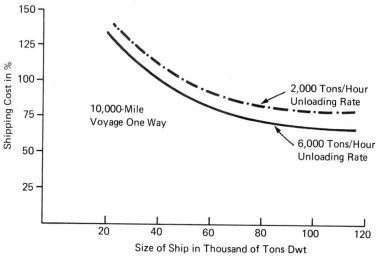

commodities. It does in fact mean that there are limits to adaptation to specific kinds of traffic. The backhaul of specialized transport equipment like hopper cars for coal or grain and tank cars and tanker vessels tends to be empty. No more than half of the downbound ore boats on the Great Lakes return to Lake Superior and Lake Michigan points with coal. Refrigerator cars usually return empty. The economic cost advantage of the specialized equipment must take into account the cost of the empty backhaul. That cost may, if the volume is large enough, be offset by the reduced loading and unloading cost of specialized equipment. A common carrier of freight is likely to have such a large variety of commodities to haul that the use of specialized equipment would not be possible for a substantial part of its business. General-purpose equipment is therefore used. This equipment includes boxcars, gondola cars, and flatcars on railroads; general commodity trailers; and containers for trucks and general cargo ships.

Compromise of equipment and service to provide flexible general-purpose capability poses a dilemma for common carriers. Shippers more and more seek equipment designed to meet their particular needs and dedicated to their service. Such demands pressed by large shippers who have alternatives open to them can rarely be resisted, but the penalty for the carrier is a high equipment investment in relation to volume of traffic and an increased ratio of empty to loaded miles. When available funds for investment in new equipment are limited, as is usual, the fleet of general-purpose equipment declines from want of replacement; and shippers dependent upon it suffer during periods of equipment shortage.

Standardization in transportation applies to way structures including terminal facilities and communication systems which are used by carriers, as well as vehicle units, both power and burden carrying. It also applies to methods of operating the carrier and carrier communications. We will briefly consider these in reverse order.

The need for standardization of communications in respect to equipment and operating methods within a carrier's scope of operations for a smooth flow of traffic and for safety purposes is obvious. Where all carriers make common use of terminal facilities and services and traffic-control centers as with ships and aircraft, uniform and standard equipment and procedures are unavoidable. Similarly compatible communications among connecting carriers which interchange freight with one another are essential to speedy movement and to recording the location of shipments and their progress toward destination.

Terminals and shops must be standardized to accord with common aspects of vehicle equipment. For example, standard floor levels of railcars and trucks should be matched by equivalent levels of platforms at terminals, warehouses, and the business establishments they serve. Before World War II, Atlantic coastal cities were served extensively in coastwise service by side-port delivery vessels, that is, sections of the hull of the vessel above the waterline could be opened to deliver and receive cargo. Wharves were built with ramps to facilitate the use of mechanized equipment for loading and unloading. It was a very superior way of handling merchandise cargo, but it never approximated its potential because spacings of side ports of vessels of the several operators and the spacing of the ramps at ports seldom permitted operation of all side ports at one time. This lack of standardization made the service less effective in competing with rail and truck service and hastened its disappearance. A similar problem exists today regarding airfreight operations with respect to level and width of fuselage doors and terminal facilities.

In general, standardization applied to equipment, terminals, and methods of operation may be as important as adaptation to meet special traffic requirements. Transport efficiency requires vigorous and balanced employment of both in optimum concert. On the whole, specialization will be resorted to when commodity movements are large and consistent and when the saving in loading and unloading costs incident upon specialization more than offsets the costs of empty backhaul. Where these conditions are absent, general-purpose equipment will tend to be used. Thus we have another example of trade-offs.

Standardization of communications, both facilities and operating rules and methods, is essential for any form of interchange or joint use of terminals. Interchange of railroad cars throughout the North American continent is made possible by a standard gauge of 4 feet

8½ inches. Except for Spain and the Soviet Union, the same is true of Europe. But free interchange of cars also requires that all cars whether railroad or privately owned have standard widths, couplings, airbrake connections, and wheels. Even the specialized cars mentioned above are compatible in these respects.

Safety in passing of ships and aircraft requires common rules of the road and special communication facilities aboard vehicles. All ship-and-shore stations, whether equipped with radio telephone or radio telegraph, have the same safety calling frequencies and signals. In congested airspace, aircraft must be monitored by controllers on the gound who are able to communicate with each plane with speed and certainty regardless of nationality.

Specialized railcars, ships, and aircraft must conform either in some aspects of design or procedures or both. Motor-transport development has involved a minimum of standardization, but the age of containerization is upon us, which is already prescribing standard dimensions, fastening devices, and transfer methods; and the motortruck trailer body is the most important container. General standards in dimensions and transfer equipment are now employed. There is great reluctance to adopt a single standard trailer-body container used in interchange, but free interchange as with railroads will require it.

Compatibility of rail track and cars and the design of ships and barges and of loading and unloading facilities used with them is necessary for the highly specialized systems of transporting bulk materials. Low cost and expeditious transfer at terminals is the result. For nonbulk freight, standard container systems provide the only way to obtain comparable time and cost of transfer. Extensive systems for handling such freight will necessarily require compatibility in equipment and transfer methods. Piggyback service has grown rapidly, but efficient through-movement and free interchange throughout the nation and continent will not be possible as long as we have several different systems of rail piggy-back (transfer between rail and highway car) operations and no agreed-upon standards for containers. Fortunately, in the interim, Flexi-Van or other container types can be placed on bogeys and handled just as are conventional semitrailers over rail piggyback ramps where end loading is practical.

COMPATIBILITY OF UNIT-LOAD EQUIPMENT

Unit load equipment should be designed to insure compatibility in combining subunits. If the 40' × 8' × 8' trailer body is the standard unit, smaller containers must have dimensions that will be compatible. They usually are of 20' × 8' × 8' or 10' × 8' × 8' outside measurement to enable them to fit into the system. The dimensions and fittings of the vehicle whether truck chassis, flatcar, or ship's deck must be adaptable to all possible combinations of units and subunits. Compatibility may be looked upon as an extension of the principle of standardization. By the same token, unit loads that are to be put into vehicles or containers should be of dimensions that will fit readily and tightly so that space may be effectively used and unoccupied space within which loads could shift be minimized. Strapped pallet loads are common for case goods and should have dimensions determined by those of the vehicles to be used.

MINIMIZATION OF DEADWEIGHT TO TOTAL WEIGHT

The minimization of deadweight to total weight of the vehicle unit of movement or the maximization of payload weight to total weight is an important principle of vehicle-unit design. The cost of fuel in transport operation is directly related to the total weight of the unit of movement, whereas revenue relates only to the payload in the vehicle. The larger the railcar, the aircraft fuselage, the ship, or the truck trailer, the more favorable the ratio tends to be.

The use of unit-load equipment in coordinated transportation, whether railcar, truck trailer or trailer body, containers, or pallet boards, produces an unfavorable ratio. The economic advantage arises because their use makes possible a better application of other principles, especially the all-important one of minimizing handling and transfer time and costs. Nevertheless, the principle of a favorable weight ratio applies to the design and construction of containers and the equipment used for their transportation. Both design and the use of lightweight materials can assist in minimizing the tendency for empty weight to grow in relation to revenue capacity.

MAXIMUM UTILIZATION OF CAPITAL, EQUIPMENT, AND PERSONNEL

Last, but certainly not least, is the principle of intensive utilization of capital, equipment, and personnel. Good utilization of capital, plant, equipment, and personnel is more difficult for a carrier than for most enterprises. As for all service industries, output cannot be stored. Available capacity must be such as to meet the demand for service at the time needed. Both freight and passenger traffic are subject to seasonal, weekly, and daily peaks and valleys. In addition to the fluctuations in time there is the imbalance of traffic between the two directions of vehicle movement—the problem of the backhaul common to freight operations. Through lower backhaul rates, vigorous promotion of traffic, rate agreements with connecting carriers, and merger, carriers try to reduce the imbalance.

The amount and kind of plant investment should be dictated by realistic estimates of volume of traffic and revenue. This problem is made greater for railroads and pipelines which, unlike other modes, must make extensive investment in way and fixed facilities. In respect to equipment, the airlines and steamship lines must replace their fleet units by much larger and more expensive equipment in accordance with the technological development of their industries. The economic and business advantage of steamship lines going to super ore boats and tankers and of airlines going to jumbo jets comes in reduced operating cost per ton-mile and cubic-foot-mile of payload capacity. But unless utilization is above the break-even point, operating losses will result.

Utilization does not refer only to load factor of the vehicle unit of movement. It refers to the total of payload ton-miles or passenger-miles produced in a given period of time. The percentage of the time that the vehicle is moving under load and its speed as well as its average load factor will determine the utilization. It is for that reason that effective management is concerned with the average hours in flight per day in aircraft operations, with loaded car-miles and locomotive-miles per day in rail operations, and with the percent of time a ship spends moving at sea under load. Only pipelines limit utilization measurement to determination of average load factor and do not need to consider standby time of vehicles. Railroads, in addition to the other measures noticed, must also pay heed to the density of traffic per mile of road per day and to the relation of throughput in terminals to the installed capacity.

As suggested above, the increasing investment in vehicle equipment of a specialized sort creates the general prospect of an empty backhaul. So adherence to the positive value of one principle may make it difficult to adhere to another. The answer is that the investment in transport facilities, its allocation and use, should be guided by a recognition of all these principles and result in the most effective accommodations for national economic and carrier performance. New incentives and new methods of sharing economies among the shippers and carriers in major traffic movements may be needed.

SELECTED REFERENCES

Bowersox, Donald J.; Smykay, Edward W.; and La Londe, Bernard J. *Physical Distribution Management.* Rev. ed. New York: Macmillan Co., 1968, pp. 140–51.

Hay, William W. *An Introduction to Transportation Engineering*, chaps. 8 and 9. New York: John Wiley & Sons, Inc., 1961.

Koopmans, Tjalling C. "Optimum Utilization of the Transportation System," In *Proceedings of the International Statistical Conferences, 1947*. Vol. 5. Washington, D.C., 1947. Vol. 5 reprinted as supplement to *Econometrics*, vol. 17 (1949), pp. 136–46.

Loree, L. F. *Railroad Freight Transportation*. New York: D. Appleton & Co., 1922.

McCallum, George E. *New Techniques in Railroad Ratemaking*, chaps. 4 and 5. Pullman: Washington State University, 1968.

Meyers, Harold B. "The Maritime Industry's Expensive New Box." In Hale C. Bartlett, ed., *Readings in Physical Distribution*, 3d ed. Danville, Ill.: The Interstate Printers & Publishers, Inc., 1972, pp. 193–202.

Norman, O. K., and Walker, W. P. *Highway Capacity Manual*. Washington, D.C.: Bureau of Public Roads, U.S. Department of Commerce, 1950.

7

Intercity Passenger Logistics

To travel faster and farther for both pleasure and profit has ever been a prime interest of human beings. It is both the means and the measure of social advancement. Travel for business and pleasure increase greatly as industrial and social life advance. Increased business travel is a concomitant of expanding goods movement required to serve an expanding market in spite of some saving from advances in the technology of communications. More travel to conventions, to political, religious, educational, and social gatherings and to resorts and places of interest is to be expected in the advanced industrial countries.

Intercity passenger logistics is a major consideration in every country, but becomes a complicated national problem in a large industrial nation. In this chapter we shall examine intercity passenger transport with particular reference to the United States. Our country has experienced three great revolutions in passenger transportation. First was that of the railroad development in the 19th century, which replaced travel by horse-drawn vehicles and passenger water craft. Second was the spread of the motor vehicle which replaced local rail services and electric interurban railroads during the early part of the 20th century. Third was the replacement of most of the intercity railroad passenger service and ocean steamship service by air transportation, a transition which occurred rapidly after 1950 and accelerated with the introduction of jet aircraft early in the 60s. In the next chapter we will look at people and goods movement in the urban context.

TRAVEL IN AN AFFLUENT SOCIETY

One of the hallmarks of a society which generates high per capita income is a complex economic system with strong agricultural and industrial bases and highly developed service industries, of which transportation is one. These highly developed economic systems are further characterized by increasingly large-scale enterprises, both business and governmental, operating not only in the national sphere but on an international, even worldwide, basis. Rapid communication by telegraph and cable, telephone, and more recently, the transmission of vast quantities of data by wire, microwave (including direct computer inputs), and by either in conjunction with communications satellites have improved the ability to conduct business over great distances. Yet, although closed circuit television is to some extent employed for conference purposes, no satisfactory substitute has been found for frequent face-to-face contact of managers, scientists, educators, and diplomats.

Improved transportation of passengers has greatly facilitated the development of organizations whose operations extend over wide areas—in particular by the saving of time. It was possible in an earlier era for far-flung business operations to be conducted—witness the British and Dutch East Indies companies or the Hudson Bay Company. But these were primarily trading enterprises in which authority was locally delegated. Contacts with the home office might be separated by months, even a year, when personnel and communications were conveyed by sailing ship.

The old-fashioned drummer who made his way from town to town by the railroads' slow-moving accommodation trains has been replaced by the salesperson who reaches the customer by automobile or aircraft. Top executives of companies that do business on a nationwide or multinational scale spend much more time in travel than hitherto, but they do it predominantly by fast air trips which avoid lengthy absences from their home offices.[1] Whether on the West Coast, in Europe, or in Latin America, the executive may reach his company's establishments in the field, conduct his business there, and be back in a matter of days. While most of this travel is by commercial airlines, the corporate aircraft has come to play an increasing role because of its flexibility in timing and the directness of its routing to points off the trunk-line air system.[2]

---

[1] Business travel represents a small portion of the whole. Prior to airline deregulation the proportion was increasing—from 19 percent of the trips in 1957 to 21 percent in 1963 and 23.9 percent in 1972 (*Statistical Abstract of the United States*). But a proliferation of reduced fares in 1978 and 1979 greatly expanded the volume of nonbusiness travel.

[2] Since deregulation the reduction of service at many smaller points and the increasing uncertainty of space availability on major routes appears to be causing increased use of corporate aircraft.

An increase of discretionary income leads to a great expansion of per capita recreational travel. Shortened work weeks and lengthened vacations contribute to the same end. But the automobile and the improved highway system, along with highway-related accommodations and recreational attractions, bear the major responsibility for channeling income into travel, especially where family groups are involved. In the United States, personal consumption expenditures for transportation stood at $7.6 billion in 1929, or 9 percent of total personal consumption expenditures. At the depth of the depression 30s, they had been cut nearly in half. By 1950 they were at $24.7 billion and by 1967 at $63.5 billion, or just under 13 percent of total consumption expenditures. A decade later the figure reached $150.1 billion. User-operated transport, that is, the private automobile, accounted for over 85 percent of these expenditures.[3]

The phenomenon of personal travel by automobile is, of course, largely confined to North America, western Europe, and Japan. In 1940, 73.9 percent of the world's passenger automobiles were in the United States. This proportion has gradually declined to 53.7 percent in 1965 and 39.7 percent in 1977, principally because of the rapid rise of motor-vehicle ownership in western Europe. Whereas in 1977 there was one motor vehicle to every 2.0 persons in the United States, the west European figures ranged from 3.0 persons per vehicle in West Germany to 5.5 persons in Ireland.[4]

In no area of travel has the impact of recent improvement in transportation been so keenly felt as in the overseas movement of passengers. Overseas travel is nothing new, but in earlier times it was confined largely to those possessed of ample time and means. In the post–World War II period, the more general spread of income and of leisure combined with the speed and economy of the aircraft has brought overseas travel within the reach of large numbers of people.

Departure of U.S. citizens for overseas destinations stood at an average of 331,500 annually in the 1936–40 period. Postwar growth has shown acceleration. See Table 7–1. The ocean cruise has been an important aspect of this travel in recent years, accounting for 144,000 passengers in 1959 when the figure was first separately stated and 914,000 in 1977. If cruise passengers are not counted, nearly half of all departures (citizen plus alien) are for Europe and another 38 percent are destined for Mexico and the West Indies.[5] In 1977 U.S. Citizen depar-

---

[3] The composition of personal consumption expenditures is regularly reported in U.S. Department of Commerce, *Survey of Current Business*, and later, in the *Statistical Abstract of the United States*.

[4] Over half the world's population resides in Asia which has, however, less than 12 percent of the motor vehicles. Thus China has 23,750 persons per automobile and 1,284 persons per motor vehicle. Automobile Manufacturers' Association, *Automobile Facts and Figures* (1979), pp. 33–35.

[5] These data exclude transits over the land borders with Canada and Mexico.

tures were 89 percent by air and 11 percent on ocean cruises, with only 44,000 going by regular-route passenger vessel.

TABLE 7–1
U.S. Citizen Departure for Overseas (000)

1941–45*	102
1946–50*	473
1951–55*	894
1956–60*	1,567
1965	2,956
1970	5,820
1975	7,109
1977	8,304

* Average.
Source: 1936–63 data from *Statistical Abstract of the United States, 1965*, p. 99; later data from Transportation Association of America, *Transportation Facts and Trends* (Washington, D.C., 1965, 1967, 1971, 1979).

THE PASSENGER CARRIERS: DOMESTIC

The growth of intercity passenger traffic, measured in passenger-miles, has outstripped both the gross national product and the growth of freight traffic. In 1978 gross national product was 2.95 times its 1947 level; population 1.52 times; freight ton-miles, 2.39 times; but intercity passenger-miles, 3.61 times.[6] Expenditures for passenger transportation including the cost of owning and operating private automobiles, have exceeded 10 percent of gross national product since such calculations were first made in 1958. These passenger expenditures also exceed the nation's estimated freight transport bill.[7] All forms of transportation (except pipelines) participated in that traffic. There are individual carriers by water, rail, highway, and air which are devoted exclusively to either freight or passenger service. Most of the so-called passenger carriers, however, handle some goods in the form of mail, express, and baggage. The strictly passenger carriers are largely confined to the urban and suburban areas.

Until 1920 intercity travel was largely by rail, although coastwise and Great Lakes steamers rendered substantial passenger services. Railway travel reached 16 billion passenger-miles in 1900 and increased at the rate of approximately 5 percent each year until a peak of 47 billion was reached in 1920. Thereafter an irregular decline set in as the electric interurban railway, the bus, and the automobile began to

---

[6] Transportation Association of America, *Transportation Facts and Trends* (Washington, D.C., July 1979), p. 2.

[7] Ibid., p. 3. Commercial passenger transport, however, is only about one ninth of the total.

make inroads upon rail passenger volume. The rapid improvement of the motor bus and the spread of good highways enabled significant growth in that form of transport. But the automobile was the principal cause of the demise of the interurban electric railway and the gradual disappearance of local and branchline passenger traffic on the steam railways. Even in long-haul services the bus substantially replaced passenger train operations.

Air passenger transport was nonexistent in 1926, except for occasional emergency passengers carried on mail planes or by chartered aircraft. After 1927, however, with suitable multiengine aircraft available, services began to be offered over an increasing network of routes. Air transportation did not become price competitive with rail until after World War II. It did, however, continually develop its speed advantage as compared with all forms of surface transportation and greatly improved its record for reliability and safety. After World War II the growth of air passenger traffic was rapid. By 1956, air, rail, and bus were sharing intercity passenger-miles about evenly. In the following year air surpassed rail, and by 1967 air volume was five times the rail volume. The comparative participation of the several modes is shown at strategic dates in Table 7–2.

Despite the rapid growth of intercity commercial passenger transport, well over 80 percent of all intercity passenger movement has been by auto since the late 1920s except during the period of wartime gas and rubber rationing. Although trustworthy statistics on passenger-miles by private car are not available, estimates are regularly made from sample data. These show the extraordinary degree to which the automobile is relied upon and the magnitude of the growth which has made it impossible to keep the highway system abreast of demands. The estimates show, also, that more than half of the automobile trips are for business purposes of various kinds. The relation between automobile and all commercial intercity passenger-miles (given in billions) is shown in Table 7–3.

TABLE 7–2
Distribution of Commercial Domestic Intercity Passenger Traffic in the United States (millions of passenger-miles)

	1926		1940		1957		1979	
	Miles	Per-cent	Miles	Per-cent	Miles	Per-cent	Miles	Per-cent
Steam and electric railways	41,210	86.9	24,766	63.9	26,200	31.8	11,600	4.6
Buses	4,375	9.2	11,613	30.0	25,300	30.7	26,600	10.5
Domestic airlines	(none)		1,041	2.7	28,900	35.1	210,300	83.3
Inland waterways	1,848	3.9	1,317	3.4	2,000	2.4	4,000	1.6
Total	47,433	100.0	38,737	100.00	82,400	100.00	252,500	100.00

TABLE 7-3
Relation between Automobile and All Commercial Intercity Passenger-Miles (billions)

	Total Commercial		Automobile	
	Passenger-Miles	Percent	Passenger-Miles	Percent
1920	40.8	86	7.0	14
1940	30.9	11	238.4	89
1960	74.8	9.5	706.1	90.4
1970	154.8	13.1	1,026.0	86.9
1975	183.5	14.0	1,123.0	86.0
1978	239.7	15.6	1,297.7	84.4

What occurred in the United States in the 1920s and 1930s has spread to many other parts of the world since World War II as discretionary income has increased and the possibility of motor-vehicle ownership has grown. In no major country, however, has the price of gasoline been as low as in the United States; hence automobile size as well as relative use have been more inhibited elsewhere than here. Finally, it should be noticed that the volume of passenger transport by private aircraft, too, has been increasing rapidly, from 1.7 billion passenger-miles in 1952 to 12.7 billion in 1977.

CHARACTERISTICS OF PASSENGER TRAFFIC

Passenger traffic has certain favorable characteristics which assist the carriers. The traffic, unlike much freight movement, is well balanced by direction. Passengers who move in one direction usually return, often by the same route and even the same carrier. While emigration is important at various times and on a number of routes, its volume in relation to total movement is usually small. Passengers also load, unload, and transfer themselves and perform a portion of the baggage handling task. Unless carriers' service fails to adhere to schedule or connecting schedules are poorly arranged, it is not necessary to "warehouse" passengers. The majority move through terminals promptly so that a minimum of waiting space is required.

High standards of service have traditionally been provided for passengers, particularly in first-class accommodations. Fast and dependable service has been sought. The fast, through "limited" trains of the railroads used to be famous for their timekeeping qualities and were given preference over all other traffic except the silk expresses on the transcontinental lines. The shift to air transport has accustomed the public to a less reliable service. Weather conditions have been a bete noir of air transport from its beginnings; and while vast progress has been made, instrument approaches to airports still reduce normal capacity in periods of poor visibility and occasion delays both in the air and on the ground. When such conditions are widespread or prolonged, the entire schedule may become disorganized as aircraft assigned to outward flights are delayed elsewhere. Growing congestion of runways, gate positions, and air space around the large metropolitan airports make delay an even more common experience for the air traveler.

Since fares between two points are generally the same by all carriers of a particular mode, competition among passenger carriers tends to concentrate on service features rather than on price. This is an area of somewhat narrow opportunity which, except for the quality of the equipment itself, is largely one of passenger amenities. The airlines emphasize quality of cabin personnel, drink, and meal service, and provide music and movies in flight. In periods of low-load factors, as in 1971, space may be set aside for lounges and more commodious seating emphasized. Fare structure has been used not so much as a competitive device among airlines as it has been used to permit tapping various potential market segments without unduly diverting first-class revenue. The institution of coach service (originally at unpopular night hours) with high-density seating and less service than is provided in first-class was one of the earliest such efforts. Since airline deregulation in 1978 much more emphasis has been placed on a variety of reduced fare packages in order to fill unused space. In competitive markets such moves by one airline are usually quickly countered by others.

The principal element in service competition among passenger carriers is the equipment itself. Railroads well understood that service competition was expensive and sought, by schedule agreements, to avoid overt competition of this type. Schedule times were agreed on the principal long-haul passenger routes; and when trains were reequipped with new sleeping, dining, and lounge cars, the principal competitive trains often blossomed out with new equipment on the same day with, perhaps, a schedule speed-up thrown in for good measure.

Equipment is even more critical in the air-transport business. The airline that secures a preferred spot on the manufacturer's delivery schedule can offer an improved plane on principal competitive routes in advance of others. Speed and range, as well as increased comfort, commonly make the new aircraft particularly attractive to passengers and confer at least a temporary advantage on the airline.[8] Competi-

---

[8] A noteworthy example is TWAs failure to have aircraft in transcontinental service that could compete with the DC-7s introduced by United and American. TWA virtually disappeared from the transcontinental first-class market. Even greater penalties fell upon the lines that were slow in introducing jets. See Paul W. Cherington, *Airline Price Policy* (Boston: Harvard Graduate School of Business, 1958), pp. 257–64; cf. Samuel B. Richmond, *Regulation and Competition in Air Transportation* (New York: Columbia University Press, 1961), pp. 54–55.

tion for a place in delivery schedules for new and superior aircraft is one of the most important aspects of airline management. It tends, among other things, to substantial overcapacity at times of major transition from one generation of aircraft to another. The new aircraft are characteristically larger and faster than their predecessors, and airlines ordinarily have no means for accomplishing agreed cutbacks of schedule frequency. Hence capacity is temporarily expanded much more rapidly than passenger traffic can grow.[9] Earnings will be temporarily reduced—red ink may even appear.

Passenger traffic, like freight traffic, is predominantly short haul. There is a direct relationship between passenger volume and the population of communities between which it is generated and the distance that separates them. The chief domestic airline services, from the point of view of volume of travel, are New York-Florida, New York-Chicago, Los Angeles-San Francisco, New York-Boston, and New York-Washington, in that order. Hence, despite the great reduction in time which air transport has produced, the average trip is not long: 487 miles in 1946 and 719 miles in 1978. Average hauls by other modes are much shorter. In 1978 rail average haul was 217 miles and bus 126 miles.

Passenger carriers face traffic variations with which it is difficult to cope. Heavy weekend volumes are characteristically the result of the large pleasure-travel component. Holidays produce marked peaks, and these are exacerbated when the holiday falls on a Friday or Monday. These periods which generate maximum highway congestion and accident toll for automobile travel also produce the greatest peaks of air, bus, and rail passenger traffic. Public carriers cannot afford to own and hold idle large amounts of equipment to service the peak demands which characterize a half dozen annual holiday weekends. Yet it is at those times that many thousands of the public have their only contact with such carriers. They experience, crowding, delays, and temporary service breakdowns which generate much ill will. Seasonal variations are, to a degree, more easily managed. July and August rank first in passenger traffic. Winter traffic tends to be light in the West and North, but heavy in the South and on the North-South routes. Hence temporary transfers of equipment from one service to another assist in accommodating the heavier flows.

FACTORS AFFECTING PROFITABLE SERVICE

The costs of operating a schedule—whether by a train, bus, aircraft, or steamship—are largely independent of the volume of revenue traffic

---

[9] For an analysis of the propensity to overschedule, see William E. Fruhan, Jr., *The Fight for Competitive Advantage: A Study of the United States Domestic Trunk Air Carriers* (Boston: Harvard Business School, 1972), chap. 5.

handled by that schedule. Crew size, fuel consumption, and maintenance expenses are all virtually unaffected by the number of passengers aboard, as is depreciation of the heavy investment involved in the equipment itself. It follows that the revenue-load factor is of extraordinary importance. It may be defined as the ratio of revenue passenger-miles to seat-miles operated. Thus an aircraft operating nonstop between two points with 144 available seats and 72 revenue passengers would have a passenger load factor of 50 percent. Half the service generated by the trip would be forever lost since it was not used for carrying passengers. At any fare level and for any type of equipment and route, a break-even load factor can be calculated at which revenue will just cover cost. Airline load factors declined rapidly after jets were introduced because capacity was added more rapidly than traffic grew. After jets had been in service for a time and operations had become adjusted to them, their break-even load factors declined as compared with the previous generation of aircraft. With break-even load factors on long hauls down near 40 percent, the penalty of operating grossly excessive capacity was materially reduced.

Passenger fares reflect mileage more than any other factor;[10] hence revenue per seat-mile does not correspond with cost per seat-mile at various lengths of haul. Because of terminal costs, including landing fees in the case of aircraft, short-haul service cost by all forms of transport is higher per available seat-mile than longer hauls. Taxiing, warm-up, and the attainment of cruising altitude represent a disproportionate part of a short flight and account for higher per-mile flying costs. The bus is least affected, since it has minimum terminal stopping costs, and is most nearly an ideal short-haul vehicle. Transport vehicles may run into increasing seat-mile costs again on very long hauls. This is particularly true of the aircraft on nonstop runs where it becomes necessary to sacrifice carrying capacity in order to increase fuel load. Short-haul airline operations rarely can achieve sufficient load factors to break even. Hence several of the high-density routes, for example, New York–Washington, tend to be unprofitable and they must be subsidized by profit generated on long-haul routes. This is one reason why the route pattern of an airline is of large significance in determining the profitability of the system.[11]

Load factor tells us how well the space in equipment is utilized when it is in revenue service. Another aspect of utilization is the number of

---

[10] Arbitraries are added in short-haul airline fares, but they affect only a partial adjustment.

[11] To some degree aircraft design can overcome these difficulties, but until recently the market for short-haul aircraft has not been large enough to attract the manufacturers. In addition, it is difficult to secure adequate aircraft utilization from aircraft confined to short routes (flying hours per aircraft day). New generations of planes have characteristically been designed primarily with the premium long-haul markets in view.

hours out of each day that a piece of equipment can be scheduled in revenue operations. Passenger travel does not spread itself evenly over the hours of the day, and there are preferred hours of departure and arrival in all classes of passenger travel. Maintenance, servicing, and turnaround time eat into the time available for revenue operation. Good utilization can be secured on transcontinental and transoceanic runs. But in short-haul service, enough equipment must be available to handle morning and late afternoon peaks. Some of that equipment must stand idle most of the day, and the average utilization of equipment (hours in revenue service per day) will fall. Cost per idle hour, representing the cost of carrying the investment, is high.

Where right-of-way and terminal facilities are in public ownership and are paid for through user charges, density of passenger traffic over particular route segments is of slight importance to the profitability of carrier operations. Once density is sufficient to enable good equipment utilization, further improvement from this factor is not likely to be achieved. The situation is otherwise with conventional railroad or rail rapid-transit operations. Here the ownership of permanent way and terminal facilities is commonly lodged with the same agency, whether public or private, that furnishes equipment and conducts operations. Moreover, unlike highways and airports, rail rapid-transit facilities and much of the plant devoted to rail commuter operations are not multipurpose but are exclusively devoted to conducting commercial passenger operations. Heavy concentrations of passenger volume are essential if these high-capacity facilities are to cover their capital costs, especially where the plant is used primarily for the journey to and from work and hence is heavily used only 20 hours a week. Characteristically, at least in the United States, peak-period passengers do not cover those costs.

PASSENGER TERMINALS

Since the bulk of intercity passenger traffic is between the large urban areas or has its origin or destination in one of those areas, concentrated volumes of traffic must be handled in the large city terminals. Railroads were accustomed to providing monumental downtown terminals for their passenger services, permitting relatively easy connection with the service of other rail lines by a short taxi trip and serving the business and hotel areas of the cities conveniently.[12] A well-located suburban stop, such as Paoli on the Pennsylvania main line out of Philadelphia, often made the long-distance trains easily accesible to

---

[12] In many of the large cities, for example, Cincinnati, St. Louis, Kansas City, Washington, and Los Angeles, Union Stations served all of the railroads jointly.

some of the suburban areas. These city terminals, although often very costly, were comparatively compact and were usually well connected with the urban transit system whether bus or rail. Underground approaches and trainshed facilities, as in New York's Grand Central and Pennsylvania Station and Chicago's Union Station, could minimize the impact upon the city center. In many instances the downtown sites were secured and developed when the cities were still relatively young and small. Hence the city could grow around and adjust to them.

Airports came later on the urban scene. They were almost invariably public enterprises, predominantly municipal, and intended to accommodate all airlines serving the area as well as general aviation operations. They required far more space than rail terminals and also long approaches clear of buildings or other obstacles that would intrude into the approach pattern used by the aircraft. Available locations were necessarily few and, as a rule, somewhat distant from the city center.[13] Although originally built in comparatively open country, metropolitan airports become surrounded by commercial and residential development within a few years thus giving rise to never-ending complaint about airport noise and pollution. Since what would ultimately be required in respect to runway length, terminal and hangar space, and parking areas could not be foreseen, the earlier airports became inadequate and could not be expanded.

The necessity to provide additional airports at major metropolitan areas arose both from traffic volumes which exceeded the capacity of the existing airports and from the inability to enlarge them, especially in runway length, to accommodate intercontinental jets. The newer airports are farther out, and travel time on the ground for most passengers becomes significant, the more so where it is necessary to make the trips during rush hours. Upward of two hours of ground time appears excessive even in connection with a transcontinental flight of five and one-half hours. Except for the recent extension of the Cleveland rapid-transit system to Hopkins International Airport and the Washington Metro to National Airport, no major U.S. airport can be reached except by bus, taxi, or automobile, or by high-cost helicopter services (from other airports in the system or from heliports). London's Gatwick, however, has frequent rail service to Victoria Station; and that service is used by more than 70 percent of the passengers moving

---

[13] Dulles International which serves Washington, D.C., for example, utilizes 10,000 acres and has two parallel 10,500-foot runways. Its 600-foot-long terminal building is capable of being expanded to 1,800 feet. By contrast, Washington Union Station, including the head house, measured 755 feet wide and approximately 1,600 feet from the front plaza to the main crossovers on the approach tracks. The coach yards and engine terminal were at Ivy City, several miles away. Its daily passenger capacity easily equalled that of Dulles.

through the airport.[14] Growing congestion of highways in all major urban centers is likely to increase ground times for air passengers and add to the uncertainty of their arriving at airports in time for their flight schedules. Yet the passenger volumes at most airports are not large enough to justify rapid transit construction solely for airport traffic. In addition, passengers come from and are destined to points throughout vast metropolitan areas which are most easily serviced by automobile.

Increased delay en route to and from airports is troublesome enough, but major airports are increasingly faced with delay of aircraft takeoffs and landings in consequence of limited runway capacity and congested air space. Both airports and air traffic control systems have tended to lag behind the growth of air traffic. Peak hours, of course, present the problem at its maximum with long lines of aircraft awaiting takeoff clearance and others in the holding pattern waiting to land. But the lead time for providing additional airport capacity is sufficiently long to indicate that the congestion will become measurably worse before expansion can begin to relieve it.[15]

Most airports are multipurpose facilities. Not only commercial passenger aircraft use them but also cargo aircraft, unscheduled charter flights, aerial taxis, and corporate and private aircraft—even, to a degree, national guard and other military aircraft. Flight training operations have not been wholly removed from major airports. In the past the private Piper Cub has been treated with the same priority as the intercontinental jet in landing and takeoff lineups. One obvious measure to relieve congestion at major airports so far as it affects scheduled passenger operations is, of course, to accord priority to the scheduled aircraft. The Port of New York Authority has sharply increased landing fees in peak hours to discourage private aircraft from using the airports at those hours. Such measures bring loud cries of discrimination from private plane owners. In the longer run, however, it seems clear that small aircraft operations must be moved out of major airports into facilities which, while adequate for them, are useless to the large transport aircraft.[16]

---

[14] Berlin-Tempelhof and Brussels airports also have rail service, while Tokyo Airport is served by a monorail. The last is poorly located, comparatively slow, and has not lived up to expectations.

[15] Lead time tends to be lengthened by the unwillingness of communities to accept new airports. Witness the long delay and controversy about a site for New York's fourth jetport. The Dallas-Fort Worth Airport is the last major airport likely to be constructed in the United States for some years.

[16] Teterboro in the New York airport system, under the management of Pan American World Airways, is making an effort to attract nonairline traffic away from major airports. More widespread employment of rational pricing policies for use of airports and the air traffic control system might assist in alleviating the conflict in use. See Jeremy J. Warford, *Public Policy toward General Aviation* (Washington, D.C.: The Brookings Institution, 1971), esp. chaps. 7–9.

DISAPPEARANCE OF RAIL SERVICE

The figures on passenger mileage already presented indicate the speed at which the railroad has been superseded as a passenger carrier. Annual passenger-train mileage operated in the United States averaged 565.4 million in the 1926–30 period. As late as 1947, 415 million train-miles were operated. By 1966, however, train mileage had declined to 164 million and train abandonment was accelerating.

In July 1969 the Interstate Commerce Commission reported that only about 500 intercity passenger trains were left and that applications to abandon some 50 of those were in hand.[17] Out of 212,000 miles of railroad operating in 1968, only 59,350 miles had any passenger service. Abandonment cases reaching the commission increasingly covered the last trains operating on particular rail routes. Both the California Zephyr and the City of San Francisco, the last trains operating on the central transcontinental run, were up for abandonment. Western Pacific reported the Zephyr to be producing annual losses of the order of $1.2 million; Denver and Rio Grande Western a loss of $1.7 million on the same train—sufficient to reduce the company's net income by 15 percent.[18] With the equipment over 20 years old and needing early replacement, the urgency of the case was plain to the railroads involved. What enterprise would invest in the reequipment of a service faced with losses of these proportions?

The plain difficulty with rail passenger transportation on the longer hauls is that is has lost any advantage over other forms of passenger movement in the eyes of most people. For the family on vacation, the automobile is cheaper, far more convenient, and fast enough on good highways to cover an acceptable amount of territory. For other types of long-distance movement, air transportation is not only much faster but at the going fares it is characteristically cheaper than first-class rail services. Dwindling numbers of people still prefer train service with its comfort and leisure, although it is possible, since completion of so large a part of the Interstate Highway System, to travel both faster and at lower cost between many points by bus.

A comparison of two specific Chicago–Denver operations made by Burlington Railroad cost analysts makes clear major differences in the economics of long-distance rail and plane travel. The California Zephyr was compared with a Boeing 727, both on the basis of recent average performance, with the results shown in Table 7-4. The 47-man

---

[17] *Traffic World*, vol. 139, no. 3 (July 19, 1969), pp. 15 ff.

[18] *Trains*, vol. 29, no. 10 (August 1969), p. 4. Southern Pacific reported that passengers handled on the City of San Francisco declined from 200 per trip in 1966 to a mere 77 during the first two months of 1969. Most transcontinental jets would handle more passengers than that.

TABLE 7–4
Comparison of California Zephyr and Boeing 727 on Basis of
Average Performance ($ unless otherwise noted)

	Zephyr	727
Average load	166 persons	72 persons
Trip revenue	5,000+	3,400+
Expenses	5,400	2,500
Profit	350	950
Labor cost	2,288	391
Fuel cost	500	300
Time	18½ hrs.	2 hrs.
Revenue per hour	290	1,727
Cost per passenger	32.57	34.88
Revenue per passenger	30.50	48.00
Labor share of operating cost	42%	16%

Source: As reported in *Trains*, vol. 28, no. 4 (February 1968), p. 4, and elsewhere in the railroad press. The CZ's load factor was substantially in excess of that of the 727.

labor requirement for the Zephyr, compared with a 6-man crew for the jet, obviously accounts for much of the difference between these operations.

While the long-distance services were disappearing, commutation traffic by rail increased. Such services are operated principally in the Boston, New York, Philadelphia, Chicago, and San Francisco urban areas. They are almost invariably operated at a loss, but public necessity requires their continuance and public aid has been provided in varying amounts in the Boston, Chicago, New York, and Philadelphia area to keep these services operating and, in some instances, to effect improvement. The Long Island Railroad, largest of the commuter operations, is now owned by the Metropolitan Transportation Authority, a creature of the State of New York. Total rail-passenger revenue declined from $963.3 million in 1947 to $444.3 million in 1968. Over the same period, however, commutation passenger revenues (included in the total) increased from $67.4 million to $153.1 million.[19] The trend continued with intercity revenues falling to $210 million and commutation revenues increasing to $340 million in the late 1970s.

In the entire period since World War II, railroad passenger services, taken as a whole, have generated very large deficits when calculated on a fully distributed cost basis. Since both freight and passenger services, for the most part, use the same trackage, engine-house facilities, dispatching services, and the like, there was much controversy as to how much could be saved were all passenger service discontinued. Perhaps the closest guide to such an appraisal is the deficit calculated on the basis of solely related expenses, taxes, and rents—a proxy for the direct cost of operating the passenger service. Despite the rapid

---

[19] Some commuter services were abandoned, notably those of the Pennsylvania Railroad in the Pittsburgh area.

pace of train discontinuance, this deficit climbed from $8.8 million in 1963 to $30.9 million in 1966 and approximately $170 million in 1968. The latter figure was roughly 30 percent of railway net income in that year, which gives some impression of the burden which railways were carrying.

AMTRAK TAKES OVER

Public realization of the likelihood that all long-haul passenger service by rail faced abandonment led the Congress, in 1970, to pass legislation which established a national rail passenger service corporation. The new corporation would establish a coordinated basic network of intercity rail passenger train service, would purchase needed passenger cars, and would undertake modernization and replacement of such cars. It would contract with the railroads for the operation of the train service that it deemed necessary and capable of ultimately operating on a self-supporting basis.[20] Railroads could buy into the corporation at sums determined in relation to their previous passenger-service deficits, making their contribution in part by turning over passenger cars to the corporation. Those railroads that joined would be permitted to abandon all noncommuter passenger service not incorporated into the corporation's network. Those which did not would not be allowed any further passenger train abandonment until 1975.

The new service, known as Amtrak, was established on schedule on May 1, 1971. All railroads then operating intercity passenger service joined except for Southern, Rock Island, and Rio Grande.[21] Despite some expansion to take care of vigorous complaint, the Amtrak service provided less than half as many intercity trains as had been operating on April 30. The others were forthwith abandoned, except for those operated by the lines not in Amtrak and a few whose intercity character was questionable. Amtrak's initial funding was inadequate, and refurbishment of equipment and promotion of the service were slow to get underway. Although Amtrak pays the railroads only what amounts to the above-the-rail costs of operating the trains (contributing nothing to maintenance of basic plant), the first-year loss of some $270 million was unexpectedly large. Only the New York–Washington service operated above a break even. Much criticism has been leveled at

---

[20] The contractual basis and its revision to afford incentives to the railroads is described in William J. Baumol, "Payment by Performance in Rail Passenger Transportation: An Innovation in Amtrak's Operations," *Bell Journal of Economics*, vol. 6, no. 1, Spring 1975, pp. 281 ff.

[21] Southern's last passenger train, the Crescent, has since been taken over by Amtrak. Rock Island and Rio Grande services have been cut back.

the operation because of slow timing of many long-distance services, poor on-time performance, and low standards of personal service on board. The railroads which actually operate the service have been accused of giving preference to their freight operations.

Despite criticism, Congress has increased the level of funding, and some additions to service have been made. French-built gas turbine trains have been placed on the Chicago–St. Louis corridor operation, and international services to Canada and Mexico have been reinstated. New locomotives and cars were ordered in considerable number. The fuel shortage, exacerbated by the Arab oil embargo in the fall of 1973, curtailed automobile travel and forced cutbacks in airline schedules. Amtrak's services suddenly acquired a new popularity, and many were booked far in advance. Similar results accompanied the fuel shortage in the summer of 1979. No significant early expansion of Amtrak's service is feasible because of the long lead time involved in building new rail passenger-carrying equipment. In the longer run it is clear that escalating fuel prices will compel increased attention in Detroit to fuel economy in the design of automobiles, lend some permanence to consumer preference for compact and subcompact cars, curtail long-distance automobile travel, and worsen the competitive posture of the airlines. For the airlines, fuel comprised 12 percent of operating expenses prior to the escalation of fuel prices. By the spring of 1974 the ratio had climbed above 20 percent and by 1979 to more than 24 percent. By contrast, the motor common-carrier ratio was in the range of 2.8 to 3.6 percent. In the circumstances, expansion of Amtrak services, particularly on the shorter hauls, appears to be fully warranted.

In 1978, however, Amtrak had operating revenues of only $321.2 million against operating expenses of $863.5 million, hence an operating loss of $542.3 million which had to be picked up through governmental appropriations. Appalled by the continued and growing losses, the Carter Administration proposed a 43 percent cutback in Amtrak's route mileage. Hardly had the implication of this proposal become appreciated when long gas lines appeared in California. By June Amtrak was turning away more than half as many passengers as it was carrying on the limited equipment available to it. In the circumstances Congress adopted a formula which would require much less pruning and appropriated larger operating and capital funds than the president desired.[22]

Meanwhile a private corporation has launched an Auto-Train Service between Lorton, Virginia, and Florida. Passengers and their

---

[22] Luther S. Miller, "America Rediscovers the Passenger Train," *Railway Age*, August 13, 1979, pp. 28 ff. Canada has followed the Amtrak pattern by establishing Via Rail Canada, but under more favorable conditions of track and equipment. Large passenger service losses are common around the world.

automobiles ride the same train overnight and are afforded attractive accommodations after the fashion long popular over the trans-Alpine crossings and on other night runs in Europe. Only a slight dent has been made in the over-the-road movement, but consideration is being given to development of similar operations on other routes. The future is clouded, however, by the decline in profitability of Auto-Train resulting from its high price in relation to air fares and the cost of car rental at destination.

MEGAPOLIS: URBAN CORRIDORS

The rapid pace of urban growth promises that some corridors will develop in which the built-up areas are nearly continuous over long distances. The prime example is the so-called Northeast Corridor from Boston to Washington. Here the congestion of highways, of airports, and of airspace caused a reexamination of the role of the railroad as a means of high-speed ground transport which would relieve the load on other modes and accommodate a significant share of the expected increase in traffic. Thirty years ago excellent train services were available: half-hourly New York–Philadelphia and hourly New York–Washington and New York–Boston. The postwar improvement of the highways, introduction of faster aircraft, and the institution of the air shuttle services rapidly eroded rail traffic. In consequence, the service was reduced; and as frequency declined, its traffic loss was accelerated. Aging equipment and reduced standards of track maintenance also compelled lengthening the schedules of several of the fastest trains on the route.

These runs are short: 226 miles New York–Washington and 229 miles New York–Boston. Ground time at both ends added to significant delays and irregularities of plane service suggested the possibility that trains might be provided that would be competitive with overall time by air. The success of Japan's New Tokaido Line which diverted large volumes of passenger traffic from the air, as well as the development of fast train services in France and elsewhere in western Europe, no doubt nourished the idea.[23] Under the High-Speed Ground Transportation Act of 1965 a project was laid out to upgrade the Pennsylvania Railroad line between New York and Washington and provide 50 new self-propelled electric cars capable of a maximum speed of 160 m.p.h. to operate a demonstration service. Not until January 19, 1969 was the first regular service instituted; by the spring of 1971, when the service was taken over by Amtrak, nine daily round trips were operating but the schedules were generally on a three-hour timing.

---

[23] On the Japanese line 54 daily nonstop trains made the Tokyo-Nagoya run of 212.4 miles in 122–23 minutes, averaging 103.6 to 104.5 m.p.h.

When Conrail was established in 1976 the Boston–Washington corridor lines were assigned to Amtrak for maintenance and operation. At the same time Congress provided $1.75 billion to upgrade track, stations, and other facilities and extend electrification from New Haven to Boston in order to enable provision of frequent high-speed passenger service in the corridor. For the limitations of the railroad prevented attaining the sustained speeds for which the "Metroliners" and the most recently acquired electric locomotives were designed. Progress has been slow. Delays and the impact of inflation have forced some curtailment of the program. Further appropriations are being sought. The rebuilding of an existing railroad whose alignment dates well back into the previous century is a difficult task—far different from the laying down of a completely new line as in Japan. But the prospect of rail service competitive with air seems, at long last, a reality.

Under the aegis of the Department of Transportation, research has been undertaken on other "far-out" concepts for high-speed ground transportation. These range from new methods of tunneling to provide an underground tube, in which cars could move on a column of air, to ground effects machines moving in air suspension over a prepared right-of-way. The linear induction motor promises fast, quiet, and polution-free transport, but requires entirely new permanent way. Neither STOL (short take off and landing) aircraft nor helicopters are being neglected. To cope with anticipated congestion over the next decade, however, requires superior application of techniques already known and in an advanced stage of development. It seems questionable whether sufficient emphasis has been placed on them. Concepts now in the design or prototype stage cannot be made operative for some decades. Even the construction of conventional transit facilities is proving to be painfully slow. It is plain, however, that whatever is done will result from government rather than from private initiative in view of the dismal financial record of ground passenger transportation in the past 50 years.

COORDINATION AND NATIONAL
PASSENGER LOGISTICS

Although Amtrak and the bus lines both enjoyed increases in traffic in 1979 traceable to the fuel shortage of the early summer and the sharp escalation of gasoline prices, passenger miles in automobiles also grew. The crisis of supply of petroleum-based fuels is likely to continue, indeed, to worsen over time. Hence it may become impossible to support intercity transportation of passengers more than 90 percent by automobile and aircraft. Some form of planning and programming national passenger logistics has become an urgent matter. What is needed is a coordination of rail (intercity and metropolitan), highway bus, and air facilities and services. Each must be employed in conjunction with the others to provide optimum service at minimum cost. Each must make use of the latest developments in fuel-saving technology in replacing and augmenting existing passenger-carrying equipment.

SELECTED REFERENCES

Caves, Richard E. *Air Transport and Its Regulators.* Cambridge: Harvard University Press, 1962.

Davies, R. E. G. *A History of the World's Airlines.* London: Oxford University Press, 1964.

———— *Airlines of the United States Since 1914.* London: Putnam & Co., Ltd., 1972.

Douglas, George W., and Miller, James C., III. *Economic Regulation of Domestic Air Transport: Theory and Policy.* Washington, D.C.: The Brookings Institution, 1974.

Droege, John A. *Passenger Terminals and Trains.* New York: McGraw-Hill Book Co., 1916.

Federal Coordinator of Transportation. *Passenger Traffic Report.* 1935.

Fruhan, William E., Jr. *The Fight for Competitive Advantage: A Study of the United States Trunk Air Carriers.* Boston: Harvard Business School, 1972.

Hultgren, Thor. *Railroad Travel and the State of Business.* New York: National Bureau of Economic Research, 1943.

Interstate Commerce Commission, Bureau of Economics. *The Intercity Bus Industry: A Preliminary Study.* Washington, D.C.: 1978.

Ladd, Dwight R. *Cost Data for the Management of Railroad Passenger Service.* Boston: Harvard Business School, 1957.

Morlock, Edward K., and Olsen, William T. "The Quality of Intercity Passenger Transportation Service in the Northeast Corridor," Transportation Research Forum, *Proceedings, Twelfth Annual Meeting* (1971), pp. 391 ff.

Ross, Daniel R. "A Critical Look at Amtrak," Transportation Research Forum, *Proceedings, Thirteenth Annual Meeting* (1972), pp. 131 ff.

Stanford Research Institute. *The Future of Rail Passenger Traffic in the West.* Palo Alto, Calif., 1966.

Transportation and Logistics Research Center, The American University. *Criteria for Transport Pricing.* Cambridge, Md.: Cornell Maritime Press, 1973.

Warford, Jeremy J. *Public Policy toward General Aviation.* Washington, D.C.: The Brookings Institution, 1972.

8

Urban Logistics: Human and Goods

Problems of central-city congestion and urban movement are not new. Seven centuries ago Leonardo da Vinci observed the traffic crunch of Renaissance cities with dismay and sketched out a system of multilevel roadways to separate different types of traffic. Variations of this approach and many other schemes have been offered over the intervening years, but little has been done until quite recent times. Indeed most of what may be looked for to provide relief is still in the planning stage. Yet the problems spawned by the automobile, by the rapid progress of urbanization, and by other trends of the last half century appear at least to have generated much more serious purpose to recognize and seek solutions. The question begins seriously to be posed: Shall we revamp urban transportation, revamp the city, or try some combination of the two?

Rural population has been declining in the United States since 1940, hence the entire population growth has been urban; and the trend is expected to continue. The urban population which stood at 74.5 million in 1940 had almost doubled by 1970. In the latter year 62.1 million lived in the central cities of the 230 Standard Metropolitan Statistical Areas, another 74.9 million in the adjacent suburban areas. Three fourths of the population growth between 1960 and 1970 was in those surburban areas. Total population in the SMSAs was slightly more than double that of the rest of the country. At the same time the number of passengers handled by all forms of urban public transit declined from 13.1

billion in 1940 to 5.9 billion in 1970, the rate of decline in each of the last two decades approximating 50 percent. Not only was the automobile relied upon to provide mobility for the increment of population, it also made sharp inroads upon established public transit operations and displaced them from the role they had long fulfilled.[1]

The logistics systems associated with an urban area are simple in functional concept but complex in their operation. A series of subsystems is accommodated, principally upon the network of streets, which provides for the movement both of people and goods including (1) the movement of people in and out in pursuit of their contacts with other parts of the country and the world; (2) the movement of people between residence and workplace; (3) internal circulation for shopping, educational, recreational, and other necessary purposes; (4) goods movement inward to supply the productive enterprises upon which the economy of the urban area is founded and to distribute their output, both within the area and to markets outside; (5) goods movement inward to meet the food and other requirements of the urban population from external sources; (6) internal goods distribution from carrier terminals, warehouses, wholesale establishments, and other points of receipt to stores, other business premises, and households; and (7) through movement of people and goods. To the extent they depend upon the motor vehicle, all of these subsystems become intermingled upon the streets and highways so that the improvement of one depends upon a general improvement of circulation. Both the demand for movement and the ease or difficulty of providing for it are greatly affected by the structure of the urban area. For some time the motor vehicle seemed to give promise of resolving problems in all of the subsystems. Why has the promise not been fulfilled?

CHANGES IN THE PATTERN OF URBAN DEVELOPMENT

Urban Sprawl

By contrast with the growing facility of movement that technology has afforded to intercity and international travel, the era of the automobile and aircraft has brought costly and baffling problems to the metropolitan areas. As pointed out in Chapter 3, urban centers were compact when they relied upon foot and animal transport. The railroad, the electrically propelled streetcar, and the electrically propelled urban-transit railroad permitted expansion, but upon well-defined and

---

[1] If the years of World War II are omitted, transit patronage had peaked at 17.2 billion in 1926 when urban population was about 60 million. The fuel crunch and the modest improvement in transit service have had some effect on transit ridership which was estimated at just over 7 million in 1976.

comparatively high-density corridors. All of these means provided for the public mass movement of passengers on fixed routes.

The automobile changes all of this. It provides flexible, individual transport which is confined to no fixed route pattern and which utilizes streets and highways at low density. It generates the potential of great freedom of movement for the individual, both as to route and timing. It provides privacy, door-to-door convenience, and comfort. And it is clear that the preference, not only of most Americans but of people all over the world, is for the automobile as the means for most urban and suburban movement as soon as it becomes available to them.

Quite apart from conferring freedom of movement, that is, freedom from the fixed routes, time schedules, and transfer points of public transportation systems, the automobile also accords a new freedom in the choice of residence. The areas between the corridors of settlement defined by rail lines can be filled out with residential development. The built-up area can expand without reference to extensions of rail transit facilities. Low density (i.e., single family) housing can play a proportionately larger role as the areas that are usable are increased by extension of the street pattern to give access by automobile.[2] The location of residence in relation to workplace need no longer take account of mass transit facilities which characteristically converged on the city center. Residence on one side of town and workplace on the other is commonplace, and the patterns of individual movement are increasingly dispersed and complex. Not infrequently they involve crosscurrents which reflect the extent to which choice of residence has been freed from any close relationship to place of work or the city center.

Footloose Industry

Prior to 1930 or thereabouts, industrial location was strongly oriented to the rail pattern, to the waterfront in port cities, and to navigable waters inland where water transportation was significant in materials movement. Industry that required or shipped materials in carload lots in substantial quantity necessarily sought locations on railroads where direct siding connections could be secured and expensive cartage to railroad public or team tracks avoided. Light industry tended to concentrate in downtown areas where maximum customer access was available, cartage distances to and from related industries were minimized, and rail freight houses and team tracks were close at hand. Wholesaling and warehousing activities followed a similar pattern.

---

[2] A strong preference both for the single family house and for greater space around it appears long to have existed and to have been enhanced by growing income. The automobile made its realization in the suburbs possible for millions of families. Federal policy, postwar, made financing more practicable. On these points, see J. R. Meyer, J. F. Kain, and M. Wohl, *The Urban Transportation Problem* (Cambridge: Harvard University Press, 1965), pp. 109–19.

Well-defined industrial and wholesale districts tended to build up, and high concentration of such activity developed. The necessity for proximity to rail facilities and to other industrial and commercial activities led to intensity of land use and a tendency for multistory construction.

While the first effect of the development of the motortruck was to increase economic cartage distances and thus free location slightly from the constricted relationship to rail facilities, it was the development of long-haul truck capability that fundamentally altered locational considerations for a substantial segment of industry. The railcar was a door-to-door method of transport only when both receiving and shipping plants were located on a rail line and had sidings. The truck had door-to-door capability anywhere on the vast network of streets and highways. Suburban, or even country, locations well oriented with respect to the highway system could service regional markets entirely by truck, utilizing rail only for the longer hauls and for the receipt of heavy materials used in manufacture or processing. Thus, while a rail location often continued to be desirable for a portion of required goods movement, that location need no longer be within the urban area. Some industries both in light manufacturing and in wholesale trade could dispense with rail-oriented location altogether.

New industrial locations, accordingly, have become unhinged from the older and concentrated industrial centers. Single-story construction on relatively cheap land with ample room for parking has become characteristic of the plants that are finding peripheral and small-town locations. The ring-like development around the periphery of Boston on Route 128 is a clear-cut example.[3] Most major urban areas have experienced a similar development in which one of the most strategic locating factors becomes nearness to major intersections on the growing system of throughways. And locations in smaller communities intermediate between major metropolitan centers have become much less disadvantageous than in the past.

Benjamin Chinitz has noted "a pervasive trend of industries to conform to population—a trend toward decentralization."[4] The Bureau of Public Roads in a study of certain manufacturing, wholesale, retail, and service industries between 1947 and 1958 found an increase of only 100,000 jobs in central cities compared with 1,600,000 jobs outside.[5] The shift of industry away from the Northeast continues. Market orientation seems to increase in importance. These shifts should not, however, be attributed principally to the development of truck trans-

---

[3] "A Golden Semicircle;" see American Trucking Associations, Inc., Highways, Trucks and New Industry (Washington, 1963), pp. 18–22.

[4] Benjamin Chinitz, Freight and the Metropolis—The Impact of America's Transportation Revolution on the New York Region (Cambridge: Harvard University Press, 1960).

[5] American Trucking Associations, Highways, Trucks and New Industry, p. 16.

port. That development has been a facilitating factor in a situation where rapid growth both of population and per-capita income has brought many additional market areas up to a size that will support manufacturing plants of sufficient scale to be reasonably efficient.[6]

Debasement of Structure

Everywhere the central city has tended to fall into decay, to lose population, and to be deprived of some of its traditional functions. The escape to the suburbs has removed much of the more affluent population and left once desirable residential sections, located belt-like around the central business district, to degenerate into slums. Retailing functions of the central city have diminished as new shopping centers have been spawned on the periphery and in the suburbs. New industrial locations, the development of R&D centers, and, to an increasing degree, even the building of new office space have occurred on the periphery. The older industrial and wholesale complexes of the central city have deteriorated and generate increased vacancy rates. Property is no longer adequately maintained, much less renewed. As land can be made available, it is more and more devoted to parking lots and garages to accommodate the change in means by which people reach the central city. Civic and cultural functions tend to remain concentrated, but in a steadily less attractive environment.[7]

Nor has the outward spread from the central city been characterized by orderly or attractive development. Fine residential sections and well-designed shopping centers are too often connected by main roads lined with an incredible conglomeration of small stores, eating establishments, filling stations, and used-car lots—at night aglow with a jumble of signs—the neon jungle. Urban sprawl often appears to resemble a mindless dispersion without structure that enormously complicates the patterns of movement and defies efforts to channel them into efficient flows.

---

[6] Los Angeles affords a striking case of industrial dispersion in an automotive-oriented environment. In 1924 industry was almost entirely concentrated in the downtown area. By 1960 it was widely dispersed over the 2,200 square-mile area. But what is especially of interest is that except for the service industries along the Wilshire corridor and into Hollywood, industrial dispersion has moved along the transport corridors carved out by the railroads. This is not to say that all industry which has located in such corridors is by any means dependent upon rail transport. In part it reflects topographic considerations (which influenced the rail location in the first place) and in part the tendency for main highway routes to develop parallel to rail routes. See Dudley F. Pegrum, *Transportation: Economics and Public Policy* (Homewood, Ill.: Richard D. Irwin, 1963), pp. 521–26. © 1963 by Richard D. Irwin, Inc.

[7] Richard B. Andrews, *Urban Growth and Development: A Problem Approach* (New York: Simmons-Boardman Publishing Co., 1962), pp. 62–77.

Congestion

The hallmark of the modern metropolitan area, virtually everywhere in the world, is congestion—the impedence and slowing of movement. The causes are multiple. Expansion of the built-up areas, increased population densities in slum areas, and debasement of structure all tend to multiply and lengthen the trips which are necessary by some means of powered transport. The problems are exacerbated by the fact that street systems must accommodate goods transportation as well as the movement of people. The great expansion in the range of goods available, the multiplication of appliances requiring servicing, and the growth in average discretionary income have increased the density of local goods transportation required to serve any given density of population. At the same time the outward spread of metropolitan areas has lengthened average hauls from freight terminals, warehouses, and industrial establishments. Few firms find it feasible to manufacture or warehouse at multiple locations even in the larger metropolitan areas. Nor do the over-the-road motor carriers which handle so large a share of the traffic that is intended for dispersion over the metropolitan area commonly find a multiplicity of terminals to be feasible. In the more congested areas the pickup and delivery of goods is becoming increasingly costly as the number of stops which can be made by peddler vehicles in any time period decreases. Growing congestion of the streets and the common lack of off-street loading areas contribute to this phenomenon.

The speed of automobile travel in American cities ranges from 16 miles per hour in Boston and St. Louis to 22 miles per hour in San Francisco and Milwaukee.[8] Public buses move at a substantially slower rate when sharing streets in common with other traffic. In the rush hours traffic slows to a crawl, with vehicle speeds of 6 to 10 miles per hour, while the urban motorist finds the problems of discovering a place to stop perhaps more serious than finding room to move.[9] Yet there is some evidence that although deterioration recurred in the early postwar years, the enhanced highway programs of the recent past have effected improvement in the quality of urban movement.[10] Dissatisfaction may sometimes stem from failure to meet expectations rather than from failure to effect improvement; for example, the freeway with flow at 35 m.p.h. instead of the anticipated 55 or 60 m.p.h.

No mode of transport that has ever been developed is comparable to the automobile in capability to provide mobility and convenience for its owner and the family. In metropolitan areas, however, increased

---

[8] Editors of *Fortune*, *The Exploding Metropolis* (New York, 1958).

[9] Wilfred Owen, *The Metropolitan Transportation Problem*, rev. ed. (Washington, D.C.: The Brookings Institution, 1966), pp. 2–3.

[10] Meyer, Kain, and Wohl, *Urban Transportation Problem*, pp. 74–81.

automobile ownership and use have created unprecedented problems of maintaining mobility. Because of the road space in square feet required per occupant (automobiles rarely show average occupancy as high as 1.5 persons even in the journey to and from work) and the absence of central control of vehicles, efficient utilization of the space provided for vehicle movement is impossible. Scheduling of movement to maximize road or street capacity as is the practice in rail operations cannot be undertaken. In the still distant future automated guideways to control vehicle tracks, speed, and spacing may be introduced on selected high-density routes. But at present driver anarchy prevails. At peak hours the capacity of the roadway actually declines and the square footage used per passenger increases as the speed of movement falls. Congestion of critical arteries builds up quickly.

THE HIGHWAY APPROACH AND THE DECLINE OF TRANSIT

We have seen that the motor vehicle opened up large opportunities for the individual, the industrial or commercial firm, and the developer. All hastened to take advantage of those opportunities. Urban spread has occurred in a short space of time, *largely without foresight or plan* and at the instance of multitudes of individuals and enterprise units. Governments fell far behind in their efforts to influence and provide for change, lacking adequate planning organs and effective zoning controls. In consequence, they have been reduced to chasing after events.

The best developed and equipped governmental agencies in the transport field were the state highway departments backed up by the Federal Bureau of Public Roads and provided with very substantial sources of funds. The most immediate response to the decentralization that began was, therefore, more highway construction. Observed trends were extrapolated forward, and highway "needs" developed in terms of anticipated traffic volumes. In general, the highway authorities had no objection to sprawl provided that new highways were built and old ones improved fast enough to keep up with it. They were convinced that the public had decisively and irreversibly opted for a highway solution.

By contrast, mass rail transportation in a few of the largest cities and public transit by bus and streetcar almost everywhere had been developed by private companies. The government structure made no provision for dealing with public passenger transportation as it did for highway construction. The private companies found ridership declining, hence unit operation costs rising, at the very time that equipment had become largely obsolete. Not only were extensions of service rarely undertaken into newly developing areas but equipment replacement was limited, service frequencies declined, and the use of public transportation became steadily less attractive. In the effort to remain solvent, fares were increased. Thus a process got underway that rapidly weakened public transportation but that the private operators were unable to reverse or even materially to slow down. The effects of traffic decline were the more serious since use of public transit for the journey to work held up better than use for other purposes. As off-peak traffic melted away, load factors worsened and plant utilization declined.

Few American cities took any action to arrest the deterioration of mass transit until financial crisis on the part of the private operators threatened complete collapse. By then the structure of public transit had been greatly weakened and the public preference for the automobile even in urban trips considerably enhanced. In a number of municipalities, principally of small size, transit was allowed to disappear. In other instances municipal ownership was undertaken. From 1959 to 1970 the number of private transit systems declined from 1,173 to 938. Public systems increased, however, from 52 to 141. Nearly all rapid transit operations were publicly owned, and the public systems accounted for at least 80 percent of all passengers handled.[11] Municipal ownership was often a rescue operation which brought little promise of early improvement in transit service. Faced with limited finances and a multitude of demands for funding, municipalities were ill equipped to absorb transit operating deficits, much less to make investment in extension and modernization.[12]

THE CITY AS A FREIGHT TERMINAL

Although recent data are not available, it is plain that the great bulk of all freight traffic moves into the urban areas, originates there, or is exchanged between urban areas. These same urban areas provide for the interface between the several transport modes. Their street networks serve as vast terminal systems upon which pickup, delivery, and transfer of freight is accommodated by motor vehicle. It is probable that some 40 percent of all freight transport costs are encountered in these urban areas. Hence the efficiency with which urban goods movement can be accomplished has a major effect upon the efficiency of freight transport as a whole. Unhappily that efficiency is low and appears to be declining.

Despite the rapid progress of urban decentralization, there is heavy

---

[11] U.S. Department of Transportation, *Economic Characteristics of the Urban Public Transportation Industry* (1972), pp. 2–3, 2–4.

[12] The decline of public transit has enhanced the importance of the taxicab. In many communities it is the only public passenger transportation available. In 1970 taxicabs hauled about 35 percent as many passengers as all forms of public transit combined.

concentration of local truck traffic in the more congested areas of cities. New York is, no doubt, an extreme case; yet it is one of the few cities in which an effort has been made to study freight movement in detail. More than one third of the truck tonnage there is accounted for in Manhattan which has only 7 percent of the city's land area, and 32 percent of that tonnage is handled in peddle trips making multiple stops with an average consignment of only 600 pounds. In the 60s thanks to larger equipment and improved highways, motor common carriers operating in intercity service were able to hold their line-haul unit costs in check, but their pickup and delivery costs increased by more than 65 percent. This reflects the reduced productivity of their city vehicles in consequence of urban congestion.[13] Truck circulation has been speeded up by throughway and arterial construction. The growing delays are encountered principally in the city streets close to the points of pickup and delivery where congestion is greatly enhanced by the characteristic absence of off-street loading docks. By contrast the newer industrial and commercial premises in suburban areas tend to make adequate provision for handling trucks.

Truck traffic is inextricably mixed with other vehicular traffic; hence urban transport plans forecast vehicular volumes as a basis for highway design. Planning does not, however, extend to the conditions encountered at actual origins and destinations of goods nor to the way in which the movement of goods is organized in the hands of large numbers of carriers, cartage operators, and industrial and commercial firms. Urban goods movement, indeed, has been little studied and is not well understood. The nature of the problem is suggested by the fact that a one-square-mile area in Brooklyn was shown to be visited by 4,000 local trucks on the average weekday delivering consignments which averaged only 165 pounds. Although many schemes have been developed for merging pickup and delivery to reduce truck movement and increase productivity, almost none have been successfully implemented.[14] Line-haul carriers protect themselves to some degree by assessing terminal arbitraries, waiting time charges, or turning the function over to local cartage concerns. But these devices do not improve the efficiency with which urban goods movement is conducted.

PROBLEMS TO BE RESOLVED

If the quality of urban life is to be improved, it is apparent that changes in transport policy may well be requisite. But a great number of ques-

---

[13] These matters are discussed more fully in Ernest W. Williams, Jr., ed., *The Future of American Transportation* (Englewood Cliffs, N.J.: Prentice-Hall, Inc., 1971), chap. 6.

[14] For a good example of a half dozen similar studies see Dennis R. McDermott, "An Alternative Framework for Urban Goods Distribution: Consolidation," *Transportation Journal*, Fall 1975, pp. 29 ff.

tions must be answered before sound policy directions can be laid out. What objectives are to be sought in respect of city structure? Is the central business district (CBD) to be preserved, even revitalized? What is to be done with the blighted areas that increasingly encircle CBDs? Is sprawl to be arrested or simply controlled? What weight is to be given to factors not readily quantifiable, such as esthetic effects of transport construction?

A more specific set of questions relates directly to transportation. What should be the relative roles of the automobile, the bus, and rail rapid transit (if any)? If mass transit is to be instituted, who will own and operate it? What service standards should be provided? If mass transit is considered an essential element in improvement, how can its use be encouraged and the strong tendency to increased automobile use discouraged? If investment is called for, who benefits, who should pay, and how? By what means is the multiplicity of political jurisdictions to be overcome to permit area-wide planning and execution of plans? Some approaches to many of these questions will be explored below.

ALTERNATIVES FOR THE IMPROVEMENT OF URBAN LOGISTICS

Whether or not the heavy investment in urban freeways and other highway improvements since 1956 has enhanced the quality of urban transport, there is widespread and apparently growing discontent with the present state of affairs. Since urbanization is expected to continue at a rapid rate, it is obvious that much must be done merely to keep abreast of demand and avoid deterioration of mobility. During the 60s added dimensions of the problem came within the understanding of the public. The automobile was recognized as the greatest contributor to air pollution in the cities, and a problem earlier thought to be confined to the peculiar geographic conditions of the Los Angeles basin was generalized. The intrusion of freeways into the heart of cities was increasingly opposed because of the property destruction required, the disruption of established communities, and the tendency for such highways to segment the community much as railway rights of way had done in an earlier era. Older and more centralized cities began to look askance at the destruction of their downtown areas and to seek ways to arrest the trend and move toward rehabilitation. Finally, it was recognized that the progressive anemia of public transit left an increasing proportion of the population stranded—the ghetto area, the elderly, and those unable to afford the automobile. The spectacle of freeways overwhelmed with traffic in the rush hours soon after their completion raised questions whether a highway solution could ever be an adequate one in the larger conurbations.

A first requisite in considering solutions is to recognize that every urban area is a special case, differentiated from all others by size, density of land use, economic structure, geographic constraints, nature of historical development, and other factors. There is a vast disparity between such cities as Milwaukee, Fort Worth, and Providence, which have 50,000 to 75,000 persons moving out of the CBD in the peak evening hours at corridor densities ranging from 6,000 to 9,000, and New York, with more than 800,000 and corridor densities exceeding 60,000. New York is unique. Its nearest rival, Chicago, has average corridor densities which do not exceed 40,000 in the peak hour. Philadelphia, Boston, and Washington are the only other cities in the United States with corridor densities exceeding 26,000. Of these all but Washington have long had rail rapid transit systems (Washington has recently acquired one) as well as rail commuter services. As will appear shortly, corridor densities are of enormous significance in determining the economic mode for accommodation of the journey to and from work which generates the peak loading.

Studies have established the general economic relationships among the various available modes of urban transport, although the results would require adjustment to fit the circumstances of any particular urban area. The estimates allow for the costs of highway or rail structures, equipment, and operating costs.[15] They show that the automobile, with a loading of 1.6 persons per car and using existing downtown streets to reach intended CBD destinations, is normally the cheapest method of performing the journey to work when peak-hour corridor volumes are less than 10,000. When this volume is reached or exceeded, an integrated bus service[16] can become more economical than the automobile. Its service characteristics can be made quite attractive, although not the equivalent in convenience of one's own car, if exclusive bus lanes are marked out in congested areas and priority of access to freeways is accorded. In the 1960s only 14 cities in the United States had corridor densities at or above this level.

Rail transit can, via subway loops, provide direct distribution in the CBD. In the suburban areas, however, it must be provided with feeder bus services and parking accommodations for park-and-ride patrons. Passenger convenience and overall journey time are both adversely affected by the necessity to transfer at suburban stations. Even where corridor densities are very high—40,000–50,000 passengers in the peak hour—it appears that special circumstances are required to make rail transit as cheap as an integrated bus system. These include high residential densities in the areas to be served, heavy generation of rider-

---

[15] Meyer, Kain, and Wohl, *Urban Transportation Problem*, chaps. 8-11.

[16] One which fans out over feeder routes in the suburbs and provides service direct to the CBD without transfer.

ship at the outward ends of the system so that good load factors are achieved, and lengthy downtown distribution (requiring a large or elongated CBD) in relation to the line-haul.[17] Where rail transit already exists, of course, right-of-way costs can be regarded as sunk and the comparative economy of rail transit improves. Moreover, even where average corridor densities are lower than may appear to justify rail transit, one or more may have the residential density and volume characteristics to support it.

The kind of urban growth that has been occurring through expansion of the built-up areas by reason of the flight to the suburbs characteristically reduces residential densities. Hence it is hostile to the provision of public transit on an economical basis and with standards of service sufficiently high to attract commuters away from their automobiles. Indeed there is evidence that the price elasticity of demand for such service is low—a very large differential below automobile costs might be necessary to induce shifts. Growing incomes, on the other hand, strengthen the urge to use the automobile even in the face of considerable congestion. The possibility may be considered, of course, that provision of high-quality transit will encourage higher density development along the corridors served. The older cities of the East and the Middle West, which developed in their downtown areas prior to the rise of the automobile, are the most logical candidates for public transit development since they retain high densities in their inner rings. The automobile-oriented metropolitan area, of which Los Angeles is the outstanding example, lacks the requisite density and the concentrated origin–destination flows to make transit economically viable.[18]

Comparative economics no longer appears to be the only governing factor in appraising solutions for urban transport needs. Such cities as Seattle and Houston, which lack present corridor densities that would justify rail rapid transit, are nevertheless considering investment in rail facilities. The first portion of a rail transit system for Atlanta commenced operation in 1979. Construction is underway in Miami. The factors mentioned at the start of this section largely account for this development. The fact that ten or more years are required to develop and construct a rail transit facility necessitates action in advance of the time when urban growth generates requisite densities.

Growing awareness of the nation's fuel supply shortage may add force to the advocacy of expanded and improved public transit. Despite emission control devices installed on automobiles, the standards fixed for air pollution levels apparently will not be met in the congested areas of many large cities. The probability that the automobile will be banned from limited downtown areas in a number of cities is clearly

[17] Ibid., p. 303.

[18] For a discussion of the Los Angeles case, see Pegrum, *Transportation*, chap. 21.

increasing.[19] Bus transit is likely to fill the need in medium sized and smaller cities. Even where rail transit is contemplated, the bus may fill a transitional requirement during development and a major feeder and supplemental function in the long run.

PEAKING AND PEAK-PERIOD PRICING

Few economic activities suffer as greatly from sharp peaking characteristics as do urban transit and rail commuter operations. These were always dominated by traffic volumes generated by the journey to and from work, hence always encountered morning and evening peaks. But work-oriented traffic has held up better than all other types of journeys in the face of automotive competition. Hence 70 to 80 percent of urban and suburban rail-passenger traffic is now work-oriented. The near universal adoption of the five-day week and the loss of weekend recreational travel further reduced the employment of plant and equipment. On the rapid transit systems of Chicago, Cleveland, and Philadelphia, 58 percent of weekday volumes are encountered in the four peak hours. Rail commuter operations in Chicago, Washington, and Philadelphia have 68 to 72 percent of weekday volume concentrated in those peak hours.[20] A large part of the plant is thus required by loads that are encountered only during 20 hours out of the week.

Since the automobile is more heavily used for types of trips other than the journey to work, peaking is not quite so marked as on public transit facilities. Yet 30 percent or more of all home-based trips are journey-to-work trips in most of the larger cities which rely heavily upon the automobile. The peak to off-peak ratios on urban expressways tend to exceed two to one.[21] And the peak traffic flow on arteries leading into the CBD is directionally imbalanced as is also the

---

[19] The National Science Foundation has offered some comparative data on fuel consumption by various modes of transport which also roughly indicate comparative propensity to generate air pollution:

	Passenger-Miles per Gallon	BTU per Passenger-Mile
Buses	125	1,090
Railroads	80	1,700
Automobiles	32	4,250
Airplanes	14	9,700

These data apparently refer to intercity transport. Rail rapid transit would undoubtedly show up better than the railroad figure here quoted because of use of electric power and attainment of higher load factors.

[20] Meyer, Kain, and Wohl, *Urban Transportation Problem*, table 30, p. 95.

[21] A range of 2.4 to 2.6 to 1 is given in Wilbur Smith and Associates, *Future Highways and Urban Growth* (New Haven, 1961), p. 93.

case with public transit. Vast expenditure has been made to provide lanes to accommodate peak flows—lanes not required at other than peak hours—inbound for the morning peak and outbound for the evening peak.

Peak-hour riders, whether on public transit, rail commuter services, or urban highways, collectively occasion the provision of facilities and equipment far in excess of that necessary to accommodate off-peak flows. The whole cost of incremental facilities is chargeable to them in a causal sense—facilities which stand idle 148 hours a week in order to be available to meet a demand concentrated in 20 hours. The rail commuter, however, has characteristically enjoyed reduced fares by comparison with off-peak riders and transit fares are almost invariably the same in peak and in off-peak hours. Both railroads and transit systems have made efforts from time to time to encourage off-peak ridership with reduced fares, but no system has attempted to recover from peak-period riders the costs attributable to them.

The case of the automobile used for the journey to work is similar. User charges may cover nationwide highway expenditures, but the user-charge receipts of major urban areas (including federal and state grants) fall far short of highway expenditures in those areas.[22] What is important here, however, is that user charges are not differentiated by time of use to fix peak facility costs on peak-period users nor are they differentiated to reflect the per-mile cost of highway construction which tends to increase sharply with land use density. Hence they cannot perform the allocative function expected of a price system. As in the case of transit operations, off-peak users subsidize peak users to some extent; while to the degree there is a shortfall in total user-charge receipts, the general taxpayer is levied upon for a contribution.

The significance of this state of affairs is that it encourages peak use, exacerbates congestion, and generates continuing demand for provision of additional costly capacity. Only the increased trip time and associated frustrations exercise any pressure to shift a journey into off-peak hours. If continuing investment in facilities occurs in response to demand, this pressure may be of little significance. Hence differential pricing is argued for, which will put upon peak users the added costs which they occasion.[23] To this proposition may be added more specific charging for use of segments of the system which reflect the higher cost of facility provision in the more heavily built-up areas. Ingenious schemes have been proposed for accomplishing these ends

[22] The proportion of highway costs that should be borne by vehicular use is very much in controversy.

[23] See William S. Vickrey, "Pricing in Urban and Suburban Transportation," *American Economic Review*, vol. 53, no. 2 (1963), pp. 452 ff. On rapid transit pricing, see William S. Vickrey, *The Revision of the Rapid Transit Fare Structure of the City of New York* (Mayor's Committee on Management Survey of the City of New York, 1952).

by differential charges against automobiles.[24] A spreading out of the peak period and a reduction in the peak-hour load would be expected to result from such pricing practices. Alternative means of reaching the workplace might also receive more favorable consideration by many who presently drive.

More attention is also being accorded congestion costs, that is, the cost of congestion which each added user of the road system imposes upon all other users.[25] Congestion prices would be a further step to close the gap between private and social costs and to condition use in peak periods upon a willingness to bear the cost occasioned by such use. In practice, each vehicle in the peak flow upon a highway is equally responsible for pushing up the hourly rate of flow; hence each vehicle is unidentifiable so far as concerns the allocation of congestion costs. Differentiating charges, however, in any or all of the ways here discussed, would bring the user-charges system into an allocative role rather than a mere cost recovery role. A more simple and direct attack might be upon parking charges at facilities within the CBD.

FEDERAL URBAN TRANSPORT PROGRAM

There was reluctance to recognize a federal role in urban transport. After World War II, the Bureau of Public Roads did urge the states to engage in planning transportation systems in their major urban areas. Provision was made for federal aid to highway construction within urban areas, including segments of the Interstate System which would provide access to and through, as well as around, major urban areas. George Smerk credits the Transportation Act of 1958 as the "catalytic event that set in motion the activities leading to the urban mass transportation policy of the federal government."[26] That act had nothing directly to do with urban transport, but it provided easier means for the abandonment of rail passenger services and commuter services of importance to a number of major cities which were among the first candidates for abandonment under the new procedures.

The Housing Act of 1961 made money available for up to two thirds

---

[24] See William S. Vickrey, "Pricing Is a Tool in Coordination of Local Transportation," in National Bureau of Economic Research, *Transportation Economics* (Princeton: Princeton University Press, 1965) pp. 275 ff; and Tillo E. Kuhn, "The Economics of Transportation Planning in Urban Areas," ibid., pp. 297 ff.

[25] Conrad J. Oort, "Criteria for Investment in the Infrastructure of Inland Transport," European Conference of Ministers of Transport, *2nd International Symposium* (1965) pp. 71–74; and John R. Meyer and Mahlon R. Straszheim, *Pricing and Project Evaluation* (Washington, D.C.: The Brookings Institution, 1971), chap. 4.

[26] George M. Smerk, "Ten Years of Federal Policy in Urban Transit," *Transportation Journal*, Winter 1971, p. 46.

136

of the cost of demonstrations in mass transportation.[27] By 1970 upward of 120 demonstration and R&D programs were being administered by the Urban Mass Transportation Administration of the Department of Transportation to which jurisdiction had been transferred. So-called demonstrations were often helpful in shoring up ailing commuter and transit operations until more permanent support could be found. The Highway Act of 1962 required comprehensive urban transport planning in all metropolitan areas having central cities with a population exceeding 50,000 as a condition to receipt of federal funds for highway construction after July 1, 1965. This proved difficult to comply with, since most such metropolitan areas transcend the bounds of any political unit. A number of states, therefore, created *ad hoc* agencies to undertake the task in major metropolitan areas. A good deal of progress was made in planning methodology, but the lack of enhanced federal funding for planning was a handicap, while community acceptance of plans which frequently opted for highway solutions has been difficult to secure.[28]

Not until 1964 were federal funds made available for capital projects involving new equipment and facilities. Up to two thirds in federal money was available if planning standards were met under the Urban Mass Transportation Act of that year. An amendment two years later provided authorization of funds for planning, training and development, and R&D of a more basic character than had been funded under the 1961 statute. The framework of a comprehensive federal transit program was thus established, though no provision for assistance with operating deficits was incorporated even though a number of cities were heavily burdened with such deficits.[29] Authorization is not appropriation, however, and federal funding was modest, necessitating careful screening and allocation of limited appropriated resources. Research and development efforts, moreover, are subject to the criticism that they are too largely concentrated on new technology which cannot be available for application sooner than a decade hence.

The 91st Congress, late in 1970, authorized a more forceful attack on

---

[27] The background of this act is discussed in Melvin R. Levin and Norman A. Abend, *Bureaucrats in Collision: Case Studies in Area Transportation Planning* (Cambridge: M.I.T. Press, 1971), pp. 34–44.

[28] On the development of planning techniques, see Roger L. Creighton, *Urban Transportation Planning* (Urbana: University of Illinois Press, 1970). The difficulties encountered and the effect upon results of the unequal strength of the highway and housing authorities are emphasized in Levin and Abend, *Bureaucrats in Collision*.

[29] The plight of major urban transit systems is suggested by the Chicago Transit Authority which is mandated to cover its operating costs from revenues. Despite increases in fares that are already among the highest, operations required curtailment. The transit industry as a whole had an estimated operating deficit exceeding $513 million in 1972. The potential for loss is demonstrated by the Long Island Railroad, principally a commuter operation (funded by the State of New York), which managed a deficit of $55.3 million on gross revenues of $243.4 million in 1978.

urban transport problems. A 12-year $10 billion transit aid act author-ized, in addition, contract authority of up to $3.1 billion over the next five years. This provided, for the first time, assurance of long-term fed-eral financial assistance. State and local matching was required, at least one dollar for each two of federal money.[30] Appropriations and obligational authority incorporated in the fiscal 1971 and 1972 budgets were, however, disappointingly small in relation to the authorized program. Despite strong opposition from highway interests a com-promise in 1973 made some highway funds available and opened other new avenues for urban support.

The 1974 amendments to the Urban Mass Transportation Act of 1964 marked a change of the first importance. Whereas federal assistance had hitherto been on a project basis, each project laboriously pre-pared, documented, and reviewed, the new act placed about one third of the funding on a formula rather than a discretionary basis and allowed the cities, at their option, to use formula grants for either operating or capital purposes. The formula method for allocating funds among the states had been a long-standing feature of the highway program. Now, on a small scale, it entered the urban transport finance picture. For the hard-pressed cities the opportunity to use formula funds to help cover operating deficits was also welcome relief.

Not until 1978 was further progress made toward federal encour-agement of mass transit redevelopment—then only after a long strug-gle between an economy-minded administration and the congres-sional advocates of increased transit funding. The president failed to appreciate the relationship of improved transit to urban redevelop-ment or even to the fuel economy he sought in his message on energy. Nonetheless the bill which ultimately emerged provided for a gradual increase in federal transit assistance from the $2,365 million actually appropriated in fiscal 1978 to $3,670 million in fiscal 1982. Significantly the formula portion would in every year exceed the provision for dis-cretionary capital assistance. The basic formula gives weight one half to population and one half to population density. A second-tier formula funding is provided at a level of $250 million per annum after 1979, 85 percent of which goes to cities of over 750,000 population. Ear-marked bus replacement and rail funding are also included within the formula totals. Interstate highway funds may be transferred to transit purposes, but with an 85 percent federal share in contrast with the 90 percent applicable to highways. For the first time the nonurban areas become eligible for operating as well as capital funds.

The president's new energy program, launched in the summer of

---

[30] Since 90 percent federal aid is available for urban portions of the highway net-work, financially hard-pressed cities may still find it more feasible to seek highway money.

1979, gave recognition to the utility of transit assistance as a means for energy conservation and proposed additional funding for transit out of receipts from the "windfall tax" on oil. When the tax was passed in 1980, however, transit advocates were disappointed. Despite the progress made with gradually increased appropriations and enlarged flexibility in the federal program, it remains true that the vast majority of the nation's population still lacks a useful alternative in the form of public transit.[31]

TOWARD A BROADER PLANNING FRAMEWORK

In earlier times the development of railroads, the extension of rapid transit lines beyond the areas of intense development, even to some extent the laying down of interurban railways tended strongly to shape the course of urban development. During much of the period since World War II, however, the highway planners have been responding, in principal part, to developments shaped by others as they endeavored to cope with volumes of road traffic generated by subdivision within the sprawling framework which the automobile made possible. Mass transit is being looked to as an alternative to further proliferation of urban freeways, as a means to relieve highway congestion, and as a help in relieving various types of pollution and in improving the quality of the urban environment.

That good public transit can reshape the character of urban development is illustrated by Toronto's subway and by the airport extension of Cleveland's transit, among other examples. Though it was long considered questionable whether even high-quality transit could induce people out of their automobiles, the success of the Lindenwold line out of Philadelphia provides hope that it can be done at least in some circumstances. The concept of subsidizing operations to permit low transit fares, even the notion of free transit, is capturing wider interest and a more receptive audience. And some progress is being made by those who argue for charges against the automobile that more nearly reflect the social costs its use inflicts.

Contemporaneously substantial progress is being made in Europe, less in the United States and elsewhere, toward concepts of municipal planning which seek livable communities in which requirements for mechanical transport are minimized. The idea of the New Town goes a long way back in British planning history, and several generations of such towns have been conceived and executed. The earlier expecta-

---

[31] For further detail on the 1978 statute see George M. Smerk, "Update on Federal Mass Transportation Policy: The Surface Transportation Act of 1978," *Transportation Journal*, Spring 1979, pp. 16–35.

tion of achieving substantially self-sufficient communities has given way to more modest aspiration, and many of the later generations of new towns and those now being conceived fall somewhat in the category of satellites to the large urban areas. Whether publicly sponsored, as often in Europe, or privately promoted as in the United States, however, they start with the assembly of a very large tract on which an entire community, planned *as a whole*, can be laid down.

Basic to the concept is the bringing of residence and workplace together in the same community, one of modest size. Shopping, educational, recreational, and cultural facilities are worked into the scheme. Variety is provided through the style of subcommunities which, themselves, are partially self-contained. Pedestrian and vehicular traffic are separated; and an effort is made, in the special arrangement of facilities, to enable walking to substitute for vehicular movement to the maximum possible extent. Industrial facilities requiring access to the trunk highway net are peripherally located to keep truck traffic out of the heart of the community. Where the community is sizable and not far removed from a major city, it may develop a traffic density to and from the city sufficient to support some form of mass transport without the severe peaking generated by the journey to work.

In the United States two major cities are in course of development—Columbia, Maryland and Reston, Virginia. The former is designed for a population of 110,000 by 1981 and is organized into 40 pedestrian-oriented neighborhoods. It is believed large enough to support the needed variety of urban institutions.[32] The New Communities Act of 1968 provided a federal guarantee to enable private developers to generate the low-interest financing necessary to pull them through the prolonged land acquisition and development phases. Its provisions were extended to public bodies by the Housing and Urban Development Act of 1970.

Though no large success with new towns has been achieved in the United States, there are some recent developments which suggest progress toward curbing urban growth and reviving the central cities. Whether these trends will be sustained it is far too early to say. There are indications that the movement from rural to urban areas has moderated if not reversed. And there is movement from the suburbs back to the city in some urban areas. Demographic trends may encourage this as the proportion of older people grows and the recognized energy efficiency of the apartment and row house may abet it. As in Toronto, the Washington Metro is demonstrating the ability of transit to shape urban growth—$970 million in private development is underway near

---

[32] "If any part of the plan has not panned out, it is the internal transportation . . . nothing appears to be able to separate the American suburbanite from his car," *Business Week*, June 30, 1973, p. 82.

Metro stations and as much as $5 billion may be inspired by the sub-way.[33] Propelled by gasoline shortages and the attraction of increased federal aid for urban development, downtown urban shopping malls are beginning to take the limelight from suburban malls. Chicago, Boston, Philadelphia, and Tulsa have benefited from such redevelopment and 15 other malls are under construction or in prospect.[34]

While some progress may be made toward alleviating the impact of the automobile upon urban areas and circulation may be improved by mass transportation development, it is rightly pointed out that efforts in these directions, standing alone, will not get to the heart of the problems suffered by most of our cities. They face severe economic and social problems, not merely problems of traffic congestion, which stem from the undisciplined way in which they have been allowed to grow in the past. The problem of creating a satisfactory urban environment transcends solutions centered only upon transportation and clearly requires a coordination of transport planning with broad community planning.[35]

SELECTED REFERENCES

Andrews, Richard B. *Urban Growth and Development: A Problem Approach.* New York: Simmons-Boardman Publishing Co., 1962.

Catonese, Anthony J., ed. *New Perspectives in Urban Transportation Research.* Lexington, Mass.: D. C. Heath & Co., 1972.

Cornehls, James V., and Taebel, Delbert A. *The Political Economy of Urban Transportation.* Port Washington, N.Y.: Kennikat Press, 1977.

Creighton, Roger L. *Urban Transportation Planning.* Urbana: University of Illinois Press, 1970.

Danielson, Michael N. *Federal-Metropolitan Politics and the Commuter Crisis.* New York: Columbia University Press, 1965.

Doxiadis, Constantinos A. *Ekistics: An Introduction to the Science of Human Settlements.* London: Hutchinson Publishing Group, 1968.

Gottman, Jean. *Megalopolis: The Urbanized Northeastern Seaboard of the United States.* Cambridge: M.I.T. Press, 1961.

Gunther, John. *Twelve Cities.* New York: Harper & Row Publishers, 1969.

Lang, A. Scheffer, and Soberman, Richard M. *Urban Rail Transit: Its Economics and Technology.* Cambridge: M.I.T. Press, 1964.

---

[33] Barbara Gamarekian, "The Boom on the Potomac," *New York Times*, October 7, 1979, Section 3, pp. 1, 9.

[34] "A Battle No Longer One-Sided," *Forbes*, September 17, 1979, pp. 129–35.

[35] On this general thesis, see the excellent little book by Wilfred Owen, *The Accessible City* (Washington, D.C.: The Brookings Institution, 1972). On a European venture in town planning, see Heikki von Hertzen and Paul D. Spreiregen, *Building a New Town: Finland's New Garden City, Tapiola* (Cambridge: M.I.T. Press, 1970).

Marion, John. H. "Urban Goods Movement-The Key to Improved Transportation Productivity." Transportation Research Forum, *Proceedings, Fourteenth Annual Meeting* (1973), pp. 161–176.

Meyer, J. R.; Kain, J. F.; and Wohl, M. *The Urban Transportation Problem.* Cambridge: Harvard University Press, 1965.

Mumford, Lewis. *The Highway and the City.* New York: Harcourt, Brace & World, 1964.

Owen, Wilfred. *The Metropolitan Transportation Problem.* Rev. ed. Washington, D.C.: The Brookings Institution, 1966.

———. *The Accessible City.* Washington, D.C.: The Brookings Institution, 1972.

Pegrum, Dudley F. *Transportation: Economics and Public Policy,* chaps. 12 and 22. Homewood, Ill.: Richard D. Irwin, Inc., 1963.

Port of New York Authority. *Metropolitan Transportation–1980.* 1963.

Smerk, George M. *Urban Transportation: The Federal Role.* Bloomington: Indiana University Press, 1965.

———. *Readings in Urban Transportation.* Bloomington: Indiana University Press, 1968.

———. *Urban Mass Transportation: A Dozen Years of Federal Policy.* Bloomington: Indiana University Press, 1974.

Stropac, Joseph A. *BART: Off and Running.* Burlingame, Calif.: Chatham Publishing Co., 1972.

Transportation and Logistics Research Center, The American University. *Criteria for Transport Pricing.* Cambridge, Md.: Cornell Maritime Press, 1973.

U.S. Department of Transportation. *Economic Characteristics of the Urban Public Transportation Industry.* 1972.

Vernon, Raymond. *The Changing Economic Function of the Central City.* New York: Area Development Committee of the CED, 1959.

Weiner, Paul, and Deak, Edward J. *Environmental Factors in Transportation Planning.* Lexington, Mass.: D. C. Heath & Co., 1972.

Whyte, William H. *The Last Landscape.* New York: Doubleday & Co., Inc., 1968.

Williams, Ernest W., Jr., ed. *The Future of American Transportation,* chaps. 2, 6, and 7. Englewood Cliffs, N.J.: Prentice-Hall, Inc., 1971.

9

Costs and Cost Finding in Transport and Distribution

Cost finding is essential to effective control of operations, the pricing of service, and the determination of investment policy. It is of growing importance in transport regulation. An understanding of cost concepts and of the state of the cost-finding art will be helpful to an understanding of the comparison of modal capabilities in the next chapter. It is essential for an exposition of rate-making principles later in the book and a necessary prelude to comprehension of regulatory controversies concerning rates. Nor are the concepts to be discussed irrelevant to distribution management—they apply as well to the warehouse function and to private carriage as they do to the conduct of for-hire transport service.

While cost concepts can be simply and clearly stated, their application to transport enterprises is difficult in the extreme. Partly for that reason cost finding in transport lagged in time behind that in manufacturing industry, received less wholehearted attention, and remains in controversy. We will look first at concepts, second at difficulties presented to the transport cost finder, and finally at the state of the art.

COST CONCEPTS

The Supply Function

The characteristic supply function shows the quantities that will be offered to the market at different prices and mirrors the cost of generating various quantities of a product or service. It presumes the producers will at least seek to cover their costs plus a normal profit. Unit costs will tend to increase as aggregate industry output mounts, since larger quantities of factor inputs must be assembled and used, for example, plant must be expanded and increased quantities of materials and of labor must be employed. Factor prices are likely to move up in consequence of increased demand for them. Hence the supply curve as usually illustrated slopes upward to the right of the origin.

Demand curves are usually portrayed as sloping downwards, that is, aggregate quantity that will be purchased in the market increases as price declines. There are recognized exceptions where a high price may determine the desirability of a product as with certain luxury goods. The nature of transport demand will be discussed at a later point, but it is useful to present the characteristic formulation here. In Figure 9-1 aggregate output and sales are determined by the intersection of the demand and supply curves.

FIGURE 9-1
Demand and Supply

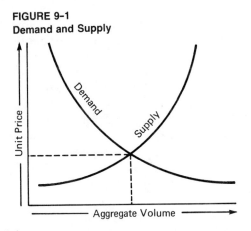

Fixed, Variable, and Total Costs

Few economic enterprises operate without encountering some costs which are fixed regardless of output and others that vary with output. Assume we have a manufacturing plant. There are costs that are fixed regardless of whether we produce nothing or a volume of product equivalent to plant capacity. These include depreciation resulting from time rather than use, amortization of investment, taxes based on plant value, and custodial costs. If we are in operation, general management costs may also be fixed over the range of output along with heat and some other general inputs. In Figure 9-2 these are shown by the straight line parallel to the horizontal axis—a body of cost which is unchanging without regard to the operating rate. The term *constant cost* can be used in place of *fixed cost*.

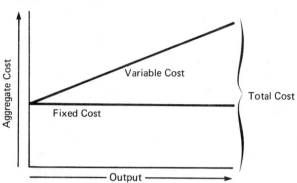

As we increase the operating rate, hence the output, various costs will increase in the aggregate with output. These include materials, operating supplies, direct labor, light, and power. Unlike fixed costs, these costs are a function of output and are therefore called variable costs. Total cost is the summation of the two categories at any level of output.

For clarity of thought it is important to note that cost *per unit* of output in the illustration of Figure 9-3 will decline as output increases. The aggregate fixed cost remains the same, but it can be spread over more units of output. Average fixed cost per unit thus declines as output increases, while variable costs per unit *may* be constant. In these circumstances average total unit cost declines.

Unit Cost Behavior

A given plant is likely to have an optimum rate of operation—one at which unit costs are minimized. It may be possible to push output beyond this point, but higher unit costs are characteristically encountered when a plant is forced beyond designed capacity. At rates of output below the optimum, the plant is not being fully utilized—excess capacity exists. Certain factor inputs, such as supervision and minimum number of machine operators, may be indivisibilities. If any output is to be secured, as much of these factors must be supplied as would support a larger output; hence average unit costs attributable to them are high at low rates of production and decline as output is increased. Within a certain range of output, even though not over the whole operating range, these costs are fixed. These circumstances plus the spread of fixed costs over larger numbers of output units as the operating rate is advanced produce a unit cost curve which is characteristically illustrated as U-shaped.

Empirical studies dedicated to the development of actual cost curves

FIGURE 9-3
Fixed and Variable Costs per Unit of Output

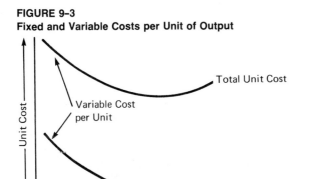

tend to show, in a number of circumstances, relatively flat cost curves except at extremely low and very high rates of output. Many types of plant installation appear to have the capability of efficient production over fairly wide ranges of output. Such plants, of course, have aggregate fixed costs that are low in relation to variable costs even at modest output rates. Some types of transport plant fall in that category—others do not.

Economies of Scale

Our discussion thus far has dealt with the behavior of costs in a given plant during its lifetime. In the long run all costs are variable, that is, plant can be scrapped and replaced by other plant. When the replacement decision is looked at, all costs of a new plant are variable since they do not come into existence unless the decision to replace is affirmative.

When the capacity of a plant is outrun by demand, it may be supplemented by adding another of similar or smaller capacity; or it may be scrapped and replaced by one of larger capacity. Which decision is appropriate will depend upon whether large plants are more efficient than small ones, that is, upon whether economies of scale exist. At any given state of technology, larger plants will in many types of production be more efficient than smaller ones, that is, capable of generating lower unit costs at or near optimum output levels. But, as in so many economic and technologic relationships, to increase plant size beyond a certain level may result in reduced efficiency. The principle may be illustrated as in Figure 9-4 which uses average total cost curves for four plants, each one of larger capacity than its predecessor. Each larger plant develops lower unit costs than its predecessor within

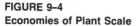

FIGURE 9–4
Economies of Plant Scale

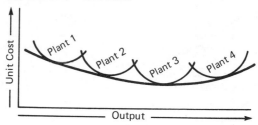

the operating range for which it is designed until plant 4 is reached. As we move from plant 1 to plant 2 and plant 3 we achieve economies of scale as long as the capacity of the plant can be reasonably well utilized. When we go to plant 4, however, we see that diseconomies of scale result. The plant is too large given the present state of the art of this industry. The curve that can be constructed around these individual plant cost curves is appropriately known as an envelope curve, and it generalizes scale economies.

It will be noted that plant 2 at very low operating rates has higher unit costs than the smaller plant 1 producing the same output. The same is true of each of the other plants. To build a larger plant that cannot be kept busy may be less efficient than to provide a smaller one which can, even though the latter, because of fluctuations in demand, may sometimes have to operate at above optimum rates.

Where scale economies exist, an industry may be said to operate under conditions of decreasing costs (increasing returns to scale). Large units will tend to drive out smaller ones. If the optimum plant scale generates all of the output the market will take, monopoly results. Plant scale is the result of technological factors. The firm, or enterprise, which may operate a multiplicity of plants can also display increasing returns to scale. Larger firms may realize economies in purchasing, in channeling a larger volume of goods through the sales organization, and in other ways. An able management team may be capable of managing an enlarged enterprise with little, if any, addition to its ranks. But enterprises can become too large for effective management, overheads may increase, and decreasing returns to scale may set in.

Marginal Cost

When unit costs are increasing or decreasing over the range of output as shown in Figure 9–3, the cost of one unit added to previous output will depart from average unit cost. If unit costs are falling, the cost of an added unit will be less than the average cost of units thus far produced. If they are increasing, the cost of an added unit will exceed average cost. The cost of producing one additional unit is referred to as marginal cost. The term *out-of-pocket cost* is frequently used by businessmen and in the transport industries to denominate the same concept. To enable the concept to be applied to various increments of output, the following definition may be employed:

$$\text{Marginal cost} = \frac{\text{Increase in total cost}}{\text{Increase in output}}$$

The marginal cost curve will intersect the average total cost curve from below at the minimum point of the total cost curve as shown in Figure 9-5. In a perfectly competitive industry all firms will be of optimum scale, will operate at that output which coincides with the intersection of marginal and average total cost, will dispose of the output at a price equivalent to that level of cost, and will realize a normal profit. Such conditions rarely exist in practice.

FIGURE 9-5
Average Total and Marginal Unit Costs

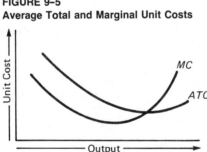

Decision Costs

Business decisions look at the future rather than the past; hence their prospective effects both on revenue and costs are the relevant issues. Cost already incurred to provide a firm's productive capacity are *sunk costs*. They are not relevant to a decision to reduce price and obtain larger volume, and thus move the operating rate closer to the available capacity. Neither are fixed costs relevant since they must be met regardless of the rate of output anticipated for such a decision. Only marginal (or incremental) costs are relevant. The increase of cost that will result from the increase of output should be compared with the increase of revenue expected from the same decision.

Where investment is contemplated for the purpose of increasing capacity, of course, the costs of putting new plant in place are not sunk but are costs incurred because of the decision taken. The prospective returns require comparison with those from other possible investments; for to make this investment, one must sacrifice placing the same re-

148

sources in some alternative, perhaps more profitable, employment. The return from the best possible alternative employment may be referred to as the *opportunity cost* of capital devoted to the contemplated purpose. The concept seldom applies to rate making since rates usually apply for an indefinite period and to an unpredictable volume of traffic.

Readiness to Serve—Standby Costs

Certain businesses, of which utilities and transportation are the most important examples, furnish services rather than tangible goods. Demand must be met the instant it occurs by a supply of electricity or of transport capacity; otherwise the public will suffer from an inadequacy of service. Tangible goods can be produced and stored in advance of peak demands (daily, weekly, and seasonal peaks are common in public-service industries), but service industries must maintain sufficient capacity to provide them with a readiness to serve at times of peak requirements.

To hold plant in readiness to serve engenders *standby costs*. The latent capacity is there to serve when the peak demand occurs. The cost of having capacity necessary to service periodic demands that exceed the normal continuous load is, therefore, attributable to the peak demand. Thus two lanes may be perfectly adequate for an urban highway during most of the day, but the morning and evening peaks of traffic engendered by the journey to and from work may require six lanes during the approximately 4 hours out of 24 when such traffic is concentrated. Should the capacity actually provided prove inadequate to permit movement at normal rates of speed, *congestion costs* will be imposed upon the users of the facility which may take the form of delay, discomfort, and added fuel costs which they are compelled to bear.

PROBLEMS OF TRANSPORT COSTING

The Unit of Output

Our simple presentation of cost concepts has, thus far, ignored numerous complexities encountered in practice. Not least is the question of the unit of output in relation to which costs are measured. Cost curves are customarily drawn for a plant which produces a single product, hence has a homogeneous output. Our plant produces "widgets," each one exactly like any other. There can be no doubt what the unit of output is, and the number of widgets can serve as the divisor, thus:

$$\text{Marginal cost of a widget} = \frac{\text{Increase of cost in dollars}}{\text{Increase in number of widgets produced}}$$

When a plant produces several products rather than one, the problem of measuring output becomes more complex.

The transportation industry, however, produces services. How are they to be measured? Characteristically we use the ton-mile and the passenger-mile—the number of tons moved one mile and the number of passengers moved one mile. These are useful statistical measures for some purposes. As compared with tons originated or tons handled, ton-miles are additive without duplication even where the tons have moved over several carriers or several modes of transport. Hence the volume of freight service performed is usually expressed in ton miles and the freight traffic share of the several modes is calculated on the basis of the percentage of ton-miles generated by each.

To use the ton-mile as a measure of output for costing purposes, however, is far from satisfactory. Weight and distance are two important measures of transport service which are incorporated in the ton-mile. But 1,000 tons moved one mile generate the same number of ton-miles as ten tons moved 100 miles, although the services are obviously very different and unlikely to generate equivalent unit (i.e., ton-mile) costs. Speed is another element of the transport service which finds no reflection in the ton-mile measure. Finally the measure treats all tons as if they are the same—100 tons of coal moved in a single ordinary open hopper car count the same as, say, 36 standard automobiles moving in three expensive 89-foot tri-level auto rack cars. Not only the investment in equipment and the costs of maintaining it but the movement costs also are substantially higher for the automobile movement. The disparity grows when the automobiles must be protected from vandalism.

Transport service is often produced in units that are quite different than the service units that must be priced. And costs are needed that correspond with prices both to establish appropriate prices in the first place and to measure profit results on traffic moving under particular rates. The rail line-haul unit of production is the train—perhaps 3,000 tons or more of revenue freight. But rates are usually stated per ton or per 100 pounds. The motor freight line-haul unit is the rig—characteristically either a semitrailer or a double bottom (one semitrailer and one full trailer). Yet each of perhaps several hundred shipments carried by such a rig must be separately priced. A 30,000-ton river tow which moves as an integral unit may comprise 30 or 40 barges, each conceivably carrying a separate consignment for which the shipper must be billed. Terminal services, too, present difficulties. A city delivery truck, for example, may make a dozen deliveries, each performed under different circumstances. Between the line-haul rig and the city delivery move, the freight must be handled and sorted over the terminal platform. Different production units are appropriate to each step in the service, but somehow they must be added to generate a total cost which can be broken down to a per-ton or per-100-pound basis.

A final complication is that costs are more directly related to the movement of equipment than to the tonnage of revenue freight carried. The costs of moving a highway rig one mile are not greatly different for a loaded rig than for an empty rig. Hence if cargo can be found to fill a rig that would otherwise move empty to a place where it is required for loading, that cargo virtually gets a free ride once the costs of loading and unloading are covered.

Multiple Services

What has already been said suggests another problem which is quite characteristic in transport. Plant is installed in order to make it possible to perform not one kind but several kinds of service. The highway is a good example. It provides access to abutting property. It conveys a variety of vehicles bent on numerous objectives—the automobile used for business or pleasure, the farmer's pickup, the long-haul common-carrier truck and bus, the telephone company's maintenance vehicle, the ambulance, military vehicles, and many others. It is a multiple-purpose facility, indivisible, but designed to meet the maximum requirements expected to be placed upon it by a composite of uses. Yet if those who use or benefit from the highway are to be called upon to bear its cost—both construction and maintenance—some means of allocating the total must be found and used.

Commercial carriers also frequently generate capacity which is utilized for several services. Most commercial aircraft carry passengers, excess baggage, mail, express, and cargo. The direct flying costs are accordingly incurred on behalf of all of these services. The mix of services will vary greatly from one flight to another. Railroad passenger trains formerly provided all these services except cargo. Intercity buses frequently carry express parcels as well as passengers and their baggage. Rail plant—trackage, signal systems, and other facilities—is often used by both freight and passenger trains. In all of these circumstances services are performed under conditions of *common costs*—costs generated on behalf of a multiplicity of services and only arbitrarily assignable to each of those services. In the same way the costs of operating a freight train or a river tow are common to the many separate consignments included.

Assignable Costs

Certain costs may be directly assignable to a particular service. Thus the cost of owning and maintaining passenger-carrying railroad cars may be assigned to the passenger service. The cost of owning, maintaining, and operating aircraft that are exclusively used in cargo service may be assigned to cargo. Directly assignable costs may be fixed or variable. Thus the amortization and taxes on a passenger terminal are fixed costs. They are also directly assignable to the passenger service. The cost of ticket sellers and baggage handlers in a large terminal may be variable, at least with large fluctuations in passenger volume. But these are also assignable costs.

Common costs are not directly assignable. Whether they fall in the category of fixed or variable costs, they are caused by, or incurred on behalf of, several services in common. They can be separated between those services only arbitrarily.[1] This process is called *apportionment*, and there are usually many bases on which it can be done. A plausible argument can often be made for each of several bases of apportionment, but none can be said to be better than another at getting at the costs that were *caused* by a particular service. They are simply ways of distributing a body of costs among services.

Joint costs are most often encountered in transport in the familiar backhaul situation. Joint costs are found when two products or services are necessarily produced together in fixed proportions. One may be said to be a by-product of the other. Thus when animals are slaughtered for their meat, the hides are a necessary by-product. In the same way the movement of trucks under load westbound in a regular-route transport operation requires their return eastbound to the origin if the service is to be maintained whether or not loads are available. Return capacity is a by-product of the loaded trip out. The round trip costs can be ascertained, but they are caused by the outbound loads which occasion the trip, and some part of them can only be apportioned to whatever loads can be found to fill backhaul capacity. Except for loading and unloading, as noted before, the movement of that backhaul traffic is virtually costless since the truck will go back in any event.

Time jointness is also encountered in transport, as in many other kinds of economic activity, but in the case of transport it is often a phenomenon of more than usual importance. No type of traffic, other than a continuous flow of liquid through a pipeline, moves at an equal rate 24 hours a day, 365 days a year. Even a pipeline stream may be slowed or accelerated, thus the rate of throughput adjusted, by changes in pumping pressure. All other types of transport encounter periodicities in the demand for service. Capacity is installed with a view to handle the peak traffic expected, as during the morning and evening peaks on an urban highway or mass transit facility. In the off-peak hours much more highway or rail capacity is available than is

---

[1] As Kahn rightly points out, under certain circumstances definable shares of common costs can *in principle* be causally attributed to each of the services. Alfred E. Kahn, *The Economics of Regulation: Principles and Institutions*, vol. 1 (New York: John Wiley & Sons, Inc., 1970), pp. 78, 85.

needed or used. Thus latent capacity is a by-product of the peak traffic requirement. The principle is the same as in the case of jointness of products.

COST FINDING

Origin of Commission Formulas

The Interstate Commerce Commission has developed formulas for cost finding for railroads, motor carriers of general commodities, and water carriers operating in domestic trade. Costs are regularly published for rail and motor carriers; and between the years when full cost studies are made, costs are updated by appropriate price indices. Carriers perform their own cost studies using the commission's formulas and also other approaches as may seem appropriate to particular purposes. The Civil Aeronautics Board, similarly, has developed cost formulas for airlines.

Cost finding was considered of little importance either for regulatory or management purposes as late as the 1930s. A report of the Federal Coordinator of Transportation which suggested cost-finding procedures for railroads late in that decade was coldly received. Pioneering work was being done by the California Railroad Commission, however; and when the Interstate Commerce Commission became convinced of the need of costs for regulatory purposes it turned to that commission for a director of its cost program. The occasion was *Class Rates, 1939*, an investigation of alleged territorial discriminations in rates for which at least broad territorial costs were seen to be needed. Rail Form A came out of that proceeding, but two limitations should be noted: (1) the original work was done in wartime and the railroads convinced the commission that many special studies sought by the cost section would divert personnel from more essential tasks and (2) what the commission needed was evidence that costs were or were not higher in Southern and Western Territories than in the Northeast (Official Territory). Costs relating to particular railroads or traffic movements were not required and were not sought. Broad territorial averages were sufficient.

Once Form A was available, however, and territorial costs were regularly published, they began to be used in rate cases and for other purposes when the costs shown tended to support the position taken by one or more parties to a proceeding. Use built up slowly, but Form A was convenient and it had some status as a product of the commission's own staff work. Financial emergency involving whole groups of motor carriers during and immediately after the war led to the development of a somewhat similar formula for motor-carrier cost finding. It became clear as time went on that formulas satisfactory for the purposes for which they were devised were gradually being applied to more specific purposes for which they were less well suited.

Important General Characteristics

Costs as developed by the commission are historical costs, and the same is true when the formulas are applied by individual carriers to their own data. For rate-making and other decision purposes, prospective rather than historic costs are required. Despite the complexity of the formulations, moreover, they are largely limited by the data available from the uniform systems of accounts prescribed for rail and motor carriers which were not designed to serve cost-finding purposes. Special studies on a limited sample basis are employed to secure some critical information not revealed by the accounts. An example is switching-engine minutes per car placed or pulled from industry sidings. The rail costs, indeed, contemplate single-car siding-to-siding movements and are thus limited in their usefulness since much traffic moves in multiple-car lots or full train loads. These sample studies, as well as those employed to enable costing of motor carrier pickup and delivery operations, fail to reveal the wide range of costs encountered in terminals of differing size, complexity, and degree of congestion.

Costs as published by the commission are averaged territorial costs. They assume movement in average-weight trains with average number of intermediate yardings and interchanges encountered by the traffic as a whole. It is probable that little, if any, traffic actually moves under such average conditions. These limitations should be borne in mind in connection with the cost comparisons offered in the next chapter. Methods are provided for adjusting these average costs to obtain costs more nearly representative of actual traffic conditions.

Concepts

The formulas are designed to generate both out-of-pocket and fully distributed costs. Critical to this process is a determination of which costs are fixed and which are variable. For this purpose cross-section analysis was employed both in rail and motor-carrier costing. Ton-miles per route mile were plotted against route-mile operating costs, a least-square line fitted and extended to the left until it intersected the vertical axis. The cost measured at the point of intersection was taken as fixed, the remainder as variable. Out of this type of analysis came the proposition that 80 percent of rail cost and some 90 percent of motor-carrier cost was variable. Be it noted, however, that cross-section analysis does not address itself to the question being asked, that is, what is the variation of cost associated with changes of traffic volume moved by a particular route or system? Instead it compares different systems which happen to have different traffic densities. Time-series analysis would appear more appropriate but is faced with a great many difficulties. It is possible to argue, however, that the percent variable for railroads is considerably overstated.[2]

The commission's rail variable-cost concept resembles a long-run variable cost, for it assumes that changes can be made in plant and equipment. It embraces from 44 to 100 percent of various classes of operating expenses, rents, and taxes. It also includes an allowance for variable cost of capital on 100 percent of the motive power and equipment and on one half of the road property. The tacit assumption is made that significant traffic increases will require a proportionate increase in motive power and cars and an increase at half that rate in terminals and trackage. The latter assumption, at least, is of dubious validity.

Fully allocated cost incorporates the remainder of operating expenses, rents, and taxes which are presumed to be fixed costs plus a return on the remaining 50 percent of road property. Both of these concepts as applied to carload freight service require a prior separation from total costs of those costs attributable to the passenger service and to the less-than-carload freight service, neither of which is any longer of great significance.

The two concepts as applied to motor carriers generate costs which are not directly comparable with the rail costs. Motor-carrier costs do not include a cost of capital. Hence they must be increased before a valid comparison with rail costs can be made. While costing of motor-truck service avoids the complexity involved in separating passenger and freight service costs, the largest part of the traffic of motor common-carriers of general commodities is less than truckload. Worse, a substantial proportion of the shipments falls in the small shipment category, including very large numbers of minimum-charge shipments. Costing must, therefore, differentiate by size of shipment. Unlike rail carload traffic, a very large part of motor-carrier business must be moved over carriers' terminal platforms both at origin and destination. Line-haul, pickup and delivery, and platform costs must be separately stated for shipments of varying size. Yet as already noted, the costs to be dealt with are in large measure common costs and the methods of apportionment are necessarily arbitrary.

OTHER COST FORMULATIONS

Costs based upon the commission's formulas used often to be employed in ratemaking proceedings where carriers wished to prove that

---

[2] Using similar methods and 1958–67 data, Harter Williams obtained a variable proportion of 49 percent. *ICC Practitioners Journal*, November–December 1969, pp. 26–31.

proposed rates were compensatory.[3] This is largely because costs so prepared are easier to prove—the formula itself is not ordinarily challenged. The costs presented are often based on a particular carrier's actual figures and are frequently recast to reflect better the characteristics of the movement to which the rate would apply. Published average territorial costs may often be used if the rates to be justified lie above them. Since the 4-R Act of 1976 introduced the concept of market dominance, the rate as a percent of variable cost has become one of the tests of market dominance in rail-rate cases. In an inflationary period, in any event, the emphasis is upon rate increases.

Multiple regression analysis has been applied to the study of carrier costs. It enables each cost category to be tested against a variety of measures of output or performance in the search for the best fit. Studies performed outside the commission, however, have commonly utilized the cross-section approach and have produced results at variance with the commission's formulation. Cross-section analyses have superior statistical qualities as compared with time-series studies, but the argument most often urged for their use is that they generate long-run data which are considered most appropriate for regulatory decision making.[4] The argument may be offered that in a well-developed industry, the plant operated by each firm should have become adapted over time to the traffic density characteristically encountered; hence each plant should be working at about the same percentage of capacity and each should represent the most efficient plant available for the level of traffic being handled. If these things are true, it would appear that the cross-section approach should generate a good approximation of long-run marginal costs. Characteristically they are not true in the rail industry. Moreover, it has been shown that even if each firm in the sample is operating at the same percentage of capacity,[5] biased estimates of long-run marginal costs will be obtained from cross-section analysis, the usual procedures leading to overestimation.[6]

Several cost studies of rail cost undertaken by the cross-section method have yielded much higher percent-variable calculations than the 80 percent used by the commission. Griliches, by separating the large from the small roads and using a logarithmic form, finds a percent variable (1957–61 average data) of 90.4 percent for the large roads

---

[3] They are also used by the commission's Board of Suspension as a test for proposed rates, and many protested rates escape suspension because they are above such costs.

[4] John R. Meyer, Merton J. Peck, John Stenason, and Charles Zwick, *The Economics of Competition in the Transportation Industries* (Cambridge: Harvard University Press, 1959), p. 43. On the methodology of statistical costing, see chaps. 2 and 3 of this volume.

[5] Capacity is especially difficult to measure in transport.

[6] John R. Meyer and Mahlon R. Straszheim, *Pricing and Project Evaluation* (Washington, D.C.: The Brookings Institution, 1971), p. 41.

and 60.3 percent for the small roads.[7] Earlier studies by Borts yielded results consistent with these while showing variations of percent variables among the main regions of the country and a higher percent variable for switching than for line-haul service.[8] Meyer et al. found surprisingly low long-run marginal operating costs—1.8 mills per gross ton-mile for the 1947–50 period and 2.8 mills per gross ton-mile for the 1952–55 period—accompanied by high threshold costs.[9] Roughly adjusted to a revenue ton-mile basis and to 1958 prices, they concluded that the typical revenue ton-mile would cost from 8 to 9 mills without capital costs.[10] Even with variable capital costs included, this would appear to imply a variability closer to 60 percent than to 90 percent. Evidently much remains to be done to improve understanding of the behavior of rail costs and to furnish the industry and its regulators with costing tools that are more adequate to the tasks placed upon them.

PUBLIC COSTS

The transport firm in developing its own policies, whether they relate to pricing, operating practice, route extension, construction, or capital investment, is concerned with costs that fall upon it and will be reflected on its books. Social costs not placed upon the firm under existing institutional arrangements, such as pollution costs, are of no concern in the decision process except as some concession may have to be made to public opinion and pressure. Costs encountered by various levels of government in providing transport facilities used by carriers are likewise of no concern except to the degree that they are placed upon the carriers through user charges or some other form of recoupment. The cost studies discussed above start with costs as reflected upon the books of the carriers. Hence they ignore public costs when these are not charged against the carriers.

Railroads and pipelines, since they own their permanent way and structures, meet the costs of owning and maintaining these facilities directly and reflect them in their accounts. Air, motor, and water carriers

---

[7] Zvi Griliches, "Cost Allocation in Railroad Regulation," *Bell Journal of Economics and Management Science*, Spring 1972.

[8] George H. Borts, "The Estimation of Rail Cost Functions," *Econometrica*, January 1960, pp. 108–31.

[9] Threshold costs may be defined as the expenditure level that must be attained before output reaches the relatively economical middle portion of the cost function.

[10] Meyer et al., *The Economics of Competition*, p. 63. Compare the percent variability of roughly 60 percent with the 57.4 percent variable asserted by the Canadian National Railways at 1958 freight volume in its submission to the McPherson Royal Commission. *Royal Commission on Transportation*, vol. 3 (July 1962), p. 355.

use basic facilities provided by governments. In the first two cases user-charge systems have long been in existence so that the accounts of air and motor carriers reflect some of the costs associated with their use of publicly provided facilities. Only in 1980, however, were user charges placed upon the water carriers which employ the coastal and inland waterways improved or made navigable by the federal government. Where user charges exist, their adequacy and fairness have long been in controversy, but these issues will be explored in a later chapter.

Two points are relevant to the present discussion. When rail or pipeline costs are compared with those of other forms, they will not necessarily generate comparisons useful for the purpose of determining the relative efficiency with which the modes can perform particular transport tasks. The extent to which they do will depend upon the accuracy with which public costs are reflected in their accounts through user-charge payments. Thus rail and water-carrier cost comparisons are biased in favor of the latter, since the water-carrier accounts reflect no public costs attributable to the navigable channels employed. Second, the characteristic form of user charges (of which the fuel tax is the most important example) converts governmental costs which have a large fixed element into variable costs so far as the carriers are concerned. Highway user charges can be avoided in the event of a traffic downturn by curtailment in the vehicle-miles operated. Railroads and pipelines cannot similarly escape costs associated with ownership of their permanent way.

ECONOMIES OF SCALE IN TRANSPORT

There is substantial agreement that there are no scale economies of consequence in truck transportation except in the less-than-truckload segment in which terminal investment is important.[11] But there are studies which find important scale economies in air transport while others reach an opposite conclusion. A similar diversity of results is reflected in studies of scale economies in the rail industry. In the face of such disparity of testimony in apparently reputable work, the student may be forgiven an impression of some confusion. Yet the matter is of large importance for its bearing upon cost behavior (and assumptions with respect to it are implicit in various of the cost studies already discussed) and for what it can tell us about important issues of public pol-

---

[11] On increasing returns to density in trucking see James C. Johnson, *Trucking Mergers* (Lexington, Mass.: Lexington Books, 1973), pp. 19–22. A useful analysis of recent scale studies is Garland Chow, "The Status of Economies of Scale in Regulated Trucking: A Review of the Evidence and Future Directions," Transportation Research Forum, *Proceedings, Nineteenth Annual Meeting (1978)*, pp. 365 ff.

icy later to be discussed, for example, the degree to which competition is workable in transport, the strength of the tendency toward monopoly in the absence of control, the desirability of mergers, and the kind of transportation organization that is most efficient. In an effort to clarify there may be merit in noting the treatment by E. A. G. Robinson which, in search for optimum firm size, seeks a reconciliation of optima of (1) the technical productive unit, (2) the managerial unit, (3) the financial unit, and (4) the marketing unit.[12] At the least it is well to distinguish changes in unit cost associated with (1) increased or reduced loading of installed plant in relation to capacity, (2) route density (technical or plant scale), and (3) size of firm.

Short-run marginal cost reflects changes in the loading of the plant—by definition of the short-run, plant can neither be expanded nor contracted. Thus if the schedule of an airline is taken as fixed in the short run, the operating cost per available seat-mile is also fixed. If the revenue load factor is 50 percent, the cost per revenue seat-mile is twice that per available seat-mile. If the load factor can be increased to 60 percent, the cost per revenue seat-mile is reduced to one and two-thirds times the cost per available seat-mile. Some small added cost associated with ticketing, baggage handling, and the like is, of course, incurred.[13] The filling of empty backhaul capacity is of like nature; and the same phenomenon may be observed upon a line of railroad. On a line having capacity to move 30 trains per day but presently handling only 10, the train-mile cost for added trains will be lower than present train-mile cost.[14]

The question of scale, however, introduces long-run considerations of efficient plant and firm size. The railroad industry has long been presumed to be characterized by increasing returns to scale. Yet several studies have cast doubt on this proposition if by scale is meant the sheer size of the railroad measured by route mileage, traffic volume, or employment. Healy's study using 1954–56 data indicated increases in wages and transportation expenses as well as lower rates of return for railroads having more than 10,000 employees. Above 19,000 em-

---

[12] E. A. G. Robinson, *The Structure of Competitive Industry* (Chicago: University of Chicago Press, 1958). The reconciliation of differing optima is discussed in chap. 7.

[13] The marginal analysis is sometimes employed in determining whether to add a flight to the basic schedule, for while the schedule as a whole must return fully allocated cost or better, the question whether profit will be improved by adding a flight is determined by marginal cost versus marginal revenue. See Leonard S. Silk and Daniel B. Moscowitz, "Marginal Analysis: The Case of Continental Airlines," in Campbell R. McConnell, *Economic Issues: Readings and Cases*, 2d ed. (New York: McGraw-Hill Book Co., 1966), pp. 148 ff.

[14] Excess capacity can be eliminated fairly quickly in air and motor transport (except as respects publicly provided basic facilities). In the rail industry, however, it has persisted over a very long period of time. Hence the time horizon associated with the "short run" may be quite long as respects some elements of plant.

ployees he found an increase in capital requirements as well. The same study showed lower rates of return on carriers having fewer than 5,000 employees, suggesting a very narrow size band within which most efficient operations were attained.[15] A study of railroad performance in the period 1872–86, which attempts to eliminate the effects of technological advance over the period, also finds an absence of evidence of increasing returns to scale.[16] Doubt has been cast, too, upon the ability to achieve anticipated savings at least in the larger mergers of the recent past.[17] Unless one argues that too little time has passed to bring economies into play, this may be tantamount to saying that increasing returns to firm scale are not to be expected in the industry.

While there has always been doubt about the ability to manage very large roads as efficiently as smaller ones, the majority of railway economists of earlier times appear to have believed that economies of plant scale were inherent in the rail technology, for example, that a double-track road nourished with adequate traffic would perform at lower unit costs that a single-track road similarly nourished in relation to its capacity. It is less than clear whether capacity utilization and plant scale were not often combined in their thinking. Recent studies have merged the issues by employing a common methodology to seek answers to each question. Thus Healy's approach to the question of plant scale is a cross-section analysis of carriers classified by density, an approach comparable to that used in examining the percent variable in response to traffic fluctuation. His conclusions are consistent with those of Borts and thus suggest only moderate plant-scale economies in the West and, perhaps, the opposite in the Northeast.

There is great difficulty in separating out the effects of the three phenomena we have identified; yet to do so is of critical importance if railway cost behavior is to be understood. At the time of Healy's study, for example, many of the eastern roads incorporated in this sample were working at little more than 55 percent of their wartime peaks of freight traffic over main routes while some of the western roads enjoyed traffic at levels 80 percent or better in relation to their peaks. As a test for the presence of plant-scale economies the cross section must compare plants working at an efficient level of loading. Clearly much more work needs to be done to clarify the issues; and it would be the part of wisdom, meanwhile, to reserve judgment.

Failure to distinguish between plant size, measurable by such fac-

---

[15] Kent T. Healy, *The Effects of Scale in the Railroad Industry* (New Haven: Committee on Transportation, Yale University, 1961), scale conclusions summarized at p. 3.

[16] Robert M. Spann and Edward W. Erikson, "The Economics of Railroading: The Beginning of Cartelization and Regulation," *Bell Journal of Economics and Management Science*, Autumn 1970, pp. 227 ff.

[17] Robert E. Gallamore, "Measurement of Cost Savings of Recent Railway Mergers," Transportation Research Forum, *Papers, Ninth Annual Meeting (1968)*, pp. 217 ff.

tors as stage length and route density, and size of firm uncorrected for that type of difference in the character of operations appear to account for differences in view about economies of scale in air transport. A number of studies find economies of scale as firm size increases.[18] Straszheim, however, finds the sharp decline in direct costs as firm size increases to be due principally to such matters as plane choice (the opportunity for which is influenced by route pattern), stage length, and density.[19] He differentiates these causes for decreasing costs from economies of scale. Other students of air transport have suggested the same explanatory factors for the observed decreasing costs, factors which we would place under the rubric "plant scale."[20]

RELATIVE ECONOMY AND FITNESS

For some 40 years a battle raged in the regulatory and legislative arenas between rail carriers on the one hand and motor and water carriers on the other, on the question of what standard should determine the level of a rate made for purposes of intermodal competition. The rails, with a higher proportion of fixed costs, sought a variable cost standard while their competitors argued for fully allocated costs. The struggle brought costs very much into the regulatory process, but the issue was not resolved until 1976 when Congress accorded freedom to the railroads to make rates down to a level that did not diminish their "going concern value." What precisely that means will, no doubt, ultimately be determined by the courts. In the interim, however, many would take it to be largely influenced by the variable cost standard for railroads, a result acceptable to many economists.[21]

At present, relief from rate regulation has been extended to railroads in perishable produce and may well be extended to other areas. *De facto* relief from entry regulation in many aspects of motor carriage may well bring rate deregulation in its train. Where greater freedom to price exists, carriers must give close attention to their own costs and to

---

[18] Jesse W. Proctor and Julius S. Duvean, "A Regression Analysis of Airline Costs," *Journal of Air Law and Commerce*, vol. 21 (Summer 1954), pp. 282 ff.; and Stephen Wheatcroft, *The Economics of European Air Transport* (London: Michael Joseph, Ltd., 1956), pp. 59–63.

[19] Mahlon R. Straszheim, *The International Airline Industry* (Washington, D.C.: The Brookings Institution, 1969), pp. 96 ff.

[20] See, for example, Paul W. Cherington, *Airline Price Policy: A Study of Domestic Airline Passenger Fares* (Boston: Harvard Business School, 1958), pp. 42–66. Cf. George W. Douglas and James C. Miller, III, *Economic Regulation of Domestic Air Transport: Theory and Policy* (Washington, D.C.: The Brookings Institution, 1974), pp. 13–18, where no economies of firm size are found.

[21] William J. Baumol et al., "The Role of Cost in the Minimum Pricing of Railroad Services," *The Journal of Business*, October 1962, pp. 1–10.

the costs of their competitors. Market research becomes of greater importance and must be informed by adequate cost work. The question whether a carrier has a cost advantage must be resolved if the types of traffic for which it is most efficient and for which it should make a price bid are to be defined. If the division of traffic is to be ruled more largely by unregulated competition, the importance of a proper reflection of public costs on carriers' books through appropriate user charges is considerably enhanced.

SELECTED REFERENCES

Banner, Paul H., ed. *The Issue of Public Costs in Competitive Transportation Rate Making.* Washington, D.C.: Southern Railway System, 1966.

Borts, George H. "Increasing Returns in the Railway Industry" *Journal of Political Economy*, vol. 62 (August 1954), pp. 316–33.

———. "The Estimation of Rail Cost Functions." *Econometrica*, vol. 28 (January 1960), pp. 108–31.

Chow, Garland. *The Economics of the Motor Freight Industries.* Bloomington: Division of Research, School of Business, Indiana University, 1978.

Healy, Kent T. *The Effects of Scale in the Railroad Industry.* New Haven: Committee on Transportation, Yale University, 1961.

Interstate Commerce Commission. *Explanation of Rail Cost Finding Procedures and Principles Relating to the Use of Costs,* Statement 7–63 (1963).

———. *Rail Carload Cost Scales by Territories* (annual).

———. *Cost of Transporting Freight by Class I and Class II Motor Common Carriers of General Commodities* (annual).

Johnson, James C. *Trucking Mergers: A Regulatory Viewpoint.* Lexington, Mass.: Lexington Press, 1973.

Kahn, Alfred E. *The Economics of Regulation: Principles and Institutions,* chaps. 3 and 4. Vol. 1. New York: John Wiley & Sons, Inc., 1970.

Meyer, John R.; Peck, M. J.; Stenason, John; and Zwick, Charles. *The Economics of Competition in the Transportation Industries,* chaps. 1–3. Cambridge: Harvard University Press, 1959.

Meyer, John R., and Straszheim, Mahlon R. *Pricing and Project Evaluation,* chap. 3. Washington, D.C.: The Brookings Institution, 1971.

Poole, E. C. *Costs: A Tool for Railroad Management.* New York: Simmons-Boardman Publishing Co., 1962.

Roberts, Merrill J. "Some Aspects of Motor Carrier Costs: Firm Size, Efficiency and Financial Health." *Land Economics,* August 1956, pp. 228–38.

Stenason, W. J., and Bandeen, R. A. "Transportation Costs and Their Implications: An Empirical Study of Railway Costs in Canada." National Bureau of Economic Research, Special Conference No. 17, *Transportation Economics* (1965), pp. 121–38.

162

Straszheim, Mahlon R. *The International Airline Industry*, chaps. 4 and 5. Washington, D.C.: The Brookings Institution, 1969.

Transportation and Logistics Research Center, The American University. *Criteria for Transport Pricing*. Cambridge, Md.: Cornell Maritime Press, 1973.

Wilson, George W. *Essays on Some Unsettled Questions in the Economics of Transportation*, esp. chaps. 2 and 4. Bloomington: Foundation for Business and Economic Studies, Indiana University, 1962.

10

Modal Cost and Service Relationships

Transport modes differ not only in service capabilities and responsibilities but also in the level and structure of their costs. Rail and air transportation are organized to constitute nationwide modal systems with appropriate international connections. Pipeline transport is closely integrated with the industries it serves, particularly petroleum production and refining. Inland water transportation and trucking do not, however, provide modal systems in the same sense as does rail transport. While many individual trucking companies have large territorial coverage and interchange of traffic and equipment is substantial, the universal interchange that characterizes the rail service has not developed. Intermodal transport, such as truck-rail-truck, has become more common but is not yet a major feature of domestic transportation. Hence it cannot be said that we have a national system of transportation in which each mode performs in accordance with its economic fitness.

Shippers buy a transportation package composed of service and cost aspects and must select that package which best meets their particular requirements. Although the American industrial system was built around common-carrier transport largely supplied by the railroads, it has become increasingly possible in recent decades for the shipper to haul for himself—by truck, by water, and even by air. Private transport can often be set up to provide the kind of service required by a particular shipper more exactly than commercial carriers, serving large numbers of shippers who have diverse requirements, may find it feasible to provide for him. Service advantage, whether secured by private operations or by the choice of a type of commercial carrier which offers different service dimensions than others, may well be accompanied by added cost. The latter must be evaluated in order to determine if the results secured by superior service are worth it. Since disparities in the cost of using several forms of transport are common, as are differences in service quality, this type of decision is important and continuing in most industrial and commercial traffic operations.

So far as the use of common, contract, or other commercial carriers is concerned, the shipper's choice of carrier is determined by the rates charged by the several competing forms of transportation plus such added costs as he may incur in using a particular mode. These last include expectancy of loss and damage in transit and the speed and adequacy of anticipated claims settlement. They include, also, the costs of particular packing requirements and the obligation to load and unload and to secure freight in the carrier's equipment by appropriate bracing and dunnage. Sometimes cartage costs must also be included because they are necessary to reach air, rail, or water carriers from the shipper's plant. The carrier's rate is, however, ordinarily the largest element in the shipper's transport costs. It is the rate which is of significance to him and which affects his choice of the means of transportation, not the cost which the carrier incurs in producing the transportation service unless that cost is accurately reflected in the rate. Where private transportation by the shipper is feasible, he, of course, compares the cost at which he can perform that service with the rates charged by the commercial carriers plus the ancillary costs noticed above.

With five primary forms of commercial freight transport and three of passenger, the relative rates of development of each of these forms became of large national significance. Public policy necessarily addresses itself to this question, for it must decide whether any forms of transport are to be promoted by public aid and what approach to apply to the control of competition between as well as within modes of transportation. Indeed the issues raised by intercarrier competition and by the largely unrealized opportunities for coordination among the modes are, today, doubtless the most live and important issues in the whole subject of transportation economics. This would not be the case were the several modes of transport broadly similar in their service and cost characteristics. But they are not similar. We must, therefore, understand their characteristics and the differences among them before we can profitably take up the subjects of rate making and regulation, or even the issues of public promotional policy, all of which are of concern to shippers and carriers alike.

SERVICE DIMENSIONS

We have noticed some of the ways in which technology determines the capacity and capability of the several forms of transport. Our concern here will be with service characteristics as they affect the usefulness of a transport mode to shippers. One such characteristic is the size of shipment which can be economically and conveniently handled. The pipeline is a continual-flow, one-way medium of transport. All other forms employ discrete units of transport capacity.[1] Even the pipeline, however, must regulate shipment size when several varieties of crude or various refined products are to be batched over the same line. This is the common practice. Minimum tenders must be prescribed which are large enough to prevent admixture between successive batches to a degree that will affect specifications when the liquids are delivered to tanks at destination. Such minimum tenders are seldom less than 10,000 barrels, usually substantially more.

Discrete units of freight carrying capacity all have two principal measures—weight and cubic. The cubic capacity controls the loading of light-density freight while the weight capacity determines the maximum amount of high-density freight that can be safely carried. Motor-carrier units are the smallest. The common over-the-road trailer is in the 40-foot category, with cubic capacity in the range of 3,000–3,600 cubic feet for van types and weight capacity ranging up to 30 tons. The 45-foot trailer is becoming more numerous as most states now permit its use. An effort is made in the design of vehicles for long-distance over-the-road service to secure maximum cubic and weight capacity within the limits imposed by state size and weight restrictions.

Railroad equipment can be built to a more liberal clearance diagram and with heavier axle loadings. Railcars of less than 50-ton capacity are rapidly disappearing from service; a nominal capacity of 100 tons is now common for dry bulk and tank cars, and 70-ton capacity is featured in an increasing proportion of the new boxcars built. In boxcars, cubic capacities range from about 3,900 cubic feet for 40-foot 50-ton cars up to 10,000 cubic feet for a limited number of 70-ton cars built to 86½-foot length. Hi-cube cars of the latter variety are especially designed for auto-part service, groceries, and large household appliances—all light-density commodities.

It is plain that there is substantial difference in the capacity of commonly employed highway trailers and railcars. Shipments which are not large enough to secure the benefit of rail carload rates may be large enough to be shipped as a truckload in a dedicated trailer. Motor

---

[1] The transport of solids in capsules floated in a pipeline stream may impart this characteristic to pipelines in the future.

carriers can also make split pickups and deliveries more cheaply and expeditiously than railroads so that two or more large, but less-than-truckload, shipments may be handled in the same vehicle even though picked up from or delivered to separate premises. There is, accordingly, a tendency for choice of mode to be affected by shipment size in relation to vehicle carrying capacity. Ship and barge capacities are much higher, ranging upward from about 500 tons, and while a barge or ship can be moved from one installation or port to another to complete loading or discharging, there is a cost associated with each such move. Hence barge and ship transportation in the bulk trades is limited to large volume movements. The cost of accumulating substantial quantities in preparation for movement must be set against the higher transport rates commonly associated with the movement of smaller quantities.

Speed of movement is also of importance. What is of concern to the shipper, however, is door-to-door time rather than the speed of line-haul movement. Transit time is a part of the order cycle required to replenish warehouse stocks and thus may be influential in determining the reorder point. Stocks in transit, moreover, generate inventory costs as do stocks held in warehouses, although the insurance costs may be less. Speed of delivery can be an important element in customer service, and a shipper must often insure that he is competitive with other suppliers in his ability to render quick service. In general, the more perishable or valuable the commodity the more importance is attached to speed of delivery.

Both truck and rail transport can render door-to-door service, for well over 90 percent of rail carload traffic moves from the shipper's siding to the siding of the receiver, most traffic requiring cartage to or from rail team tracks having long since deserted the railroads. The movement of truckload traffic is, however, generally faster than the movement of rail carloads over any length of haul. For the truck is the unit of movement and once loaded may proceed directly to destination; whereas the railcar must be transferred to a terminal yard, incorporated into a train, the train often reclassified at one or more intermediate points and ultimately broken up at destination to permit individual cars to be switched to receivers' sidings. Door-to-door elapsed time for the car can be very great in relation to the running time between terminals. Despite the customary circuity of the river routes and the slow movement of barge tows on inland rivers, overall time between shippers and receivers located on the rivers may be good by comparison with rail carload traffic. For these tows, unless interrupted by lockages, are normally in movement 24 hours a day, barges being cut in and out by harbor tugs while tows are in motion.

In theory any two major points in the United States may enjoy overnight air cargo service. Yet shippers and receivers are not, with a few exceptions, located at airports. Pickup and delivery of airfreight by truck, ground handling time, and, in the case of international traffic, time required for clearance through customs all add substantially to door-to-door time. Hence the margins between door-to-door speed of truck and air transport will frequently be less than might be supposed. Nor will an increase in airport-to-airport speed have any measurable effect upon total elapsed time in most instances. Both in respect of speed and cost, the major problems for air cargo operations are on the ground except for very long flight stages.

Regularity of service, which implies availability on demand and predictability of arrival times, is usually judged to be more important than speed. A distribution system can be adjusted to slow transportation services, provided the delivery times are assured; and the cost associated with slow movement can be reckoned and appraised. When, however, transit times are irregular and unpredictable, buffer stocks must be carried at destination in order to insure against stockouts, and the cost of this practice may balloon rapidly. It is not uncommon, for example, for rail transit times to vary between 5 and 14 days over the same route of movement and without pattern. If shipments are equally spaced at origin, substantial bunching will occur at destination; and whereas no cars will be received on some days, more than can be unloaded or even accommodated on the siding will be received on other days. Similar variance in transit time of less-than-truckload shipments is not uncommon, particularly where multiple-line hauls are involved. Truckload services, on the other hand, tend to be substantially more reliable than rail service.

Rail piggyback service can offer both greater speed and superior regularity of movement than conventional carload service. This is especially true where volumes are sufficient to permit solid scheduled piggyback trains to be operated between principal points. On some routes and over relatively long hauls, piggyback can equal or improve upon the speed of motor-carrier service, though its ability to do this has been restricted by the speed-up in highway services which the spread of the Interstate System permitted. The capacity and flexibility of the terminal facilities which load and unload highway trailers is strategic, for the reaction time of the terminal determines how soon trailers must be received to make an outbound train schedule and how promptly delivery can be made at the other end. Direct piggyback service to smaller intermediate points which requires piggyback flatcars to be handled in conventional trains which switch intermediate stations offers little advantage. Many railroads are reexamining their small terminals and considering the advisability of alternate arrangements.

Run-through trains have been placed in service in growing numbers since 1966. Such trains bypass most intermediate terminals and are interchanged as a whole, including motive power, between connecting railroads. Long-distance schedules can thus be considerably expedited. The problem of insuring that any given car gets into the train for which it is intended has not yet been fully resolved, however. And it is the car rather than the train with which the shipper is concerned.

The effort to ship regularly may also be frustrated by an inadequate supply of carriers' equipment, whether trailers, freight cars, or barges. Freight car shortages of some consequence have occurred at one or more times during every year since 1939. Mines, lumber mills, steel plants, and various other types of manufacturing enterprise are without significant storage capacity at the shipping end. They are dependent, accordingly, upon regular equipment supply in order to avoid shutdowns. While deficiencies of equipment supply have plagued most forms of transport, none have been so persistent and disabling to shippers as these shortages of freight cars. It appears likely that railroads have lost traffic in consequence—some to commercial competitors of other modes and some to private transportation. Motor-carrier equipment tends to be in more adequate supply, and a shift to truck may afford some relief in the face of rail shortages. Where long hauls of relatively low-grade commodities are involved, however, the comparatively high cost of truck transport makes a shift to that mode impractical.

Comparative service of individual carriers and of modes is also measured, in part, by the proportion of loss and damage encountered and the speed with which claims for such events are paid. Despite extensive efforts to reduce loss of and damage to goods moving in transportation, there is little to suggest that overall improvement is being secured.[2] Shortages plus known theft-pilferage accounted for 45.6 percent of all motor claim payments. In general, rail cargo is subject to greater risk from rough handling, shocks, and vibration encountered in transportation than is motor freight; and greater expense in packaging, loading, and securing the freight may be necessary in the effort to minimize such risks. The high value and ready disposability of much of the consumer goods traffic moving by truck makes that mode especially vulnerable to pilferage and to hijacking.

The loss of cargo on the docks in ports is a worldwide problem. Such losses in the Port of New York alone have been estimated at as high as $160 million per annum. Nor are the airlines exempt. Indeed the problem has been growing rapidly with them. Because of the high average value of air cargo, the fact that it moves primarily as small shipments which must be handled at airports, and the exposure which occurs at airport terminals, the air cargo record in relation to revenue appears to

---

[2] The ratio of claims to revenue varies from year to year in the range of 1.2 to about 1.8 percent of operating revenues.

be substantially worse than that of motor carriers.

Shippers take account of their loss and damage experience and carriers' claims-settlement practices both in choosing carriers and routes and in selecting the mode to be employed. They take account, also, of the costs of providing protection through the design of packaging, or otherwise, that the risks associated with a particular mode require. Railroads are more active than other modes in claim prevention, frequently on a basis of cooperation with shippers that is designed to improve packaging and loading. In air and water transport the liability of the carriers for loss and damage is far more limited than in other modes; hence the shipper must also recognize the costs of cargo insurance.

COMPARATIVE LEVELS OF COST BY TYPE OF CARRIER

Surprisingly little study has been made in the United States of the comparable costs of performing transportation by the several types of transport. This results partly, no doubt, from our insistence upon keeping them largely insulated from one another and in competition with one another. Costs are compared in critical competitive rate proceedings before regulatory bodies, but in the atmosphere of an adversary proceeding where the object is to prove a point rather than to promote an understanding of comparative cost performance. The absence of study results, also, from the nature of the transportation service and the inherent difficulties, touched on in Chapter 9, which stand in the way of determining the cost of particular segments which it may be desired to compare.[3] We will start, therefore, with some consideration of averages.

Rail-Motor Comparisons

Rail and motor transport alike extend to every part of the country and are capable of hauling almost any type of freight that may be offered. Hence there is the physical possibility of competition between them in the handling of most types of freight everywhere. Water transport on a port-to-port basis is limited to the coasts, the Great Lakes, and the improved inland waterways; hence it touches only a part of American industry and very little of its agricultural, timber, and mineral produc-

---

[3] The outstanding work on the subject is still John R. Meyer, Merton J. Peck, John Stenason, and Charles Zwick, *The Economics of Competition in the Transportation Industries* (Cambridge: Harvard University Press, 1959). Complexities of the problem are discussed in George W. Wilson, *Essays on Some Unsettled Questions in the Economics of Transportation* (Bloomington: Foundation for Business and Economic Studies, Indiana University, 1962).

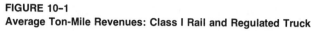

FIGURE 10-1
Average Ton-Mile Revenues: Class I Rail and Regulated Truck

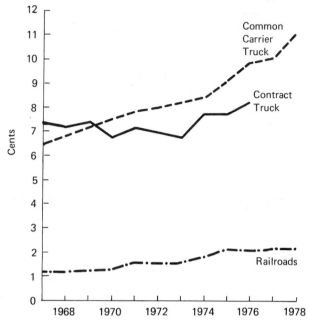

tion.[4] Pipeline transport is severely specialized by commodity, although the prospect of increased movement of solids in pipelines has had some competitive impact. Air transport remains a high-cost form, still regarded by most shippers as premium transportation that is only competitive with surface transport when trade-offs in the nontransport areas of distribution cost offset the higher transportation charges. The bulk of our analysis will, therefore, be devoted to an examination and comparison of rail and motor transport.

Figure 10-1 compares average revenues per ton-mile of railroads, motor common carriers, and motor contract carriers. It will be apparent at once that the difference in the level of revenues per unit of freight service performed suggests that these two types of transport are of markedly different service and cost characteristics. Average revenues reflect, of course, both the rates charged and the character and composition of the traffic, including length of haul. Since motor common-carrier rates for the same commodities over similar hauls have long been approximately the same as rail rates, the sharp difference in average revenue reflects primarily a difference in the composition of traffic for the two types of transport in respect to shipment size, com-

---

[4] Substantial volumes of grain, ores, coal, and other commodities are fed onto the water system by other modes of transport.

modities carried, and lengths of haul. It is plain that the ton-mile, although convenient in comparing performance, is not a homogeneous output unit and is, therefore, of limited usefulness in analysis.[5]

The set of relationships can be more clearly understood if consideration is given to the extent to which each of these types of transport normally penetrates various levels of the "traffic stratum." A diagram can be constructed which conveys a general impression, although it can lay no claim to accuracy in its detail. Thus we may observe that although bituminous coal is seldom hauled more than 75 miles by truck, it moves 450 miles and more by rail; anthracite, a more valuable but rapidly declining commodity, has moved as far as 130 miles by truck, but will move beyond 600 miles by rail; iron and steel sixth class, which includes ingots, pigs, slabs, blooms, and billets, may move beyond 200 miles by truck, but by rail it will sometimes move to distances exceeding 1,000 miles; iron and steel fifth class, which is more valuable per ton and includes such primary mill shapes as sheet, plate, and structurals, will move up to 350–400 miles by truck and almost limitless distances by rail; finally, high-class articles rated second class and above are capable of moving up to full transcontinental hauls by either rail or truck.

The relationship of rates to prices tends to preclude the movement of lowgrade commodities over great distances unless special circumstances are present, as in the movement of low sulfur western coals over exceptional distances in order to meet environmental requirements. Closer sources or substitutes, even though the commodity may be of lower quality, will tend to be used as more economical than transportation over great distances. The rail line in Figure 10-2 shows roughly the maximum ability of commodities to move at rail rates. Motor transport of volume traffic is more costly than rail, and the disparity between the two grows as the length of haul increases. Hence motor carriers do not penetrate the traffic stratum as deeply as do the railroads. Were we to rely wholly on truck transportation, patterns of distribution for the great bulk of all freight (measured in tons, not value) would be considerably restricted and would approximate the motor-carrier line shown in Figure 10-2. Truckload costs have, however, been declining in relation to rail costs, hence the trucks' ability to penetrate the spectrum improves.

At all lengths of haul, for other than bulk traffic, the division of traffic between truck and rail is also affected by shipment size. The relationship between carload and truckload quantities has already been commented upon. In general, rail participation in the available traffic increases both with the lengthening of the haul and the increase of

---

[5] On this point see Wilson, *Essays on Some Unsettled Questions*, pp. 14–23, and recall the discussion in Chapter 9.

FIGURE 10-2
Rail and Truck Penetration of Traffic "Stratum"

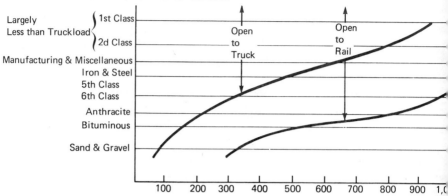

shipment size. The average rail carload originated in 1977 was 61.1 tons, while the average load of regulated trucks in common carriage of general freight was 13.5 tons. Data developed by the Census of Transportation for manufactured goods illustrate the affect both of shipment size and length of haul on rail participation. For example, in the machinery category, the railroads obtained only 13.8 percent of the tons in the weight bracket 10,000–19,999 pounds, while trucks secured 85.7 percent of that traffic. In the 20,000–29,999-pound bracket, however, rails secured 29.6 percent of the tons, and for shipments over 30,000 pounds they had 59.8 percent of the tons. The importance of length of haul in combination with shipment size is suggested by the data in Table 10-1. It is plain that rail average hauls exceeded those of motor carriers in all weight brackets.

Regulated motor carriers, in fact, are predominantly carriers of less-than-truckload traffic, and this is especially true of the common-carrier segment of the industry.[6] More than 78 percent of the revenues of regulated motor carriers in 1976 came from less-than-truckload traffic, whereas railroads derived less than 0.1 percent of their freight revenues from less-than-carload business. Both types of transport participate in small-shipments traffic tendered them by freight forwarders and shippers' associations, but this traffic has already been consolidated into truckload and carload lots by those agencies.

Where disparities in function are so great, comparisons of cost between the two modes are useful only in respect to traffic of kinds for which they do or might compete. Both forms, however, respond in the same direction, if not at the same rate, to certain phenomena which affect their costs: (1) unit costs decline as the haul lengthens, (2) unit costs decline as the average vehicle load increases, and (3) unit costs

---

[6] There are many specialized heavy haulers, some of which transport machinery and structural items that are too large for convenient movement by rail.

TABLE 10-1
Importance of Length of Haul in Combination with Shipment Size

	Rail Percentage	
Weight Bracket	Of Tons	Of Ton-Miles
Under 1,000 pounds	2.9	5.2
1,000–9,999 pounds	3.8	8.1
10,000–19,999 pounds	13.8	24.1
20,000–29,999 pounds	29.6	40.8
30,000 pounds and over	59.8	72.0

Source: Department of Commerce, *1963 Census of Transportation*, Commodity Transportation Survey, Machinery (Except Electrical and Industrial). The 1967 Census shows little change in this phenomenon.

decline with improved balance of direction of traffic. Rail unit costs will tend to decline with three additional phenomena not available to motor carriers: (1) with an increase in train loading, (2) with the receipt of traffic in multiple-car lots, and (3) with the increase of ton-miles produced per mile of road operated. The term *unit cost* refers, here, to the cost per ton-mile encountered in the handling of specific types of traffic.

The function of producing freight-transportation service by any form of transportation breaks down into two elements: the service required to initiate and to conclude the movement, and the actual movement from point of origin to point of destination. The former we call terminal service and the latter line-haul movement. We may make a division of costs accordingly between terminal and line-haul. Motor and rail carriers contrast strongly in the relationship of these two elements. When a shipment is a truckload, the motor carrier need only spot its over-the-road rig at the shipper's dock and lend the assistance of the driver in loading the vehicle. Once loaded, the vehicle can proceed at once in line-haul movement to destination. The railroad, however, gains great economy in line-haul movement by assembling large trainloads of freight for movement as single units. Hence its terminal operations are much more complicated. It must select a car suitable for the shipper's needs in its terminal yard, switch this car to the shipper's siding, subsequently pick it up when loaded with another switching locomotive, consolidate it with other loaded cars in an industrial yard, transfer it to a classification yard where road trains are made up, switch it along with hundreds of other cars until a train of 50 to 150 or more cars has been assembled. Then the car enters upon line-haul movement as an element of a road train. Rail terminal costs may, therefore, represent 40 to 60 percent of the whole, and line-haul costs the remainder, depending principally upon the length of haul.

The data in Table 10-2 will illustrate the relationship of the two forms

TABLE 10–2
Relationship of Terminal Costs and Line-Haul Costs

	Rail Boxcar (50-ton load)		Highway Rig (25-ton load)	
200-mile haul:				
Terminal	$120	$2.40/ton	$ 35	$1.40/ton
Line haul	70	1.40/ton	70	2.80/ton
	$190	$3.80/ton	$105	$4.20/ton
400-mile haul:				
Terminal	$120	$2.40/ton	$ 35	$1.40/ton
Line haul	140	2.80/ton	140	5.60/ton
	$260	$5.20/ton	$175	$7.00/ton

in a general way—the heavier load of the typical rail unit, the proportion of terminal expense, and the disparity of line-haul cost per ton. The terminal costs for both forms of transport actually vary considerably from one location to another, depending upon the size and complexity of the area, the degree of congestion, and other factors. Line-haul costs also vary as among route segments. Averages will not, therefore, provide a guide to the cost of any particular haul even though they may disclose the general nature of the cost behavior and convey some impression of magnitude. Where the traffic moves in lots of less size than the unit of movement, that is, in less-than-truckload or less-than-carload lots, both types of transportation must perform costly pickup and delivery service and must handle the freight over terminal platforms from the pickup trucks, sort it, stow it into outbound road vehicles, and repeat the operation in reverse at destination. One or more interchanges between carriers or transfers en route may also be required. As average shipment size falls, terminal cost per 100 pounds increases. Moreover, with heterogeneous small shipments it becomes increasingly difficult to obtain good loading of the line-haul trailer with the consequence that line-haul costs per ton will grow.

The railroad's economy in line-haul movement arises from the limited inputs required to move freight. A 6,000-horsepower locomotive will move from 5,100 to 17,000 gross trailing tons or from 3,000 to 12,000 tons of actual freight depending on the profile of the line and the speed required with a four or five-man crew. Three thousand tons of freight would require at least 100 tractor-trailer combinations, a similar number of drivers, and some 25,000 horsepower for the over-the-road movement. Hence railroads minimize fuel and labor inputs in the line-haul movement in comparison with trucking operations at the expense of heavy inputs for the assembly and breakup of trains, since traffic is usually received in carload units from shippers. The terminal cost per car is reduced when multiple-car units are tendered by shippers—to about 62 percent with two-car cuts and to about 51 percent

TABLE 10-3
Southern Territory Costs (cents per 100 pounds)

| Miles | Rail Fully Distributed Cost, Plain Box | | | Rail Piggyback 34-Ton Load | Truck Out-of-Pocket Cost–30,000 Lbs. and Up |
	25-Ton Load	50-Ton Load	70-Ton Load		
30	13.5				13.8
50	15.5	9.4	7.7		16.4
100	18.2	11.4	9.4	28.2	22.7
200	23.9	15.4	13.0	31.9	35.1
300	29.7	19.5	16.6	37.5	47.6
400	35.4	23.5	20.1	43.2	59.7
500	41.1	27.6	23.7	48.8	70.8
1,000	69.8	47.9	41.6	77.1	130.8

with three-car cuts. When solid trainloads are tendered, the terminal cost per car is minimal.[7]

It is from considerations of this sort that the early expectations that motor carriers would be confined to short-haul freight arose. And they have, in fact, become the predominant haulers of most types of traffic in short-haul service except for siding-to-siding movements of low-grade bulk commodities in large quantities and in areas where intraharbor barge service is available for such commodities as coal, petroleum, sand, and gravel. Our understanding may be reinforced by examination of the data in Table 10-3 which are excerpted from Interstate Commerce Commission published costs. These are, again, average costs derived for a particular territory. They cannot be applied precisely to other territories or to any particular haul. The rail costs are shown on a fully distributed cost basis, whereas the motor-carrier costs are out-of-pocket and would be increased approximately 10 percent to put them on a fully distributed basis. Even then, because of differences in cost concepts which underlie the Interstate Commerce Commission's rail and motor-carrier cost formulas from which these data are derived, they would not be fully comparable. The comparison shown here puts truck costs in a favorable light because they are shown on an out-of-pocket basis; yet at all distances beyond 30 miles with a 25-ton load the rail costs are lower. The services, though door-to-door in both instances, are not fully comparable since shippers will almost invariably encounter greater expense per ton for loading boxcars than for loading highway trailers. Overall, therefore, the truck may have a cost advantage at somewhat longer hauls. The table also demonstrates the

---

[7] See J. William Vigrass, "An Evaluation of Multiple Car Volume Rates for Railroads," in Transportation Research Forum, *Papers, Third Annual Meeting (1962)*, pp. 90–91. In unit-train operations for coal or ore, the road locomotives may remain attached while the train moves slowly under the loading mechanism. A similar operation may be feasible at destination, but not if car dumpers are employed.

great economy that can be secured with heavier loading of the rail-cars.

Piggyback costs, it will be observed, are substantially higher than boxcar costs; and boxcar transportation can still enjoy advantage where both shippers and receivers have rail sidings. The piggyback costs do not include the cost of moving the highway trailers from the shippers' premises to the rail terminal nor of the delivery at destination. To make them comparable with truck costs, approximately 9 cents per hundred pounds would need to be added. Hence, on a door-to-door basis, piggyback costs in Southern Territory do not become comparable with truck costs until a haul of 300 miles is reached—thereafter they lie increasingly below truck costs as the haul lengthens.

The rail average haul has moved upward almost continually since 1949, from 412 miles in that year to 587 in 1978. Motor-common-carrier hauls have been more variable, but reached 301 miles in 1978. Contract-carrier hauls on the average are substantially shorter. Much motor-carrier traffic moves over distances far exceeding the average haul; and in general, the volume of long-haul truck traffic has shown vigorous growth characteristics. Under a structure of rates very closely approximating that developed by the railroads during a period when none but rail transport was available for general purposes, motor carriers necessarily confine their holding out to business which enjoys rates under the rail structure which will cover their costs.[8]

Competitive Overlap and Rate Relationship

The Transportation Census, the continuing traffic studies of certain of the motor-carrier conferences, and other data outputs permit greater specification of motor-rail relationships than hitherto. One analysis of such data[9] shows that 10 percent of manufactured tonnage leaves the factory in less-than-truckload shipments, hence is not eligible for rail movement. A third of outbound tonnage is in lots of more than 45 tons and is clearly rail freight. Thus about one half of manufactured tonnage is competitive between the two modes so far as shipment size is concerned. Roughly 59 percent of tonnage is competitive on a distance basis, representing the middle distance mileage blocks.

The same study develops a number of interesting points by comparison of rail and motor rates from waybill data. It appears that for the period 1965–67, shippers paid approximately an 18 percent premium

---

[8] Motor-carrier rate levels have moved above rail levels in the postwar period, a differential on much traffic being acceptable to shippers in view of motor-carrier service advantages and less ancillary costs. This differential may be expected to increase markedly because of rapidly rising fuel and labor costs for motor carriers.

[9] Alexander Lyall Morton, "Truck-Rail Competition for Traffic in Manufacturers," Transportation Research Forum, *Proceedings, Twelfth Annual Meeting (1971)*, pp. 151 ff.

for the superior service characteristics offered by truck transportation. The premium appears to be greater on smaller shipments for which the rails do not actively compete. And it appears to decline with increases in length of haul up to 250 miles. Apparently motor carriers are able to exploit their advantage in delivery times on short hauls by rates that are more than an average differential above rail rates.

The Bulk Carriers

Carriers by water and pipeline more nearly resemble the railroads in respect to the level and character of their costs than they do the motor carriers. Ocean and Great Lakes vessels and inland-waterways tows are large units of port-to-port movement comparable to the trainload. Lake vessels may handle 26,000 or more tons of cargo,[10] and inland water tows handling 20,000 to 40,000 tons of freight are becoming common on some segments of the river system. In the late 1960s rail ton-mile costs for line-haul operation ranged as low as 0.25 to 0.3 cents per ton mile in the trainload movement of bulk commodities. Bulk lake ships operated with line-haul costs in the range 0.12 to 0.18 cents per ton-mile.[11] Larger ocean bulk ships achieved yet lower costs, while inland waterway tows had costs in the range between lake ships and rail trainload operations. Pipelines of 24 to 30-inch diameter have ton-mile costs approximating those of ocean-going tankers in the 25,000 to 30,000-ton range. Water routes, by comparison with rail or pipeline, are often circuitous so that more ton-miles must be generated in order to move a given volume of freight between two points. Comparative costs in 1969 for various types of carrier in petroleum products service for hauls of typical length for each type are given in Table 10–4.

TABLE 10–4
Cost of Gasoline Transportation

Type	Miles	Tons per Shipment	Cost per Ton-Mile (cents)
Coastwise tanker	2,200	29,600	0.12
30-inch pipeline Gulf to East Coast	1,400	1,387*	0.15
Barge tow (Mississippi River)	1,163	8,322	0.19
20,000-gallon tank car	130	66	2.52
7,500-gallon tank truck	67	25	5.23

* Tender or batch.
Source: Littleton H. Fitch, "Planning Transportation use in Petroleum Distribution, Transportation Research Forum," *Papers, Tenth Annual Meeting (1969)*, p. 176.

[10] Vessels of 1,100-foot length and 60,000 tons capacity have been designed to take advantage of the dimensions of the new Poe Lock at the Saulte.

[11] John L. Hazard, *The Great Lakes—St. Lawrence Transportation System: Problems and Potential* (Washington, D.C.: Upper Great Lakes Regional Commission, 1969), p. 40.

Costs of all transport modes have escalated rapidly, particularly since 1973, in consequence of high rates of inflation and OPEC-induced price increases for fuel. This process is continuous and, since labor, fuel, and materials are used in different proportions in the several modes, cost relationships are changing and will continue to change. Long-haul unit-train coal rates were, in early 1979, of the order of 1 to 1.15 cents per ton mile at the level of full cost plus 7 percent. Barge costs, which were of the order of 3.3 mills per ton mile in 1972, may well be double that figure today. The development of data on comparative costs lags well behind the events which govern their upward movement.

Nearly all Great Lakes and coastwise traffic represents the movement of bulk commodities; petroleum, coal, ore, grain, and stone in full shiploads.[12] These commodities are loaded and unloaded mechanically by high-capacity facilities made possible by the great volume of the bulk-traffic flows which these carriers serve. The traffic is normally concentrated and dispersed by other forms of transport. Ships and pipeline operations are not a substitute for other forms of transportation except where particular conditions prevail, for example, an ability to concentrate at a particular point of transfer sufficient volume of a bulk commodity to justify the investment in expensive transfer equipment or to support the constant flow which a pipeline requires for economical operation and amortization of the investment.

Inland barge operators confine themselves to the handling of traffic in full transportation units. The unit of movement, the barge, is much smaller than a bulk ship and usually ranges from 500 to 1,400-ton capacity. Like a railroad, a barge line can gather a large number of barges in order to form a tow and thus achieve maximum economy in line-haul movement. To assemble 10 to 40 barges into a tow is, however, a less difficult and costly task than to assemble an average train; and it requires no investment in and maintenance of such a facility as a railroad classification yard. The separation of the carrying unit (barge) from the power unit (towboat) is an advantage, for only the barges need lose time for loading and unloading. Double-crewed towboats are kept in service 24 hours a day in order to maximize use of the heavy capital investment which they represent. This advantage is being gradually introduced into the lake and coastal trades, though ocean-going barges tend to be much larger and a tug may tow only one barge.

The pipeline is the only one-way method of transport and thus has no problem of balancing equipment back to origin. It is also a con-

---

[12] General cargo moves between the Atlantic and Gulf and in the intercoastal trade in containerships on a basis of rates that is highly competitive with rail. Most general cargo moved on the Lakes is in export-import traffic via the St. Lawrence.

stant-flow mechanism with an enormous delivery capacity even though it may pump at pressure which moves the stream only two to four miles per hour. Like other forms of transport it must perform both line-haul and terminal operations; yet the pipeline system is so closely integrated with refining operations that the terminal problem is minimized. Nevertheless, crude from producing wells must be accumulated in lease tanks until a minimum batch is available for movement over a gathering line which feeds into the trunk-line system. Products pipelines, receiving a continuing flow, must pump into storage and hold a supply of all product specifications from which they can deliver to railcars or tank trucks on demand. The line-haul costs of pipelines do not become comparable with those for the average coastwise tanker until diameters of 24 inches and over are reached.[13] Such large diameters of pipe, requiring a daily throughput of 250,000 barrels and more, are rarely feasible because flows of this size concentrated over a particular route are seldom encountered.[14] Lines of as little diameter as six inches can, however, often compete with normal rail petroleum rates for movement in tankcar lots in relatively shorthaul service. The level of pipeline costs per ton-mile clearly depends upon the volume of traffic available on a continuing basis over the projected life of the line, for that volume determines the size of the line which it is economically practicable to install. In no other form of transport is the level of unit costs so responsive to the volume of available traffic.

DIFFERENCES IN MODAL COST STRUCTURES

We have already observed that the cost structure of any carrier is made up of fixed and variable elements. How large a portion will be fixed will depend upon the time span and the amount of change in the volume of traffic we have in mind. If a reduction of traffic is in view, the question is: What expenses can be reduced and in what measure? If neither the plant nor the management and supervisory organization can be cut in size, their costs are fixed in aggregate amounts and become higher per unit at the reduced level of traffic. Declines in traffic are often accompanied by reduced equipment-load factors; for exam-

---

[13] Investment per mile in a pipeline is sufficiently high to result in a larger proportion of investment cost than is true even for a railroad. Labor cost, however, is unusually low since pipeline operations can be fully automated. Hence the proportion of fixed cost is higher than any other mode. Pipeline rates are thus expected to be less affected by inflation than rail rates—one argument offered for slurry pipelines in lieu of rail service for coal transport.

[14] Rich producing fields may generate such flows to tidewater or to refineries. The heavy eastern U.S. product consumption led to the use of 36-inch diameter pipe in the main trunk of the Colonial Pipeline. The line from Alaska's North Slope is 48 inches and may handle up to 1.2 million barrels a day.

ple, vehicle or train-miles cannot be cut as rapidly as traffic falls. Hence operating expenses, although variable, are not variable *in proportion* to the decline of traffic volume.

The reverse of these events is likely to be encountered with traffic increases. Vehicle or train loading improves. There is almost always unused capacity available in some elements of the transportation plant, and the overhead organization can usually cope with added volume without adding to the ranks of management and supervision. Hence these costs are fixed, as before, but with volume up unit costs decline. Large increases in volume will, however, if they are expected to continue, require investment in plant to relieve bottlenecks and overcome congestion. Over the very long run any transportation plant may be changed completely and all costs may become variable.[15]

Small increases in traffic may require no investment in fixed property or equipment: they may even be capable of being absorbed by the existing service without an increase of vehicle-miles. If a bus of 44-passenger capacity is being operated with an average load of 30 passengers, an increase of 14 passengers per trip will cause no visible increase in expense. Up to this limit, all costs may be said to be fixed. If all passengers are to be seated, however, an increase beyond this point will require the operation of another vehicle, all costs will have become variable, and excess capacity will again have been created. Railroads usually have ample trackage and major terminal facilities to handle any likely increase of traffic. Motor and air carriers, for the most part, lack this element of fixed cost because their basic facilities are provided at user charges which are variable with the volume of operations conducted. Nevertheless, all types of transportation tend to have overhead, general, and financial expenses which are approximately fixed with moderate changes in the volume of traffic, whether upward or downward.

The fact that cost structures of various types of transport differ in respect to their fixed and variable elements is a cause of great difficulty in regulating their competitive relations one with another. The fact that much transportation is conducted at common costs makes it difficult to secure acceptable estimates of the cost of handling any particular traffic by any type of carrier. Such cost studies as are available are open to a wide variety of objections, especially with respect to railroads because of the variety of traffic which they handle, the size and complexity of their operations, and the presence of large elements of fixed costs. A block of traffic which, if added to that already handled by a railroad, might represent an increase in volume of 1 percent could occasion an increase of 20 percent if obtained by a motor carrier. The

---

[15] The long run may be very long. Most American rail routes are on the original alignments, with most tunnels and many bridges still in use, though they were laid out and built from 70 to 140 years ago.

motor-carrier aggregate costs might increase by 19 percent in consequence, but the rail costs only 0.5 percent or less. The increase in rail cost would be difficult to detect and to attribute to the increase in traffic as the causative factor.

SELECTED REFERENCES

Barriger, John W. *Super-Railroads for a Dynamic American Economy.* New York: Simmons-Boardman Publishing Co., 1956.

Baumol, William, Jr., and associates. "The Role of Cost in the Minimum Pricing of Railroad Services," *The Journal of Business,* vol. 35 (1962), pp. 357 ff.

Cushman, Frank M. *Transportation for Management.* Englewood Cliffs, N.J.: Prentice-Hall, Inc., 1953.

Emerson, H. N. "Oil Transportation Preferences—Their Bases." Washington, D.C.: American Petroleum Institute, 1957.

Meyer, John R.; Peck, Merton J.; Stenason, John; and Zwick, Charles. *The Economics of Competition in the Transportation Industries.* Cambridge: Harvard University Press, 1959.

Milne, A. M. *The Economics of Inland Transport.* London: Sir Isaac Pitman & Sons, Ltd., 1955.

Morton, Alexander Lyall. "Truck-Rail Competition for Traffic in Manufactures." Transportation Research Forum, *Proceedings, Twelfth Annual Meeting (1971)* pp. 151 ff.

Nelson, James C. *Railroad Transportation and Public Policy.* Washington, D.C.: The Brookings Institution, 1959.

Sargent, J. R. *British Transport Policy.* Oxford at the Clarendon Press, 1958.

Williams, Ernest W., Jr. "Some Aspects of the Problem of Intercarrier Competition," *Vanderbilt Law Review,* vol. 11 (October 1958), pp. 971–85.

Wilson, George W. *Essays on Some Unsettled Questions in the Economics of Transportation.* Bloomington: Foundation for Business and Economic Studies, Indiana University, 1962.

Wycoff, Daryl D. *Organizational Formality and Performance in the Motor Carrier Industry.* Lexington, Mass.: Lexington Books, 1974.

11

Service Obligations and Liabilities of Public Carriers and Warehousemen

The demand for and the supply of transportation are influenced by actions taken in the purported public interest. For centuries the vital importance of transportation to the social, political, and economical welfare of the community has been recognized. On the supply side there have resulted many examples of public aid in the development of transportation ways (highways, waterways, airways, and, in some instances, railways) over which private commercial carriers were permitted to operate. On the demand side, which is our concern in this chapter, there has developed a framework of legal standards and restrictions to protect the traveler and shipper. The difference in the liabilities among the several modes should be known by a physical-distribution manager in choosing carriers and routes to avoid unnecessary costs and losses. Likewise rights and remedies should be fully understood by the manager in the event of loss or damage in the course of transportation or storage.

CLASSES OF CARRIERS AND THEIR LIABILITIES AND SERVICE OBLIGATIONS

The extent of the public interest is reflected in the legal requirements which are imposed upon the several classes of carriers. If a private individual owns a vehicle which he uses to carry himself and family or his own property (not serving others for hire), he is a "private" carrier. The restrictions imposed upon his operations are very few, if any. If the private carrier operates over his own way, there are no public restrictions. If he uses a public way, he normally has to have a vehicle license and to comply with traffic, safety, and accident regulations. Farmers, merchants, and manufacturing plants use their own motortrucks to carry their goods. The great preponderance of motortrucks are privately owned. Many hotels have their own buses. Manufacturing and mining establishments may own short railroads or steamships, and oil companies regularly use their own pipelines. A "private" carrier is organically a part of the business which owns it and is usually specialized in character to meet the peculiar operating needs of the business. The primary business test is strategic in differentiating between private and for-hire carriage. Thus a manufacturing concern may deliver its products to customers and charge for the transportation service, but its primary business is manufacturing and the transportation is incidental to that business.[1] Direct control of the transportation is essential.[2]

If a carrier is engaged in a "for-hire" operation carrying the goods of other than the owner by individual contract or agreement, it is known as a *contract* carrier. Such a carrier of traffic does not offer to give service to the public at large, but the service is tailored to the requirements of only one or a few particular shippers. It is usually a specialized type of carrier that uses a modified design of equipment suited for transporting only a certain class of traffic, or renders a service tailored to the particular requirements of the shipper. The motortruck as a vehicle lends itself to specialization. For example, contract motor fleets may use tank trucks designed only to haul milk, gasoline, or other liquid products. A large part of motor transportation for hire is performed by contract carriers. Their obligations and liabilities are fixed by their contracts with individual shippers.

OBLIGATIONS TO SERVE: COMMON CARRIER

Unlike a contract carrier, a common carrier holds itself out to serve the general public rather than a few shippers of its own selection. The duty of a common carrier to give service without discrimination is old and well established in common law. The duty to serve has been stated as follows: "It is the common-law duty of a common carrier, on being

---

[1] L. A. Woitishek, *Common Carrier Application*, 42 MCC 193 (1943); *Lenoir Chair Co., Contract Carrier Application*, 48 MCC 259 (1945), 51 MCC 651 (1950); and *Schenley Distillers Corp., Contract Carrier Application*, 44 MCC 171 (1944), 48 MCC 405 (1948).

[2] *Schenley Distillers Corp.* v. *United States*, 326 U.S. 432 (1945); *Brooks Transportation Co.* v. *United States*, 93 F. Supp. 517 (1950), 340 U.S. 925 (1951). See William H. Borghesani, Jr., "Parent-Subsidiary Transport in Schenley Case Examined," *Private Carrier*, issues of September 10, 1969, and September 25, 1969.

tendered a reasonable compensation, to receive at reasonable times and carry all goods offered to it for transportation, within the line of its business or of the kind which it undertakes to transport. Having room or the facilities for transporting the goods, and holding itself out to the public as ready and willing to carry goods for all persons indifferently, the law imposes upon it the duty of receiving and carrying them over its established route."[3]

Ordinarily a carrier which does business with all shippers is eager to take all shipments which are offered. Common carriers solicit traffic to utilize capacity and to increase revenues. However, extraordinary business volume, war, or other unusual conditions may stimulate enough traffic so that some carriers will prefer not to carry the less profitable traffic items. To unjustly discriminate is contrary to common law and is now usually prohibited by statute. The Commission and courts have held that the carrier must accept a shipment of any commodity tendered if that commodity is included in the category of goods which the carrier, through its published tariffs or other wise, holds itself out to carry. These prohibitions are no longer strictly applied in Great Britain, France, and Canada, where railroads may grant lower rates to shippers who contract to give all, or a minimum volume of traffic over a year, to a railroad. British railways, indeed, have been generally relieved of their common-carrier obligations in respect to freight traffic. In recent years the Interstate Commerce Commission has approved special contracts which do not involve intercarrier and shipper competition. Motor freight carriers have long endeavored to discourage undesirable traffic through high rates on bulky low-grade commodities and in late years on shipments under 500 pounds.

RIGHT TO REFUSE SERVICE

A common carrier can specifically exclude certain types of goods. Railroads may refuse to take dogs as baggage[4] or refuse to accept shipments of money or jewels as baggage or freight.[5] Some carriers may not have the facilities to handle livestock, explosives, or other commodities requiring special care. In the absence of published tariffs covering such a commodity, the carrier cannot be required to provide the necessary equipment to handle it. In general, however, a common carrier cannot select the types of traffic which it chooses to carry but

---

[3] D. C. Moore, *A Treatise on the Law of Carriers*, 2d ed. (Albany: Matthew Broder & Co., 1914), pp. 116–17.

[4] *Memphis News Publishing Company* v. *Southern Railway Company*, 75 S.W. 941 (1903).

[5] 70 Cal. 169 (1886).

must carry all commodities offered for which facilities are available. Furthermore, it must provide facilities to handle commodities covered in its tariffs, without additional charge beyond the regular freight charge.[6]

The carrier can refuse to accept any shipment if it is not offered at the right time or place or not properly packed for shipment. It may not be reasonable for the carrier to pick up freight or to receive it at a freight house at all hours of the day. A carrier may require the goods to be delivered to a certain platform, siding, pier, or station; and in door-to-door pickup service, it may require the goods to be on a platform at the street level. The carrier may set up reasonable requirements for the packing of a shipment as a condition for accepting it. Related to these is the requirement that reasonable notice must be given when requesting transportation service, that is, for the delivery of a car, barge, or trailer for loading or for pickup service.[7] No shipper who refused to comply could hold the carrier liable for commercial loss which might result from such a refusal.

The franchise or the certificate of convenience and necessity prescribes the route and points to be served by the carrier and may limit the types of commodities which may be handled and the direction of movement. For example, many interstate motor carriers are limited to the transportation of certain commodities between points by the provisions of the certificates of public convenience and necessity under which they operate. The carrier with a limiting certificate cannot be compelled to carry commodities not included in the certification. Most common carriers, however, have no such limits specified in their certificates or charters.

By statute the railroads' transport service has been extended to include the sizes and types of cars and facilities and services incidental to transportation, such as elevation, storage, care of livestock in transit, and various other in-transit and terminal services. Facilities and services cannot be abandoned without permission of a regulatory authority. A service which is held to be essential to public convenience and necessity cannot be dropped merely because it is unprofitable to the carrier.

ADEQUATE SERVICE

The common law holds that a common carrier must provide adequate facilities and service to handle the traffic that it holds itself out to carry.

---

[6] *Covington Stockyards Company* v. *Keith*, 139 U.S. 128 (1891).

[7] The principle is established in Part 4, Sect. 1 of the Interstate Commerce Act. Also see *Davis, Agent* v. *Henderson*, 266 U.S. 92 (1924).

Adequate service has been interpreted to mean that (1) the available facilities (cars, trucks, and so on) must be sufficient to take care of the usual amount of business; (2) the kind of equipment (cars, and so on) which must be provided includes that which is normally supplied and excludes equipment which the carrier has specifically stated in published tariffs would not be supplied; and (3) the carrier is obliged to perform the transport service with reasonable dispatch. Failure to provide service with dispatch may cause commercial loss to the owner of the goods. In times of a marked shortage of equipment of any type, the carrier is required to exercise diligence in supplying equitable service and is prohibited from discriminating in the equipment or service made available to individual shippers. A case in point is the provision of Section 1 of the Interstate Commerce Act which requires that the distribution of coal cars among mines in times of shortage be according to the production ratings of the mines. This has led to recent challenge of the growing practice of assigning cars to unit-coal-train operations.

LIABILITY OF WAREHOUSEMAN AS BAILEE

Both warehousemen and carriers are liable as bailees for loss and damage of goods and equipment owned by others and entrusted to their care. English common law in this way sought to protect the owner who had surrendered physical possession of his goods. The warehouseman is therefore liable for goods in his possession which are stolen or damaged unless he can show that such loss occurred in spite of his exercise of due care in handling, storing, and protection of the goods. The owner therefore may prove negligence. To protect his liability the warehouseman may insure the goods in his own name. The warehouseman, on the other hand, is protected in collecting his charges by a lien on the stored goods.

Warehouse receipts are frequently used as negotiable instruments in the transfer of ownership of the goods in storage. The warehouseman, however, does not have to deliver the goods unless: (1) the charges are paid, (2) the bill of lading or warehouse receipt is surrendered, and (3) the person taking delivery signs a receipt. Many states and the District of Columbia have adopted a uniform warehouse receipt.

LIABILITY OF A CARRIER AS BAILEE

The liability of a carrier, if a common carrier, usually extends beyond that of bailee according to both common and statute law. If a contract carrier, however, the terms of the contract may modify the liability above or below that of a common-law bailee. For example, when a ship is leased for a voyage or for a period of time, a contract known as a *charter party* sets forth at length the obligation and liability of the charterer and the ship's owner.

Leasing of vehicles such as motor-carrier trailer units, railroad cars, ships, barges, and aircraft is extensive among the several modes of transportation and among the several types of carriers—common, contract, and private. The lessee carrier as a bailee is liable for the exercise of ordinary diligence in the care of vehicles leased. He is not an insurer and therefore is not liable for loss arising from accident or matters beyond his control if ordinary care has been taken. Neglect must be shown. The lease may specifically outline the obligations and liability of both lessor and lessee.

LIABILITY OF RAIL AND HIGHWAY COMMON CARRIERS

Common-carrier liability for goods carried includes, with certain exceptions, any loss or damage to the goods while in the possession of the carrier whether or not resulting from an act of or from the neglect of the carrier. In other words, the carrier is virtually an insurer of the goods in its possession. This unusual liability was first imposed on common carriers by the common law because collusion between carriers or employees of carriers and thieves was very frequent in the early days of horse-drawn highway and sailing-ship transport. Theft of valuable cargoes of modern motortrucks in which drivers are found to be accomplices occasionally occurs today. Pilferage remains a serious problem, particularly at seaports. The difficulty of proving negligence and of placing responsibility for loss among connecting carriers, and the ease with which blame can be placed on others, is perhaps the impelling premise for the more strict obligation imposed upon common carriers. By statute the liability of rail and motor common carriers has been extended to cover loss arising from a drop of price in the market which resulted from delayed delivery.

LIMITATION OF CARRIER LIABILITY: THE EXCEPTIONS

In medieval England the carrier was exempt from liability for loss and damage arising only from "acts of God" or "acts of the enemy of the King." Today, the exceptions include (1) an act of God, (2) an act of the public enemy, (3) an act or default of the shipper, (4) an act of public authority, and (5) an inherent defect or nature of the goods. An *act of God* refers to some extraordinary and unavoidable event such as flood, lightning, or tornado, and does not include bad weather conditions which the carrier might reasonably expect to experience in the route over which it operates. *Act of the public enemy* refers to acts of organized armed forces and not mobs, riots, and strikes. *Act or default of the shipper* covers any neglect of the shipper to mark accurately or to pack or load the goods according to accepted standards and regulations. *Act of public authority* applies to attachment for debt or other seizure by legal process or in conformity with regulations. *Inherent defect or nature of the goods* includes disease of plants or animals and damage to merchandise occurring before shipment. It also includes injuries to livestock resulting from goring or kicking.

Liability for damage resulting from delay is confined to negligent delay. A carrier is exempt from liability for damage or loss from delay that may arise from "acts of God" or unusually bad weather conditions such as ice or snow, strikes, and conditions of traffic congestion, if no negligence of the carrier can be shown. If the delay can be proved to exceed that which is reasonably necessary, the carrier is liable for the damage resulting therefrom. Loss occurs from delay when a higher price or other financial benefit might have accrued to the consignee had the goods been delivered with reasonable promptness.

Common-carrier liability is limited in respect to when it begins and ends in any given instance. It does not begin until the carrier has the goods in fact in its custody and has an executed contract of carriage which provides full transportation instructions. It ends on delivery to the receiver or after a given length of time at or in its terminal awaiting action of receiver to get the goods or have them delivered. For the railroads the time is 48 hours after the first 7:00 A.M. following arrival at the terminal. Other common carriers have different time limits. After the designated time has passed, the carrier's liability becomes only that of a bailee.

UNIFORM BILL OF LADING

When a shipper turns over the custody of a shipment of freight to a rail or highway motor-carrier, he obtains a receipt which is called a uniform bill of lading. In times past, carriers operating overland regularly gave a receipt to the shipper. It stated the ownership and value of the shipment. In the course of time this receipt was replaced by a bill of lading.

A bill of lading contains on its face a description of the shipment, the names and addresses of the consignor and consignee, the value of the shipment, and the rate which is to be paid. The bill of lading description of the shipment is used by the carrier in making up the waybill and other operating papers used in the handling of the shipment to destination. On the back of the bill of lading is a printed detailed statement of the responsibility and liability of the carrier and of the owner of the shipment. This printed statement, after the shipper and the carrier have signed the bill of lading, becomes a contract which establishes the liability for the loss or damage of the shipment while in the hands of the carrier. Short-form bills of lading commonly incorporate the contract terms and conditions by reference.

The amendment of the Interstate Commerce Act known as the Bills of Lading Act of 1916 gave the Interstate Commerce Commission the power to prescribe the form of the railroad bill of lading. In a later amendment the Motor Carrier Act of 1935 gave the same power with respect to common carriers engaged in interstate highway transportation. The commission accordingly has prescribed a uniform railroad bill of lading and a uniform motor highway bill of lading. These are fundamentally alike and impose comparable liabilities on the carriers The bills of lading used for intrastate shipments by rail or motor are essentially the same as those for interstate carriers.

There are two types of railroad uniform bill of lading, namely, the *uniform straight bill of lading* and the *uniform order bill of lading*. The straight bill of lading is used when the delivery of the shipment to the consignee is not conditioned by a financial transaction covering the payment for the merchandise. The person to whom the carrier is liable when a straight bill of lading is used is the owner of the shipment, who may be the consignor or the consignee. The order bill of lading is used when the consignor as owner does not want delivery made to the consignee until financial settlement has been made for the merchandise. The order bill of lading is therefore sent by the consignor to a bank designated by the consignee where payment for the shipment is required before surrender is made of the bill of lading. When the order bill of lading is used, the holder of the bill of lading is the one who can claim the goods and to whom the carrier is liable. The order bill of lading is, therefore, a negotiable paper that is evidence of ownership. The transfer of such a bill, properly endorsed, has the effect of passing title to the goods covered by the bill to the holder of the bill. Different colors are used to distinguish the two types of bill of lading to avoid the error of an unauthorized delivery of a shipment by a carrier's employees.

INSURANCE NEEDS OF SHIPPER USING RAIL AND MOTOR COMMON CARRIERS

Since a rail or motor common carrier is a virtual insurer of goods handled by it, usually it is not necessary for the shipper to cover his shipment by a cargo insurance policy. However, he may desire to have insurance to cover it before the carrier takes possession or after the carrier ceases to be liable as a common carrier, that is, when the goods are kept on the property of the carrier after the expiration of free time, in which case the carrier's liability is that of a warehouseman. Or the shipper might decide to protect himself against loss or damage that might occur at the time of transfer from one carrier to another, the transfer not being covered by a through bill of lading. In this event warehouse-to-warehouse inland marine insurance coverage may be obtained.

COORDINATE LIABILITY OF CARRIERS

Prior to 1906 it was necessary for the owner of a shipment which was lost or damaged to file his claim against the railroad on which the loss or damage occurred, if there were a number of connecting carriers which handled the shipment. This imposed upon the shipper the difficult and often impossible problem of determining where and when the damage occurred. The Carmack Amendment of 1906 made the initial carrier liable for payment of a claim, and the second Carmack Amendment of 1930 made the delivering carrier, as well as the originating carrier, liable. So today the owner of a shipment lost or damaged may file his claim against the originating or delivering carrier as an alternative to filing against the carrier on whose lines the loss or damage occurred. The carrier which settles the claim may collect from the carrier responsible if the loss or damage did not occur while the shipment was in its possession; or if the locus of damage cannot be ascertained, the participating carriers will prorate the claim.

LIMITING CARRIER AND WAREHOUSEMAN'S LIABILITY

Carriers have frequently sought to limit their liability by (1) the terms of a special bill of lading, (2) tariff provisions, or (3) special contract. The limitations sought were generally of two sorts, namely, (1) exemption from loss or damage not caused by the carrier's negligence or (2) restriction of the amount of damages recovered to a sum below that of the value of the loss or damage. The incentive provided to the shipper was often in the form of reduced rates which are generally called *released rates*.

Released rates were prohibited by the Cummins Amendment of 1915, which declared that the carrier accepting a shipment is liable "for full actual loss, damage or injury to such property" caused by it or its connections "notwithstanding any limitation of liability."[8] However, one year later, the second Cummins Amendment restored the power

---

[8] Interstate Commerce Act as amended, April 1, 1941, Part I, Sect. 20, Par. 11. The same provisions apply to motor carriers, Part II, Sect. 219.

to make released rates but only when "expressly authorized or required" by the Interstate Commerce Commission. Animals "valuable for breeding, racing, show purposes or other special uses" could be shipped at released rates, but there could be no released rates for transportation of ordinary livestock. The act also requires that the released value of a shipment be declared in writing by the shipper and that the tariffs published governing the released rates make specific reference to the commission's order with respect to the rate.

The Interstate Commerce Commission has not permitted many rates to be based upon the declared value of the shipments. Most of the rates which have been approved apply to household goods, certain ores, express traffic, and livestock for breeding, racing, or show purposes. No federal laws similarly prevent contracts which limit liability of warehousemen.

LIABILITY OF WATER CARRIERS

Because of the hazards of navigation, especially of sea navigation, custom and statutes relating to water carriers have exempted them from many of the liabilities that apply to land carriers. As a bailee, a water carrier, like any carrier, is liable for damage or loss resulting from gross negligence or action of the carrier or its employees. The usual common-law exemptions which apply to water carriers are (1) acts of God; (2) acts of the public enemy; (3) inherent defect, quality, or vice of the thing carried; (4) seizure under legal process; (5) insufficiency of packing; and (6) other acts or omissions of the shipper.

Additional exemptions from liability which apply to water carriers include (1) hazards of the sea or other navigable waters, (2) errors in navigation, (3) efforts to save life or property at sea, and (4) fire. To get the benefits of these exemptions there must be no evidence that gross negligence or design accompanied any or any combination of the four hazards. Furthermore, the law states that in preparation for voyage the carriers must exercise due diligence to (1) so load or stow the vessel as to make it seaworthy and to prevent damage from fire, spoilage, or impregnation of freight; (2) have vessel and equipment in condition and properly supplied for voyage (reasonable inspection required); and (3) employ competent personnel to command and man the vessel. The carrier is similarly liable for damage incidental to handling of cargo including the loading and unloading of the vessel.

The basic act of Congress limiting the liability of water carriers in domestic and foreign service is the Harter Act of 1893.[9] A uniform bill of lading is not required for U.S. water carriers. Each has its own form of bill of lading. But the statutes of water-carrier liability do not permit a

---

[9] 27 Stat. 445.

carrier to limit its liability for loss or damage arising from negligence by any provision in the bill of lading. The Carriage of Goods by Sea Act of 1936 repeats some and amplifies other provisions of the Harter Act as it applies to the foreign shipping of the United States.[10] There is a provision in most ocean bills and tariffs limiting liability to $500 per package. Efforts to apply this limit to containers have instigated litigation with the result that such limitation must be clearly stated in the tariff. The only important amendment to the principles established in the Harter Act is the provision that places the burden of proof on the carrier when damage to its cargo has resulted from unseaworthiness of the vessel. Over and beyond these liabilities declared by statute and common law, the liabilities assumed and covered in the bills of lading vary widely among carriers. The development of large and powerful compartmented steel-hulled vessels, new navigation instruments including the gyrocompass, radio equipment including the radio direction finder, radar, and two-way radiotelegraph and radiotelephone communication with other ships and the shore have greatly reduced the risks at sea, but the traditional exemptions continue. Because the liability of water carriers is so limited between ports, once the voyage is begun, marine insurance is required to protect the owners of goods transported by water.[11] As the risks at sea have declined, insurance rates have naturally fallen.

A common carrier in the ocean trade issues regular "ocean bills of lading" and "through export bills of lading." The former cover only the water movement from port of loading to port of unloading. This means that the shipment is normally handled in separate bills of lading by land carriers to the port of loading and from the port of unloading respectively. By joint arrangement between land and water carriers, a through bill of lading is often used to cover the movement of the shipment from an inland point of origin to an inland point of destination. Each phase of movement is covered by a separate part. One may be a railroad bill of lading, the second an ocean bill of lading, and the third another railroad bill of lading covering the foreign rail haul. The through bill of lading provides for the transfer from one carrier to

---

[10] 49 Stat. 1208. The act, for example, establishes the liability of the carrier to make holds and refrigerating and cooling chambers firm and safe for reception, carriage, and preservation of cargo. Other carrier requirements include (1) a complete description of shipment and condition when received, (2) issuance of "shipped" bill of lading instead of a "received" bill of lading after cargo is loaded, which specifies the ship on which the shipment is loaded and date of shipment if required by the shipper, (3) avoidance in a bill of lading of provision for insurance of cargo to benefit carrier, and (4) placing the burden of proof on the carrier when damage has resulted from unseaworthiness of the vessel. The liability of the shipper for accurate description, packing, and marking of a shipment is made specific and complete.

[11] In domestic rail-water shipments the tariff may state that the rate covers the insurance for the portion of the haul that is by water. If it does not, the shipper must take out an insurance policy as he does in regular ocean service.

another. This provision makes it unnecessary for the shipper or receiver to have representatives at the port to take care of the transfer and reshipment.

The charter party covering a tramp ship voyage is a contract between the owner or operator of a vessel and someone who wants to lease the vessel.[12] If it is for a period of time, it is a *time charter;* and if it is for one or more specified voyages, it is called a *trip charter.* The charter party specifies what the owner or operator will furnish in the way of supplies and personnel, if anything, including crew, fuel, and supplies in addition to the vessel itself. It specifies who shall be liable and under what conditions for port fees and canal dues and for loss and damage at port or at sea to vessel and cargo. However, it must be remembered that in the absence of any express limitations, the carrier as bailee is liable for loss or damage resulting from his negligence.

LIABILITY OF AIR CARRIERS

The common-law status of the air carrier as a bailee is basically no different from that of any other carrier. As with other common carriers, a ticket is a contract of carriage. Within the law a carrier may write in provisions restricting or limiting its liability. But a carrier or its servants cannot be released from negligence, although a reduced rate may have been tendered.[13] The airlines as certified common carriers have the usual property exemptions including damage or loss from acts of God, acts of the public enemy, inherent defects of the goods, fault of the shipper, and so on. An airline is liable for damage or loss resulting from negligence or acts of the carrier or its employees. However, the exact liability status of air carriers in the United States cannot be stated since there is no federal statute or Supreme Court decision defining it.

Liability for loss of life in international air service has been definitive since the Warsaw Convention of 1929. Liability for loss of life was at first limited to $8,292. In the Hague Convention of 1934 it was raised to $16,584 a person, but a court may award higher indemnity if the carrier or its personnel are shown to be guilty of willful misconduct. The United States is not a party to the Hague Convention. The signatories of the Montreal Agreement waived the Warsaw Convention (both discussed below) limits and agreed to accept a limit of $75,000 for the death of a passenger. Under conditions of absolute liability this amount is likely to become standard. Recourse beyond this limit is

---

[12] A line may lease a vessel through a *time charter* and place the vessel in common-carrier line service. On the other hand, it may be rechartered on a *trip* or *voyage charter.*

[13] *Curtiss-Wright Flying Service, Inc.* v. *Glose,* 66F (2) 710 (1933).

possible in a suit brought under the Warsaw Convention when the airline is found guilty of willful misconduct, recklessness, or gross negligence.[14] The international airlines serving the United States have thus become virtual insurers of their passengers, although domestic airlines do not assume this degree of liability.

Most of the United States laws and court decisions defining the liability of air carriers have related to their liability for death or injury to passengers rather than to property. Airplanes have been primarily passenger carriers, although the importance of air express and air cargo has increased rapidly in recent years. There is a well-defined tendency in this country to make all passenger carriers for-hire common carriers rather than to give distinctive status to airline and charter carriers. Taxi service is really a contract service rather than a scheduled service over a given route, but most of the states consider taxicabs and airplanes engaged in this service as common carriers.

Some state laws and some court decisions have attempted to impose the principle of "absolute liability," denying the air carriers the usual common-law exemptions of liability.[15] Under this principle, only by a showing of negligence on the part of the person injured could the carrier escape full liability. The principle of absolute liability was adopted in the Montreal Agreement of 1966, on the part of all airlines serving the United States. Only sabotage was excepted from full liability for loss. At the other extreme is the Maryland statute which relieves the air carrier of liability unless design or negligence can be shown.[16] This law in effect grants to aircraft the exemptions set forth in the Harter Act for water carriers.

The decisions of courts in the United States respecting air loss and damage have for the most part fallen somewhere between these two extreme points of view. The Warsaw Convention as amended in 1934 in the Hague Convention has set up the standards of liability for the airlines of the nations who are parties to the conventions respecting international service.[17] The conventions lean toward a strict but limited liability. The carrier has the burden of proving that it was not guilty of negligence as a cause of the damage or loss. This would include proof that the aircraft was in airworthy condition, that it was adequately manned by qualified and certificated crew members who could be expected to deal with unfavorable conditions of navigation, and that all reasonable precautions had actually been taken. Liability for prop-

---

[14] John E. Stephen, "The Reshaping of the Warsaw Convention," *Airline Management and Marketing Including American Aviation*, October 1969.

[15] See Rowland W. Fixel, *The Law of Aviation*, 4th ed. (Charlottesville, Va.: Michie Co., 1967), chap. 4.

[16] Laws of Maryland, 1931, chap. 403.

[17] The Warsaw Convention, "International Convention of Certain Rules Relating to International Carriers by Air," 1934.

erty damage or loss also has been more definitive in international air freight and express service. Under the Hague Convention damage and loss of property are limited generally to $331.67 per kilogram of weight or actual value, whichever is less.

Domestic airbills currently limit liability on freight and express to $9.07 per pound or fraction thereof, but not less than $50 per shipment. Added liability for higher valued pieces is subject to shippers' payment of applicable charges for actual value. Carrier liability extends to transportation charges or actual damages, whichever is least in amount. Tariff publication is no longer required and, therefore, cannot be used in liability determination. The Civil Aeronautics Board, under a rule enacted in 1978, requires that an air carrier must notify the shipper of the extent of his insurance coverage.[18] Many domestic carriers, no longer bound by the CAB's earlier ruling, have cut back their maximum liability to 50 cents a pound.

CONCLUSION

The legal requirements imposed on common carriers and warehousemen for the most part are old and well defined. They constitute an important element in the demand for transport service. The liability imposed varies among land, water and air carriers. However, in each case it stems from the common-law liability of the bailee and yet goes beyond that because of the circumstances peculiar to the transportation business. Advancing technology and the development of the functions of a carrier prevent these liabilities from remaining fixed. New equipment and services require adjustments by legislation and legal interpretation. As safety at sea advances because of larger, more powerful, sturdier vessels equipped with better navigation aids and radio communications, there is a tendency to increase the liabilities imposed on ocean carriers on the part of courts by a stricter interpretation of negligence. However, legislation may lag behind technological developments. In spite of the great advance in safety at sea, the liability of water carriers is quite limited in comparison with that of land carriers.

The legal restrictions imposed upon carriers reflect the social importance attached to transport service. The demand for transportation service is shaped and limited by these regulations. Through them the carrier is relieved of the burden of attempting to meet unreasonable demands for service. However, the requirement to provide what a regulatory authority considers a safe and adequate service in the public interest imposes additional operating costs and investment on the

---

[18] CAB 43 FR 53635, November 16, 1978.

196

carrier in its efforts to supply transport service. It is important that legal requirements be reasonable and subject to change. Otherwise the burden of higher costs to the shipping public may well be out of proportion to the benefits of the protection secured.

SELECTED REFERENCES

Bugan, Thomas G. *When Does Title Pass.* Dubuque, Ia.: Wm. C. Brown Co., 1951.

Buglass, Leslie L. *Marine Insurance and General Average in the United States: An Average Adjuster's Viewpoint.* Cambridge, Md.: Cornell Maritime Press, 1973.

Cushman, Frank M. *Manual of Transportation Law.* Dallas: Transportation Press, 1951.

Dykstra, Gerald O., and Dykstra, Lillian G. *The Business Law of Aviation.* New York: McGraw-Hill Book Co., 1946.

Elliot, B. K. *A Treatise on the Law of the Railroads.* Indianapolis: Bobbs-Merrill Co., 1922.

Fixel, Rowland W. *The Law of Aviation.* 4th ed. Charlottesville, Va.: Michie Co., 1967.

Guandolo, John. *Transportation Law,* chap. 49. Dubuque, Ia.: Wm. C. Brown Co., 1965.

Higgins, Alexander P. *The International Law of the Sea.* London: Longmans, Green & Co., 1943.

Miller, John McKnight. *Law of Freight Loss and Damage Claims.* 3d ed. Dubuque, Ia.: Wm. C. Brown, 1967.

Powers, C. F. *A Practical Guide to Bills of Lading.* Dobbs Ferry, N.Y.: Oceana Publications, Inc., 1966.

Wilson, G. Lloyd. *Interstate Commerce and Traffic Law.* Englewood Cliffs, N.J.: Prentice-Hall, Inc., 1947.

12

Freight Service for Production in Logistics Systems

In almost every industry's or firm's logistics system, transportation in total cost is the most important function. In this chapter we are concerned with the volume movement of basic materials to processing and manufacturing plants and interplant volume movements, whereas in the next chapter we will focus on the freight service attached to the distribution of finished materials and products as merchandise to the ultimate industrial and consumer markets. Here we are concerned with the logistics requirements of production-oriented industries. Raw materials from mine, farm, and forest generally move to the first processing plant as unpackaged bulk materials. The intermediate movement to subsequent processing plants or storage en route to processing, as with iron, plastic pellets, and flour and grain feeds, may be in bulk. However, many of the intermediate production shipments of processed materials are packaged or otherwise assembled by count, such as structural items, leather, textiles, and parts for assembly.

ECONOMIC CHARACTERISTICS OF FREIGHT SERVICE DEMAND

The demand for transport service, whether that of bulk or merchandise freight, is a derived demand because it depends on the demand of industrial and consuming centers for raw and basic materials and manufactures.[1] Associated with the geographic specialization and the related large scale of modern industrial enterprises is the growth of concentration of population in the great urban centers. Cities depend for nearly every essential commodity including food, textiles, fuel, and the great range of durable consumers' goods, on the bulk-freight service. They are tied to the agricultural areas by it, hence depend upon it for their very life, drawing staples from farm areas sometimes thousands of miles away. Similarly, their manufactures of clothing require that cloth be brought in by the carload, and the fiber from which such cloth is manufactured may in turn come partly from other continents. While geography, resources, and scope of economic activity of a vast nation such as the United States set the stage and overall need for extensive bulk transportation service, the specifics in terms of routes, carriers, and services are determined by the logistics requirements in the aggregate of the industries being served. In moving raw materials from farms, mines, or forests, the first objective is to provide for volume movement to the first and often to succeeding steps in processing. In coal and ore mining, volume movement by barge or solid trainload is possible at the location of the individual mine. In agriculture, forest, and petroleum industries, relatively short hauls for assembly to accomplish volume movement is required. Trucks are used to bring grain to local elevators from individual farms, livestock to stockyards, logs to a local sawmill, and pulpwood from surrounding wooded areas to a railroad siding. Gathering lines of four to six inches in diameter bring petroleum from individual wells in an area to large tanks and major pipeline terminals from which extended movement by barge, tanker, or trunk pipeline to refinery takes place.

Volume bulk movement may be required beyond the first processing plant. Much iron ore from the Mesabi Range in Minnesota moves in volume by rail to sintering plants on the shore of Lake Superior where most of the foreign matter is extracted from the ore. From the plants the sintered ore is moved in volume by lake vessels and railcars to storage and finally by railroad to steel mill locations. When important sources of raw material become exhausted, an industry may have to depend on more distant sources of supply. This has been notably true in the United States with respect to lumber, petroleum, and iron ore. When an industry must depend on distant sources of raw material, more efficient transport systems are sought to keep down the cost of delivered production materials.

---

[1] The nature and some of the consequences of derived demand will be discussed in chapter 16.

PRODUCTION FREIGHT TRAFFIC

The portion of production freight traffic that consists of fuels, raw supplies, and materials moving to the first stage of processing and manufacturing substantially exceeds that of the intermediary movement between stages of processing and manufacturing. Petroleum and its refined products are the exception. Coal and coke are consumed while raw materials of farm, forest, and mines lose considerable volume and weight, particularly in the initial processing. Except for petroleum, which is largely transported by pipeline, railroads are the leading transporters of production supplies. The volumes transported by rail and pipeline in 1976 are shown in the accompanying table. The

	Tons
Petroleum and petroleum products	
(of which 2,324,369 tons were by rail)	1,449,229,172
Coal including anthracite	397,064,418
Nonmetallic minerals, except fuels	133,299,080
Farm field crops (of which wheat	
and corn totals 88,279,184)	129,337,072
Chemical and fertilizer minerals	48,535,474
Forest products	648,850
Livestock and livestock products	216,243
Total	2,158,330,309

Source: Interstate Commerce Commission, *Freight Commodity Statistics, Class I Railroads, Year Ended December 31, 1976*, and *Transport Statistics Part 6, Pipe Lines for Year Ended December 31, 1976*. (Barrels reported are converted into tons in the above listing.)

dominance of petroleum and its products would be even greater if we included the barge and coastwise-tanker tonnage not duplicated in the pipeline and railroad tonnages. Motor carriers have become important in short-haul carriage of raw materials, farm field crops, and livestock. Except for the inclusion of petroleum products, the tonnages listed are essentially supplies for initial processing.

Although the extent of production-freight movement is explained by the size of the country and a high degree of regional specialization, the patterns of this movement cannot be visualized without observing the remarkable concentration of both origin and destination at a limited number of localities. The major part of the traffic is concentrated over a relatively few important mainline routes, with the rest of the transport system serving primarily to feed through traffic into the mainlines and to distribute traffic from them. A surprising proportion of the bulk freight traffic, however, terminates in a few of the largest cities; and a considerable portion of the intermediate traffic originates in the same centers. Studies of the Federal Coordinator of Transportation in the early 30s demonstrated that 22 percent of rail freight originated and 46 percent terminated in 86 large metropolitan terminals. More recent studies of this kind are lacking, but an even greater concentration probably prevails today.

Because of the broader distribution of sources of raw materials and fuels, freight origination of these materials is naturally more scattered than its termination at processing centers. However, some sources permit concentration into major traffic flows. The Chesapeake and Ohio, for example, is one of the largest originators of coal traffic among the railroads, handling in a normal year some 70 million tons. Yet the greatest part of this coal originates on the mainline and branches within the short stretch between Ronceverte, West Virginia, and Huntington, a distance of 181 miles. At each end of this district, in the large classification yards at Russell, Kentucky, and Clifton Forge, Virginia, the coal is assembled into solid trains for westward and eastward movements, respectively. Many of the other bulk raw materials are similarly concentrated in origin.

REQUIREMENTS OF BULK TRANSPORTATION SERVICE

The economic advantages of geographic specialization and large-scale production cannot be obtained without much long-distance movement of bulk freight. It is a primary phase of production in the modern industrial economy. Large-scale enterprise concentrates on the movement of traffic in relatively homogeneous flows of large volume at low cost. To minimize the transportation costs, appropriate specialization of transport facilities and operation has developed for various types of commodities.

The transportation characteristics of the commodity as well as the market pattern shape the distinct service requirements of traffic movement from a production source to final processing. Is the product perishable, flammable or nonflammable, fragile or sturdy, bulky or dense relative to weight, very large or easily accommodated in standard equipment, very heavy or easily handled? These characteristics, the amount of output of the product, and market conditions tend to set the service standards of a given industry. Assuming these standards can reasonably be met, the cost is the primary consideration in choosing the carrier and carrier service. What are the respective rates among the carriers and routes that might be employed? The ability of any carrier to meet specific service and cost requirements depends in the first place on the mode of transport it represents and the operating conditions that prevail. For example, water carriers generally offer cheaper service, but the service may be much slower, less frequent, and less dependable in keeping schedules. The service requirements include (1) adequacy, (2) economy (cost), and (3) quality of service. The last includes safety, dependability, and speed.

ADEQUACY

Adequacy and economy are the paramount and universal requirements which are imposed upon the carriers and routes where major commodity flows to processing centers take place. Adequacy involves (1) availability to serve all desired areas of the market; (2) capacity of route and plant to accommodate peak movements; and sometimes (3) regularity of operations, that is, the ability to operate at all seasons. Adequacy is the quantitative aspect of freight service for production.

Adequacy for grain transport is focused on availability of suitable cars, box or closed hopper, to move the grain during the harvest season from local elevators and other storage facilities to the primary grain markets. For the coal industry, adequacy relates to the availability of cars and barges for loading at mines. For petroleum, the capacity of pipelines and tankers to maintain the flow of crude oil to refineries is vital. The movement of fruits and vegetables to processing plants may largely depend on availability of motortruck equipment. In steel production there are three vital bulk traffic flows, namely: iron ore, coal, and limestone. The availability of ore vessels during the navigation season of the Great Lakes must be sufficient to provide the year's supply of ore from Minnesota and Labrador. Throughout the year the mills of Ohio, West Virginia, and western Pennsylvania must depend on hopper-car supply to move the ore from Lake Erie stockpiles to the mills.[2] Raw lumber usually moves from sawmills to finishing and processing plants by rail for long distances and by truck for shorter distances. Cotton from gins usually moves by rail, and the supply of boxcars at harvest time is crucial. The movement of livestock to packing houses is largely by truck, whereas the movement of meat to principal markets is mainly by refrigerator cars and refrigerated trailers in rail piggyback service. There is a substantial seasonal peak in all perishable traffic and some for almost all movements of raw material to processing plants. Fortunately, in agricultural traffic the seasonal peaks in southern states may precede those of more northerly areas.

The supply of bulk-transport capacity is not always adequate. Crippling car shortages were encountered in World War I, but careful management of the car supply avoided a repetition in World War II. The intervening years were characterized by a generally sufficient car supply. The last 20 years, however, have been marked by growing concern over car supply. The grain, lumber, coal, and steel industries have all felt the impact of car shortages at various times. Methods of car hire have been adjusted in an effort to provide incentive for increased car ownership, but the declining earning power of an impor-

---

[2] Since the advent of taconite pelletization it has been practicable to ship by rail in the winter for, unlike direct-shipping ores, pellets do not freeze in the cars and, because of higher Fe content, they can stand higher freight costs.

tant segment of the industry, principally the lines of the Northeast, has held down capital expenditures for new equipment.[3] Periodic shortages of tankers and dry-bulk ships in the ocean trades are marked by sharp upward moves on trip-charter rates and heavy bookings of new tonnage with the shipbuilders. But the shipbuilding cycle is a long one, and new tonnage often comes from the outfitting basin after the peak of demand has passed.[4]

A transport plant includes many components. Mere addition of cars in the railway system will not cure the phenomenon we call a car shortage. Motive power, track and yard capacity, and terminals must be in balance with the car stock lest congestion impede flow and lengthen car turnaround. Shippers and receivers, too, must have the capability to load and unload at a faster pace. The car shortages associated with a 1972–73 export grain movement 50 percent above the prior year were greatly exacerbated by plugged terminal elevators at the ports and accumulations of cars awaiting unloading.

ECONOMY (COST)

If several carrier routes are available and adequate, a shipper is likely to make his choice on the basis of cost. Only those modes of transport which are by nature volume carriers can produce service to accommodate the transportation of bulk freight over considerable distances. Both investment and operating costs must be included in determining ton-mile cost. Water, rail, and pipeline carriers can realize low ton-mile costs through good utilization of equipment and a favorable load factor. The price range for the movement of bulk materials is usually low. This results in part from market requirements that the traffic move at low rates and in part from the fact that bulk freight traffic usually makes possible good utilization and hence lower cost.

Next to availability and adequacy, the rate is the major factor determining the distribution of bulk freight among carriers. The cost characteristics of the several modes were presented in Chapter 10. It will be recalled that water and large diameter pipeline ton-mile costs are stated in mills, whereas railroad costs will normally average over 1 cent per ton-mile. Truck costs when moving full truckloads may ap-

---

[3] Incentive per diem on plain boxcars has resulted in an increase in supply of this type of car which some regard as excessive. Railbox, a subsidiary of Trailer Train (which is owned by the principal railroads), has provided a fleet of free-running boxcars. Leasing companies, through ownership of short-line railroads, have placed a large number of plain box in service.

[4] Since 1973 reduced rates of increase in the demand for petroleum and generally depressed conditions in the world steel industry have generated significant surpluses of both types of ship. So large and prolonged a surplus is unprecedented and it has resulted in charter rates at unprofitably low levels.

proximate 3 cents per ton-mile. Thus truck transport of bulk material is limited to relatively short distances, although truck movement of intermediate production goods extends over a wide range of distances. There are exceptions, as in lumber and fresh fruits and vegetables, which frequently move over very long distances by truck because of superior service.

QUALITY OF SERVICE

Under the caption of the quality of service, dependability, safety, and sometimes speed are considerations. The quality of service requirement varies widely according to industry and product. Safety is paramount when the bulk commodity is flammable or combustible, as is true with petroleum, liquified petroleum gas, nitrate of soda fertilizer, and a wide range of bulk chemicals. Generally, receivers of bulk shipments like to be assured, within reasonable limits, of the time to expect delivery. Use of the lower cost carrier or route usually means that more time will be required in transit. If delivery schedules are dependable, the receiver can estimate his needs and arrange his orders so as to allow sufficient time; hence dependability rather than speed is what counts. Sometimes extended time in transit saves storage costs to the shipper or consignee. Railroads and pipelines are usually more reliable than water carriers because they are less affected by unfavorable weather conditions. Water operations may be imperiled by ice, fog, or severe storms. Unless the commodity is one that is subject to contamination from other commodities which are in proximity or which require good ventilation, there is a minimum of damage while in transit by water. Much damage arises in rail transportation incidental to switching operations. However, the damage during loading and unloading is likely to be higher for barge carriers when carload freight is loaded by the shipper and unloaded by the consignee, whereas water cargo in seaboard operations and in bargeload shipments is handled by stevedores under contract with the water carrier. For long distances the railroad is generally faster than a water carrier.

PRODUCTION CARRIERS' SERVICES

Production-freight service often presents real problems to the carriers that conduct the service. Seasonal variations in production and shipment are generally pronounced. Although agricultural traffic and utility coal may be relatively stable despite varying levels of economic activity, the steel and construction industries are notably cyclical. The source of raw materials may shift because of exhaustion of certain resources or the discovery of others. Because of this, carriers which have thrived on hauling a basic material in the past may find themselves deprived of their traffic base. The anthracite railroads are a case in point. A description of the volume-freight services of the several modes follows.

Railroads operate several kinds of freight trains and offer special services in connection with some of them. Trains may be classified as (1) drag, (2) scheduled prior classified, (3) solid bulk, (4) expedited symbol, and (5) unit. Drag trains, which were the prevailing type before World War I, moved from one division terminal to another without schedule when there were enough loaded cars to make up the train to the full tonnage rating of the locomotive. Reclassification at each terminal was the rule. Scheduled prior classified trains which now prevail move on schedule between distant major terminals with blocks of cars to be dropped off and added at important terminal points, the train retaining its identity while on a given railroad and sometimes, by changing locomotives or with the use of pooled power and cabooses, to points on connecting lines. Solid bulk trains have long been used in coal, ore, and other mining regions, moving from one mining operation to a coke plant or smelter, or to an urban area where they are classified for delivery to various local consignees. Expedited symbol or "red ball" trains, once used for silk trains from the West Coast and for petroleum from the Southwest, still move perishables and sometimes are employed in expedited intermediate production and distribution transport. Passenger train speeds are normal for these trains and intermediate yarding is held to a minimum.

The unit train is a post-World War II development. This service is distinguished by the fact that there is only one shipper and one receiver, thereby reducing switching to a minimum and eliminating any need for interchange or classification. Solid coal trains to power plants or export loading docks operate at costs that permit rates to be approximately half of the regular carload rates. In some cases the cars are owned by the mining companies or by the utilities—in one case, that of Detroit Edison operating from Waynesburg Southern origins in northern West Virginia, the motive power is also owned by the utility. The unit train has been extended to iron ore, phosphates, grain, and other commodities where volume permits.

Special railroad intransit services include cooling, heating, and ventilation of perishables, loading, unloading, watering and feeding of livestock, diversion, and reconsignment. Mechanical refrigerator cars have largely replaced the old ice-cooled cars, which required perishables from the West Coast to be stopped and switched to reice several times before reaching eastern markets. Livestock movement to packing houses has largely gone to trucks. This industry has moved westward towards the feeding lots, making for a practical shorter distance for motorcarrier service. Livestock *drift* (loss of weight) is less. This new locational pattern, however, gives the railroads a longer haul of packinghouse products to eastern markets.

Reconsignment and diversion are essential services for farm products such as grain and for lumber which leaves the mills prior to sale. We have noted the locational impact of transit privileges in Chapter 5. These arrangements permit milling, fabrication, and other types of processing to be performed at one or more intermediate points between the source of raw materials and the ultimate destination of the finished or semifinished product while they protect the through basis of rates. Access to a given market may not be possible without transit privileges because they permit a manufacturer to meet the delivered price of a competitor. Railroads are not required to accord transit. But if the service is accorded to some or is available at certain points to some shippers and not to others, a carrier may be compelled to provide the service to others or at additional points to prevent a charge of unjust discrimination. The processing in transit that is permitted is limited. The processed product must not be completely unlike the original product in transportation characteristics or form. Wheat may be processed into flour and feed, but the flour may not be converted into bakery goods. Cotton may be compressed in transit but not converted into thread or cloth. Logs may be sawed into lumber and slabs, but further processing into furniture or other finished forms would not be permitted. The weight of the inbound carload (which is usually heavier than the outbound processed commodity) and the rate applicable to the outbound commodity (which is higher than the original rate if not the same) are used in billing through charges. The full local rate to the transit point is paid at time of original shipment. When the shipment departs from the transit point, either the balance of the through rate is paid, as in the grain trade, or the second local rate is paid and the owner makes an intransit reclaim for the difference.

Water transportation freight service takes several forms including (1) barge tow on rivers and canals carrying both dry and liquid cargoes; (2) dry-bulk and tanker lake vessels on the Great Lakes; and (3) ocean vessels including (a) dry general-cargo, (b) dry bulk-cargo, (c) tankers, and (d) unit-load vessels carrying containers. All of these are involved in production-transport service. However, much of the merchandise in containerships may be finished goods in distribution to the market. Except for conventional general-cargo vessels, postwar technical development in all these categories has been remarkable. The modern diesel towboat of 3,000 to 7,500 horsepower pushes tows of 20 or more barges which aggregate 10,000 to 40,000 tons. The standard bulk dry-cargo and tanker vessels of 100,000 gross tons and more offer the most economical transport ever developed. Modern containerships, especially the cellular type which accommodate over 200 tractor-trailer bodies, represent a revolution in terms of both service and cost in ocean general-cargo transport. Heavy industries and power plants have responded in scale of operation and location to the economy made possible by the postwar advances in freight movement by water.

Pipelines have, since the onset of World War II, introduced a revolution in the economy of long-distance movement of liquid products. The difference has not been pronounced in the collecting lines moving the crude to refineries or to tank farms for transshipment to deepwater tankers, but rather in the increased diameter adopted for the newer long-distance lines. Throughput increases as the square of the diameter at equivalent pumping pressure; hence unit costs decline rapidly with larger-line pipe. Coastwise water movement of products has been partly displaced by large-diameter lines. New lines into the midwest supply liquified petroleum gas as well as anhydrous ammonia. Extension of the pipeline net is, of course, closely tied to the opening of new crude production and to expansion of refining capacity.

Motor carriers have come to play an ever growing part in production-freight movement. Over limited distances grain, livestock, logs, lumber, and pulpwood are taken to storage centers or to processing plants. Highly-specialized equipment over modern highways enhances the economy of such operations. In respect to intermediate production freight, the range of motor-carrier operations is much greater because of the higher value of processed or semimanufactured goods. In this vast traffic they are more and more competitive with railroads in services and sometimes in rates, hauling large tonnages of mill shapes and forms of iron and steel, bulk chemicals, cement, and other commodities.

Among the several modes, railroads remain the principal bulk carrier within the continental area accounting for over 35 percent of all ton-miles of freight. A not inconsiderable amount of bulk freight service is performed by private carriers, and there is a tendency for private transport to increase. Most of the ore boats, tankers, and barge tows belong to owners of the products carried and therefore come in this category. Many pipelines are essentially private carriers in fact though common carriers at law. Some short railroads are owned by industrial concerns and derive a large part of their traffic from the parent companies (although most render common carrier service for others as well), and private transportation of many types of bulk by motor vehicles has developed rapidly in recent years.

INDUSTRY DEMAND AND TRANSPORT PATTERNS

Industry production and marketing requirements determine the broad patterns of logistics and traffic flow patterns of production-oriented industries. However, as we shall see, transportation facilities available and rate structures may influence these patterns of production sources and distribution. These relationships can be demonstrated by examples of four industries having extensive flow patterns. They are in order: coal, petroleum, steel, and grain.

COAL

A more striking example of the effects on production, use, and transportation which can result from shifts to substitutes is not likely to be found. Well into the present century, coal was the predominant fuel for industry, utilities, and domestic heating. Gas for the stove and the water heater, except in the Southwest, was usually a product of the local gas works and derived from coal. Coal was the largest single item of traffic for the railroads and a major item in the Atlantic coastwise and Great Lakes trades. The anthracite railroads serving Pennsylvania, the great eastern trunk lines and the Pocahontas roads of the Virginias and Kentucky depended upon coal for the largest part of their revenue.

Cheap oil, convenient as a household fuel, and abundant natural gas made available to the Northeast and Midwest after World War II by large diameter pipelines, rapidly displaced coal from the household market and from much of the industrial and utility markets as well. Railroad coal-car loadings declined from 8,937,856 in 1944 to but 4,487,000 in 1973. Demand for metallurgical coals for the steel industry and for export held up, but alternate fuels took the lead from steam coals. Much of the disaster that overtook the railroads of the Northeast is attributable to the rapid loss of the coal business.

After 1970 additional impetus to conversion from coal, particularly in the utilities market, came from the imposition of environmental controls. Emissions of particulate matter and sulfur dioxide, characteristic with the burning of coal, could only be rendered acceptable by the costly installation of precipitators and stack scrubbers. Hence a further shift to low-sulfur oils and, until a tightness of supply was recognized in 1972, to natural gas.

Although coal is widely distributed in the United States it varies greatly in quality—suitability for metallurgical coke, heating value per ton, and sulfur content. The high-quality deposits occur in restricted areas, fortunately not far from the heavy consumption areas of the Northeast and North Central states. The great bulk of the fuel produced followed a few predominant routes to market. One large, well-defined flow originates in the Pennsylvania, Maryland, Virginia, and West Virginia mines and moves to tidewater at Philadelphia, Baltimore, and especially at the Hampton Roads ports of Norfolk and Newport News.[5] A substantial amount was formerly transshipped into coasting steam-

---

[5] U.S. coal exports in recent years have averaged about 40 million tons annually, mostly metallurgical coal. The great bulk of it moves via Hampton Roads.

ers and barges for distribution up and down the Atlantic coast. Destinations for export include Japan, Europe, and the countries of South America. Another flow is from the central and western Pennsylvania mines and those of Maryland and northern West Virginia all-rail to New York State, New England, and Canada via the New York gateways, and to the cities of the eastern seaboard. Westward, from all of these states and from Kentucky, coal moves into what has been known as the lake cargo market. Such coal was largely dumped into vessels at Lake Erie ports for movement to Detroit, Milwaukee, Chicago, and other lake ports, as well as to the head of the lakes at Duluth. Some utilities at these points are now served all-rail by unit trains.

Coal has moved west on the Great Lakes since the opening of the Cleveland and Pittsburgh Railroad in 1854. In 1971, however, an experimental shipment was made eastward using the Burlington Northern ore docks at Allouez, Wisconsin, for transfer to lake boat. This movement has grown. More important, coal mining which had become moribund in Wyoming and Montana after railroads switched from steam to diesel power has been resumed and greatly expanded. This rather sudden development is traceable first to the growth of environmental concern and second to the now demonstrated weakness of the nation's reserves of natural gas and crude petroleum along with uncertainties and delays in atomic power generation.

Steam generating stations were required in the Southwest when it became apparent that the potential of atomic power had been overestimated and when planned hydro installations were blocked because of probable adverse effects upon the Grand Canyon and other natural features. Antipollution standards characteristically forbid the use of coal or oil containing more than 1 percent of sulfur by weight unless expensive stack scrubbers are installed to remove the excess. Heavier freight costs are being accepted in order to use western coal to meet these standards. Finally, although energy policy has been in disarray, the pressure is on to burn coal in new generating plants and to convert existing plants from oil to coal.

Low-sulfur coal capable of economic strip mining is virtually exhausted in the East, only about 4 percent of the nation's coal reserves of this type being located in West Virginia and eastern Kentucky. Fortunately, railroads have been prepared to move expanding western production to remote markets in Texas, Oklahoma, the Central States, and elsewhere on hauls that often reach 1,000 to 1,500 miles. The unit train is the means. In 1970 western unit-train operations were insubstantial. By 1977, however, 40 services were being operated which involved an average daily frequency of 29.5 trains and an annual movement of 66.4 million tons of coal.[6] Expansion continues and the

---

[6] See the listing in William D. Warren, "The Unit Train and the Development of Low Sulfur Coal Resources in the Western Interior Region," *Transportation Journal*, vol. 18, no. 4 (Summer 1979), pp. 53 ff.

greatest growth is believed still to be ahead as the nation's reliance on coal for energy expansion accelerates.

Much of the movement is over single-track lines which were never intended for large volume bulk movement. Large sums have been spent in track rehabilitation, the lengthening of sidings, and the improvement of signal and train-control systems. The longest new rail line constructed in the United States since 1932 is Burlington Northern's 115-mile coal route between Gillette, Wyoming, and Orin which, when fully completed and signalled, is expected to have a capacity of 125 million tons a year. It greatly shortens the routes to potential markets. This is only a beginning on the capital investment likely to be required to accommodate anticipated volumes. Faced with the need to expand, railroads have sought high rates on western coal and have generally obtained decisions from the Interstate Commerce Commission which insure a return above the full cost of the service. Utilities have responded with appeals and court litigation.

Confronted with these railroad-rate policies and the knowledge that, as a labor intensive industry, railroads face continuing escalation of costs in an inflationary era, various interests have sought to promote slurry pipelines as an alternative. These are not only opposed by the railroads. Their economics are unclear because no lines of the diameter and length proposed are operating today. Moreover, their heavy demands for water generate environmental opposition because they would draw water from areas that are sparsely supplied. The desirability of slurry lines remains in controversy.

PETROLEUM AND PETROLEUM PRODUCTS

No freight movement, measured in ton-miles, approaches that of petroleum and its products to and within the United States. Pipelines and water transport dominate the transportation both of crude petroleum and refined products. Indeed, half the tonnage moved in international commerce is oil.

The crude petroleum movement is featured by the import of some 8 million barrels per day in ocean tankers from OPEC countries and some other sources abroad to the refining centers in the Northeast and Gulf Coast port cities. Since no U.S. port will accommodate the very large crude carriers, transshipment to smaller vessels for some of this volume occurs in the Caribbean.[7] Crude produced in North America is moved primarily by pipeline from the Texas, Oklahoma, and Louisiana region and south central Canada to the refineries in the North Central area. California refineries are fed by local pipelines,

---

[7] An off-shore unloading facility capable of handling such vessels is under construction off the Louisiana coast.

and the combined pipeline-tanker service from the Alaskan North Slope production. There is also substantial coastwise tanker operation between the Gulf producing area and the East coast refineries.

The general shape of the crude and products pipeline networks is quite different, but both are highly concentrated in the Eastern half of the continental United States. Product pipelines, which now range up to 38 inches in diameter, were developed after 1930. They now carry much of the flow, but coastwise tanker service from the Gulf to the Northeast market continues, although the volume moved is not quite as large as that of the parallel pipelines. Tank-barge movement up the Mississippi system to the North Central market is substantial. Some products, however, still move by rail tank cars and by small coastwise and river tankers or tank barges to conveniently located bulk stations, whence access to filling stations and other consumers is by truck. In some areas of the country, particularly on the Pacific coast and in the Northwest, where limited quantities are consumed in comparatively broad areas, long-distance movement of petroleum products to bulk stations by truck has developed in substitution for rail or water movement. In the Columbia River valley intense competition developed between motor, barge, and rail transport of this commodity. In the Southwest, rail movement from Bakersfield and other refining areas into Arizona and New Mexico was largely superseded by truck. In the 1950s, however, the Southern Pacific Railroad built a pipeline into this area for the distribution of products.

The petroleum industry makes use of all kinds of surface transport between the producing well and the ubiquitous gas station. A representative sequence of movement of crude petroleum to the refinery and of gasoline through the bulk station to the retail outlet is shown in Figure 12-1. It will be observed that the long haul between producing area and refinery is performed by trunk pipeline or ocean tanker. Between the refinery and the bulk station all kinds of for-hire surface transport are used. Comparative costs for typical distances were shown in Chapter 10.

THE STEEL INDUSTRY: IRON ORE

The steel industry affords an excellent example of the growth of demand for bulk transportation and of the reciprocal relationship between the demand for and the supply and character of the transport. The early iron industry grew upon the site of local ores which could be mined on the spot in sufficient quantities to supply a small furnace. Charcoal from neighboring woods provided the fuel. The small daily production was made into bar iron, castings, gun barrels, utensils, fireplace hardware, nails, and other rudimentary products for trans-

FIGURE 12-1
Representative Petroleum Movement

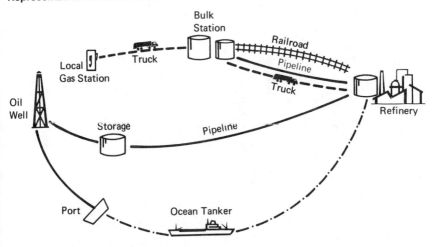

port by riverboat, wagon, or pack train to supply a relatively limited market. The advent of the railroad made coal deposits accessible, permitted marketing over a wider area because of the lower cost of transport, and thus made possible the establishment of larger furnaces and much more economical production. These factors combined to reduce the price of iron in the market and so considerably to increase its uses, thus expanding the market both in territorial extent and in the volume of per capita use. Cheaper iron permitted the manufacture of a wider variety of iron products, demand mushroomed, and large-scale production and transport became possible, bringing about further declines in cost and in market price. These reciprocal relations go on continually. They are accompanied by technological improvement in manufacturing and in transportation which reinforce the tendencies toward centralization to secure the benefits of specialization and large-scale production.

Today the iron and steel industry in a normal year uses about 130 million tons of ore, 75 million tons of coal, many million tons of flux stone, and numerous other items. Of the 130 million tons, about 90 million are domestic ore and 40 million are imported. The ore produces some 94 million tons of finished and semifinished products for the market. Transportation is required for every ton of the raw and finished product and is vital to the integrated functioning of both the basic steel and steel fabricating plants. Figure 12-2 shows the flow of ore on the Great Lakes to steel mills in 1976 and the import through North Atlantic ports.

Western mills at Minnequa, Colorado, Provo, Utah, and Fontana, California, rely primarily on railborne domestic ores. The decline of

FIGURE 12–2
Iron Ore Movements by Water, 1976

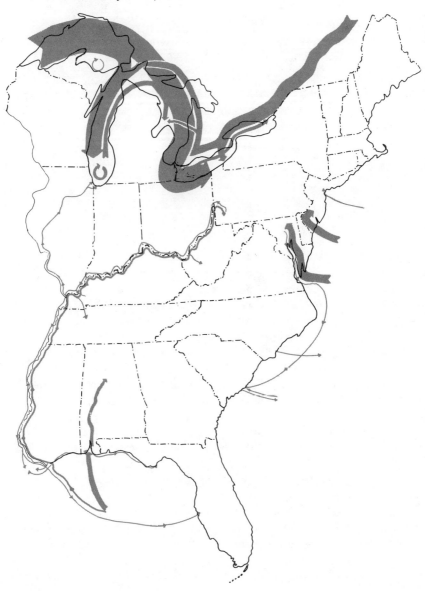

Wyoming production has led to the establishment of the longest unit
train movement in the United States—taconite pellets from the Minnesota ranges to Minnequa. The shipment of pellets, which, unlike
direct-shipping ores, do not freeze in the cars, has also permitted
winter rail movement to Chicago and other centers when the Great
Lakes are closed to navigation by ice.

Iron and steel in semimanufactured form constitutes a major item of production freight. The traffic is handled largely by the railroads from major producing centers—Pittsburgh, Chicago, Gary, Cleveland, Youngstown, Buffalo, Baltimore, and others—and distributed widely. Major streams of the traffic follow Conrail and the Baltimore and Ohio east and west out of Pittsburgh, and the Pittsburgh and Lake Erie north. The various roads out of Chicago distribute the product of that district in every direction. Both Pittsburgh and Chicago make considerable use of river barges in distribution, especially of pipe and oil-country goods on the long haul to Texas and Louisiana points. The truck has become of major importance in the short-haul distribution of steel and competes strongly, particularly in moving sheet and strip for automobile and appliance manufacture and in the movement of structurals for delivery to construction sites.

Mill shapes and forms were once an important export for the American steel industry. In recent years, however, the industry has been assailed by a growing volume of imports in an increasing range of products. In considerable part this results from the growing obsolescence of a substantial portion of American steel-making capacity at a time when Japanese and European facilities, rebuilt since World War II, have taken advantage of the most modern technology. Some developing countries, such as Taiwan, Korea, Brazil, and Mexico are also moving into export markets. The response of American steelmakers is the closing down of a number of obsolete mills along with modernization of others. Some traditional centers of steel production are likely to disappear from the transportation landscape with resulting changes in product flows.

GRAIN

The role of the railroad in opening the west to grain agriculture was pointed out earlier. The movement of grain was a main element in the business of the railroads in the vast territory between the Mississippi and the Rockies. It remains of large importance to this day. But the seasonal character of the crop and the fluctuation in export volumes from year to year make it a difficult type of traffic to handle to the satisfaction of farmers, grain dealers, and overseas customers. Car shortages have been endemic over a long period of years and blocked port elevators are common during heavy export movements. Unmoved grain piles up in country elevators and eventually backs up into storage on the farm, sometimes on the ground for lack of bin capacity.

Railroads remain the mainstay of the grain movement into primary markets and into export position, primarily through Gulf ports. But the Mississippi system has become a more significant channel than formerly, especially for export movement. River barges are fed by both rail and truck. Consistent car shortages, too, have put more of the movement on trucks with hauls that have gradually lengthened to as much as 350 miles. Important export volumes also go into ocean ships at Duluth on Lake Superior and, for the Canadian crops, at Thunderbay. The north Pacific ports, too, have increased their participation in the export of grain from the western margin of the U.S.-Canadian spring wheat region.

Over the last several decades rail movement of grain has changed significantly. The boxcar fitted with grain doors has largely been replaced by the covered-hopper car which loads from the elevators through top hatches and self-unloads through bottom hoppers. These cars are now most commonly built to 100-ton capacity compared with half that for the average boxcar formerly employed. The railroads inability to finance sufficient cars for this seasonal business has been partly offset by lease or purchase of cars by the major grain companies. The unit train has become a regular feature in the grain movement as a means to shorten car-turnaround time and thus improve availability.

A major problem for the grain traffic is the obsolescence of the rail gathering system. The growing territory was crisscrossed with branch lines in the period before the truck and good roads made obsolete the proposition that grain could be moved by wagon only about ten miles from the farm to country elevator. Deprived of passenger and general freight traffic by highway competition, these lines long ago became a drain on the railroads most heavily committed to the grain-growing regions—Chicago and Northwestern, Milwaukee, and Rock Island. Abandonment of lines has been resisted, though the economics of the unit train make it sensible to concentrate grain by truck into fewer larger elevators on main lines which can load grain in trainload quantity. At long last a restructuring of railroads within the corn belt appears likely with long bankrupt Rock Island under court order to liquidate and bankrupt Milwaukee far advanced on a plan to reduce its mileage to a limited core system that may be able to sustain itself. To prosperous and well-maintained railroads like Santa Fe and Union Pacific, grain remains an important element of profitable traffic.

Since the grain farmer has long been heavily dependent on rail movement to reach his markets, freight rates on grain have been a sensitive subject. Western agricultural interests sought to inhibit rate increases by the burden of proof placed on railroads by the Mann-Elkins Act in 1910. The agricultural depression of the early 1920s prompted the Hoch-Smith Resolution which sought the lowest possible level of rates for agricultural products. Canadian railroads still suffer the burden of the statutory Crow's Nest Pass rates on grain which are fixed at the level established in 1892. Most recently U.S. railroads, using the authority granted by the 4-R Act of 1976, imposed seasonal rates on grain, a very logical step considering the sharp seasonal fluctuation in volume and the failure of steady year-round rates to support the cost of carrying sufficient equipment to cope with fall peaks. Congress, however, repealed the authority for this type of rate in 1980.

SELECTED REFERENCES

Barriger, John W. *Super Railroads for a Dynamic American Economy.* New York: Simmons-Boardman Publishing Co., 1955.

Bencord, Harry. *General Cargo Ship Economics and Design.* Cambridge, Md.: Cornell Maritime Press, Inc., 1965.

Constantin, James A. *Principles of Logistics Management,* chap. 1. New York: Appleton-Century-Crofts, 1966.

Droege, John A. *Freight Terminals and Trains.* 2d ed. New York: McGraw-Hill Book Co., 1925.

Farris, Martin T., and McElhiney, Paul T. *Modern Transportation: Selected Readings,* chaps. 7, 8, 27, and 28. 2d ed. Boston: Houghton Mifflin Co., 1973.

Hazard, John L. *The Great Lakes—St. Lawrence Transportation System: Problems and Potential.* Washington, D.C.: Upper Great Lakes Regional Commission, 1969.

————. *Transportation: Management—Economics—Policy,* sect. 3. Cambridge, Md.: Cornell Maritime Press, 1977.

Illinois Central Railroad. *Organization and Traffic of the Illinois Central System.* Chicago, 1938.

Loree, L. F. *Railroad Freight Transportation.* New York: D. Appleton Co., 1922.

National Transportation Policy Study Commission. *National Transportation Policies through the Year 2000: Final Report.* Washington, D.C.: U.S. Government Printing Office, 1979.

Perle, Eugene D. *The Demand for Transportation: Regional and Commodity Studies in the U.S.* Chicago: University of Chicago Press, 1964.

Phillips-Birt, D. *The Future of Ships.* St. Ives, Huntingdon, England: Imray Laurie None & Wilson Limited, 1970.

Plowman, E. Grosvenor. *Elements of Business Logistics,* chaps. 1 and 2. Stanford: Stanford University, Graduate School of Business, 1963.

Ullman, Edward L. *American Commodity Flow.* Seattle: University of Washington Press, 1957.

13

Freight Service in Physical Distribution Systems

NATURE OF DISTRIBUTION FREIGHT SERVICE

In this chapter we are concerned with freight transportation service involved in the distribution of products in the market. These include manufactured goods and perishables. The conditions and requirements of this service generally differ markedly from those associated with freight service for production. Packaging is usually required for shipment.[1] Loss and damage is a serious problem. Expedition and careful handling are necessary. Perishable freight will deteriorate unduly if fast service is not provided. Customers of nonperishable products need fast, safe, and dependable delivery to avoid the costs and risks of large inventories. It is, therefore, a quality service. Except for livestock transported to packing houses, only an occasional emergency will require similar expedition in transporting unpackaged supplies to storage or processing plants to meet production needs. Expedited bulk freight service may be regularly provided when it is incidental to either low-cost volume vessel loading and unloading facilities for ore, coal, grain, and so on, or to volume shipments direct from one shipper to one receiver as prevails in unit-train operations. Generally, expedited and scheduled freight service is expensive and is accorded to distribution service rather than to production-transport service.

---

[1] However, in recent years wine has gone from the West Coast by tanker to East Coast markets, orange juice by tank car in trainloads from Florida to the Northeast, flour in bulk in covered hoppers for packaging close to the market.

IMPORTANCE OF DISTRIBUTION FREIGHT SERVICE

Since the volume of bulk materials moving to storage or directly to processing plants is so large and since they often move extended distances, the volume of bulk freight service far exceeds that required for distribution. Of the more than 5.5 billion tons moved intercity in the continental United States in 1977, it is estimated that approximately 1.3 billion tons were involved in distribution. This amounts to less than 25 percent of the total tonnage. That the tons transported in the supply function so far exceed those in the distribution function is explained by the consumption of coal, coke, and fuel oil in processing operations and the great loss of weight of ore, logs, lumber, and livestock in the course of processing prior to the transportation of the finished products. However, in terms of the value of commodities involved, the revenue received by the carriers, and the cost of rendering the service, the importance of distribution traffic rivals that of production traffic.

As we progress in the arts, with an emphasis on the variety of consumers' goods for plant, office, and household use, distribution freight service and merchandise freight service in particular have greater economic importance. This arises, also, from the trends in methods of doing business. More and more finished goods are distributed in the market in small lots. Both producer and distributor tend to keep inventories at a minimum; and, therefore, they order shipments to meet day-to-day needs. The wholesaler who once ordered in carload quantities for local distribution to retailers has in many lines disappeared, and more small-lot shipments go from the manufacturer's plant or warehouse direct to the retailer, often for a substantial distance. Motor-freight service since 1925 has become a major transportation industry, largely because of the increasing volume of this type of freight in the conduct of American business. The postwar development of physical distribution management has focused enhanced attention on the speed, dependability, and efficiency of merchandise service. Application of the systems concept makes clear the ancillary costs which slow and irregular service inflicts upon shippers.

CATEGORIES OF DISTRIBUTION TRAFFIC

A great variety of commodities is involved in distribution transport service. They differ greatly in nature—perishable or nonperishable, solid or liquid—as well as in the quantities in which they move. All carrier modes are involved in attempting to provide the speed, dependability, and safety needed for distribution service. The principal categories of commodities and the nature of their movement are as follows:

1. Fresh fruits and vegetables, fresh meats and fish, and horticultural items move directly in full refrigerator carloads or truckloads to principal urban market centers where local jobbers and merchants obtain daily supplies and chain warehouses distribute to their retail outlets. Some, of course, move to canning, freezing, and other processing plants, also in truckload and carload quantities. Less perishable fruits and vegetables, such as apples, pears, and potatoes, may move in carload and truck volume to warehouse storage from which distribution is made over a period of months.

2. Refined liquid products include petroleum products and chemicals. Gasoline and fuel oils, the principal petroleum products, may employ extensive systems of pipelines, tank ships, and barges to move them from refinery to important market centers from which tank trucks make delivery to retail outlets and distributors. Local barge operations are sometimes employed in metropolitan areas where refineries are located. Lubricating oil and chemicals of all kinds usually move in carload and truckload quantities or in barge loads between plants and to distribution terminals.

3. Manufactured nonperishables include a vast variety of commodities such as agricultural, industrial, and mining machinery and equipment; office equipment and supplies; military hardware; automobiles; household appliances and supplies; processed foods and beverages; and transportation and communication equipment. Several steps are usually involved in the distribution of these products. Manufacturers and processors move products in volume shipments by barge, railcar, and truck, or a combination of two or all three, to the principal market areas. The shipments are consigned as a rule to distribution-area warehouses or wholesalers from which local distribution is made. However, large industrial, construction, and military equipment will likely go by special railcar or truck to the industry, shop, or other location where it is to be installed. Railroads and motor carriers dominate this volume movement of nonperishable solid goods and therefore account for most of the vast amount of ton-miles performed in distribution. Private, contract, and common carriers participate; and piggyback is of growing significance.

However, a large proportion of merchandise shipments moves in less-than-carload-or-truckload quantities. While large plants dominate the market, there are many small factories and shops turning out specialized equipment, such as typewriters and precision instruments, which will normally move in less-than-volume shipments. Moreover, the great supply of goods going to distribution warehouses and wholesalers must be distributed from those locations to retail outlets or to ultimate customers. For this phase of distribution, as well as for back orders with manufacturers designed to overcome stock-outs in market-oriented warehouses, less-than-carload-and-truckload shipments may prevail.

SMALL SHIPMENTS TRAFFIC

The provision of economical transport service on small shipments has been a serious problem. Retailers have gone in for smaller and smaller inventories, thus requiring frequent delivery of small orders. Rail, motor, and air vehicles have continued to increase in size. Therefore, the tasks of assembly and disassembly for movement involve extensive handling and clerical work. Spiraling postwar labor costs have served to increase the relative costs of less-than-volume shipments. The cost problem grows the smaller the shipment. Motor carriers, which carry the overwhelming share of these shipments, increasingly prejudice smaller shipments by steeply graduating the rates inversely with the weight of the shipment and even by refusing to carry the lower grade commodities, especially if they are of light density. Shipments under 1,000 pounds are particularly affected, and they constitute the serious small-shipments problem. The alternative to truck freight rates is the higher rates of any express service. Shipments of 100 pounds or less are classed as parcels. The parcel services are United Parcel Service and parcel post.[2]

The break-bulk intercity carriers, both direct and indirect, handling shipments of under 10,000 pounds and the tonnage handled by them in 1976 was as estimated below:

	Tons
Motor carriers	85,000,000
United Parcel Service	4,865,000
Airfreight	3,330,000
Rail LCL	550,000
Water carrier	305,000
Bus express	281,000

Source: Transportation Association of America, *Transportation Facts and Trends*, 15th ed. (Washington, D.C., July 1979), p. 11.

The rail less-than-carload lot (LCL) had declined from 22,164,000 tons in 1950 and is expected to decline further if not to vanish. Motor, air, and United Parcel Service traffic continues to expand. It should be noted that local metropolitan transportation of break-bulk shipments of less than 10,000 pounds is extensive and not included above. Local service is performed either by private truck or local transfer motor-carrier firms.

The indirect carriers who assemble such shipments in truckloads, plane loads, or carloads and their relative importance in 1976 were: freight forwarders, 4,400,000; parcel post, 875,000; air parcel post, 217,000.[3]

---

[2] UPS limits its parcels to 50 pounds or less. Parcel post weight limit to first-class post offices is 40 pounds, and in dimension the limit is 72 inches of length and girth combined.

[3] Transportation Association of America, *Transportation Facts and Trends*, 15th ed. (Washington, D.C., July 1979), p. 11.

In addition to these indirect carriers, shippers' associations have been growing rapidly. These enable shippers in a locality to cooperate in assembling a carload of their shipments going to a common destination area. This tonnage in 1976 amounted to 7,127,827, roughly double the freight-forwarder figure and more than twice the volume a decade earlier. Mail-order and variety store chains having many shipments below 10,000 pounds going to a number of outlets in a local area often make up "pool" cars and thereby get a carload rate and expedited service.

The most economical quality transportation service for distribution, except for very short distances, is movement in carload quantities from the siding of the shipper to that of the receiver. Expedited service is possible if both are located on the same railroad, avoiding delays and costs of interchange, or where special through interline service is provided as it is in the perishable trains from the West, Southwest, and South to Northeastern markets and in the increasingly numerous run-through trains which move over the lines of several railroads without reclassification. Rivaling such services is that of pipeline, tanker, and barge in the distribution of petroleum and other liquid products. Full truckloads going from the dock of the shipper to that of the receiver are superior in speed and often comparable in cost to rail carloads for limited distances of 500 miles or less. Only as changing and increasingly competitive marketing conditions made it necessary to depart more and more from the use of these large-lot services, especially in the final link of distribution systems, did it become apparent that we had a small-shipments problem of considerable magnitude.

We will now review the principal developments to accommodate this usual and less fortunate traffic in distribution freight service in order to provide the fast, dependable, and economical service which industry requires. The cost and delay problems include: (1) handling involved in assembly, transfer, and dispersion; (2) frequent congestion in freight terminals; (3) congested street traffic for trucks engaged in collection and delivery; (4) low utilization of vehicles in both line-haul and local operations; (5) damage from breakage and spoilage; (6) pilferage of shipments; and (7) cost and time loss incurred in interchange between carriers.

MOTOR FREIGHT SERVICES

The first conquest in the substitution of truck for rail service was in the relatively short-haul movements of LCL railroad freight. As highways improved and the motor freight vehicle increased in size and dependability, the size of shipments it could accommodate increased and the range of overnight delivery became much greater, recently going up to 500 miles. The average haul of merchandise is much less than that. The range of merchandise that the motor carriers will accept in intercity hauls has widened, but because trucking is a relatively high-cost mode of transportation with vehicles of limited size, intercity general commodity carriers often either refuse to include low-grade items in their tariffs or quote prohibitive rates.

The pervasiveness of the industry has greatly expanded the commercial area of the nation which once consisted only of areas within 10 or 20 miles of a railroad or waterway. Trucking has continued to grow, surpassing the railroads in gross freight revenue by 1964. In 1977 the comparison was estimated at $19.3 billion for the railroads and $31 billion for regulated commercial motor freight in intercity operations only. In ton-miles of intercity freight, trucking is exceeded only by the railroads and, between 1964 and 1976, by the pipelines. The estimated percentage of total ton-mileage in 1978 was 35.8 percent for the railroads, 23.3 percent for the pipelines, and 24.7 percent for trucks.

However, the basic nature of intercity motortruck merchandise service has changed. When the industry was young and the vehicles and carriers were small, trucking companies usually operated on a door-to-door basis. The principal carriers now maintain fleets of pickup and delivery vehicles in the larger cities. These feed traffic into and deliver it from terminals in which the shipments are sorted and transferred between pickup vehicles and the much larger line-haul trailers. The congestion of city streets, the larger size of major metropolitan areas, and the dispersion of customers result in low productivity of city delivery trucks. Hence some motor carriers with a large proportion of less-than-truckload traffic own more pickup trucks than line-haul vehicles. A vast amount of motor-carrier terminal construction has been carried out, particularly since 1950, and some very large installations, with the latest equipment available for materials handling, have been built by the principal carriers at major cities.

The increasing concentration of less-than-truckload freight through terminals makes for economy in line-haul truck operations, but terminal expenses and delays are becoming steadily more important. Operating costs of terminal operations of Class I and II general freight common carriers rose from $1.17 per ton in 1945 to $4.83 in 1967 and $16.50 in 1977.[4] Long hauls will often require interchange between lines which have made rate and operating arrangements for that purpose. In this way many of them can accept freight going to any section of the nation. Where it is accomplished over the platform in transfer rather than by the exchange of full trailers, delay, irregularity, and higher costs result.

---

[4] American Trucking Associations, Inc., *American Trucking Trends* (1969 and 1978), and Chapter 10.

Common-carrier motor lines are important transporters of dry and perishable freight, but petroleum and other liquid products are largely handled by contract carriers who specialize in tank-truck equipment. Nevertheless, some common carriers offer liquid freight service. Contract carriers also predominate in the delivery of new automobiles and are frequently used by manufacturers and distributors to provide more effective service to retailers than is ordinarily available from common carriers. Private truck operations are often used for the same reason.

Flexibility ranks first among the distinctive characteristics of motor-truck service. The size and design of the vehicles can be fitted to meet individual needs of any enterprise, and their ability to go wherever a highway of any kind exists makes this the most flexible of all modes of freight transport. Just as the private automobile gives the maximum of convenience in passenger service, so does the truck in merchandise service. Speed of delivery also ranks high among its advantages. Industries, commercial houses, and the armed services have often resorted to motortruck service for emergency shipments.

As we saw in the previous chapter, the role of the truck in handling materials for production is significant, especially for collection for volume movement or other relatively short hauls. The major role of the motor freight carrier is, however, in the movement of products in distribution to the market. Of the more than 600 billion ton-miles of freight transportation in intercity service by truck in 1968, probably more than 450 billion ton-miles were involved in the distribution process. The ton-mile cost of motortruck freight compared with that of rail freight reflects the truck emphasis on service quality and the predominance of small shipments in its traffic. In 1978 the estimated average revenue per ton-mile in intercity movement by Class I motor carriers was 11.2 cents as compared to 2.4 cents by rail. The difference between rail and motor rates may be slight for highgrade traffic, the spread, if any, varying with the distance of movement. Railroad piggyback has grown steadily in recent years, especially on the longer hauls, because that kind of operation can approximate both motor-carrier service quality and rates.

PIGGYBACK SERVICE

The growth of railroad trailer on flatcar (TOFC), commonly called *piggyback*, has expanded since 1950 into a very major service. It may be said to be the third effort, but the first really successful one, of the railroads to regain and develop less-than-carload traffic as well as to get back into the market for potential carload business of off-rail shippers or receivers.

The first effort on the part of the railroads was to introduce container service and to provide universal less-than-car-load lot pickup and delivery service. While these methods provided a door-to-door service they did not prove competitive with motor carriers either in expedition or cost. Then came a significant development of merchandise trains often involving two or three railroads in interline through service. The trains moved on passenger schedules giving overnight pickup and delivery service at all main terminal cities. Almost 100 of these trains came into being between 1930 and 1950. But, in time they too proved not to be the answer.

Piggyback has been a very successful effort. Solid piggyback trains between major terminals are operated over most of the larger railroads today. The trailers are assembled at the terminals for train movement and then distributed by highway tractor. The trailer or trailer body is loaded at the shipper's platform and delivered to the consignee's platform. Especially designed flatcars equipped to fasten down the trailer or trailer body are necessary. The transfer of trailers at the rail yard was once generally effected by end loading over ramps in a roll-on and roll-off fashion with the flatcars in position and "bridged." Now, however, the transfer of trailers or trailer bodies is usually accomplished by specially designed mobile or gantry cranes or by jumbo fork-lift trucks. This system provides more flexibility and often reduces cost.

Piggyback transportation began in 1926 when the Chicago North Shore and Milwaukee Railroad, an electric line, established the service between Chicago and Milwaukee.[5] However, the extension of service among the major railroads has largely come about since 1950. As of June 30, 1957, no less than 57 Class I rail carriers were offering the service, using some 4,000 trailer units and over 200,000 railcars.[6] The service has continued to grow, the number of trailer and container units hauled reaching 2,032,000 in 1969.[7] Volume peaked in 1969, dipped in 1970 and 1971, partly in consequence of the economic recession, recovered forcefully the following year, but declined again in the recession of 1975. Recovery has been rapid and 1978 loadings stood 45 percent above those of 1967.

There are six types, or plans, of piggyback service in operation today. Plan I is a service offered to commercial truckers who can use it in lieu of over-the-road line-haul operation. On long hauls it may materially reduce fuel and labor costs and may avoid ton-mile taxes and license fees, as well as low limits on size and weight of a state traversed en route. The freight moves on a motor-carrier bill of lading. Plan II is a door-to-door railroad service in which the railroad uses its own container or trailer equipment and contracts with local truckers to

---

[5] Harold L. Johnson, *Piggyback Transportation: An Economic Analysis* (Knoxville: University of Tennessee, 1956), p. 4.

[6] Interstate Commerce Commission 71st *Annual Report*, 1957, pp. 60–61.

[7] Interstate Commerce Commission 84th *Annual Report*, 1970, pp. 42–43.

assemble at originating terminal and deliver from destination terminals. Plan II½ is a railroad service in which the railroad supplies the trailer or container unit and the shipper performs the service to and from the rail terminals. Plan III differs from Plan II½ since the shipper supplies his own trailer or container equipment. Plan IV requires the shipper to provide the railcars as well as the highway equipment and operation. Plan V is a joint motor-rail or rail-motor service involving an established through route and a joint single-factor rate. Plan II has always been the most used service, but Plan II½ has had a remarkable growth since it relieves the shipper from ownership of the trailer and the management of its return haul, yet gives him control over and a chance to expedite movement to and from rail terminals.

Though piggyback has been a growth area in the railroad industry, it suffers from handicaps both of economics and of management. Conventional piggyback which takes the full highway trailer (including undercarriage and brake system) aboard the flatcar generates about 31 tons of equipment weight per trailer moved compared with 13 tons of tare weight if the same trailer is moved over the highway. Even fuel economy disappears when adverse terrain is encountered and the combination of weight and air resistance greatly narrows the advantage in level terrain. With the cost of handling trailers to and from rail facilities rapidly growing, the break-even distance compared with over-the-road movement may well surpass 500 miles. Management on too many railroads still fails to accord piggyback a preferred position as a segregable service entitled to its own dedicated train schedules and to allot sufficient funds for adequate terminal development.

A breakthrough may well be in the making. The container is far better than the trailer both for weight and air resistance. New car concepts, some providing double-deck stacking of containers, another a skeleton articulated car of reduced weight, may significantly alter the relationships. An experiment conducted jointly by the Association of American Railroads and the Federal Railroad Administration may demonstrate the feasibility of short, fast, dedicated trains operated with reduced crews. Should increased traffic be generated by these means, union cooperation on crew consist may be forthcoming. For the moment, however, skepticism is warranted when proposals are voiced for large shifts of traffic from highway to rail.

POOL-CAR SERVICE

Rail "pool-car" service has continued its popularity since World War II because it combines the economy of railroad carload service with expedited delivery service. A shipper who has a number of less-than-carload shipments for customers in a given local area places them in one car; and if he has enough to meet the carload minimum, gets a mixed-carload rate. At destination the shipper's representative dispatches the merchandise to the several customers by motor carrier. Several shippers might cooperate in a pool-car service including arrangements for delivery. However, usually there is one shipper. The service is much used by mail-order houses and manufacturing plants. Consolidation of shipments of several shippers may be performed by a freight forwarder or by shippers' associations, which have grown in number in recent years. The shipper-owner pays the regular mixed-carload rate which a forwarder gets. The pool-car shipper or forwarder saves the difference between the carload and the less-than-carload rates less the cost of loading and unloading the equipment.

FORWARDER SERVICE

Some years ago the freight-forwarder service came into being to provide a more convenient and economical service. The forwarder is a common carrier in relation to the shipper and arranges for the billing and handling of the shipment. By assembling several less-than-carload shipments into one car, the forwarder gets a "mixed-carload," or per-trailer, piggyback rate which permits him to give the shipper a rate no higher than, and often not as high as, the less-than-carload rate which he would pay if he shipped independently. The spread between the mixed-car rate and the less-than-carload rate is the source of the forwarder's compensation. The car is made up for destination, avoiding the necessity of transfers in transit. In recent years the forwarders' service has ceased to be exclusively a station-to-station one. It includes pickup and delivery by motortruck between rail assembly stations and premises of the consignor and consignee. It involves, moreover, assembly and distribution at major centers by the use of connecting motor-carrier services. The forwarder is a specialist who provides an economical and expeditious service. Nevertheless, domestic-forwarder traffic has been stagnant in recent years, and forwarders saw little promise of growth unless they were permitted to contract with railroads for underlying service on a wholesale basis. This right was finally accorded by the Motor Carrier Act of 1980.

EXPRESS SERVICE

It was in 1839 that an enterprising young man named William Harnden began a special expedited-package-delivery service between Boston and New York City carrying parcels by hand aboard passenger trains from sender to receiver. The service grew rapidly, requiring vehicles to pickup and deliver packages to and from designated express cars moving on passenger trains. Numerous express companies developed which by the last quarter of the 19th century were consolidated into the Adams, American, Southeastern, and Wells-Fargo companies. As their rivalry increased, pickup and delivery service for the prevailing small shipments proved so costly that competition had to be reduced. Moreover, greater coverage, extending to the entire railroad system was desirable.

The advent of the parcel post system in 1913, handling many small shipments at lower rates, injured the express business and made the competition that existed among the four large companies too costly. In 1919 these companies were merged under the name of the American Express Company except that express service on the Southern Railway continued under the Southeastern Express Company. In 1929 the American Express Company was taken over by the Class I railroads of the nation and renamed the Railway Express Agency. Several years later it ceased to be essentially a railroad service by getting permission to use trucks, buses, and aircraft in its service. Later the Class I railroads sold their interest and it became REA Express. The company reorganized its service by the establishment of modern terminals at key points and substituting its own truck operations for discontinued rail passenger trains that formerly carried express. Nevertheless it moved into bankruptcy and was liquidated in 1974.

One factor in the demise of REA was the unwillingness of the Civil Aeronautics Board to approve renewal of its long-standing arrangement with airlines for the exclusive conduct of express service by air. As an alternative, a number of airlines offer express or preferred freight service under their own tariffs, rules, and regulations. But there is no longer a universal nationwide and international air-express service.

UNIT LOAD DEVELOPMENT IN WATER TRANSPORTATION

In the deep-sea trades the developments in unit-load operations for handling merchandise have been remarkable. Seatrain Lines was the pioneer, when in 1929 it began coastwise service between Atlantic and Gulf-coast ports and, for a time, between New York and Havana, Cuba, with large vessels with tracks on four decks to accommodate a train of 100 railroad cars. In the postwar period the focus has been on the development of ships to accommodate demountable trailer bodies as containers or trailers on wheels by the roll-on and roll-off methods.

Atlantic Container Lines combines both methods on its ships. Sealand Service, Inc., introduced the cellular type all-containership in the 50s. In addition to the solid containerships, many general-cargo ships take deck loads of containers. The service spread from the coastwise to intercoastal and then to transatlantic and transpacific operations. The containership is rapidly replacing the conventional general cargo vessel, providing superior service and lower costs. The rate of growth is phenomenal. In 1969 the container traffic in the North Atlantic was 80 percent above that of 1968 and the rate of increase in the Pacific was greater.[8] In 1970 the capacity of vessels in the trades increased from 65,000 to 105,000 containers of 20-foot length, aggregating 1.8 million gross register tons. Growth has continued with 8.7 million tons in service in 1978.[9] To accommodate this revolution in deep-sea shipping, major ports of the United States, Europe, and Japan installed waterfront container terminals backed up by large open yards for assembling the containers which are speedily moved to and from shipside to expedite loading and unloading of the increasingly large and expensive containerships.

The roll-on and roll-off system employed by the military during World War II was the first container system used in overseas commercial operations. In the 40s this method was employed by the Alaska Steamship Line in the Seattle–Alaska service and the TMT ferry service between Miami and Puerto Rico. Because of its flexibility in serving smaller ports without adequate terminal facilities to handle demountable trailers and containers and its economy in short trades, the roll-on and roll-off system persists in some circumstances and has shown growth in intra-European operations.

But the introduction of the cellular ship by the Pan Atlantic Lines in coastwise service in the 50s prepared the way for the recent rapid expansion of container service. This ship, converted from a break-bulk vessel and using shipboard gantry cranes fore and aft, permitted placing of 220 trailer bodies four deep in 55 cells. In each cell the trailer bodies fitted neatly between corner posts like an elevator in its shaft. Rapid transfer between ship and open wharf was achieved by the gantries and, of course, a deckload of containers supplemented the below-deck load. By contrast, modern containerships carry from 700 to over 1,400 containers and utilize shoreside cranes for loading and discharge. Sealand Service entered the coastwise and then the intercoastal service in the late 50s, and Seatrain extended its service to accept containers as well as railcars. Matson Navigation Company

---

[8] Address of Andrew E. Gibson, U.S. Maritime Administration, before the National Foreign Trade Convention in New York, reported in *Container News*, June 1971, p. 24.

[9] Organization for Economic Co-operation and Development, *Maritime Transport, 1970*, pp. 15, 64; ibid., 1978, p. 66.

began containership service between the West Coast and Hawaii in 1958. Sealand Service, Inc., successor to Pan Atlantic, developed a very successful service between the ports of New York and Hampton Roads and Puerto Rico. The late 60s saw the extension of containership service to Western Europe, the Mediterranean, Asia, and Australia. New York and Rotterdam have become the preeminent container ports with Oakland, California, taking first rank on the U.S. Pacific coast. The year 1978 saw the establishment of container service between Australia and the Peoples Republic of China.

The growth of containership service is explained by the substantial benefits that flow from it. These include: (1) greatly expedited service, (2) reduced costs because of higher utilization of vessels and reduced labor costs ashore and aboard ship, (3) greatly reduced damage, (4) protection from pilferage, (5) reduced packing costs, (6) reduced ocean rates, (7) reduced insurance premiums, and (8) easier tracing of a shipment. Not all of these advantages have yet been realized in full potential measure. Problems include: (1) lack of standardization of equipment and methods of transfer; (2) inadequate port facilities, causing congestion and delay; (3) delay from customs and other government inspection procedures; (4) lack of arrangements for through billing and coordinate liability; and (5) lack of adequate control of the return of containers. Relatively, the economics of the service are greater for such shorter ocean hauls as are found in coastwise, Puerto Rican, and Hawaiian services where the advantage of rapid port turnaround is so pronounced. The service to Puerto Rico has been a great boon to its trade with the East Coast and, therefore, to its economy. Yet dissatisfaction with ocean freight rates continues and the government of Puerto Rico has taken over a large portion of the operation in a corporation of its ownership.

AIR MERCHANDISE SERVICE

Until the late 1930s airfreight took the form of express only. Thereafter air cargo service offered directly by the airlines provided transportation on passenger schedules at rates substantially below those charged for air express. Volume grew rapidly enough to require the scheduling of some all-cargo flights in the early 40s. All-cargo services are now carrying growing volumes of general-merchandise freight, and the 747, DC-10, and L1011, as they came into use generated a substantial increase in belly capacity. Growth rates approximating 20 percent per annum were achieved in the 60s, but 1974 and 1975 saw a temporary decline of volume. A rapid recovery occurred in 1975 but current expansion is restrained both by lagging growth in the economy and the sharp upward trend in air-cargo rates. Airfreight is expensive in relation to surface modes and will probably remain so. Air transport is particularly vulnerable to high fuel costs and to other inflationary impacts. Average ton-mile revenue held in the 20–24-cent range from 1950 to 1973 but has moved upward since at a rapid rate, reaching 37.1 cents in 1978. Deregulation of air cargo in that year was promptly followed by rate increases designed to allow more adequately for the inflation of cost than the Civil Aeronautics Board had previously permitted. While new aircraft are more fuel efficient, no major technological breakthrough is anticipated in the near term.

The merchandise services provided by air include air parcel post, parcel services offered by some trunk airlines and specialized carriers, and airfreight. Together they reach all parts of the United States and most principal foreign points. Air Cargo Inc. is a jointly owned subsidiary of the certificated airlines which serves as agent for the owning lines. It solicits freight and contracts with local motor-freight operators to perform pickup and delivery service. The several services offered the shippers include (1) airport-to-airport service, (2) an added pickup and delivery service, (3) a pickup without delivery or delivery without pickup, and (4) connecting truck service where the distance of pickup or delivery is extended to points distant from air terminals. The rates vary accordingly. Air rates for door-to-door service usually limit pickup and delivery to 25 miles from airports. Beyond this distance a motor carrier participates in joint or combination rates.

A unique parcel service was developed by Federal Express to provide overnight service between all principal points. Freight is gathered from all points and flown to a transfer facility at Memphis, Tennessee. There it is resorted and dispatched to destination. Emery, largest of the airfreight forwarders, has developed a competitive service. Traditionally an indirect air carrier, Emery has been forced to introduce aircraft operations of its own because the major lines, faced by excess belly capacity on daytime flights, reduced their overnight all-cargo operations.

Airfreight sets a new standard of speed of delivery of merchandise freight. It makes possible first-morning delivery between any two traffic centers in the United States. Long-distance shipments whose value, urgency of delivery, or perishability is such as to justify a high rate will provide an increasing traffic. The possible economic effect on inventory practices of manufacturers and merchants who use it should be substantial. Wastage from spoilage of flowers and choice fruits and vegetables may be eliminated, the saving in many instances being more than enough to cover air costs. The production and marketing patterns of many commodities may be greatly changed, providing a demonstration of the economical significance of speed in transport of the manufactured products of farm, mine, and factory. Rates are changing rapidly with fuel-cost escalation and, since airfreight deregulation, they differ among the several forwarders and airlines available on a route. A comparison of some of the rates available in April

1978 on a 50-pound package between New York and Los Angeles follows:

Airfreight forwarder	$59.02
Greyhound bus	43.00
Air cargo	40.33
United Parcel Service:	
Surface	14.85
Air	29.15
United States Postal Service	45.10

PARCEL TRANSPORTATION SERVICE

There are two principal intercity parcel services, namely, the Parcel Post Service of the U.S. Postal Service which in 1971, as a public corporation, replaced the 195-year old U.S. Post Office Department, and the United Parcel Service, a private corporation. The Parcel Post Service takes parcels up to 40 pounds, whereas, the United Parcel Service sets an upper limit of 50 pounds. Parcel post is nationwide, extending to every hamlet and home and place of business for delivery within the 50 states. Parcels must be delivered to a post office for sending. The United Parcel Service now also has nationwide operating authority. The service includes scheduled pickup and delivery, for business patrons, by motor equipment operated by the UPS in conjunction with its terminals. These terminals are highly automated for selecting, assembling, and dispatching of shipments by destination. Intercity movement is provided by special over-the-road equipment except that long-distance movement between the Eastern United States and the West Coast is by contract with airlines. The service has been excellent and profitable, providing the only really bright spot in dealing with the small shipments problem.

The United Parcel Service provides a prime example of the efficiency attainable by application of the principles stated in Chapter 6 on a level not previously employed. The key to success is limitation of dimensions and weight of parcels accepted in order to provide a homogeneity of traffic composition which permits automated sorting and handling in terminals, adaptation of vehicles to traffic, and simplified rates and billing. The use of areawide rather than route motor-carrier authority in I.C.C. certificates of public convenience and necessity and the avoidance of service in the more thinly populated areas also play a role.

CARRIER SERVICE IN DISTRIBUTION SYSTEMS

As producers and distributors of merchandise devise distribution systems in terms of modern business logistics, carriers are more and more called upon to provide scheduled deliveries. This requirement provides a new marketing target for carrier decisions in regard to service, rates, operations, and equipment. Whether or not a carrier works with a shipper in designing its distribution system, it should know what the system is and work with the shipper in its execution. Otherwise the traffic will likely go to another carrier or be transported by the shipper's own fleet of trucks, barges, or aircraft.

The receiver of manufactured goods wants his needs met with the minimum of inventory on his part. This requires the supplier to have a stock of goods located where delivery can be prompt and dependable. Whether the stock of goods for distribution is maintained at the plant or at a field warehouse, a shipper requires expedited and dependable door-to-door delivery. For less-than-carload shipments, motor-freight carriers can generally provide such a complete service. Other modes often require motortrucks to originate and deliver at both ends of a line-haul. Trailer-on-flatcar (TOFC) operations have enabled the railroads, in conjunction with motor carriers, to provide a coordinated scheduled service. Air and water carriers, like the railroads, now use containers or tractor-trailer bodies in a coordinated service to facilitate direct door-to-door service in both domestic and overseas service.

The distribution of products of most manufacturing industries involves two or more carrier movements. The finished product first moves either to a field warehouse, a public warehouse, or a chain or mail-order company's warehouse from which deliveries are made. Rail carriers may prevail in the first step, especially if the haul is a long one, while motor carriers prevail in the final step from warehouse to customer. In overseas service there will be a transfer at the seaboard from rail to ship or aircraft, but motor-freight carriers will likely make final delivery at destination.

In some instances the requirements may reasonably be met by establishing through routes and joint rates with other carriers. Schedules should be strictly maintained. But delays and divided responsibility at interchange points may dictate central control by merger, lease, or contract. Since interchange so frequently involves carriers of different modes, intermodal container service is often required to reduce transfer time to the minimum. Again, there should be central control to provide coordinated operations whether by contract, lease, or common ownership.

Because large shippers may obtain barges, ships, trucks, and planes to insure control of time and cost of delivery, the penalty to a for-hire carrier for delay in response to the demands of business logistics may be very great. The record of carrier management in meeting new needs is not encouraging. The lag in response led to third parties intervening in the shipper-carrier relationship. They have in the past included railway express companies, freight forwarders, carloading companies, and private car lines. In recent years the growth of private and exempt carriage has come to threaten the common and contract-carrier systems. The future of the common carrier as the base of our transportation system is at stake in their willingness and ability to meet the needs of modern business logistics.

SUMMARY AND A LOOK AHEAD

Distribution-freight service is an increasingly important part of freight service, the cost of which represents a large part of the national income. Except for the movement by carlot shipments moving from siding to siding on one railroad system, avoiding interchange delays, and the direct movement in trailer lots and piggyback service door-to-door without transfer of lading, distribution transportation presents an increasing problem in both service and cost.

A number of direct and indirect carriers are involved in the transportation of less-than-trailer-lot shipments. Wages for labor required for assembly, transfer, and breaking bulk go higher and higher; and the smaller the shipment the greater the penalty. The consolidation of carlot shipments by pool cars of one company, by freight forwarders, and by shippers' associations has proved very helpful in combining good service and moderate costs. Containerization in both domestic and foreign freight service has demonstrated notable possibilities. Finally, the United Parcel Service and, to a less degree, a number of semiautomated airline freight terminals at airports have demonstrated that automation of terminals and scheduled service offer much hope.

However, the small shipments problem is becoming more serious because small inventories held by dealers tend to push up the costs of this traffic and carriers' rates tend to rise more rapidly than for larger shipments. Billing costs are virtually the same for small as for large shipments, pickup stops cost nearly as much for a small as for a large shipment, and platform costs per 100 pounds are heavier for smaller than for larger shipments. Yet the traditional minimum charges designed to insure a base revenue fail to cover these costs which have been increasing out of proportion to the increase in line-haul costs. The efforts of motor carriers to cut their losses on the very small shipments by imposing arbitrary surcharges have been strongly resisted by shippers, such as mail-order houses and wholesalers, which have a large volume of such traffic. The competition of parcel post, air express and cargo, freight-forwarder service, motor-carrier service, and United Parcel Service is especially sharp in the area of small shipments. The dispersion of the traffic among so many agencies with the resulting duplication of pickup and delivery and terminal services results in inefficiency, inadequate standards of service, and high costs.

There is much to be done in terms of technology, organization in conducting transportation service, and removal of government constraints. Standardization of piggyback equipment and methods and of containers, ships, and port facilities to handle them have a long way to go. Joint rates and through routes are often lacking. In foreign container service, clearance and inspection procedures cause delays, through billing is often not available, harbor fees here and abroad are involved, cumbersome documentation prevails. These and lack of standardization all stand in the way of efficient merchandise service overseas. Until transport companies, free to use any combination of carrier equipment and service they may find useful, become commonplace, the freight forwarders may be expected to play a larger role in the solution of the problem of less-than-carlot and less-than-trailerlot shipments in the distribution process.[10]

SELECTED REFERENCES

Barriger, Forrest C.   *Freight Costs in the Smaller Business.* Sunnyvale, Calif.: Barr Co., 1963.

Brewer, Stanley H.   *The Utilization of Motor Common Carriers of General Freight in Distribution Patterns.* Seattle: University of Washington Press, 1957.

Constantin, James A.   *The Characteristics of Motor Freight Movements by General Commodity Carriers in Oklahoma.* Norman: Bureau of Business Research, University of Oklahoma, 1963.

Cushman, Frank M.   *Transportation for Management,* chap. 3. Englewood Cliffs, N.J.: Prentice-Hall, Inc., 1953.

Gifford, Gilbert L.   "The Small Shipment Problem." *Transportation Journal,* Fall 1970, pp. 17 ff.

King, Charles W.   "How Total Costs Affect Ratemaking." *Distribution Age,* December 1965, p. 25.

Lewis, H. T., and Culliton, J. T.   *The Role of Air Freight in Physical Distribution.* Boston: Harvard Business School, 1956.

Longman, Donald R., and Schiff, Michael. *Practical Distribution Cost Analysis.* Homewood, Ill.: Richard D. Irwin, Inc., 1955.

Oi, Walter Y., and Hurter, Arthur P., Jr. *Economics of Private Truck Transportation.* Dubuque, Ia.: Wm. C. Brown Co., 1965.

Railway Systems and Management Association. *Costs and Decision Making in Transportation.* Chicago, 1965.

---

[10] Of particular utility to many exporters is the nonvessal-operating common carrier (NVOCC) which also has domestic forwarder authority. Such a carrier may consolidate small shipments and forward to a foreign destination on a through bill of lading and single-carrier responsibility.

Roberts, Merrill J. *Economics of Consolidated Transport*. Pittsburgh, Pa.: University of Pittsburgh Press, 1967.

Ruppenthal, Carl M. *New Dimensions in Business Logistics*. Stanford: Stanford University, Graduate School of Business, 1963.

Schneider, Lewis M. *The Future of the U.S. Domestic Air Freight Industry: An Analysis of Management Strategies*. Boston: Harvard Business School, 1973.

Stephanson, Frederick, Jr. "The Night-Freighter Controversy." *Transportation Journal*, Summer 1976, pp. 15 ff.

Taff, Charles A. *Management of Physical Distribution and Transportation*. 6th ed. Homewood, Ill.: Richard D. Irwin, Inc., 1978.

Wein, Harold H. *Domestic Air Cargo: Its Prospects*. East Lansing: Michigan State University, 1962.

14

Inventory Management, Storage, and Materials Handling

FUNCTIONS ANCILLARY TO TRANSPORTATION

Our outline of systems of goods movement in Chapter 4 makes clear that despite the importance of transportation as the connective in the economic system, many related functions must be discharged in order that transportation can be carried on and its purposes achieved. We have just looked at transport services under two broad heads—those involved on the assembly side of the productive processes and those most directly associated with distribution of the resulting product to ultimate customers. Transportation, materials handling, and inventory holding and management enter into both sides of the total productive process. While empirical evidence is limited and of doubtful quality, it is generally accepted that the assembly and distribution process taken together account for some 20 percent of the gross national product. Distribution costs alone, from the end of the production line to the point of final sale (excluding markups of middlemen and retailers), amount to as much as 25 percent of net sales in such areas as foods and food products and primary and fabricated metals. Transportation is the largest single item in assembly and distribution costs and may account for as much as half of the total. But other elements which are closely related to transport and are the source of potential trade-offs which may contribute to a reduction of total cost, also are important.

Distribution of finished product is ordinarily a more complex process than assembly of raw materials and components for manufacture, although the latter may present challenging problems when hundreds of

FIGURE 14–1
Simple Distribution Handling Cycle

1. End of production line → packaging for shipment and palletizing → handling of materials to point of rest in factory warehouse.
2. Picking of items for outbound order → handling to tailgate of truck or gangway of railcar → stowing in line-haul vehicle.
3. Unloading inbound vehicles at distribution center → movement to assigned place of warehouse storage → stacking pallet loads.
4. Order picking → repalletizing broken pallet orders → movement to tailgate of outgoing truck → stowing in vehicle.
5. Adjustment of stock record and placing of reorder on factory.
6. Unloading at customer's premises → movement to work or storage space → breaking pallet loads → breaking cartons → placing in shelf or display space.

components must be brought together to nourish an assembly line as in the automotive and numerous other industries which supply consumers' or producers' durable goods. Many successive stages are involved before goods are displayed for ultimate sale. Figure 14–1 indicates the successive steps involved in handling a product through simple distribution channels that reach direct from manufacturer to retail outlet. With the exception of item 5, all of these steps involve the movement or manipulation of the goods. Except for item 5, all the clerical and record steps are omitted. Inventory is held at the factory, the distribution center, and the retail outlet. Distribution channels can be much longer than the one illustrated here and correspondingly more complex, costly, and time consuming.

Two successive transportation moves are involved here—from the plant to the distribution center and from the distribution center to the customer. Unless private transport is employed, there are interfaces between shipper (the manufacturing company) and carriers at the shipping dock of the plant, at the receiving dock of the distribution center, and at the shipping dock of the distribution center. There is an interface between the carrier and the retailer at the latter's receiving dock. Compatibility between carrier's equipment, dock design, and materials handling equipment is essential at each of these four interfaces if a low-cost, expeditious movement is to be secured. What applies to the physical handling of the goods applies also to the execution of necessary paper work.

THE FUNCTIONS OF STORAGE

The simple distribution system illustrated above revealed storage being carried out at manufacturing plant, distribution center, and customer's premises. The manufacturing plant would also maintain stocks

of raw materials and components and, quite possibly, of partly manufactured items (goods in process) between each of several stages of
production. In the aggregate considerable capital would be tied up in
inventory held at these numerous successive stages. Moreover, each
instance of holding stock requires materials handling to place goods
into stock and, subsequently, remove them from stock. Each also requires a system of records and control. The costs of manipulating and
holding inventory are sufficient so that inventory levels are under increasingly rigorous scrutiny. Storage is, however, an indispensable
element in the productive and distributive systems for a variety of
reasons. These have been briefly noticed in Chapter 4.

Storage designed to spread a supply seasonally produced over the
year frequently involves successive storage at points along the channels of movement which connect sources and markets. Grain is a good
example. The initial surge of the harvest is absorbed by the country
elevators spotted throughout the growing areas. Their limited capacity
is quickly plugged, however, unless prompt movement can be secured
to the larger terminal elevators at central market points which provide
major holding capacity. Thence movement is made to milling centers
and into export position. Terminal elevators at ports serve primarily to
adjust the inbound flow from railcars, barges, and trucks to the outbound movement of full ship cargoes. Where receipt is by the trainload
of, say, 5,000 tons, and vessels of up to 100,000 tons are to be loaded
outbound, the accumulation of cargoes becomes a major function.
Storage capacities both at milling centers and ports, however, assist in
the spread of seasonal supply. Excess production in relation to the
capacity of the transport and storage system to absorb it will lead to
storage on the farm, including temporary ground storage.

Facilities employed in such a system are provided by various institutions—elevator companies, grain-marketing organizations, port
authorities, and carriers. In the lake grain trade, major storage
facilities are provided by the railroads which serve not only to assist in
coping with seasonal production but also to carry grain over the winter
when lake transportation is halted. In similar fashion railroads customarily provide storage at lower lake ports for iron ore destined to
interior mills and feed it inland during the period of interrupted navigation.

When seasonal markets are encountered and a compromise is
made between relatively even production over time and a buildup of
stocks against the peak selling period, the responsibility for carrying
stock may be shared between the manufacturer and distributors, but
its locus is primarily a consequence of relative bargaining power in
relation to the market. In view of the wide stock fluctuations involved,
public warehousing may have a significant cost advantage for a large
part of the function since it permits avoidance of investment in

warehouse facilities whose occupancy will be low during a significant part of the year.

In the adjustment of production to sale, temporary storage as an incident to transportation may play an important role. Fruit and vegetables, lumber, and other products are not infrequently shipped toward likely market areas prior to sale. Diversion and reconsignment, temporary interruption of movement for track storage on cars, and the selection of slow or fast routings as occasion may demand can assist the process of placing products in the most advantageous markets while affording time to effect sale without holding at the point of production.

Continuous process manufacturing, such as petroleum refining, can adjust output to changing demand rates (seasonal or cyclical) by altering the rate of operations. Where multiple-plant systems are involved or individual plants contain multiple units for performing one or more of the processing stages, the shutdown of less efficient units is another possible response. Costs are characteristically associated with these production alternatives. Storage to take up output when demand is lagging is a complete or partial alternative to adjusting the operating rate of the manufacturing facility. Costs attach, also, to this alternative; hence a weighing of the possibilities in search of a least-cost combination is appropriate.

Noncontinuous production encounters the problem of economical lot size. Setup costs are involved in shifting a production line from one product to another. Downtime is encountered while equipment is cleaned, machine tools are adjusted, and other necessary changes are accomplished. These costs are minimized per unit of output the longer the production run that is undertaken.[1] The conventional approach would seek to minimize manufacturing cost. But production in excess of the rate at which sales of the product are accomplished requires inventory carrying which ties up space and capital, requires custodial services, may result in a tax liability, and runs the risk of product obsolescence. These costs must be weighed against the unit-manufacturing economies to determine economical lot size. While the economic order quantity model is frequently used, it fails to take account of the effect of frequent line changes on annual productive capacity.[2]

In all of the instances thus far described, *storage,* the holding of

---

[1] See John F. Magee, *Industrial Logistics: Analysis and Management of Physical Supply and Distribution Systems* (New York: McGraw-Hill Book Co., 1968), p. 174, on costs related to quantity. On scheduling and its relation to inventory control, see J. L. Heskett, Robert M. Ivie, and Nicholas A. Glaskowsky, Jr., *Business Logistics* (New York: The Ronald Press Co., 1964), chap. 12.

[2] For an alternative formulation see John E. Bishop, "Integrating Critical Elements of Production Planning," *Harvard Business Review*, September–October 1979, pp. 154 ff.

goods over time, is the function that is employed to balance production with sale when the timing of the two functions differs. Storage is also employed for speculative purposes, especially in the commodity markets where price changes may be anticipated and storage costs can be offset against price gains. Routine inventory control, however, employs inventory in a distribution system primarily to deal with two kinds of uncertainty: (1) imperfections in synchronization of successive stages of operation, including transportation; and (2) inaccuracy of demand forecasting. In these situations inventory serves a balancing function as does storage in the cases discussed above, but it partakes heavily of the nature of insurance of effective performance at the customer end of the distributive process.

INVENTORY MANAGEMENT: KEY TO DISTRIBUTIVE EFFICIENCY

In the past, transportation and warehousing were commonly looked upon as sources of cost—unavoidable but necessary functions, hence to be accomplished at lowest possible cost. Realization has grown, however, that the distribution service which a company is capable of rendering is an element in its marketing mix—an asset which can be employed to expand the territorial reach of the market and to improve market share in each market segment serviced. Quality of distribution service is important; hence cost is to be weighed against the marketing purpose that can be accomplished. Performance of the system is to be measured, not merely cost. And since cost is often inversely related to the quality of service rendered by a distribution system, desirable service standards must be determined and a system designed to provide them at minimum cost.

Two major sets of influences, product proliferation and reluctance to hold inventory, have tended strongly to reshape attitudes toward distribution in the period since 1950. The first applies especially in consumer goods industries; the second potentially affects all industries which market out of stock rather than manufacturing to order. The grocery, drug, and appliance trades are the best examples of the first and represent the industries in which the earliest major efforts were made to examine and reform distribution practices. Both influences were strengthened by the growth in size and complexity of manufacturing and retailing organizations: the manufacturers continually taking on new lines of product, often by acquisition of established firms, and frequently resorting to divisionalized manufacturing and selling organizations; the retail chains expanding their market coverage, broadening product lines, shifting into larger stores, and developing more sophisticated control of their selling space.

Competition for shelf space became the order of the day. Retail outlets provided display, but the selling functions shifted in larger part to the manufacturers. Packaging had to become a selling tool in order to attract the attention of prospective customers when accorded shelf space. Advertising had to be designed to pull the product through the retail establishment by leading customers to urge retailers to stock it. Turnover was the key to access to shelf space without which sales could not be achieved. Product shelf-life shortened, and product obsolescence came at a faster pace. Contemporaneously retailers, faced with small and declining margins, became less and less willing to back up shelf display with inventory held in their stores or warehouses. Store managers were evaluated on their profit performance, and that depended in very large part on turnover in relation to space used. The old method of periodic order taking with shipment a week or ten days later on an unpredictable cycle became inadequate to the task.

Business had long worked with comfortable inventory levels. Early in the 50s stock levels of 30 days and more were not uncommon in manufacturer's warehouses. Stock levels had not been adjusted to the capabilities of transport which could resupply in five days or less and large savings in inventory cost could be made by such adjustments.

Growing competitive pressures and the cost-price squeeze corresponded in the 50s with a belief—inaccurate as it turned out—that economies in production had been exhausted. Many managements turned their attention for the first time toward distribution as a "last frontier" for cost cutting and began to restructure their organizations in the search for increased efficiency in product distribution. The move happened to coincide in timing with the development of methods capable of providing better control of operations and improved coordination between production and distribution. Electronic data processing, computer capability, and analytic programs for examining inventory policies, warehouse locations, and other functions came into being within a comparatively short space in time. As reform of distribution processes got under way, the original cost-cutting objectives were often superseded by more positive approaches which took account of the possibilities for enhancing sales volume and improving market share. Price policy is capable of being met quickly by competitors. Product development and the creation of efficient distribution systems require both time and money and are not capable of being countered with equal dispatch.

These developments have put pressure on traditional channels of distribution. The tendency has been to shorten the chain between manufacturer and customer by establishing more direct channels which increasingly eliminate the wholesaler and jobber. Thus some of the older marketing institutions become partly obsolete, and the number of interfaces between independent business establishments is reduced. Control of distribution comes increasingly into the hands of the manufacturer, and he is placed in position to manage inventory in a way to assure desired levels of customer service.

COMPONENTS OF THE DISTRIBUTION SYSTEM

Especially in large multiple-product firms marketing nationwide or, indeed, on a multinational basis, physical distribution is a complex function. We can do no more in this introductory treatment than to note certain of the more critical elements and relationships embraced within the function.[3] Those elements include: (1) the points of production, (2) the points at which inventory will be held in the market area, (3) the transportation services connecting these and tying inventory centers to customers, (4) the production scheduling and inventory policies to be applied, and (5) the information system which guides and controls performance. In the short run all of these must be taken as fixed elements in the operation of the system. Over time all can be changed, some more quickly and at less cost than others. System planning contemplates such changes and involves both structure (design) and performance.

The process may be viewed as starting with a marketing plan and with sales forecasts based upon that plan by product and by market area. This defines the amount of product that must be supplied and the timing and location of delivery in broad terms. Production scheduling follows in order to provide a flow of each item in the product line to replenish inventory as sales to final customers occur during the forecast period. When multiple manufacturing plants are involved in the system and where two or more of those plants are capable of producing the same product, the transportation model (a form of linear programming) may be used to assign production quantities to each plant. Production costs must be known as well as the behavior of costs with changes in volume of output. Likewise transport costs from each plant to each warehouse in the system must be specified. Given an appropriate rate of production at the plants, an inventory model can be used for each market-oriented warehouse (or distribution center) to govern the flow of product between the plants and the warehouse.

As we noted in Chapter 4, warehouses stand astride the channels of distribution between factory and customer in order that product may be moved in quantities (often straight carloads) that insure economical transportation between the plant and a point convenient to the cus-

---

[3] The pioneering text on the subject appeared in 1961. Since then a formidable literature has developed part of which is noted in the selected references appended to this chapter and to Chapter 4.

FIGURE 14-2
Warehouse Inventory Level

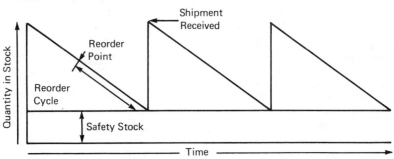

tomer and in order that stock may be available close to the customer to provide, say, overnight delivery of orders. An inventory policy is designed to insure an acceptable ability to fill customer's orders as they arrive while holding to a minimum the costs of inventory carrying, warehousing, transportation, and reordering against the factory. Hence an inventory system must insure supply for customer orders which vary in rate over time, while utilizing economical reorder quantities, the latter determined in principal part by the cost of placing an order on the factory and the transport cost associated with various sizes of shipment. With a constant rate of sale from the warehouse, the process will look like that shown in Figure 14-2. This illustrates the principle of inventory models, but linear rates of sale are rarely encountered in practice and actual reorder performance is not a constant either. Likewise forecasts are more or less inaccurate and the timing of actual sales can be expected to differ from forecast timing.[4]

Safety and buffer stocks are introduced in order to insure against these variations. Safety stock acts as a buffer to provide for unusual concentration of demand in time or slower response to a reorder than is normally expected. If the reorder cycle is 14 days (time elapsed from triggering an order on the factory until actual receipt and placement of the goods within the warehouse stock), then the reorder should be placed 14 days in advance of prospective stock exhaustion. What is the probability, however, that sales will exceed the normal or forecast rate during those 14 days and by how much? Past experience may provide a guide which enables a schedule of probabilities to be drawn up. The carrying of stock is costly, both in terms of capital tied up and space required; hence safety stock is not designed to provide absolute assurance of ability to supply. A policy decision must be made which bal-

---

[4] Forecasts of aggregate sales are likely to be more accurate than forecasts for the sale of an individual product in a particular market area. It is the latter that is significant for inventory policy.

ances the cost of safety stock against the loss of sales which an out-of-stock situation may precipitate.

The cost to a firm's market position which poor inventory management may generate has only recently been subjected to investigation. Where the customer is the retail store, retaliation can be expected when deliveries are late. It may take the form of delisting the product, refusing shelf space to new products, or refusing to participate in the manufacturer's planned promotions. In one study a four-day out of stock at the warehouse was found to result in 25 percent of the stores going out of stock. Both the cost of lost sales and of retailers' retaliation could be calculated and set against the costs of a more liberal inventory policy.[5]

Note was taken in Chapter 10 of the importance of reliability in transportation service. We shall see in Chapter 15 that a lack of quality control has been characteristic of freight service, especially in the railroad industry, and that variation in delivery time is the rule rather than the exception. One important reason for instituting private transport operations is the inability to secure desired reliability in delivery times from commercial carriers.

The reorder cycle is made up of the time required to prepare and transmit an order to the factory, the time required at the factory to assemble and load the goods called for in the order, the transit time from factory to warehouse, and the time required to unload and move the goods into stock position at the warehouse and update warehouse records. All elements except transit time are within control of the shipper. A sample study of carload movements disclosed that 35 percent required more than the median time for delivery, 3 percent being more than five days late. The possibility exists, therefore, that in a given case the actual reorder cycle may not be 14 days but 19 days or more. Without a buffer there is a good chance that the warehouse may be out of stock and that in order to provide minimum customer satisfaction, recourse may be had to expensive small shipments direct from factory to customer or from more remote warehouse stocks. On relatively high-value products the gross safety stock cost *per carload* may escalate at the rate of $10 per day of delay beyond median transit time.[6] In a large distribution operation it may become prohibitively expensive to insure against transit variability by buffer stock and it may be preferable to use a different transport mode even though at higher transport cost. This is the basis for the "planned emergency" in which air cargo is used to avoid the necessity for excessive stock levels.

---

[5] Harvey N. Shycon and Christopher R. Sprague, "Put a Price Tag on Your Customer Servicing Levels," *Harvard Business Review*, July–August 1975, pp. 71 ff.

[6] See Don P. Ainsworth, "Implications of Inconsistent Railroad Service," in Transportation Research Forum, *Proceedings, Thirteenth Annual Meeting (1972)*, pp. 498 ff.

It is plain that the reorder cycle is critical in determining stock levels required; hence also in determining the efficiency of the distribution system. If the cycle can be cut, stock levels and cost can be reduced without detriment to customer service. An important key to that objective is found in high-speed data processing and communications. The time-honored method in many businesses was to have salesmen call on customers at regular intervals, take orders, and mail them to the central office for processing and credit check, after which they would be mailed to the appropriate warehouse. Ten-days elapsed time was not unusual before a warehouse could ship. Warehouse reorders were similarly mailed to the factory. Under these circumstances more time was often involved in paper preparation and flow than in the actual movement of the goods once the shipping order became available.

The problem of slow order response was tackled from both ends. The distribution center concept made the warehouse in each market area not only the holder of a company's complete product line in stock even when produced in several geographically separated plants but also the locus of customer service. Each customer was assigned to a particular distribution center. Customer orders went there direct, and all processing including credit check was performed there. Thus the delivery cycle was considerably reduced. The computer was called upon to provide continuously updated stock records, and programmed to respond to the reorder quantity for each stock item by writing an order on the appropriate factory for wire transmission, thus providing close to instantaneous reorder on the factory. Electronic data processing plus high-speed communications have probably contributed more to reducing the reorder cycle than any improvements in transportation. But, as we shall see, order picking and material-handling processes have also been speeded materially. As communications are improved, the system moves closer to a real-time basis, buffer stocks are reduced, and the problem of forecasting demand is minimized.[7] In these circumstances unreliable transportation stands out like a sore thumb and rouses a shipper's ire.

DESIGN OF DISTRIBUTION SYSTEMS

In the light of the principles suggested in Chapter 4, the efficiency of a distribution system depends heavily upon the number and location of warehouses spotted in market areas and the transport linkages employed. Hence they are primary elements in the design of a distribution system. Efficiency must finally be measured, however, as cost per

---

[7] In short-period forecasting, exponential smoothing of recent actual stock disappearance may replace the judgmental methods required for longer time horizons.

sales dollar in relation to a standard of customer service, for example, 85 percent of customers receive goods within three days of order 90 percent of the time. Sight should not be lost of the fact that the standard of service provided will have an impact on sales volume, hence on profit potential.[8] Standards of customer service are not necessarily uniform over a nationwide market but will tend to be less exacting in the more lightly populated areas depending upon the character of competition encountered from other suppliers. Design commences, then, with a standard of customer service that in relation to competitors' activities serves the marketing purpose. The problem becomes at the outset one of determining the minimum number of warehouses that will provide that service and their locations.

Two major principles govern the solution of this problem: (1) concentration of inventory at a minimum number of locations reduces total stock required, hence inventory cost; and (2) warehousing as close as possible to each customer minimizes the small-shipment transport cost of delivering to him. Clearly these two principles are opposed and must be compromised—inventory cost traded off against transport cost with a view to minimize total cost. Whereas in earlier times it was not uncommon for large national distributors of consumer products and various types of industrial goods sold off the shelf to employ 100 or even 200 or more warehouses to cover their markets, the recent trend has been to reshape such distribution systems drastically. From 4 to 12 distribution centers are often found to be capable of providing satisfactory service to the great majority of customers.[9] Figure 14-3 suggests that the minimum cost point is somewhere in this area.

If customer service capability is to be squared with cost, the choice of location for each distribution center in the system is of obvious importance. The locational decision is usually founded upon a market analysis which provides a picture of the geographic distribution of sales. From that, prospective market areas for each distribution center can be blocked out on the basis of transit times characteristically available from the carriers. If short-line distances are used as a proxy for transport cost, a mathematical determination of optimal warehouse location within the market area can be secured. Since actual freight rates depart considerably from short-line distance relationships, this involves a good deal of simplification. But it can inform the search for an actual workable location—one at a major transport hub with good rail and highway access and competitive service by both transport modes. The available locational models have cost minimization as

---

[8] For an argument on *profitable* distribution see Richard F. Poist, "The Total Cost vs. Total Profit Approach to Logistics System Design, " *Transportation Journal*, Fall 1974, pp. 13 ff.

[9] The spread of comprehensive motor-carrier service has had much to do with this development.

FIGURE 14-3
Transportation, Inventory, and Total Costs

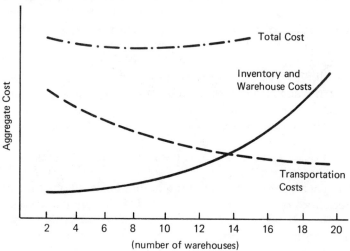

their objective. Yet we have emphasized the importance of customer service as a sales-building tool; and the object of distribution system design should, of course, be maximum contribution to profit. James Heskett has suggested that a time-oriented model, tailored to the peculiarities of each firm, may become a more appropriate tool than those which are now available.[10]

Simulation, utilizing computer capability, can be a powerful tool for comparing alternative plans for a distribution system. A simulation program does not, however, develop the alternatives to be compared; neither does it optimize. Its virtue is the ability to run through, say, a year's sales a large number of times on different assumptions with great speed and print out comparative results. As compared with this capability, the design and calibration of a simulation model to cope with a complex system is both costly and time consuming. Like other sophisticated techniques in business analysis, it is not to be recommended unless the program to be studied is of large scale and continuing usefulness can be foreseen, for the number of variables that must be examined is very large even in a moderate-sized business operation. Moreover, some of them, including a few that are critical to the results, are difficult to quantify, for example, market strategy, employee motivation, and customer service requirements.[11] A model

[10] James L. Heskett, "A Missing Link in Physical Distribution Design," in Donald J. Bowersox, Bernard J. LaLonde, and Edward W. Smykay, *Readings in Physical Distribution Management: The Logistics of Marketing* (New York: Macmillan Co., 1969), chap. 14.

[11] For a brief account of the technique and its application, see George A. Steiner, *Top Management Planning* (New York: Macmillan Co., 1969), pp. 440-51.

capable of adaptation to a variety of distribution circumstances has, nevertheless, been developed.[12]

THE REVOLUTION IN WAREHOUSING AND TERMINALS

Since World War II there has been a veritable revolution in the design and operation of warehouses and terminals. The emphasis has shifted from a concept of indefinite storage to accomplish appropriate adjustment of inflow and outflow to one of maintaining fluidity through the terminals and through the warehouses. This revolution has been largely the result of rapidly mounting labor costs involved in handling the goods at warehouses and terminals. Also, producers and merchants both have desired to decrease inventory costs and risks. Finally, those who receive the goods have been more insistent upon prompt and dependable delivery. New service standards have come into existence.

To deal with higher labor costs it has been necessary to change the design and operation of warehouses and terminals so as to make effective use of improved materials-handling equipment, such as lift trucks, conveyor belts, and tractor-trailer operations. There is little similarity between the modern warehouse and that of prewar which, for centuries before, reflected the fact that a warehouse was considered to be a place for storage for indefinite periods of time without regard for labor and handling costs. It was, accordingly, a multistory structure to maximize utilization of the space required for the building, with small elevators which accommodated one or two hand trucks, and with low ceilings on each floor. Before the days of lift trucks when freight had to be handled and stored by hand, it was not practical to have high piling of goods on any given floor. By contrast, the modern warehouse is normally a one-story structure with a high ceiling permitting the stacking of pallet loads, providing adequate aisle space and facilities for transfer to and from the warehouse platforms, and with wide door openings and smooth floors for the operation of modern materials-handling equipment. It reflects the new concept of a warehouse as a distribution facility adapted to rapid turnover of inventory and the maintenance of flow in the market.

CATEGORIES OF WAREHOUSES

Open storage is standard for coal, ores, and lumber, and for heavy machinery and equipment at dockside in seaports and elsewhere.

---

[12] See Donald J. Bowersox, *Dynamic Simulation of Distribution Systems* (East Lansing: Division of Research, Graduate School of Business Administration, Michigan State University, 1972).

Otherwise, the function of storage generally involves warehouses. Industry-owned warehouses which are adapted to the product line which the industry produces have come to dominate the warehouse business, but the public warehouse is still important and is adapting its service offering to changes in distribution practices.

Warehouses may be classified in terms of goods handled as (1) cooler and cold storage, (2) household goods, (3) general merchandise, or (4) special product warehouses. Unless an industry or commercial establishment has sufficient volume to justify its own warehouses, it will generally call upon the public warehouse to provide services. Public warehouses are usually located in the general vicinity of important metropolitan areas. As the term implies, the public warehouseman serves a number of customers and has full responsibility for operation of his facility. An alternative to the industry-owned warehouse and the public warehouse is the leasing of warehouse space by an industry which permits it to have exclusive use of a portion of the warehouse. These rented areas are sometimes referred to as field warehouses. Warehouses may also be classified according to the nature of the commodities which they handle. Most warehouses may be termed as general merchandise warehouses. In port cities they may be bonded warehouses, which means that the importers may place goods in these warehouses under bond and avoid paying duty unless and until they sell the merchandise within the country. In case the goods are reexported, no duty is paid. In addition, there are specialized storage facilities, such as grain elevators, cement silos, and other bulk storage facilities for basic materials which must be protected from the weather.

WAREHOUSE EQUIPMENT

Economy in the operation of warehouses depends largely upon (1) location, (2) design and layout, and (3) mobile equipment. The controlling factor in the design and location of warehouses is providing an efficient environment for the operation of modern mobile equipment. This equipment includes conveyor belt facilities, tractors, and the ever-present lift truck. Only by the high-speed operation of modern equipment in a single-story warehouse can labor costs be kept down. It was the development of the lift truck operating on smooth floors that made modern warehouses economical. The small lift platform, known as the pallet, which usually is four-feet-by-four-feet or four-feet-by-six-feet has come into general use for stacking goods.[13] Lift trucks come

---

[13] Slip sheets are sometimes used in place of pallets, and fork trucks can be adjusted to handle them. One form of lift truck will grip the load, requiring neither pallet nor slip sheet.

in various varieties as to design, size, and power to meet the requirements of the kinds of loads to be handled and the height required to
stack pallets.

Because of their advance in capacity and speed, lift trucks have
tended to take the place of earlier operations conducted by small
gasoline tractors hauling a train of flat trailers. It is entirely possible
that the increasing use of conveyor belts will replace the lift truck in
many operations. An important development in loading facilities at
plants and warehouses has been the automated assembly of pallet
loads which generally requires a system of conveyor belts. Some of the
more important airfreight terminals at principal airports make wide
use of conveyor belts for the distribution of freight received to facilitate
assembly for various destinations and for the movement of the freight
from the specific locations to the loading dock of the airport. The drag
line, either overhead or beneath the floor, has been a feature of most of
the larger modern motor-carrier terminals.[14]

As labor costs have mounted—each warehouseman now costing
from $18,000 to $25,000 a year including fringes—the cost of machinery
for the automation of materials handling has declined. Hence the
trade-off of investment for labor becomes more attractive. Automated
operations have become possible for certain kinds of goods, embracing computer-controlled routing over a conveyor system to selected
points of storage. Since order picking is one of the more costly
warehouse operations, automatic retrieval from stock can be important
to efficiency. One such installation in a General Motors plant has eight
levels of gravity-storage lanes. Each day it moves some 16,000 boxes of
700 different automotive parts which were formerly handpicked from
bins and loaded on hand trucks. Manpower requirements have been
reduced by 70 percent, and the former accumulation of back orders
has been eliminated.[15]

The same principle is used in many air-cargo terminals where storage of cargo is required prior or subsequent to line-haul movement.
Automatic sorting is also an important key to the efficiency of United
Parcel terminal operations where the size and weight limitations imposed by the carrier produce a sufficient homogeneity in packages to
permit its application. Automated-warehouse or terminal facilities,
however, involve heavy investment. They lack the flexibility of conventional operations. Hence care should be taken to insure that the
pattern of traffic which they are designed to handle is likely to continue

---

[14] The degree to which man-hour productivity is increased by this device is questionable. In addition, productivity shows little improvement after a terminal exceeds 20,000
square feet of dock area, presumably because average hauling distance increases with
terminal size. See D. Daryl Wycoff, "How Management Terminal Decisions Can Influence Motor Carrier Productivity," *Traffic World*, November 13, 1972, pp. 90 ff.

[15] *Business Week*, September 9, 1972, pp. 92–93.

at the location in question for a considerable period of time, at least sufficient to permit amortization of first cost.

Warehouse costing presents some of the elements we have already noted in connection with transportation costing. Fixed costs are present, associated with the space occupied (whether owned or leased). Overhead costs associated with management and operations are, in principal part, common costs. Direct operating costs are often assignable to particular products handled. Whether simulation or less formidable techniques are to be employed in the analysis of warehouse operations or the design of distribution networks, appropriate cost functions must be developed which will reflect the response of cost to volume of throughput. Average costs per unit handled may be useful in comparing operations of one period with another or of one facility with others, but they are of little use in systems design.

Certain features of cost behavior are worth noting, however. Order-processing costs are practically independent of the size of the order. Broken case lots ordered by customers generate the highest handling costs in relation to volume. Case lots impose a smaller penalty, but require the breaking of pallet loads in which goods are customarily received and stored. The advantage of being able to sell in complete pallet loads is, therefore, clear. And the importance of order size in relation to distribution operations is present in the warehouse as well as in transportation.

ADAPTATIONS OF PUBLIC WAREHOUSING

As distribution methods have changed, the more progressive public warehousemen have moved to modify and expand their services. Several nationwide networks have come into existence which permit the servicing of a manufacturer's entire market by a single public warehouse organization. Modern public warehouse operations are equipped to service the manufacturer's customers, picking and assembling orders, maintaining inventory records, and placing reorders on the factory. Such services are even offered in the export markets by some of the foreign freight forwarders which will process customer orders from overseas, fill those orders out of portside stocks, and reorder against the supplier. In performing these functions the warehouseman or forwarder acts as the agent of the manufacturer and substitutes his facilities and services for the manufacturer's own distribution center.[16]

---

[16] Walter F. Friedman, "Physical Distribution: The Concept of Shared Services," *Harvard Business Review*, March–April 1975, pp. 24 ff.

Transloading services are provided by carriers to enable full vehicle loads to be broken into several smaller shipments for diverse destinations. Warehousemen may perform similar break-bulk functions. These operations are the reverse of the manufacturers effort to minimize transport cost by arranging pool cars in which shipments representing several product lines or several divisions of a decentralized company are married to take advantage of the lowest carload rates or of incentive minimum weights. In some instances, notably in the drug and cosmetic trades, specialized public warehousemen receive branded products from a number of manufacturers, maintain stocks, and fill orders from retail stores with a mixture of products sought by the retailer. Substantial economies are realized in making deliveries to the stores when all products, no matter who their manufacturer, can be combined in a single delivery. These operations are to be distinguished from those of wholesalers since they do not carry stock for their own account nor undertake the selling function. There appears to be some revival of the jobber for the same purpose of joining distribution of several brands of like products.

The variety of methods and devices available to the distribution manager is continually broadening. Hence his opportunities to improve the efficiency of his function are growing. At the same time the complexity of the task is enhanced and the stature of distribution management grows. Rapid increase of cost and high rates of interest during a period of double-digit inflation enhance the concern of management for effective conduct of the function. Problems of organization and of relationship to the other functional areas of business will be noticed in Chapter 18.

SELECTED REFERENCES

Ackerman, Kenneth B.; Gardner, R. W.; and Thomas, Lee P. *Understanding Today's Distribution Center.* Washington, D.C.: The Traffic Service Corp., 1972.

Attwood, Peter R. *Planning a Distribution System.* London: Gower Press, 1971.

Ballou, Ronald H. *Business Logistics Management.* Englewood Cliffs, N.J.: Prentice-Hall, Inc., 1972.

Bowersox, Donald J. *Food Distribution Center Location Technique and Procedure.* Marketing and Transportation Paper No. 12. East Lansing: Bureau of Business and Economic Research, Michigan State University.

———. *Logistical Management.* New York: Macmillan Publishing Co., Inc., 1974.

———; Smykay, Edward W.; and LaLonde, Bernard J. *Physical Distribution*

Management: Logistics Problems of the Firm. New York: Macmillan Co., 1968.

Briggs, Andrew J. *Warehouse Operations, Planning and Management.* New York: John Wiley & Sons, Inc., 1960.

Enrick, Norbert Lloyd. *Inventory Management: Installation, Operation and Control.* San Francisco: Chandler Publishing Co., 1968.

Frederick, John H. *Using Public Warehouses.* Homewood, Ill.: Richard D. Irwin, Inc., 1957.

Jenkins, Creed H. *Modern Warehouse Management.* New York: McGraw-Hill Book Co., 1968.

Magee, John F. *Production Planning and Inventory Control.* New York: McGraw-Hill Book Co., 1958.

————. *Industrial Logistics: Analysis and Management of Physical Supply and Distribution Systems.* New York: McGraw-Hill Book Co., 1968.

Marlow, W. H., ed. *Modern Trends in Logistics Research.* Cambridge: M.I.T. Press, 1976.

Schiff, Michael. *Accounting and Control in Physical Distribution Management.* Chicago: National Council of Physical Distribution Management, 1972.

Smykay, Edward W. *Physical Distribution Management.* 3d ed. New York: Macmillan Publishing Co., Inc., 1973.

Starr, Martin K., and Miller, David W. *Inventory Control: Theory and Practice.* Englewood Cliffs, N.J.: Prentice-Hall, Inc., 1962.

Taff, Charles A. *Management of Physical Distribution and Transportation.* 6th ed. Homewood, Ill.: Richard D. Irwin, Inc., 1978.

15

Management, Labor, and the Efficiency of Carrier Operations

Despite the considerable extent to which many firms rely upon private transport for a part of their requirements, commerce and industry are heavily dependent upon commercial carriers for most of the freight and long-haul passenger transport which they need. The efficiency with which these services are performed is, therefore, of large consequence to industry since it affects the level of rates they must pay, the quality of delivery services which they can render to customers, and the availability of service when required. With transport making up so large a part of the gross national product, its efficiency is also of concern to the nation because of its repercussions upon the nation's economic health. Inadequate transportation can impede the growth of the economy. Inefficient conduct of the service can tax the nation by diverting resources from other segments of production.

The quality of management is critical in transport as in all economic enterprise. While government policy can create conditions favorable to or restrictive of management performance, only the respective carrier managements are in direct control of operations, finance, marketing, and the other customary management functions. One of the reasons for the recurrence of proposals over the last 30 years for the relaxation of regulation is to generate greater freedom for management performance and an environment better calculated to stimulate innovative management. The management texts counsel an identification of external constraints and the maximization of a firm's performance within those constraints. Yet the best management talent—and good management is a scarce resource—does not go into industries where important areas of policy are beyond the control of the firm. The very importance of the transport industries and the fact that there seem to have been major problems within those industries over most of their history has resulted in continuing criticism of transport management.

We cannot hope in a single chapter to probe the area thoroughly, but we can touch upon some of its more important elements.

DIFFERENTIAL CARRIER PERFORMANCE

Motor carriers can be found with operating ratios in the low 80s, others with ratios above 100. Major eastern railroads moved into bankruptcy in the early 1970s while some of the large southern and western roads were showing results as good as or better than at any time in their history. Some large airlines generated heavy losses, while others continued to show highly profitable operations. These conditions were not peculiar to the 1970s—they had occurred many times previously. Differences in performance of this sort are often attributed to differences in management quality. Yet no two transport enterprises are alike; hence the appraisal of management by intercarrier comparisons is difficult and perilous. We shall see some of the reasons why this is so.

Location and Route Pattern

Railroad plant is fixed in location. A line of railroad cannot be picked up and placed somewhere else where traffic opportunities are greater. Except for terminals, the plant of motor, water, and air carriers is principally composed of moving equipment. Yet regulated carriers of these types are institutionally constrained—their certificates prescribe the points and routes they may serve and the kind of service that may be rendered. The regulatory authorities also affect the amount and vigor of the competition to which they may be subjected.[1] The market for the services of a particular carrier depends, therefore, upon the economic activity in the area which it serves—both the level and kind of activity—and is affected by shifts in that activity. Changes can be adjusted to only slowly, expensively, and with difficulty, for both route extensions and service abandonments require government approval and lack of profit does not necessarily indicate that public need for a service has disappeared.[2]

---

[1] Thus United Air Lines saw its Hawaiian operations turned from a $14 million annual profit to a deficit of $17 million in 1971 as a result of opening the route to five new competitors in CAB's transpacific route awards of 1969. (*Fortune*, March 1972, p. 73.) Whether United could have done more to influence the result is unclear.

[2] Airline deregulation in 1978 produced important changes in that industry, the results of which cannot yet be appraised. But many carriers were able to extend their route patterns easily by picking dormant rights. The CAB has expanded its certifications on international routes and airlines will be able to add new route segments without certification proceedings. Total discontinuance of service is still somewhat restrained until substitute service can be arranged.

The differential performance of railroads is a good case in point. The rail industry as a whole has experienced a declining share in the nation's freight and passenger traffic since the 1920s, except for the interruption of the trend during World War II. The nation's economic growth has been much more rapid in the South and Southwest than in the Northeast. The center of heavy industry, the type which produces freight traffic for which railroads are best adapted, has been shifting westward. Industrial growth in the Northeast has been largely in research-oriented and light industry which is productive of little rail business. Hence rail freight traffic has declined in the Northeast while it has grown in the South and West—the thrust of economic growth was powerful enough there to more than offset the decline in rail market share.[3] Eastern roads have faced other burdens in greater measure than roads elsewhere, for example, doing business in highly congested urban areas where costs have been escalating, contending with a large proportion of short-haul traffic for which motor carriers are most competitive, and carrying heavy and long-continued passenger deficits associated with commuter services around the large cities. These difficulties do not exempt management from criticism, but they do provide a point of departure for appraisal.

If the relation of the route structure to the market in a geographic sense is important, so also is the makeup of that structure. Since common carriers are obliged to accept all traffic offered them within the range of their holding out and since it is difficult to retire from a service once begun, such carriers can best improve their prospects by seeking route segments that promise good profit margins. Where carriers can seek new authority with some chance of success, as in air transport, or have good prospects for approval of acquisition of other carriers, as in motor transport, an important element in management policy may be the improvement of the route structure with a view to offset existing unprofitable segments or to improve overall margins.

The costs of terminal and short-haul services have been rising more rapidly than those of long-haul movement. Competition is often most severe in short-haul markets. Available transport equipment is often better adapted to the longer hauls, as has been notably the case with jet aircraft. Perhaps more important, rate structures have traditionally been closer to or even below cost on short hauls; and it has been difficult to increase them in a way at all proportionate to the recent rise in costs. Carriers heavily involved in short-haul traffic which do not have service in profitable long-haul markets are, therefore, likely to

---

[3] For some revenue and traffic composition comparison, see Ernest W. Williams, Jr., "Traffic Composition and Railroad Earning Power," *Transportation Journal*, Fall 1969, pp. 17 ff.

show poorer results than those with a more favorable route pattern.[4] Yet the bulk of traffic, both freight and passenger, is offered in the short-haul markets. Hence competition for operating rights in long-haul markets can be quite sharp, and the risk is always present that too many carriers will be certificated for the available volume. Whatever the comparative quality of operating management, route structures will often be found to be a principal explanatory factor in differential carrier performance.

Adjusting Route Pattern and Traffic Composition

Railroads have little latitude in correcting an unsatisfactory route pattern except through the process of abandonment. Much less mileage has been abandoned over the years than would have been desirable for the economic health of the industry. Although securing the right to abandon is a slow, expensive, and uncertain process, it appears the railroads have been much too slow in proposing large-scale abandonments. Managements have not been anxious to reduce the extent of their operating control nor to turn traffic over to others except in cases of gross unprofitability. In 1972 the trustees of the bankrupt Penn Central contended that some 9,000 miles (nearly 45 percent) of lines must be abandoned because they were unproductive. If the trustees were right, where were the managements of the three underlying carriers on this issue prior to merger? New Haven had already been in bankruptcy for many years prior to inclusion in Penn Central. Both the Pennsylvania and New York Central had curtailed maintenance sharply after 1954 and argued that merger (consummated in 1968) might be a way of averting insolvency. None sought actively to reduce their properties to a size which shrinking traffic might support.

Many trunk airlines have enhanced their profitability by applying for authority to operate in long-haul markets characterized by comparatively high traffic densities. This has brought new competition to the larger trunk lines which were already established in those markets. At the same time the CAB evidenced little willingness to approve route extensions for the largest of the airlines whose route patterns were substantially shaped at an earlier period in technology and traffic development. While the initiative is with the managements, constraints are greater for some than for the others. Foresight in attempting to fill out route patterns and prevent intrusion of competitors on existing high-profit routes as well as skillful conduct of the regulatory battles are of obvious importance. The larger and more successful motor car-

---

[4] At the 1972 annual meeting, the president of Eastern Airlines reported that only 20 percent of Eastern's routes were profitable on a consistent basis, 40 percent more or less break even, and the remaining 40 percent are consistent losers. (The Wall Street Journal, April 26, 1972, p. 7).

riers, too, have put large emphasis upon expanding into long-haul markets, principally by acquiring other motor carriers and tacking the acquired operating rights on to their own. In both industries a major thrust of the effort has been to increase the number of points between which single-line service could be rendered and the territorial coverage which could be offered to shippers and passengers.

A variety of traffic is handled over any route segment, and it reflects the economic activity adjacent to the route. The composite result may be materially affected by the proportion of the traffic which is handled at a loss. A mark of good management in any line of business is the effectiveness with which the product line is "pruned" of loss items. Common carriers are, however, required to handle the traffic offered, although they certainly are not required to solicit traffic which can only be handled at a loss. They may attack the problem by reducing the cost of handling such business, discouraging it, seeking increased rates of more nearly compensatory character, and seeking improved divisions of the through rates where joint-line traffic is involved. To some extent they proceed in all of these ways. To improve rates or divisions, however, normally requires a regulatory proceeding in which significant opposition will be encountered, and the former necessitates cooperation with other carriers in the territory. Concentration on the active solicitation of profitable traffic is often a more promising course, and it is to widen the opportunity to do so that route-pattern extensions are frequently sought.

Despite the extent to which carrier fortunes may be governed by the territory served, the route pattern, and traffic composition, it remains true that effective management can turn in a superior performance in the face of such constraints. Where the trends are unfavorable, as for the Eastern railroads, the best of management performance may be inadequate to the task of arresting financial anemia given the constraints within which management must labor. Thus highly effective and progressive management was provided on the New York Central under Al Perlman; yet after a decade the long-term prospect still seemed to be a slide into bankruptcy—hence a willingness to merge. It is often the case that relatively poor management develops in the face of long-continued unfavorable conditions. The growing financial bind leads to cost cutting, deferral of maintenance, the curtailment of management development, and a failure to produce service innovations, market research, and other steps needful to the maintenance of a competitive posture. Time is bought, but the ultimate reckoning made the more sure, and a point of no return may have been passed before the carrier's board of directors moves to change management.[5]

---

[5] Penn Central's board was still declaring dividends a year before the carrier filed under Section 77 of the Bankruptcy Act.

Peculiarities of Carrier Management

In many respects carrier management presents problems that are not often encountered in like magnitude in other types of industry. With the exception of bulk water carriers and pipelines, all types of carriers are labor intensive—50 percent and more of their operating expenses going as payments to labor. Airlines and railroads have the misfortune to be capital intensive as well, the latter affected by a painfully slow capital turnover. Only a few of the railroads and airlines are large enterprises, as measured by earnings or capital investment, when compared with the largest industrials. But their plant is spread over a vast geographical territory—nationwide in the case of some trucking concerns and globe spanning for some airlines and steamship companies. Operations throughout the territory served are interrelated. Failure to turn an aircraft promptly at New York may disarrange schedules across the continent or the Atlantic Ocean. Operations are continually exposed to weather conditions and other hazards beyond the control of management; rail trackage is exposed to natural hazards, and equipment of all sorts performs subject to the elements. Widespread property is difficult to protect against vandalism, pilferage, and sabotage—risks all too rapidly growing in modern society.

A substantial portion of the operating task is performed outside the immediate reach of supervision, unlike the situation on the factory floor. The condition is suggested by what a Pan American World Airways captain calls anarchy aloft. "Every flight crew is a shape up," he says, "with personnel constantly shifting from flight to flight. At the point where the public and the product come together—in a $24 million facility—no member of management is present. The captain, nominally in command, is strapped in a cubicle remote from the customers; he and the remainder of the crew belong to three separate unions."[6] The case of the train crew is not greatly different, though after recent mergers only two unions are likely to represent the men comprising the crew. But engineers, firemen, brakemen, and conductors are assigned from separate seniority rosters. The conductor, perhaps 150 cars behind the engine, is in charge; and on most main lines he is in radio contact with the engineer and the dispatcher. Trainmasters charged with train operation can ride but a few trains; road foremen of engines charged with supervision and instruction of engineers are similarly limited. Many trucking companies employ patrol cars to observe and assist their rigs between terminals, but only a portion of such operations can come under surveillance. Heavy reliance must be placed upon reports and upon recording devices.

---

[6] *Fortune*, March, 1972, p. 37. The first cost of the aircraft has about doubled in the period since.

Safety is a major consideration in all transport operations. It necessitates high regard for the rule book, introduces rigidity in operations, and deters innovation.

No operation can be properly controlled unless performance can be effectively measured. Feedback is the means by which deficiencies of performance are detected and corrected. But performance measurement is especially difficult in transport operations. Problems of costing, arising largely out of the widespread presence of common and joint cost conditions, have been discussed earlier (Chapter 9). While control in most industries is based upon profit results, that has not generally been true of transport enterprise. Instead, performance has usually been measured through operating statistics—train and vehicle loading in relation to capacity, speed between terminals, fuel consumption, cars handled per switching engine hour, and like measures. All such statistics are partial rather than comprehensive measures. They lead to optimizing some factor inputs without regard to the effect upon others. A good illustration is the common practice of railroads to hold cars in yards until a full-tonnage train can be made up. Train operating costs may thereby be minimized per car-mile, though that proposition has yet to be proved.[7] If the cost of cars held idle in the yard awaiting tonnage were brought into the reckoning, a different picture would emerge. But the cost of car time is nowhere accounted for in the statistics used for control. Individual carriers have made progress toward measurement of performance in profit terms, but the majority of managements have been laggard in attacking what is a critical problem and central to effective control, despite its difficulty.

Railroads especially—other carriers to a less but increasing degree—must fit their operations into a system of transport. This deprives the individual carrier of a good deal of the latitude that its management might be supposed to exercise. Equipment must be standardized in critical respects in order to be interchangeable and widely employed. New equipment must be compatible with old. Most rail carload shipments move over the lines of two or more railroads. But once a loaded car leaves the line of the originating carrier, that road loses control. Unless connecting lines provide acceptable service it may be impossible to hold traffic against competition. The breakdown of performance on the Penn Central in 1969–70, representing 10 percent of the nation's rail mileage, therefore affected all railroads adversely by producing diversion of business to other modes as well as by failure to return cars to the owning roads in order to meet their loading requirements. Even in rate matters, the right of independent action preserved under Section 5a agreements may be more theoretic than real. Joint

---

[7] A recent study does find no material cost advantages for TOFC (piggyback) trains exceeding 20 cars in length.

rates may not be made or changed unless agreed by the connecting carriers involved. Rates over the line of a single carrier may, if changed, produce an unlawful discrimination in relation to joint rates in which that carrier participates. Independent action may bring from connecting carriers threats to divert joint-line traffic. In all matters touched by regulation, competitors will endeavor to use regulatory procedures to impede change.

Ocean carriers over most of their history operated with little concern about their connecting inland carriers. The development of the containership, however, forced new ways of doing business. Since it is no longer necessary to break bulk at the seaboard, through services from the interior to destinations within the country of import are easy to envisage. Such developments require close coordination with rail and truck carriers, however, which necessitates some compromise of the interests of all concerned. Standardization of container dimensions, fittings, and transfer mechanisms becomes necessary. Management of containers in multimodal operations must be arranged. Joint liability and through-rate arrangements require negotiation. The pace of all these developments is slow, and the influence which ocean-carrier managements can exercise is limited. Like problems assail all carriers that seek to promote intermodal services.

ORGANIZATION FORM AND MANAGEMENT ATTITUDES

Pioneers in Corporate Organization

To people today it may come as a surprise that railroads were pioneers in large-scale organization. In the 1850s, however, railroads were the largest business organizations in the land and the first to face the problems of controlling great numbers of men spread over hundreds of miles of line and utilizing physical plant of large monetary value. The departmentalized and divisional form of organization pioneered by Benjamin Latrobe on the Baltimore and Ohio and by Daniel McCallum on the Erie was brought to substantial perfection by John Edgar Thompson on the Pennsylvania—all before the outbreak of the Civil War. Significantly all three were engineers, concerned primarily with efficiency of operations and security of revenues collected all over the line by agents and conductors. From the start of rational organization, therefore, railroads were heavily production oriented. But it was in railroad organization that line and staff concepts were first clarified and defined and the principles of delegation of authority worked out. While the resemblance of railroad to military organization has often been remarked, it appears that Latrobe and the others "did not borrow; they approached their brand new problem of building an administrative structure in much the same rational and analytical way as they approached that of building a railroad or a bridge."[8]

McCallum provided passenger and freight departments for the pricing and securing of traffic in those two broad classes. He recognized the need of statistical cost information as a guide to profitable pricing. Railroads pioneered in accounting as in organization; yet the costing of the individual traffic movements which required to be priced was never effectively taken in hand. Traffic officers worked from average costs separated between freight and passenger and from a general understanding of the direction of departure of costs for particular hauls from the average. Rate making became far more an art than a science; and with the growth of traffic associations for the joint consideration of rates, the development of rate relationships designed to equalize competition, and the accretions of precedent, it became increasingly institutionalized.

Departmental Coordination

Under the divisional plan of organization, the major operating functions—train operation, maintenance of equipment, and maintenance of way—were well coordinated. Care had been taken to insure that result. The operating department was by all odds the largest; and until quite recent times, rail presidents characteristically came up through its ranks. As the art of rate making became more complex and arcane when the impact of regulation added volumes of administrative law to the background required by the rate maker, the traffic department, too, acquired a new independence in regulatory and legislative matters. Chief executives became more and more extensions of the operating department and exercised steadily less control over the traffic and legal aspects of the business. It was possible to regard some railroads as triple headed—the president supreme in operations, the vice president of traffic in rate making, the general counsel in legislative matters. But the primary fact was that the operating department too often determined the character and quality of service rendered in accordance with its own measures of operating efficiency. The traffic department was compelled to price and sell a service over which it had no control and little influence. And the law department was likely to see obstacles on the regulatory front whenever innovations were nonetheless brought forward. Chief executives trained in operations found the complexities of rate making and regulation repelling if not incomprehensible and were little inclined to overrule their experts in these areas.

---

[8] Alfred D. Chandler, Jr., "The Railroads: Pioneers in Modern Corporate Management," *Business History Review*, Spring 1965, p. 36.

A house thus divided was not well prepared to meet competitive challenges. The latter required service and price packages addressed to shipper and passenger requirements—packages which could only be developed by close departmental cooperation. Moreover market research was critical to a determination of what would meet the competition, including careful study of competitors' capabilities. Even traffic departments were little inclined to take on tasks of this sort, especially since chief traffic officers were conditioned by long years of exposure to traditional rate-making and solicitation techniques attuned to the task of securing an appropriate share of the business in a transport scene largely monopolized by railroads. To import personnel trained outside the industry for tasks whose significance was not fully appreciated was hardly an acceptable course. Market research made progess on some roads, beginning in the 1950s, and jointly in connection with several of the rate bureaus. The promising and, in many respects, pioneering market research activity of New York Central was dismembered following merger. The industry remains weak in this critical area, though there are important exceptions.[9]

The basic functions represented by departments in other forms of transport resemble closely those found in railroads. Like the railroads, too, they have tended heavily to emphasize operations to the comparative neglect of the marketing functions and to place predominant emphasis upon their line-haul operations to the neglect of the terminals. Passenger carriers, of course, both airlines and intercity bus companies, devote much more attention to advertising and promotion than do the freight carriers. With minor exceptions the nonrail carriers have not found recourse to a divisional plan of organization either necessary or desirable. Airlines tend to be highly centralized in their organizational structure, hence faced with a long chain of command. Motor carriers have found, in many instances, that their large terminals afford desirable points of coordination for local operations, maintenance, and sales activity and for the control of their traffic composition. A large portion of their freight traffic stems, however, from national accounts which must usually be approached at their headquarters. And central dispatch of their line-haul equipment is generally considered a requisite to insure high utilization and effective response to equipment demand. Steamship companies engaged in far-flung general cargo services tend, however, to use subsidiary companies to operate major trade-route areas.

[9] On the problems of railroad management and efforts to improve, see D. Daryl Wycoff, *Railroad Management* (Lexington, Mass.: Lexington Books, 1976). The successful methods of Southern Railway are given emphasis.

Absence of Profit Responsibility

What has been said about organization and performance measurement will suggest that profit orientation has been weak in transport companies. In the normal railroad organization no one has profit responsibility short of the president.[10] The division is not a profit center—it is not even a true cost center. The handling of receipts and disbursements is centralized. Divisions are operating units not responsible for the cultivation of revenue. Nor are they assigned those important elements of cost attributable to ownership of road and equipment. Peter Drucker has asserted flatly that a railroad is not capable of profit-center decentralization after the fashion of many successful manufacturing and merchandising companies.[11] The reorganization of the Pennsylvania Railroad Company in the mid 1950s on a regional plan fell far short of such an objective. Since operating and traffic departments were brought together at the regional level, it may have improved coordination, but as in the case of most railroads, some 80 percent of the freight volume was controlled by a few dozen major corporations whose chief traffic officers continued to deal with the system traffic department. The lack of profit accountability and the use of nonprofit measurements of performance leads to suboptimization, to shift of responsibility from one division to another, and to department rivalry.

The better-managed motor carriers have come much closer to achieving profit orientation than most transport operations. That is undoubtedly a major factor in their ability to achieve below average operating ratios with consistency. The principal key is a careful classification of traffic by commodity, length of haul, customer, and other critical parameters, the costing out of each traffic class, and the measurement of terminal managers and salesmen against profit yardsticks.[12] The same methods were employed by New York Central in its flexi-van service (container on flatcar) by using New York Central Transport, the motor-carrier subsidiary, to manage the service. Transport was charged for terminal and rail line-haul services to make it effectively a profit center.

The profit crisis of 1970–71 produced reorganization of at least one major airline partly for the purpose of extending profit responsibility deeper into the organization. Catering was pulled out from the mar-

---

[10] Herbert Harwood, Jr., "Making Money in the Railroad Business Means Finding the Missing Men," *Trains*, vol. 31, no. 8 (June 1971), pp. 18 ff.

[11] Peter Drucker, *The Practice of Management* (New York: Harper & Bros., 1954), p. 217.

[12] It will be recalled that because of the high ratio of variable cost the problem of costing motor-carrier freight is less intractable than in the case of railroads.

keting department and established as a profit center. Operations were separated into three broad territorial divisions, each charged with its own marketing and terminal functions and responsible for its own balance sheet. As in other industries, the plan was expected to develop general managers short of the chief executive's post, a process which traditional transportation organization does not foster.

Need for Quality Control

Well-managed carriers frequently achieve reasonably consistent on-time performance by their line-haul units. The majority have been satisfied with that measure of service control. It is of small comfort to the rail shipper, however, to know that on-time performance of scheduled freight trains is good if his car is left behind in the yard. The movement of carload shipments is too often slow, irregular, and unpredictable.[13] Deliveries are frequently bunched so that receivers find difficulty in unloading cars promptly. Less-truckload freight suffers from similar disabilities and, in addition, is difficult to trace when delayed or lost. In both rail and truck service, irregularity is compounded when the traffic must be interchanged between two or more carriers. In short, quality control, when it is applied, relates to the unit of movement rather than to the shipper's traffic unit. Complaints on the subject have been long, loud, and increasing over the past 30 years.

On the other side of the coin, shippers are often far from cooperative. Failure to provide shipping papers in timely fashion and to properly mark freight is too frequent. Motor carriers specialize in door-to-door service. Congestion at shippers' and receivers' docks, refusals to accept freight at particular times, division of traffic among too many carriers, and other failures push costs and delays upon the motor carriers. To a surprising extent receivers of trailers in rail piggyback service fail to make timely pickups from rail carriers' terminals. An undue amount of import air-cargo sits for days at J. F. Kennedy Airport awaiting consignee's willingness to accept delivery, though expensive airport cargo terminals should perform as flow-through rather than storage facilities. Carriers can do little beyond urging improved practices and the assessment of charges for delay.

In rail operation the problem of service quality control is closely tied to that of improving car utilization. Perhaps no single matter is of larger current importance both for improving the rail competitive position and securing a faster turnaround of capital devoted to freight-carrying equipment. As Lewis Sillcox points out, half of the industry's total depreciated investment is working only 10.91 percent of the time to pro-

---

[13] A 1969 survey showed that a rail shipper had only a 33 percent opportunity of getting his shipment from origin to destination on a consistent basis compared with a 95 percent expectation of consistent and faster service by truck. Department of Transportation, *Report on Cybernetic Techniques* (1970).

duce profits. "Unless and until the railway industry learns how to manage and make its freight-car fleet perform, there simply is no hope for any success in effectively meeting its competitive challenge."[14] Fast communication and computerized data manipulation should hold the answer, as in a wide variety of scheduling and distribution problems. Much time and money has been spent along these lines in the last 15 to 20 years by the major individual roads. Some have achieved good control on their own lines. Yet car utilization, despite the growth of unit and run-through trains, increased only 8.3 percent in the decade since 1969. The coupling of the systems of individual roads is looked to for future results, but progress is painfully slow and industrywide funding uncertain. Motor carriers, in 1971, launched an attack on their interchange problems through a pilot study at Indianapolis. The success achieved has led to extension to additional terminals. Despite the importance and long-standing recognition of the problem, it must be said that far too little management attention has as yet been allocated.

Short-Period Viewpoints

Long-range planning has become an accepted practice, in one form or another, in a majority of large industrial corporations.[15] Accelerating change, growing lead times for major capital investments, and an increasingly complex environment have compelled that development. Most transport organizations continue, however, to operate on a short time horizon and to devote managerial attention overwhelmingly to current operations. Maintenance is adjusted almost from month to month in accordance with revenue fluctuations on far too many properties. Sustained equipment purchase is virtually unknown—few industrial markets can dry up as rapidly or universally as that for freight cars. Major improvement projects are slowed, accelerated, and slowed again before completion. The pipeline industry is a major exception; and the airlines, operating in an industry where the aircraft itself is a major competitive tool in a consumer market—that for passengers—and is also a long lead-time item, have gone farther than others in equipment planning.[16]

---

[14] Lewis K. Sillcox, *Mileage Is Time and Time Is Money* (mimeo), presented before Northwestern University Graduate School of Management, January 24, 1972.

[15] See E. Kirby Warren, *Long-Range Planning: The Executive Viewpoint* (Englewood Cliffs, N.J.: Prentice-Hall, Inc., 1966), pp. 2, 40.

[16] Forecasting is not accurate enough to date critical cyclical turning points. Hence wide-bodied jets, justifiable in the longer run, came into the fleets just as traffic growth stagnated and earnings plummeted. Before traffic recovery permitted development of the wide-body inventory to the intended level, the fuel crisis, beginning late in 1973, compelled schedule reductions. A number of wide bodies were grounded, some orders were canceled, and other deliveries were stretched out. Many economists expected recession in 1978, then reversed their forecasts to place it in 1979, but in early 1980 the downturn finally appeared.

A major reason for the short-term outlook is the narrow financial margin on which so much of transport works. Programmed maintenance must be supported by adequate cash flow. In the railroad industry, plant improvement, such as yard construction, can rarely be financed except out of internal cash flow. Even the airline industry, when committed equipment purchases coincide with depressed traffic and earnings, as in 1970–71, is compelled to defer delivery of some aircraft—even cancel some orders. Motor carriers, with short lead-time and short-lived equipment, are much less constrained. But the short-term outlook is not confined to maintenance and capital programs which require large outlays. It is felt also in the traffic-building activities and the research programs upon which improved future performance heavily depends.

Though it is understandable that management may ignore longer term requirements when those of the present cannot be satisfied, the failure to look forward stands in the way of development of appropriate priorities. Moreover it generates a major failure in communications to the public and prevents any adequate understanding of the consequences of the present carrier position. A recognized function of management in the present era is the management of change. But that counsels a forward look and a disengagement from preoccupation with current operating problems—a virtual impossibility under the organizational forms current in the transportation industries.

LABOR-MANAGEMENT RELATIONS

Few areas of management concern have exhibited greater or more lasting difficulty. The labor-intensive and far-flung operational characteristics of the transport industries, plus the fact that they have faced inflationary circumstances during most of the period since the economic crisis of 1907, makes the question of labor relations of more than usual importance for these industries. Much of the period has been marked by a struggle to keep ever-mounting wages and fringes from eroding margins unduly; for example, great emphasis has been given to the application of laborsaving technology in order to improve productivity somewhat in accord with man-hour costs. The regulated segments of the industry face the added problem that rate increases can only be successfully sought after labor settlements have been reached and the added costs can be appraised. Substantial delay may then develop before increases are approved, though it is fair to say that the regulatory bodies (especially the Interstate Commerce Commission) have expedited their procedures in considering general rate-level increases.[17] Wage awards, moreover, are often retroactive to a date some months prior to the contract settlement whereas rate increases can only be prospective.

Multiplicity and Traditions of Unions

Railroads, airlines, and water carriers all suffer from the fact that their unions are largely organized on a craft basis (unlike the usual pattern abroad). Prior to the merger of two unions with the Brotherhood of Railroad Trainmen to form the United Transportation Union,[18] the railroads dealt with 21 standard railroad unions plus a few others that had representation rights for some employees. The situation in the ocean trades, in respect to shipboard personnel, is almost as bad. Airlines generally face three unions aloft and several others on the ground, including railroad clerks who have extended their jurisdiction into the airline industry. By contrast, the motor carrier industry deals almost wholly with the Teamsters' Union so far as operating personnel is concerned.

Under these circumstances a class of work, sometimes narrowly defined, comes to "belong" to members of a particular union. The phenomenon is especially troublesome in the mechanical trades where management has little flexibility in the use of skilled employees. And the urgency of maintaining a hold on a particular class of work becomes more and more important as employment and union membership shrink, especially in trades which involve nontransferable skills; hence resistance to change tends to become more stubborn. Rail employment has declined from the level of 1.4 million in the late 40s to less than 500,000 today, a level that is too small to comfortably maintain so large a number of unions.[19] Merger among operating unions has not been paralleled by a similar development among the nonops. Jurisdictional fights occasionally flare up, as between the Brotherhood of Locomotive Engineers and the UTU. The seagoing unions have also found attrition as the active American merchant marine has declined and automation has come along. Although air transport has been

---

[17] This general problem is referred to as *regulatory lag*. See an appraisal of its impact on the railroads in the 1950s in James C. Nelson, *Railroad Transportation and Public Policy* (Washington, D.C.: The Brookings Institution, 1959), pp. 125–31. Motor carriers have been somewhat dismayed by the fact that the commission has recently enunciated and applied more rigorous standards of proof in rate-level cases and, in a rate-making proceeding, threatens a change in the long accepted operating-ratio standard for judging the adequacy of earnings.

[18] Into which the Brotherhood of Locomotive Firemen and Engineers also later merged.

[19] A case in point is the Order of Railway Telegraphers. The ranks of the sleeping car porters' union have also been decimated.

growing, some occupations have become superfluous, for example, the flight engineers, and threaten the continued existence of a union. All three of these industries have been plagued by a succession of strikes and threatened strikes.

Rail and airline labor relations are subject to the Railway Labor Act, while the other transportation industries are governed by the labor law applicable to industry in general. Under the Railway Labor Act, threatened strikes which are judged of national importance may be headed off by appointment of an emergency board to investigate and recommend. Such a board has 30 days to investigate and report, and a strike is barred for 30 days thereafter. The report is not binding. Strikes in other transport industries are subject to the Taft-Hartley procedures, and Taft-Hartley injunctions are often sought in maritime disputes.

Bargaining is substantially nationwide in the rail industry and in trucking since the Teamsters' Union moved in that direction in 1964. Nationwide interruption either of rail or truck transportation has such rapid impact upon industrial production and the national economy that such strikes cannot be tolerated. Hence a strike, or the threat of one, impels presidential interference. Until recent years the president had, under war powers legislation enacted during World War I, the authority to seize the railroads in order to prevent a strike. As such power no longer exists, resort to Congress for special legislation is increasingly the rule. The likelihood of ultimate recourse to the White House and the Congress is not conducive to settlement of issues through collective bargaining, mediation, or emergency-board procedure. Faced with the risk that a nationwide strike will precipitate congressional action, rail unions have resorted to selective strikes.[20] Both railroads and certain airlines have protected themselves, in part, from the effects of selective strikes by what amount to mutual-aid pacts. When the Norfolk & Western was struck by the Brotherhood of Railroad and Airline Clerks for an extended period in 1978, the strike was ultimately extended to other roads on the grounds they were supporting the struck carrier through payments under the pact. Continuance is, therefore, in doubt.

Management Initiative in the Adjustment to Technological Change

Differences among and within the several transportation industries are noticeable in their approach to major issues of labor relations. On the

---

[20] This tactic, pursued by the UTU in 1971, led to a separate settlement on the Chicago & North Western and later to a nationwide agreement worked out with a group of rail presidents under the pressure of White House intervention. Presidential support for transport labor legislation was suddenly withdrawn in the summer of 1972, presumably for political reasons, just as the chances for passage appeared improved.

whole, however, transport management has left the initiative to the unions. Union proposals have been countered with management proposals, but serious bargaining and ultimate determination has most often hinged on accession to union demands. The power to curtail or to interrupt service resides with the unions; the overriding public interest is in continuous service; and when government pressure is ultimately exerted, it is most often management that must give way. Such a situation counsels early identification of circumstances that require change and iniation of efforts to find an accommodating formula. But a successful approach of that type has rarely been observed in practice. The attention of top management, indeed, has been too little directed toward labor problems—most nearly, perhaps, in trucking where national bargaining is placed with a committee of chief executives.

Of largest economical importance has been the adjustment of crew consist and other work rules to changing technology. The problem plagues the rail and maritime industries especially, although it has been felt in air transport as well. In general, practices described as *featherbedding* have been less common in the trucking industry. In rail operating departments, three types of practice, once well warranted by conditions, have come under attack: (1) the standard five-man crew consist in road and yard service, (2) the 100-mile standard for a day's work (150 miles for passenger trainmen) with accompanying confinement of crews to divisional bounds, and (3) the inability to use road crews for yard work without penalty. All of these affect labor costs adversely. Perhaps more important they impede service improvement and render some types of service patently uneconomical. Since the diesel engine began to be used in yard service in 1926 and the first road-freight diesel was road tested in 1940, one might have expected an early examination of the necessity to continue the use of firemen on these locomotives with a view to bargaining for the cessation of hiring and the phasing out of the existing personnel by the process of attrition. Not until the late 50s however, with the roads almost completely converted to diesel power, was a serious effort made to get the firemen off. Then a major public relations effort was mounted which was hardly conducive to creating the conditions for successful bargaining. After a special Presidential Railroad Commission reported on this issue in 1962, it was necessary for Congress to intervene and legislate compulsory arbitration for the use of firemen and the crew-consist dispute only.

Changes in work rules are not easily negotiated and, of course, they must be bought. An exercise of judgment is called for to determine what it is worth paying for greater freedom in the assignment and use of men. The West Coast longshore settlement of some 15 years ago opened the route to technological innovation with very little impediment at the cost of substantial payments into a fund designed to compensate displaced workers. The route to efficient containerization was effectively opened up in the Pacific maritime trades, productivity in longshore operations moved rapidly upward, and the settlement was generally looked upon as a constructive one. Less stable conditions on the East Coast and far less astute bargaining stood in the way of an equally efficacious settlement. The accomodation reached encountered an adverse decision by the National Labor Relations Board which, in 1980, was still being litigated in the courts.

Both the bankrupt Milwaukee and the deficit-ridden Conrail concluded agreements with the UTU in 1978 designed to afford greater flexibility in the size of freight-train crews. These agreements were generally judged too expensive to be of significant value to the carriers. Late in the year, however, a much more liberal agreement was reached between UTU and Canadian National under which only 25 percent of the savings go to employees and then only for a period of ten years.[21] A number of specific agreements have been reached for reduced crews in short-train turnaround service and in the high-frequency piggyback experiments lately conducted by Milwaukee and Illinois Central Gulf with Department of Transportation sponsorship and partial funding. Agreement is by no means impossible where mutual interest can be identified, but it tends to come with painful delay.

Perhaps the most critical failure of management over the long run is a failure of communications on the part, especially, of the railroads. Despite the fact that this is a heavily regulated industry about which a vast amount of information is available from government sources, there is continuing distrust by labor of what it is told about the economic and competitive condition of the industry. There is lack of faith, too, in the good intentions of management when it comes to carrying out the spirit of an agreement. On the economic health of the industry, the perceptions of employees are widely disparate from the facts. The general public reacts in much the same way.

Negotiation of Merger Arrangements

Two recent mergers out of which came the nation's largest railroads—Burlington Northern and Penn Central—illustrate the latitude that is open in negotiation and the different results that may come from different perceptions of the problem to be solved. Labor opposition was encountered in both merger cases—special labor agreements were negotiated in both. Burlington Northern, however, achieved an agreement which was well adapted to enable it to carry out the pur-

---

[21] See *Railway Age*, January 29, 1979, pp. 29-30.

pose of the merger. It acquired great flexibility in the assignment and relocation of men, in the merging of seniority rosters, and in other respects without undue cost penalties. Penn Central's agreement, spearheaded by the management of the Pennsylvania Railroad, was designed to buy off labor opposition rather than to facilitate the coordination of the merged properties. It not only lacked flexibility and assessed inordinate costs for relocating personnel but it required rehiring some 5,000 employees that had previously been terminated. After merger, labor costs exploded and combined operations were impeded.[22]

SIZE, MERGERS, AND THE CAPACITY TO MANAGE

The Penn Central debacle led to fresh concern about the ability to manage very large transport enterprises—even to proposals for a moratorium on further railroad mergers. Our earlier discussion sheds some light on why it may be more difficult to effectively manage a large transport organization than to manage an industrial organization of equivalent size. There are various measures of size. Burlington Northern is larger than was Penn Central when measured by operated line mileage and territorial reach. It is smaller if measured by revenues, traffic volume, or number of employees. Perhaps much more important, its operations are less complex since it is substantially free of passenger service and must commit a much smaller portion of its resources to terminal operations. Penn Central was about twice as large as Southern, one of the most profitable railroads in the United States. A critical difference between them is illustrated by the accompanying table. Penn Central was a massive terminal complex with a range of operating problems without parallel on any other system.

	Penn Central	Southern
Yard crews	2,636	511
Number of yard crew locations	381	77
Locations having ten or more crews	79	15

Management crises are not unusual when growth proceeds more rapidly than the development of management capability. Since acquisition of other carriers is the most practicable method for rapid growth, management crisis is often associated with a merger movement. Consolidated Freightways, Spector Mid States, and other motor

---

[22] Because different unions represent employees other than those in the cockpit, Pan American World Airways is likely to have serious difficulty in meshing its operations with those of National Airlines, which it acquired. See "Meshing Problems for Pan Am and National," *Business Week*, January 21, 1980, pp. 56 and 60.

carriers have experienced the problem. Greyhound replaced a chief executive officer when it appeared to the board that growth in the bus company might get out of hand. Many years went by before Associated Transport, a merger of eight smaller motor carriers, could be made to perform efficiently and profitably; and the carrier ultimately failed and was liquidated. Norfolk & Western ran into unanticipated and serious difficulties before securing control of car movement and service quality after it absorbed Nickel Plate and Wabash. Merger of transport undertakings usually requires an actual merger of both organization and operations. The problem is not the same as acquiring a manufacturing company which can continue to operate as a separate entity. In all instances cited, however, as well as in many others, problems were overcome and effective control secured. Some of these carriers are now among the best performers in their respective industries. Burlington Northern, despite its size, has encountered none of the more serious difficulties experienced by Penn Central, and its merger appears to be on the way toward achievement of anticipated results.[23]

Penn Central was a very special case, and its difficulties should not prejudice examination of other merger proposals. Pennsylvania and New York Central, the moving parties in the merger, were both among the largest railroads in the United States. To an unusual degree they paralleled one another throughout Official Territory and served nearly all principal cities (outside of New England) in common. From the late 1850s they had been sharp and tenacious competitors. As noted above, both were on a downhill course in revenues and profit potential. In theory a large-scale parallel merger of this sort should have permitted a maximum of economies, but since the carriers proposed to avoid major line or service abandonment in an effort to forestall opposition, the estimated annual economies (after the fifth year when labor protection provisions would expire) were a mere $86 million. Nevertheless the hope was expressed that these economies and potentially appreciable improvements in service would mitigate declining fortunes.[24]

In the end, Penn Central proved impossible to reorganize as a private corporation. So, also, did Erie-Lackawanna, Reading, Central of New Jersey, Lehigh Valley, and Lehigh and New England. The North-

---

[23] The record of correspondence between actual and anticipated results of rail mergers is not especially reassuring. Appraisal is difficult, but see Robert E. Gallamore, "Measurement of Cost Savings of Recent Railway Mergers," Transportation Research Forum, *Papers, Ninth Annual Meeting (1968)*, pp. 217 ff. For a discussion of major issues in railroad mergers see Marvin L. Fair, "Railroad Mergers and the Public Interest," *Transportation Journal*, Winter 1966, pp. 5–15.

[24] The merger was an unpopular one, but judged by its proponents as competitively necessary in the light of expected approval of the control of B&O by C&O and the enlarged N&W system.

eastern rail system was faced with declining traffic potential, and was overbuilt, obsolescent, and grossly undermaintained. Congress resorted to a takeover of these systems in 1976 and their merger into the Consolidated Railroad Corporation (Conrail). Unfortunately it refused to take the politically hazardous step of permitting sufficient abandonment of light traffic and duplicative line to create a core system which would have the prospect of becoming self-sustaining. And it established the possibly dangerous precedent of underwriting lifetime security for displaced rail personnel. With over $3 billion of federal money poured into the system, major rehabilitation and service improvement have taken place. Yet, though deficits have been pared, a breakeven is not in sight. Conrail counts on further major-line abandonment, additional labor concessions, and substantial deregulation of railroad rate-making as necessary to this end. The last was legislated in 1980 and is already being utilized. The others remain remote prospects. Meanwhile, Conrail is larger than Penn Central, dominates rail transport in the Northeast, and affects performance of the whole rail system of the continent. Nor has it been demonstrated that a system of this size and complexity can be effectively managed.

The tools available for the management of large enterprises have been vastly improved. Carriers have at their disposal high-speed communications and data processing, a wide range of relatively new analytical techniques, and the powerful potential of operational simulation. Very large operations in all forms of transport are being conducted with success. More important, they are showing improvement. The capability to recentralize many management functions exists. Hence it would be unwise to conclude that size limits need to be set on carriers because of incapacity to manage. Despite the early use of computers and the historic availability of captive communications systems, however, most carrier managements have moved slowly to accept and adapt the output of management science to their needs. The distinction between route density and firm size made in Chapter 9 and the findings of Healy noted therein should not be overlooked.

INTERMODAL MANAGEMENT

One of the reasons offered by the former Pennsylvania management for diversifying into nontransport activities was an inability to offset the low earning power of the railroad through diversifying within transportation. U.S. law frowns upon control of motor, water, and air carriers by railroads. Many other railroads have moved in the same direction; and William Johnson, chairman of Illinois Central Industries, offers another reason—the ability to manage in the nontransport area without the impediment of regulation. The transformation of railroads into conglomerates, however, has given rise to criticism and alarm lest the resources of the railroads be drained and the public interest suffer.[25] As in the case of the Pennsylvania, most railroads which have sought to exploit the diversification route are among the less profitable whose areas of service show little prospect for rail traffic growth.[26] The exceptions are carriers like the Union Pacific and Santa Fe which have been able to exploit the mineral and timber resources on their landholdings.

Many railroads do have motor-carrier subsidiaries, but their motor-carrier operations are generally confined to the offering of service which is ancillary to rail service. Southern Pacific is a partial exception: its Pacific Motor Transport is one of the largest motor carriers in the land. Within California, which is a very large state, PMT is able to operate as any other motor carrier would in handling intrastate traffic. Elsewhere the carrier is generally subject to the usual restrictions. Southern Pacific also has a controlled pipeline and an airfreight-forwarder operation. These three ancillary enterprises are organized and run with substantial independence under operating managements of their own. Coordination with the parent company is, of course, close.

Canada lacks the kind of restriction that is imposed on U.S. railroads. Both Canadian Pacific and Canadian National have extensive highway, air, and water operations; both control hotel chains, telegraphs, stockyards, and other related enterprises. They are the closest approach to transport companies in North America. Both are very large rail organizations with continentwide service. It is significant that they have found it desirable to segregate the several transportation modes in separate operating organizations and to conduct them somewhat in competition with one another. This does not prevent a degree of intermodal coordination that goes beyond that with which we are familiar. Indeed intermodal control gives these roads the opportunity, which they have exploited, to move more quickly and forcefully in the development of intermodal services. The differences among the several transport technologies, however, counseled an organizational form that is anything but a close integration.

The Canadian experience and that of Southern Pacific cast some doubt upon the theoretical justification sometimes offered for "transport companies"—that the transport company itself can best determine the mode or combination of modes appropriate to each shipment and thus can better serve the shipper. Many factors that affect modal choice are

---

[25] See the frank criticism by Perry M. Shoemaker, "Should Railroads Diversify for Growth and Profit?" *Transportation Journal*, vol. 9 (Fall 1969), pp. 5 ff.

[26] Kenneth R. Graham, "Rail-Based Holding Companies—Alternative to Intermodal Ownership," Transportation Research Forum, *Proceedings, Twentieth Annual Meeting* (1979), pp. 238-244.

peculiarly within the knowledge of the shipper, for example, what quality of service is required within his distribution system, inventory and customer service policies, and what it is worth paying for such service. What the shipper needs is a variety of appropriately priced services, and the transportation company can make a contribution toward meeting that need. Even the Canadian roads, however, have been able to move only slowly in adjusting rates on truck, piggyback, and rail-carload services in a way to reflect the relative costs involved in these services. The principal argument for greater freedom to offer intermodal service seems, therefore, to be the greater facility with which coordinated services can be developed when the several modes are under a common control.

SELECTED REFERENCES

Barriger, John W.   *Super-Railroads for a Dynamic American Economy.* New York: Simmons-Boardman Publishing Co., 1956.

Chandler, Alfred D., Jr.   *Henry Varnum Poor.* Cambridge: Harvard University Press, 1956, chap. 7.

———.   The Railroads: Pioneers in Modern Corporate Management." *Business History Review,* vol. 39 (Spring 1965).

———.   *The Visible Hand: The Management Revolution in American Business.* Cambridge: Harvard University Press, 1977.

Cochran, Thomas C.   *Railroad Leaders, 1845–1890.* Cambridge: Harvard University Press, 1953.

Daughen, Joseph R., and Binzen, Peter.   *The Wreck of the Penn Central.* Boston: Little, Brown and Co., 1971.

Drucker, Peter F.   *The Practice of Management.* New York: Harper & Bros., 1954.

Dunlop, John T.   "Manpower in Operating Classifications on the Railroads." *Transportation Economics,* pp. 423 ff. National Bureau of Economic Research, 1965.

Fruhan, William E.   *The Fight for Competitive Advantage: A Study of the United States Domestic Trunk Air Carriers.* Boston: Harvard Business School, 1972.

Healy, Kent T.   "Management and Technological Change." *Technological Change and the Future of the Railways,* pp. 126 ff. Evanston, Ill.: Transportation Center at Northwestern University, 1961.

Levinson, Harold M.; Rehmus, Charles M.; Goldberg, Joseph P.; and Kahn, Mark L.   *Collective Bargaining and Technological Change in American Transportation.* Evanston, Ill.: The Transportation Center at Northwestern University, 1971.

Middleton, P. Harvey.   *Railways and Organized Labor.* Chicago: Railway Business Association, 1941.

Nelson, James C. *Railroad Transportation and Public Policy.* Washington, D.C.: The Brookings Institution, 1959.

Romer, Sam. *The International Brotherhood of Teamsters.* New York: John Wiley & Sons, Inc., 1962.

Sobel, Robert. *The Fallen Colossus.* New York: Weybright and Talley, 1977.

Welty, Gus. "Burlington Northern's First Year." *Railway Age,* vol. 170 (February 22, 1971), pp. 22 ff.

————. "Burlington Northern: Marketing, the Profit-Center Way." *Railway Age,* vol. 171 (September 27, 1971), pp. 24 ff.

16

Principles of Rate Making

Rates that move traffic, like prices that sell products, must be adjusted with regard to the effective demand in the market served. If they are to generate profit they must also take account of supply conditions, that is, the cost of producing the service in the amount demanded. Hence both supply and demand conditions enter into the making of rates. In a competitive market, price fixed at the intersection of supply and demand curves will clear the market and, in equilibrium, result in efficient production of a quantity consistent with demand at a price that generates a normal profit for all producers serving the market. In practice, markets rarely approximate the model of pure competition—the stock market and the grain market are two examples that come very close. In transport, however, competition in many markets is notably imperfect, although workable competition has become increasingly possible with the development of alternative services. We have given some attention to supply factors in Chapter 9. Demand conditions in transportation remain to be explored before rate theory can be satisfactorily discussed.

TRANSPORT DEMAND

Derived Demand

Freight transportation is a service, not a commodity. It has no value except as it is used to enable the production and distribution of goods desired for ultimate consumption or capital investment. Freight transport is an input in the process of production and of distribution. The demand for the transportation of a commodity may, thus, be said to be derived from the demand for that commodity in its final market (which is a direct, rather than derived, demand). Other inputs in the production process also encounter derived demand. Intermediate products, such as steel shapes and forms intended for fabrication into end products, are of this class.

In respect to final products sold to ultimate consumers, a reduction of price is ordinarily expected to cause an increase in the number of units sold. A service produced to meet a derived demand is, however, one or more steps removed from final demand. A reduction in price for that service will only have effect upon the demand for the commodity being transported if it is passed through to the final consumer; yet the transport service is but one of several factors of production involved and its price may be only a small part of the cost of production. If the "commodity" is a major appliance, say a refrigerator priced at $600, and the freight charge from factory to retail outlet is $60, a reduction of 10 percent in the freight charge, that is, $6, may not occasion a downward adjustment in retail price. Even if the reduction is fully passed on to the consumer, the new price of $594 is unlikely to generate an increase in refrigerator sales.

Demand for passenger service, like freight demand, is usually a derived demand. People travel for the purpose of reaching a destination and doing something there—transacting business, visiting relatives or friends, enjoying a national park or recreation facilities. For many, travel itself may contribute to the enjoyment of a visit or vacation, but journeys are rarely taken by commercial carriers for the mere pleasure of the journey. That there are exceptions does not nullify the general rule.

Price and Elasticity of Demand

What effect a change in price will have upon the amount sold, whether of a good or a service, is obviously of importance in price policy. The net revenue which an enterprise seeks to maximize is the result of price times volume sold less average unit cost times volume. In greater or less degree volume sold is a function of price and the term *price elasticity* is used to refer to the change in volume which will result from a change in price, all other things remaining undisturbed. As we have noted, demand curves are characteristically downward sloping indicating that a reduction of price will result in an increase in volume sold—an increase of price in a reduction of volume.[1]

---

[1] A demand curve, or demand schedule, indicates what volume will be bought at each possible price just as a supply curve indicates what volume will be offered by producers at each possible price. At high prices there may be fewer buyers, and each of those may be prepared to buy less than at a lower price.

Demand is said to be elastic when a reduction in price will generate a sufficient increase in volume of sales to cause an increase in gross revenues. It is said to be inelastic when a price reduction causes an upward reaction in volume which is not sufficient to preserve the gross revenues attained with the earlier and higher price. Thus with an inelastic demand a price *increase* may cause little decline in volume and may result in greater gross revenues. An increase of gross revenue by price reduction when demand is elastic does not, of course, indicate that a price reduction is desirable for producers. The added volume will occasion an increase in aggregate production cost. Marginal revenue must at least equal marginal cost if the producer is to be equally well off.

The price elasticity of particular products depends upon a number of factors. Thus the demand for necessities, such as food, is relatively inelastic in the aggregate. Yet price reductions may lead to a shift from less expensive to more expensive food items, imparting an elastic demand to the latter. Strictly speaking there has been a shift in the demand curves for the several products making up the foods category in consequence of a general reduction in prices. Commodities or services for which there are reasonably good substitutes may be expected to show higher elasticities than those for which there are no or poor substitutes.

Where demand is derived, as in the freight service, the elasticity of demand for transportation of any product will tend to be determined by the elasticity of demand for the product itself. Hence demand for the transport of staples will tend to be inelastic *because* demand for staples is itself inelastic. In general, the smaller the ratio of the freight cost to the price of the product in the market, the more inelastic will be the demand for transport of that product as in the refrigerator example cited above. Where the ratio of freight cost is high in relation to market price of the product, transport demand may prove to be more elastic than that for the product itself. In these circumstances freight rate reductions may bring more distant producers into the market by reducing the transport cost barrier which they formerly faced. Thus despite little increase in the amount of product sold in that market, transport volume may increase considerably because of a lengthening of the average haul. In effect more remote sources for the commodity have been partially substituted for nearer sources. These phenomena will be explored further at a later point.

The discussion thus far has concerned *aggregate* demand for the freight service and has said nothing about how that demand may be shared among competing modes or competing carriers within a mode. Aggregate demand for freight service may be expected to be price inelastic in the short run. Transportation by one mode is, however, often substitutable for transport by another mode. Hence *modal* demand can be more price elastic than aggregate demand, and the same is true of the demand schedule faced by an individual carrier within a mode. Price reductions can divert traffic from one carrier to another or one mode to another without having any noticeable effect upon *aggregate* freight transport demand.

Income Elasticity

Price elasticity, as discussed above, refers to the effects upon volume when only price changes and all other circumstances remain the same. Aggregate demand for transport is also affected by changes in income. Recovery from a recession is marked by an increase in economic activity and an increase in aggregate income. Gross national product moves up, as does the index of industrial production. More goods are being produced. Aggregate freight volume follows production up, and this phenomenon may be denominated as an income effect, not one generated by changes in price.[2] Income elasticity may be defined as the change in aggregate transport demand associated with a given change in an appropriate indicator of aggregate income of a region or nation.

Long-term economic growth is associated with an increase in *per capita* GNP. That is to say that the output of the economy grows more rapidly than does the population—the average citizen is better off in availability of economic goods and services. Price inflation, which tends in modern experience to be associated with economic growth, must be separated out to provide an appropriate income measure. Growth of per capita income alters the preferences of consumers; hence the composition of the national product. In recent decades the most notable such effect, so far as transport demand is concerned, has been an increase in the proportion of services in the national product. Services seldom generate outputs that require transportation; hence ton-miles per billion of GNP have shown a tendency to decline. The opposite may be true of an economy at an earlier stage of development where increases in income are directed to increased purchases of goods—most probably goods at a higher stage of manufacture or processing than formerly, hence possibly embodying more transport per unit of value.

Income changes occasion changes in demand schedules. A decline in aggregate income, such as may be associated with an economic recession, will shift the entire demand schedule to the left, as from D to D_1 in Figure 16-1. Less will be bought at each price. A strengthening of

---

[2] In practice, of course, price changes will be occurring at the same time so that the effects produced by changing income and those stimulated by price changes may be difficult, if not impossible, to separate out.

FIGURE 16-1

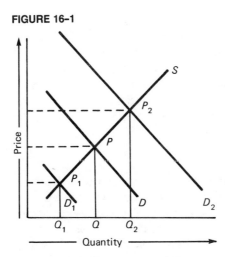

demand, however, which might result from a sharp recovery will shift the schedule to the right (D_2). If the supply schedule (S) remains unchanged, an unlikely event in the course of an economic cycle, price and output will shift—both declining during recession (P_1, Q_1) and both increasing during recovery (P_2, Q_2). Stickiness of prices will result in lower sales than with complete price adjustment.[3]

Changes in the Economic Structure

We have noted that the price elasticity of demand for transport can exceed that for the commodity transported when distant sources of supply are induced to compete in markets hitherto supplied locally or from nearby sources. Unless excess productive capacity exists, little of this type of substitution of sources is likely in the short run. Cross penetration of markets may, however, be stimulated with resulting crosshauls of product. In the longer run capacity can be expanded at points where manufacturing cost is lower than it is at or near the market if long-haul freight rates are sufficiently reduced to make the delivered cost competitive with local production cost. This produces a shift in the demand schedule for transportation[4] without the necessity of any shift in demand for the product being transported.

As noted in our discussion of industrial location, structural change in an economy will affect the aggregate freight transport demanded in relation to total goods output. A tendency toward centralization of pro-

---

[3] The aggregate supply function (S) is of the sort consistent with constant or increasing average unit costs of output. As noted earlier, a substantial portion of transport industries operate within the range of decreasing unit costs.

[4] This is true if transport output is measured in ton-miles rather than in tons carried.

duction will shift the demand schedule for transport to the right. De-centralization will produce the opposite effect. Changes in transport rates which are expected to continue in effect, or a decline in transport cost relative to other inputs which is believed to represent a continuing trend, can influence decisions on industrial location and on plant scale. Hence long-run demand for transport can be affected more sharply than short-run price elasticities would suggest.

Cross Elasticity

If the demand schedule for rail transport is drawn upon the assumption that the rates of all other modes will remain unchanged, that schedule may well be price elastic within the ranges of price where other modes are good substitutes. Rail rate-reductions in relation to the rates of other modes may, while having little or no effect upon aggregate transport demand, divert business from other modes. One mode, how-ever, is seldom a perfect substitute for another mode because the product is not identical. Service quality will differ in a number of re-spects, and shippers will not agree on the values which they place upon service differences. Since transport service is multidimensional, as already pointed out, and there is no good measure of output, the competitive relationships are complex and difficult to explicate.

Let us imagine, however, a commodity which moves between two points 500 miles apart in carload quantities where rail, motor-carrier, and water-carrier services are all available. Let us then attempt to construct a demand schedule for rail transport on the assumption that the motor and water rates, and the relative service qualities, remain unchanged. Rail is employed here because rail transport does com-pete with both motor and water transport under certain circumstances; yet it is rare to find a commodity that utilizes all three modes between the same points.

In Figure 16–2 demand for rail service at rates between R_1 and R_2 is very small and highly inelastic. Few, if any, shippers will use rail service at a rate above the motor-carrier rate. A reduction to parity with the motor-carrier rate may attract some business from shippers having rail sidings and for whom the loading of rail equipment is for some reason easier than loading motor-carrier equipment. When the rate is reduced below the motor-carrier rate, as at R_3, demand for rail service may become increasingly elastic—highly elastic as the margin between the two grows—until at R_4, all motor-carrier traffic except that tied to motor carriers by special circumstances has been diverted. Rail demand then becomes inelastic again until further reduction brings the rate close to the water-carrier rate. Since rail service may be superior in speed and frequency to water service and, for users having sidings, will not require trucking to and from terminals, rail demand

FIGURE 16-2

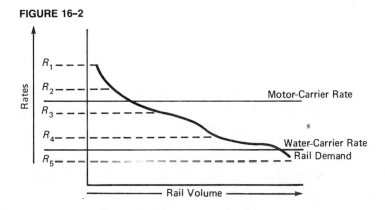

may turn elastic at a rail rate above the water-carrier rate level. It is entirely possible, indeed, that most water-carrier traffic may be diverted at such a rail rate level. The motor-carrier and water-carrier demand schedules will shift to the left as each rail rate-reduction is made within the range of substitution. The critical factor is the degree of substitutability of the service in relation to shippers' needs. To some shippers rail service will be a more adequate substitute for truck service than it is in the minds of others.

Commodities, also, are frequently substitutable for one another, hence there is cross elasticity between them. Coal, gas, and oil can frequently be quickly substituted for one another in utility burning equipment as price relations shift. In the longer run, long-distance transmission of electricity can be substituted for the movement of fuel by locating new generating capacity at the mine mouth. In such circumstances the elasticity of demand for transport of any one of the fuels may be high. Cement and asphalt are fairly good substitutes in highway surfacing, although under certain conditions of climate and subgrade, one will be preferable to the other. Yet in this, as in many other cases of imperfect substitutes, a sufficient disparity of price may offset the imperfection in the minds of purchasers.

Measurement of Elasticity

Statistical demand curves and measures of elasticity are ordinarily developed from time series.[5] More work has been done on passenger than on freight demand, but despite the importance of price elasticity for pricing policy, surprisingly little study has been accorded the ques-

---

[5] A cross-section approach has been employed by W. Bruce Allen and Leon H. Moses, "Choice of Mode in U.S. Overseas Trade: A Study of Air Cargo Demand," Transportation Research Forum, *Papers, Ninth Annual Meeting (1968)*, pp. 235–48. The appropriateness of the method requires further demonstration in this context.

tion in transport. Practicing rate-makers work from belief rather than knowledge, and successful pricing in a given situation can furnish little guidance that is useful in other situations. That aggregate price elasticity is considered to be low is not surprising in the light of our discussion up to this point. Rate makers will pay far more attention to the possibilities of diverting traffic from competitors and accept the proposition that the aggregate volume will be little affected by their rate-making activities. Even developmental rate-making is largely of this character, since it seeks to put a new source of supply within a market by displacing present sources in whole or part.

As Baumol points out, the demand function is a tricky concept which defies definitive approaches. Only one point on a demand curve can be observed with any confidence—that which represents present price and resulting sales. While we attempt to get data to plot another point, the whole curve may shift without our knowing it. More fundamental, the relationship deals with potential consumer behavior—what number of units will be bought if a different price is charged or some different marketing effort is employed? But, as he also says, "the demand function must ultimately play a critical role in any probing marketing-decision process, and there is really no way to get away from it."[6] The rate maker seeks information from shippers as to their reaction to changes under consideration and information as to the total volume of traffic moving and its distribution by modes. In the latter quest he is hampered by the fact that comprehensive commodity statistics for all modes of transport (including private carriage and transport exempt from regulation) are unavailable.[7] Hence, he works in greater or lesser degree in the dark.

Studies of price elasticity do lend some confirmation to the proposition we have advanced. They face the difficulties that available time series are often too short to be fully serviceable; they require deflation to remove the effect of price increases, income effects must be isolated, changes in relative technological progress of the modes ought to be allowed for, and shifts from one mode to another may turn out to be subject to a "learning curve," or face delay because distribution systems must be altered. The implicit assumption is made that past relations between price and volume will persist in the future. The estimated elasticity, moreover, relates only to that range of rate fluctuations that is reflected in the time series—greater increases or reductions in rates might have larger effects upon volume than the computed elasticity suggests. The statistical process itself will face the

---

[6] William J. Baumol, *Economic Theory and Operations Analysis*, 2d ed. (Englewood Cliffs, N.J.: Prentice-Hall, Inc., 1965), p. 211.

[7] The three censuses of transportation so far conducted shed light on broad classes of manufactured products.

problem of multicolinearity—interdependence among the variables to be examined.[8]

A study of demand for transportation in the United States for 1946–61 produced the following price elasticities: rail, 0.842; motor transport, 1.872 (insignificant); and inland water, 0.264 (insignificant). Income elasticities were found to be: rail, 0.976; truck, 0.342 (insignificant); and water, 1.305.[9] Sletmo finds a price elasticity of 0.376 for rail, truck, and air combined.[10] These findings tend to confirm the proposition that aggregate transport demand is price inelastic and that rail and water transport volumes, at least, tend to be significantly affected by general economic conditions.

Doubt is cast by Sletmo's investigations upon the general assumption that price elasticities for air cargo are high. He finds aggregate demand for airfreight worldwide to be inelastic and elasticity on the North Atlantic route close to unity, that is, a rate reduction leads at best only to the preservation of gross revenues. In United States domestic airfreight, however, he finds demand price elastic with estimates ranging from −2.2 to −1.1.[11] Evidently air and truck services are much better substitutes than air and ocean services; hence reductions in air-cargo rates have greater promise of diverting traffic in the domestic trades. Indeed high cross-price elasticities are found between domestic truck and airfreight.

All of these studies, be it noted, deal with freight traffic in the aggregate measured in ton-miles. Prices (rates) are made for the movement of particular commodities, or groups of commodities, between particular points or areas. The demand function of consequence to the rate maker is that applicable to the movement of a commodity in a particular transport market. If the econometrician has difficulty in estimating price elasticity for transport *in the aggregate*, what can be said for the problem that faces the rate maker?

RATE-MAKING PRINCIPLES: COST OF SERVICE

If transport operated as a perfectly competitive industry, there would be little reason to discuss its pricing principles, nor would pricing be in

---

[8] A useful summary of prior work, methodological difficulties, and results of both static and dynamic models applied to air cargo is Gunnar K. Sletmo, *Demand for Air Cargo: An Economic Approach* (Bergen: Institute for Shipping Research, The Norwegian School of Economics and Business Administration, 1972).

[9] Haskel Benishay and Gilbert R. Whitaker, Jr., "Demand and Supply in Freight Transportation," *Journal of Industrial Economics*, vol. 14, no. 3 (July 1966), p. 253.

[10] Gunnar K. Sletmo, *Demand for Air Cargo*, p. 70.

[11] Ibid., p. 92. A range of estimates develops from the fact that static and dynamic models generate different results.

controversy. The producer under perfect competition can
can produce at a price which, in equilibrium, returns cost
mal profit. Any higher price will exclude him from the market,
er one will convey no advantage. But transport is a world of
perfect competition. Moreover, the present situation which generates a great deal of intermodal competition as well as sharp competition within some modes is an outgrowth of a period when the railroad
industry, as long as its organization held reasonably together, had a
monopoly position in most transport markets. Finally, pricing is one of
the most important objects of regulation, and rate-making principles
must play a large role in the regulatory scheme.

Competitive Rates

The cost-of-service principle brings supply considerations to bear upon
the rate-making process but, as we know, supply alone does not determine price. A. C. Pigou, one of the few theoretical economists to
devote extended attention to railroad pricing, equated the cost-of-
service principle to simple competition and said, "It is generally
agreed that simple competition would tend to bring about a system of
uniform rates per ton mile for similar services" through the equating of
aggregate demand with supply.[12] He notes, however, some of the
numerous differences in cost of service that would produce differences
in rates per ton mile. Rates would be high in areas of difficult and
costly construction—high also in areas of light settlement because the
demand schedule there is low and the expenses involved in building
and working a railroad adapted for a small volume of traffic are high.
Small consignments would take higher rates. Long-haul rates per
ton-mile would be lower than short-haul rates because of better utilization of plant. Seasonal or periodic differences in rates might develop
because fluctuations in volume would produce differences in cost and
therefore of supply price. A wide variety of other differences in cost
would produce differences in ton-mile rates for superficially similar
services.

It is generally possible to say with some assurance that one transport service costs more to provide than another, but how much is the
difference in cost? The wide variety of circumstances under which
service is performed quickly provides cost justification for a multitude
of departures from uniform per ton-mile rates. How is one to know that
those differences are cost based and not the result of some other prin-

---

[12] A. C. Pigou, *The Economics of Welfare*, 4th ed. (London: Macmillan & Co., Ltd.,
1948), p. 291. The book was written originally in 1920 when railroads were still of predominant importance in internal transport in England and when regulatory questions
had been freshly raised in connection with restoration of railroads to private control after
World War I.

ciple or of the whim of the rate maker? How can the results
competition be approached in practice if the supply sched
particular service is as obscure to the rate maker as is the
schedule? Everyone accepts that an enterprise will not knowingly
a good or service below cost except for a promotional or a com
tively destructive purpose. How, then, could the trustees of Penn C
tral have contended that the carrier was losing $80 million a year
below-cost rates? Or that the president of a major motor-carrier coul
assert that shipments under 500 pounds in weight (70 percent of all
shipments) generated a loss of $380 million for motor carriers in 1969?[13]

Part of the difficulty stems from the problems of finding appropriate
costs which were touched on in Chapter 9. Part stems from the fact that
costs change over time and that rate adjustments tend to lag because
carriers cannot give continuing surveillance to the vast number of
rates in force; and when they do, they face shipper opposition to increases and regulatory delay. But there is also a lack of accord as to
the concept of cost that is appropriate to particular rate-making situations—even as to the concept that would produce the most desirable
results for economic efficiency. And there is concern lest short-term
pricing, based appropriately on incremental cost, may become imbedded in the rate structure and persist over the long term. It is easy to
say that no rate should exist that falls below the variable cost of the
particular service to which it applies and that all rates, taken together,
should generate revenue sufficient to cover total cost plus a reasonable
profit.[14] Such a policy is far from easy to carry out in practice.

Standards of Cost

We have earlier defined fixed and variable costs and the concepts of
marginal cost and average total cost. We have observed that the cost
structures of the several modes differ so far as the proportion of fixed to
total cost is concerned at characteristic levels of output. Rail and motor
carriers provide good examples, especially since they are competitive
with one another over a considerable range of hauls. The effects which
changes in volumes have on total cost, given such differences in cost
structure, can be illustrated in several ways, as in Figure 16–3. More
instructive, perhaps, is a numeric example which illustrates that under
certain circumstances, the diversion of traffic from a carrier having low
fixed costs to one having high fixed costs by pricing below average
total cost may result in improved profit for the latter and, at the same
time, reduce total transport cost to the shipping community.

---

[13] *Traffic World*, May 1, 1972, p. 35.

[14] This implies discrimination, a matter to be explored below under Rate-Making
Principles: Value of Service.

A has a cost structure similar to that of a
of a motor carrier. Assume the set of
erage total cost is higher for carrier

	Carrier A	Carrier B
. . . .	300,000	300,000
. . . .	5¢	5¢
. . . .	$15,000	$15,000
. . . .	$10,500 @ 3½¢	$13,500 @ 4½¢
. . . .	4,350	1,200
Total	$14,850	$14,700
erage total cost per ton-mile	4.95¢	4.9¢
Profit	$150	$300

A than for carrier B, but that carrier A's average variable cost (3½
cents) is 1 cent per ton-mile lower than that for carrier B. Each carrier
can contend that it is the low-cost carrier by choosing that measure of
cost that proves its point. Now if fixed costs have been properly identified and measured, they remain the same for any volume that can be
handled by the existing plant. Variable costs will remain the same per
unit unless the traffic handled moves outside the range of efficiency.
Assume that carrier A finds a particular commodity being handled by
carrier B which is distinguishable from all other traffic so that it can be
separately priced. There are 50,000 ton-miles generated in moving this
commodity, and a reduced rate of 4 cents per ton-mile diverts the
whole of it. Now we have:

	Carrier A	Carrier B
Total ton-miles	350,000	250,000
Rate per ton-mile	300,000 @ 5¢	5¢
	50,000 @ 4¢	
Revenue	$17,000	$12,500
Cost:		
Variable	$12,250 @ 3½¢	$11,250 @ 4½¢
Fixed	4,350	1,200
Total	$16,600	$12,450
Average total cost per ton-mile	4.8¢	4.98¢
Profit	$400	$50

Note that carrier A has increased its profit by 166⅔ percent though total
profit of the two firms remains unchanged. Carrier A now has lower
average total cost than carrier B—the reverse of the situation before
the traffic diversion. Shippers now pay the two carriers $29,500 as
compared with $30,000 before the rate change, and the total costs
incurred by the two carriers combined have fallen from $29,550 to
$29,050. Evidently the traffic is now being handled more efficiently
than before. But carrier A has resorted to discrimination—to what carriers call selective pricing.

problem of multicolinearity—interdependence among the variables to be examined.[8]

A study of demand for transportation in the United States for 1946–61 produced the following price elasticities: rail, 0.842; motor transport, 1.872 (insignificant); and inland water, 0.264 (insignificant). Income elasticities were found to be: rail, 0.976; truck, 0.342 (insignificant); and water, 1.305.[9] Sletmo finds a price elasticity of 0.376 for rail, truck, and air combined.[10] These findings tend to confirm the proposition that aggregate transport demand is price inelastic and that rail and water transport volumes, at least, tend to be significantly affected by general economic conditions.

Doubt is cast by Sletmo's investigations upon the general assumption that price elasticities for air cargo are high. He finds aggregate demand for airfreight worldwide to be inelastic and elasticity on the North Atlantic route close to unity, that is, a rate reduction leads at best only to the preservation of gross revenues. In United States domestic airfreight, however, he finds demand price elastic with estimates ranging from -2.2 to -1.1.[11] Evidently air and truck services are much better substitutes than air and ocean services; hence reductions in air-cargo rates have greater promise of diverting traffic in the domestic trades. Indeed high cross-price elasticities are found between domestic truck and airfreight.

All of these studies, be it noted, deal with freight traffic in the aggregate measured in ton-miles. Prices (rates) are made for the movement of particular commodities, or groups of commodities, between particular points or areas. The demand function of consequence to the rate maker is that applicable to the movement of a commodity in a particular transport market. If the econometrician has difficulty in estimating price elasticity for transport *in the aggregate*, what can be said for the problem that faces the rate maker?

RATE-MAKING PRINCIPLES: COST OF SERVICE

If transport operated as a perfectly competitive industry, there would be little reason to discuss its pricing principles, nor would pricing be in

---

[8] A useful summary of prior work, methodological difficulties, and results of both static and dynamic models applied to air cargo is Gunnar K. Sletmo, *Demand for Air Cargo: An Economic Approach* (Bergen: Institute for Shipping Research, The Norwegian School of Economics and Business Administration, 1972).

[9] Haskel Benishay and Gilbert R. Whitaker, Jr., "Demand and Supply in Freight Transportation," *Journal of Industrial Economics*, vol. 14, no. 3 (July 1966), p. 253.

[10] Gunnar K. Sletmo, *Demand for Air Cargo*, p. 70.

[11] Ibid., p. 92. A range of estimates develops from the fact that static and dynamic models generate different results.

the realm of controversy. The producer under perfect competition can sell all he can produce at a price which, in equilibrium, returns cost and normal profit. Any higher price will exclude him from the market, a lower one will convey no advantage. But transport is a world of imperfect competition. Moreover, the present situation which generates a great deal of intermodal competition as well as sharp competition within some modes is an outgrowth of a period when the railroad industry, as long as its organization held reasonably together, had a monopoly position in most transport markets. Finally, pricing is one of the most important objects of regulation, and rate-making principles must play a large role in the regulatory scheme.

Competitive Rates

The cost-of-service principle brings supply considerations to bear upon the rate-making process but, as we know, supply alone does not determine price. A. C. Pigou, one of the few theoretical economists to devote extended attention to railroad pricing, equated the cost-of-service principle to simple competition and said, "It is generally agreed that simple competition would tend to bring about a system of uniform rates per ton mile for similar services" through the equating of aggregate demand with supply.[12] He notes, however, some of the numerous differences in cost of service that would produce differences in rates per ton-mile. Rates would be high in areas of difficult and costly construction—high also in areas of light settlement because the demand schedule there is low and the expenses involved in building and working a railroad adapted for a small volume of traffic are high. Small consignments would take higher rates. Long-haul rates per ton-mile would be lower than short-haul rates because of better utilization of plant. Seasonal or periodic differences in rates might develop because fluctuations in volume would produce differences in cost and therefore of supply price. A wide variety of other differences in cost would produce differences in ton-mile rates for superficially similar services.

It is generally possible to say with some assurance that one transport service costs more to provide than another, but how much is the difference in cost? The wide variety of circumstances under which service is performed quickly provides cost justification for a multitude of departures from uniform per ton-mile rates. How is one to know that those differences are cost based and not the result of some other prin-

---

[12] A. C. Pigou, *The Economics of Welfare*, 4th ed. (London: Macmillan & Co., Ltd., 1948), p. 291. The book was written originally in 1920 when railroads were still of predominant importance in internal transport in England and when regulatory questions had been freshly raised in connection with restoration of railroads to private control after World War I.

ciple or of the whim of the rate maker? How can the results of simple competition be approached in practice if the supply schedule for a particular service is as obscure to the rate maker as is the demand schedule? Everyone accepts that an enterprise will not knowingly price a good or service below cost except for a promotional or a competitively destructive purpose. How, then, could the trustees of Penn Central have contended that the carrier was losing $80 million a year on below-cost rates? Or that the president of a major motor-carrier could assert that shipments under 500 pounds in weight (70 percent of all shipments) generated a loss of $380 million for motor carriers in 1969?[13]

Part of the difficulty stems from the problems of finding appropriate costs which were touched on in Chapter 9. Part stems from the fact that costs change over time and that rate adjustments tend to lag because carriers cannot give continuing surveillance to the vast number of rates in force; and when they do, they face shipper opposition to increases and regulatory delay. But there is also a lack of accord as to the concept of cost that is appropriate to particular rate-making situations—even as to the concept that would produce the most desirable results for economic efficiency. And there is concern lest short-term pricing, based appropriately on incremental cost, may become imbedded in the rate structure and persist over the long term. It is easy to say that no rate should exist that falls below the variable cost of the particular service to which it applies and that all rates, taken together, should generate revenue sufficient to cover total cost plus a reasonable profit.[14] Such a policy is far from easy to carry out in practice.

Standards of Cost

We have earlier defined fixed and variable costs and the concepts of marginal cost and average total cost. We have observed that the cost structures of the several modes differ so far as the proportion of fixed to total cost is concerned at characteristic levels of output. Rail and motor carriers provide good examples, especially since they are competitive with one another over a considerable range of hauls. The effects which changes in volumes have on total cost, given such differences in cost structure, can be illustrated in several ways, as in Figure 16–3. More instructive, perhaps, is a numeric example which illustrates that under certain circumstances, the diversion of traffic from a carrier having low fixed costs to one having high fixed costs by pricing below average total cost may result in improved profit for the latter and, at the same time, reduce total transport cost to the shipping community.

---

[13] *Traffic World,* May 1, 1972, p. 35.

[14] This implies discrimination, a matter to be explored below under Rate-Making Principles: Value of Service.

In this example, carrier A has a cost structure similar to that of a railroad, carrier B one like that of a motor carrier. Assume the set of facts given in the table. Note that average total cost is higher for carrier

	Carrier A	Carrier B
Total ton-miles	300,000	300,000
Rate per ton-mile	5¢	5¢
Revenue	$15,000	$15,000
Cost:		
Variable	$10,500 @ 3½¢	$13,500 @ 4½¢
Fixed	4,350	1,200
Total	$14,850	$14,700
Average total cost per ton-mile	4.95¢	4.9¢
Profit	$150	$300

A than for carrier B, but that carrier A's average variable cost (3½ cents) is 1 cent per ton-mile lower than that for carrier B. Each carrier can contend that it is the low-cost carrier by choosing that measure of cost that proves its point. Now if fixed costs have been properly identified and measured, they remain the same for any volume that can be handled by the existing plant. Variable costs will remain the same *per unit* unless the traffic handled moves outside the range of efficiency. Assume that carrier A finds a particular commodity being handled by carrier B which is distinguishable from all other traffic so that it can be separately priced. There are 50,000 ton-miles generated in moving this commodity, and a reduced rate of 4 cents per ton-mile diverts the whole of it. Now we have:

	Carrier A	Carrier B
Total ton-miles	350,000	250,000
Rate per ton-mile	300,000 @ 5¢	5¢
	50,000 @ 4¢	
Revenue	$17,000	$12,500
Cost:		
Variable	$12,250 @ 3½¢	$11,250 @ 4½¢
Fixed	4,350	1,200
Total	$16,600	$12,450
Average total cost per ton-mile	4.8¢	4.98¢
Profit	$400	$50

Note that carrier A has increased its profit by 166⅔ percent though total profit of the two firms remains unchanged. Carrier A now has lower average total cost than carrier B—the reverse of the situation before the traffic diversion. Shippers now pay the two carriers $29,500 as compared with $30,000 before the rate change, and the total costs incurred by the two carriers combined have fallen from $29,550 to $29,050. Evidently the traffic is now being handled more efficiently than before. But carrier A has resorted to discrimination—to what carriers call selective pricing.

FIGURE 16–3

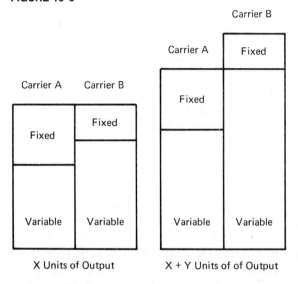

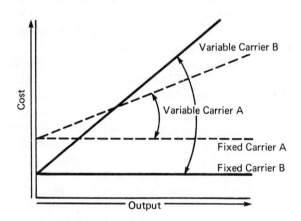

Under competition excess capacity in time tends to be eliminated. Price falls, volume increases, and inefficient enterprises are forced out of the industry and their capacity disappears. Excess capacity has existed in the railroad industry, however, from the beginnings of the industry until the present time. There is nothing to indicate that the excess will be eliminated in the foreseeable future unless major changes in corporate structure and public policy occur.[15] Motor and

---

[15] This point and its consequences for pricing policy is forcefully made in William J. Baumol et al., "The Role of Cost in the Minimum Pricing of Railroad Services," *The Journal of Business*, vol. 35, no. 357 (October 1962), pp. 1–10.

water carriers, on the other hand, can and do adjust their capacity fairly quickly to changes in volume; hence they do not experience excess capacity of major proportions over extended periods of time as do the railroads. This difference of circumstances produces quite different perceptions as to the cost-of-service principle among the modes, leading railroads to advocate marginal (out-of-pocket) cost pricing while motor and water carriers contend for average total (fully distributed) cost. Whatever standard is employed in competitive situations, however, rates as a whole must generate sufficient revenue to cover total cost and yield a profit if transport operations are to be successfully carried out by private firms without subsidy.

Common Costs

Use of cost as a rate-making principle is greatly complicated by the presence of large portions of common cost within the outlays of transport firms.[16] In general the proportion of directly assignable cost will be larger, the larger the unit of shipment to be priced. Thus few costs will be directly assignable to a 500-pound truck shipment. If we wish to take the trouble, we may be able to assign a cost to the pickup truck movement from the last customer to the one offering the 500 pounds,[17] the waiting time involved in getting the consignment loaded, and the billing cost. We can hardly segregate out a portion of the platform handling cost or of the line-haul cost. Only an arbitrary apportionment can be made. On the other hand, a large proportion of cost can be directly assigned to the movement of a trainload of coal in unit-train service on a repetitive daily basis. Both motive power and cars may be exclusively assigned to this shuttle movement, crew costs can be precisely determined, special trackage at origin and destination may be used only by these trains. There still remain common costs of some importance, for the lines traversed are used by trains in other services and supervision costs are incurred in common for all of the services rendered.

Common costs, then, are usually substantial in relation to total cost and can rarely be entirely avoided. They must be arbitrarily apportioned, and this can be done in a variety of ways. A physical measure or a combination of such measures may be used, for example, tons, ton-miles, vehicle-miles. Or common costs may be apportioned as a ratio of directly assignable costs. The method employed will result in different estimates of cost for the same service, whether the cost to be used is out-of-pocket or fully distributed. Despite the fact that, as Pigou

---

[16] The reader will recall that fixed as well as variable costs may be partly directly assignable to particular services and partly common to all services.

[17] But that will differ depending upon whether a shipper close by happens to have traffic on the same day and on the skill with which the dispatcher coordinates pickups.

rightly points out,[18] joint and common costs are not the same thing, their effect upon the cost finder and the rate maker is without practical difference.[19] In both cases an arbitrary apportionment becomes necessary. There remains the possibility that the rate maker may choose to apportion on the basis of demand conditions and that brings us squarely upon the value-of-service principle of rate making.

RATE-MAKING PRINCIPLES: VALUE OF SERVICE

Demand conditions as they bear upon the rate-making process are usually referred to by the term *value of service* or *what the traffic will bear*. The rate maker may be unaware of the demand schedule for a commodity and ignorant of the term *price elasticity*. He does know from experience that a rate can be made high enough to *dry up the traffic* when a lower rate might permit traffic to move *freely*. Thus, though he uses terms different from those of the economist, he is aware of the effect which rates can have upon the amount of service shippers will buy. To the extent that he can experiment by changing rates over time, he may reach an approximation of the rate that will attract the largest volume of traffic. If that rate produces vehicle-mile earnings that are near or above average, he is likely to conclude that the rate is compensatory and is in the interests of the carrier.

Determinants of Value of Service

One might suppose that the value of service rendered in transporting commodity X from point A, where it is produced, to point B, where it is used or consumed, is measured by the difference in price at the two points. If the price at B is $2 per unit higher than the price at A, then the value of the transport service is $2 and any rate at or below that level will cause commodity X to move between the two points. Unfortunately matters are not so simple, for freight rates are both price determined and price determining. If a rate of $1 were named between the two points, the price at B might decline by $1, by 50 cents, or not at all.[20] But if the price did decline we would be led to conclude that the value of service is now less than $2, although nothing but the freight rate has changed.

Many products are sold nationwide at a uniform price, yet the freight charges incurred between the producing plants and the many

---

[18] See the summary of his discussion with F. W. Taussig in Pigou, *Economics of Welfare*, pp. 295–300.

[19] Roy P. Sampson and Martin T. Farris, *Domestic Transportation: Practice, Theory and Policy*, 2d ed. (Boston: Houghton Mifflin Co., 1971), p. 157.

[20] The degree to which a freight rate-reduction would be passed on to consumers at B depends heavily on the elasticity of demand for product X in market B.

markets served vary a great deal. Many products are crosshauled. A manufacturer in Houston may sell on the West Coast while a San Francisco manufacturer penetrates the Texas market. Grain is an exceedingly competitive commodity. If our original proposition held, one would expect to see the price paid at each country elevator lower than that at the central market by the amount of the freight rate. Empirical studies show a broad general correspondence to this pattern, but they do not show agreement in detail.[21] Evidently the freight rate is not the only factor affecting price at the country elevator. There will, however, tend to be a closer correspondence between price differences and freight rates for relatively homogeneous low-grade products where the freight rate is a large part of the delivered price than for higher valued and more differentiated items.

What will be paid in freight at market B to import commodity X from source A will depend upon the demand schedule for commodity X at B. That demand schedule will depend, among other things, upon the substitutes or near substitutes that are available for commodity X. And the transport demand schedule derived from it will depend upon the cost of producing X at B, if that is feasible, and the cost of procuring X from other sources than A. It will depend, too, on the decisions of business firms who handle commodity X at B. In order to fill out a product line and enhance their total sales, they may accept a smaller margin on X, but at some point the margin may be so low that they are quite prepared to drop X from their stocks.

The matter may also be looked at from the point of view of the producer at A—indeed producers are commonly the moving parties in competitive distribution. The value of the service between A and B to him is measured by whether his net revenue will be improved by shipping into that market. If he can get a price at B that is above his production and selling cost plus the freight rate, he may see advantage in entering the market. At the least the added volume may assist in absorbing overhead. A reduction in the rate would improve his margin but not his sales at B nor the amount of transport he buys. An increase in the rate might lead him to stop selling at B unless he can increase his price there (but if he had thought it would improve his net revenue he would have charged a higher price in the first instance).

Value of Service Differs among Shippers

Our producer at A may have several competitors there who also produce X. He is, however, the low-cost producer. A rate that will induce him to market in B will not induce his competitors to do likewise since

---

[21] See, for example, W. T. Jackman, *Economic Principles of Transportation* (Toronto: University of Toronto Press, 1935), pp. 561-63; and D. Philip Locklin, *Economics of Transportation*, 7th ed. (Homewood, Ill.: Richard D. Irwin, 1972), pp. 59-63, and citations therein. © 1972 by Richard D. Irwin.

they would realize no improvement in net revenue. In effect the rate is so high that it excludes them from the market at B. At some lower rate, however, they would be prepared to ship into market B. In short, the value of service is not the same for all shippers. There may be other reasons than a difference in cost. The competitors may be better established in other more profitable markets, for example, and working close to their production capacity. At any rate that does move traffic there are likely to be some shippers who would be willing to pay a higher rate before they would cease to ship. Others may find the rate too high for their purposes. Those shippers who would pay more realize what Alfred Marshall called *consumers' surplus*—the difference between the rate they pay and the higher rate they would be willing to pay.[22]

The concept of consumers' surplus is useful in considering price discrimination, which will be discussed below. Some economists have argued that rate policy should seek to maximize consumers' surplus, hence that rates should be based upon marginal cost and the difference between marginal and average total cost should be governmentally subsidized (at least in the railroad industry, where decreasing costs are the normal expectation).[23] An argument for government ownership of the railroads has even been made on this basis. Be it noted that for most freight services the immediate consumer is a business firm of some sort or another, either the shipper or receiver of the goods. As the above discussion suggests, the freight rate may or may not be passed on to the ultimate user of the goods in whole or in part in individual marketing circumstances.[24]

Ability to Bear Transport Charges

Since the value of the commodity has often been taken as at least a crude index of the value of the service, it is important to consider the ability of commodities of varying value to bear transport charges. Since transport rates are universally based on weight, except for ocean and air rates where a measurement (cube) unit may alternate, it is value per unit of weight that is usually proper for comparison with the freight rate. The value of the commodity is its selling price which, if we assume workable competition in the markets for most commodities,

---

[22] Alfred Marshall, *Principles of Economics*, 8th ed. (London: Macmillan & Co., Ltd., 1920), pp. 124–33. For a lucid description of the application of the principle to transport rates, see C. Colson, *Transports et Tarifs* (Paris: J. Rothschild, 1890), chap. 6.

[23] Harold Hotelling, "The General Welfare in Relation to Problems of Taxation and of Railway and Utility Rates," *Econometrics*, vol. 6 (1938), p. 242; and R. H. Montgomery, "Government Ownership and Operation of Railroads," *Annals of the American Academy of Political and Social Science*, vol. 201 (1939), p. 157.

[24] The incidence of the freight rate is analogous to the incidence of a tax. See, for example, Marshall, *Principles of Economics*, pp. 413–15; and Kenneth E. Boulding, *Economic Analysis* (New York: Harper & Bros., 1941), pp. 239–43.

is a reflection of demand and supply conditions in the markets. The mere fact that one commodity is priced higher than another per unit weight tells us nothing about the price elasticity of demand for the commodity. It does, however, tell us something about the effect of the freight rate upon the final price.

The movement of indispensable commodities that are available only from a distance clearly will not be deterred by transport charges that are high relative to their value. Demand for such commodities is highly inelastic. Yet they are comparatively few, and the aggregate transport demand generated by them is small. The more common circumstances are those which permit (1) one staple to be substituted in part for another, (2) necessary stocks of a commodity to be secured from nearer rather than farther sources, or (3) local production to be arranged at costs only somewhat higher than production costs at other places. All such possibilities place limits upon the ability to bear transportation charges.

The fact remains, however, that the range of commodity values per ton is great—from a few dollars in the case of sand, gravel, coal, and other bulk items to thousands of dollars in the case of a wide range of manufactured goods and appliances. It is freight charges *relative* to final price rather than the absolute level of freight charges that determines what influence freight charges may have on price and, therefore, on demand. The range of transport rates is much less wide than the range of commodity values; hence relative transport charges tend to be lower as commodity values go higher even though the freight rate per ton mile increases. The more valuable commodities can and do bear higher absolute transport charges and still move freely. Given a transport monopoly, therefore, commodity value is a useful guide for determining which commodities can be assessed higher charges without serious risk of inhibiting their movement.

Discrimination

Discrimination may be defined as the sale of two or more similar goods or services at prices which are in different ratios to marginal cost.[25] Discriminatory prices yield a larger revenue than a single price system, but certain conditions are essential to create the ability to discriminate. The basic condition which permits the sale of different units of product at different prices is that the market be split into separate sections and that it be difficult to transfer product or service from one

---

[25] The inequality of $P_1/MC_1 \neq P_2/MC_2$. Some economists prefer the proposition that prices are discriminatory if the difference in price is not equal to the difference in marginal cost, that is, $P_1 - MC_1 \neq P_2 - MC_2$. See George J. Stigler, *The Theory of Price*, 3d ed. (New York: Macmillan Co., 1966), p. 209.

section of the market to another.[26] The rule of profit maximization in discriminating monopoly is that marginal revenues be the same in all markets where the monopolist sells.[27] Under any other situation it could shift product from one market to another with profit. In dealing with discrimination in the transport service, Pigou adds to the proposition that no unit of service sold in one market can be transferred to another market where a different price may prevail, the following additional condition: No unit of *demand* proper to one market can be transferred to another market as would occur if different rates from origins A and B enabled the favored origin to increase its production and, therefore, its demand for carriage.[28]

Pigou defines three degrees of discriminating monopoly as follows: first degree, price exacted from each purchaser equal to that purchaser's demand price and no consumers' surplus left to any buyer; second degree, n separate prices devised in such a way that all units with a demand price greater than x were sold at a price x, all with a demand price less than x and greater than y at a price y, and so on; third degree, distinction of buyers among n different groups, separated from each other by some practicable mark, with a separate monopoly price charged to the members of each group.[29] Some consumers' surplus would accrue to buyers under second and third degree discrimination; hence only the first degree would maximize the revenue of the monopolist in the light of demand conditions. Because of the cost and difficulty of administering the first and second degrees, Pigou considers that in real life only the third is found.[30] As a practical matter since railroads have been subjected to regulation, published tariffs plus efforts to prevent rebates rule out first and second degree discrimination.

Third degree discrimination amounts to segregating the market as much as possible into categories which have different demand elasticities. Inelastic markets can then be charged high rates well above the cost of service. Those markets having price elastic demands can be accorded low rates designed to maximize revenue above marginal cost. Total traffic may well be larger than under uniform rates, for if uniform rates are high enough to cover average total cost no traffic will be developed from many of those markets which have an elastic demand. Discriminatory pricing among alternatives early commended

[26] Baumol, *Economic Theory and Operations Analysis*, p. 323.

[27] Ibid., p. 324.

[28] Pigou, *Economics of Welfare*, p. 275.

[29] Ibid., p. 279.

[30] Ibid., p. 280. It appears, however, that the rebate system practiced by the Southern Pacific in California may have approximated the first degree at least for large shippers. See Stuart Daggett, *Chapters in the History of the Southern Pacific* (New York: The Ronald Press, Co., 1922), pp. 250–256.

itself to railway managers since their minimum plant generated capacity in excess of the traffic volume which could be encouraged at uniform rates. By pushing up rates for traffic on which demand was inelastic, revenues in excess of average cost could be extracted from such traffic. On the other hand, the reduction of rates on types of traffic having elastic demand toward marginal cost could bring added volume that would make a contribution to overhead. Added volume would take up excess capacity, reduce average unit cost, and thus permit lower *average* rates for all traffic under discrimination than the uniform rates required at the lower traffic volume that would be attracted by such rates.

Pigou found social justification for discriminatory rates in the railroad service up to a point. Specifically he considers discrimination in the third degree preferable when no uniform price can be found which will cover the expenses of producing *any* quantity of output, but a system of discriminatory prices is practicable that will make some output profitable and thus make possible the provision of improved transport. This he believes most likely to occur under conditions of decreasing supply price (decreasing unit costs) and where demand is relatively elastic, conditions he believes to be satisfied with railroad construction in areas hitherto unprovided with transport until considerable economic development has taken place. A certain intermediate range of population and economic activity is necessary to make rail service possible at uniform prices. Hence if discrimination were not permitted or a subsidy provided, certain lines would not be built until the country had developed to the level required to support such lines under competition.[31] Pigou has in mind, of course, governmentally required pricing of the competitive form, for it is clear that a territory that will barely support one railroad will not support several lines in competition one with another.

Types of Discrimination

Railroads did not originate rate discrimination. Some forms already existed in the operations of wagon, canal, and water transport, for it was early discovered that profitable freighting required the tapping of a broader spectrum of traffic than could be attracted at uniform rates. Crude classifications were in use that extended lower rates to less valuable commodities and singled out some more valuable items for higher charges. Classification of commodities, indeed, readily meets the requirement for barring the transfer of demand from one market to

---

[31] Pigou, *Economics of Welfare*, pp. 308–12.

another. Copper bar cannot easily be made to masquerade as coal; hence different rates are entirely practicable.

Railroads brought commodity discrimination to a high degree of perfection. Faced with a high potential capacity even on a primitive line of road in comparison with the traffic previously moved by wagon or canal, they understood the need for downward discrimination to bring to the line commodities that had not previously moved. Such commodities need only contribute something above the direct cost of handling them to improve the carriers' position. Overhead could be recouped, at least in large part, by upward discrimination on commodities with good ability to bear transport charges. In effect the fixed and common costs were apportioned among commodities somewhat in proportion to their ability to bear transport charges.

Since freight moves from one place to another, transport markets can also be geographically distinguished. Freight moving from point A to point C cannot be made to masquerade for freight moving from point A to point B. But there are limits, since if C lies beyond B on the same line of road, the rate to B cannot be higher than the rate to C plus the rate from C back to B, otherwise shippers will employ an agent at C to reship back to B. Geographic discrimination usually developed where competitive circumstances external to the railroad appeared at one point and not at others, for example, the competition of water carriers between A and C but not between A and B. A lower per-mile rate above direct cost from A to C might permit the railroad to divert some traffic from the water carriers thus improving its contribution to overhead. Shippers between A and C would be afforded a transport alternative formerly unavailable to them at a competitive price. Shippers at B would suffer no harm provided their rates were not increased, for all that the railroad had done at C was to secure a share in traffic already moving by water at lower rates. C had a natural advantage (presence of the navigable waterway) which B did not enjoy. If geographic discrimination had been limited to such circumstances, less criticism of it would have developed.

Transport markets can also be distinguished by direction of travel. Traffic flows quite commonly are directionally imbalanced with the result that empty equipment must be moved in one direction. Lower rates in the direction of light traffic were early tried as a means of encouraging better loading. Finally, shippers themselves could sometimes be classified on the basis of their location in relation to the transport facility; for example, shippers without a rail siding could be distinguished from those which had a railside location and, perhaps, afforded an allowance to cover the cost of draying the freight to the railroad. In sum there are numerous ways of segregating transport markets in order to permit discriminatory pricing.

Monopolistic Competition in Transport Markets

The type of competitive railroad development by private corporations that occurred in the United States and in Great Britain resulted in several railroads operating in competition between the larger urban centers, but left most points with service by only one railroad. Price competition could and did break out between the competitive points and affected large volumes of traffic. But railroads sought by agreement to terminate such price competition; and ultimately, when regulation had come to their assistance, price competition was brought under reasonably effective control. A value-of-service rate structure was, therefore, perfectly practicable and quite thoroughly practiced. Grafted upon those discriminations which railroads might have perpetrated in their own interests were others encouraged by public policy, including relatively low rates on agricultural commodities and on the movement of staples into export position.

Whatever might be said of the desirability of such a system, it was comparatively stable and could, by the adjustment of the level of rates with changing economic conditions, be made to support the rail system. It was, however, highly vulnerable to competition from outside the rail industry. Apportionment of overheads in accordance with the value of the service results in rates on high-valued traffic that are well above the costs of producing the service, sometimes by several multiples. It was no accident that the development of motor transport resulted in the diversion of large volumes of such high-valued traffic. Motor-carrier costs need not be nearly as low as rail costs to permit profitable rates to be made that would equal or undercut above-cost rail rates on a wide variety of traffic. Hence motor-carrier penetration of rail business tended to commence from the top of the traffic stratum under value-of-service pricing. Motor common carriers, in turn, themselves having adopted substantially the rail classification and rates, found some of their own high-rated volume traffic vulnerable to private trucking. For the shipper who trucks his own traffic obtains the service at cost regardless of the rate structure which public carriers may seek to impose.

Carrier traffic officers have found it difficult to recognize that a changed concept of the value of service by any mode is now appropriate. Where competition by one mode with another has become feasible, the value of service by one mode may be fixed by the cost of generating comparable service by the other mode. Where the services are not such good substitutes as to leave the shipper indifferent as to which mode he employs, some differential between the rates of the two modes may be needful to offset the difference in service quality. These principles were long recognized in rail-water competition, but primarily to the benefit of the water carriers by permitting or requiring rail rates differentially above the water rates without regard to the relative costs of service by the two modes. These principles were not readily extended to the case of rail-motor competition.

Commodity discrimination has continued and is entirely supportable between two modes operating under published and regulated rates. The regulatory authorities, indeed, have worked hard to prevent rate reductions on high-valued traffic in the belief that the maintenance of such rates is essential to the continuance of adequate service on low-grade traffic and that the latter is essential to the health of the economic system. As soon, however, as shippers are capable of resorting to private trucking of desirable high-value traffic flows, public carriers will suffer an erosion of the better-paying traffic. Much such erosion has in fact occurred. We may add a corollary, therefore, that for those shippers willing and able to truck privately the value of common-carrier service to them is fixed by their own cost of trucking.

In earlier times the burden of proving what rate a particular movement was "entitled" to within a value-of-service rate structure could be left to the shipper. In today's more competitive scene the shipper often has several alternatives. Market research, formerly considered unnecessary, has become increasingly essential if carriers are to conduct their pricing activities in the light of actual demand-and-supply circumstances. Costing procedures badly need improvement. More comprehensive and detailed data on traffic flow must be provided. Carriers of one mode must develop an understanding of their own costs and those of others. Service quality control must be coordinated with pricing policies. To this end a number of the carriers have instituted market research programs; yet 40 years after the beginnings of significant intermodal and private competition these efforts must still be looked upon as modest and incommensurate with the size of the task.

SELECTED REFERENCES

Ackworth, W. M.   *The Elements of Railway Economics*, chaps. 8 and 9. Oxford at the Clarendon Press, 1924.

———.   "The Theory of Railway Rates," *Economic Journal*, vol. 7, no. 317 (1897).

Baumol, William J., et al.   "The Role of Cost in the Minimum Pricing of Railroad Services." *Journal of Business*, vol. 35, no. 357 (October 1962).

Hadley, A. T.   *Railroad Transportation: Its History and Its Laws*, chaps. 4–6. New York: G. P. Putnam's Sons, 1885.

Kahn, Alfred E.   *The Economics of Regulation: Principles and Institutions*. vol. 1, Part II. New York: John Wiley & Sons, Inc., 1970.

Lansing, John B. *Transportation and Economic Policy*, chaps. 4 and 19. New York: The Free Press, 1966.

Lardner, Dionysius. *Railway Economics*. London: Taylor, Walton and Maberly, 1850.

Locklin, D. Philip. *Economics of Transportation*, chap. 7. 7th ed. Homewood, Ill.: Richard D. Irwin, Inc., 1972.

Nelson, James R., ed. *Criteria for Transport Pricing*. Cambridge, Md.: Cornell Maritime Press, 1973.

Pegrum, Dudley F. *Transportation: Economics and Public Policy*, chaps. 7 and 8. 3d ed. Homewood, Ill.: Richard D. Irwin, Inc., 1973.

Pigou, A. C. *The Economics of Welfare*, chaps. 14–18. 4th ed. London: Macmillan & Co., Ltd., 1948.

Ripley, W. Z. *Railroads: Rates and Regulation*. New York: Longmans, Green & Co., 1912.

Roberts, Merrill J. "Transport Pricing Reform." *Transportation Journal*, Spring 1973, pp. 5 ff.

17

Rate Making in Practice

All carriers subject to regulation, whether rail, motor, water, pipeline, or air, are required to publish their rates in tariff form together with the rules and regulations that govern the application of the rates and the performance of the services to which they apply. These rates, rules, and regulations must be adhered to; departures constituting violations of law. Great complexity has developed in tariffs over the years, especially those for rail and truck freight. Upward of 1 trillion rates are estimated to be contained in the tariffs currently in effect. As many as 12 tariff publications may sometimes have to be consulted in order to find the rate applicable to a particular shipment and the routing restrictions and other regulations that may surround its use. Something approaching $1 billion annually is thought to be the cost to shippers and carriers which result from the use of so complex a system.

Shippers frequently perform both a preaudit and a postaudit of freight bills beyond a nominal sum. The audited bills are then commonly sold to professional freight-bill auditors who find their profit in retaining 50 percent of the overcharges which they successfully claim from carriers. In principal part these overcharges stem from the use of a rate, in calculating freight charges, that turns out to be higher than the applicable rate even though it may have seemed to have had the benefit of good tariff authority. The problem has been enormously complicated during the several post-World War II inflationary periods by the issuance of master tariffs which provide a way of applying general increases to rates. Two or three such master tariffs may have to be applied during a considerable period of time before the basic tariffs are reissued to incorporate the increases. And tariffs are quite commonly supplemented extensively before reissue.

FREIGHT CLASSIFICATION AND COMMODITY RATES

The task of pricing transportation is more complex than pricing goods in a store or warehouse where the question essentially depends on one thing, what the object to be sold is. The service for which a rate (price) is set depends on (1) what is being transported, (2) how much is being moved, and (3) where it is being transported (between what points). A fourth factor may be involved if a special service is rendered. Rate making is the application of rate-making principles and the basic elements of rate structure in the determination of the actual rates to be charged. The for-hire carrier of freight has the task of setting many hundreds or perhaps thousands of rates covering a wide range of commodities, packed in a variety of ways, and moving in different quantities over various distances and in several classes of service.

A carrier desires to set a rate in any given instance that is low enough to encourage the traffic to move via its facilities, yet high enough to be profitable. It seeks to maximize its net revenue from freight service. Thus, whenever possible, a rate should not only cover special costs assignable to the traffic and a proportionate share of the common costs, but also contribute to a net return to the stockholders. Where this is not possible a rate that merely covers special cost and contributes something to common costs may nevertheless be a "profitable" rate if it reduces losses or at best permits a broader spreading of the common costs, leaving a larger net income after all charges. A high rate which substantially reduces traffic may be less profitable than a lower one. As pointed out long ago by William Z. Ripley, "Not until a rate has been put into effect, can its results be known."[1] In making rates the individual carriers cooperate in determining the division of through interline rates. The two aspects of rate making are (1) classification of commodities into groups for rating purposes and (2) preparation of rate scales and their application in tariffs. These two aspects will be discussed in this order. In the first we are concerned with what is shipped and in the second with where it is shipped.

Development of Rail Freight Classification

This extensive task of pricing thousands of commodities moving over so many possible routes would be all but impossible if they were not grouped into "classes" for rate-making purposes. All commodities in a

---

[1] William Z. Ripley, *Railroads: Rates and Regulation* (New York: Longmans, Green & Co., 1912), p. 101.

given group or class are treated uniformly, the rate being the same for a given haul.

For some years the early railroads followed the example of their predecessors and competitors, the canal boat and wagon train operators, and had relatively simple classifications, if any. As commerce and the railroads expanded, individual railroads developed more elaborate classifications. But this still left the shipper who had a shipment going over several lines en route to destination in a state of confusion trying to determine the through charges. It has been estimated that there were as many as 138 distinct classifications in what is termed today the *Eastern Trunk-Line territory*.[2]

Regional uniformity began in 1882 with the *Joint Western Classification*, a forerunner of the *Western Classification*. By 1888 the railroads in the East, West, and South had set up the organizational basis for the well-known *Official* (eastern), *Southern*, and *Western Classification* territories. The formation of the three great classification regions was a big step toward uniformity and afforded great relief to shippers and carriers. But these three separate major classifications, with many differences in the description of articles and rules as well as differences in ratings, continued as separate publications until 1919, when the United States Railroad Administration in cooperation with the Interstate Commerce Commission brought the three principal classifications together in one volume known as the *Consolidated Freight Classification*. Uniformity of descriptions of commodities and rules was established, but the identity of the three classification territories and ratings was retained.

The move to attain a national uniform classification was launched by an Interstate Commerce Commission investigation of class rates in all territories east of the Rocky Mountains, a proceeding known as *Class Rate Investigation, 1939*. On May 15, 1945, the commission ordered the railroads to begin work on a uniform classification with a view to eliminating discriminatory relationships and simplifying rate procedure.[3] By commission order growing out of the last of these proceedings, *Uniform Freight Classification No 1* was issued to go into effect February 1, 1952. Until late 1955,[4] it applied only to the rate territories east of the Rocky Mountains.

---

[2] H. H. Shannon, "History of Freight Classification," *Traffic World*, January 31, 1931, p. 283.

[3] 262 ICC 447 (1945). The report of this case presents a thorough treatment of the development and principles and practice of rail freight classification. The order was later modified in the supplementary proceedings 264 ICC 41 (1945); 268 ICC 577 (1947); 281 ICC 213 (1951).

[4] 296 ICC 555 (Docket Nos. 30416 and 30660, 1955). The decision from this proceeding of October 19, 1955, required the extension of the Uniform Classification to the Rocky Mountain-Pacific territory and to transcontinental rates. However, an interim basis of rates was allowed rather than the 28,300-rate scale, effective east of the Rocky Mountains.

The *Uniform Freight Classification* like its predecessor presents the classes by number and the classification rules. There are 30 classes as follows: Classes 400, 300, 250, 200, 175, 150, 125, 100, 92.5, 85, 77.5, 70, 65, 60, 55, 50, 45, 40, 37.5, 35, 32.5, 30, 27.5, 25, 22.5, 20, 17.5, 16, 14.5, and 13. Class 100 corresponds with the old Class I. The other classes are multiples of Class 100 if they are a higher number, or a percentage of Class 100 if lower, as the number of the class indicates. For example, Class 40 is a rating that is just 40 percent of Class 100 for a given haul for all commodities rated in Class 40.

Items are listed alphabetically in the classification as shown in the section of a page of the *Uniform Classification* which is reproduced as Figure 17-1. There are three columns opposite each item, showing the less-than-carload ratings, carload minimum, and carload ratings, respectively. The rating shown is the class to which a commodity is assigned. Less-than-carload ratings are usually higher than carload ratings for a given commodity class or item. Some ratings are "any-quantity" ratings and, therefore, are the same for carload and less-than-carload quantities. The amount which must be shipped in order to get the lower carload rating is designated as the carload minimum quoted in thousands of pounds. It is a matter which is influenced by the density of the goods; size, type, and capacity of the car; number of tiers which may be loaded without damage; size of shipment common to the trade (commercial quantity); and competition of other carriers, particularly motor carriers. For example, the carload minimum weight is much lower for furniture than for building lumber.

A commodity shipped loose is likely to take a higher rating than if it is packaged, and the more secure the packing, the lower the rating tends to be. Lower ratings are obtained on "knocked-down" articles such as furniture or vehicles. These are all adjustments based on the cost-of-service principle to reflect costs associated with density of the commodity and risk as packed for shipment. Articles which are especially subject to loss or damage take higher rates in recognition of the cost of claims settlement. However, the assignment of higher ratings to finished goods than to unfinished goods reflects the value-of-service principle.

The *Uniform Freight Classification* and the old *Consolidated Freight Classification* include the classification rules and regulations which apply generally to marking, packing, and other requirements in the application of ratings. To meet the competition of motortrucks, the railroads in 1932 introduced the "all-freight rate." This applies to a carload shipment of mixed commodities, regardless of the regular classification of any of the commodities included. For years, rule 10 of the *Consolidated Classification* had provided for mixed-carload shipments which ordinarily take the rating of the highest rated commodity and the highest carload minimum applying to any commodity. The first "all-freight

FIGURE 17-1
Typical Page from Ratings Section of *Uniform Classification*

31240-31660 UNIFORM FREIGHT CLASSIFICATION 4

Item	ARTICLES	Less Carload Ratings	Carload Minimum (Pounds)	Carload Ratings
31240	**Cottonseed hull fibre or shavings, other than bleached or dyed,** see Notes, items 31241 and 31242: In bags, barrels or boxes In machine pressed bales	85 70	20,000R 29,000R 40,000R	45 37½ 27½
31241	**Note.**—Section 2 of Rule 34 will not apply.			
31242	**Note.**—If charge computed at the higher CL rating subject to the lower CL minimum weight exceeds the charge computed at the lower CL rating subject to the higher CL minimum weight, the lower CL rating subject to the higher CL minimum weight will apply.			
31250	**Cottonseed hulls,** not ground, in bags, barrels or machine pressed bales; also CL, in bulk	50	36,000	17½
31260	**Cottonseed hulls,** ground (**cottonseed hull bran**), LCL, in bags; CL, in packages or in bulk	50	40,000	17½
31270	**Cottonseed hulls, cake or meal in mixed carloads:** Where cottonseed hulls are shipped in mixed carloads with cake or meal or with cake and meal, the rates to be applied based upon a carload minimum weight of 40,000 lbs. shall be those which would be applicable if the commodities were shipped separately in carload lots, the deficiency in carload minimum weight, if any, to be charged for at the rate applicable to cottonseed hulls.			
31280	**Couplings,** brass or bronze, other than pipe fittings, in barrels or boxes	77½	30,000	50
31300	**COVERS:**			
31310	**Barrel,** burlap, in bales	70	30,000	40
31320	**Barrel,** cotton, in bales	70	30,000	40
31330	**Barrel, basket, box or pail,** wire, in packages	100	24,000R	55
31340	**Barrel, box, can, pail or tub,** display, **noibn,** in barrels, boxes or crates	100	24,000R	55
31350	**Basket or hamper, noibn,** with rim, in packages; also CL, loose	100	24,000R	55
31360	**Basket or hamper, noibn,** without rim, in packages; also CL, loose	70	36,000	32½
31370	**Cooling box,** rubber composition or synthetic plastic; or rubber composition or synthetic plastic and steel combined, in boxes or crates	85	24,000R	55
31380	**Food, noibn,** synthetic plastic, with or without metal parts, in boxes	200	10,000R	100
31390	**Ice cream can or milk shipping can,** steel, in boxes or crates	85	24,000R	55
31400	**Meter box,** cast iron, with or without fasteners, loose (LCL, only if weighing each 25 lbs. or over), in packages	50	40,000	35
31410	**Rayon yarn cake** (covers in tubular form, knitted rayon or knitted cotton or a mixture thereof), in bales or boxes	100	20,000R	70
31420	**Shipping** (covers for freight during transportation), canvas, cloth, rubber or tarpaulin, in packages	85	24,000R	55
31430	**Shipping** (covers for freight during transportation), paper, printed, in packages	70	36,000	37½
31440	**Shipping** (covers for freight during transportation), paper, not printed, in packages	55	36,000	32½
31450	**Tank thief-hole,** aluminum and iron combined, in barrels or boxes	100	24,000R	45
31465	**Covers, discs, fillers, partitions, platforms,** see Note, item 31471, **or wrappers, for packing,** or **interior packing forms, noibn,** fibreboard or paper, corrugated: Other than flat, KD flat, folded flat or nested, in packages Nested, in packages Flat, KD flat, folded flat or nested solid, in packages	150 100 65	24,000R 24,000R 24,000R	35 35 35
31470	**Covers, discs, fillers, partitions, platforms,** see Note, item 31471, **or wrappers, for packing,** or **interior packing forms, noibn,** fibreboard, paper or woodpulp, not corrugated: Other than flat, KD flat, folded flat or nested, in packages Nested, in packages Flat, KD flat, folded flat or nested solid, in packages	150 100 55	36,000 36,000 36,000	35 35 35
31471	**Note.**—Flat covers, discs, fillers, partitions or platforms, not printed, made of one piece of fibreboard or paper, not further finished than cut to shape, not scored, slotted nor perforated, will be rated same as fibreboard or paper from which cut.			
31480	**Crampons or ice creepers, boot or shoe,** in boxes	85	30,000	55
31490	**Crochet hooks,** in boxes	100	20,000R	70
31500	**Crosses,** wooden, in the white, in boxes	70	30,000	35
31510	**Crucibles, noibn,** in barrels, boxes or individually bolted to wooden lift truck platforms	85	24,000R	55
31520	**Crucibles or muffles,** abrasive material, in barrels, boxes or crates; also CL, packed in excelsior, hay, straw or similar packing material and securely racked and braced in car	85	24,000R	55
31530	**Crucibles or scorifiers,** clay, in barrels or boxes	70	30,000	37½
31540	**Crude petroleum treating compound, noibn,** for separating water from crude oil, or preventing corrosion of oil well equipment, in barrels; also CL, in tank cars, Rule 35	65	36,000	37½
31550	**CUPRO-NICKEL, see Note, item 31551:**			
31551	**Note.**—Ratings apply on metal or metal articles composed of copper and nickel containing more than 50% copper.			
31560	**Blanks (unfinished shapes),** in barrels, boxes or tubs	60	30,000	45
31570	**Castings, noibn,** as from the mold, except that fins, sinker-heads and gates may be removed, and castings may be cleaned or rough turned to ⅛ inch of finished size, loose (LCL, only if weighing each 50 lbs. or over), or in packages	60	30,000	45
31580	**Forgings, in the rough,** as from the hammer or press. They may have the flash or excess metal removed and may be annealed, cleaned or tumbled but not machined; bolt or center holes may be made but not threaded, loose (LCL, only if weighing each 25 lbs. or over) or in packages	60	30,000	45
31590	**Ingot, pig or slab,** LCL, in barrels, boxes, crates or tubs; CL, loose or in packages	60	30,000	40
31600	**Plate or sheet,** LCL, in barrels, boxes, crates or tubs; CL, loose or in packages	60	30,000	45
31610	**Rod,** LCL, in barrels, boxes, crates or tubs; CL, loose or in packages	60	30,000	45
31620	**Scrap,** loose (LCL), only if in pieces weighing each 50 lbs. or over), or in packages	55	40,000	27½
31630	**Shot,** in barrels or boxes	60	30,000	45
31645	**Cups, cartridge case or bullet jacket,** metal, in bags, barrels or boxes	60	30,000	40
31650	**Curios, noibn,** consisting of **bead work, prehistoric implements, images and Chinese or Japanese curios,** in barrels or boxes	200	10,000R	100
31660	**Curtain pole or rod fixtures,** bone, metal or wooden, in boxes	85	30,000	55

rate" took a rate that was 70 percent of first class, but in more recent years such rates have declined to as little as 50 percent and sometimes less.

No other class of carrier has a classification task equal to that of the railroads, because other carriers have a more limited variety of traffic. The intercity motor freight lines most nearly approximate the railroads in this respect. Many of these carriers use the *Uniform Freight Classification;* others use special motor freight classifications, most commonly the *National Motor Freight Classification.* This classification, for the articles listed, conforms closely to that of the rail carriers with which the motor lines compete. Rules and regulations are similar except that less stringent packing requirements apply to some commodities and rate breaks are commonly provided at various shipment weights. Truckload minimum weights are generally lower than carload minimum weights, and separate ratings are supplied for various shipment weights between minimum charge shipments and truckload lots. This provides a gradation of rates by shipment size that does not exist in rail service.

The coastwise and inland water carriers have generally adhered to the rail classifications. The intercoastal lines employ many of the rules and regulations of the *Uniform Classification,* but the rates applied are commodity rates. In domestic shipping the short ton of 2,000 pounds is used. Ocean carriers, on the other hand, use a general commodity rate, weight, or measurement at ship's option, and supplement it with numerous commodity rates special to each trade.

Airlines abandoned a simple commodity classification in 1946, introducing instead a single scale of general commodity rates which treated varying densities of freight by equating 250 cubic inches to the pound. Thereafter special commodity rates proliferated, largely for competitive reasons. Various weight breaks were provided and special rates were accorded to traffic tendered by shippers or forwarders in containers of various sizes. Since air-cargo deregulation in 1978, the CAB has ceased to require the publication and filing of tariffs on cargo except in international movement or within Hawaii and Alaska. Without regulation of cargo rates, airlines are free to change rates without notice and are no longer obliged to adhere to such rates as they may publish. Shippers complain since they are no longer able to ascertain in advance what air-cargo charges will be.

Classification of articles handled in freight service is the first step in the application of rate principles. The assignment of articles to classes, therefore, recognizes both cost-of-service and value-of-service factors. The principal cost-of-service factors are: (1) space occupied in proportion to weight; (2) risks and hazards of handling incident to the inherent nature and value of the commodity and the method of packing; (3) special services required, including icing, ventilation, need of special equipment, cleaning, fumigation, diversion, and other intransit privileges and forwarding services; (4) handling costs incident to method of packing and unusual size or weight of the article; and (5) volume, regularity, and direction of movement.

The motor-freight lines of New England use a classification which is based essentially on the weight density of articles, although some fragile or bulky articles take higher ratings than under strict density rules in recognition of the greater risk of carriage. Five regular classes were incorporated, into which commodities were introduced in accordance with the following plan:

	Pounds per Cubic Foot
Class 1	1 to 6
Class 2	6 to 10
Class 3	10 to 15
Class 4	15 to 20
Class 5	20 and over

The density schedule was intended to insure approximately the same revenue for a highway rig no matter what the combination of articles with which it might be loaded; hence the rates reflected the ratio of cube to tonnage capacity of the rigs commonly in use. The classification received wide shipper support and was well regarded by the Interstate Commerce Commission.[5] Traffic into and out of New England, however, moves principally subject to the *National Motor Freight Classification*.

The principal value-of-service factors in classification include (1) market value of the shipment, (2) market competition of shippers served by other carriers, (3) competition of other carriers, and (4) development of new production and markets. The competitive factors, 2 and 3, are influenced by the volume, regularity, and direction of movement which were listed above as basically cost factors. In fact, the volume, regularity, and direction of flow between certain points may be such as to justify a rate or charge which is below the class rate. Competition often serves to force this lower rate for volume traffic, perhaps forcing a different set of rate relationships for the commodity in question. The commodities are, therefore, assigned "commodity" rates which remove them from the application of the class rates.

Exceptions and Commodity Rates

Every commodity handled by the railroads is covered in the *Uniform Freight Classification*. Similarly, the *National Motor Freight Classifica-*

---

[5] *New England Motor Carrier Rates,* 8 MCC 287, 290–93, 321 (1938). A further description and discussion is found in Frank M. Cushman, *Transportation for Management* (Englewood Cliffs, N.J.: Prentice-Hall, Inc., 1953), pp. 208–11.

308

tion embraces all commodities carried by the motor lines.[6] In the absence of an "exceptions rating" or commodity rate, a shipment in its movement will be governed by the published class rates based upon its rating under the applicable classification. (For the convenience of the student a brief glossary of terms is contained in the Appendix to this chapter.)

Competitive conditions often compel railroads and other carriers to move much of their volume traffic on exceptions or on commodity rates. A common form is the classification exception which substitutes a different rating or rule for that contained in the classification. The exception sheet may apply to one article or to a number of articles in the same general class having different classification ratings; again, it may apply to an entire classification territory or only to traffic between a few points. The class rates still apply, but the exceptions rating, which is usually lower, supersedes the classification rating. The increase in the number of classes in the *Uniform* and *National Motor Freight Classifications* was designed to reduce the need for exception ratings. Frequently, exceptions are published along with rates in the class rate tariffs, but some separate exceptions tariffs exist. Class rates govern the movement of a wide range of commodities moving normally in small shipments and of all irregular and occasional traffic, and they shape the general pattern of rate relationships throughout the nation.

Although class rates govern the larger number of shipments, the bulk of traffic flow is subject to commodity rates. A commodity rate is a published rate which governs the movement of a specified commodity between named points of origin and destination. It is usually, although not always, below the class rate and applies to carload, truckload, or other quantity of shipment. To get such a favored rate, the commodity must move in substantial volume with some regularity. The carload or truckload minimum is often higher than would apply under the class rate. Commodity rates encourage the commodity to move in volume, especially where long distances are involved. They facilitate control of routing by the originating carrier.

There is at any time only one legal rate between any two points on any given commodity description. The *Consolidated* or *Uniform Classification* and the class rates published by railroad and motor-carrier rate bureaus in conjunction with it provide a rate upon every commodity between every pair of points on the railroad and motor-carrier systems, although single-factor rates are not always available and combinations may have to be built up on rate-base points to secure the

---

[6] Where the commodity is not specifically described in the classifications, it is governed by the "rule of analogy," which gives it the rating of the commodity most nearly resembling it.

charges for a through movement. Yet there may be half a dozen different named rates between those points and innumerable possible combination rates. Among the welter of available rates, the rules of priority contained in the tariff circulars of the Interstate Commerce Commission and the more specific rules in particular tariffs determine the legal rate. Occasionally tariff ambiguities give rise to disputed interpretations of priority. As will be pointed out later, the legal rate is not necessarily a lawful one, but it is the one the carrier is required to charge and the shipper to pay in the first instance. Complaint of unlawfulness may later be made, and the prescription of a new rate for the future and reparations on past shipments sought. In the absence of other rates, the class rate or the lowest combination (if no single-factor rate from origin to destination is available) is the legal rate. But carriers and groups of carriers frequently, because of particular situations affecting their territory and traffic, may make other rates which take priority over the class rates. The lowest available rate between any two points is not necessarily available via all routes. Tariffs may be open routed or they may contain routing restrictions.

FREIGHT TARIFFS AND RATE SCALES AND STRUCTURES

In this second part of the chapter on rate practice we are concerned with the second and final step which is the naming of the rate for a given haul of a commodity whether it moves on a class or a commodity type of rate. Classifications only supply ratings; the rating must be used with a class-rate tariff to secure the applicable rate.

Freight Tariffs

Aided by the groupings of the freight classification and the systematic relationships of territorial rate scales, the carriers perform what would otherwise be an impossible task, namely, the setting of the rates for the movement of thousands of commodities between thousands of pairs of points. The actual rates charged are published in the form of listings called *tariffs*. A tariff may also show applicable ratings, rules and regulations governing service, the routings available under the tariff, special service charges, demurrage, and other related matters. Tariffs vary in size from a single page to a volume of 1,000 or more pages, depending upon the number of points between which the tariff applies.

Class rate publication is relatively simple since the class to which a commodity belongs is determined by the applicable classification and only the exceptions need be published in the class tariff. An index of points from which the rates apply and an index of points to which they apply give the key to two sets of symbols which, combined in a relatively short table, make possible the discovery of the rate-basis number. This is usually a number corresponding to the first-class rate in cents per hundred pounds.[7] All that then remains is to publish the rates of each of the other classes corresponding to the rate-basis numbers. Such a tariff is complicated in form but reduces the space required for rate publication enormously. A tariff of 150 pages constructed on this plan may have only 8 or 10 pages devoted to showing the actual rates. Many other methods of simplified publication are employed. A typical page of a simple class tariff gives the "Station from Which" listed on the side of the page and the "Station to Which" listed along the top so that the appropriate "rate reference number" appears in a square found by the intersection of the lines from the stations of origin and destination. Figure 17–2 shows a more complicated, but common, form of commodity tariff.

Joint rates are for the most part published by rate bureaus or associations through publishing agents. Thus the number of tariffs is greatly reduced, for a single agent may publish the rates via all routes between one large area and another. The publishing agent receives his authorization in various forms of concurrences or powers of attorney which are filed with the Interstate Commerce Commission and listed in the resulting tariffs. Such agency tariffs may contain exceptions which limit the application of rates to certain routes or to traffic of some carriers and not of others. Similarly, the routes over which rates apply may be restricted by specific note in the tariff or by making the tariff subject to a separately published routing guide (also a tariff).

The making of joint rates must, of course, be a cooperative enterprise since the several carriers making up a through route must agree on the rate in which each of them will concur and upon a division among them of the revenues from that rate as well. Most of the making and changing of joint rates is therefore done through rate bureaus and associations, and where interterritorial rates are involved, more than one association will come into the picture and will conduct joint proceedings. In such circumstances the rate proposal is usually docketed simultaneously with the two bureaus concerned. Local rates generally cannot be made independently, for many hauls that are local to one carrier are subject to competition of through routes composed of competing carriers and publishing joint rates. The carrier publishing the local rate may indeed participate in some of those through routes. Nevertheless the Railroad Revitalization and Regulatory Reform Act of 1976 prohibits joint consideration of single-line rail rates.[8]

---

[7] Motor-carrier tariffs may contain several sets of rate scales, since it is not uncommon to apply higher rates on joint-line hauls.

[8] The Motor Carrier Act of 1980 similarly prohibits discussion of or voting on single-line truck rates after January 1, 1984 and the Staggers Rail Act of 1980 tightens the prohibition against group railroad rate making. See the discussion in Chapter 19.

FIGURE 17-2

Freight Tariff No. 23-L.

Item No.	COMMODITIES In carloads, unless otherwise provided with the commodity named below.	FROM Stations shown on pages 38 to 86, taking the following Index Numbers, Names or Rate Bases.	TO Stations shown on pages 87 to 177, taking the following Index Numbers, Names or Rate Bases Numbers.	Rates in Cents	PER, In pounds, except as otherwise indicated.	Route Number (Item 270.)
[T33] 3035	PULP, viz.: Cotton Seed Hull Shavings, in bags, bales or bundles. Minimum weight 40,000 pounds.	Hopewell................Va.	Nitro................W. Va.	27	100	
3040	PYRITES, Iron................ Minimum weight 50,000 pounds.	(Stations shown in Note 60, taking: Baltimore Basis............ Philadelphia Basis............ Edwards................N. Y. Emeryville................N. Y.	Pittsburgh................Pa. Pittsburgh................Pa. Josephtown................Pa. Newell................Pa.	277 299 277 277	2,240 2,240 2,240 2,240	S253a S253a
3045	PYRITES, Iron................ Minimum weight 56,000 pounds.	Edwards................N. Y. Emeryville................N. Y.	Alton................Ill. Belle................W. Va. Charleston............W. Va. Dunbar................W. Va. Elk................W. Va. Fairmont................W. Va. Malden................W. Va. Nitro................W. Va. Owens................W. Va. South Charleston....W. Va. South Ruffner........W. Va. Streator................Ill. Watts Street................W. Va. West Charleston......W. Va. Witcher................W. Va.	594 506 441 506 550 506	2,240	
3050	REFUSE ASPHALT LUBRICATING GREASE, mixed with mill cinder, mill scale or dirt................ Minimum weight 60,000 pounds.	Conshohocken................Pa.	Carnegie................Pa. Canton................Ohio Granite City................Ill.	19 19 29	100	
3055	REFUSE, Cork Waste, ground in bags, minimum weight 20,000 pounds, subject to Rule 34 of Official Classification................	Camden................N. J.	Beaver Falls................Pa.	36	100	
3070	RICE BRAN AND RICE HULLS, physically mixed and partially prepared (a product of Rice Mills), requiring further preparation for human consumption, in bags................ Minimum weight 36,000 pounds.	Stations shown in Note 60 taking Baltimore Basis. † Will not apply on tra	†Pittsburgh................Pa. ffic originating on the P. R.	29 R. when	100 for P. R.	Y78 R. delivery.
3075	ROCK, Ganister, not ground, in open top cars, minimum weight 90% of marked capacity of car, except when car is loaded to cubical or visible capacity, actual weight will apply................	Barree................Pa. Berkeley Springs........W. Va. Brooks Mills................Pa. Hannah................Pa. Harbison Walker Refractories Co. 16........Pa. Madley................Pa. Moore's Mills................Pa. Mt. Union................Pa. Reedsville................Pa. Wolfsburg................Pa.	Hubbard................Ohio Hubbard................Ohio Hubbard................Ohio	209 220 209	2,000 2,000 2,000	Y146

For Explanation of Reference Marks and Notes, see pages 178 to 351, inc.

Since the number of railroads is small, railroad rate bureaus are compact and their standing rate committees include representatives of all member carriers. It is otherwise with motor-carrier bureaus which typically have hundreds of members with diverse interests. An element of complexity in motor-carrier tariffs arises from the widespread practice of individual carriers to "flag out" provisions of an agency tariff. A motor carrier may refuse to go along with an increase of one or more rates applying on traffic which is of particular importance to it.

Numerous carriers provide for a higher class as a minimum than applies regularly or bar the application of rates for their account to other than single-line hauls. As so much motor-carrier traffic is in the small-shipments category, minimum charges are an important feature of motor-carrier class tariffs. In the face of escalating pickup, billing, and platform costs, the old simple rule of the classification that the minimum charge would be for 100 pounds at the first-class rate proved inadequate. Flat minimum charges were named, and the various bureaus treat the problem of minima in a variety of ways. In some territories more than 40 percent of the *number* of shipments move subject to minimum charges.

All tariffs are published subject to the requirements of the Interstate Commerce Commission as to form and content and are governed by the rules of the commission's tariff circulars. The title page carefully states the name of the carrier or agent publishing it, the Interstate Commerce Commission and state commission numbers, the previous issues canceled by this tariff, the effective date, the kind of tariff (e.g., local, joint, or proportional class rates; commodity rates; export or import rates), and the areas or stations from and to which it applies. If it is a commodity tariff, the commodities or kinds of commodities covered will be stated.

Since most rail and considerable truck traffic moves on commodity rates, tariffs naming such rates are of extraordinary importance. Some commodity rates are published in the same tariff with class rates. More commonly they are published in separate tariffs. Of these, some deal with a particular commodity. Others name rates on a great number of commodities. Some may adopt a rate scale or use a class-tariff "column." Others name a specific rate on a particular commodity between only two or a very few points where there happens to be a movement in volume.

Because one of several kinds of tariffs may apply to a shipment between two points, it is well to know something of their priority. First, if a special rate such as joint, import, export, or proportional exists, it takes precedence over the standard combination of class or commodity rates. Second, if a commodity rate is applicable, it takes precedence over the class rate. And finally, in applying class rates, a published "exception" rating naturally supersedes the classification rating. Since the application of general increases at different levels in the several territories sometimes brings joint rates above the lowest combination, such a combination is usually protected by special rule in the tariff.

Besides the regular point-to-point tariffs there are those which relate to switching and other terminal services and to in-transit services such as icing, reconsignment, storage, and concentration. The rates for terminal and some in-transit services are published as uniform rates per car regardless of the commodity handled. Tariffs covering some in-transit services, including storage, compressing, and milling, specify the commodities to which they apply.

Basic Factors of Rate Structure (Applying the Principles)

Rates are set forth in conformance to a scale or system that has been formulated carefully by the carriers individually or collectively in rate associations. To understand the types of rate structures which are employed, it is first essential to know the basic factors used in their formulation. These include such cost-of-service factors as (1) quantity shipped, (2) distance, and (3) operating conditions, and such value-of-service factors as (1) equalization and (2) competition.

Rates must be made for varying sizes of shipments, the rates per 100 pounds for larger shipments tending to be less than for small ones. This is not an exceptional price policy since manufacturers and other suppliers often give merchants and consumers lower prices on large-scale purchases. Carload rates are well below less-than-carload rates for most commodities carried by a railroad. However, carriers do publish some "any-quantity" rates. In addition to the less-than-carload and carload rates, there are Plan II piggyback rates between large numbers of points which are closely oriented to competitive truck rates. Many railroads offer Plan III and/or Plan IV piggyback rates between principal points which are, in effect, all-commodity rates subject to the requirement that not more than 60 percent of the trailer load be of any single commodity. These rates are usually published on a per-trailer basis, subject to additional charges for excess weight. Shippers having a vessel load, or a good portion of one, to offer as a single shipment can usually get rates substantially lower than for smaller cargoes. Motortruck lines give volume as well as regular "less-than-truckload" rates. Highway common carriers of household goods and regular freight make a similar difference between quantity and smaller shipments, employing a scale by which the rate varies with the poundage offered. Tramp vessels and contract-motor and air carriers usually quote rates below those of regular common carriers partly because of the lower cost inherent in volume shipments. Within recent years the railroads have obtained permission of the Interstate Commerce Commission to publish trainload, multiple-car, and annual-volume rates in a variety of circumstances involving bulk commodities.

A large proportion of coal traffic today moves on rates which apply only to unit trains. Multiple-car rates for coal got their start in the East because of the threat of slurry pipeline construction. But they soon proved their value for large volume movements because equipment utilization could be controlled in an operation dedicated to a particular mine-to-customer movement. They could be tailored also to the size and frequency of delivery and to various arrangements for the supply of equipment—whether by the mine, the utility, or the railroad. Multiple-car rates were later extended to grain, phosphate rock, sulfur, and various fertilizer materials.

These differences in rates for quantity and smaller shipments are justified by the carriers on the cost-of-service basis because the clerical costs of checking, billing, and collecting are the same regardless of the size of shipment. The cost of loading, unloading, and transferring a shipment varies, but not directly with the size of shipment. A better average utilization of vehicle is provided by large shipments. In rail service with few exceptions, such as livestock loaded at public stockyards by the carrier, the shipper loads and the consignee unloads carload freight, relieving the carrier of all such cost. The regulatory agencies have on that basis upheld the differences between less-than-carload and carload rates.

Since the task of transportation service is to convey a shipment from one point to another, it is to be expected that the rates will increase with distance—a measure of the amount of transportation performed. The cost of rendering the service tends to vary with distance. However, if distance scales are set up to reflect the cost of service, the rates will not vary in proportion to distance. Terminal costs, as pointed out in Chapter 9, are significant in all forms of transport and, on average, may represent 30 percent or more of total costs. Origin terminal costs for a particular consignment are not affected by the length of haul. They are the same whether the consignment is to move 10 miles or 1,000 miles. Similarly, destination terminal costs are not affected by the distance over which freight moved before the haul was terminated. A fixed element must, therefore, be incorporated in a rate scale to reflect terminal costs.

Line-haul costs do, of course, vary with length of haul. For some modes, such as single-line motor-carrier operations, they increase almost in direct proportion to mileage. There are numerous factors, however, which may result in something other than a linear line-haul function. Equipment utilization is generally improved as the haul lengthens so that equipment costs per mile are reduced. In the rail service longer hauls frequently permit preblocking of trains for long distances and consequent reduction of intermediate classification costs. Higher average speeds and heavier trainloads are also commonly achieved—both tending to reduce ton-mile costs.

Rate scales ordinarily give weight not only to the probable cost function but also to value-of-service considerations. The purpose of devising a scale is to produce a reasonable relation of rates for varying lengths of haul that may be applied over a broad territory. The intent is, therefore, to reflect average rather than specific transportation conditions, to simplify the task of rate construction, and to reduce the complexity of rate publication. When a first-class or Class 100 scale is designed, a spectrum of related scales ranging from 13 percent to 400 percent is determined, for all of the other scales stand in a mechanical relation to Class 100. Terminal costs are much more affected by the character of the commodity than line-haul costs, but classification at best can only roughly insure that the commodities rated column 13 have a cost approximating 13 percent of those rated at Class 100. To the extent that rating itself is affected by value-of-service considerations, departures from cost relationships will be insured.

The progression of rate scales normally departs from the probable-cost function out of regard for value-of-service principles. It is held undesirable to place full terminal costs on very short-haul traffic; hence a rapid early progression is provided to absorb those costs. Very long-haul traffic is held less able to bear its full cost than is traffic over intermediate distances; hence the policy of encouraging more distant sources of competitive products into markets counsels a favorable taper on the longer hauls. Scale construction, therefore, commonly contemplates that middle-distance traffic will subsidize traffic at both ends of the distance profile—very short-haul business may be handled at a loss while very long-haul traffic makes less than a full contribution to overhead and profit. Rate scales, once promulgated, tend to remain in effect for a long period of time, subject perhaps to percentage increases. When terminal costs increase more rapidly than line-haul costs, the range of short hauls priced below cost will be extended, and this has occurred in recent years.

Since there are large numbers of routes between major points separated by any substantial distance, it is necessary, when applying a scale, to determine also the "rate-making" distance between any two points. This is usually the distance over the shortest practicable route between the two. The rate for that distance will then be applied over all routes, or over all that do not exceed some specified percentage of circuity. The level of the rate scale must, accordingly, be high enough to cover the cost of average circuity in movement, that is, short-line routes will take above-cost rates while the longest routes command rates below full cost.

It will be apparent that a great deal of averaging is resorted to in the construction and application of distance scales of rates. While the form of the scale appears to reflect cost relationships at varying lengths of haul, considerable disparities will occur between rates and costs for specific hauls. Perhaps more important, however, is the practice of applying such scales uniformly over broad areas with only minor exceptions. This results in the same rates being charged for hauls of like length on low-cost high-density routes and on routes of extremely low density, including light-traffic branch lines, on which unit costs are substantially above average.[9] The method has long been considered reasonable and has often been prescribed by the regulatory authorities. Indeed a single scale was prescribed for application throughout the country east of Mountain Pacific Territory upon a showing that *average* freight service costs in the three broad classification territories were not notably disparate. Rates that depart upward from the cost of the service to which they apply often attract unregulated competition and, when such business is lost, the ability to subsidize below-cost rates is diminished. Where rates are below cost, they promote the continuance, even the growth, of uneconomic traffic flows and may encourage businesses to locate at points where service can only be rendered at above average cost and, therefore, at noncompensatory rates.

Operating conditions are seldom responsible for a change in the level or rate of progression of rate scales in one area as compared with another. To make a marked deviation because of a local condition of terminal congestion or difficult grades would be contrary to the purpose of having a scale apply to a considerable area in order to simplify the making of tariffs and to avoid local discrimination. Even where a difficult route of some length exists, it is usually not practical to allow a higher level or more rapidly progressing rate scale because of the competition with another somewhat more favorable route. In limited areas higher scales of rates may be applied as in the case of the former mountain differential in Canada or the multiple scales formerly applied to intrastate motor-carrier traffic in California. Higher rate scales are also sometimes provided for in areas of low traffic density.

Intense and incomplete competition of carriers if uncontrolled leads to rate wars and unjust discrimination in rates because each competitor seeks not equalization but an advantage over its rival. To prevent cutthroat competition, rate structures may be adjusted to enable competing carriers, routes, producing areas, shipping points, and market centers to share in the flow of traffic to or from important markets. This may be effected either by voluntary agreement of the carriers or by regulatory action. An adjustment to permit sharing of traffic and trade opportunities is called *equalization*. It has come to be a very important element in rate structures. It may take the form either of equal rates for unequal distances or of carefully adjusted differences called *differentials*. The latter may be designed to minimize the difference in rates of competitors of unequal distance from the market or to aid a less favorable (slow or indirect) route with a rate lower than that of the more favorable competing route. Equalization not only per-

---

[9] What are middle-distance hauls for railroads may be long hauls for trucks. Terminal costs are also widely disparate and are generally higher in the larger cities. To cover the more extreme situations of this kind motor carriers sometimes publish terminal arbitraries to be added to the line-haul rates. In New York these arbitraries are zoned.

meates the entire railroad commodity-rate structure of the United States but also is a prevailing principle in steamship rates to and from competing ports. Equalization is not so widely applied by motor, water, and air carriers. Highway rates may be influenced by equalized rail rates, but there is no general systematic practice of equalization in rate structure comparable to that of the railroad. Air carriers have been largely passenger, mail, and express-carriers and have not adopted the practice in their freight operations. The adoption of uniform transatlantic rates for all North Atlantic ports by the North Atlantic conference is a notable example of equalization in port-to-port water-rate structures.

Rate Structure

Freight-rate structures have developed in consequence of traffic and transportation conditions within and between the several rate-making territories. A rate structure is an interrelated system of rates constructed in response to competitive factors as they relate directly to a given transport situation. Structures may be territorial, that is, they may apply to movements within a freight-rate territory, large or small. They may be interterritorial, that is, they may apply to movements between the rate-making territories. They may be class- or commodity-rate structures. Commodity structures may merely cover a system of rates built around the factors of competition for the supply of a single market area with one commodity from a number of producing points, or they may embrace movements the country over. Thus we may refer to the lake-cargo coal-rate structure which essentially related to the rates from a number of producing fields to Lake Erie ports for transshipment by water, or we may refer to the sugar-rate structure, having in mind the country as a whole.

Whether a shipment moves under a class-rate tariff or a commodity-rate tariff, the actual rate for a shipment is based on some systematic arrangement or scale that is prepared by the individual carrier or group of carriers, or prescribed by a governmental agency. The arrangement or structure of the rate may be essentially (1) a distance rate scale, (2) a differential arrangement, or (3) a group system involving key points. Distance scales are coming more and more to be used and are now the almost universal basis for class rates.

The most extensive scale in application is the Docket 28300 scale which serves as a basis of class rates in all of the country east of the Rocky Mountains (see Table 17–1). As originally prescribed, the Class 100 rate started with 40 cents ($8 per ton) for the initial 5 miles and the scale extended up to 2,500 miles. The scale employs 5-mile blocks up to 100 miles, 10-mile blocks from 100 to 240 miles, 20-mile blocks from 240 to 800 miles, and 25-mile blocks from 800 to 2,500 miles. It illustrates the

TABLE 17-1
Scale of Class 100 Rates Prescribed for Application in All Territories Governed by Docket 28300

Miles	Rate	Progression per 100 Miles	Miles	Rate	Progression per 100 Miles
5	40		1,300	253	13
100	70	30	1,400	266	13
200	90	20	1,500	278	12
300	110	20	1,600	290	12
400	115	15	1,700	302	12
500	140	15	1,800	313	11
600	155	15	1,900	324	11
700	170	15	2,000	334	10
800	185	15	2,100	344	10
900	199	14	2,200	353	9
1,000	213	14	2,300	361	8
1,100	227	14	2,400	368	7
1,200	240	13	2,500	375	7

Source: This is the original scale prescribed in 262 ICC 766, appendix 10. Subsequent adjustment incident to rate level increases substantially increased the rates and changed the rate of progression. The revised scale in 296 ICC 662, appendix 4, extends the scale to 3,000 miles.

character of a graduated distance scale. A 500-mile haul costs just twice the 100-mile haul instead of being five times that amount. Although the rate of progression starts at 20 cents per 100 miles after the first 100 miles, it declines at intervals to 7 cents after 2,300 miles. Instead of the 2,400-mile rate representing 12 times the 200-mile rate, it is only a little over 4 times that rate.

Substantial disparity once existed between rate scales of the many rate territories and subterritories or zones. But east of the Rocky Mountains the uniform rate scale just described was applied simultaneously with the Uniform Classification on May 30, 1952. The former zones of low-traffic density in New England, Michigan, and Florida were allowed adjustments through arbitraries added to the standard scale. Commodity rates that are "column rates" (a percentage of a given class, usually of first class) have a similar profile in any given area of application. Some commodity rates are based upon independent distance scales which are often marked by irregular rates of progression. Other commodity rates are purely competitive point-to-point rates of limited application, the simple pattern of which does not reflect a distance scale. Still others are parts of commodity-rate structures in which the relationship of one rate to another is determined less by distance than by competitive factors.

To simplify rate making and to allow for variety of competition, the distance scale is often modified in its application so that a number of points take the same rate. This is brought about by local grouping of points with a key major city or concentric zones. In fact, there may be some departures from the distance scale in the modified systems.

FIGURE 17-3
Rate Structure Profiles

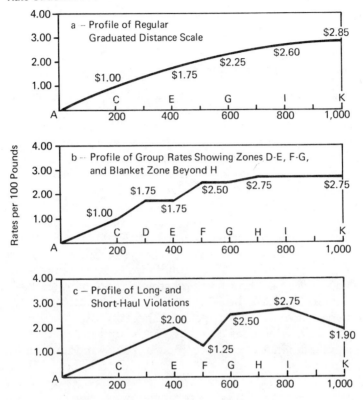

Distance from A at 200 Mile Intervals

Compare the rate structure profiles in Figure 17-3. These departures are to meet the unusual conditions of water and rail competition. However, distance-scale rates used by motor carriers adhere generally to the point-to-point basis.

The order of the Interstate Commerce Commission in *Ex Parte 270* (December 11, 1970) led to the abandonment of the rigid strictures of the old modified distance-scale system for commodity rates in favor of a more flexible rate adjustment based on cost of service. Nevertheless, the geographic patterns of long-standing rate structures such as the MacGraham percentage scale for rates between the Central Freight Association territory and the Trunk-line territory and the Transcontinental zone system have served as broad outlines from which departures have been made.

Ex Parte 270 criticized general percentage increases because they have the effect of misaligning rate relationships, a process which may alter competitive relationships of shippers in reaching their markets and which may not provide incentive for the service improvements which they need. A close relation of commodity rates to cost of service was emphasized as a desirable objective. Sensitivity of tariffs to the needs of specific commodity traffic was advocated.

Equalization and Differentials

Equalization, especially as applied in railroad commodity-rate structures, rivals the distance principle in importance. It is reflected in practice in uniform rates via various available routes except those that are excessively indirect. It is a means by which competing market centers, such as central grain markets standing between the growing areas and points of export or consumption, can each be afforded equivalent transportation costs between the origins of the products which they handle and the markets they wish to service. It is a means, also, by which sources of production at disparate distances from processing or consuming areas can be placed competitively into those areas. Where costs of transportation differ too greatly as between production areas close to markets and those farthest away, outright equalization of rates may be impossible. Differentials for the farther sources over rates from the nearer may, however, be established on a level much below the cost disparity. Especially where cost of production at the farther sources is relatively low and the quality of output high, such differentials may accomplish a substantial equalization of delivered cost and permit the farther sources to compete. The principles are important in rate structures because they provide a basis for systematically recognizing and reflecting competitive forces encountered in the marketing of commodities in the rate structure, thus neutralizing pressures for changes in rate relationships.

Equality of opportunity among competing terminals and markets may be obtained by equal rates where the nonrate competitive factors are similar in character.[10] There are many examples of this in the railroad rate structure. Since 1894 the rates between the Missouri River crossings (Kansas City, Omaha, and Sioux City) and the Mississippi River crossings (Dubuque, Fort Madison, Hannibal, and St. Louis) have been generally the same, although the distance varies from 200 miles between Kansas City and Hannibal to 414 miles between St. Louis and Omaha. Furthermore, the rates between the Mississippi crossings and Chicago are equal, although Dubuque is but 172 miles from Chicago and St. Louis is 284 miles, as shown in Figure 17–4.

A type of equalization of interterritorial routes of special interest is the "proportional rate." Figure 17–5 shows competing routes between

---

[10] R. W. Harbeson, "The North Atlantic Port Differentials," *Quarterly Journal of Economics*, vol. 46 (1932), pp. 669 ff.

FIGURE 17–4
Equalization of Missouri and Mississippi River Crossings

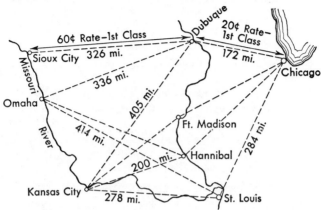

A in one territory and point F in the adjoining territory. The indirect route composed of connecting railroads P and Z cannot share in traffic between points A and F unless the through rate is no lower than that via the more direct route. The problem is especially acute for railroad P, whose local (territorial) rate is 15 cents above the local rate from A to B. Accordingly railroad Y may establish a rate to C of 55 cents (shown by a dotted line) which applies only to interterritorial traffic going to point F. The intraterritorial rate scale remains unaffected. Since road Y

FIGURE 17–5
Proportional Rates

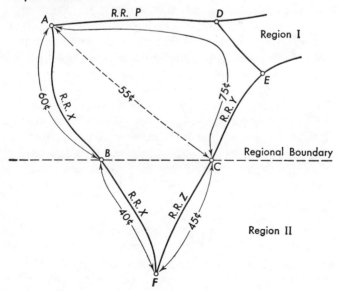

cannot control the local rate of Z, the 20-cent reduction is the sure way to make the combination rate of $1, as it is by the direct route. Such a rate is a proportional rate. A proportional rate cannot be used for a local shipment but only in combination with another rate.

When the nonrate competitive factors of alternative routes are not equal, the equalization of opportunity requires the setting up of "differential" rates. The North Atlantic port differentials have occupied a most important place in the nation's rate structure. Export and import traffic moving between the North Atlantic ports and the interior area west of the Appalachians was generally controlled by differentials designed to equalize Boston, Philadelphia, Baltimore, and Norfolk with New York by giving Portland, Maine, and Boston the New York export and import rates with Montreal, Philadelphia, Baltimore, and Norfolk enjoying differentials on such traffic below the New York level. The carefully adjusted differential did not result in equal sharing of traffic by competing routes but was designed to spread the traffic in some degree among them. The importance of the differentials declined as freight-rate levels increased, and they were maintained at an absolute level in cents per 100 pounds. Moreover, they were successfully attacked by New York interests which sought a parity with the ports to the south. The relative decline of the North Atlantic ports in favor of the Gulf and South Atlantic ports in respect to export traffic originating in the Middle West reflects the fact that the equalization of New Orleans with Baltimore and favorable rate treatment of other southern ports enabled those ports to exhibit other advantages open to them, in general at the expense of New York and more northerly ports.

The opening of the St. Lawrence Seaway produced a new set of competitive circumstances which affected both Atlantic and Gulf coast ports. While the effect of the Seaway upon general cargo has been minimal, it has been important in a limited range of commodities. On many of these, reduced rates unrelated to the earlier rate structure have been named by the railroads in an endeavor to retain their long-haul traffic. Many commodity rate structures have been subjected to nonrail competition in the last 40 years. Modification has been necessary, but has usually been deferred until traffic volume has been seriously affected. Despite the fact that nonrail competition is usually quite uneven in its impact, the earlier form of major rate structures has often been surprisingly well maintained.

Tariff Computerization

A complex pricing system which involves so much work for the mere determination of the applicable legal rate suggests the possibility of major cost reductions both in the compilation and use of tariffs if the capability of the computer is brought to bear. For nearly 90 years the skilled rate clerk has been indispensible to shippers and carriers alike in order to cope with the problems of finding rates, pricing shipments, making comparative rate analyses, compiling tariffs, supplements, and reissues thereof. Memory and the capacity for meticulous discharge of endless routine tasks are two essential qualifications of the rate clerk. Twenty-five years ago the prospect of cutting through all of these processes by tariff computerization was held out in glowing terms. Progress, however, has been modest. Tariffs ought to be capable of being supplied on tape, tariff files of large shippers maintained in that form, and small shippers serviced via tariff bureaus whose data banks can be queried directly. Preparation of bills of lading and freight bills ought to be no more complicated than purchase orders which are now frequently generated by computers as an incident to inventory control systems. At present, the demand for computerized tariffs remains small.

Some motor-carrier rate bureaus calculate their class rates by formula in the computer. Some also calculate by computer a so-called pony tariff which provides a ready reference to weight breaks by class of traffic, weight of shipment, and distance. Figure 17-6 shows part of a page from such a class rate tariff and part of a page from the Mac-Master Pony which incorporates rate breaks and minimum charges in each weight category. The computer has also found a good deal of application in connection with traffic studies and in the simulation of the probable effect of proposed rate changes.

A number of computer-produced rail commodity tariffs are on file. Figure 17-7 is a fairly typical page from such a tariff. These, as a rule, are tariffs applicable to one or a few commodities rather than general commodity tariffs. The computer program cumulates and alphabetizes the list of stations from which and to which rates apply and the commodity descriptions for print-out of the necessary indexes. Station listings and rates on individual sheets are columnarized and paged by the program so that the resulting print-out can be duplicated and thus made to serve directly as tariff material. The program calls attention to errors and inconsistencies, thus greatly reducing tariff editorial work and eliminating the proofing of printed tariffs. Supplemental matter can be introduced into memory, and a new printout will reflect the most recent rates and rules, thus enabling reissue at minimum cost.

If progress in computerizing tariffs has been slow, the problem of keeping up with tariff changes resulting from increases to overcome inflation and surcharges to deal with escalating fuel costs, has given impetus to efforts to capture existing rates in computer memory and continuously update them. The military services pioneered in this kind of activity. A few large companies like Exxon and Dow have been able to develop in-house systems. But more and more companies, unable to cope with tariff complexity by manual methods, are turning to service

FIGURE 17-6
Illustration of Class Rate Tariff and MacMaster Pony

MT 28 — MAC MASTER TARIFF 28 PONY — MT 28

RATE BASIS	MIN. CHGE	MIN. WT.	APPLI-CATION	500	400	300	250	200	175	150	125	110
41	$7.15	0 TO 499	MC WT	39	49	65	78	98	112	131	157	179
			RATE	1815	1452	1089	908	726	635	545	454	399
			MAX WT M	484	484	484	484	484	485	484	484	484
			S	473	471	466	462	457	453	447	440	434
			MAX CHGE	$88.00	$70.40	$52.80	$44.00	$35.20	$30.80	$26.40	$22.00	$19.35
		500	RATE	1760	1408	1056	880	704	616	528	440	387
			MAX WT	906	906	906	906	906	905	907	906	906
			MAX CHGE	$159.50	$127.60	$95.70	$79.80	$63.80	$55.80	$47.90	$39.90	$35.10
		1000	RATE	1595	1276	957	798	638	558	479	399	351
			MAX WT	1,605	1,605	1,605	1,604	1,605	1,605	1,603	1,604	1,606
			MAX CHGE	$256.00	$204.80	$153.60	$128.00	$102.40	$89.60	$76.80	$64.00	$56.40
		2000	RATE	1280	1024	768	640	512	448	384	320	282
			MAX WT	3,554	3,554	3,554	3,554	3,554	3,560	3,554	3,562	3,546
			MAX CHGE	$455.00	$364.00	$273.00	$227.50	$182.00	$159.50	$136.50	$114.00	$100.00
		5000	RATE	910	728	546	455	364	319	273	228	200
42 43	$7.15	0 TO 499	MC WT	38	48	64	77	97	111	129	155	176
			RATE	1835	1468	1101	918	734	642	551	459	404
			MAX WT M	485	485	485	484	485	485	484	484	485
			S	474	471	466	462	457	454	448	441	435
			MAX CHGE	$89.00	$71.20	$53.40	$44.50	$35.60	$31.15	$26.70	$22.25	$19.60
		500	RATE	1780	1424	1068	890	712	623	534	445	392
			MAX WT	907	907	907	907	907	906	906	907	905
			MAX CHGE	$161.50	$129.20	$96.90	$80.80	$64.60	$56.50	$48.50	$40.40	$35.50
		1000	RATE	1615	1292	969	808	646	565	485	404	355
			MAX WT	1,609	1,609	1,609	1,608	1,609	1,610	1,608	1,608	1,611
			MAX CHGE	$260.00	$208.00	$156.00	$130.00	$104.00	$91.00	$78.00	$65.00	$57.20
		2000	RATE	1300	1040	780	650	520	455	390	325	286
			MAX WT	3,576	3,576	3,576	3,576	3,576	3,582	3,576	3,584	3,583
			MAX CHGE	$465.00	$372.00	$279.00	$232.50	$186.00	$163.00	$139.50	$116.50	$102.50
		5000	RATE	930	744	558	465	372	326	279	233	205
44	$7.15	0 TO 499	MC WT	38	48	64	77	96	110	128	154	175
			RATE	1855	1484	1113	928	742	649	557	464	408
			MAX WT M	485	485	485	484	485	485	484	484	485
			S	474	471	467	463	458	454	448	441	436
			MAX CHGE	$90.00	$72.00	$54.00	$45.00	$36.00	$31.50	$27.00	$22.50	$19.80
		500	RATE	1800	1440	1080	900	720	630	540	450	396
			MAX WT	908	908	908	908	908	907	909	908	909
			MAX CHGE	$163.50	$130.80	$98.10	$81.80	$65.40	$57.20	$49.10	$40.90	$36.00
		1000	RATE	1635	1308	981	818	654	572	491	409	360
			MAX WT	1,614	1,614	1,614	1,613	1,614	1,615	1,613	1,613	1,611
			MAX CHGE	$264.00	$211.20	$158.40	$132.00	$105.60	$92.40	$79.20	$66.00	$58.00
		2000	RATE	1320	1056	792	660	528	462	396	330	290
			MAX WT	3,598	3,598	3,598	3,598	3,598	3,603	3,598	3,606	3,603
			MAX CHGE	$475.00	$380.00	$285.00	$237.50	$190.00	$166.50	$142.50	$119.00	$104.50
		5000	RATE	950	760	570	475	380	333	285	238	209
45 46	$7.15	0 TO 499	MC WT	38	47	63	76	95	108	126	152	173
			RATE	1875	1500	1125	938	750	656	563	469	413
			MAX WT M	485	485	485	485	485	485	484	485	484
			S	474	472	467	463	458	455	449	442	435
			MAX CHGE	$91.00	$72.80	$54.60	$45.50	$36.40	$31.85	$27.30	$22.75	$20.00
		500	RATE	1820	1456	1092	910	728	637	546	455	400
			MAX WT	909	909	909	909	909	908	910	909	910
			MAX CHGE	$165.50	$132.40	$99.30	$82.80	$66.20	$57.90	$49.70	$41.40	$36.40
		1000	RATE	1655	1324	993	828	662	579	497	414	364
			MAX WT	1,619	1,619	1,619	1,618	1,619	1,620	1,617	1,618	1,620
			MAX CHGE	$268.00	$214.40	$160.80	$134.00	$107.20	$93.80	$80.40	$67.00	$59.00
		2000	RATE	1340	1072	804	670	536	469	402	335	295
			MAX WT	3,619	3,619	3,619	3,619	3,619	3,624	3,619	3,626	3,610
			MAX CHGE	$485.00	$388.00	$291.00	$242.50	$194.00	$170.00	$145.50	$121.50	$106.50
		5000	RATE	970	776	582	485	388	340	291	243	213
47	$7.15	0 TO 499	MC WT	37	47	62	75	94	107	125	150	171
			RATE	1895	1516	1137	948	758	663	569	474	417
			MAX WT M	485	485	485	485	485	485	485	485	485
			S	474	472	467	464	459	455	449	443	437
			MAX CHGE	$92.00	$73.60	$55.20	$46.00	$36.80	$32.20	$27.60	$23.00	$20.25
		500	RATE	1840	1472	1104	920	736	644	552	460	405
			MAX WT	910	910	910	910	910	909	911	910	911
			MAX CHGE	$167.50	$134.00	$100.50	$83.80	$67.00	$58.60	$50.30	$41.90	$36.90
		1000	RATE	1675	1340	1005	838	670	586	503	419	369
			MAX WT	1,623	1,623	1,623	1,622	1,623	1,624	1,622	1,622	1,620
			MAX CHGE	$272.00	$217.60	$163.20	$136.00	$108.80	$95.20	$81.60	$68.00	$59.80
		2000	RATE	1360	1088	816	680	544	476	408	340	299
			MAX WT	3,639	3,639	3,639	3,639	3,639	3,644	3,639	3,647	3,645
			MAX CHGE	$495.00	$396.00	$297.00	$247.50	$198.00	$173.50	$148.50	$124.00	$109.00
		5000	RATE	990	792	594	495	396	347	297	248	218

FIGURE 17-7
Page from Cast Iron Pressure Pipe and Fittings Tariff

1110   **TARIFS E-702-A**   1115

SECTION 1
STANDARD ALL RAIL RATES
(FOR APPLICATION, SEE ITEM 1000)
RATES IN DOLLARS PER 2,000 POUNDS, SEE ITEM 220

ITEM 1110

List of commodities as described in Item 800
Applying on Cast Iron Pressure Pipe and Fittings

FROM

STATION	CODE		STATION	CODE
IL Kewanee	F11	PA	Monongahela	F9
NJ Phillipsburg	F7		South Greensburg	F9
OH Warren	F10	VA	Radford	F8
PA Hamburg	F12			

TO (ITEM 200)

STATION	CODE		STATION	CODE
CT Canaan	T1	IL	Barstow	T15
Danbury	T2		Bloomington	T16
Hartford	T3		Brownfield	T17
New Haven	T4		Cairo	T18
New London	T5		Carmi	T19
Stamford	T6		Carthage	T20
Waterbury	T7		Centralia	T21
Willimantic	T8		Champaign	T22
DE Dover	T9		Chicago	T23
Georgetown	T10		Danville	T24
Seaford	T11		De Kalb	T25
DC Washington	T12		Decatur	T26
IL Aurora	T13		Dixon	T27
Barry	T14		East Burlington	T28

TO (Item 200)	FROM					
	F7	F8	F9	F10	F11	F12
T1	8.06	17.19	14.38	14.83	22.47	9.09
T2	7.80	15.85	13.93	15.39	22.81	8.58
T3	9.09	17.19	15.39	15.85	22.81	9.87
T4	8.06	16.29	14.83	16.29	23.03	9.35
T5	9.35	17.19	15.85	17.19	23.26	10.12
T6	6.84	15.39	13.93	15.39	23.03	8.31
T7	8.31	16.74	14.83	15.85	22.81	9.35
T8	9.35	17.19	15.85	16.74	23.03	10.12
T9	6.59	11.94	11.16	12.96	22.36	6.84
T10	7.80	12.96	11.94	13.93	22.59	8.06
T11	7.54	12.44	11.94	13.48	22.47	7.80
T12	8.31	+B-I 7.44	10.12	10.90	21.47	8.06
T13		F1 16.85	13.93	12.44	. . . .	19.89
	21.23					
T14		F1 19.55	17.64	16.74	. . . .	22.36
	22.47					
T15		F1 19.55	16.74	15.39	. . . .	21.91
	22.13					
T16		F1 16.41	14.83	13.48	. . . .	20.79
	21.47					
T17		F1 15.51	16.74	16.29	. . . .	21.91
	22.36					
T18		F1 17.64	17.19	16.74	. . . .	22.13
T19	22.47					
	21.69	15.51	14.83	14.38	. . . .	21.23
T20		F1 19.89	17.98	15.73	. . . .	22.36
	22.59					
T21		F1 16.41	15.39	14.83	. . . .	21.47
	21.69					
T22		F1 15.51	13.48	12.44	. . . .	19.89
	20.79					
T23		F1 16.41	12.96	11.42	. . . .	19.44
	20.34					
T24		F1 14.49	12.96	11.94	. . . .	18.98
	20.34					
T25		F1 17.30	14.38	12.96	. . . .	20.79
	21.47					
T26		F1 16.41	14.38	13.48	. . . .	20.79
	21.47					
T27		F1 18.20	15.39	13.93	. . . .	21.23
	21.69					
T28		F1 19.55	17.19	15.85	. . . .	22.13
	22.36					

EXPLANATION OF REFERENCE MARKS

I   Applicable only to points in Virginia taking Washington, DC rate basis. To other points taking Washington, DC rate basis apply rate of $9.87.

SECTION 1
STANDARD ALL RAIL RATES
(FOR APPLICATION, SEE ITEM 1000)
RATES IN DOLLARS PER 2,000 POUNDS, SEE ITEM 220

ITEM 1115

List of commodities as described in Item 800
Applying on Cast Iron Pressure Pipe and Fittings

FROM

STATION	CODE		STATION	CODE
IL Kewanee	F11	PA	Monongahela	F9
NJ Phillipsburg	F7		South Greensburg	F9
OH Warren	F10	VA	Radford	F8
PA Hamburg	F12			

TO (ITEM 200)

STATION	CODE		STATION	CODE
IL East Clinton	T29	IL	Harvard	T42
East Dubuque	T30		Jacksonville	T43
East Louisiana	T31		Jerseyville	T44
East St Louis	T32		Jonesboro	T45
Edgewood	T33		Kankakee	T46
Eldorado	T34		Keithsburg	T47
Forman	T35		La Salle	T48
Freeport	T36		Lincoln	T49
Galena	T37		Litchfield	T50
Galesburg	T38		Marion	T51
Galva	T39		Mattoon	T52
Gibson City	T40		Metropolis	T53
Gladstone	T41		Morris	T54

TO (Item 200)	FROM					
	F7	F8	F9	F10	F11	F12
T29	22.13	F1 19.10	15.85	14.83	. . . .	21.69
T30	22.36	F1 19.89	16.74	15.85	. . . .	21.91
T31	22.47	F1 19.10	17.64	16.74	. . . .	22.13
T32	22.13	F1 17.76	16.74	15.85	. . . .	21.91
T33	21.47	F1 16.41	14.38	13.93	. . . .	20.79
T34	21.91	F1 15.55	15.85	14.83	. . . .	21.47
T35	22.13	F1 15.95	16.74	16.29	. . . .	21.91
T36	21.91	F1 18.88	15.85	14.38	. . . .	21.47
T37	22.36	F1 19.89	16.74	15.85	. . . .	21.91
T38	22.13	F1 18.88	16.29	14.83	. . . .	21.69
T39	21.91	F1 18.88	16.29	14.83	. . . .	21.69
T40	21.23	F1 15.55	13.93	12.44	. . . .	20.34
T41	22.47	F1 19.55	17.19	15.85	. . . .	22.13
T42	21.47	F1 17.76	14.38	12.96	. . . .	20.79
T43	22.13	F1 17.76	16.29	15.39	. . . .	20.34
T44	22.36	F1 18.88	17.19	16.29	. . . .	21.91
T45	22.47	F1 17.76	17.64	16.74	. . . .	22.13
T46	20.34	F1 15.95	12.96	11.42	. . . .	19.44
T47	22.47	F1 19.55	17.19	15.85	. . . .	22.13
T48	21.47	F1 17.30	14.83	13.48	. . . .	20.79
T49	21.69	F1 16.85	14.83	13.53	. . . .	21.23
T50	21.91	F1 17.30	15.85	14.83	. . . .	21.47
T51	22.13	F1 17.19	16.74	15.85	. . . .	21.91
T52	21.23	F1 15.95	13.93	13.48	. . . .	20.34
T53	22.36	16.74	16.74	15.85	. . . .	21.91
T54	20.79	16.85	13.93	12.44	. . . .	20.34

organizations which can supply rate retrieval from data banks. One such service company spent $3 million over two and one half years to develop its data bank which comprises most air, rail, and truck rates. Subscribing companies use such a service not only for up-to-date rate information, but also sometimes for payment of freight bills after a computerized audit process.[11] The prospect that rate bureau activities may be cut back by reducing the scope of antitrust exemption suggests the likelihood of a flood of individual carrier tariff publications. Such a development will widen the scope for tariff service companies.

APPENDIX: GLOSSARY OF TERMS

Agency tariff   A tariff published by an authorized publishing agent on behalf of a number of carriers, frequently all those members of the rate bureau to which the agent is attached.

Class rate   A rate, almost always published in cents per 100 pounds, which is to be applied in conjunction with a classification rating when no more specific rate, such as a commodity rate, is available.

Classification   A tariff publication which lists rules and regulations, commodity descriptions, and the ratings to be applied to each commodity to determine what class rate is applicable. Each tariff which names rates contains a rule which specifies the classification to which it is subject. The classification itself does not contain rates.

Combination rate   A rate which results from adding two or more rates, for example, a rate from A to B plus a rate from B to C to generate a rate between A and C. Used when no single-factor rate A to C is available or when the applicable tariff by rule specifies that a combination will take precedence over a single-factor rate if the combination produces lower charges.

Commodity rate   A rate made to move a particular commodity, often between a few named points, designed to meet the special conditions surrounding the movement of that commodity. It normally takes priority over the class rate between the same points for the same commodity as rated in the classification.

Concurrence   A power of attorney filed with the publishing agent and the regulatory body which empowers the agent to publish rates on behalf of the carrier which gives it.

Exceptions   Rules, regulations, or ratings published in the tariffs naming rates or in a separate exceptions tariff which take priority over those in the classification to which these tariffs name exceptions.

Flag out   The term applied to a notation in an agency tariff that says the rule, regulation, charge, or scale of rates does not apply for the account of the

---

[11] "Saving Money When Freight Rates are Computerized," *Business Week*, February 26, 1980, pp. 111 and 114.

particular carrier which requests that notation. An alternative provision applicable to that carrier may be included in the same tariff.

Fourth section departure The charging of more for a shorter than a longer haul over the same route in the same direction when the shorter is included within the longer haul. This is prohibited by the fourth section of the Interstate Commerce Act except when permission, known as *relief*, is granted. See Chapter 22.

Independent action Publication by or on behalf of a carrier or group of carriers of a rate which differs from that published in a bureau tariff on behalf of most member carriers. See Flag out.

Joint rate A rate made by two or more connecting carriers between a point on the line of one carrier and a point on the line of another carrier and published as a single sum between the two points. The carriers agree how the proceeds of the rate shall be shared among them, the shares being known as *divisions of the rate*.

Local rate A rate between two points on the line of a single carrier. When to a junction point with another carrier it may be used with a local rate of that carrier to form a combination between an origin on the first carrier and a destination on the second.

Long- and short-haul violation See Fourth section departure.

Master tariff A tariff, usually of broad territorial application, which describes the method by which the rates in existing tariffs are to be increased following a proceeding in which the carriers demonstrate that they need more revenue. In time the regular tariffs are reissued to incorporate the increases.

Minimum charge The charge to be assessed even though the applicable rate applied to weight would produce a lower charge. Small shipments frequently pay the minimum charge.

Minimum weight Weight at which the truckload or carload rate applies. Any lesser weight is paid for as though the minimum were shipped. If the weight of shipment exceeds the minimum it is charged at actual weight unless incentive minimums are published which provide lower rates for tonnage above the minimum.

Proportional rate A rate which may not be used for local traffic between the points to which it applies, but may only be used in combination with one or more other rates to develop charges for a through shipment.

Publishing agent See Agency tariff.

Rate break A method of classifying shipments by weight, commonly used in air and motor transport, which accords lower rates as shipment size increases. Thus shipments of 499 pounds or less might take one rate, those 500 to 1,999 pounds a lower rate, and so on.

Rate scale A method of relating rates systematically to length of haul so that rates are always higher the longer the haul, although the rate of increase with mileage may decline as length of haul increases (taper).

Rating A designation which indicates where a specific commodity stands in relation to others for determining class rate application. A commodity rated 85 will take rates 85 percent of those applied to a commodity rated 100. See Classification.

Tariff   A publication filed with the appropriate regulatory agency, posted in a carrier's public tariff file, and made available to shippers with or without charge, which specifies the rules, regulations, ratings, or rates applicable to transportation. The applicable tariffs are made a part of the contract of carriage and must be adhered to.

SELECTED REFERENCES

Colquitt, Joseph C.   *The Art and Development of Freight Classification.* Washington, D.C.: National Motor Freight Traffic Association, Inc., 1956.

Cushman, Frank M.   *Transportation for Management*, chaps. 6–8. Englewood Cliffs, N.J.: Prentice-Hall, Inc., 1953.

Daggett, Stuart, and Carter, John P.   *The Structure of Transcontinental Railroad Rates.* Berkeley: University of California Press, 1947.

Fair, Marvin L.   *Economic Considerations in the Administration of the Interstate Commerce Act*, chaps. 4, 5, and 6. Cambridge, Md.: Cornell Maritime Press, 1972.

Flood, Kenneth U.   *Traffic Management*, chaps. 4–7. 2d ed. Dubuque, Ia.: William C. Brown Co., 1963.

Healy, Kent T.   *The Economics of Transportation in America*, chaps. 20, 21, and 22. New York: Ronald Press Co., 1940.

Interstate Commerce Commission.   *Class Rate Investigation*, 262 ICC 447 (1939).

Joubert, William H.   *Southern Freight Rates in Transition.* Gainesville: University of Florida Press, 1949.

Mansfield, H.   *The Lake Cargo Coal Rate Controversy.* New York: Columbia University Press, 1932.

Ripley, William Z.   *Railroads: Rates and Regulation*, chaps. 4, 5, 10, and 11. New York: Longmans, Green & Co., 1912.

Shinn, Glenn L.   *Freight Rate Application.* Washington, D.C.: Traffic Service Corp., 1948.

Taff, Charles A.   *Management of Physical Distribution and Transportation.* 6th ed. Homewood, Ill.: Richard D. Irwin, Inc., 1978.

————.   *Commercial Motor Transportation*, chaps. 14 and 15. Cambridge, Md.: Cornell Maritime Press, 1975.

Wager, Charles H.; Colton, Richard C.; and Ward, Edmund S.   *Practical Handbook of Industrial Traffic Management*, chaps. 1, 5, 6, and 15. 5th ed. Washington, D.C.: The Traffic Service Corp., 1973.

Whitten, Herbert O., and Shira, John L.   "The Impact of Ex Parte Rate Increases on Tariff Complexity." *Transportation Law Journal*, vol. 3, no. 1 (1971).

18

The Management of Logistics
in Industrial Firms

THE TASK: APPLYING A CONCEPT

We have earlier catalogued the functions included within the logistics operations of the firm, observed the fact that they are interrelated and that trade-offs are possible among them in order to achieve objectives. We have explored at greater length the transportation, warehouse, and inventory functions and have noted the central position of stocks and their location in distribution operations. All of these functions, taken together, constitute a subsystem within the firm. The total cost concept affords a basis for their organization and management. The usefulness of the distribution system as a competitive tool for the expansion of sales and of market share has also been pointed out. The objective of the firm is measured in profit; hence both cost and market aspects must be brought within the logistics management task.

What is called for, then, is the coordination of a variety of functions in response to a concept of management. These functions are spread across the traditional structure of the firm and, in one way or another, affect all major departments. Production, marketing, and finance are all involved; and, the reader will recall, their separate functional concepts are disparate and require compromise—that, indeed, is a major element in the task of top management. Since many of the important differences among departmental objectives, however, concern issues dealt with in logistics management—for example, the level, composition, and location of stocks—the logistics concept itself can become an important coordinating device. A fresh point of view is brought to bear, relationships are specifically recognized, and the concept, when properly defined, can be made consistent with the overall objectives of the firm.

Many difficulties stand in the way. The functions to be coordinated are essential to the conduct of the business and therefore already exist. They are, however, fragmented under the jurisdiction of the various traditional departments; and their costs are often buried under an accounting system which was not designed to break them out. Such an important element as the cost of funds tied up in inventory is not reflected in the accounts at all. Top management characteristically, therefore, does not know what magnitudes are to be dealt with or what potential advantages may reside in a reorganization of functions. Purchasing, raw materials stocks, inplant materials handling, and finished goods stocks at the plants are likely to be under the jurisdiction of the production (or manufacturing) department. Field warehouses and their stocks may be under control of marketing. The traffic manager, taking care of all transportation outside the plants, may report to either of these, to finance, or to top management. He may seem to be the logical candidate to pull together a logistics subsystem, but few traffic men aspire to such broadened responsibilities. Top management may, therefore, have no obvious place or person within the organization to which to turn when it seeks to make the concept operational.

The vital distribution functions must, of course, continue to be performed while change and improvement are in contemplation or execution. The traditionally fragmented administration of these functions fails to contribute to profit objectives and may subvert them in principal part because (1) costs cannot be identified and trade-offs considered; (2) elements of the distribution function are subordinated to other major functions and discharged in the interest of those functions; and (3) performance, notably of the traffic department, is measured on cost-minimizing principles which are suboptimal if trade-off opportunities exist. Though it may appear that the total-cost concept of distribution management could be applied under any organizational form, the organization structure most often proves to be an indispensible element in the effort to secure the desired coordination.

ORGANIZATION: A TOOL OF MANAGEMENT

Many firms manage their logistics effectively without an organization structure that identifies the function and makes formal provision for its discharge. This is because logistics is understood from top management downward and cooperation takes the place of defined logistics responsibilities. By contrast, firms can be found which recognize the

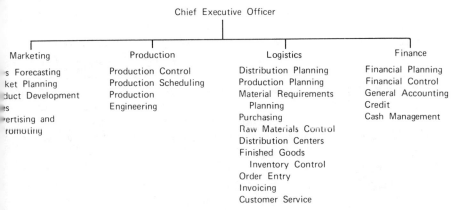

ᴺURE 18-1
ᴺctional Organization of the Firm

Chief Executive Officer

Marketing	Production	Logistics	Finance
ᴺs Forecasting	Production Control	Distribution Planning	Financial Planning
ket Planning	Production Scheduling	Production Planning	Financial Control
duct Development	Production	Material Requirements	General Accounting
ᴺs	Engineering	Planning	Credit
ᴺertising and		Purchasing	Cash Management
romoting		Raw Materials Control	
		Distribution Centers	
		Finished Goods	
		Inventory Control	
		Order Entry	
		Invoicing	
		Customer Service	

function in their organizational assignments, yet fail to apply the concepts in practice. Organization is not a substitute for understanding nor can it change the outlook of people and reform their behavior to that contemplated by the chart. Cooperation is easier in the smaller and less complex firms, and the chief executive officer has a better opportunity to encourage it. For larger organizations a carefully planned structure may be essential even though it cannot, by itself, accomplish the ends sought.

Status is accorded by location within the organization, access to the chief executive officer, and the organizational level in relation to the other major functions of the business. We earlier noted that functional departments are likely to look upon logistical questions from differing points of view depending on their respective objectives—inventory policy was cited as an example. Hence there is a good deal to be said for gathering all logistical activities under a top-level executive who is on a par with those heading the other major functions of the business and who has direct access to the chief executive officer. Such a pattern is laid out in Figure 18-1. Such a plan also makes it possible to coordinate the flows of authority with those of information, an objective not achieved when the management information system is developed without appropriate organizational adjustment.[1]

Outside the industrial firm the carriers, public warehousemen, and other enterprises which are relied upon for much of the work of goods movement have comparable problems. As the logistics concept takes hold among their customers, they must adjust their own approach to shippers. Traditional concepts of selling services must give way to

---

[1] Harrison H. Appleby, "Organizing the Logistics Function to Optimize Benefits," National Council of Physical Distribution Management, *Annual Meeting, 1978*, pp. 178 ff.

concepts which recognize the shipper's enlarged view and his contemplation of trade-offs. More important, the long-standing production orientation of carriers must be modified, for carriers' marketing departments must be capable of offering service and rate packages rather than working only price as a tool for securing business. Reorganization may be indicated. Size is, again, of importance. That shippers often find more satisfaction in dealing with small than with large carriers traces to their ability to reach top management in the small carrier with correspondingly better prospects for securing action. The sales or marketing departments of large carriers are too frequently powerless to affect the operating plan which determines service quality.

Distribution management cannot dispense with experienced specialists. Traffic management, warehouse management, locational analysis, packaging engineering all require technical skill of a specialized and high order. On the carrier side, rate and cost men now require augmentation in the marketing departments by industry specialists who can come closer to understanding customer requirements in particular industries, often because they are recruited from those industries. Industrial departments charged with inducing industries to locate plants in the carrier's territory require much greater sophistication in an era of power shortage, environmental concern, and need for high standards of service performance.

Within the organizational plan these specialists, on whom reliance is placed to get things done, must be appropriately related to one another and to a planning process which enables the logistics concept to be given force. They must be measured by their contribution to optimal logistics performance rather than, as formerly, on the basis of success in minimizing the cost of their respective functions. This often means reduced independence. The traffic manager, in particular, is likely to be found at a lower level in a logistics organization than was his former status.

THE ORGANIZATIONAL FORM

The kind of organization that is appropriate and effective will depend heavily upon the size of the firm, the territorial scope of its operations, the nature of the business and its complexity. Diversity is therefore the rule as each enterprise seeks a form appropriate to its own circumstances. Several broad classes may be observed, however, within which organizational responses tend to show some similarity.

Some industries are production oriented. This is generally true of the petroleum, primary metal, bulk chemical, and other industries heavily reliant upon raw material sources and supplies. For these, procurement, inbound transport, and materials management are of primary importance. Traditional organization left these functions to the production department except for transportation which was consigned to a traffic department often headed by a vice president. This form tends to persist in the steel and some of the other primary metals industries. Where it exists a penalty tends to be paid in the form of unnecessarily high raw materials inventories and occasional mismatch of grades of material with plant requirements. In effect, production seeks insurance against the performance of traffic which it does not control. A further aspect is lack of coordination between mining and refining.

The petroleum industry has gone far in the development of effective logistics control of its crude production, allocation to refineries, and transportation on a worldwide basis. Owned and controlled tanker fleets are closely tied to these operations. In petroleum, as in the other raw-material oriented industries, a clean break is commonly made between inbound logistics and distribution. The latter is appropriately decentralized except for major policy concerns, such as rate negotiations, facilities locations, and motor-carrier operating authorities. Market areas encounter diverse conditions, and the plant which supplies such an area provides a good basis for locating a distribution unit. Some raw-materials oriented concerns which have an exceptionally complex line, often including consumer as well as industrial products, find decentralization of line authority in distribution essential in consequence of that complexity. Some of the major chemical companies fit this pattern.

Distribution comes into its own in market-oriented firms, primarily those which serve consumer markets in the grocery, drug, appliance, and other trades. Here, in the face of keen competition and short shelf-life at the retail level, customer service becomes of predominant importance and centralization of the distribution functions is most likely to be found. Distribution centers carrying a complete stock mixture from the numerous manufacturing plants operated by the firm may be a key feature. Since reaction time becomes competitively important, order processing, credit check, and information channels may be brought into the system. Finished inventory control is critical; hence the distribution organization must have a strong role in production scheduling. Thus functions traditionally belonging both to production and marketing departments are impinged upon in the interest of securing required service at acceptable cost. A centralized plan of organization is sketched out in Figure 18–2.

The larger firms of the class just discussed have relied heavily upon profit-center organization to secure efficiency and motivation in their several product lines. A major problem, therefore, is to hold divisional managers charged with manufacture and sale of a product line responsible for profit performance when so important an area as physi-

334

FIGURE 18-2
Distribution Organization in Consumer Goods Firms

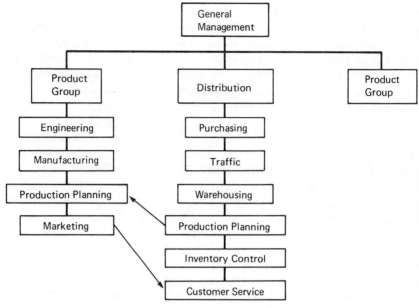

cal distribution is outside of their direct control. The distribution organization which controls inventory and goods movement to accomplish the customer service that is so important to the success of the products in the market, stands as a service agency in relation to the divisional managers (or profit centers). To decentralize distribution, however, is to sacrifice the advantage of a single point of contact for customers on service matters, consolidation of stocks, and volume shipments of multidivision orders to customers. Centralization, too, affords far greater bargaining power in relation to carriers in matters of equipment, service, and rates. Nevertheless, organizational compromise is frequently found which places distribution more in a staff than a line relation to operating divisions and requires negotiation of pool car arrangements, joint distribution centers, and other devices by which goods flows can be consolidated. In these circumstances advantage to the firm as a whole is not sufficient—divisional interests must be shown to be congruent with them.

MANAGING THE TRANSPORT FUNCTION

Scope of Control

The function of transportation (or traffic) management, while it occupies a position subordinate to the distribution manager in firms which have reorganized to reflect the logistics concept, remains of very large importance. Indeed when it must be managed with an eye to broader objectives than mere minimization of transport costs, the function assumes a more complex and strategic character. As we have noted, when measured by cost, transport is often the largest single element in the distribution system. It is also one which, more than others, is indirectly rather than directly controlled by management. In most firms a large part of transportation costs represents purchased transport furnished by commercial carriers with which the traffic manager's relationship is one of choice and negotiation. In effect the traffic manager is a highly specialized purchasing agent.

Where new distribution systems are in the design phase or changes of existing systems are in contemplation, the traffic manager must supply alternative transport-cost and service packages which can be incorporated in the analysis for the exploration of trade-offs expressed in time and cost. This may involve the compilation of rates over the hauls involved, the estimation of transit times (including variations around the average), or the estimation of rates that can be secured from carriers when those presently in the tariffs are not realistic for the purpose at hand. The latter is especially likely where new plant or warehouse locations are contemplated in some of the hypothetical systems to be compared. The traffic manager can and usually does provide the judgmental basis for selection, so far as transportation affects the choice, of points of location to be tested. In this connection he is concerned with the availability of carriers, their route patterns and territorial coverage, and the rate circumstances (rate group within which located, whether inside switching limits or motor-carrier commercial zones, whether branch line or main line), among other factors.

Within the functioning system, of course, it is the job of the traffic manager to insure the actual flow of goods required by the inventory-control system and customer service standards established. This includes purchasing and monitoring commercial transportation, including expediting and tracing when required, as well as supplying private transport service in the firm's own vehicles as a supplement or replacement of commercial services. Emergencies, whether breakdowns of customary transport, interruptions of production, or stockouts generated by unanticipated demand, may require to be dealt with by the purchase of premium transportation, sometimes even the charter of an aircraft. The planned emergency is an increasingly common element in distribution systems—a concept which trades off high-cost service (commonly air cargo) against inventory savings achieved by limiting stocks of slow moving or very high value items or providing for exceptional fluctuations of particular product demands. Routine functions include the work necessary with carriers to insure adequate supply of proper equipment, damage prevention activities, placing and processing of claims, freight-bill auditing, and the maintenance of records of service rendered by each of the carriers employed.

The maintenance of tariff files and their continual updating is a vital function. Computerized storage and retrieval are coming into vogue in many instances, but new rate information must regularly be entered into the system. Where actual shipment is in the hands of traffic managers at plants and installations, rate and routing guides must be furnished and kept up to date by the central traffic department in order that policy be known and followed. Quite apart from insuring that information is up to date, rate changes must be watched as a guide to action. Changes may open opportunities to secure more favorable treatment or disclose situations which should be taken up with carriers for correction. Rates of competitors must be watched to make sure that no transportation advantage is secured by them without all available steps being taken to prevent or rectify such a result through equalization of the advantage or a restoration of earlier rate relationships. Rate research, especially when successive general rate increases are being applied through publication of master tariffs, may disclose combinations which make available a lower basis of charges. New or changed products may necessitate securing rates or ratings suitable to permit their being marketed.

The right of the shipper to route traffic, not simply by selecting the originating carrier but also by selecting intermediate and delivering carriers as well as specifying points of interchange, is a principal tool for securing desired service performance. Some routes, both rail and motor carrier, have a record of faster and more reliable transit times than others. Many joint motor-carrier routes that are open under tariff provisions are, in fact, not workable routes if transit time is of consequence. In addition, routing is an element in the shipper's bargaining power. Hence the authority to route traffic is usually centralized along with the authority to negotiate rates and service arrangements in the firm's chief traffic officer. Such concentration of authority enables the full weight of the firm's traffic volume to be brought to bear and issues of reciprocity to be explored in their fullest dimensions.

While negotiation of rate or service matters may be necessary or desirable under various circumstances, they become essential when new locations for plants or distribution centers are in contemplation. The time to negotiate is in advance of an irrevocable decision, for once the latter has been made, bargaining power related to the choice of location vanishes. One group of carriers can no longer be played off against others associated with a possible alternative location. While the majority of rate and service matters are settled directly with carriers or through the rate bureaus, traffic managers must be prepared to use the regulatory processes, by complaint or otherwise, when redress is open under the governing statutes even though not voluntarily accorded by the carriers.

It is plain that a traffic manager to be effective must have detailed understanding of regulatory statutes and their interpretation, carrier and regulatory institutions and their established procedures, tariff construction and interpretation, bills of lading, and other specialized contract forms. He needs an understanding, also, of carriers' routes and service capabilities, equipment, loading and clearance limitations, and other technical factors. A wide acquaintance with carriers' traffic and operating officers is advantageous. The distribution manager to whom he may report requires general knowledge of traffic work if he is to make effective use of his traffic department and draw its expertise fully into the task of maximizing the profit contribution of the distribution function. He must be in a position to lend support when transportation adjustments are sought whose purpose is to serve broader distribution objectives.

Rate Negotiations

As one recognized work on transportation management points out, "No one needs to sit by idly and complain that he cannot do anything about his rate situation, for all sorts of remedies are available to him. To be sure, his views will not prevail in every case, but if he has a good understanding of how these things take place he can avoid many situations that might otherwise be extremely troublesome."[2] The remedies begin with the carriers and their rate bureaus.

Regulated carriers of all modes subject to the Interstate Commerce Act, as well as most ocean carriers subject to the Shipping Act of 1916 as amended, perform their rate-making and rate-adjustment work in the first instance cooperatively through the rate bureaus (sometimes known as conferences or associations). Antitrust exemption is extended under both statutes for joint rate-making activity. Similarly, international airfreight rates are largely fixed by unanimous consent of the member airlines through the traffic conferences of the International Air Transport Association. A number of American airlines have withdrawn from IATA and all of them from its traffic conferences on order of the Civil Aeronautics Board. Its future is somewhat clouded. Rate bureaus and conferences in domestic surface transportation have a long history, but they attained their exempt status in 1948 by virtue of the Bulwinkle Amendment (Section 5a) to the Interstate Commerce Act.

Each railroad rate bureau has a defined territorial jurisdiction (ocean conferences are generally organized by trade route), and its member carriers are those which have service within that territory. The major motor-carrier bureaus follow similar principles, but upward

---

[2] Charles H. Wager, Richard C. Colton, and Edmund S. Ward, *Practical Handbook of Industrial Traffic Management*, 5th ed. (Washington, D.C.: Traffic Service Corp., 1973), p. 101.

of 100 motor-carrier bureaus exist and many overlap. Separate classification committees deal with classification rules and ratings. Action to approve rates or changes in rates is usually taken upon majority vote. Following favorable action the rate or rates go to the bureau's tariff publishing agent to be published and filed on behalf of all member carriers in what is known as an agency tariff, the agent operating on the authority of concurrences filed by the member carriers. The right of independent action is preserved for every member carrier by the terms of the agreement under which the bureau operates. The agreement must be filed with and approved by the Interstate Commerce Commission.

Even before the Bulwinkle Amendment, procedures were worked out between the National Industrial Traffic League (representing shippers) and the rail carriers on rate bureau procedures designed to give proper notice of proposals and pending actions and to confer on interested parties a right to be heard. In general, proposals may be made by a shipper directly or, at his request, by a carrier member of the bureau, or by a carrier or the bureau on its own behalf. Such proposals should contain all the information necessary for consideration and decision, and some bureaus provide farms for this purpose in order to assist the preparation of properly supported proposals. A synopsis of the rate proposal must be publicized in a recognized traffic publication so that all shippers who may have an interest are informed. Written submissions may be made in support or opposition, and a public hearing may be requested by any interested party.

A staff group of the bureau, often called the standing rate committee, analyzes all proposals and makes recommendation. Unless objections have been entered by shippers or carriers or a request made for hearing, such recommendations usually stand. Otherwise the rate-making committee composed of carrier traffic officers reviews the matter, conducting hearings if necessary. Committee action is taken without shippers present, the vote is confidential, and the secret ballot is sometimes employed. Appeal to a committee of the carriers' chief traffic officers is provided for. Where a proposal covers rates between points in the territories of two or more bureaus, concurrent or successive action may be required by the several bureaus concerned. Most bureaus publicize a synopsis of approved proposals along with advice of disposition. Publication in tariff form, filing with the commission, and distribution to interested shippers follow.[3]

Rate bureau procedures tend to be time-consuming. Motor-carrier bureaus may dispose of issues within 50 to 100 days from submission of

---

[3] The procedures of the principal rate bureaus differ in detail. They are described in G. E. Lowe, *Practice and Procedure before Rate-Making Associations* (Washington, D.C.: The Traffic Service Corp., 1967). Members of ocean conferences generally publish their own tariffs.

a proposal. Rail actions tend to average six months or more. Independent actions and flag outs are far more common in motor-carrier than in rail bureaus. The latter have only a small number of members and are relatively close-knit. The former may have 1,000 or more members representing a diversity of interest and opinion. In earlier years, when independent action was taken, it was not uncommon for the bureau which had filed the tariff on behalf of one or more of its members to lodge a protest with the commission and seek suspension. Shippers interested in the independent action might then wish to intervene. The 4-R Act of 1976, however, removed railroads from the ambit of Section 5a and created a new Section 5b. This prohibits joint action on single-line rates and permits voting on joint-line rates only by carriers which may "practically" participate in the traffic. Further it prohibits any joint (i.e., bureau) protest of an independent action.[4] The commission administratively applied a similar prohibition of bureau protests to motor carriers which, by the Motor Carrier Act of 1980, was given the force of statute. Both legislation and Commission action seem designed ultimately to dismantle group rate making through rate bureaus. Shippers face the prospect of losing an instrument which has been of considerable value to them in the past.

Common shipper procedure is to work out a proposal with one or more of the carriers serving the firm. The carrier can then initiate and sponsor the proposal with the appropriate bureau. Naturally the carrier must be convinced that for competitive or other reasons, the proposed rate change will be of advantage to it. Likewise it must be convinced that the rate sought is a lawful one that can be defended before the commission if need be. The possible repercussions of a rate change on other rates is always of concern to a carrier; hence proposed rates that fall within the historic pattern of development of the rate structure are more readily accepted than those which would make a departure and, perhaps, precipitate demands for changes in other rates to preserve relationships. Where a traffic manager believes that rates filed with the commission may prejudice the business of his firm and sees reason to suppose they may be unlawful in some respect, he may, of course, lodge a protest with the commission and seek their suspension and investigation. The 1980 rail and motor carrier legislation, however, considerably limits the Commission's power to suspend. When rates are suspended, the burden of proof as to their lawfulness is upon the carrier or carriers that filed them. A protesting shipper nevertheless should be prepared to make a showing as to the unlawfulness alleged.[5]

---

[4] For a discussion see R. J. Rooney, "The RRRR Act—Some Implication for Railroad Rate Bureaus," *Transportation Journal*, vol. 17, no. 2 (Winter 1977), pp. 17 ff.

[5] After rates are in effect a shipper who believes them unlawful may lodge a complaint. The burden of proof is on the shipper in such a complaint proceeding.

Private Transport

Large shippers have always been able to employ ships and barge tows for the handling of their own traffic. Few were able to afford railroad construction to meet their own transportation requirements except as plant railroads in large industrial complexes or short lines to tap forest or mineral resources and connect them with the common-carrier rail system. The development of the motortruck, however, made it possible even for small enterprises to consider meeting some of their transport needs with private vehicles. Many major industrial firms operate large private truck fleets when the nature of the trans-portation activity lends itself to efficient handling by this method. Such a large fleet may be organized as a separate trucking department.

Discovery of use for private transport and initial analysis of its feasi-bility may be expected to come from the traffic department. Entry into private transportation, however, raises issues of broad corporate pol-icy which require decision at the top. Is it desirable to divert some managerial effort to an enterprise which is alien to the company's main business? Is anticipated return on investment as attractive as in the company's primary business? If trucking is contemplated, will entry invite the Teamsters' Union into the company's labor bargaining structure? Since fine lines must be drawn around a private operation to insure its legality, does the proposed operation meet the tests of the law? What weight is to be accorded the strengthened bargaining power a private operation will provide in dealing with commercial carriers? If commercial carriers are important customers of the com-pany, what will be the effect on sales? If a private operation is begun and its reason for existence is later weakened, what difficulty will be encountered in curtailing or discontinuing it?

While the impetus to investigate the feasibility of private transport may arise from dissatisfaction with the service of commercial carriers, few such operations are instituted without a showing that transport cost will be reduced. Private carriers escape certain costs that fall on com-mercial carriers, for example, the costs associated with regulation and with marketing the service. More important, well-managed private operations are highly selective of the traffic which they handle, seek-ing the regular flows and leaving the fluctuations and dispersed movements to commercial carriers. Thus they may secure more inten-sive use of equipment and manpower than do commercial carriers. Backhaul is a problem, for without return loads, good utilization is impossible. Interplant flows, deliveries to customers who are also suppliers, and engaging in exempt transportation on the backhaul are among the devices available to deal with this. In 1979 the possibility of hauling regulated commodities for hire by seeking commercial au-thority was opened by the Interstate Commerce Commission. In 1980 the scope of lawful private carriage was expanded by permitting a corporate entity to haul for compensation traffic of 100 percent controlled subsidiaries.

What makes private transportation attractive, more than any other factor, is the rate structure of regulated carriers. The private operator secures transportation at cost. The value-of-service rate structure of regulated carriers with its widespread averaging and cross-subsidization confronts the shipper with rates that often depart widely from the cost of furnishing the particular services required. The private carrier service will, therefore, be used selectively to handle traffic for which commercial-carrier rates are above cost, while leaving to commercial carriers that traffic on which the commercial-carrier rates are below the cost of operating a private service. The "profits" of private carrier operations are normally measured by the savings achieved in comparison with published commercial rates.

Private carriers sometimes use rail piggyback plans II½ and III which provide a ramp-to-ramp service. The existence or threat of private carriage is, of course, used in rate negotiations. The commission normally permits regulated carriers greater latitude in reducing rates to meet private or exempt competition than it does to meet the competition of other regulated carriers. Nonetheless the commission is often skeptical of the costs at which shippers say they can perform transportation with their private fleets. Commercial carriers continually complain that shippers deceive themselves as to the true costs of private carriage. Well-managed private fleets are, however, carefully accounted for and carry not only their direct costs but appropriate allocations of corporate overhead.

MANAGING INVENTORY LOCATION AND FLOWS

The strategic importance of inventory location, level, and composition, and the rudiments of inventory control were touched upon in Chapter 14. It remains to note some of the interfunctional relationships which distribution management may be called upon to explore. These are intended more as examples of expansion out of the logistics subsystem as normally designated than as a comprehensive list of relationships with other functions.

Materials management in multiplant firms which employ localized raw-material sources, such as for crude oil, ores, or timber, may move deeply into production scheduling by the route of materials allocation. Refineries or processing plants may have different cost functions, raw material hauls will differ by plant, and the markets assigned to plants are subject to change with resulting alteration of outbound transport costs. Whenever operations are at less than capacity, therefore, the question is presented of how to place in customers' hands the quantity sought at least total cost. This requires determination of which plants should curtail operations and by how much. Such allocation questions can be dealt with mathematically. Organizationally both analysis and decision may be vested primarily in the logistics organization.

At the output end, physical distribution analysis brings to light many opportunities for profit improvement that can only be realized by the cooperation of other functional areas. Sales performance is normally measured on gross volume or on the margin between selling price and cost of goods sold. The latter does not ordinarily include transportation and most other physical distribution costs appropriate to the particular sales transaction. Markets may be actively cultivated which are too remote from production sources to be served at a profit, or products may be pushed which have higher than average distribution cost and hence realize little or no profit in some markets. A system which charges salespeople with distribution costs specific to their sales can stimulate improved allocation of sales activity.[6]

The marketing department usually seeks both a full product line and high inventory levels since these assist in providing a quality of customer service that eases the sales task in its effort to build volume. Many of the costs, however, fall upon the distribution department. Small-volume and slow-moving items may turn out to be losers, and their importance in the line to promote the sale of other products may well be exaggerated. Inventory costs can be reduced by using the planned-emergency approach or some other method of minimizing stock requirements. But the distribution department will seek to eliminate as many of these items from the line as possible.

For many years the conventional wisdom in marketing has counseled market segmentation in order to satisfy customer needs more precisely and improve market share. Recession in the mid-70s, accelerating inflation with accompanying loss of discretionary buying power, and the growing cost of carrying inventories has led to a partial reversal. As customers become increasingly concerned with value in relation to price, and manufacturers with profit margins rather than market share, product proliferation is slowing and product-line simplification more often seems an acceptable marketing strategy.[7] To the extent this occurs, the interests of marketing and distribution managers move closer together.

Small orders are the bane of any distribution operation, for there are substantial fixed costs associated with processing an order regardless

---

[6] This approach is argued by Michael Schiff, *Accounting and Control in Physical Distribution Management* (Chicago: National Council of Physical Distribution Management, 1972).

[7] Alan J. Resnik, Peter B. B. Turney, and J. Barry Mason, "Markets Turn to 'Counter-segmentation,'" *Harvard Business Review*, September–October 1979, pp. 100 ff.

of its size. Order-picking and shipping costs also escalate in relation to sales price as orders decline in size. Full pallet loads are much cheaper to handle per pound than broken pallet loads—case lots than broken case lots. Customers will ignore these differences in the supplier's costs unless pricing practices reflect economies of order size. From the customer's point of view, larger orders may mean increased inventory costs, hence a price incentive and active work by the sales force to induce a change in ordering practices may be needed. Such proposals logically originate with the distribution department.

INFORMATION SYSTEMS, FEEDBACK, AND CONTROL

In logistics systems as well as in transportation operations, communications, data origination and flow, data processing, and the preparation and movement of paper are of critical importance. Impedence of customer service, indeed, is probably more often generated by delays in information flow (including processing) than by inability to move goods promptly. A service standard that calls for delivery within three days of order placement upon the warehouse is anomalous if a week has already been consumed in paper processing since receipt of order. Similar in principle is the case of the railroad rushing a train at 70 m.p.h. over the road when the cars composing it are already three and more days old before leaving the initial terminal. These conditions reflect a lack of balance in the system—the existence of congestion and delay at one or more stages. Information systems require balance of capacity at all points of processing just as a system of goods flow must be designed to avoid bottlenecks.

Major objectives in design of information systems include (1) acceleration of consumer-service reaction time, (2) reduction of reorder-cycle time, (3) shortening the forecast period in inventory management, (4) improving capacity to readjust stock locations and to deal with emergencies, and (5) providing a more adequate data base and analytic capability for distribution system redesign and improvement. Approximation of real-time reporting of actual stock disappearance from distribution centers can provide much more effective inventory control (with consequent reduction of safety stocks) than working against sales forecasts, no matter how laboriously generated. Exponential smoothing which gives heavy weight to recent sales levels may prove both simpler and more accurate. A centralized summary of actual stock and order position at the close of each day will enable immediate matching of orders with stock at alternative locations and permit prompt inventory repositioning.

While emergencies may arise from unexpectedly-heavy sales, they more commonly result from failures or irregularities in transport performance. In such instances the carriers' information systems become of great importance to shippers. Years ago, many railroads developed systems for reporting delays to carload shipments, especially to meet requirements of automotive assembly plants and other like circumstances where delays to shipments of components might mean plant shutdowns. More modern systems turn on a central computer installation which continuously updates car-location reports and can be queried for location and status of any car in the system, including direct queries from shippers who are equipped to communicate with the carrier's computer. Many individual railroads have good reporting capability, but interline shipments are still not always easy to trace.

Stock and order reporting constitute a species of feedback which enable the performance of the system to be monitored and evaluated. In increasing measure, control systems are being incorporated which permit automatic response to data on the basis of decision rules. Reorders placed on the basis of trigger-stock levels provide an example. They may be generated against one of the company's factories for warehouse replenishment or against an outside supplier. In such systems the manager delegates some of his decision-making responsibility. He may, in consequence, lose control over the efficiency of the operation since the validity of the decision rules may not persist indefinitely over time nor may rules designed for average circumstances treat particular situations effectively. As Ronald Ballou points out, "Loss of control over computerized inventory systems offers far too frequent an example of this."[8]

The vast amount of data required to describe the flows of materials and products stood in the way of effective analysis of complex distribution systems prior to the development of electronic data processing. Both analytic and simulation techniques depend heavily on computer capability. They permit optimization of subsystems and rapid comparison of numerous alternatives. On the carrier side improved information systems bid fair to provide the tools for service quality control and more intensive equipment utilization that have hitherto been lacking.[9]

THE STATE OF LOGISTICS MANAGEMENT

Despite several decades of increased attention to the logistics function, organizational change, and success stories from individual firms,

---

[8] Ronald H. Ballou, *Business Logistics Management* (Englewood Cliffs, N.J.: Prentice-Hall, Inc., 1973), p. 58. Inventory control is one of the functions most commonly computerized, but the proportion of firms doing so declined slightly between 1971 and 1975. See Ballou, "Computer Methods in Transportation—Distribution," *Transportation Journal*, vol. 16, no. 2 (Winter 1976), pp. 72 ff.

[9] On the effective development of computer programs for distribution, see Alan D. Wheeler, "The Computer: Triumph or Terror for Transportation Managers," *Transportation Journal*, vol. 15, no. 4 (Summer 1976), pp. 39 ff.

overall accomplishment leaves a great deal to be desired. Inventory management was one of the first areas to be studied and reformed—inventory models were applied and the services of the computer employed. Yet nationwide results appear worse rather than better. Between 1967 and 1977 inventories increased by 190 percent while sales grew only 156 percent, hence the ratio of sales to inventories declined by 11 percent. Six out of ten major food companies showed a declining ratio of sales to inventories. Nor does the behavior of inventories cling closely to sales experience. At one time sales skyrocket while inventories grow sluggishly. At another time the opposite occurs. Profits per dollar of sales have declined 53 percent over the decade.[10]

A recent productivity study suggests the prospect of $40 billion in annual savings from the nation's $420 billion distribution bill. Progress is conceded in acceptance of the logistics concept and in organizational reform. But measurement is said to have barely begun and control to remain largely an objective for the future. The application of techniques adapted from industrial engineering is advocated—the use of measures of physical inputs against physical measures of output in place of the usual accounting in dollar terms.[11] Productivity, of course, has become a nationally recognized problem, especially in the service industries of which transportation is a notable example. It is quite possible that productivity is poorer at the procurement end than it is in distribution.[12]

INTERFACES OUTSIDE THE FIRM

The systems of materials management and physical distribution are characteristically designed to produce good results within the reach controlled by the firm. They come to an end at the interfaces with suppliers, common carriers, and customers. At the distribution end the interface, depending on channels used, may be with the final customers, with retail outlets, or with middlemen. The firm's system design is affected by requirements at the interface, but the assignment of responsibilities may depend on relative bargaining power between the firm and the next link in its marketing channel. Were the physical distribution system to embrace all links in the chain, despite one or

---

[10] Burr W. Hupp, "Profit Opportunities—and Strategics—in Distribution," National Council of Physical Distribution Management, *Annual Meeting (1978)*, pp. 486, 537–38.

[11] Wendell M. Stewart and James E. Morehouse, "Improving Productivity in Physical Distribution: A $40 Billion Game," National Council of Physical Distribution Management, *Annual Meeting (1978)*, pp. 1–32. See also Kenneth B. Ackerman and Bernard J. LaLonde, "Making Warehousing More Efficient," *Harvard Business Review*, March–April, 1980, pp. 94 ff.

[12] For a vivid discussion see Arthur W. Todd, "Impact, Knowledge and Choice—One Company's Management of Inbound Transportation," Transportation Research Forum, *Proceedings, Twentieth Annual Meeting (1979)*, pp. 269 ff.

more changes of title en *route* to final customers, inventories might be differently distributed among the several stages and total costs reduced. As it stands each successive enterprise seeks its own profit maximization without regard to the effect on adjacent firms in the chain. Commercial carriers, standing between installations that are part of a firm's logistics system, interface twice with the firm's operations; at the manufacturing plant of origin and at the distribution center of receipt. Carriers serving a firm's customers from its distribution centers have relationships with both parties to a transaction which involves passage of title.

It is logical that the first stage in the development of physical distribution management should focus inside the bounds of the business enterprise. Improvement in productivity of the distribution sector of the nation's economy, however, transcends the limits of particular firms. Interorganizational solutions will increasingly be required and sought.[13] In present circumstances individual enterprises, whether by design or inadvertence, thrust burdens upon others. This is especially evident in the experience of carriers which are compelled to do business in circumstances where shippers and receivers fail to provide adequate dock and handling space, hence force significant delay on carriers' equipment and drivers or even necessitate call-backs in order to effect delivery. It is evident, too, in the propensity for many shippers to distribute traffic among a multitude of carriers when a few would suffice, thus compelling pickups of small quantities and inviting congestion and delay at the docks. The costs which fall upon carriers must, of course, be recouped in higher levels of rates which fall upon all shippers. Broad-gauged distribution managers recognize these problems and their converse—carriers' bunching of arrivals in consequence of irregular service performance—and often move some distance toward their resolution. There are limits, however, when carriers find regulatory obstacles in the way of rate structure adjustments which would enable a sharing of the savings generated by cooperative effort. Institutional change, indeed, will be the price of progress toward extending the distribution concept outside the boundaries of the enterprise. In some lines of business the wholesaler is returning to favor because of his ability to combine distribution of many manufacturers' products. More generally third-party firms, sometimes built around public warehousing, seem to have a future.

SELECTED REFERENCES

Armitage, Howard M., and Dickow, James F. "Controlling Distribution with Standard Costs and Flexible Budgets," National Council of Physical Dis-

---

[13] For some suggestions see James L. Heskett, "Sweeping Changes in Distribution," *Harvard Business Review*, March–April 1973, pp. 123 ff.

tribution Management, *Proceedings, Sixteenth Annual Meeting (1979)*, pp. 99–122.

Ballou, Ronald H. *Business Logistics Management*. Englewood Cliffs, N.J.: Prentice-Hall, Inc., 1973.

Bowersox, Donald J.; Smykay, Edward W.; and LaLonde, Bernard J. *Physical Distribution Management: The Logistics Problems of the Firm*. Rev. ed. New York: MacMillan Co., 1968.

Bucklin, Louis P. *Competition and Evolution in the Distributive Trades*. Englewood Cliffs, N.J.: Prentice-Hall, Inc., 1972.

Crosse, Charles, and Kriesberg, Martin. *Procedures for Evaluating Delivery of Wholesale Food Distributors*. U.S. Department of Agriculture Bulletin, 1960.

Deakin, B. M., and Seward, T. *Shipping Conferences: A Study of Their Origins, Development and Economic Practices*. Cambridge at the University Press, 1973.

Flood, Kenneth U. *Traffic Management*, chap. 2. 2d ed. Dubuque, Ia.: William C. Brown Co., 1963.

———. "Decision Making in Private Carriage." *Private and Unregulated Carriage: Selected Papers*. Evanston, Ill.: Transportation Center at Northwestern University, 1963.

———. "Questions in Company Operated Transport." *Harvard Business Review*, January–February 1961.

Heskett, James L.; Glaskowsky, Jr., Nicholas A.; and Ivie, Robert M. *Business Logistics: Physical Distribution and Materials Management*. 2d ed. New York: The Ronald Press Co., 1973.

Lowe, G. E. *Practice and Procedure before Rate-Making Associations*. Washington, D.C.: The Traffic Service Corp., 1967.

Magee, John F. *Industrial Logistics*. New York: McGraw-Hill Book Co., 1968.

Marlow, E. H., ed. *Modern Trends in Logistics Research*. Cambridge: M.I.T. Press, 1976.

Oi, Walter Y., and Hurter, Arthur P., Jr. *Economics of Private Truck Transportation*. Dubuque, Ia.: William C. Brown Co., 1965.

Schiff, Michael. *Accounting and Control in Physical Distribution Management*. Chicago: National Council of Physical Distribution Management, 1972.

Shycon, Harvey N., and Maffai, Richard B. "Simulation—Tool for Better Distribution." *Harvard Business Review*, November–December 1960.

Taff, Charles A. *Management of Physical Distribution and Transportation*. 6th ed. Homewood, Ill.: Richard D. Irwin, Inc., 1978.

Vreeland, Barrie. *Private Trucking from A to Z*. New York: Commerce and Industry Association, 1968.

Wager, Charles H.; Colton, Richard C.; and Ward, Edmund S. *Practical Handbook of Industrial Traffic Management*, chaps. 5 and 14. 5th ed. Washington, D.C.: Traffic Service Corp., 1973.

19

Regulation of Transportation: Origin and Scope

EARLY RAILROAD REGULATION

The 1870s saw the beginning of public activity to establish control over railroads, first by the states and then by the federal government. For four decades railroads enjoyed comparative freedom from regulatory restrictions. Their expansion brought much needed transport service to isolated communities and areas; hence they had received generous aid from all levels of government. But praise changed to denunciation; public aid gave place to development of a comprehensive scheme of regulation.

Rapid and competitive building created rail capacity well ahead of the growth of traffic. Hence the general level of rates had to be high if any profit was to be realized. Between the larger cities the competition of two or more rail routes was generally available. Thousands of points were, however, served by only a single line; and these included the country stations whence came most of the nation's agricultural produce. Competition between major points led to rate cutting, but no like pressure existed at the noncompetitive points. Discrimination became widespread. Between 1869 and 1874 Illinois, Wisconsin, Iowa, and Minnesota inaugurated mandatory provisions to control railroads by establishment of maximum rates, prohibition of local discrimination in rates and combination of competing lines. The earlier statutes prescribed maximum rates, but later laws of Illinois and Minnesota provided that a commission would set maximum rates, providing for judicial determination in the light of specific facts and flexibility to meet changed conditions.

Except for the Illinois Act of 1873 these laws were short-lived, but with accompanying litigation they laid the basis for effective positive control of railroads. Through a series of six cases decided by the Supreme Court in 1877, the right to regulate rates and service was established.[1] All were railroad cases except *Munn* v. *Illinois* which related to an Illinois Act of 1870 requiring public warehouses to obtain licenses and subjecting them to stated maximum rates for the storage and handling of grain. Nevertheless, this case proved most important in railroad regulation because the Court clearly set forth the principles of law pertaining to common carriers, treating them as "affected with public interest," hence subject to positive control. Regulation by the states could not effectively control interstate commerce, although the states were at liberty to attempt such control in the absence of congressional action until, in 1886, the Supreme Court ruled that the commerce clause of the Constitution gave Congress the exclusive right to regulate interstate transportation.[2]

EARLY FEDERAL REGULATION

The Windom Committee reported in 1874 that the primary rail shortcomings were (1) insufficient facilities, (2) unfair discrimination, and (3) extortionate charges.[3] Meanwhile the character of the railway problem was changing. The resumption of rapid building after the Panic of 1873 had subsided, the intrusion of one road into the territory of another, and the continued weakness of earning power in the light of growing overcapacity precipitated new rate wars. Efforts of the railways to curb them through agreements to maintain rates and even through pooling proved ineffectual.[4] Hence, while railways had generally opposed the state efforts, they began to swing toward some form of federal regulation as a means of accomplishing rate stability.[5] Powerless to control their own rate-cutting proclivities and faced with continuing declines of ton-mile revenues, they sought to shape the pending bills in a way that would permit the control of competition without subjecting them to undesired supervision. The power of the large shippers, which had been growing with the industrialization of the country and the development of trusts, was a major cause for the shift in rail-

---

[1] *Munn* v. *Illinois*, 94 U.S. 113; *Chicago, Burlington and Quincy* v. *Iowa*, 94 U.S. 155; *Peik* v. *Chicago and Northwestern Railway Co.*, 94 U.S. 164. Other cases include 94 U.S. 179; 94 U.S. 180; and 94 U.S. 181.

[2] *Wabash, St. Louis and Pacific Railway Company* v. *Illinois*, 118 U.S. 5.

[3] *Report of Senate Select Committee on Transportation Routes to the Seaboard, 1873–1874*, 43d Cong., 1st. sess. Senate Report No. 307 (1874).

[4] The best account of a pool operation is Julius Grodinsky, *The Iowa Pool: A Study in Railroad Competition, 1870–1874* (Chicago: University of Chicago Press, 1950).

[5] Gabriel Kolko, *Railroads and Regulation: 1877–1916* (Princeton: Princeton University Press, 1965), documents this at length, chaps. 1 and 2.

road viewpoint. The Cullom Committee in its report of January 1886 found discrimination between persons, places, and commodities to be the paramount evil.[6] Rebating was widespread; published rates existed only for the small shippers and for those at noncompetitive points. The large industrialists, capable of shifting their traffic on short notice from one railroad to another, enjoyed a power with which railroads were unable to contend.

The Act to Regulate Commerce of 1887 has remained the foundation statute of what is now called the Interstate Commerce Act which defines the jurisdiction of the Interstate Commerce Commission over domestic transportation. This is particularly true of Part I of the act, relating to railroads and pipelines. Part II concerning motor carriers was added in 1935; Part III which applies to water carriers in 1940; and Part IV covering freight forwarders in 1942. Only air carriers among interstate transportation agencies are outside the commission's province.

Part I now consists of 25 sections covering 12 principal subjects, 9 of which describe functions of railroad operation which are subject to regulation. The subjects and sections which relate to them in whole or part are as follows:

Area Subjects	Sections
a. Rate levels; maximum-minimum rates and basis for determination	1, 15, 15a, 19a, 22
b. Discrimination in general; personal, local, traffic	3
c. Personal discrimination; in rates, rebates	2, 10
d. Local discrimination; long-and-short-haul violations	3, 4
e. Combination; pooling and consolidation	1, 6, 7
f. Through routes and service; interchange	3
g. Safety of services	25
h. Service; rules, joint use of facilities, emergencies	1, 3
i. Finance; securities	20a
j. Extension and abandonment	1

Implementation Subjects	Sections
k. Interstate Commerce Commission; organization authority and procedures	11–14, 16–19, 24
l. Reports, publication of tariffs, accounts, statistics	6, 20, 21
m. Legal rights and liabilities of shippers and carriers	3, 8, 9, 10, 23

The development of the act, as it relates to railroads, is traced in Figure 19-1 which shows the principal features of each enactment under the headings listed above.[7]

---

[6] 49th Cong., 1st sess., Senate Report No. 46.

[7] A recodification of the act was signed into law on October 17, 1978, under which sections are now numbered in five digits, for example, section 1(1) becomes 49 U.S. Code 10501. A conversion table for the recodified act appears in *Traffic World*, July 30, 1979, pp. 25–31, and as an appendix in Marvin L. Fair and John Guandolo, *Transportation Regulation*, 8th ed. (Dubuque, Ia.: William C. Brown Co., 1979).

EXPERIENCE WITH THE ACT OF 1887

It is plain from Figure 19-1 that the substantive provisions of the act were stated in very broad and general terms. Nowhere is a just and reasonable rate nor an unjust discrimination defined, nor is there any grant of a power to prescribe a rate in the place of one found unlawful. For some time there was general compliance with the commission's orders and little contest of its powers. But in the early 90s some of the imperfections of the act were made manifest. The railroads were strongly inclined to appeal commission decisions; the courts to review in matters of fact as well as law and to receive new evidence.

Important attacks were made upon the substantive provisions of the act. The Social Circle Case[8] and the Maximum Rate Case[9] made it clear that the commission had the power to prescribe neither an actual nor a maximum rate. Hence the carrier could set the rate a bit lower and, should the shipper complainant be prepared to litigate further, the proceedings would have to start all over again. Finally, the long-and-short-haul clause was emasculated when the Court found that all differences in competitive conditions would justify departures.[10]

The decline of rate levels continued through the 80s and 90s. With pooling outlawed, the roads had even more trouble than formerly in the effort to maintain rates. Moreover, their rate associations came under attack as violating the Sherman Act and were found to be unlawful.[11] Yet, after 1899, there was a rise in freight rates which exceeded the rise of other prices and reflected the efforts of railroads to secure some control by means of consolidation.[12] The community of interest plan in the East and the bringing together of the Harriman and Hill systems in the West contributed to this end; yet the old evils of unjust discrimination were still extensive, local discrimination was rampant, and the rebating evil had, if anything, grown apace. The railroads, indeed, convinced that they were powerless to control rebating were themselves actively seeking legislation that would bring the power of the government to their aid.[13] The Elkins Act of 1903, which made any departure from the published tariff a misdemeanor and assessed fines against the receiver as well as the giver of rebates, was the result. Secret rate cutting was substantially reduced for a time,

---

[8] *Cincinnati, New Orleans and Texas Pacific Railway Company v. Interstate Commerce Commission*, 162 U.S. 116 (1896).

[9] *Interstate Commerce Commission v. Cincinnati, New Orleans and Texas Pacific Railway Company*, 167 U.S. 479 (1897).

[10] *Interstate Commerce Commission v. Alabama Midland Railway Co.*, 168 U.S. 144

[11] *United States v. Trans-Missouri Freight Association*, 166 U.S. 290 (1897); *United States v. Joint Traffic Association*, 171 U.S. 505 (1898).

[12] See *Report of the United States Industrial Commission*, vol. 19 (1902), pp. 272-91; and Interstate Commerce Commission, *Railways in the United States in 1902*, part II, "A Forty-Year Review of Changes in Freight Tariffs," (1903).

[13] On this, see Kolko, *Railroads and Regulation: 1877-1916*, pp. 90-101.

FIGURE 19–1
Development of Railroad Regulation

Principal Statutes	I (a) Rate Level (Reasonable Rates)	II (b) Discrimination in General	III (c) Personal Discrimination	IV (d) Local Discrimination	V (e) Combination
Act to Regulate Commerce, 1887	All rates must be "reasonable and just" (Sec. 1).	Any "undue or unreasonable preference or prejudice forbidden" (Sec. 3).	Special rates or rebate for like service forbidden (Sec. 2).	Forbidden to charge more for shorter than a longer haul except under "substantially similar circumstances and conditions" (Sec. 4).	
A. Elkins Act, 1903 B. Expediting Act, 1903			A. Railroad Co. as well as employee liable for rebate violation. Receivers of rebates liable. Any departure from published tariff a misdemeanor. Fine up to $20,000 rather than imprisonment.		
Hepburn Act, 1906	Maximum rates could be set by ICC on complaint after hearing for 2-year period—and division of rates.		Indirect rebating by allowances or car rental prohibited. Passes restricted. Notice for change of tariff set at 30 days.		"Commodities Clause" Railroad forbidden to transport the market article it owns.
Mann-Elkins Act, 1910	ICC could set maximum rates on its own motion.		No deviation	No deviation of long-and-short-haul prohibition except by express authorization of ICC (see text for limitations on fourth-section relief).	

VI ...rough ...ce Routes	VII (g) Service	VIII (h) Finance	IX (i) Extension and Aban- donment	X (j through m) Implementation Subjects
...ovide ...er and ...l facilities ...terchange ...ffic .3).				j. ICC of 5 members—6 year terms. Power to subpoena witnesses. To enforce orders could seek injunction in federal court. l. Tariffs must be published and 10 days' notice for change. Prescribe accounts, but not to audit or inspect. Annual reports of railroads required.
				A. Elkins Act l. See personal discrimination column. B. Expediting Act k. Circuit courts to expedite ICC appeals. Direct appeal to U.S. Supreme Court.
...uld compel ...ugh routes ...division of s.				k. ICC of 7 members—7 year term. Order, unless appealed to go into effect in 30 days, putting burden of appeal on carriers. l. Enforce, examine, and audit accounts. 30 days' notice for increase in rates.
				k. ICC could suspend proposed rates 120 days + 6 months if necessary. Commerce court created to handle appeals. m. Shipper has legal right to route shipments.

FIGURE 19–1 *(continued)*

Principal Statutes	I (a) Rate Level (Reasonable Rates)	II (b) Discrimination in General	III (c) Personal Discrimination	IV (d) Local Discrimination	V (e) Combination
A. Panama Canal Act, 1912 B. Valuation Act, 1913 C. Commission Division Act, 1917	B. ICC to make valuation of railroads as basis for rate regulation.				A. Railroads could not operate c have inte est in wa⬛ carriers u⬛ ing Panaı Canal or ı other con petitive w⬛ ter carrier except wi ICC approval.
The Transportation Act of 1920	Rule of rate making recognized need of rates to yield fair rate of return. ICC could set minimum rates. ICC could divide joint rates according to revenue needs.			Bases required for fourth-section relief 1. Long-haul rate must be compensatory. 2. Water competition must be actual. 3. Exception for circuitous route only when distance to intermediate point exceeds that of entire more direct route.	Pooling allowe with ICC ap⬛ proval. ICC to draw u⬛ consolidatio plan. Lease or stocı control with ICC approva
The Hoch-Smith Resolution, 1925	ICC in regulating rates should consider condition of the industry and market conditions.	ICC to investigate rate structures to determine amount and kind of discrimination.			
Denison Act, 1928	ICC to set minimum differential between competitive all-rail and water-rail rates.				

VI (f) Through Service Routes	VII (g) Service	VIII (h) Finance	IX (i) Extension and Abandonment	X (j through m) Implementation Subjects
				C. Commission Division Act j. ICC of 9 members organized into divisions which could issue orders subject to whole commission.
	Must file car service rules for ICC approval. ICC can compel joint use of terminals in "emergency." ICC can embargo or reroute traffic.	ICC must approve issues of all securities. Recapture of one-half earnings above 5+% used as revolving loan fund.	No construction of line without certificate. ICC could require extention to provide adequate service. No abandonment of line without certificate.	k. ICC increased to 11 members.
CC could compel through rail-water routes using inland water routes and set division of rates.				

FIGURE 19–1 *(continued)*

Principal Statutes	I (a) Rate Level (Reasonable Rates)	II (b) Discrimination in General	III (c) Personal Discrimination	IV (d) Local Discrimination	V (e) Combination

A. Emergency Transportation Act of 1933
B. Sec. 77B Uniform Bankruptcy Act, 1933
	A. New rule of rate making in rate level control.
	ICC to consider:
	  1. Effect on traffic
	  2. Need for adequate service
	  3. Need for revenue.
	Recapture clause abolished.
					B. Sec. 77B. ICC to submit plan of reorganization.
					Two-thirds vote of any class creditors bind all of that class.

The Transportation Act of 1940	ICC to give special consideration to rates on agricultural exports. Amended rule of rate making. ICC to consider only effect on traffic of carrier at issue.	ICC to investigate interterritorial freight rates.			
Miscellaneous Postwar Laws A. Reed-Bulwinkle Act, 1948 B. Railroad Modification Act, 1948 C. S. 937 Public Law 85–99, 1957				C. S. 937 Public Law 85–99 (1957) Long-and-short-haul relief in connection with circuitous routes without prior approval of ICC.	A. Reed-Bulwinkle Act Railroad rate bureau not subject to antitrust. Under broad control of ICC only.

VI) Through rvice Routes	VII (g) Service	VII (h) Finance	IX (i) Extension and Aban- donment	X (j through m) Implementation Subjects
	Set up office of Federal Coordinator of Transportation to make broad study of railroad conditions.		Stock and lease control must conform to consolidation standards. ICC given control over railroad holding companies.	
ailroads should establish more through rail-water routes and joint rates.	Preamble of Act A statement of transportation policy for ICC Act. Land grant rates to civilian agencies abolished. Board of Investigation and Research set up for transport study.	The equidistant provision in fourth section in respect to circuitous routes dropped. Matter for ICC permission on merits of case.	ICC relieved of consolidation plan requirement conditions for approval of a confirmation stated (see text).	
		B. Railroad Modification Act (1948) Terms of railroad security issues may be changed if approved by ICC and 75% of holdings of given issue.		

FIGURE 19–1 *(continued)*

Principal Statutes	I (a) Rate Level (Reasonable Rates)	II (b) Discrimination in General	III (c)	IV (d)	V (e) Combinatio...
Transportation Act of 1958	Amends rate making rule re minimum rates. Where competing modes involved ICC to consider traffic conditions of carriers to which rate is applicable, not protection of traffic of competing modes.				
Rail Passenger Act of 1970					Provided for a national rail passenger system owned and operated by Amtrak
Regional Rail Reorganization Act of 1973					Provided for "Final System Plan" for Northeast roads receivership under a Consolidated Rail Corporation "Conrail" (freight operated
Railroad Revitalization and Regulatory Reform Act of 1976	ICC cannot find minimum rate unreasonable if it covers variable cost or maximum rate unless market dominance is proved. A rate which reduces going concern value may be revised to support it if otherwise just and reasonable. Reaffirmed Section 15a (3) forbidding holding up of rate to protect carrier of other mode if such rate contributes to going concern value. Standards for adequate revenue level to cover expenses and attract capital required.	ICC in considering rate increases or decreases will consider alleged effect on commodity relationship, shipper discrimination or preference and destructive competion.			The secretary of Transportation may prepare plans and make proposals for restructuring the rail system and hold informal hearing to be reported to ICC. Final approval of merger remains with ICC but must obtain opinions of secretary of Transportation and the attorney general

VII (g) Service	VIII (h) Finance	IX (i) Extension and Abandonment	X (j)–(m)
	Federal government may guarantee loans to a railroad for 15 years if for capital investment, equipment, and maintenance up to $500,000. Total loans up to $500,000,000.	ICC can authorize abandonment of any intrastate service if any state fails to act and if found in the public interest.	
	Provided for government loans to National Railroad Passenger Corporation.	The AMTRAK Corporation may discontinue train service on 30 days' notice if not required by public convenience and necessity.	
The ICC is authorized to direct other railroads to provide service for 180 days which a carrier has discontinued.	U.S. Railway Association and DOT may authorize security issues of Conrail and make loans for necessary supplies, equipment and services.		
In order to promote freight car supply, distribution and utilization, the ICC is authorized to establish rules and regulations for computation of just and reasonable demurrage charges.	Act provides for a railroad rehabilitation and improvement fund in the U.S. Treasury, administered by secretary of Transportation who may guarantee security for issues of notes and bonds. Public offering of securities, except equipment trust certificates, is subject to concurrent jurisdiction of ICC and SEC. Notes of less than two years' maturity do not require approval.	Abandonment or discontinuance of a service is forbidden unless ICC has issued a certificate holding present or future public convenience does not require it. Abandonment of an intrastate service, if no state action within 120 days, may be appealed to ICC.	

360

FIGURE 19–1 *(concluded)*

Principal Statutes	I (a) Rate Level (Reasonable Rates)	II (b) Discrimination in General	III (c)	IV (d)	V (e) Combin
Railroad Transportation Policy Act of 1980	Market dominance is defined. No market dominance, hence no ICC authority to prescribe if rate does not exceed specified percentage of variable cost through October, 1984 and a cost recovery ratio thereafter. Burden of proof falls on carrier if these limits are exceeded. A zone of rate flexibility provided based on cost adjustment factors published by ICC.	Contract rates permitted, but essential terms must be available to public. Challenge on grounds of discrimination sharply limited to respect of contract rates and rates independently made within zone of flexibility for distinct services or over different routes.			Mergers of Cl or III railroad a Class I ca are not subj regulation. A ties of rate bureaus cur No discussi singleline ra No discussic joint rates e> by carriers v can particip the covered fic.

yet indirect rebating through "midnight" tariffs, switching allowances to large shippers, and excessive mileage payments to the private car lines of packers and other industries developed to continue the drain on revenues.

The Hepburn Act of 1906 finally conferred the maximum rate power on the commission, struck down "midnight" tariffs by requiring 30-days' notice of rate changes, and dealt with switching allowances and private car lines. In addition, it brought petroleum pipelines under regulation.[14] The fourth section was not strengthened until the Mann-Elkins Act was passed in 1910. That act required the prior approval of the commission before a long-and-short-haul departure might lawfully be made and it struck out the phrase "under substantially similar circumstances and conditions." In addition, the commission was permitted to suspend for investigation increased rates on complaint or upon its own motion.

---

[14] See Figure 19–1 for a summary of its provisions.

VI *Through Service Routes*	VII *(g) Service*	VIII *(h)*	IX *(i)*	X *(j through m) Implementation Subjects*
arrier participating in joint rate may add a urcharge without oncurrence of the ther carrier or carers participating in he rate.	A declaration of rail policy seeks to promote competition, minimize the need for regulation, promote safe and efficient rail transportation by allowing adequate revenue. ICC may require reciprocal switching where practical, in the public interest and necessary to provide competitive rail service.			Limited liability rates may be approved by declaration of the shipper or by written contract between shipper and carrier. ICC may exempt from regulation railroad services that are limited in scope or that do not require protection of shippers from abuse of market power. But this does not authorize intermodal ownership. State regulatory standards and procedures are subject to ICC certification to insure conformity with interstate practices. Provides for a Railroad Accounting Principles Board and establishes guidelines.

THE PERIOD OF RESTRICTIVE REGULATION: 1906–1917

The object of the laws passed in this period was to protect the public by adequate restrictions on railroad earnings and discriminatory practices. The larger objective of an adequate and efficient transportation system was pushed into the background. The Hepburn and Mann-Elkins Acts made the commission a powerful administrative agency. This was especially true after the Supreme Court upheld and interpreted the Hepburn Act in 1910.[15] The Court limited judicial review to evidence that the commission's order (1) had violated the Constitution, (2) was arbitrary because not in accordance with facts presented in evidence, or (3) had gone beyond the powers conferred by statute.

The commission in two decisions in 1911 gave evidence of intent to exercise its newly won power.[16] It allowed very meager increases in

---

[15] *ICC* v. *Illinois Central Railroad*, 215 U.S. 452, 470. ·

[16] *Advances in Rates, Eastern Case*, 20 ICC 243 (1911); and *Advances in Rates, Western Case*, 20 ICC 307 (1911).

rates to meet significant increases in wages and prices of materials and took the carriers to task for inefficiency. The policy of the commission during this period reflected the letter and spirit of the statute; the elimination of abuse by adequate restraint on railway practices. On April 6, 1917, the United States entered World War I. By late autumn the railroads proved far from adequate to deal with the unusual traffic demands, in part because the restrictive rate policy had limited their investment in plant during the preceeding ten years. On December 28, by proclamation of President Wilson, the government took control of the railroads.[17]

RAILROAD REGULATION SINCE 1920

Resumption of private operation was accompanied by a change in the objective and framework of regulation. The restrictive philosophy of the first 30 years gave way to one in which development of an adequate and efficient transport system was primary. Since railroad earning power had been seriously weakened by inflation and physical deterioration during the war, it was necessary to develop a plan of regulation that would permit restoration of plant and earning power. Since lack of capacity had threatened to limit the war effort, it was plain that future policy should seek a railroad development more in accord with the nation's need for service.

The Transportation Act of 1920 provided for transition from government to private operation and established a positive and comprehensive framework for regulation. A rule of rate making was included which stated that "the Commission shall initiate, modify, establish or adjust such rates so that the carriers as a whole or in a given territory will under honest, efficient and economical management and reasonable expenditures for maintenance . . . earn a net railway operating income equal, as nearly as may be, to a fair return upon the aggregate value of the railway property . . . used in the service of transportation."[18] To prevent erosion of revenue from competitive reductions of rates, the power to prescribe minimum and specific rates was conferred. Proposed reduced as well as increased rates could be suspended.

Provision for commission control over car service rules, joint use of terminals, and, in emergency, over the distribution of equipment and routing of traffic arose largely from prewar developments. Related to

---

[17] On the period of restraint prior to 1917, see Albro Martin, *Enterprise Denied* (New York: Columbia University Press, 1971). On wartime control, see Walker D. Hines, *War History of American Railroads* (New Haven: Yale University Press, 1928).

[18] This was the first effort of Congress to provide a tangible guide for the level of rates.

this was the requirement that commission approval be obtained before extension of or abandonment of any line. Control over abandonment did not extend to partial discontinuance of service, such as of one or more passenger trains. That authority remained with the states until 1958 when the power to approve even intrastate abandonment was given to the commission.

Investigations by the Interstate Commerce Commission had exposed financial manipulations of major import.[19] A carrier's need for higher rates might stem in principal part from an effort to earn a return upon an inflated capitalization. If rates were kept down to provide only a fair return upon the fair value of needed and useful transportation property, then the carrier must either neglect maintenance and jeopardize service or risk loss of credit standing and close the door to capital funds for improvement and extension. Hence commission approval would be required for the issuance of securities or the assumption of obligations.

The enlarged power over rates, coupled with a rule of rate making designed to secure adequate earning power, was not expected to work effectively without change in the structure of the rail industry. Rate levels would have to be fixed for groups of railways in view of the competitive relations among them. Recapture was but a temporary expedient which enabled part of the excess earning power of the strong to be placed at the disposal of the weak. Consolidation of the weak with the strong was viewed as the permanent solution; hence the commission was directed to develop a plan of consolidation into a limited number of systems of equal earning power while preserving to the maximum possible degree the channels of traffic movement and competition among railroads.[20] Combinations would require the approval of the commission. The 1920 act, whose provisions are summarized in Figure 19-1, came close to completing the structure of railroad regulation. That the objectives were largely unattained resulted, in considerable measure, from changes in transportation which Congress had not foreseen.

Much of the legislation since 1920 which relates to railroads was designed to (1) modify or scrap features of the 1920 act which proved unworkable, (2) deal with the emergency generated by the depression of the 30s, and (3) coordinate rail regulation with that of other modes which were brought under government supervision. The Hoch-Smith Resolution of 1925 indicated that the Congress, while it desired an adequate rail system, was nonetheless concerned to insure the lowest

---

[19] See, for example, 27 ICC 560 (1913) concerning manipulation in New York, New Haven and Hartford Railroad Co.

[20] The standard work on the history of the effort is W. N. Leonard, *Railway Consolidation under the Transportation Act of 1920* (New York: Columbia University Press, 1946).

possible basis of rates to agriculture and to other depressed industries.[21] But no major legislation was passed until the Emergency Transportation Act of 1933 which sought to: (1) eliminate waste and preventable expenses by (a) avoiding duplication of services and facilities and (b) promoting joint use of terminals, (2) promote reorganization of the railroads to reduce fixed charges and improve credit, and (3) provide for a broad study of the means of improving transportation conditions. A Federal Coordinator of Transportation was to provide leadership, but few of his proposed projects were carried out in view of the opposition of the railroads and because of the labor-protective provisions.

The onslaught of the depression, the development of competitive forms of transport, and the failure to accomplish mergers of the strong and weak roads all made plain that the 1920 act was in need of revision. The rate-making rule, Section 15 of the act, was changed to delete reference to fair return on fair value and substitute a less definite standard of "due consideration, among other factors, to the effect of rates on the movement of traffic; to the need . . . of adequate and efficient railway transportation service at the lowest cost consistent with the furnishing of such service; and to the need of revenues sufficient to enable the carriers, under honest, economical, and efficient management to provide such service." The recapture clause was repealed retroactively. The rule of rate making was again revised in 1940, 1958, and in 1976. The commission's authority in respect to combinations was considerably strengthened by subjecting holding companies used to acquire railroads to regulation in respect of accounts, reports, and securities.

EXPANSION OF THE REGULATORY SCHEME

Some indirect regulation of domestic water carriers was provided in the act of 1887 which extended to common carriers "partly by railroad and partly by water, when both are used under a common control. . . ." The Hepburn Act gave the commission authority to establish through routes and joint rates for rail-water services, the power to fix maximum joint rates, and the authority to fix divisions of such rates. The Panama Canal Act of 1912 forbade railroads to own or control any

---

[21] The effect of the resolution is discussed in D. Philip Locklin, *Economics of Transportation* (Dallas: Business Publications, 1935), p. 478. An interesting interpretation of the resolution in relation to the general policy of the Congress in respect to discrimination in favor of low-grade and long-haul freight is offered by Robert A. Nelson and William R. Greiner, "The Relevance of the Common Carrier under Modern Economic Conditions," in National Bureau of Economic Research, *Transportation Economics*, Special Conference, vol. 17 (1965), pp. 351 ff.

water carrier operating through the canal and to control any water carrier that competed or might compete except with commission approval.

Regulation of water carriers operating port-to-port services or wholly independently of railroads was, however, highly incomplete. The Shipping Board Act of 1916 prohibited unjust discrimination and required maximum rates to be filed. In 1933 larger powers were conferred in respect to common and contract carriers operating in intercoastal service via the Panama Canal. This act was amended in 1938 to confer power upon the Maritime Commission, which had superseded the Shipping Board, over coastwise and Great Lakes carriers. Minimum rates could be prescribed for domestic deep-sea carriers.

Motor transport had been developing rapidly and gave evidence of becoming the most threatening competitor of railroads because of its impact upon the high-rated traffic. The states had begun to regulate motor carriage; but a growing proportion of the traffic was interstate, and the Supreme Court had ruled that the states could not restrict carriers engaged in interstate commerce except to make reasonable safety regulations and appropriate charges for the use of highways provided by the states.[22] The large number of small truckers, including thousands of owner-operators, did business without published rates and bid for traffic at whatever rates might be required to fill their trucks. Although there were many failures, new entrants promptly appeared. The state regulating authorities, the larger motor carriers, and the organized shippers joined the railroads in seeking the extension of regulation. A bill suggested by the Federal Coordinator was passed as the Motor Carrier Act of 1935. Unlike railroad regulation, motor-carrier regulation required a classification of carriers, for the Court had determined that a private carrier could not be converted into a public utility by legislative fiat,[23] nor could a contract carrier be regulated in the same manner as a common carrier.[24]

Provisions of the Motor Carrier Act

The act established a comprehensive framework for the regulation of common and contract carriers. Important exceptions include: school buses and taxicabs; truck operations within a city and its surrounding commercial zone; highway services supplemental to other forms of transport; and, most important, carriers of farm products, fish, and newspapers. A common carrier must secure a certificate of public

---

[22] *Buck* v. *Kuykendall*, 267 U.S. 307 (1925); *Bush Company* v. *Maloy*, 267 U.S. 317 (1925).

[23] *Michigan Public Utilities Commission* v. *Duke*, 266 U.S. 570, 577 (1925).

[24] *Frost* v. *Railroad Commission of California*, 271 U.S. 570, 583 (1926). *Smith* v. *Cadson*, 283 U.S. 553 (1931).

convenience and necessity while a contract carrier must secure a permit as a means to limit the entry of new firms and thus the number of carriers to those which the commission finds required in the public interest. A grandfather clause was included to protect existing carriers, those in *bona fide* operations on June 1, 1935 (July 1 for contract carriers), being entitled to certificates or permits covering operations actually performed by them on and after the grandfather date. In granting operating rights the commission must find that the proposed operations serve the public convenience and necessity. It would, therefore, consider the adequacy of existing service, including the competence and attitude of the carriers as public servants, and the effect of the proposed operations upon the traffic and revenues of existing carriers. Consolidation, mergers, or acquisitions of control require the commission's approval on a finding that the proposed transaction will be consistent with the public interest. Likewise issuance of securities is subject to approval under Section 20a of Part I which had previously applied only to railroads.

Comprehensive rate regulation is provided along the lines of railroad rate regulation. Motor common carriers are required to establish reasonable rates and charges, classifications, and rules and regulations, and to adhere to them. Passenger carriers are required to establish through routes and joint rates with other motor common carriers of passengers. Motor carriers of freight might, but they were not required to, establish through routes and joint rates with other such carriers and with rail and water lines.

All forms of discrimination are forbidden along the lines of the similar proscription of Part I. However, there is no comparable emphasis upon local discrimination and no long-and-short-haul clause. The commission may, if it finds any rate or charge unlawful, prescribe the maximum, minimum, or actual rate. Unlike its rate-regulatory powers as applied to railroads, however, the commission is here specifically precluded from prescribing intrastate rates in order to remove discrimination against interstate commerce. Rates must be published, filed, and posted; and only the rates specified in tariffs lawfully on file may be collected. Thirty-days' notice is required for changes in rates, rules, or regulations; and the commission may suspend such changes for investigation of their lawfulness.

The scope of regulation imposed upon contract carriers is less than that applied to common carriers. They were required only to file their minimum rates, and they might not change these on less than 30-days' notice. An amendment of 1957, however, requires them to file the rates actually charged. The commission, if it finds any such rate unlawful, may prescribe only the minimum rate. It may not give preference or advantage to a contract carrier in competition with any common carrier.

Safety regulation extends to private and exempt carriers as well as to regulated carriers. The commission was authorized to prescribe reasonable safety regulations including qualifications of employees, maximum hours of service, and standards of equipment. These powers, along with those relating to railroads, were transferred to the Department of Transportation when that agency was created.

Problems in the Administration of the Act

The distinction between private and for-hire carriage has given difficulty; so also has the distinction between common and contract carriers. It must be found in the nature and scope of a carrier's business and in the extent of its "holding out" to shippers, for the bill of lading used by common carriers is as much a contract as the instrument used to define the relationship between a contract carrier and a shipper. As the commission put it in one case, "In view of applicant's holding out to carry for any shipper, within the limits of his facilities, his status is that of a common carrier."[25] With the passage of time many contract carriers added to their customers and tended to create the impression of a holding out to the general public. In 1954 the commission found that one such carrier, which had 69 customers in that year compared with only 1 in 1950, had unlawfully converted its operations to common carriage.[26] The Supreme Court, however, overruled the commission and held that a contract carrier is free aggressively to solicit new business within the scope of its permit.[27] The confusion resulting from this decision led to an amendment of the law which provides that a contract carrier is "one who conducts its business other than as a common carrier under continuing contracts with one person or a limited number of persons for the furnishing of transportation services through the assignment of motor vehicles for a continuing period for the exclusive use of each person served. . . ." Specialization thus became a definite statutory test of contract carriage.

The agricultural exemption, too, gave difficulty and occasioned revision of the statute. The act exempted from economic regulation "motor vehicles used in carrying ordinary livestock, fish (including shell fish), or agricultural (including horticultural) commodities (not including manufactured products thereof). . . ." Under this exemption a substantial unregulated-transportation business has been built up in which about one third of all intercity trucking is conducted. Regulated

---

[25] *Warren C. Marshall, Common Carrier Application,* 27 MCC 252 (1940). Cf. *N. S. Craig, Contract Carrier Application,* 28 MCC 629, 632–34 (1941); 31 MCC 705 (1941). A carrier's holding out and actual performance may be limited to a few articles only, in which case it is a common carrier, but only of a restricted list of commodities.

[26] *Motor Ways Tariff Bureau v. Contract Transportation Co.,* 62 MCC 413 (1953).

[27] *United States v. Contract Steel Carriers,* 350 U.S. 409 (1956).

carriers, both rail and motor, find it difficult or impossible to compete with exempt carriers because they have not the flexibility in rate adjustment required. The commission instituted an investigation and promulgated a list of commodities on the assumption they were exempt until changed "to possess new forms, qualities, or properties, or result in combinations."[28] Thereafter in numerous court decisions various commodities were added to the list, including fresh and frozen dressed poultry and frozen fruits and vegetables.[29] In the Transportation Act of 1958 the exemption was modified to prevent further growth and to return to regulation frozen fruits, berries, and vegetables, as well as a number of imported commodities.

The Transportation Act of 1940

Competitive conditions, together with the lingering effects of the Great Depression, caused general concern over the present and future financial status of the railroads and their relationship to the other carriers. Mounting competition arose not only from the advance of technology in the several modes of transport but also from increasing public aid for the development of highways, waterways, and airways. A principal purpose of the 1940 act was to bring all interstate water carriers under the Interstate Commerce Commission and to make common carriers by water subject to a pattern of regulation comparable to that of rail and motor lines. The whole was introduced with a statement of national transportation policy which was designed as a preamble to the entire Interstate Commerce Act. It directed the commission to administer all regulation of the several carriers under its jurisdiction in an equitable manner to the end of preserving the inherent advantages of each while fostering a coordinated transportation system.[30]

The most outstanding feature of Part III is that the transportation of petroleum and products in bulk is exempt, as is that of dry bulk commodities when not more than three are handled in any one vessel or tow. In consequence, something over 90 percent of all water transport on the inland and coastal waters is exempt both from entry controls and rate regulation. Only a small number of common and contract carriers operate under commission authorization on the basis of tariffs

---

[28] *Determination of Exempted Agricultural Commodities,* 52 MCC 511 (1951).

[29] *Interstate Commerce Commission* v. *Allen E. Krobbin, Inc.,* 113 F. Supp. 599 (1953); *Interstate Commerce Commission* v. *Frozen Food Express,* 128 F. Supp. 374 (1955); *Interstate Commerce Commission* v. *Hume Transfer and Storage Company,* 352 U.S. 884 (1956).

[30] Because there are certain inconsistencies within the policy and between it and specific provisions of the act, administration has proved troublesome. Some of these matters will be touched on in chapter 24.

filed with it. The regulation of operations to Alaska, Hawaii, and Puerto Rico remains vested in the Federal Maritime Commission.

The principal problem of water-carrier regulation has concerned the relationship between rail and water rates and the establishment of effective through routes between the two types of carrier. Section 2 (4) of Part I of the act was amended in 1940 to declare that "it shall be the duty of common carriers by railroad subject to this part to establish reasonable through routes with common carriers by water subject to Part III." Railroads have been unrelenting in adjusting rate structures to meet and destroy competition. Principal procedures have been (1) long-and-short-haul exceptions with fourth-section relief, (2) depressed rates on important competitive traffic, (3) high local rates to and from water connections accompanied by relatively low through rates, (4) refusal to enter into joint rates over through rail-water routes, and (5) restriction of proportional rates to all-rail traffic.

Congress provided for joint rail-water rates in 1920; and the commission, responsive to the Dennison Act of 1928, authorized such joint rates where the distance over the water portion of the route did not make the route excessive compared with the competing all-rail route.[31] Yet the commission has been reluctant to prescribe joint rail-water rates differentially below all-rail rates even where long barge hauls and efficient transfer facilities might seem to show that the rail-water routes are the more efficient and, on a cost basis, deserving of differentially lower rates.[32] The commission has also been reluctant to disrupt a delicately balanced competitive rail-rate structure in order to open up the proportional structure to water-carrier competition or to prescribe joint rail-barge rates.[33] The Supreme Court has, however, concluded that the barge lines are entitled to rail factors comparable to the divisions of through rail rates.[34]

The Freight Forwarder Act of 1942

Part IV of the act covers freight forwarders using surface forms of transportation in interstate commerce. Such forwarders arrange for the transport of merchandise freight from the shipper's door to the receiver's door, using rail, motor, or water carriers to perform the intermediate transportation. The forwarder takes advantage of the difference between carload and truckload rates and less-than-carload or

---

[31] *Ex Parte 96*, 156 ICC 129 (1929).

[32] *American Barge Line Co. et al., v. Chicago & Eastern Illinois Railroad Co. et al.,* 287 ICC 403 (1952); 291 ICC 422 (1954).

[33] *American Barge Line v. Alabama Great Southern Railroad Company,* 296 ICC 247 (1955); 303 ICC 463 (1958).

[34] *Arrow Transportation Co. v. United States,* 176 Fed. Supp. 411 (1959).

-truckload rates. Small consignments are assembled from numerous shippers at one point, consolidated, and forwarded at carload rates to a destination point at which distribution is made to numerous receivers. Such carriers after 1942 required permits from the commission and were required to file tariffs and to adhere to the rates contained therein. They are, under the statute, common carriers in relation to shippers but, in effect, shippers in relation to the underlying carriers. They were required to pay the published tariff rates, except that motor carriers could publish for their use special "assembly and distribution" rates. Until the Motor Carrier Act of 1980, forwarders might not contract with rail or water carriers for transport at rates less than those available to shippers generally, despite the large volume of traffic they might control.

It should be noted that bona fide shippers' cooperatives that consolidate and ship for their members are exempt under the act. They require no authority, nor need they publish tariffs. Since the great curtailment of rail less-carlot service, the growing inadequacy of service on small shipments, the increase in size of carriers' equipment, and the proliferation of incentives for the heavier loading of equipment, shippers' cooperatives have flourished.

Reed-Bulwinkle Act

Attention has been called earlier to the efforts of railroads to secure the right to pool as a means of controlling rate competition. No such right was conferred, the limited authority to pool with specific commission approval granted in 1920 being intended for special purposes, such as the pooling of passenger services. After the rate associations had been successfully attacked under the Sherman Act in the 90s, they were reformed and group rate-making through rate bureaus became the universal practice. It had the tacit approval of the commission and, in view of the development of comprehensive rate regulation after 1906, it was thought to be immune to antitrust prosecution. Rate bureaus not only developed in the motor-carrier industry after it was subjected to regulation but they were encouraged by the commission. Nevertheless, suits were brought against both eastern and western railroads in 1940 claiming unlawful price fixing through the rate bureau activities. They were rendered moot by passage of the Bulwinkle Amendment, Section 5a of the Interstate Commerce Act, in 1948. Rail, motor, or water carriers could now lawfully agree upon rates under the terms of agreements filed with and approved by the Interstate Commerce Commission.[35]

---

[35] Freedom from prosecution under the antitrust acts is also available to ocean carriers under conference agreements approved by the Federal Maritime Commission. Similarly the Civil Aeronautics Board may confer immunity on air carriers.

The Transportation Act of 1958

After the Interstate Commerce Commission received authority to regulate motor carriers it followed the practice, with few exceptions, of forbidding railroads to make rates lower than contemporaneous motor-carrier rates. Railroads could meet, but not undercut, competition. That their costs might be lower was generally held irrelevant and, as motor-carrier service was generally superior, railroads felt deprived of the opportunity to compete. This came to be known as the *umbrella theory* of rate making. Section 15 (a) (3) sought to correct it by saying that the rates of one mode should not be held up to protect the traffic of another. The section was made subject to the declaration of policy, however, and there developed prolonged litigation which left unsettled what standard of cost should be applied in rate cases which involved intercarrier competition. Neither the Interstate Commerce Commission nor the courts resolved this issue and it was not laid to rest until the 4-R Act of 1976 resolved the ambiguity. Railroads obtained some benefit from the 1958 act, however, for it accelerated the abandonment of unprofitable passenger services and brought a halt to the rapid expansion of the agricultural exemption for trucks.

Department of Transportation Act of 1967

Although not directly involved in economic regulation, two important adjustments in the structure of federal transportation policy occurred in the 60s; namely, the Urban Mass Transportation Act of 1964, and the Department of Transportation Act of 1967. The first provided for direct grants to local and state governments for comprehensive planning and for low-interest loans for improvement of mass transportation. The second established the Department of Transportation. It transferred jurisdiction over safety of rail and motor transportation from the Interstate Commerce Commission to the Department of Transportation. Major units responsible for highway and air promotion and air safety were transferred from the Department of Commerce. Overall planning and administration of transportation policy were given to the department.

Administrative agencies in the department include: the Federal Railroad Administration, the Federal Aviation Administration, the Federal Highway Administration, the Urban Mass Transportation Administration, the St. Lawrence Seaway Development Administration, the United States Coast Guard and, for budget purposes, the Transportation Safety Board.

REGULATION OF AIR TRANSPORTATION

Although the regulation of air carriers is, in many respects, patterned after the regulation of surface carriers, it is embraced in a separate statute and delegated to a separate agency. Like control of ocean carriers, air-transport regulation is joined with promotional activity. The activity of the federal government in aviation falls into four main categories: (1) safety regulation; (2) promotion, including aid in the development, maintenance, and operation of airway and air navigation facilities, airports, air traffic control, and weather services; (3) subsidy to airlines; and (4) economic regulation. Safety regulation includes a number of activities, such as the licensing of pilots, certification of aircraft, promulgation and enforcement of air-traffic regulations, approval and inspection of air navigation aids, and the investigation of accidents.

Air transportation in the United States began with transport of the mails by the Post Office. The transition from direct government operation to the fostering of commercial aviation, conducted by private concerns with government aid and under regulation, required the establishment of machinery to continue the development of airways and to establish safety controls. The Air Commerce Act of 1926 provided for these functions and placed them in the Department of Commerce. The more immediate aids to air-transport operators were through mail pay administered by the Post Office Department.[36] The Air Mail Act of 1934 sought materially to reduce the power of the Post Office and placed rate jurisdiction, after the negotiation of temporary contracts, in the Interstate Commerce Commission which was to fix fair and reasonable rates for each route.

The 1934 act was recognized as a temporary expedient only, and the years prior to passage of the Civil Aeronautics Act of 1938 saw discussion both of the content and locus of air-transport regulation. The question whether air-transport regulation should be delegated to the Interstate Commerce Commission or to a separate independent regulating agency was resolved in favor of the independent agency. The original organization provided by the act was shortly superseded when the president sent reorganization plans 3 and 4 to the Congress, effective June 30, 1940. Under those plans there was created the organization that lasted until the Federal Aviation Act of 1958, comprising a Civil Aeronautics Administration in the Department of Commerce and a five-man Civil Aeronautics Board.

Until 1958 the Administrator of Civil Aeronautics consolidated in his office the functions of promoting civil aviation; issuing airworthiness certificates to aircraft; examining and registering pilots; inspecting and certifying flying schools, aircraft factories, and service stations; and administering all safety rules and regulations—all in addition to pro-

---

[36] For an account of the authority of the Postmaster General and its exercise, see F. A. Spencer, *Air Mail Payment and the Government* (Washington, D.C.: The Brookings Institute, 1941), chaps. 3 and 4.

viding, maintaining, and operating the airways system, including its navigation aids and air-traffic control. In that year the Federal Aviation Agency was created, following several serious accidents which raised questions about the performance of the administration, and given independent status. The functions of the administration were transferred to it, and closer coordination with the Department of Defense was provided for on the grounds that the air-navigation system was a common civil-military system. When the Department of Transportation was activated in 1967, the agency was incorporated in the department.

The Civil Aeronautics Board has remained an independent regulatory agency and has retained all economic regulatory authority. Its powers over the certification of carriers, the development of route patterns, and mergers are discussed in Chapter 20. Until the deregulation of air cargo in 1978 its powers over rates were essentially the same as those of the Interstate Commerce Commission in respect to the common carriers subject to its regulation, but the board has been much less called upon to deal with rate-making issues other than those having to do with the adequacy of the rate level. Faced with a continuing decline in airline earning power after 1955, the board conducted a general investigation of passenger fares which it completed in 1960.[37] It concluded that the adequacy of the fare level should be measured by return on investment and that a return of 10.5 percent, on the average of good and bad years, would be reasonable. Airlines as a whole have seldom obtained such a return and will tend to do so only in the interval between equipment cycles.

In respect to mail rates as a means of subsidy to trunk and international airlines, the board's work is now of historic interest, since both types of carrier have been off direct subsidy for a number of years. Local-service airlines remain heavily dependent upon subsidy. The Federal Aviation Act provides for determination of subsidy rates upon the basis of the revenue need of each carrier after other revenues are considered, including mail revenues at the service rate which all carriers receive. The subsidy is paid by the Civil Aeronautics Board out of monies appropriated to it for that purpose.

Prior to 1961 the board determined the "need" of each airline separately and subsidized local-service lines on a plane-mile basis. Then the board adopted a formula based on density which was revised in 1963. Certain routes may also be designated as no-subsidy routes, while an effort has been made to discontinue stations which do not develop a minimum of passenger traffic, the so-called use-it-or-lose-it policy. The class system of subsidizing the lines, together with efforts at

---

[37] *General Passenger Fare Investigation*, 32 CAB 291 (1960).

rationalizing their services, have been followed by a gradual reduction in the annual subsidy.[38]

THE PERIOD OF DEREGULATION AND AID TO THE RAILROADS

The postwar decline of the railroads that precipitated the supportive features of the 1958 act gave rise to agitation for a reexamination of the nation's transportation policy. The Weeks' Committee report of 1955 presaged preoccupation with an excessive degree of regulation that weakened the railroads in an increasingly competitive environment. This inquiry was followed by the Senate study on national transportation policy, which also recommended a reduction of the restrictions on railroad rate making and acquisition of other modes to effect coordinated transportation. It also emphasized the need to consider urban transit as a significant aspect of the nation's transport system. The Urban Transportation Act of 1964 represented a constructive adjustment and the Department of Transportation Act of 1967 provided a framework for coordinating national policy.

Fear of disaster for the railroads led to a broad change of policy which began to look toward the deregulation of all modes and the provision of financial assistance to the railroads. A first and important step which relieved the rails of the heavy burden of passenger deficits was the establishment of Amtrak, discussed in Chapter 7.

Regional Rail Reorganization Act of 1973

The act designated a "final system plan" for the northeastern area of the country, consisting of most of the eastern railroads in trusteeship under the Bankruptcy Act: Penn-Central, Erie-Lackawanna, Lehigh Valley, Reading, Central of New Jersey, and Lehigh and Hudson River. Conrail was created to have direct control over the system, but subject to the United States Railway Association governed by a board of directors representative of the federal agencies involved and various other public and private interests. The Association (USRA) authorized Conrail to issue debentures, preferred stock, Series A and B common stock, and contingent notes. Debentures and preferred stock were to be issued to USRA and other securities to persons and railroads incident to acquisitions and leases. USRA, at its discretion, was authorized to make loans to Conrail for necessary supplies, equipment, and services. The act authorized the Interstate Commerce

---

[38] On these matters, see George C. Eads, *The Local Service Airline Experiment* (Washington, D.C.: The Brookings Institution, 1972).

Commission to direct other railroads to provide services which were threatened with discontinuance, but not for more than 180 days duration.

The Railroad Revitalization and Regulatory Reform Act of 1976

The act represented the first major effort towards deregulation by giving the railroads more freedom in rate making. It limited the authority of the Interstate Commerce Commission over rates by declaring that:

1. No rate contributing to the going concern value of a railroad can be found unjust or unreasonable on the grounds that the rate is below just or reasonable minima.
2. A rate equalling or exceeding the variable costs of providing the service is presumed to contribute to going-concern value. (This can be rebutted by clear and convincing evidence.)
3. No rate can be found unjust or unreasonable on the ground that such rate exceeds just or reasonable maxima unless the ICC first finds that the railroad has "market dominance" over such service. "Market dominance" has reference to an absence of effective competition from other carriers or modes of transportation for the traffic or movement to which a rate applies. (See Section 1(5) (c). However, a finding that a railroad has market dominance does not create a presumption that the rate exceeds a just and reasonable maximum. This has to be proved.
4. A railroad may increase a rate from a level which reduces going-concern value to a level which contributes to going-concern value so long as the rate is otherwise just and reasonable.

The act reaffirmed the principle of Section 15a(3) that a railroad rate cannot be held up to protect a carrier of another mode, but added the qualification that the commission not find that the rate at issue would reduce the going-concern value of the carrier.

On the other hand, the commission, in a proceeding involving a rate increase or decrease, will consider any alleged adverse effect on commodity rate relationships. Unjust discrimination, undue preference or prejudice, and destructive competition remain prohibited. Moreover, the commission is called upon to establish reasonable standards and procedures for the maintenance of revenue levels for railroads which, under honest and efficient management, will cover expenses and attract equity capital.

Independent of the control of the Interstate Commerce Commission, the act provides for a railroad rehabilitation and improvement fund in the Treasury of the United States to be administered by the Secretary of Transportation. A billion dollar guaranteed loan program was provided by the act. The fund is to provide security for notes and bonds that the secretary may authorize railroads to issue. The fund may also be used to purchase redeemable nonvoting shares of railroads at par. These provisions are intended to assist those railroads which have inadequate earning power to finance rehabilitation and improvement of plant and equipment.

Public offerings of securities other than equipment trusts are subject to concurrent jurisdiction of the Interstate Commerce Commission and the Securities and Exchange Commission, for economic and disclosure purposes respectively. Notes of less than two years maturity, if they do not result in an aggregate debt exceeding 5 percent of the par value of outstanding securities, do not require approval.

Abandonment or discontinuance of service on a line is forbidden unless a certificate has been issued by the Interstate Commerce Commission that present or future public convenience does not require continuance of the service. Abandonment of an intrastate service requires application to the state involved, but if no action is taken in 120 days, the railroad may appeal to the Interstate Commerce Commission. Advance notice of intention to abandon is provided through required publication by railroads of maps showing the lines under consideration for such action.

Final authority in mergers and acquisition of control remains with the commission, but the act gives the Secretary of Transportation an important role. He has authority to prepare plans and proposals, including "comprehensive restructuring of the rail system." The results of informal hearings must be reported to the commission, which cannot act on any application without obtaining opinions of the Secretary of Transportation and the Attorney General. The act establishes time limits for commission action. The only addition to the regulatory authority of the commission provided by the act directs it to establish rules and regulations for the computation of just and reasonable demurrage charges in order to promote freight car supply, distribution, and utilization.[39]

Airline Deregulation

Air-cargo transportation was effectively deregulated, except in Alaska and Hawaii, by a 1977 enactment. Entry is no longer subject to a public convenience and necessity criterion, but only to a showing of fitness, willingness, and ability. Certificates may not restrict the points to be served or the rates to be charged. The board may remove rate discriminations but has no other authority over cargo rates in domestic air commerce.

---

[39] A later statute, the Department of Energy Organization Act of 1977, transferred the authority of the ICC over transportation of oil by pipelines to the Federal Energy Regulatory Commission which, for budgetary purposes, is lodged within the new department. That authority stems from the Hepburn Act of 1906 and remains in its original form.

The Airline Deregulation Act of 1978 completes the plan for deregulation of this industry. It reduces the authority of the Civil Aeronautics Board prior to its demise on January 1, 1985. At that time the regulation of certification and rates will cease and other responsibilities of the board will, under the "Sunset Provisions," be transferred to other federal agencies as follows: (1) provision of compensation for air service to small communities and (2) authority of the board with respect to foreign air transportation to the Department of Transportation, (3) the determination of the rates for carriage of the mails in interstate and overseas transportation to the Postal Service (which had it before the Act of 1934), and (4) authority respecting mergers and agreements to the Justice Department. The expiration of the Civil Aeronautics Board on January 1, 1985, will remove the antitrust protection the industry had.

Among the restrictions and limitations of the board's authority prior to its demise are: exemption from regulation of routes and rates of commuter service by planes under a load capacity of 56 passengers or cargo service with a maximum pay load of nine tons (Alaska excepted); elimination of regulation of fares, rates, and services where planes employed have a capacity of less than 30 passengers; exemption from regulation of other air services if the board finds it to be in the public interest. Copies of applications for merger, lease, or purchase must be given to the Secretary of Transportation and the Attorney General.

Entry of new carriers and additional routes for existing carriers are to be encouraged and authorized. After notice to the public of an application for entry or extension, the board has only 150 days to issue a recommended decision and 90 days thereafter to make its final decision. Application for reactivation of now dormant routes by existing and new carriers is permitted and a rush by carriers to procure such rights developed on the effective date of the act. If the applicant is found to be fit, willing, and able, and the proposed service is in the public interest, the board is to grant the certificate or amended certificate, as the case may be. In the years 1979, 1980, and 1981 existing carriers were entitled to add one route without proof beyond its fitness to render the service.

Belatedly and happily, the ambiguous term *supplemental carrier* was replaced by *charter carrier*. Service regulation was liberalized to permit airlines to commingle individual and group fares, but not with charter passengers. Foreign airlines will be authorized to employ fill-up service for one flight per day between domestic United States airports except those in Hawaii. The act sought to prevent reduction of safety and monopoly which some have held would result from free competition in entry, rates, and services. Accordingly, safety is given priority in policy and the terms of Section 7 of the Clayton Act are invoked to prevent the lessening of competition.

The act forbids any agreement between airlines limiting capacity or setting rates or fares except joint rates, fares, and charges. Curiously, the board is given added responsibility for determining subsidy needs of carriers serving small communities and the factors it is called upon to consider in rate decisions are increased to a total of 13. The solicitude for commuter lines serving the smaller points reflects the expectation, since realized, that the major trunk airlines would drop many of the less profitable points from their route patterns.

The government is seeking actively to extend its "open skies" policy to the international sphere. Several new bilateral agreements with other nations have enhanced the opportunities for entry of additional carriers in international markets. A liberalizing renegotiation of Bermuda II with the United Kingdom has even been achieved. Participation of American-flag airlines in the rate-making activities of the International Air Transport Association is no longer permitted, though many U.S. lines participate in the other functions of that association.

The Motor Carrier Act of 1980

Administrative deregulation of the motor-carrier industry following rule-making proceedings by the commission proceeded rapidly in the period 1978–80. Some of these steps are recounted in Chapter 20. The Carter Administration was urging further movement in this direction and seeking comprehensive legislation. The organized trucking industry, the International Brotherhood of Teamsters, and important elements in Congress thought the commission was going too far. Hence, while the 1980 act contains important regulatory reform, it also admonishes the commission to go no farther with deregulation than the statute provides.[40]

Entry into both common and contract carriage is eased. Dual rights are not only permitted, but common and contract freight may now be mixed in the same vehicle. In the interest especially of fuel economy, the commission is directed to eliminate, within 180 days after passage of the act, gateway restrictions and circuitous route limitations. It must also process expeditiously carrier applications designed to broaden commodity authority, to serve intermediate points, to provide round trip authority, and to eliminate unreasonably narrow territorial restrictions.

Exemptions are enlarged. In the interest of improving the lot of the owner-operator hauling presently exempt agricultural commodities, the movement of livestock and poultry feed, agricultural seeds and

---

[40] In 1979 the commission also took the important step of exempting the transportation of fresh fruits and vegetables by railroad from regulation of rates and tariffs. The exemption was later extended to some other commodities of an agricultural nature. Thus the railroads were put in better position to compete with exempt truckers and the results have been encouraging.

plants, is now exempt when transported to the site of agricultural production or of sale for agricultural purposes. Only a fitness test is required to transport food intended for human consumption as well as soil conditioners and fertilizers. Hence the backhaul problem should be ameliorated. Owner operators are given additional protection by providing for prescription by the commission of simple forms of written contract to replace the oral agreements that have been common in the past. The movement of passengers and cargo becomes exempt when it is a part of a continuous movement in conjunction with an airline. Private carrier opportunities are extended by making it lawful to haul for compensation for wholly-owned subsidiaries within a corporate structure.

Substantial rate-making freedom is accorded, for the commission may no longer suspend or disapprove rate increases or decreases which do not exceed 10 percent from the rate in effect on July 1, 1980, or one year previous to the effectiveness of the changed rate. The commission may enlarge the zone by 5 percentage points if it finds that competition is adequate to regulate the level of rates. In addition, upward adjustment is allowed to account for inflation—initially 5 percent, two years later and thereafter on the basis of the Labor Department's producers' price index. The commission retains the right to suspend and investigate on an allegation of unjust discrimination or predatory pricing practice. Rate bureaus are curbed, as noted in Chapter 17, but general increases and classification changes can still be processed by the bureaus with antitrust immunity. Motor carriers may now file released value rates without obtaining approval.[41]

Because of concern about inadequate enforcement of motor-carrier safety regulations and the possibility that greater freedom of entry and increased competitive pressures might worsen an already bad situation, the Congress enacted minimum insurance provisions which may well prove onerous, especially to small carriers. The Secretary of Transportation shall by regulation require a minimum of $1,000,000 of financial responsibility for any vehicle operating in interstate commerce for hire ($5,000,000 in the case of certain hazardous materials). For a period of two years the secretary may reduce this to not less than $500,000. Penalties are provided for violations.

Railroad Transportation Policy Act of 1980 (Staggers Rail Act of 1980)

Although passed only a few months apart, the motor carrier and rail acts differ substantially in approach. This reflects the fact that congres-

---

[41] Contrary to the general deregulatory thrust, the commission is now empowered to require through routes and joint rates between motor carriers and between motor and water (but not rail) carriers.

sional reorganization assigned the two forms of transport to different committees in Congress. No longer is it possible to expect a comprehensive act covering all principal modes of surface transport as in the Transportation Act of 1940. In view of the barriers to entry into rail transportation, however, it is not astonishing that most of the 1980 act relates to rates and rate making.

Rail carriers are given specific statutory authority to make contract rates with shippers. As the Conference Committee report says, the act establishes a separate class of service and enables railroads to become contract as well as common carriers. With some exceptions, once a contract has been approved by the commission, the service provided under it is exempt from all regulation and all of the requirements of the Interstate Commerce Act. In order to preserve their common carrier capability, however, railroads may not commit more than 40 percent of their car supply under contract. Prior to approval a shipper may complain that the proposed contract unduly impairs the ability of the carrier to discharge its common carrier obligations or a port may complain that unreasonable discrimination against the port will result. In the case of agricultural products, forest products, and paper, a shipper may complain of unreasonable discrimination because of failure of a carrier to enter into a similar contract with that shipper.

The act builds upon the 4–R Act in respect of rates. Thus it provides that a rate that equals or exceeds variable cost is conclusively presumed to contribute to going concern value. Market dominance is now specifically defined rather than left to the commission. There is no market dominance, hence no commission authority over the maximum level of a rate, if the rate is less than 160 percent of variable cost until September 30, 1981; 165 percent during the following year; 170 percent for the year ending September 30, 1983; and 175 percent in the year ending September 30, 1984. Thereafter a cost-recovery percentage of variable cost will apply designed to secure coverage of both fixed and variable cost. For this purpose, cost is defined to include a return on equity at a rate equal to the embedded cost of capital. One exception is included to hold the rate on coal from Wyoming to San Antonio at a lower level until 1987.

A zone of rate flexibility is provided, tied to the base rate at the time of passage of the act, adjusted quarterly by an index of railroad cost. A carrier may increase its rates by 6 percent a year over the adjusted base rate without challenge provided that the increases in the first four years do not bring the rate above 118 percent of the adjusted base. After October 1, 1984, increases of 4 percent are authorized unless the carrier is found to have adequate revenues. Such rates may be challenged on complaint if they exceed the applicable revenue-variable cost percentage for the particular year by 20 percentage points or 190 percent, whichever is lower. These provisions are effective only for rates established by independent action by a carrier. Provision is made, however, for inflation adjustments applicable to group-made rates should they be required. These provisions may well resolve the problem of regulatory lag which has plagued rail carriers during most of the past three decades.

The burden of proof of unreasonableness remains on the complainant as in the past unless the parameters described above are exceeded. In the event that they are exceeded, the burden falls on the carrier making the rate. Thus, where there is statutory market dominance or a rate that falls outside the limits of flexibility, the carrier must prove reasonableness when challenged.

The opportunity of challenging a rate as generating an undue discrimination is greatly abridged. Apart from the provisions which relate to contract rates, charges of discrimination are precluded in the cases of separate rates for different services, rates applicable to different routes and surcharges assessed by one participant in a joint rate. With restrictions of this sort it remains to be seen to what extent antitrust jurisdiction may supersede that of the Interstate Commerce Commission. The exception is the retention by the commission of authority over discrimination within or among ports. State commissions are dealt with harshly in their jurisdiction over intrastate rates. Unless certified by the commission in respect of their procedures they lose jurisdiction over intrastate rates, classifications, rules, and practices. Even if so certified they have no jurisdiction over general rate increases, inflation-based increases or fuel adjustment surcharges. No proof of discrimination against interstate commerce is required in such situations as used to be called for under Section 13 of the act.

The act hits group rate making and railroad rate bureaus severely after January 1, 1984. The commission is likely to do so at an earlier date. Carriers may not discuss single-line rates nor joint rates in which they cannot practicably participate. Joint rates over competitive routes may not be discussed by disparate carriers making up several such joint routes. General rate increase proceedings may, however, continue until April 1, 1982. Rate bureaus may continue to serve as publishing agents with antitrust exemption. But since labor protection provisions are included, it is evidently expected they will shrink in size.

Both the commission and rate bureaus are placed under strict time limits in various classes of proceedings. Some of these may prove difficult with which to comply. In view of the importance placed on revenue-cost relationships as rate-making standards, provision is made for a railroad accounting principles board composed of the Comptroller General of the United States and six appointees chosen to meet specific statutory requirements. It is of interest here that the Comptroller General is an agent of the Congress, not of the Executive Branch. Pending new findings Rail Form A costs, adjusted as required in particular proceedings, will continue to be acceptable.

The act provides for the expedition of merger applications by the commission. It also encourages ownership and operation by other parties of lines scheduled for abandonment.

THE GREAT EXPERIMENT IN BRIEF REVIEW

Regulatory history to date shows three major periods of substantive regulation. Let us briefly recapitulate the three periods.

I. *Restrictive Regulation, 1887–1917*

Legislation was designed to deepen and strengthen the regulation of rates and discrimination. Four subperiods may be identified:

A. *The Beginning, 1887–97.* The Act to Regulate Commerce provided significant legal basis for regulation and for an independent federal commission to administer the Act. Despite challenges to its authority in the conduct of hearings and enforcement, considerable regulation was in fact exercised.

B. *The Period of Doldrums, 1897–1906.* The initial showing of strength was cut short when Supreme Court decisions emasculated the most important substantive provisions of the act.

C. *Strengthened Regulation, 1906–1917.* Rehabilitation of regulation began in the Elkins Act, but effective control over rates and local discrimination came with the Hepburn Act and Mann-Elkins Act. Provision for the audit of accounts and suspension of rates made the commission a powerful regulatory body.

D. *World War I.* Shortage of transport capacity resulted in federal operation of railroads to clear up congestion and produced a change in attitude toward the character of regulation.

II. *Period of Positive and Extended Regulation, 1920–1970.*

During this half century Congress, more or less in order; (1) saw the prime importance of adequate rail transportation and the need of a fair rate of return and increased scope of regulation to assure it, (2) extended regulation to other modes of transportation, (3) established more flexibility in railroad regulation, and (4) provided for reexamination of regulation and broadened transportation policy administration. Four subperiods may be noted.

A. *The Transportation Act of 1920.* This act sought to make it possible for the railroads to have a rate of return that would assure their adequacy and at the same time to reduce wasteful competition through a general program of consolidation. It extended regulation to service, finance, and the construction of new lines.

B. *Extension of Regulation to Other Modes, 1933–1940.* During the decade of the 30s, Congress passed the basic acts of regulation for all other modes of transportation. In 1933 the Intercoastal Shipping Act established comprehensive regulation of domestic deep-sea shipping. In 1935 the Motor Carrier Act was passed. In 1936 the basic maritime act was passed, which incorporated the regulatory provisions of the Shipping Act of 1916. While the shipping acts provide for comprehensive surveillance of foreign shipping, they do not give the maritime agency specific authority to set maximum or minimum rates or to control entry of nonsubsidized shipping. The Civil Aeronautics Act was passed in 1938 and the Transportation Act of 1940 extended Interstate Commerce Commission control over common carriers on inland waters except those restricted to harbor operations.

C. *Increased Flexibility, 1933–1962.* The Emergency Transportation Act of 1933 liberalized the rate-making rule, abolished the recapture clause, and established an office to promote rail coordination. Section 77B of the Bankruptcy Act, which was passed the same year, facilitated reorganization of bankrupt railroads. The Transportation Act of 1940 further liberalized the rule of rate-making, set up a preamble for the Interstate Commerce Act, and relieved the commission from promulgating a consolidation plan for the railroads. The Act of 1958 provided for government guarantee of rail credit and provided means of facilitating abandonment of unprofitable operations while limiting agricultural exemption for motor transport. Yet, we find in this period some strengthening of the commission's administrative powers.

D. *Reexamination of Regulation and Broadened Federal Transportation Administration, 1955–1970.* The deterioration of the competitive position of the railroads and regulatory difficulties in general led to congressional provision of reexamination of the government's regulatory policy and a broadening of the scope of its administrative functioning in transportation. The report of the Weeks' Committee in 1955, under the sponsorship of the Department of Commerce, was followed by the report on National Transportation Policy, under the auspices of the Interstate Commerce Committee of the Senate in 1961.

The Urban Transportation Act of 1964, for the first time,

involved the federal government in the study and support of urban transit needs. The Department of Transportation Act which followed in 1967, was designed to coordinate government administrative support and safety in transportation.

III. *Period of Deregulation and Aid to Railroads.*

As shown in Figure 19-1, recent acts of Congress include: (1) The Rail Passenger Act of 1970, (2) the Regional Reorganization Act of 1973, (3) the Railroad Revitalization and Regulatory Reform Act of 1976, (4) the Airline Regulation Act of 1978, (5) the Motor Carrier Act of 1980, and (6) the Railroad Transportation Policy Act of 1980. The latter includes additional funding for Conrail and further modernization assistance to other railroads.

SELECTED REFERENCES

Beard, William. *Regulation of Pipe Lines as Common Carriers.* New York: Columbia University Press, 1941.

Caves, Richard E. *Air Transport and Its Regulators.* Cambridge: Harvard University Press, 1962.

Cherington, Paul W. *Airline Price Policy: A Study of Domestic Airline Passenger Fares.* Boston: Harvard Business School, 1958.

Dixon, F. H. *Railroads and Government.* New York: Charles Scribner's Sons, 1923.

Douglas, George W., and Miller, James C., III. *Economic Regulation of Domestic Air Transport: Theory and Policy.* Washington, D.C.: The Brookings Institution, 1974.

Fair, Marvin L. *Economic Considerations in the Administration of the Interstate Commerce Act.* Cambridge, Md.: Cornell Maritime Press, Inc., 1972.

————, and Guondolo, John. *Transportation Regulation.* 8th ed. Dubuque, Ia.: William C. Brown Co., 1979.

Hilton, George W. *The Transportation Act of 1958: A Decade of Experience.* Bloomington: Indiana University Press, 1969.

Hudson, William J., and Constantin, James A. *Motor Transportation: Principles and Practices.* New York: The Ronald Press Co., 1958.

Johnson, Arthur M. *Petroleum Pipelines and Public Policy: 1906-1959.* Cambridge: Harvard University Press, 1967.

Kahn, Alfred E. *The Economics of Regulation: Principles and Institutions.* 2 vols. New York: John Wiley & Sons, Inc., 1970.

Keyes, Lucile Shepperd. *Federal Control of Entry into Air Transportation.* Cambridge: Harvard University Press, 1951.

Kolko, Gabriel. *Railroads and Regulation of Transportation: 1877-1916.* Princeton: Princeton University Press, 1965.

Lawrence, Samuel A. *United States Merchant Shipping Policies and Politics,* esp. chap. 7. Washington, D.C.: The Brookings Institution, 1966.

Locklin, D. Philip. *Railroad Regulation Since 1920*. New York: McGraw-Hill Book Co., 1928.

Morgan, C. S. *Regulation of Domestic Water Transportation*. Washington, D.C.: Interstate Commerce Commission, 1946.

National Transportation Policy Study Commission. *National Transportation Policies through the Year 2000*, esp. chap. 2. Washington D.C., 1979.

Nelson, James C. "The Motor Carrier Act of 1935." *Journal of Political Economy*, vol. 44, no. 464 (1936).

Pegrum, Dudley F. *Transportation Economics and Public Policy*, chaps. 11–15, 17. 3d ed. Homewood, Ill.: Richard D. Irwin, Inc., 1973.

Richmond, Samuel B. *Regulation and Competition in Air Transportation*. New York: Columbia University Press, 1961.

Sharfman, I. L. *The Interstate Commerce Commission*, part 1. New York: The Commonwealth Fund, 1931.

Taff, Charles A. *Commercial Motor Transportation*, chaps. 5, 17–18. 4th ed. Homewood, Ill.: Richard D. Irwin, Inc., 1969.

———. *Operating Rights of Motor Carriers*. Dubuque, Ia.: William C. Brown Co., 1953.

Taneja, Nawal K. *The Commercial Airline Industry*, chaps. 10–13. Lexington, Mass.: Lexington Books, 1976.

Wolbert, George S. *American Pipe Lines*. Norman: University of Oklahoma Press, 1952.

20

The Control of Carrier Structure
and Services

No set of facilities which must be used in connection with a logistics or physical distribution system is more important to that system than the structure of the nation's carrier facilities and operations. It is therefore very important for those who manage and operate these systems to understand the content of national policy with regard to the changing structure of the carriers and the service which they perform and the degree of regulation which may protect or advance the interest of the shipping and traveling public.

The United States has been devoted to privately owned carrier development and operation to the extent that national planning of the transportation system has been almost absent. Only in air transport and the merchant marine has there been any semblance of national planning.

The Civil Aeronautics Act of 1938 committed the Civil Aeronautics Board to "the encouragement and development of an air transportation system properly adapted to the present and future needs of the foreign and domestic commerce of the United States, of the postal service and of the national defense." Happily, the directive to the Civil Aeronautics Board came early in the development of air commerce, giving the board an opportunity to give some guidance and supervision to an orderly development of the nation's air system.

Similarly the Merchant Marine Act of 1936 declares that "it is the policy of Congress to have a merchant marine sufficient for the national defense and foreign and domestic commerce of the United States and that the shipping devoted to foreign trade should carry a substantial portion of the water-borne export and import foreign commerce and serve all foreign trade routes essential for the maintenance of the flow of such commerce." The United States Maritime Commission formulated a worldwide system of "essential trade routes" of which there are now 36. This system has provided the commission and its successors the framework for authorizing American flag operators to receive operating and construction subsidies. In spite of extensive nonsubsidized operations incident to the Korean and Vietnam wars and the advent of nonsubsidized container operations, this authority of the Maritime agency has largely influenced the structure of U.S. flag-line operations and transoceanic trade to date.

With respect to other modes of transport there has been no clear statement of national objective or direction with respect to structure. This has meant that the railroad, motor-carrier, domestic water, and pipeline structures, like Topsy "just grew." Regulation of these carriers, in respect to structure, has been limited to a case by case approach in granting, amending, or revoking common carrier certificates of convenience and necessity and contract-carrier permits governing entry or extension of service (by means of construction in the case of railroads). The same fragmented approach has been used in approving mergers and applications for control of one carrier by another and in passing upon discontinuance of operations or service.

CARRIER STRUCTURE REGULATION

Certificate Regulation: Entry, Extension, Discontinuance, Abandonment

Certificate regulation was first applied to natural monopolies in the public utility field and later extended to transportation, especially for those modes which tend to be excessively competitive. The objective has been to restrict the service of a given mode to responsible persons and companies and to limit competition in the interest of investors and operating efficiency. When applied to the public utilities, the objective has been to recognize the natural monopoly character of these industries, realizing for the public the economic advantage of monopoly and at the same time protecting the consumer of the service by adequate regulation of rates and service. Until the advent of deregulation in the late 1970s transportation certification sought to avoid excessive duplication and competition which has been a natural tendency in waterway, highway, and air transport. In passing upon applications, the regulatory authorities gave preference to existing carriers on a given route or service even though they use publicly provided ways. The chief guiding principle in certificating entry and extension of service was to restrict and limit competition. A carrier desiring entry or extension of operating rights was generally called upon to show that the existing carrier or carriers on the proposed route were not in a position to increase their service to meet the public need or had been failing to perform the service for which they were certificated.

Railroad Construction and Extension. The first federal application of regulation by certificate was provided for in the Transportation Act of 1920 respecting railroad construction. The act set up provisions which would restrain railroads from construction of tracks and facilities which would wastefully duplicate existing rail facilities and, on the other hand, would require under certain conditions the construction of way facilities to provide adequate transport service. No railroad subject to the act shall construct any facilities or additional trackage without a certificate of public convenience and necessity obtained from the commission and the commission may deny an application for such a certificate or may grant it with such conditions attached as in its judgment public convenience and necessity may require. A rail carrier is, however, free to build switch and track connections and may even be required to do so in order to connect with a shipper or another carrier.

Between 1880 and 1920 there had been considerable wasteful duplicate railroad construction in the United States. By the time the act of 1920 was passed, the rail network of 230,000 miles was essentially complete. Furthermore, increasing highway competition began to be felt in the decade of the 20s and has increased since. For these reasons, the railroad industry has had little interest in extension. As a matter of fact, railroad mileage in the United States has steadily declined since the early 20s. While over 3,000 added miles have been approved to round out the system, many more miles have been abandoned.

Railroad Abandonment. The Interstate Commerce Commission can similarly grant or withhold a certificate to abandon railroad services operated in interstate and foreign commerce. Jurisdiction over intrastate service is limited to intrastate facilities used in the conduct of interstate and foreign commerce or to circumstances when continuance of purely intrastate service would impose an undue burden on interstate and foreign commerce.[1] The commission does not have jurisdiction if (1) the railroad lies entirely within a state, (2) is independently owned, (3) does not participate in interstate or foreign commerce, and (4) its continued operation would not impose an undue burden on interstate and foreign commerce.[2] The reason for abandonment is generally a reduction of traffic because of exhaustion of resources such as lumber, coal, and products or mines, or because

[1] 254 ICC 745, 763 (1944); 271 U.S. 153 (1926); 320 U.S. 685, 690 (1944).
[2] 258 U.S. 204 (1922).

of removal of plants, commercial establishments, or government facilities, or competition of other modes of transportation. There also are abandonments designed to increase efficiency of operation. For example, a tunnel may cut off a longer route and heavy grade. Reduction of gradient may also come from reconstruction of a section or as a result of merger of parallel facilities which permits concentration of traffic on the line that has the lower controlling gradient. Serious decline in railroad traffic, because of motor truck competition, has caused the rail carriers to seek abandonment of many branch lines. The 4-R Act of 1976 sought to facilitate this. For a line wholly within one state application must first be made to the state, but if there is no action within 120 days appeal can be made to the Interstate Commerce Commission which may rule that public convenience no longer requires operation of the line.

Discontinuance of Rail Service. The decline of both passenger and freight traffic has invited many efforts to discontinue service in recent years. As in the case of abandonment, a certificate is required which affirms that public convenience and necessity no longer require the service. The Rail Passenger Act of 1970 authorized Amtrak, subject to the provisions of Section 13a, to abandon train service not required by public convenience and necessity or which would impair its ability to perform other services.

The 4-R Act of 1976 set forth conditions for discontinuance of freight service over the northeastern lines involved in receivership and reorganization. Conrail, which operates these lines, is authorized to discontinue a service after 60-days' notice of intent and notification of the states involved by showing that revenue does not cover avoidable costs and a reasonable return on the value of the properties involved. Unless the Interstate Commerce Commission within 120 days finds that the service is compensatory, the service may be discontinued.

Motor-Carrier Entry. The regulation of entry and operating rights has dominated the task of motor-carrier regulation. Indeed, it constitutes the major workload of regulation. Of the cases coming before the commission, over 80 percent relate to motor-carrier entry and operating rights. Section 206 of the Interstate Commerce Act requires that any common carrier operating in interstate commerce obtain a certificate of public convenience and necessity issued by the commission authorizing such operations. Section 209 similarly requires contract carriers operating in interstate commerce to obtain a permit showing need and fitness to operate. Section 212(b) requires that any sale or transfer of operating rights must be approved by the commission.

The service performed by common carriers could be restricted as to:

1. Route.
2. Commodities carried.
3. Direction given commodities may be carried.

4. Points served.
5. Size of shipments.
6. Types of trucks or containers.
7. Season of operation.
8. Class of service.
9. Classes of shippers served.

There has been much controversy among transportation economists as well as managers of the carrier industry and government officials as to the need for regulating entry into an industry that tends to be very competitive. The dynamics of the industry are reflected by the fact that the commission handles from 12,000 to 15,000 applications yearly relative to entry and operating rights. Administrative action by the commission (1979 saw 99.5 percent of applications for authority granted) and the Motor Carrier Act of 1980 have greatly diminished the restraint imposed upon new entry into the industry or extensions of existing operations. To understand the change that is being effected we must look briefly at the standards which had been in effect for 40 years after passage of the Motor Carrier Act of 1935.

The granting of a certificate of public convenience and necessity for entry or extension of common-carrier service required an affirmative showing of public convenience and necessity by the applicant. The applicant need not only show that the public convenience and necessity required that the proposed services be instituted, but also that the existing carriers in the route area were not able to provide this service. The protection of existing carriers was an important criterion in this regulation and the applicant could gain no favor by a promise of lower rates. The applicant must be fit, willing, and able. To be fit one must have adequate financial resources and must be free of past serious violations under the act. Willingness is evidenced by appearance before the commission and a showing of property investment.

The contract carriers in highway transportation must obtain a permit to operate or to change the character of their services. The requirements for obtaining a permit or a revised permit were virtually identical with those required by common carriers in obtaining a certificate of public convenience and necessity. The applicant was required to show that there were shippers who would use his service if he were given a permit and that the granting of the permit would not have an injurious effect upon carriers in the route area. The effect upon the applicant of denying the permit was also a consideration. The applicant was required to show that he was fit, willing, and able to perform the service called for in the permit and that he was prepared to conform to the requirements, rules, and regulations of the commission. A requirement peculiar to the granting of permits was that the number of shippers to be served must be so limited that the service would not approach that of a certificated common carrier. After 1958 this became the Rule of 8, that is, a contract carrier ordinarily might not perform service for more than eight shippers.

Dual operations involving both common- and contract-carrier service were greatly restricted by the act to those cases where there was a clear showing that the public interest would be served. The act clearly discouraged joint ownership or control of common- and contract-carrier service in the same territory. Where the commission permitted the same firm to engage in dual operations, the firm conducted each type of service over different routes or in disparate areas.

Much of this has given way to new interpretations by the commission as it now seeks to promote a more competitive environment in transport. Though some of its decisions have inspired criticism in the courts and others are in litigation, the removal of restraint upon entry into the business is well underway. It is no longer of no avail to argue that lower rates will be offered by an applicant. Harm to existing carriers is usually perceived as offset by the public advantage of enhanced competition, the Rule of 8 has been stricken as a restraint on contract-carrier expansion through acquisition of new customers, and dual operations are no longer regarded as contrary to the public interest. Even the long standing bar against conduct of for-hire operations by private carriers has been struck down and common and contract authority has been granted to some private carriers.[3]

Some of these proposals were given statutory force by the Motor Carrier Act of 1980. Applicants for a certificate must still prove fitness, willingness, and ability. But they no longer must prove public convenience and necessity. A *prima facie* showing that a public purpose will be served shifts the burden of proof to opposing parties, limited to carriers which have authority already and have participated in the traffic at issue during the prior year, to show that issuance of the certificate sought would be inconsistent with the public convenience and necessity. This is a fundamental change which greatly reduces the likelihood of successful opposition. Moreover, the diversion of revenue or traffic from an existing carrier is not to be deemed inconsistent with public convenience and necessity.

Only fitness need be shown to serve any community not regularly provided with motor-common-carrier service, to replace an abandoned rail service, to transport for the U.S. Government, (except household goods and hazardous materials) or to transport shipments under 100 pounds in weight when no one package in the vehicle exceeds that weight. These provisions reflect the concern of Congress that, under reduced regulation, service to small localities and for small packages might be jeopardized.

---

[3] *Toto Purchasing & Supply Co., Inc., Common Carrier Application,* MC–141414 Sub. 1 (March 24, 1978), reversed *Geraci Contract Carrier Application,* 7MCC 369.

Water-Carrier Certificates.   The provisions of Part III of the act with respect to inland and coastal water carriers are much the same as those applicable to motor-carrier certificates and permits. Because of the wide area of exemption noted in Chapter 19, however, only a small number of cases has come before the commission under Part III. The majority involve extension of service to·newly improved waterways; and, as in motor-carrier extensions to new service points, a number of competing carriers is usually certificated.

Air Carrier Certificates.   The Civil Aeronautics Act of 1938 gave the Civil Aeronautics Board authority similar to that of the Interstate Commerce Commission in the certification of highway carriers. The same basic requirements must be met for a certificate of entry or for extension of operating rights. As in the case of highway and water carriers, grandfather rights were to be recognized. Carriers in bona fide operation on and after the grandfather date specified in the act were to be entitled to certificates covering such operation without any proof other than that of actual operation during the relevant period. Such certificates were carefully limited to cover continuance only of operations shown as to routes and points served as well as types of traffic handled.

Foreign airlines seeking to serve the United States are required to secure a permit rather than a certificate. The Civil Aeronautics Board is required to get concurrence from the President of the United States before granting a permit. The same concurrence is required for the suspension or revocation of a permit. Foreign carriers must be shown to be under control of nationals of the country whose flag they fly.

The Civil Aeronautics Board has been less opposed to permitting increased competition when an additional carrier sought to enter a given route service than the Interstate Commerce Commission has been with respect to a motor-carrier entry. An additional carrier on a route has often been allowed by the board even though the stability of existing carriers might be reduced and government subsidy required.[4] This difference arose from the act's emphasis on competition, the need for subsidy for some carriers, and the rapid growth in demand for air service.

However, the flood of applications and sharpening of competition for many routes moved the board to adopt some general principles or guidelines to which it gave weight as seemed appropriate in pro- ceedings before it. The most important were:

1.   The one-carrier principle.
2.   The local- or regional-system principle.
3.   The principle that direct competing carriers would be certified

---

[4] 8 CAB 487, 516 (1947).

where the volume of traffic was or might become sufficient to support them.

4. The principle that the board is not required to equalize carriers' systems in respect to their traffic opportunity.

In general the board sought a balance between the service potential of a single carrier and competition to encourage efficiency.[5] Prior to 1948 the board leaned towards competition in route extensions where sufficient traffic was in prospect for an added carrier.[6] However, after 1948 the board leaned mostly toward preserving earnings which would permit removal of a carrier from subsidy or the reduction of subsidy. This change of policy was influenced in part by the nature of the air system and the problems of financing the rapidly changing technology of jet aircraft.

The Airline Deregulation Act of 1978 ushered in a third period of certificate regulation. Commuter passenger service by planes under a load capacity of 56 passengers or cargo service with a pay load capacity of nine tons are exempt from regulation. Alaska is excepted. The act instructs the board to encourage and authorize additional routes to all lines which apply and grants the board only 90 days to make a decision in the public interest. Multiple awards for new carriers on routes already served have become the rule though the majority of newly authorized services have yet to be activated.

The extension of operating rights of U.S. flag lines in foreign service, like the granting of permits to foreign flag lines, is subject to concurrence by the President of the United States. The granting of certificates and permits for international operations usually involves reciprocal arrangements incorporated in bilateral agreements with each nation involved in the route. For example, the approval of Aeroflot's service between Moscow and New York involved arrangements for Pan American to provide a parallel service.

The Airline Deregulation Act provided for the transfer of the authority of the Civil Aeronautics Board over foreign service applications to the Department of Transportation on January 1, 1985, when the CAB is to expire. Meanwhile, the board utilizes every opportunity to place additional American flag competitors on principal international routes.

CARRIER MERGERS AND CONSOLIDATION

Railroad Consolidation

Importance.   In relation to the public interest, there is no problem of transportation structure that compares with that of railroad consoli-

---

[5] 7 CAB 27, 35 (1946); 8 CAB 487, 521 (1947); 9 CAB 414, 431 (1948); 7 CAB 83, 100 (1946); 8 CAB 536, 541 (1947).

[6] 2 CAB 353, 396 (1940); 4 CAB 254, 264 (1943); 9 CAB 38, 55 (1948).

dation. The situation faced in the 80s is critical. Although the railroads carry more ton-miles of freight by far than any other mode, the future of the railroad industry in the total transport system of the nation is in jeopardy. The development of other modes, stimulated greatly by billions of dollars of government expenditures and promotion, has resulted in a diversion of traffic that makes much rail service and structure uneconomical and obsolete; yet dependence on the industry for volume movement of freight over great distances remains. Motor carriers working in conjunction with railroad operations can more economically and expeditiously assemble and distribute freight in unit loads at major terminals and can entirely replace railroad service in light-density traffic areas in a coordinated service. The result is the need for an adjustment in structure, operation, and management control which transcends, perhaps, the need ever confronted by any major industry. If the adjustment is not successful, it may well bring an end to private ownership and operation of the nation's prime transportation agency.

Accordingly, the railroads face the challenge of streamlining their facilities, services, and methods of operation in the face of the increased competition of other carriers. This involves sloughing off unprofitable mileage, shrinking certain services, but above all, integration and modernization of plant and operations, reduction of terminal handling to a minimum, and the use of the most economical and best routes between traffic centers. General consolidation of the railroads is not an immediate solution of all railroad ills, but a necessary first step, the framework within which the industry can gird itself for the growing competitive struggle and for its potential role in coordinated transport. After 1955 there was renewed interest in combination of railroad properties both through consolidation and stock control. In the year 1956 alone there were 12 applications of railroads to absorb subsidiary lines and an increase in the number of applications to obtain control through purchase of stock. Delay in the adjustment threatened to result in a shrinkage of rail facilities and service far below the level which the inherent economy and fitness of rail transportation as well as national defense considerations would justify. In view of the skepticism generated by the Penn Central failure and some ten years of abortive proceedings in the proposed Union Pacific acquisition of the Rock Island, such delay did develop. But a more favorable attitude has appeared in response to additional bankruptcy and the travails of Conrail.

Advantages of Consolidation. The potential advantages of consolidation of the railroads into a limited number of systems include (1) simpler regulation of rates and service, (2) reduction of expenses, (3) improved service capability, and (4) enhanced coordination. Consolidation of the railroads became a national policy in 1920 before competition of other modes had become serious.

Facilitation of Regulation of Rates and Service. The Interstate Commerce Commission had found it impossible to set or approve rate levels in any region that would enable the weak roads to earn a rate of return that would permit adequate maintenance while not allowing the strong roads in the same region to earn more than a fair rate of return. Merger of weak roads with larger and stronger systems would facilitate regulation and assure adequate facilities and service. That this objective is still an active one is shown in recent requirements imposed on the Norfolk and Western and Penn Central systems to absorb certain weak roads.

Reduction of Expenses. Depending, of course, on the number, size, and physical relationships of the railroads consolidated in any instance, substantial savings in organization expenses are to be expected. The general offices of the smaller roads are abolished, and the number of staff officers is greatly reduced. Merging or the extension of operating divisions results in fewer division superintendents and other division officers, which can result not only in substantial savings but also in more flexible operating conditions.

Each railroad must keep a record of its own cars wherever they are on the 500-odd railroads of the United States, Canada, and Mexico, and of the "foreign line" cars on its lines in order to determine at the end of each month its credit or debit position. The maintenance of car records and accounts, which is a major task of present railroad organization, would be greatly simplified. Control of car location and movement which has been seriously inadequate should be materially improved.

The economies relating to traffic activities are among those most likely to be realized. Competition in the solicitation of freight and the operation of duplicative traffic offices is eliminated. Fewer tariffs and exceptions to the classification naturally result. Sales and rate work can be addressed more to the competition of other modes rather than toward obtaining a share of traffic already moving by rail.

The principal potential economic advantage of consolidation, however, is lower operating costs incident to better utilization of roadway and rolling stock and elimination of wasteful duplication of facilities and service. Fewer routes between important traffic centers are required. This permits the concentration of traffic on the more direct and more efficient routes. Where consolidation results in combining two parallel main-line routes of similar quality, they may be used as a double-track operation resulting in an increase in capacity substantially greater than when operated separately. Where the consolidated railroads serve a common terminal or interchange point, duplication of piggyback facilities, team tracks, and yards may be eliminated. Increased utilization of the best trackage and stations is permitted and, perhaps, the abandonment of expensive and burdensome investment in facilities and real estate. Shops may be consolidated into large-scale plants with modern equipment and specialization which would otherwise be impractical.

Greater efficiency in the handling of traffic should be obtained. There would be more single-line trains free from the delays and expense of interchange. This would be particularly fruitful where consolidation results in joining an important source of traffic and an important destination terminal, a common objective in end-to-end and branch-line consolidations. Car distribution should be improved, resulting in better handling of peak loads. Because of this as well as more direct hauls and fewer interchanges, there should be less empty-car mileage and faster turnaround, thus a saving in the number of cars required.

A consolidation of schedules is possible where the merged roads are operating train service between the same terminals, for many such trains are operating light to maintain competitive service. A reduction in unremunerative train mileage should result, with the concentration of traffic as largely as possible in heavy through trains requiring no intermediate yard work. There also would be a unification of switching operations affording better utilization of locomotives and a reduction in crew and fuel expenses. Since locomotives continue to improve rapidly with respect to power, speed, and mileage obtainable between service stops and shopping, consolidation may be in some instances the only means to exploit their potentialities in railroad operations. Finally, the standardization of signals, yards, ruling grades, and operating rules which in time would result from consolidation would greatly facilitate train operation. The general level of equipment standards would be raised.

The ultimate target of consolidation is the recasting of the operating pattern and corporate structure so as to permit full exploitation of modern technology in the production of the lowest cost and most efficient railroad service. Critical to this is the concentration of traffic upon select lines and of the limited funds available for investment on the upgrading of those same lines and their attendant facilities.

Improved Service Capability. Perhaps no handicap of the railroads in competition with their principal adversary, the motor carrier, is as serious as their inferior service capability. So much of rail service involves interchange that rail service capability is in no sense comparable to that of the motortruck. Where interchange occurs, the originating railroad cannot guarantee scheduled delivery. Consolidation, especially end-to-end, permits an expedited and dependable single-line haul both in carload and piggyback services.

Promote Coordination. We live at the onset of the age of coordination of the modes to provide a more economic and efficient transport service in which transport companies will dominate common-carrier service, at least where substantial distances are involved in traffic movement. Rail, air, ship, and pipeline will presumably serve as the trunk lines or main stems which would necessarily employ motor carriers for assembly and dispersion around principal terminals. Coordination, in many instances, may be made economical and practical by the employment of through routes and joint rates in line-haul service or by contractual arrangements for assembly and dispersion at terminals. The railroads of the United States offer by far the largest number of potential trunk-line operations and, therefore, in the aggregate, the main base for the age of coordination. How the railroads are consolidated will determine whether or not the base for coordination approaches the most economic one. The complete service capability of the motor carrier assures its continued growth as a carrier for short and medium distances and occasionally for substantial distances for high-grade traffic.

Development of National Policy on Consolidation. In the Transportation Act of 1920 the Congress made consolidation of the railroads a national policy. It was considered basic to the attainment of the general objective of an adequate transportation system. The act not only established the general principle of consolidation but also provided for the formulation of a complete plan of consolidation. The Interstate Commerce Commission at the earliest practicable time was to prepare and adopt a plan for the consolidation of the railroad properties of the United States into a "limited number of systems" in such a way as to (1) preserve competition as fully as possible, (2) maintain existing routes and channels of trade wherever practicable, and (3) produce systems that, whenever possible, would earn substantially the same rate of return under a uniform system of rates. The section, it is important to note, provided for acquisition of control on commission approval short of consolidation without these limitations. Furthermore, the commission was not given the authority to require consolidation according to the plan. The initiative in execution was left with the railroads subject to the approval of the commission.

In the Transportation Act of 1940 Congress relieved the Interstate Commerce Commission of the responsibility of requiring consolidation to conform to a general plan. Each proposal for consolidation or acquisition of control was to be decided on its own merits after the commission had considered (1) the effect upon adequate transportation service, (2) the total of resulting fixed charges, (3) the interest of the employees affected, and (4) the desirability in the public interest of including other railroads in the region of the combination. Any approval of a proposal must specify that during a period of four years from the date of the order, no employee of any railroad involved shall be placed in a "worse position" with respect to employment. Born of commission and industry frustration and the Great Depression, the

1940 policy has remained unchanged despite the radical alteration of economic and transport conditions in the postwar period.

The 4-R Act of 1976 provided for sharing merger policy direction with the secretary of transportation and the attorney general. The former is authorized to study the possible restructuring of the rail system and to conduct hearings at the request of the carriers. While the Interstate Commerce Commission retains the final authority, it must consult the secretary and the attorney general. Moreover, it now operates under statutory deadlines which are designed to prevent the inordinate delays which characterized some earlier merger proceedings.

Recent Merger Developments. The incursion of other modes into the traffic spectrum of the railroads by the 1950s threatened the ability of many railroads to maintain service and especially to find capital for modernization; hence it precipitated a merger movement. The petroleum traffic was lost to the pipelines; the passenger traffic to the automobile and air transportation; and livestock, merchandise, and much perishable traffic to motor carriers. The so-called recent merger movement began in 1955, bringing about extensive combinations, especially in the East, Southeast, and Northwest.

The movement began with the acquisition by major carriers of secondary railroads in which they already held financial interest. Most of these acquisitions were in the Middle West between 1954 and 1957, but one of the more important was a merger of the Nashville, Chattanooga, and St. Louis with the Louisville and Nashville in 1957. Two important applications for end-to-end combination were denied soon thereafter: control of the Central of Georgia by the St. Louis-San Francisco Railway in 1957 and the acquisition of the Florida East Coast by the Atlantic Coast Line in 1958. Since 1959 the commission has approved most applications, but often after much delay. The "ice was cracked" apparently by the acquisition of the Virginian by the Norfolk and Western. There followed a number of mergers, starting with the Erie-Lackawanna. Larger scale efforts soon resulted in the formation of three dominant systems in the East: the Norfolk and Western system which now includes the Nickel Plate and the Wabash, the Chesapeake and Ohio-Baltimore and Ohio system, and the Penn Central system (now much enlarged as Conrail). In the Southeast, two of the three coastal trunklines, the Atlantic Coast Line and the Seaboard Airline, were merged into the Seaboard Coastline system. In the Northwest the Great Northern, Northern Pacific, Burlington and Spokane, Portland and Seattle were merged into the Burlington Northern to become the largest railroad system of the nation when measured in mileage and territorial coverage.

Although merger of the Illinois Central and Gulf, Mobile and Ohio was approved in 1972 and the Louisville and Nashville acquired the Monon in 1973, the postwar wave of mergers came to a practical end with consummation of Penn Central in 1968. The increase of merger and acquisition activities in 1976, however, suggested that a second wave of consolidation had begun.[7] The corporate simplification of Missouri Pacific by merger into the parent of its controlled Texas and Pacific and Chicago and Eastern Illinois was accomplished in 1976.[8] Two applications for acquisition of the Detroit, Toledo and Ironton were filed in 1977 and control by Grand Trunk Western was approved two years later. In December 1977, an application was filed for merger of Burlington Northern and St. Louis-San Francisco. A 1978 attempt of Southern Pacific to acquire control of Seaboard Coastline was blocked by the commission because of failure to secure approval prior to substantial purchase of stock. Soon thereafter the Chessie system and Family Lines (Seaboard Coastline, Louisville and Nashville, and Clinchfield) sought approval for common control. In 1980 Union Pacific sought authority to control Missouri Pacific and Western Pacific while various lines were seeking to acquire portions of the Rock Island which was in the process of liquidation. These moves precipitated a proposal to merge Southern and Norfolk and Western.

Thus, the restructuring of the nation's railroads through the initiative of rail carrier applications before the commission, goes on. Decisions by the commission are made case by case without benefit of either a national plan looking toward an adequate and sound railroad system or even of guidelines that were set forth in connection with the plan called for in the 1920 act. The third guideline, the maintenance of existing routes and channels of trade wherever practicable, has been followed all too much, perhaps. The first two might have been modified in the act of 1940 to read: (1) "preservation of competition so far as practicable" and (2) "arrangement of systems to have comparable financial and traffic strength so far as possible." These principles or guidelines would appear to be essential in the broad national interest. They have not been employed, with the result that we have some weak and wobbly merged systems, a serious reduction of competition, and a number of excluded railroads which face a bleak if not disastrous future.

These principles were ignored in the Penn Central merger and in the subsequent Final System Plan for the northeast which resulted in the formation of Conrail. Penn Central was bankrupt and faced with a negative cash flow in less than three years. Conrail has encountered continuing deficits and may again be compelled to undertake the dangerous expedient of deferring maintenance. In the northwest the Milwaukee and the Rock Island for over a decade "dangled in the wind" of bankruptcy in the absence of a definitive governmental pol-

---

[7] Interstate Commerce Commission, *Annual Report, 1978*, p. 24.

[8] *Missouri Pacific Railroad Company Mergers*, 348 ICC 414 (1976).

icy. After the application of Burlington Northern to merge with Frisco, 14 competing railroads entered the proceedings seeking protection from anticipated diversions of traffic.[9] These conditions are hardly in the public interest. The end result could be the necessity for the government to take over the railroads.

Motor Carrier Mergers

The Motor Carrier Act of 1935 in Section 5(2) requires approval of the commission for the merger of two or more motor carriers when the aggregate operating revenue exceeds $300,000. Smaller carriers whose aggregate revenue is less than $300,000 may merge without authorization by the commission. This is usually effected by the transfer of a certificate or permit according to rules and regulations of the commission.

The commission has been liberal in granting permission for mergers in recognition of the fact that from the outset there has remained an excessive number of motor freight carriers. The result has been that the number of interstate motor carriers reporting to the commission has been reduced from some 21,000 to 14,000. Systems have developed, primarily by merger, which have broad territorial coverage. Many operate transcontinentally; a few have almost nationwide coverage of principal points.

The commission's alacrity in permitting motor-carrier mergers has been the subject of much criticism. The number of competitors on many routes has been sharply reduced. Despite lack of measurable economies of scale, motor carriers do gain competitive strength as their territorial coverage is enlarged and the number of points given single-line service multiplies. Small carriers may find themselves at a growing disadvantage. The greater ease of securing extensions of a carrier's route pattern under the 1980 act should make merger less essential as a means of carrier growth.

Airline Mergers and Control

The Civil Aeronautics Act of 1938 gave the Civil Aeronautics Board comprehensive control over airline mergers, acquisitions of control, or operating agreements. The act prohibits the ownership and control of airlines by aircraft manufacturing companies. Any person seeking approval of a merger, purchase, lease, or operating contract must apply to the Civil Aeronautics Board. After public hearing the board may approve or disapprove according to whether it finds the object of

---

[9] An improvement over the 49 carriers that appeared in the Union Pacific-Rock Island case a decade before. Interstate Commerce Commission, *Annual Report, 1978*, p. 29.

the application consistent with the public interest. The only restraint on the board is that it cannot approve a merger which will result in monopoly or jeopardize an air carrier not a party to the plan. The jurisdiction of the board in such matters corresponds to that of the ICC in that the approved acts are immune from antitrust attack. As of January 1, 1983, the Department of Justice will assume jurisdiction.

Air carriers are required to file a copy of contracts or agreements involving their cooperation and coordination. In recent years there has been an increasing tendency to provide for sharing of equipment so as to give the passenger through service. This has even involved interchange between domestic and international carrier operations. For example, an interchange agreement between Delta Airlines and Pan American provides for a Pan American plane departing from New Orleans as a Delta schedule with one stop at Dulles Airport in Washington. Thence it leaves for London as a Pan American scheduled flight.

Mergers, until recently, have been comparatively few in the airline industry, but the acquisition of Colonial by Eastern, of Chicago and Southern by Delta, of Capitol by United, and of American Overseas by Pan American are examples. In most instances weak carriers were acquired by larger and stronger systems and the subsidy burden was reduced. The poor financial showing of the industry in 1970 and 1971, involving heavy losses for a number of major carriers, seemed to revive interest in merger discussions. Northwest Orient declined, however, to go through with a proposed absorption of financially troubled Northeast when the board conditioned its approval with a denial of the right to institute service over a Miami-Los Angeles route for which Northeast had a certificate. Thereafter a home was found for Northeast in Delta's system, an event which was followed quickly by improvement of Northeast's service in the Florida market to the discomfiture of the other carriers on the route.

The Airline Deregulation Act of 1978 appears to have stimulated what has been referred to as merger fever.[10] Merger of North Central and Southern has been approved. Competing applications by Texas International and Pan American World Airways for control of National were resolved in favor of Pan Am. A merger of Flying Tiger with Seaboard World has been consumated. Baumgartner reasons that the fever arose from a combination of strong earnings (service greatly reduced), deregulation, the fears of small carriers and, for some larger carriers, the desire to hold some secondary hubs such as Denver, Houston, and Memphis. Nevertheless, the administration to date has opposed any substantial reduction of competition. But to some air carriers deregulation may mean to grow or to die.

---

[10] James D. Baumgartner, *Air Transport World*, September 1978, pp. 43–46.

SERVICE REGULATION

The regulation of railroad service contrasts sharply with the regulation, or rather the lack of it, with respect to service by the other modes of transportation. This, no doubt, is largely historical because of the almost complete dependence of the country on the railroads prior to the mid-20s. Furthermore, the railroads do not tend to be as competitive within their own industry as do other modes.

Railroad Service Regulation

Car Service. The Interstate Commerce Act did not specifically lay upon the Interstate Commerce Commission responsibility for adequacy of service or facilities prior to the Act of 1920. The exception, of course, was the requirement for interchange of cars which antedated the Act of 1887. The fact remains that the burden of regulation from 1887 to 1920 related largely to matters of rates and safety. The Esch-Pomerene Act of 1917 was the first to assign to the commission responsibility for car service and car-service rules. The car-service obligation of the railroads since 1920 is set forth in Section 1, Paragraph 10, of the act, which states:

> The term "car service" in this part shall include the use, control, supply, movement, distribution, exchange, interchange and return of locomotives, cars, and other vehicles used in the transportation of property, including special types of equipment, and the supply of trains, by any carrier by railroad subject to this part.

This is followed by Paragraph 11 which states:

> It shall be the duty of every carrier by railroad subject to this act to furnish safe and adequate car service and to establish, observe, and enforce just and reasonable rules, regulations, and practices with respect to car service; and every unjust and unreasonable rule, regulation, and practice with respect to car service is prohibited and declared to be unlawful.

In almost identical language the same obligations are placed upon motor carriers in Part 2, Section 216, Paragraph b.

The emergency powers permit the commission to change car service rules, to require joint use of terminals, to establish embargoes and priorities with respect to traffic movement, and to reroute traffic regardless of the original routing and ownership of the railroads making up the routes involved.

In connection with its administration of the car service regulations, the commission has held that it is the duty of carriers to furnish all necessary facilities for transportation of freight, including cars,[11] and to

---

[11] *Lumber Rates through Ohio River Crossings,* 29 ICC 38.

accept and transport all commodities tendered to them for carriage which they hold themselves out to carry, provided a reasonable compensation for the service is tendered.[12] The duty to provide adequate service is not absolute; ordinarily it is based upon reasonable demand for such service. The shipper is not entitled to more cars than he can reasonably load, and the carrier is not liable if its failure to furnish cars was the result of sudden and great demands which it had no reason to anticipate and which it could not reasonably have been expected to meet in full.[13]

The commission has been unable to hold individual carriers to providing adequate car service in times of car shortage, unless it is clearly shown that negligence or undue discrimination or preference in response to reasonable requests for service was involved. Adequate car service depends on total adequacy of the supply of cars by type, their proper distribution, and their use. The commission has not held that it should or could legally set a target for annual construction of cars and assign it by carrier. Only encouragement to construct was employed until efforts in the ealry 1970s at incentive per-diem arrangements.

The commission's main efforts have been in the better distribution and use of cars. Car service rules are subject to ICC approval, but the structure of the rules has been largely left to the carriers through the Association of American Railroads. However, the commission did hold hearings on adequacy of car service rules. Two principal developments followed: that the railroad industry must file car-service rules with the commission and that there should be added as an appendix provision for rules applying to shipments requiring prompt handling. Subsequently the rules were made mandatory, but exemption was granted to particular carriers from time to time. In 1980 primary jurisdiction over the car service was returned to the AAR.

Demurrage, per Diem, and Car Supply. The principal actions of the commission that affect car supply are those that relate to demurrage, including free time allowances, and recently to incentive per-diem charges. Demurrage charges beyond free time are designed as a penalty for delay in loading or unloading cars. The commission has held that the primary purpose of demurrage is to promote equipment efficiency through a penalty for undue detention of cars, but such a charge is not to be regarded as a source of carrier revenue.

Poor utilization of cars resulting from maldistribution and unnecessary car detention and empty movement represents a very important drawback to railroad efficiency. Except for certain carrier-owned special types of cars, the owning railroad finds its equipment beyond its control most of the time. There is no central management of cars in

---

[12] *Harp* v. *Choctaw, O.&G.R. Co.*, 125 Fed. Supp. 445. See also ICC 594; 4 ICC 131; 5 ICC 415; and 13 ICC 69.

[13] *Pennsylvania Railroad Co.* v. *Puritan Coal Mining Co.*, 237 U.S. 121. See also 139 ICC 324; 87 ICC 113; and 68 ICC 541.

interline movement. Carrier delays incident to interchange are significant, but car detention by the shipper with or without a carrier's concurrence is the principal reason that the average number of car-miles per day is pitifully small. In 1978 it was only 59.5 miles compared with 54.9 a decade earlier. Shippers' delay in loading and unloading, the deliberate use of cars for warehouses from which deliveries are made, and liberal regulations of free time cause cars to spend more time at rest than in performing transport service. The commission has not only generally supported higher demurrage rates proposed by the industry, but has also been active in their enforcement. In the spring of 1967, the Commission in *Ex Parte* No. 252, *Incentive Per Diem Charges*, ordered incentive per diem on a seasonal basis, later extended to year-round application. Receipts were to be used for the purchase or reconstruction of ordinary plain boxcars, a type of equipment in consistent short supply. Leasing companies responded by acquiring short-line railroads as a basis of boxcar ownership. The development of an apparent surplus of plain boxcars has resulted in reexamination.

Adequate transport service requires sufficient way facilities, motive power, and car supply. The latter involves the number and kinds of cars in good order and the car utilization obtained. Car utilization is affected by car distribution in relation to demand, expedition in handling by carriers, preventive maintenance of cars, and prompt turn-around by shippers and receivers. A program of the Association of American Railroads may, by extending computerized car reporting and record procedures to all railroads and rendering the systems of each railroad compatible one with another, ultimately provide centralized control of the entire car stock for the first time.

Service Regulation of Motor and Air Carriers

Air carriers, like bus lines but unlike highway common-carriers of freight, often engage in dual operations. They may engage in regular common-carrier line service and on approval of the board engage in charter service which is provided for under Section 401(b). Charter operations have been of special importance to the all-cargo carriers and afford a means by which passenger carriers can compete in the market for group travel. In addition, a group of supplemental air carriers has developed which rely upon charters, both domestic and international. Their position was considerably strengthened by legislation in 1962 and 1968 which provided the basis for inclusive-tour charters sold by tour operators and travel agents. Since then supplementals have grown rapidly and supply sharp competition in major tourist markets. The Airline Deregulation Act of 1978 established the supplementals as "Charter Carriers" and liberalized the service regulation of common-carrier airlines to commingle individual and group fares.

Specific regulation of service of other modes of transportation is largely conspicuous by its absence. Part II of the Interstate Commerce Act does provide that a certificate or permit of a motor carrier may be suspended if, after due notice, the carrier has failed over a period of time to provide the service called for in its certificate or permit. The carrier is given an opportunity to justify its failure to perform the service or to correct its inadequacies prior to a suspension. New entries on a route may also be certificated when existing carriers fail to render adequate service.[14] The regulation of air carriers by the Civil Aeronautics Board gives the board similar power after appropriate notice and hearing to suspend a certificate upon failure of the carrier to comply with the requirements of the certificate.

With respect to abandonment of service, the regulation of air carriers is more nearly like that of railroads than of motor carriers. Once the Civil Aeronautics Board has certified a given service and that service has been instituted, the carrier cannot suspend any part or all of the service involved without permission of the board. Suspensions are, however, approved at light traffic points; and shifts between trunk and local service carriers often occur in order to improve the efficiency of the service. The Airline Deregulation Act of 1978 directed CAB to entertain applications for reactivation of now dormant routes by existing or new carriers.

Provisions forbidding discrimination in service are to be found in all federal acts relating to domestic and foreign transport. Determination of service standards or enforcement of them to meet shipper and passenger requirements is not specifically provided. The federal commissions, nevertheless, can and do receive complaints from shippers and travelers for inadequacy of service and can bring substantial pressure on carriers to improve service even though no authority exists for specifying what the minimum service shall be except as may be provided in the certificate.

SELECTED REFERENCES

Adams, Walter, and Hendry, J. G. *Trucking Mergers, Concentration and Small Business: An Analysis on Interstate Commerce Commission Policy.* 85th Congress, 1st Session, Senate Select Committee on Small Business (1957).

Barriger, John W. *Super-Railroads for a Dynamic American Economy.* New York: Simmons-Boardman Publishing Corp., 1956.

---

[14] In one instance the trucking subsidiary of the Rock Island Railroad was granted extensive motor common-carrier authority because of failure of existing motor carriers in the territory to render adequate service at the smaller points. This precedent has been followed in several other applications by rail subsidiaries.

406

Caves, Richard E. *Air Transport and Its Regulators*, chaps. 8–11. Cambridge: Harvard University Press, 1962.

Cherington, Charles Richards. *The Regulation of Railroad Abandonments.* Cambridge: Harvard University Press, 1948.

Conant, Michael. *Railroad Mergers and Abandonments.* Berkeley: University of California Press, 1964.

Fair, Marvin L. "Railroad Mergers and the Public Interest." *Transportation Journal,* Winter 1966.

——. *Economic Considerations in the Administration of the Interstate Commerce Act,* chaps. 6–8. Cambridge, Md.: Cornell Maritime Press, 1972.

——, and Guondolo, John. *Transportation Regulation,* chaps. 6–8. 8th ed. Dubuque, Ia.: William C. Brown Co., 1979.

Fruhan, William E. *The Fight for Competitive Advantage: A Study of the United States Domestic Trunk Air Carriers,* chap. 4. Boston: Harvard Business School, 1972.

Grodinsky, Julius. *Railroad Consolidation: The Economics and Controlling Principles.* New York: D. Appleton-Century Co., 1930.

Healy, Kent T. *The Effects of Scale in the Railroad Industry.* New Haven: Committee on Transportation, Yale University, 1961.

Interstate Commerce Commission, Bureau of Transport Economics and Statistics. *Railroad Consolidation and the Public Interest–A Preliminary Examination* (1962).

Johnson, James C. *Trucking Mergers.* Lexington, Mass.: D. C. Heath & Co., 1973.

Kahn, Fritz R. "Motor Carrier Reform—Fait Accompli." *Transportation Journal,* vol. 19, no. 2 (Winter 1979), pp. 5–11.

Keyes, Lucile Sheppard. *Federal Control of Entry into Air Transportation.* Cambridge: Harvard University Press, 1951.

Leonard, William N. *Railroad Consolidation under the Transportation Act of 1920.* New York: Columbia University Press, 1946.

Pegrum, Dudley F. "The Chicago and Northwestern-Chicago, Milwaukee, St. Paul, and Pacific Merger: A Case Study in Transport Economics." *Transportation Journal,* Winter 1969.

Simnett, William Edward. *Railway Amalgamation in Great Britain.* London: The Railway Gazette, 1923.

Taff, Charles A. *Interstate Commerce Commission Policy Relating to Operating Rights of Motor Carriers of Property.* Dubuque, Ia.: William C. Brown Co., 1952.

U.S. Department of Transportation. *Western Railroad Mergers: A Staff Study.* Washington, D.C.: 1969.

21

Reasonable Rates and Discrimination

Reasonable rates and discrimination ever have been the prime matters in the regulation of transportation. They were most dominant in the first laws to regulate railroad rates by states and the nation. Because of a degree of monopoly or incompleteness of competition they have remained central in the regulation of railroads and pipelines. Because of the more competitive nature of water, highway, and air carriers, reasonableness and discrimination have not been major objectives in their regulation.

REASONABLE RATES

Until 1920 the issue of reasonable railroad rates was confined to maximum rates. The severity of this regulation, however, helped to usher in the control of minimum rates.

The problems of maximum rail rates early gave rise to serious legal and economic issues. The stringency of regulation by the Granger states raised the question of how severe such regulation could or should be. The railroads went to the federal courts for a judicial review of state commission decisions, contending their right to a fair rate of return. Although a rail carrier may have other income from investments, it generally depends upon revenue derived from fares and rates which it charges to pay all expenses and to yield a return on investment in carrier property. The amount of this income depends on the volume of traffic and the level of its rates as a whole.

In 1886 the Supreme Court ruled in *Stone* v. *Farmers' Loan and Trust Company* that the power to regulate is not the power to confiscate or destroy.[1] The principle of review of mandatory decisions on the reasonableness of rates was first affirmed by the Supreme Court in 1890[2] and the limits of legislative or commission action were set forth in the case of *Smyth* v. *Ames* in 1897.[3] The Court in this famous case reaffirmed the right of corporate persons to obtain protection against confiscation. The right to a "just compensation" was recognized, and the Court stated what has come to be the generally accepted "rule" of reasonableness as follows: "What a (railroad) company is entitled to ask is a *fair return upon the value of that which it employs for the public convenience.* On the other hand, what the public is entitled to demand is that no more be exacted from it for the use of a public highway than the services by it are reasonably worth."[4]

The Court went on to specify that in calculating the basis for fair value, consideration should be given to (1) the original cost of construction, (2) the amount expended in permanent improvements, (3) the amount and market value of bonds and stocks, (4) the present as compared to the original cost of construction, (5) the probable earning capacity of the property under particular rates prescribed, and (6) the sum required to meet operating expenses. These are to receive such weight as may be just and right in each case.[5]

In the computation of a fair rate of return of a carrier, the value and rate of return figures are reciprocal. A just or adequate compensation may be calculated by a low value if a generous rate of return is allowed or, if the value is high, by a lower rate of return. Either a 10 percent return on a valuation of $1 million or a 5 percent return on a valuation of $2 million would permit an annual return of $100,000. Therefore, in the employment of any rate base, the rate of return to be allowed must be looked upon "as its complement."[6] Because of the large investment involved, valuation appeared to be the logical basis for determining a fair rate of return for railroads which would serve as a guideline in the determination of maximum reasonable rates.

Valuation

Congress passed the Valuation Act of 1913 requiring the commission to "investigate, ascertain and report" the value of property owned or

---

[1] *Stone* et al. v. *Farmers' Loan and Trust Co.*, 116 U.S. 307, 331, 347 (1886). The statement relative to the point was given as *obiter dicta* rather than as part of the decision.

[2] *Chicago, Milwaukee and St. Paul Ry. Co.* v. *Minnesota*, 134 U.S. 418–466 (1890).

[3] 169 U.S. 466.

[4] Ibid., pp. 545–47. Italics ours.

[5] Ibid.

[6] I. L. Sharfman, *The Interstate Commerce Commission*, (New York: The Commonwealth Fund, 1935), part III-A, p. 317.

used by every common carrier subject to the act. In the pursuit of this end, the commission was required not only to make a complete inventory of all railroad facilities as a basis for determining a present value allowing for depreciation, but also to examine the accounts and financial history of each carrier to determine original and historical investment costs.

It was not until the Transportation Act of 1920 that Congress specified that valuation should be used in the regulation of rates. The commission was directed in a "rule of rate making" in Section 15A to regulate rates "so that carriers as a whole, or those in a given rate group, will under honest, efficient, and economical management and reasonable expenditures for maintenance of way, structures and equipment, earn an aggregate annual railway operating income equal as *nearly as may be to a fair return upon the aggregate value of the* . . . railway *property* . . . used in the service of transportation." (Italics supplied) Unlike the rule established in *Smyth* v. *Ames*, which was followed by court and commission action in adjusting individual rate schedules to prevent confiscation of the property of a given railroad, this rule was to apply to adjustments in the entire rate structure of a group of carriers in order to insure adequate transportation.

The work of the Interstate Commerce Commission and the railroads to value the property of the carriers progressed with increasing interest and anticipation until the O'Fallon decision in 1929.[7] This was a test case of a valuation formula which had been established by the ICC in a recapture clause action relative to a small railroad nine-miles long in St. Louis. Neither Congress nor the courts had seen fit to give the commission any directive in the relative weight to be attached to the several factors cited by the Court in *Smyth* v. *Ames*. In the instant case the Court rejected the single-sum value fixed by the commission.

This decision proved to be a crippling blow to the whole valuation enterprise. The enforcement of the recapture clause was clearly impractical, and contest in its administration was not again risked by the commission. In accord with these developments the Emergency Transportation Act of 1933 practically eliminated valuation as a criterion in regulation under the Interstate Commerce Act. Reference to fair return on fair value was removed from the rule of ratemaking. The commission was simply instructed to adjust rates giving consideration to (1) effect on movement of traffic, a provision which was amended in the Transportation Act of 1940 to specify that it applied only to the carriers for which the proposed rates are being considered; (2) adequacy to maintain needed service at the lowest cost consistent with service; and (3) need of revenue under honest, economical, and efficient management to provide such service.

---

[7] *St. Louis & O'Fallon Railroad Co.* v. *U.S.*, 279 U.S. 461 (1929).

Nevertheless, the Interstate Commerce Commission continues to keep valuation of the railroads up to date for possible use for both maximum and minimum rate regulation. The severity of the Mann-Elkins Act regarding maximum rate control and decreased railroad competition, led to a provision in the Transportation Act of 1920 for the regulation of minimum rates. When water, motor, and air transportation were subjected to regulation, their competitive nature was recognized and led to an emphasis on minimum rate regulation far more than control of maximum rates. Between World War II and the severe inflation which got underway in 1973, intermodal competition developed to such intensity that minimum rate regulation was a necessity. Operating ratios have played a more important role in the regulation of reasonableness of motor-carrier rates than has return on investment.

Rate of Return of Class I Railroads

Except for the period of the great depression of the 30s, the volume of the nation's traffic as well as its population has continued to increase. However, since the mid-20s railroad passenger and freight traffic have declined largely because of the rapid growth of highway transportation. The depression saw 30 percent of rail mileage slip into bankruptcy. World War II brought a revival, especially in freight traffic, and an increase in revenue. The business recession of 1967–68, although moderate, precipitated a recurrence of extensive railroad receiverships including the nation's largest system, the Penn-Central. How Conrail was established in the Act of 1973 to operate the bankrupt railroads in the northeast was explained in a previous chapter. Table 21–1 shows what has happened to the rate of return for Class I railroads since 1943.

It makes little difference to the rate of return whether the commission's valuation or the value shown on the books of the carriers is used for the computation. For example, in *Ex Parte* 166, the net property investment reported by the carriers was $22,548,967,331 compared with a valuation estimate of $20,622,713,588 by the commission. The estimated net operating income for 1947 was $586 million, which would be a rate of return of 2.84 percent on valuation and 2.60 on the net capital investment. In its decision the commission observed that these amounts were much "closer together than is usually the case when the aggregate value of the property is involved."[8]

In no single year since the 1920 Act was passed, except for the war years of 1942 and 1943, have the railroads as a whole approximated

---

[8] *Increased Freight Rates, 1947*, 269 ICC 33, 47–49 (1947).

TABLE 21-1
Rate of Return on Net Investment of Class I Railroads, 1943–1978

Year	Percent	Year	Percent
1943	5.71	1961	1.97
1944	4.71	1962	2.74
1945	3.77	1963	3.12
1946	2.75	1964	3.16
1947	3.44	1965	3.69
1948	4.31	1966	3.90
1949	2.88	1967	2.46
1950	4.28	1968	2.44
1951	3.76	1969	2.36
1952	4.16	1970	1.73
1953	4.19	1971	2.12
1954	3.28	1972	2.34
1955	4.22	1973	2.33
1956	3.95	1974	2.70
1957	3.36	1975	1.46
1958	2.76	1976	1.52
1959	2.72	1977	0.89
1960	2.13	1978*	0.24

In spite of reduced mileage, estimated net investment has increased over the years from $22.8 billions in 1947 to $28.2 billions in 1977. Rate of return figures, beginning with 1971, reflect ICC modifications requiring inclusion of deferred taxes. Beginning with 1975, the return is based on net investment less deferred taxes (Sch. A, line 21b) and NROI less investment tax credit (Sch. A, line 12b).

* First six months.

Source: Interstate Commerce Commission, *Transport Statistics in the United States* (and *Statistics of Railways*), annual reports of railroads (R-1) and RE&I reports, except that the percent for 1975–78 is computed from Schedule A summaries.

the rate of return of 5¾ percent to which the commission declared them to be entitled. The net earnings of the railroads have been erratic as well as generally low. Railroad executives and the Interstate Commerce Commission have continued to experience frustration in their efforts to realize a fair return, at least in the long run, for the railroads.

In the 1980s the financial situation facing the nation's rail industry is so serious that it is not likely that the recent legislation, including such deregulation as was contained in the 4-R Act of 1976 and the Railroad Transportation Policy Act of 1980 will result in appreciable improvement. The energy crisis calls for a new look at railroad potentials, but the readjustment in regulation and railroad structure called for to prevent a government takeover seems most unlikely to occur in the near future. With other modes, restructuring and rate adjustments to provide a fair rate of return are comparatively simple. In any event, unlike the railroads, their traffic share continues to increase and they can more readily accommodate to regional changes in the traffic origination which result from shifts of population and industry.

Unlike the situation during most of the period since motor carriers were brought under regulation in 1936, the 70s saw growing concern with general increases in their rates, hence resort to the maximum rate power in revenue proceedings. Inflation necessitated a series of general upward adjustments, seemingly without end. Shippers regularly contested carrier proposals in the belief that lesser increases would generate a sufficient level of carrier earnings. The commission sought new guidelines for return on investment, but that issue remained in controversy. The zone of rate freedom and the inflationary adjustments provided for motor carriers in the 1980 Act may make general increase cases less necessary in the future and the act calls for phasing them out.

THE CAUSES AND IMPORTANCE OF DISCRIMINATION

We have observed that three of the first four sections of the Act to Regulate Commerce (1887) dealt with discrimination. We have also observed a pattern for strengthening the powers of the regulatory authorities to deal with discriminatory practices, evidenced especially in the 1903 and 1910 enactments. In Chapter 16 we presented a definition of discrimination and discussed, as well, some of the difficulties of detecting and quantifying it in the transport industries. In Chapter 17 we observed some of the more common practices in actual rate making, many of which necessarily involve some measure of discrimination among the rates for particular hauls. We propose to examine here what limitations have been placed upon discriminatory pricing in transport, what circumstances are held to justify discrimination, and what are some of the consequences of permitted or required discrimination.

Congress has never prohibited discrimination as the economist defines it. Mere departure from cost is not sufficient to show an unlawful discrimination. The prohibitions of the statutes, indeed, rest as much upon legal as upon economic precepts, even though motivated by the observed economic consequences of discrimination as practiced before effective regulation. What was proscribed was *undue* preference and prejudice and *unjust* discrimination. The sole exception to the proposition concerns so-called personal discrimination, treated in Section 2 of the act, which is one of three recognized types of discrimination. The others are local or place discrimination, of which long-and-short-haul discrimination is a special form, and discrimination among the commodities shipped. Each will be separately discussed below. There are three approaches in the law: prohibition, prohibition with exceptions for special situations, and approval if not undue or unreasonable. Personal discrimination is prohibited, long-and-short-haul discrimination is prohibited subject to relief by the commission in specific cases, and other local and commodity discriminations are permitted if not unduly preferential and prejudicial.

Importance of Discrimination

The financial and economic impact of discrimination may be very beneficial to the carrier or carriers involved and the shippers and communities which are favored, but disastrous to others. Many businesses have been made to flourish because of the advantage discriminatory rates gave them over their competitors. A famous example is that of the Standard Oil Company which established its dominance in Ohio by an arrangement with the Marietta and Cincinnati Railroad whereby independent shippers paid 35 cents per barrel while Standard paid only 10 cents. Furthermore, the railroad turned over 25 cents collected from independents to Standard Oil.[9]

Before the motor carrier, competition faced by railroads was largely limited to pairs of points served by at least two railroads with comparable directness of haul between them. Otherwise competition was limited and often nonexistent at the smaller intermediate localities. Until regulation was developed to control it, the effect of lower rates between larger towns than for comparable hauls to or from intermediate localities was to induce a concentration of industry in larger cities. Rate differences that discriminate may determine what industry, what wholesaler, what market area, or what locality prospers. Similarly, it can well decide which seaport is favored in the traffic flow to and from interior points.

The economic power inherent in discrimination caused it to be the first and foremost reason for regulating carriers. Today, when competition among carriers is so pervasive, many advocate deregulation, but few would remove all control over discrimination. Yet, as a practical matter, the control of discrimination would be difficult, perhaps impossible, under some of the more extreme proposals for deregulation. Since transportation cost is usually the largest factor in total physical distribution cost, the success of the best-designed system may be jeopardized if the competing distributor obtains an advantage through discriminatory rates or service. Knowledge of the possibilities and of the available remedies is therefore important to managers of distribution and logistics.

Why Discrimination Practices Vary among the Modes

The problem of discrimination varies markedly among the modes. It has been greatest in the railroad industry because of the heavy investment required and the incompleteness of the competition a railroad tends to face either with another railroad or a water carrier.

---

[9] See *Report of Commissioner of Corporations on the Transportation of Petroleum*. (Washington, D.C.: U.S. Government Printing Office, 1906.)

Rail-water competition is usually limited to terminal points between which the railroad faces no water competition. The striking incompleteness of interrailroad and water competition and the extraordinary impetus to rate cutting at competitive points arising from excess capacity and heavy fixed charges were responsible for the rapid growth of various forms of discrimination in the rail industry.

Three circumstances may be distinguished. Given excess capacity and decreasing costs, rates based upon marginal cost would fail to cover total costs. As Pigou argued, uniform rates designed to cover total cost would fail to attract sufficient volume to generate required revenues since much potential traffic (in low-grade commodities with limited ability to bear transport charges) would be repelled. Hence commodity discrimination would become essential. Second, at competitive points railroads would be induced to seek volume from one another in the effort to take up their excess capacity and hold unit costs in check. Variable costs would theoretically set a floor; but in the effort to improve market share against the time when an agreement might restore rate levels and in the absence of reliable cost information, rates could well fall below that level. No like reductions would be impelled at noncompetitive points. Third, an exception to this last proposition might arise from the economic power of large shippers who, in consideration for shifting traffic at competitive points, might also obtain reduction at noncompetitive points which would be unavailable to shippers lacking similar bargaining power.

The factors leading to discrimination are much less compelling in most other types of transportation. Except where an artifical monopoly could be secured, the waterways were open highways and the investment required in boats was not sufficiently heavy to produce a serious burden of fixed costs in the coastwise and inland water trades. Until reduced by railroad aggressiveness, competition was quite active to virtually all points on navigable waters that offered traffic sufficient to justify boats calling. Rate wars developed as one operator or another attempted to drive competitors off the run; but because of the completeness of the competition, they were characterized by a lowering of the rates all along the line, and comparatively little discrimination developed. The shippers had protection, too; for the waterway is a public highway, free to all, and the investment required to operate on the rivers or in coastal waterways was not so great as to preclude their purchase of a vessel. For this reason competition in water transport is potential even where it is nonexistent.

Motor transport, as it developed, was similarly free from heavy overhead, for only the vehicle was needed to start a small business. Some discrimination developed; but both the incentive to discriminate and the range within which it could be practiced were limited, for most of the costs were direct costs which must be covered if a cash loss was to be avoided. To charge substantially above cost would soon bring new firms into the business by the prospect of profit. Even where competition of for-hire carriers is not established, there is the ever-present threat of private trucking over the public highway.

It is otherwise with pipeline transportation, for there a heavy fixed investment appears. More important, most pipeline construction has been done by large producers or refiners of oil primarily for the movement of their own crude to their respective refineries and refined products to their own markets. Discrimination against other oil companies, usually the smaller ones unable to protect themselves by pipeline ownership, develops as the owning company seeks to exclude its competitors in the oil business from access to cheap transport. This is a use of a transportation facility to discriminate for other reasons than the self-interest of the pipeline as a transportation company and was a principal cause for the extension of regulation to this type of carrier in 1906.

Air transportation, in ease of entry into public and private service on a public highway, is not unlike water and motor transport. If free from regulation, an operator can fly anywhere that public airport and airway facilities are available. Discriminatory policies will attract new operators to areas where rates are high and expel them from depressed rate points, thus placing a check upon place discrimination. The plant is mobile, though not as much so as in motor transport because of the higher first cost of the airplane. However, in the incompleteness of competition, the established services resemble the railroads. Direct competition is assured at large airport centers but may not exist at intermediate airports served by local airlines. Excess capacity provides incentives for differentiation in classes of traffic, both passenger and freight.

PERSONAL DISCRIMINATION

Nature and Causes

This type of discrimination takes many forms. Strictly speaking it refers to the charging of different amounts to different persons for the performance of the same transportation service or the performing of substantially more service for one person than for another, but without charging more or enough more to be commensurate with the additional service performed. Also the discrimination may take the form of making available a superior service to some persons which is not available to others, even though a compensating rate may be charged. Lower volume rates open to all are not now considered discriminatory in principle.

Although rates have been published in one form or another since the beginnings of common-carrier service, the advent of competition among railroads gave rise to a rapid development of personal discrimination through bargains with individuals to perform service at something less, and often substantially less, than the published rate. Only the small and irregular shipper, commanding little traffic of interest to the carrier, and the uninitiated were compelled to bear the published tariff. Rate publication was itself of restricted scope, not covering all possible traffic movements, since there was no requirement that rates be published. The widespread and flagrant character of personal discrimination was one of the major complaints leading to the demand for state and later federal regulation. It included the granting of passes to favored shippers and their employees, but discrimination in freight rates was the principal economic evil.

Types of Personal Discrimination

Discrimination among persons took a wide variety of forms. The simplest was a mere departure from the published rate in favor of a particular shipper or shippers. This practice was sometimes facilitated by blind billing and by settlement of accounts through the general office rather than through the local agent of the carrier.[10] More common was the custom of rebating which more sharply introduces the element of secrecy, since the shipper is billed at the published rate and the fact of returning to him a portion of the rate paid may be concealed in many ways. The rebate system, moreover, had the advantage of facilitating exclusive contract with a shipper whereby, in consideration of the rebate, he would guarantee to route all of his business via the particular carrier's lines. In the steamship business the rebate was commonly deferred until the expiration of a stated period during which it might be ascertained whether the shipper had lived up to his part of the agreement, and this was a mainstay of the monopoly position of the major steamship conferences. But in the ocean trade the motives of the carriers were primarily to impede the entry of additional steamship lines or to kill off newcomers, not members of the conference, and thus protect conference lines against new competition. Rebates were available to nearly all regular shippers of freight; hence personal discrimination was minimized. In the behind-the-scenes competition of railroads, however, personal discrimination was an almost universal result of the rebating practice. The same result could be secured by fostering underclassification or false billing. Closely analogous is the payment of false claims for loss and damage.

---

[10] A practice common in the Standard Oil discriminations. See *Report of the Commissioner of Corporations on the Transportation of Petroleum* (1906), pp. 76–78, 101–6, 261, 333–34.

Much traffic moves by railroad in private cars, especially refrigerator, covered hopper, coal, and tank cars, though in the past important numbers of stock cars have been privately owned. Excellent opportunities to discriminate in favor of the larger shippers fortunate enough to own such cars existed through the medium of an excessive allowance for their use. Since the railroad is obligated to furnish cars, the provision of cars by the shipper obviously entitles him to a reasonable allowance.

Effects of Personal Discrimination

In practice these discriminations have usually involved the favoring of a few shippers at the expense of the great body of shippers. And the interests of the carriers have generally dictated that the shippers so favored should be the larger ones which control substantial volumes of traffic and which have alternative carriers available to them. The force of personal discrimination has, therefore, been to favor the large firms and thereby to facilitate their further growth, increase their control upon markets and prices, and render the carrier less and less able to eliminate the discrimination even if it should so desire.

This type of exercise of power is wholly inconsistent with the accepted obligations of common-carrier and public-service enterprises, long recognized in the common law. The railroad is a common carrier affected by the public interest. The very name *common* carrier implies equality; it signifies common to all—the servant of the public. The adoption of the vocation carries with it the assurance imposed by one of the elementary principles of the common law—that every customer shall be served alike. But under the common law the shipper discriminated against had scant chance before the courts. The complexity of the rate structure and the secrecy surrounding most personal discriminations made it difficult to discover actual cases of discrimination. The proof that analogous traffic had moved, at about the same time and under substantially similar circumstances and conditions, for another shipper at a lower rate was well-nigh impossible. Even if the facts could be secured, the small shipper faced the ranks of expert corporation and railroad counsel ready to pursue the furthest legal appeal with resulting costs and delays hard for him to bear.

Personal discriminations by the carriers fostered monopoly, crushed the weak and the newcomer, and placed the future of many a business at the mercy of the carrier. It played a large role in the growth of the Standard Oil monopoly and in the building up of the great steel companies, and it fostered the control over agriculture achieved by the grain and meat-packing interests. It reached its height in the 1880s but persisted for long years after.

Widespread discrimination was deleterious to the carriers as well as to the public, for it depressed rates on large volumes of business and thus reduced revenues. But no single carrier was able to withdraw once the practice had been begun, for to cease discriminating was to lose business to a competitor. Concerted action proved impossible as a method to control a practice fraught with secrecy and suspicion. Only effective regulation could put a stop to it.

Control of Personal Discrimination

Sections 2 and 3 of the Interstate Commerce Act contain broad prohibitions against discrimination, making it unlawful by any device to charge or collect from any person a greater or less compensation for any service rendered than it receives from any other person for doing a like and contemporaneous service in transporting a like kind of traffic under similar circumstances. The prohibition of Section 2 is absolute, leaving no discretion in the commission, although the language of Section 3, pertaining to place discrimination, makes only undue or unreasonable preference or prejudice unlawful. By Section 6, rates and fares were required to be published, posted, and filed with the commission. Adherence to the published rates is called for, and 30-days' notice of changes is required, save when the commission may, on petition, permit publication to take effect on shorter notice. The published rate is the only legal rate, and it must be collected even if it is clear that an error of publication has occurred in the tariff. If the carrier misquotes a rate or bills a shipper at an erroneous rate, it must nevertheless collect the full charge when the error is discovered, even though the shipper has relied on a lower quotation. Such are the provisions which, by eliminating all possibility of lawful movement of traffic on other than the published rate, seek to rule out discriminations among shippers. Nearly identical provisions are imposed upon water and motor carriers by Section 216, 217, 305, and 306 of the Interstate Commerce Act.

Section 1 of the Interstate Commerce Act makes the granting of free passes to other than certain designated classes of persons unlawful, and similar restrictions apply to motor and water carriers. Section 1 also contains the commodities clause, seeking to prevent a railroad from transporting any article which it has produced or owned, but which is not for use of the railroad in the operation of its transportation service. Likewise, jurisdiction is given to the commission over accessorial facilities and services in order to prevent excessive allowances for supplies or services or discrimination in the provision of such services.

Severe penalties are provided in Section 10 and in the Elkins Act which prohibits the granting or receiving of rebates or the offering or solicitation of rebates. The receivers as well as the givers of rebates are made liable. False billing, classification, weighing, and so forth, are made unlawful; and these prohibitions are extended also to motor and water carriers in Sections 222 and 317. Finally, the extension of credit, which might give rise to discrimination, is regulated by Sections 3, 223, and 318 for the three types of carrier coming under the act. Except under regulations prescribed by the commission, shipments must not be delivered at destination until all transportation charges have been paid.

Under the statute law as interpreted by U.S. courts, competition does not justify differences in the treatment of shippers as it does, to a considerable degree, in the treatment of localities. In *Wight* v. *United States*[11] the Supreme Court held that discrimination between persons must rest upon differences in the conditions of carriage and that the presence or absence of competition did not create such a dissimilarity of conditions as to justify different treatment of the two persons involved. One party had a private siding on one carrier on which he was accustomed to receive shipments. Desiring, however, to use another railroad with which his siding did not connect, he reached an arrangement with this carrier to make him an allowance for trucking his freight from the latter's public team track. Another receiver of the same commodity who lacked a private siding, when unable to get a similar trucking allowance because he would have to truck from either carrier's tracks and so could bring no pressure on either railroad, alleged discrimination. The Court held that differences in the circumstances of competition affecting several shippers of the same commodity at the same point could not serve to justify difference in charges.

The United States Shipping Act of 1916 and the Intercoastal Act of 1933 also prohibit personal discrimination by requiring adherence to published rates. The Federal Maritime Commission has recently discovered substantial rebating in deep-sea service. The Shipping Act of 1916 and succeeding acts have long permitted dual rates set by steamship conferences, providing lower rates to shippers signing a contract to use only the conference lines. This was held to be an acceptable competitive alternative to the rebating practice of foreign flag lines.

LONG-AND-SHORT-HAUL DISCRIMINATION

Forms

Long-and-short-haul discrimination is a type of place discrimination which has received special emphasis in regulatory legislation, no doubt because it appears patently unreasonable. It refers to the in-

---

[11] 167 U.S. 512 (1897)).

stance in which a carrier charges more for a shorter haul than for a longer haul over the same line and in the same direction. A simple illustration is shown in the accompanying diagram:

	$1.00		$0.80
A		B	C
0 Miles		100 Miles	125 Miles

A carrier handling traffic from A to B and C charges a rate of $1 a ton for the 100 miles to B: but after carrying the freight through B and 25 miles beyond to C, it charges only 80 cents a ton. Such a situation grows out of the fact that the carrier faces competition at C and not at B. B appears patently to be discriminated against. If the rate to C is a reasonable one, the rate to B is excessive; and if the rate to B is reasonable for the haul of 100 miles from A, then the rate to C for a greater haul is clearly low. B is discriminated against and placed at a disadvantage as compared with C in the purchasing of goods from A. The rate advantage at C may cause business to gravitate there and to grow, whereas business at B may be forced to contract by the disadvantage to which it is subjected.

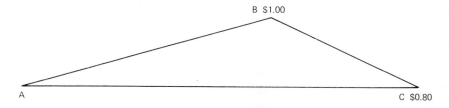

In some instances the discrimination is justified since it creates no greater disadvantage at the intermediate point B than would exist in any event. Consider, as in the other diagram, two routes between A and C, one considerably longer than the other. Assume that the 80-cent rate at C is a reasonable one for the short-line haul and that a reasonable rate, reflecting fully the cost of transportation, would be $1.25 via the longer route. But at this rate no traffic will move between A and C via the longer route. If the long route is to participate in the traffic from A to C, it must meet the 80-cent rate. This it can profitably do if 80 cents will cover the direct cost of handling the additional traffic which it gets by the rate reduction and contribute something to overhead, as may well be the case if the line is a railroad. This is no disadvantage to B, for the long route serving B can only meet the rate or accept the loss of the through traffic. C's advantage is one of location of which it cannot be deprived by any action the long route takes. It is to the possible advantage of B and other intermediate points to have the long route meet the competition of the short line at C, for any resulting contribution to the carrier's overhead may enable some reduction of the rates to B and other intermediate points. Similar circumstances may arise where a railroad feels compelled to meet water competition at one or a few points on its line—competition beyond its control and representing an advantage of location to those points having water service.

Some of the more significant areas of extensive violation of the long-and-short-haul principle were those encountered in the southern basing-point system and those characterizing the intermountain portions of Transcontinental Territory, which long since have been outlawed. Such violations were at the heart of those systems. But they were not uncommon elsewhere, though in less regular and embracing fashion.

Economic Results

The economic results of long-and-short-haul discrimination were far-reaching. They produced a powerful preference of competitive points, fostered their development at the expense of other points, and forced business into a more concentrated locational mold. The concentration of wholesaling and warehousing as well as of manufacturing was advanced by such principles of rate making, and the development of the smaller and noncompetitive points was inhibited. A less discriminatory rate structure would doubtless have produced greater dispersion of business activity and would have inhibited the rapid and perhaps excessive growth of some of our urban centers. Likewise, the functional concentration of business in large integrated firms was no doubt fostered by rate discrimination. It is by no means certain that such concentration did not in some cases pass the point of technical advantage arising from scale of production.[12]

Control of Long-and-Short-Haul Discrimination

It is not strange that the many communities which daily saw traffic hauled through them to more distant points at rates lower than they were able to secure agitated strongly for legislation prohibiting this type of discrimination. The spectacle of rates from Chicago to Spokane as much as 80 percent higher than the contemporaneous rates from Chicago to Seattle is but one example of severe maladjustments which gave ample cause for complaint.[13] Section 4 of the Act to Regulate

---

[12] See Ralph L. Dewey, *The Long and Short Haul Principle of Rate Making* (Columbus: Ohio State University Press, 1935), p. 12.

[13] Eliot Jones, *Principles of Railway Transportation* (New York: Macmillan Co., 1924), pp. 106–7.

Commerce, 1887, contained the original form of federal long-and-short-haul prohibition. It was made unlawful for railroads to "receive any greater compensation in the aggregate for the transportation of passengers or of like kind of property, under substantially similar circumstances and conditions, for a shorter than for a longer distance over the same line, in the same direction, the shorter being included within the longer distance." But, although there was considerable sentiment for an absolute prohibition, Congress recognized that there might be exceptions by authorizing the commission to grant relief from the fourth section.

Since this type of discrimination was widespread, the commission was faced with a vast number of petitions for relief on the grounds of differing "circumstances and conditions" of transport which the carriers hoped would permit continuance of the practice. As the commission was unable to deal with more than a portion of the petitions before it, it sought to define conditions under which carriers could act on their own initiative without seeking commission approval. In so doing it drew a distinction between competition with carriers not subject to the act (water carriers, foreign railroads, and so on) and competition with carriers subject to the act. The latter type of competition was held not to create such a dissimilarity of circumstances as to justify a departure from the fourth section, except on the basis of affirmative relief granted by the commission.[14] Carriers were thus free to meet water competition by fourth-section departures without specific approval.

In general, the railroads accepted the interpretation placed by the commission on the fourth section and voluntarily applied it except in Southern Territory where this type of discrimination was basic to the existing rate structure. Southern carriers refused to make the necessary adjustments and urged railroad competition in justification as constituting a sufficient dissimilarity in circumstances and conditions. The commission found otherwise in the Alabama Midland case,[15] but was overruled by the Supreme Court. The Court held that competition between carriers subject to the act (railroads) as well as water competition created a dissimilarity of circumstances and conditions sufficient to justify carriers in departing from the fourth section without specific approval of the commission.[16] The effect of this decision was to render the fourth section inoperative, for few, if any, fourth-section departures arose out of conditions other than the competition which was here held to justify them.

---

[14] *In re Southern Railway & Steamship Association*, 1 ICR 278, 288 (1887); *Annual Report of the Interstate Commerce Commission* (1897), pp. 40–41.

[15] *Board of Trade of Troy, Ala.* v. *Alabama Midland Ry. Co.*, 6 ICR 1 (1893).

[16] *Interstate Commerce Commission* v. *Alabama Midland Ry. Co.*, 168 U.S. 144 (1897).

The situation was not allowed to rest there. In 1910 the Congress undertook important amendments by enacting the Mann-Elkins Act. The words "under substantially similar circumstances and conditions" were stricken from the act. The effect was to make the clause applicable unless relief were secured from the commission on a proper showing. Carriers were permitted, however, to continue existing rates in force until the commission should act upon them, provided they made application for relief within five months of the passage of the amendments. The commission was now free to develop a reasonable control of this type of discrimination which would restrict its use to those instances in which adequate grounds could be demonstrated by the carriers.

Further amendment to the fourth section took the form of adopting in the statute certain important principles which the commission had largely established in practice. In 1920 the act was amended to require the commission to ascertain (1) that the reduced through rates covered by fourth-section relief were reasonably compensatory; (2) that relief would not be granted to meet merely potential rather than actual water competition, and (3) that when relief was granted to a circuitous route, higher charges would not be allowed at intermediate points on the circuitous line where distances were not greater than the through distance via the direct line. This last became known as the equidistant clause and was quickly found to lack merit, for a greater transportation charge for the same distance might well be justified by different transport conditions (heavier grades and curvature, lighter density, etc.) other than distance. Repeal was accomplished in the Transportation Act of 1940 which also brought water carriers subject to Part III of the act under the restraint of the fourth section.

Although fourth-section relief has been important as a device for meeting water competition, and more recently in a few instances motor-carrier and pipeline competition, its most common use has been to enable circuitous rail routes to meet rates made by direct routes and thus to share in the through traffic. The necessity to secure relief when adjusting rates via the short routes, if the longer routes were to participate in the business, led to delay and great complexity in rail tariffs. Hence the fourth section was further amended in 1957 to permit longer rail routes to meet the rates of short rail routes without prior action by the commission.

The Motor Carrier Act of 1935 contained no long-and-short-haul clause. This type of discrimination has not been important in motor-carrier rates, primarily because so large a proportion of motor-carrier costs are direct. Moreover, the charging of higher rates for a shorter than for a longer haul over the same route is regarded as *prima facie*, unreasonable, and can, therefore, be attacked on complaint by affected shippers or carriers.

OTHER PLACE AND COMMODITY DISCRIMINATION

Place Discrimination under Section 3

We earlier considered the importance of transport rates in affecting the location of economic activity and in shaping the structure of the economy. We emphasized that the rates are the transport costs from the point of view of shippers faced with locational and plant-size decisions. If rates depart from the costs incurred by carriers in providing the services for which they are named, therefore, economic development may be diverted from the course which actual transport cost relationships might dictate. Inefficiencies may thus unwittingly be imported into the economic system. Rates from one location which stand at a lower ratio to the cost of performing the service than do rates from other locations may encourage the growth of industry at the preferred location despite the fact that higher actual transport costs will be incurred and must be covered by the general level of rates. Rates on raw materials lower in relation to cost of service than rates on finished goods will artificially weight the scales in favor of market-oriented industrial locations and higher aggregate transport cost. Section 3 makes unlawful any undue or unreasonable preference or advantage to any locality, port, gateway, or to any particular description of traffic; and it is largely duplicated in the motor and water legislation of later date.

By these regulatory provisions not every discrimination in rates but only those that are undue or unreasonable are made unlawful. A measure of discrimination may be justified by differing cost factors and even by value-of-service considerations. It is therefore the measures of undueness or unreasonableness that become significant in the practical administration of Section 3. It is rate relationships that we are here concerned with, not the reasonableness of each of the rates considered in the abstract.

The proscription of Section 3 against place discrimination has been held to apply only to such discrimination as the individual carrier has the power to remove; hence, it cannot eliminate all unreasonable local discrimination.[17] Thus if two points of production serve a common market and both are on diverging lines of the same carrier entering the market, the rates from these two points are under that carrier's control and it may be required to eliminate any unreasonable discrimination in the relationships of rates from the two points. But if each of them is served only by the line of a different railroad company, the two railroads converging at the common market, each railroad can control

---

[17] As discussed below, the interpretation to be placed upon the section is more or less obscure at present because of *obiter dicta* of the Supreme Court.

only the rate from the point on its line. There is no common control; and as neither railroad is responsible for the action of the other, neither can be said to discriminate against one point or the other. "What Congress sought to prevent . . . was not differences between localities in transportation rates, facilities, and privileges, but unjust discrimination between them by the same carrier or carriers,"[18] said the Supreme Court; and the commission embodied this view in the so-called Ashland Rule, saying that "the test of the discrimination is the ability of one of the carriers participating in the two through routes from the two points of origin to the same point of destination to put an end to the discrimination by its own act."[19]

When, therefore, is the removal of the discrimination controllable by a single carrier, and therefore subject to removal by order of the commission? Even though a road may serve both points, it may not be able to remove the discrimination, for competition from other roads not themselves discriminating may exist at one or both points. But in the absence of such outside competition at one or more of the points in question, a carrier may be in a position to remove the discrimination by its own action even though it does not serve all the points involved. Such a situation would arise where a carrier is a party to joint rates over through routes serving the points and where it can correct the relationship by refusal to continue to cooperate with connections on the existing discriminatory basis.[20] Such control does not ordinarily exist where competition which the carrier meets is competition by water. However, a carrier which elects to meet competition and create a discrimination not unlawful because of its lack of control may nevertheless be required to pursue the same policy of meeting competition at other points where similar competition is encountered.

For a complaint under the third section to have adequate foundation it must demonstrate (1) that the localities involved in the alleged discrimination are in a competitive relationship, (2) that actual injury has occurred as a result of the rate relationship complained of, and (3) that the discriminatory relationship is inexplicable on grounds of differing conditions of transportation. It should be observed, too, that discrimination may exist even if the rates are the same, for there may be such a difference in the circumstances and conditions of transportation as to require a lower rate at one point than at another if undue prejudice is to be avoided.[21]

---

[18] *Central Railroad Co.* v. *U.S.*, 257 U.S. 247, 259–60 (1921).

[19] *Ashland Fire Brick* v. *Southern Ry. Co.*, 22 ICC 115, 120 (1911); and the 1920 amendments giving the commission minimum rate powers have not changed this rule.

[20] *Indiana Steel & Wire Co.* v. *C. R. I. & P. Ry. Co.*, 16 ICC 155 (1909).

[21] *Milk Producers' Protective Assoc.* v. *Delaware, Lackawanna & Western R. R. Co.*, 7 ICR 92 (1897); *Southern Kansas Grain Assoc.* v. *Chicago, Rock Island & Pacific Railway Co.*, 139 ICC 641 (1928).

In many cases the commission has held that a competitive relationship must be shown between the movements to which the rate adjustment complained of applies. And this means essentially the competition of differently located shippers or receivers of freight, not competition of carriers. Behind every complaint of local discrimination is some business interest seeking an opportunity to expand its market and so increase its business or, by reducing its transport cost in relation to competitors, to increase its profit margin. If the alleged discrimination affects a particular shipper only, it is likely to be initiated by him as a complaint; but where the wholesale trade of a community generally or an important and predominant industry in a community is involved, complaint may be made by the local chamber of commerce or similar organization.

Although in rare cases the commission has been moved to act by potential injury from a rate relationship, it has generally required proof of actual damage. This is often difficult; and it causes correction to wait upon damage, which if it takes the form of loss of firms in a locality and the more vigorous growth of business elsewhere, it is very hard to compensate by a mere subsequent rate adjustment. Injury may be shown by proof of financial loss in the conduct of business, diversion of business to competitors, or reduced ability to compete which can be traced back to the rate relationship complained of.

Export and Import Differentials

The application of the equalization principle in rate differentials was set forth in Chapter 17. Strictly speaking, differential rate structures are discriminatory, but regulation has been limited to preventing undue preference and prejudice as in all permissible discrimination. Export and import differential rates are set well below the domestic rates for the same rail haul. They are found at almost all port areas serving foreign trade. They are designed to encourage that trade and to equalize ports and port areas.

The export differential to West coast ports from the Middle West in respect to Pacific trade represents a substantial discrimination in rates but has been held lawful. It represents a joint arrangement between the Pacific Steamship Conferences and the western trunkline railroads to meet the aggregate rail and ocean rates from Atlantic and Gulf ports. These rates are known as *overland common point* (OCP) *Rates*. Steamship lines quote the through rate but must file the railroad portion with the Interstate Commerce Commission and the ocean portion with the Federal Maritime Commission. A through export bill of lading is used which is subject to transit privileges. The rail tariff specifies that the rate includes wharfage and terminal charges. Traffic must be moved within 14 days. Terminal charges are absorbed by a joint arrangement of rail and ocean carriers, usually on a 50–50 basis except on traffic to and from Hawaii. The import differentials apply to traffic taken inland whether under auspices of motor carriers, railroads, or freight forwarders; but terminal charges are not absorbed on imports.[22]

With ocean general cargo shifted largely to movement in containers, import and export rates have lost much of their application. Differentials, too, are fading. Railroads increasingly base their rates on loaded ocean containers on rail mileage between ports and inland points. This tends to restore to a port the advantage of location which it may have lost under a system of equalizing differentials.

Regional Discrimination

Local discrimination takes on much broader scope when it is alleged that whole regions are subjected to undue prejudice by a classification and rate structure higher than that prevailing in other regions. Such complaint was made on behalf of the entire South and West east of Mountain Pacific Territory as compared with Official Territory in the East. The vigor and breadth of this complaint reflected the rapid industrialization of the South and West which called into question rate structures dating in many essentials from the era when agriculture and mining were the predominant interests of these areas. The heart of the controversy rested upon the fact that thousands of items in the Southern and Western Classifications took higher ratings than in the Official Classification and that the class-rate scales in the South and West produced higher rates for equivalent distances than in the Northeast. On the other hand, the bulk of the traffic moving in the South and West was handled under exceptions and commodity rates which had grown up to meet the needs of the economy in those areas. Thus the staple agricultural products, minerals, and forest products were accommodated by commodity rates designed to open full facility for their marketing. Such an adjustment, it was contended, fostered a continuation of the conditions of the past and imposed a barrier to the spread of industrialization away from the Northeast. The rate structure prior to 1947 favored the movement of industrial raw materials into the Northeast and the marketing of finished manufactures produced in the East throughout the South and West, but imposed a barrier to the marketing of southern and western manufactures in the highly populous markets of Official Territory. As large-scale industrialization must depend, at least in considerable part, upon sales in the Northeast, this situation was considered to prejudice unduly the opportunities for development of a more balanced economy in the South and West.

The commission, after introducing into the record cost studies pre-

---

[22] For discussion of history and nature of OCP rates and absorptions, see 12 FMC 184, 208 (1969).

pared by its staff, reached findings and issued an order of broad scope. It found the present classification ratings as a whole unjust and unreasonable for the future and required the promulgation of a uniform classification, holding out the Official Classification as a model. It found both intra- and interterritorial class rates unjust and unreasonable in violation of Section 1 of the act and prescribed maximum class rate scales. The relationship of interterritorial rates to Official Territory rates was, moreover, found to work undue prejudice against interterritorial shippers in violation of Section 3. Northern interests saw their position imperiled. Spearheaded by the governor of New York, northeastern states and several western railroads took an appeal to a statutory three-judge federal court sitting at Utica, New York, and obtained a temporary injunction restraining carriers from making the changes required of them and the commission from enforcing its order. After further hearing, the court upheld the commission but continued the injunction pending appeal to the Supreme Court. By a vote of seven to two the Court upheld the commission and shortly thereafter denied a rehearing.[23] Justice Douglas wrote the majority opinion and seems not merely to have sustained the commission but also to have broadened its interpretation of Section 3 as revised by the 1940 amendment. For although the commission was careful to confine its findings of discrimination to the relationship between the interterritorial rates and Official Territory rates—both groups being in a sense under the control of Official Territory carriers since they both made the intraterritorial rates and concurred in the interterritorial rates—the majority of the Court drew no such sharp distinction and spoke as if all the adjustments might have been made on findings of discrimination. What does this do to the Ashland doctrine already somewhat eroded by later decisions?

Commodity Discrimination

The prohibitions of Section 3 against undue or unreasonable discrimination extend to discrimination between commodities. We have noted that such discrimination is the very basis of classification and is fully accepted as a necessary and desirable practice in rate making. What, then, constitutes the measure indicating at what point it becomes undue or unreasonable, and therefore unlawful? The principles are very similar to those noted in respect to local discrimination. The commodities whose rate relationship is complained of must be in competition, and actual injury must be shown. Moreover, given these conditions, justification may yet be found in the relative cost of service, relative value of the service, or in competitive forces beyond the car-

---

[23] New York v. United States, 67 Sup. Ct. 1207 (1947); 67 Sup. Ct. 1527 (1947).

rier's control. For commodities to be in a competitive relationship they must have a significant degree of substitutability in important uses. Various of the vegetable oils, for example, which can be substituted for one another in a variety of uses have been found to be competitive. But common sand and silica sand do not serve the same purposes and are not in competition; hence one is not injured by taking a higher rate than the other, both rates in themselves being reasonable. It has been argued in recent cases that aluminum is competitive with steel, hence should be accorded a similar basis of rates; but aluminum rates as yet remain substantially higher. The mere existence of some competition between commodities is not sufficient unless supported by proof of actual injury.

Many differences in rates may be justified on grounds of differing cost, and this may be an adequate explanation even among commodities shown to be in a competitive relationship. That one commodity can be loaded more heavily in a given size car than another, or that one is much more liable to loss and damage are all cost factors likely to be relevant in justifying rate differences in a particular case. The commission has also held that a difference in the value of two commodities may justify different rates for them. As in local discrimination, compelling competition in the movement of a commodity which is beyond the carrier's control may also be offered as a factor tending to disprove an undueness or unreasonableness in discrimination.

Economic Effect of Other Place and Commodity Discrimination

As we have observed, a carrier may initiate or attempt to initiate a discriminatory rate of some sort to increase its traffic in competition with another carrier of like or unlike mode and incidentally to favor shippers, communities, industries, or seaports located on its route. The economic effect of place discrimination, other than long and short haul, and of commodity discrimination is not usually so decisive as that which may result from personal and long-and-short-haul discrimination; but the disadvantage created may in the long run be equally fatal if not corrected. Adequate regulation of rate differences not justified on a cost basis is designed to protect the competitive position of a carrier, shipper, locality, or port from injury arising from unduly prejudicial and preferential rates. Similarly, on the positive side, natural advantage in efficiency or location is protected by not permitting the less efficient to receive equal rates. However, the commission has given frequent approval, in the form of differentials, to rate differences which are proportionately less than the comparative production and transport costs.

Complications may develop when one of the communities has certain advantages other than those afforded by a rate discrimination. The carrier is not warranted in placing a handicap upon a business or a locality having certain natural advantages in order to permit less favored communities or businesses to compete in the market on more-or-less even terms. Yet this practice was fairly widespread before regulation. As J. M. Clark has pointed out, a natural reaction of unfettered railroad management to the situation of competing localities of differing efficiencies serving the same market is to equalize them.[24] It was this sort of situation that the commission early sought to correct in the Eau Claire case. Because Eau Claire possessed certain advantages in the production of lumber as compared with nearby rival producing points, carriers fixed lumber rates from Eau Claire sufficiently higher than from competing points to allow all to share in the market. The commission found that the fixing of rates "in inverse proportion to the natural advantages of competing towns, with the view to equalizing 'commercial conditions' . . . is a preposition unsupported by law and quite at variance with every consideration of justice. . . ."[25]

Quantity Discounts

Until recent years the Interstate Commerce Commission denied approval of volume rates below the regular carload rate because they favored the large shipper and were unjustly discriminatory to the small shipper. However the commission has come to recognize the lower costs involved in volume traffic and has approved lower rates for multiple-car shipments[26] and for the movement of minimum annual tonnages of coal in unit trains.[27]

Efforts by large shippers to obtain contract rates and agreed charges in line with practices in Great Britain and Canada were flatly denied by the commission as unjust and unreasonable and likely to result in destructive competition.[28] By 1979 that policy had been reversed. The commission is now actively encouraging railroads and shippers to develop contract rates and the 1980 act specifically au-

---

[24] J. M. Clark, *Standards of Reasonableness in Local Freight Discrimination*, vol. 97 (New York: Columbia University Studies in the Social Sciences, 1911), pp. 77–78.

[25] *Eau Claire Board of Trade v. Chicago, Milwaukee & St. Paul R. R. Co.*, 4 ICR 65, 77 (1892).

[26] For years the only instance was *Molasses from New Orleans, La., to Peoria and Pekin, Ill.*, 235 ICC 485. Later authorization included multiple-car rates on limestone, 276 ICC 381; on coal in 304 ICC 269 and 308 ICC 217; and more recently on grain in *Grain in Multiple Car Shipments–River Crossings to the South*, I&S Docket 7656.

[27] *Coal from Kentucky, Virginia and West Virginia to Virginia*, 308 ICC 99: *Coal from Illinois, Indiana and Kentucky to Illinois and Indiana*, 308 ICC 673; and *Coal to New York Harbor*, 311 ICC 355.

[28] *Contract Rates on Rugs and Carpeting from Amsterdam, N.Y., to Chicago*, 313 ICC 247. Affirmed in *New York Central R.R. Co. v. U.S.*, 194 Supp. 947 (368 U.S., 349).

thorizes them. As noted in Chapter 19, few opportunities are left to challenge contract rates on grounds of discrimination.

DISCRIMINATION IN CAR SERVICE

Supply of Equipment

Discrimination in supplying cars and other freight-vehicle service to shippers, especially at times of transportation shortages, may be quite as serious as discrimination in rates. Favoritism in car supply has been the most common and most damaging form of service discrimination. Many industries depend for their uninterrupted operation upon steady and adequate car supply. Interruptions will occasion curtailment of production or complete shutdown with consequent losses. Mines are notable in this class, for since they commonly have no storage space aboveground, they must regulate operations in accord with the number of cars available for loading. In earlier years where railroads had extensive ownership of coal mines and when officials for certain carriers were interested in mining enterprises, it was not uncommon for favoritism to be shown by railroads in supplying cars during periods of shortage. Thus favored mines were enabled to continue full-scale operations, whereas others were forced to curtail. Similar conditions prevailed in the grain trade, where the railroads favored in car supply railroad-controlled or -affiliated country elevators and deprived independents of an adequate car supply.

This sort of discrimination is both difficult to detect and, when detected, to control, for periods of car shortages are featured by widespread overordering of cars by shippers who seek by such inflation of orders to secure at least the number of cars they need. In the coal-mining industry the evil has been curtailed by assigning mine ratings to each mine representing its capacity to produce. When cars are short, they may then be distributed equitably among the mines in a percentage of the mine rating. Even under this system, however, assigned cars for railroad-fuel service and private cars which a few mining companies owned were not counted in distributing cars ratably. Hence some mines were favored and corrective regulatory action was required. Ample car supply is, of course, the most satisfactory method for avoiding these difficulties, but occasional shortages in periods of brisk traffic are to be expected.

The steady tendency toward dedication of cars, usually specialized, to particular shippers may well come under attack. Litigation is under way to review the mine-rating system. The question is whether the dedication of cars to unit-train service out of certain mines while coal cars are in short supply constitutes an unlawful prejudice of mines not involved in unit-train service. Similarly the dedication of cars to unit-train service of grain has caused complaint by small elevators. Contracts which not only specify rates, but also guarantee car supply, may enlarge the problem.

A carrier can show preference to some shippers and prejudice to others in the way the service is performed. The carrier may supply equipment in good condition to a large shipper who can be conveniently served by another carrier while being negligent in the condition of that supplied to a small shipper who is dependent on the carrier for direct and adequate service. Furthermore, the carrier may do more to expedite delivery for some shippers than for others. Such aspects of service discrimination hardly lend themselves to legal definition and are therefore not specifically covered in the legislation. The Shippers Advisory Boards have proved very effective in reducing such discrimination, because the quarterly meetings offer an open forum for small shippers who have reason for complaint. In some cases the holding of cars without assessing demurrage or the movement of cars in local rather than in through train service to accommodate shippers who are not prepared to make delivery has been detected and condemned. The commission invites complaint of service refusals or service deficiencies on the part of motor carriers, especially in respect to small shipments where such failures have been widely alleged.

DISCRIMINATION IN AIR TRANSPORT

The Civil Aeronautics Act treated discrimination comprehensively in a single section, 404(b), by prohibiting any undue or unreasonable preference or advantage to any particular person, port, locality, or description of traffic, or any unjust discrimination or undue or unreasonable prejudice or disadvantage. The section applies to discrimination both in rates and service, but there is no long-and-short-haul clause nor any distinction between personal and place and commodity discrimination of the sort created by Sections 2 and 3 of the Interstate Commerce Act. In 1938 when the act was passed, airlines were primarily carriers of passengers and the mails and the difficulties of freight-rate regulation which plagued the Congress in its original approach to railroad control were not anticipated, nor have they yet emerged. Issues of discrimination before the Civil Aeronautics Board often tend to become confused with issues of reasonableness, in considerable part because they are most often dealt with in connection with new tariff filings by the air carriers in which some departure from accepted practice is proposed. In general a tariff may be disapproved if it proposes different fares for nearly identical services, if it proposes similar service at different fares to nearly identical persons or groups, or if it prejudices a city by fares that do not recognize locational advantage.

Differences in cost and differences in the competition encountered from surface or from unregulated air carriers may justify departures from accepted practices. Thus the board refused to countenance common fares to all Hawaiian destinations from the continental United States,[29] but approved common fares to west-coast points served on the transcontinental routes because of the long-standing practice of making rail fares on that basis.[30] Custom and competition justified common fares in the latter case, but not in the former. While the board has been fairly stiff-necked about group-fare reductions, it has always approved reduced family fares. Its treatment of the relationship of first-class to coach fares appears to have been vacillating, the question of nondiscriminatory fares based on cost differences becoming obscured by the revenue effects of diversion of business travel from first class to coach. Late in 1972, faced by the cost-revenue squeeze encountered by airlines and reluctant to approve general fare increases, the board found youth standby, youth reservation, and family fares unjustly discriminating and ruled that they should be canceled after further proceedings. Deregulation has been followed by a plethora of new fare plans and discriminatory practices which the board seems no longer inclined to control.

SELECTED REFERENCES

Bigham, Truman, C., and Roberts, Merrill J. *Transportation: Principles and Problems*, chaps. 12–15. New York: McGraw-Hill Book Co., 1952.

Clark, J. M. *Standards of Reasonableness in Local Freight Discrimination*. Vol. 97. New York: Columbia University Studies in the Social Sciences, 1911.

Commissioner of Corporations. *Report on the Transportation of Petroleum*. Washington, D.C.: U.S. Government Printing Office, 1906.

Crumbaker, Calvin. *Transportation and Politics: A Study of Long-and-Short-Haul Policies of Congress and the Interstate Commerce Commission*. Eugene: University of Oregon Press, 1940.

Daggett, Stuart. *Principles of Inland Transportation*, chaps. 14, 20, and 21. 4th ed. New York: Harper & Bros., 1955.

Dewey, Ralph L. *The Long and Short Haul Principle of Rate Regulation*. Columbus: Ohio State University Press, 1935.

———. "Interterritorial Freight Rates." In *Law and Contemporary Problems*, Summer 1947.

---

[29] *Hawaiian Common Fares*, 10 CAB 921 (1949).
[30] *West Coast Common Fares*, 15 CAB 90 (1952).

Fair, Marvin L. *Economic Considerations in the Administration of the Interstate Commerce Act*, chaps. 4, 6, and 10. Cambridge, Md.: Cornell Maritime Press 1972.

Hillman, Jordon Jay. *Competition and Railroad Price Discrimination.* Evanston, Ill.: The Transportation Center at Northwestern University, 1968.

Joubert, W. H. *Southern Freight Rates in Transition.* Gainesville: University of Florida Press, 1949.

Kahn, Alfred E. *The Economics of Regulation.* Vol. 1, chap. 5; and Vol. 2, chap. 5. New York: John Wiley & Sons, Inc., 1970.

Locklin, D. Philip. *Economics of Transportation*, chaps. 20–22. 7th ed. Homewood, Ill.: Richard D. Irwin, Inc., 1972.

————. *Report on Interritorial Freight Rates.* 78th Cong., 1st sess., House Doc. 303 (1943).

Nelson, Robert A., and Greiner, William R. "The Relevance of the Common Carrier under Modern Economic Conditions." In National Bureau of Economic Research, *Transportation Economics*, 1965.

Pegrum, Dudley F. *Transportation: Economics and Public Policy*, chap. 8. 3d ed. Homewood, Ill.: Richard D. Irwin, Inc., 1973.

Sharfman, I. L. *The Interstate Commerce Commission.* Part III–B. New York: The Commonwealth Fund, 1936.

Vanderblue, H. B., and Burgess, K. F. *Railroads: Rates, Service, Management*, chaps. 6, 9, and 12. New York: Macmillan Co., 1924.

22

Coordination in Transportation

Coordination is the placing of separate units in such a position as to permit the establishment of a harmonious relationship among them. The need to coordinate presupposes (1) a plurality of units and (2) a relationship of the functions of these units.

In transportation, coordination is a very broad term which covers a variety of arrangements.[1] It can be effected by a single carrier or by a number of carriers operating in concert. It can relate to facilities of only one mode of transportation or to those of two or more modes. A carrier may enhance coordination of its operations by an improved terminal. It may employ facilities of another mode to supplement its services as in pickup and delivery or to substitute for certain operations in feeder or branch-line functions. It may enter into cooperative arrangements for interchange with carriers of the same mode or with carriers of an unlike mode or modes. Merger or consolidation of carriers of a given category will likely advance coordination of the facilities merged. However, coordination has often been advocated as an alternative to merger in the improvement of carrier operations. In recent years emphasis has been placed on coordinated use of facilities of different

[1] *Coordination* has been used by students of transportation to include consolidation, combination, integration, and rationalization of transportation facilities, organization, and methods of operation. In fact, it has been employed to cover any major efforts to improve the organization and functioning of transportation of all kinds. Note the treatment of the National Resources Planning Board, *Transportation and National Policy* (1942), part I, sec. 4, p. 140. General definitions are given by G. Shorey Peterson in "Transportation Coordination: Meaning and Purpose," *Journal of Political Economy*, vol. 38 (1930), p. 680.

modes. Our primary interest at this point is in intercarrier coordination and integration, especially when different modes are involved.

The cooperative arrangements between carriers may either be intramodal, that is, arrangements between carriers of the same mode, or intermodal, that is, between carriers of different modes of transportation. If it is intramodal the arrangement may involve: (1) through routes and joint rates; (2) interchange of equipment; (3) joint use of facilities; (4) reciprocal railroad switching service; (5) trade associations; (6) pooling of equipment, funds, or traffic; (7) scheduling of vehicle movement to facilitate interchange; and (8) joint operating arrangements, particularly at terminals for interchange of equipment. If the arrangement is intermodal, it may involve: (1) through routes and joint rates in unit-load operations or break-bulk operations; (2) contractual arrangements to complete delivery, especially where pickup and delivery service is involved; or (3) an intergration of equipment of several modes under a single management.

Intramodal cooperation and coordination

Over the years there have developed various examples of intramodal coordination. The pipeline industry has perhaps provided the most adequate demonstration of both intramodal and intermodal coordination. The intramodal operations involve the coordination of gathering lines, crude trunk-pipeline movement to refineries, and in some instances pipeline transportation of products to major market centers. The railroad industry has provided the greatest variety of cooperative arrangements. The free interchange of freight cars between railroads was made possible shortly after the Civil War by the standardization of the gauge of tracks, giving the country, in the physical sense, a single railroad system. This was followed, near the end of the 19th century, with the development of time zones throughout the country to provide for the coordination of railroad schedules. Through routes and joint rates early became standard practices. Through the Association of American Railroads and its predecessors, the industry has developed cooperative arrangements in such matters as service rules, standardization of equipment, and representation of the industry in Congress and in the state legislatures. The Shippers Advisory Boards, formed in the early 1920s, involved coordinated efforts of the railroads to work with the shippers in each region of the country and in the nation as a whole in order to provide a more efficient distribution of railroad equipment. Cooperation through the use of Pullman service, which prevailed for many years, declined after World War II. Sleeping, dining, and parlor car service came to be operated by the individual railroads. It is now under the general administration of Amtrak. The Railway Express Agency, which was formed some years ago, was a creature of the Class I railroads and served as a central agency for the conduct of express service. The pooling of traffic and revenue of competing railroads became illegal in the Act to Regulate Commerce of 1887. Although such arrangements may be approved under the Transportation Act of 1920 by the Interstate Commerce Commission, little resort has been made to this provision.

Joint use of local facilities by two or more railroads is common. These include stretches of running track, bridges, yards, passenger stations, engine terminals, and freight stations. Among the more far-reaching cooperative arrangements was the development between 1923 and 1940 of interline passenger trains, merchandise trains, and expedited long-distance freight trains. Few of the first two exist today, but through unit trains for bulk commodities and containers are increasing in number as are scheduled freight trains handling miscellaneous traffic in carloads over several connecting railroads without intermediate classification or change of power and cabooses. Pickup and delivery by motor carrier became general in the late 30s in connection with through package car services, but break-bulk LCL is now virtually extinct.

Unified freight terminal arrangements are to be found in a number of our larger metropolitan areas including San Francisco; New Orleans; Charleston; St. Louis; Houston; Galveston; Chicago; Toledo; Indianapolis; Kansas City; Minneapolis-St. Paul; Potomac Yard, Virginia; Birmingham, Alabama; and New York City. No fewer than ten trunk line railroads prior to recent mergers were involved in the ownership of the Belt Railway of Chicago—a larger number in the Terminal Railroad Association of St. Louis.

In air transportation there are arrangements for interchange of equipment to provide through service, the honoring of tickets of other airlines, trade associations with respect to both domestic and international operations, and through routes and joint rates. Motor carriers have limited their cooperative arrangements to trade associations, traffic associations, interchange of trailers, and provisions for through routes and joint rates. Barge lines on our rivers have cooperated with respect to pooling of barges in certain instances to supplement interchange among them and in the formation of trade and traffic associations.

The Intramodal Terminal Problem

In the development of most modes there tends to be a recurrent terminal problem. As technology introduces larger vehicle units, a mode finds that its terminals become obsolete. Traffic-volume increases may often also make terminals inadequate to handle the larger number of vehicle units. In the case of railroads, the problem has been particularly acute for many years because of increasing size of trains and growing volume of traffic. The principal classification yards of the railroads represent the heart centers of rail operations because it is there that interchange takes place among divisions and routes of a given railroad or between different railroads. Usually major classification yards have both intracarrier and intercarrier trains to be broken up and formed.

Railroad Terminals. The terminal problem existed for many years before the public of the United States realized it. In the larger transportation centers the railroads had experienced increasing difficulties in the development of their terminal facilities to take care of the growing volume of traffic. It was the unhappy experience of congestion of traffic at important terminal centers during World War I which brought about a national awareness of the problem. Conditions became so bad at one time that 145,000 cars were accumulated at eastern terminals. The congestion reached as far back into the interior as Pittsburgh and at times to points in the Middle West. Congress was mindful of this in the passage of the Transportation Act of 1920. Not only did the act provide for a plan of general consolidation of the railroads but it also gave the Interstate Commerce Commission power to require, on certain conditions, joint use of a terminal.

The acuteness of the railroad terminal problem was a natural outgrowth of our reliance on competing railroads to serve our growing cities. Great difficulty arose from the competition of the cities and the railroads for space. Most of the important railroad centers of the United States were small when the first railroads were built. As the number of railroads increased and the cities grew in size, competition for space became more and more intense. Each railroad entering a city desired to serve every section of the metropolitan area. Therefore, it developed a full complement of facilities including running tracks, industrial yards, classification yards, freight houses, team tracks, and, in a port city, a set of waterfront facilities. The more advantageous locations were grabbed up by the first roads to enter the city area so that some railroads had a monopoly advantage over others. Yet the city closed in around these facilities as it grew; and when more space was required to cope with increased traffic, it was not to be had.

The wasteful duplication of facilities in terminal areas has been a great burden to railroad management and has offered a serious threat to the adequacy and efficiency of the railroads serving the nation. During the middle and late 20s the railroads made certain improvements in their operation which greatly relieved the threat of congestion at the terminals. Rail terminals were severely tested during World War II and for the most part proved to be adequate. The lessons of World War I were well learned. Everything was done to keep the terminals fluid with the result that it was only occasionally that congestion was experienced in an important terminal.

Since World War II, the railroads have continued to improve their terminals. Longer receiving and departure tracks to accommodate much longer freight trains have been installed, and major classification yards have been modernized with electronic devices for the weighing of cars and computer control of the retarders and switches in the classification of cars. A number of entirely new yards which have the latest in electronic controls have been built at strategic points. Overall capacity is adequate, and few cars are now "lost" in the yards since yard records are often computerized; advance consists are received, and automatic scanning of cars provides in and out records. But substantial delay and irregularity in interchange remains a handicap in competing with motor carriers in expedited scheduled delivery.

Air and Motor Terminals. In recent years the airlines have experienced a rapidly increasing airport problem both because of the development of air technology as reflected in the increased size and weight of aircraft and higher landing speeds and the increased volume of traffic. Unlike railroad terminals, major airports are provided by public agencies, both local and federal. They are unique also in the fact that they are jointly used by a number of airlines as well as general aviation. As the pressure of various kinds of traffic increases at our principal airports, the problem of extension, relocation, and allocation of the several kinds of air-service facilities increases.

Motor carriers have found the terminal problem to be one of increasing importance as the average size of tractor trailers has been enlarged and the amount of traffic carried has become so much greater. The development of adequate motor-carrier terminal platforms and facilities has failed to prevent higher costs and increased delay in service. Indeed the larger terminals required at major points by increased volume tend to generate higher unit costs in consequence of longer average hauls within the terminal. Ocean ports are by nature intermodal and for that reason will be discussed later.

Intramodal Equipment

Pooling of Freight Cars. To insure a better distribution of freight cars, many people have recommended at one time or another the formation of a national pool. The Federal Coordinator of Transportation made such a recommendation and submitted a plan for carrying it out. Free interchange of freight cars regardless of ownership has long been established throughout the United States, Canada, and Mexico. Management has on occasion stated that the cars already constitute a pool. However, the cooperative interchange arrangement is quite different from a real pool in which, as in the Pullman service, the cars would be subject to central direction by a separate agency. In the two decades preceding World War II the railroads made steady advances in loaded car and loaded train performance, but empty-car mileage tended to increase. This wasteful condition was the target of the proposed pool. Furthermore, railroads are prompt in the return of empty cars to the "home" road in conformance with the car-service rules to save per-diem charges on empty cars when traffic is light; but when the demand for cars is heavy, these rules fail to assure prompt return, and the distribution of cars at the most critical times is unsatisfactory. Plans for proposed boxcar pools have been more numerous because the boxcar is an all-purpose car which should have a small proportion of empty mileage. Moreover, it is the type of car that has most consistently been in short supply. In the operation of specialized cars including tank, refrigerator, and coal cars, almost half of the mileage is necessarily empty mileage. Although rail managements have not looked with favor upon car pools in the past, the increasing cost of cars and the difficulty of financing an adequate car stock led to change.

The development both of TOFC and auto-rack service for assembled automobiles has been conducted almost wholly with flat cars provided by Trailer Train Corporation, a wholly-owned subsidiary of railroads and freight forwarders. These cars move freely nationwide and are intensively utilized. Trailer Train manages their maintenance and distribution. Subsequently Trailer Train established two subsidiaries— Railbox and Railgon—to provide standard general purpose box and gondola cars. These are free-running cars. They may be loaded to any point on any railroad without regard to car-service rules. In consequence their utilization is high and their operation has proved to be remunerative. A few railroads have also cooperated with one another to treat their cars as "at home" on the lines of any participant. This, too, has expedited car movement. As mergers proceed, cars will become free running over the enlarged systems.

Nonrail Interchange. In motor-carrier operations, the exchange of trailer equipment of connecting lines to facilitate trailer lot deliveries may be expected to expand. Through routes and joint rates have been set up by a good number of motor-freight carriers, but there has been a recent tendency to attempt to close such routes to undesirable traffic such as furniture and small shipments. The commission has now been empowered to require through routes and joint rates, as it may between rail and water lines. However, rapid territorial expansion of some of the larger motor carriers, predominantly through merger, provides an increasing range of single-line routes which obviates the necessity for a great deal of interchange which was necessary in the past. Through-route and joint-rate arrangements found in both barge and pipeline industries are apparently satisfactory and little more is expected.

In air transportation, expansion of interchange of equipment between connecting trunk lines may occur as an alternative to single-line route authority. Leasing of aircraft from another line that has different peak periods or from a central leasing enterprise may be expected to increase because of the rapid rise in the cost of aircraft and persistent peaking of air-passenger traffic. Through ticketing of local and regional airlines with trunk lines may be expected to grow. The reciprocal honoring of a ticket covering movement between points served by competing airlines has been a great service to passengers and may be expected to become a general arrangement. Until the wide-bodied jets appeared, the interchange of cargo containers and pallet loads was minimal because these units had to be configured for particular aircraft types. New container designs are suitable for the B-747, DC-10, and L-1011 aircraft.

INTERMODAL COORDINATION

Postwar Interest in Intermodal Coordination

Prior to World War II, there was little recognition of the need to coordinate the several modes of transportation. Private enterprise, with more or less public encouragement and support, was exclusively directed to the promotion and development of each mode without regard to any relation to other modes or to an optimum transport-service system. The Congress in connection with the Transportation Act of 1940 inserted a so-called Statement of National Policy as a preamble to the entire Interstate Commerce Act, to the effect that the Interstate Commerce Commission should henceforth regulate the modes under its jurisdiction so as "to recognize and preserve the inherent advantages of each." But this policy was directed to equity rather than advancement of physical or management coordination. None of the provisions in the act that discouraged or forbade coordination were modified.

It remained for wartime experience of the armed services and the development of containerization and shipper interest in more effective physical distribution to start the postwar coordination movement. Many recognize it as the "new frontier" in the development of transportation. Technical developments in containers, demountable trailer bodies, conveyors, special railcars and ships, warehouse design, and methods of materials handling have responded to efforts of all parties concerned to cope with continually escalating wages by reducing the amount of labor required in handling shipments. These methods are especially fruitful when employed in a well-designed system intended to assure expedition as well as economy.

Recent Developments in Unit-Load Systems

The technical developments mentioned, among others, have made possible considerable expansion of coordinated intermodal transportation. The trailer-on-flatcar service (piggyback) stands out in domestic transport improvement since World War II. The transfer arrangements include lift-on-lift-off, roll-on-roll-off, and flexivan-swivel transfer of the former New York Central System. The latter is being phased out through conversion of the cars to accept conventional trailers loaded by overhead crane, while the 89-foot piggyback flatcar is now available with retractable trailer hitches and movable container mounts so that it can carry almost any combination of containers and trailers. All major railroads offer the service, thus providing rail-highway coordination over much of the rail mileage of the country. Piggyback has served to keep the railroads in long-haul less-than-carload service as well as to render them more competitive for truckload lots of high-rated tonnage. In 1977 nearly 6 percent of all rail carloadings were in piggyback service and continuing growth seems likely. The types of piggyback service were described in Chapter 13. A recent study revealed that TOFC or piggyback "has yet to achieve a dominant foothold in the containerized freight traffic market."[2] Critical changes needed to realize the service's potential were cited. They included:

1. Maintenance of a high service standard.
2. To meet all-motor carrier competition, high standards of equipment and maintenance.
3. Need to upgrade railroad terminal facilities to serve TOFC.
4. Balance traffic flows by pricing action and selective sales development.

There are added restrictions of ICC regulations. The TOFC movement by rail must be 85 percent of the total distance that the shipment moves. Railroads are seldom allowed to provide their own truck service and the route of a participating motor carrier must follow its regular route although the 1980 act removes the restriction that interchange be only at points the motor carrier is authorized to serve.

Coastwise and intercoastal containership service was developed in the 1950s by the Sea-Land and Seatrain companies. Seatrain began operations in 1929 using railcars as containers on ships equipped to handle 104 railcars. In the 50s this company added facilities to handle container units in addition to railcars. During the decade of the 60s deep-sea containership operations became extensive. Since 1965 no fewer than 16 companies and consortia have entered into transatlantic container service. Some of these same companies and others operate in the intercoastal, Hawaiian, and transpacific services. Barge-carrying ships have come into service on some routes. While the technical

_____
[2] M. J. Keale and J. B. Riker, *National Intermodal Network Feasibility Study* (3 vols.) prepared for the Department of Transportation, (Greenwich, Conn.: Robert Reebie Associates, 1976), vol. 3, pp. 1 and 2.

problems of barge-trailer operations are relatively simple, experiments to date have not been as promising as rail piggyback and container-ship operations. General cargo has largely left the barge lines. Also, there are traffic-flow system problems in coordinating infrequent schedules of long-distance barge operations with truck service.

The highway trailer unit provides the most important container for coordinated transportation because virtually all shipments which lend themselves to containerization originate and end via motor carrier. Only recently in the wide-bodied jets do we have aircraft that can accommodate trailer bodies. Many airlines use "in-house" containers, often designed with a concave top to fit into the fuselage, but these are operational only between airports. Several types of smaller containers are available to shippers, but most airfreight is containerized either by airfreight forwarders or by the airlines at their terminals. Hence the air-cargo container is still used more as a means of getting cargo on and off aircraft quickly than as a device for intermodal transfer of cargo.

Organization and Management of Coordination

The organization which manages a coordinated service may be that of a shipper, an association of shippers, a single carrier, a combination of carriers, or a third party or "middleman." A shipper such as a mercantile firm may assemble shipments for pool-car movement and have them delivered from rail destination to his consignees in the area by his own motortruck equipment or by arrangements with a local contract or common motor carrier. Similarly shippers in an area with compatible commodities may form an association for use of multiple-carload rates between rail terminals and arrange for motortruck distribution at the destination.

Historically the express service was the earliest transport coordinator. Today the freight forwarders and, in the ocean trades, the nonvessel-operating common-carriers, arrange for through service including pickup and delivery from rail and air terminals by highway vehicles. However, the notable postwar developments recited above were those initiated directly by carriers. Carriers may effect intermodal coordination by arrangements for through routes and joint rates, by contractual arrangements for pickup and delivery, or by acquisition of facilities of other modes for a centrally-managed coordinated service. The last is often referred to as common ownership.

Requirements for Advancing Intermodal Coordination

Requirements for enhanced coordination include the positive factors of management initiative and technological development and the negative factor of removing institutional constraints where carriers of unlike modes are involved. The mere bringing together of several carriers of unlike modes to perform a through service on a single billing may be an important step in coordination. The cost may be reduced, and the quality of service improved.

In Chapter 20 a major advantage cited for consolidation of the railroads was that it would serve as a basis of advancing coordination. Actually the major trunk lines would serve as the main stems of a coordinated national system. Only by maximizing single-line rail operation in piggyback service is it possible to attain a service standard necessary to compete with an all-motor truck service.

However, initiative in the coordination of transportation should contemplate innovation in equipment and methods of operation. Innovation is often a prerequisite to coordination, especially when the unit-load principle is involved. For example, the Seatrain operation, which was the first distinguished success in this area, required new concepts in the designing and construction of ships. In the words of the founder, the ship architect was asked to "build a ship around a hundred cars" and not to build a ship and then try to find some way to get the railroad cars onto the ship. The success of Sea-Land operations similarly resulted from the designing of a ship with cellular compartments, in place of conventional hatches and holds, into which specially designed demountable tractor-trailer bodies would neatly fit. Deck gantry cranes were required to transfer the trailer bodies between the wharf and cellular openings where they were stacked four deep. The recent development of containerships set up new requirements for port facilities quite unlike those needed to serve conventional ships. Other notable examples of innovation that made success in coordination possible are to be found in the system of handling cement which involves differential-pressure railcars, special terminals, and special trucks. Innovative management is therefore a central requirement for the establishment of coordination.

Technological development of all facilities and equipment which may be involved is an obvious requirement whose importance cannot be overemphasized. Such a need is likely to be successfully met only when management resorts to adequate effort in research and systems analysis to determine the optimum equipment and methods to be employed. Simulation studies may be very useful in checking out alternative types of equipment and methods. Compatibility is a key word in coordination, especially when unit loads are involved. The ideal logistics system provides compatibility all the way from packaging of merchandise through pallet loads, containers, tractor-trailer units, railroad cars, aircraft, warehouses, and ships.

Institutional constraints may be those of private corporate enterprise, labor organizations, or government. Corporations often continue to follow established practices and find it difficult to develop new patterns either because of conservatism within or the fear of possible retaliation from competitors. The employment of a new system of transport involving palletization or containerization may necessitate changes in the internal operations of plants and central warehouses. These may involve investments which conservative managements are reluctant to make.

The constraint of labor organizations is easily understood because coordination will generally reduce the number of jobs and the amount of labor needed to perform a given number of ton-miles or even passenger-miles of transport. Labor has been a critical problem in both Seatrain and containership operations. It was not until an understanding was worked out with the longshore unions that the Matson containership service was made possible. Despite major progress, the problems associated with labor displacement have not yet been fully resolved in the longshore trades. There the 50-mile rule on the stuffing of containers applicable on the east coast is still in litigation. The rule requires restuffing at the port or a penalty payment if consolidated containerloads were not stuffed by longshore labor within a radius of 50 miles from the port.

Although management and labor both may be flexible, constraints imposed by government policy may be very difficult to change. The constraints of regulation by government may relate to the control of and rates for containerization, limitation on extent of terminal service by motor vehicles connected with rail line-haul operations, and restrictions on common ownership and control. Other government constraints relate to documentation, customs requirements, and charges which may be assessed in ports. Later in this chapter the regulatory policy will be reviewed.

INTERMODAL COORDINATION: THE PROBLEMS OF INTERFACE

Intermodal coordination may be advanced by improvement of transfer facilities at important terminals or by development of container (unit-load) systems involving two or more modes of transportation. The interface or transfer problem at railroad terminals is largely confined to accommodation of piggyback operations which involve transfer between highway and railcars. The provision of a running track set aside for such transfer has become a regular feature at major rail classification yards and is to be found at many lesser rail terminals. The provision for such a track or tracks with highway approach alongside and adequate transfer cranes or other equipment has not proved to be a difficult problem except in the larger urban areas where large capacity is required and space is at a premium. Otherwise the principal problem of railroad coordination is intramodal in the interchange of cars. Not so with seaports and airports where interface between modes is the basic problem in handling freight, express, mail, and, to a lesser degree, passenger traffic.

Seaports

There are three categories of freight handled at seaports, and an equal number of classes of facilities is required to accommodate them. The first is bulk cargo which requires large, specialized and highly mechanized facilities. Second is break-bulk general cargo requiring covered and open wharves alongside. Third is container- or unit-cargo freight requiring space for accumulating containers to fill a ship and special cranes or cradles to effect transfer between ship and open wharf.

Coordination, particularly for general cargo, is difficult because there is a wide difference in the size of vehicle and frequency of scheduled movement between inland and ocean carriers and because the structure of general-cargo vessels results in a slow rate of loading and unloading. The usual ocean vessel holds from 9,000 to 18,000 tons of freight, whereas the inland freight car, motortruck, or plane carries only 5 to 120 tons. Two trainloads may fill a vessel, but that requires the switching of some 200 cars into position for loading or unloading. Again, inland transportation approximates a continous flow in contrast to the occasional movement of large vessels. General-cargo vessels are usually loaded and unloaded through openings on deck called hatches. A vessel may have four to seven holds, with one hatch opening for each, and three to five freight-carrying decks. At U.S. ports, cargo is lifted in and out of the hatches in sling loads called *drafts*. The average draft may be 1,000 pounds, which means that 24,000 drafts will be required to load and unload a large vessel. The handling of 30 drafts per hatch-hour is an average performance. Full loading at a single port often requires two or more days.

The problem of handling break-bulk general cargo at ports prior to World War II arose in part because of the inadequacy of waterfront facilities. The wharves themselves, especially in North Atlantic ports which had depended on railroads serving the port to build piers, were for the most part grossly inadequate for large modern vessels. At New York and some other ports modern ships were being served by tiny finger piers designed for smaller ships of the last century. Since then public port authorities on all seaboards have developed new and adequate wharf facilities. The irony of this belated development is that a large part of general cargo is today moving in containers on board specially designed containerships. Already the proportion approximates 70 percent in the North Atlantic. This traffic has no need of the facilities required for handling break-bulk general cargo. For cellular type containerships only an open wharf with gantry cranes and good access is required at shipside. Nearby, there must be a paved field of 10 to 20 acres to permit the assembly of hundreds of inbound and outbound containers which generally are demountable trailer bodies. Roll-on and roll-off systems may require a more elaborate waterfront terminal facility to permit direct loading or unloading of more than one deck of the ship.

For many years the commerce of the country has had the benefit of excellent bulk loading and unloading facilities. The ore docks for loading iron ore in the upper Great Lakes region are among the most spectacular and most efficient. Trains of hopper cars carrying the ore are pushed onto a high long dock. The hoppers are opened, and the ore drops into giant pockets each of which is equipped with a metal spout that can be lowered into one of the many hatch openings of a lake ore steamer. More recent facilities use conveyer belts and mechanical trimmers. At down-lake ports bucket conveyers dip out the ore in 8 to 16 tons at a grab and drop the ore into railcars or barges for movement to mills or onto a large stockpile in anticipation of the closing of navigation in early December.

Immense coalcar dumping equipment has long been featured at major northeastern and some Gulf ports as well as lower Great Lakes ports. The loss of the coastwise coal trade, however, resulted in retirement of some of these facilities and deterred modernization of others. Now, as export coal movement grows, transfer capacity is inadequate.

Grain elevators in the Mississippi system, through the use of conveyer belts and spouts, rapidly load river barges with grain. Some ports on all seaboards and on the Great Lakes have even larger elevator facilities for rapid loading of vessels with grain which they transfer from railcars, barges, or both.

Most efficient transfer of all has been accomplished by the petroleum industry whose pump and pipe systems make for fast and inexpensive loading and unloading. However, the prospect of floating docks located a half mile or more from the waterfront of port areas to accommodate the supertankers may serve to add appreciably to the investment cost. This recourse is directed by the inadequacy of port channels to accommodate the draft of these vessels which, in some cases, exceeds 80 feet when port approach channels often do not exceed 40 feet. One such facility is nearing completion off the Gulf Coast.

The port problem is complicated by the fact that several or all of the railroads and a number of truck lines serving a port will normally share the delivery or receipt of a vessel's cargo. All facilities at a port should be developed and operated in close coordination. At many ports of the United States this coordination is impossible because of one or more of the following conditions: (1) lack of an adequate port authority which can plan and finance general improvements, (2) lack of modern wharves to handle general cargo, (3) absence of a belt line to make each wharf readily accessible to each railroad, (4) lack of adequate highway facilities including loading and unloading platforms at wharves, (5) absence of a wide marginal highway belt line along the waterfront reaching all wharves, (6) lack of wide highways radiating from the port, and (7) division of responsibility for handling cargo between the ship's hold and the inland carrier. Those participating in only 100 or 200 feet of transportation connecting the inland carrier and the ships often include (a) the railroad or highway carrier serving the port, (b) a carloading and unloading firm, (c) the owner of the wharf, (d) the stevedore, and (e) the ocean carrier. The result of this division of management in the operation of a set of facilities which are uncoordinated and obsolete is that vessels may require seven to ten days to discharge and load cargo, and the cost may exceed that of 1,000 miles of transportation at sea. Lack of economy at the nation's seaport gateways imposes an economic burden on the nation and retards the development of the merchant marine under the American flag. Imports cost the public more, exports face a handicap in developing markets, and domestic shipping is unable to realize its possibilities in giving cheaper transport. An efficient means of transfer at terminal areas is the minimum essential of coordination in transportation. Despite rapid development of containerization and of new terminals to accommodate it, much general cargo will continue to require conventional handling.

The Airport Problem

The airport problem is as old as air transportation, but it has become so acute since 1960 that it threatens to slow down and limit progress in the industry. Congestion causing increasing delays of aircraft in landing and departure is serious at all major airports, and they accommodate the largest part of the nation's commercial traffic. Few airports can accommodate the new generation of jumbo-sized aircraft. Ground transportation for both passengers and freight is grossly inadequate in capacity and efficiency.

The fact that volume of traffic and increasing size of units of vehicle movement outgrew the airports in the 50s and 60s is reminiscent of what happened in the development of the acute railroad-terminal problem between 1910 and 1930. Aviation has the advantage which the railroads lacked of having its terminals located well away from crowded city areas, but it has more difficult problems, including the limits of the air space over and near the airport, of multiplying capacity over time. The railroads could and did relocate terminals, and by adding trackage and equipment that went with it, they solved their problem. In the case of aviation, the multiplicity of carriers served and their special interests make coordinated efforts difficult. Inadequate highway access is found at many airports. This is also reminiscent of the seaport problem. The environmental problem, involving not only highway and street routes but also the noise and pollution of jet aircraft, is of increasing concern. As a result of route extensions following deregulation, gate space has become a major limitation at some large airports.

A distinctive feature of airport development is the participation of the federal government in financing enlargement and improvement and in providing important services. The Airport and Airways Act of 1970 committed the government to spend $16 billion during the next ten years through a trust fund nourished by excises and taxes upon passenger tickets and airfreight bills. Reenactment of these taxes was under Congressional consideration later in 1980. This is help that was never available to the railroad terminals and seaports. But it also adds another party to the responsibility for the solution of airport problems. These parties already include a state or bistate commission, a city or county government, the airport authority, the airlines, and various peripheral interests, such as parking concessions, at the airport.

Unit-Load Systems (Containerization)

The second method for dealing with the problem of coordinating carriers of different modes is participation in a unit-load system whereby transfer can be effected without costly and time-consuming break of bulk. The unit load may be a pallet load, a container, a motortruck trailer body, a trailer on its chassis, a railcar, or a barge. The system employed may be owned and controlled by one carrier as an integrated operation, but the system of through movement of the unit load may be effected by contractual arrangements, accompanied by through billing and joint rates either between carriers or as arranged by a freight-forwarding agency.

While the so-called age of containerization is just beginning, it has some old and interesting antecedents. The canal-boat sections on flatcars of the Pennsylvania Public Works in the 1830s were essentially containers. Curiously, they were used for passengers as well as freight. There is record of a wooden boxlike container invented in 1846 by a Captain Powell in England which was used to facilitate the transfer of miscellaneous goods from horse-drawn vehicle to railroad wagons and between wagons of railroads having different gauges.[3] Prior to the recent rail-motor container service, the most significant example in the United States was the reported use of containers from 1847 to 1896 by the New York, New Haven, and Hartford Railroad to

---

[3] *Railway Age*, vol. 84 (1928), p. 1252, editorial.

coordinate rail and water operations via the Fall River Steamship Line.[4]

Beginning in the early 1920s, container service was developed by a number of railroads of the United States as a means of coordinating rail and motor transport. It was a valuable adjunct in pickup and delivery service where a number of commodities were being shipped by one consignor to a consignee. The New York Central and the Pennsylvania developed extensive container services after 1922. The advantages in reduction of damage and theft and in economy of movement of merchandise which lends itself to containers is very great. However, container services were dropped as railroads phased out of the less-than-carload business. TOFC replaced them.

When Sea-Land began containership operations in the Puerto Rican trade, coordination with highway transport was a major objective. Faster and more reliable service, reduced pilferage, and greatly reduced cost of transfer between truck and ship were to be the major benefits. With expansion of container services to all major trade routes, some cargo continues to be containerized in the ports, but to an increasing extent ocean cargo moves between inland origins and destinations in containers utilizing rail and truck for the inland hauls. This has posed major problems in the supply of containers, their interchange among modes and their locational control. Steamship ownership predominates, but pooling of containers through leasing organizations which have worldwide coverage, communications networks, and computerized container-locating systems is making rapid progress.

The fast turnaround of containerships in port has led to increased sea speed and larger size for these vessels. The business becomes capital intensive rather than labor intensive, as in conventional break-bulk operations. Concentration of service between a few major ports with high frequency of sailings and fast transit time are sought to improve service quality and generate high utilization for these costly vessels. Multiple port calls are avoided. Hence rail and truck transportation are more and more used to feed containers to and distribute from a few select ports. Thus transpacific traffic is delivered at Oakland or Los Angeles and handled by rail in trainload lots to Houston and other Gulf ports (called a minibridge) rather than bringing the ship through the Panama Canal to Houston to deliver traffic destined for Texas points. Rail service is also used to bridge the continent both in the United States and Canada on traffic between Europe and the Far East. This is effective intermodal coordination.[5] It is frequently accom-

---

[4] *Railway Age*, vol. 69 (1920), p. 515.

[5] There is also a landbridge between Europe and the Far East via the railways of the USSR.

plished by solid container trains furnished by railroads under contract with steamship companies.

Two designs of ship which take barges as well as containers on board have been developed. These have great potential where ports are backed by inland waterway systems. Thus barges can move from points on the Mississippi River system to European points on the Rhine without rehandling of the cargo either at New Orleans or Rotterdam. The same concept can be used to gather in cargo from smaller ports where protected coastal waters are available.

Integration of Transportation

Integration is defined as *formation of a whole from constituent parts.* Integration employing different modes of transportation may be related to the structure of a national system which employs each mode according to its economic fitness or to the establishment of a transportation enterprise employing two or more modes under a unified corporate control. Therefore, in national policy it represents the ultimate in composition of the national transportation system. In carrier service it represents a centralized control that can provide the maximum coordinated service among the several transport technologies. Transportation companies are developing and should increase if private management is fully to exploit the economy of integrating modes into a unified and controlled transport service. Conceivably, such a carrier would offer various combinations of integrated service between two major centers depending on the cost and service package a shipper chooses to buy. Common ownership can justify the investment necessary to provide new and specialized equipment to effect an innovation in service. However, differences in vehicle movements of two modes or in the volume and pattern of traffic may produce circumstances that will not justify such an investment in the modes involved. Therefore, coordination by establishing through routes and joint rates or contract with a carrier of another mode, or perhaps reliance on a third party such as a freight forwarder, may be more economical and practical.

REGULATION OF COORDINATION

Intramodal Coordination

The Transportation Act of 1920, it will be recalled, gave the Interstate Commerce Commission four directives designed to effect service coordination. The provisions covered (1) the consolidation of the railroads, (2) emergency car-service control, (3) control over car-service rules, and (4) joint use of terminals. Since the discussion in this chapter has been concerned with coordination short of consolidation, the present analysis will be confined to the last three provisions.

Emergency Provisions and Car-Service Rules. In time of emergency, declared by the president of the United States, the Interstate Commerce Commission was empowered to place embargoes on traffic movement, route traffic, and distribute car equipment, regardless of ownership of the facilities, route preference of shippers, or existing rules and regulations bearing upon car service. The emergency provisions were designed to compel coordination to relieve any areas of serious congestion and car shortage. The control over car-service rules does not give the commission direct power to establish standards of service, but it simply provides that all car-service rules affecting the interchange and distribution of equipment must be submitted to and approved by the commission. The Car Service Division of the Association of American Railroads has administered the car-service rules. The commission has, also, generally asked the association to administer embargoes which are found to be necessary. When congestion once becomes serious in a terminal district or area, or some important route is crippled by a flood or otherwise, traffic must be diverted to prevent more serious conditions. The two car-service provisions of the 1920 act have proved to be practical and particularly valuable in time of war or other emergency.

Joint Use of Terminals. The power of the Interstate Commerce Commission to require joint use of railroad terminals was also established by the Transportation Act of 1920. A carrier owning a given set of terminal facilities may be required to permit another railroad in the vicinity to share in the use of the facilities if (1) the proposed joint use is in the public interest, (2) it will not impair the ability of the owning carrier to handle its own traffic, and (3) a reasonable compensation is agreed upon. In the event an agreement cannot be reached on compensation, the commission can decide the terms which in its judgment are just and reasonable, but the charges must be based upon the "principle controlling condemnation proceedings." This means a high rate based on the value to the owner in damages resulting from the use of the property. The compensation requirement, together with the commission's interpretation of "public convenience," has made the provision virtually nonoperative. Since the owning carrier is jealous of the advantage which its terminal facilities give it over its competitor, a high value is bound to be claimed. The commission first tried to apply the provision when it ordered the Chicago, Milwaukee and St. Paul to extend to the Chicago, Burlington and Quincy the use of its terminal facilities at Hastings, Minnesota, following agreement on the compensation.[6] Because of the failure of the parties to agree on compensation,

---

[6] *Hastings Commercial Club* v. *Chicago, Milwaukee & St. Paul Ry. Co.*, 69 ICC 489 (1922).

the case came before the commission again in 1926.[7] It reversed its previous decision on a different interpretation of the carriers' interest and that of the public. The later decision emphasized the possible loss to the Milwaukee Railroad and possible inconvenience to the public which might result from the joint use. The question of constitutionality of compulsory joint use of terminal facilities was raised by the owning carrier. However, the commission held that the provision is "but an extension of the general principle that the interest of the public imposes important qualifications on the manner of use of property employed in carrier service."[8] In any event, the provision is now unworkable. Joint use of terminals is not required of other modes.

Interchange Regulations. The provision of facilities for interchange between railroads and their regulation has a direct bearing on coordination. The common-law obligation of a carrier does not compel interchange of freight with another carrier or of equipment incident to that interchange. As railroads grew and their services were extended, the need of free interchange became obvious. Self-interest in giving through service caused the practice among the rail carriers to become common prior to the legal requirement in the Act to Regulate Commerce in 1887 which provided that "any common carrier subject to the provisions of this act shall . . . afford all reasonable, proper and equal facilities for the interchange of traffic." Seldom has a railroad sought to obstruct free interchange. On occasion, when a railroad has insisted upon a transfer of freight from one car to another, the commission has ruled that a shipper has a right to through movement of carload freight without the delays and cost of transfer at junction points.[9]

Special aspects of interchange which have occasioned more controversy in regulation include (1) switching of competitor's freight in terminals, and (2) construction of extensions to effect interchange. Railroads have often refused to switch freight at terminals which has arrived by way of a competitor's line. Section 3 of the Act to Regulate Commerce, after stating the obligation to interchange without discrimination, continues ". . . but this shall not be construed as requiring any such common carrier to give the use of its tracks or terminal facilities to another carrier engaged in like business." This has been interpreted by the commission to permit a carrier to refuse switching service at a given terminal provided it treats all carriers alike.[10] This

---

[7] 107 ICC 208 (1926).

[8] 69 ICC 489 (1922); and 107 ICC 208 (1926).

[9] 26 ICC 226, 234 (1913). A railroad cannot require transfer to keep its cars on its own tracks. See 47 ICC 532 (1917).

[10] *Waverly Oil Works v. Penna. R.R. Co.*, 28 ICC 621 (1913). See also 29 ICC 114 (1914); 26 ICC 226 (1913); 31 ICC 294 (1914); 33 ICC 76 (1915); 46 ICC 464 (1917); 31 ICC 550, 551 (1914). The right of a carrier to protect its monopoly advantage by declaration of a closed terminal is explored in *Port Arthur Chamber of Commerce & Shipping v. Texarkana & Fort Worth Ry. Co. et al.*, 73 ICC 361 (1922).

interpretation has led to the distinction of an "open terminal" and a "closed terminal." If a carrier offers to switch cars over its tracks for one railroad, it must do so for all. An "open terminal" does not imply joint use, but simply that it is open to the handling of traffic for all connections by the owning road's locomotives and crews. The 1980 act gives the commission the right to require reciprocal switching, in effect to create open terminals, under certain conditions noted in Table 19-1.

The construction of a connection by a railroad when necessary for interchange can be required under Section 1 of the Hepburn Act of 1906. This requirement is operative on three conditions: (1) if such connection is found to be practical, (2) if public safety will not be endangered, and (3) if the volume of business justifies the expense of construction and maintenance. The Panama Canal Act of 1912 extended this requirement to connections between railroads and waterfront terminals of water carriers. However, motor carriers have greatly lessened or limited the dependence of water carriers on direct rail connection. The power granted the commission in 1980 to require through routes among motor carriers and between them and water carriers does not include power to require interchange of trailers.

Rate Regulation in Intramodal Coordination. The power of the Interstate Commerce Commission to prescribe joint rates and routes also came with the Hepburn Act and was strengthened in succeeding amendments to the Interstate Commerce Act. Through routes and joint rates develop together. Where two carriers have agreed to quote a rate between two points on their respective lines via a specified junction point, a through route comes into existence. Often the through rate agreed upon is less than the sum of local rates. Where traffic justifies and it is necessary to prevent discrimination, the Interstate Commerce Commission can require the establishment of a through rate and route and specify the division of the through rate. This authority may be used to facilitate coordination in carrier operations. The Mann-Elkins Act of 1910 specified that a carrier could not be required to participate unless the route included substantially the entire length of its line between the points concerned, that is, a carrier could not be required to short-route itself. The only exception to this prior to 1940 was where the through route would be unreasonably long compared with another practicable route. Many carriers have refused to perform terminal service at origin or destination of a proposed through route, insisting on a substantial portion of the line haul. The Transportation Act of 1940 gave the commission power to require a carrier to enjoy less than substantially the maximum length of its line in a through route needed to provide efficient transportation. Yet the commission is instructed to give reasonable preference to the originating carrier.

The Interstate Commerce Act similarly requires water carriers subject to Part III to establish through routes with other water carriers and with railroads. Under Part II of the act, motor-bus lines are required to establish through routes, and motor-freight lines, since 1980, may be required to establish through routes. The Civil Aeronautics Act requires air carriers to establish through routes and joint rates and fares. Through routes and rates are required, therefore, between carriers of each mode of transportation and are permissive between two carriers of unlike modes of transport except for rail and water, and motor and water where they may be required. The scheme of regulation of interstate transportation, aside from the rail interchange and car-service provisions of the Transportation Act of 1920, has not been effective in promoting needed coordination.

Regulation of Intermodal Coordination

Through Routes and Joint Rates. Intermodal through routes and joint rates are purely voluntary except when a showing of public interest requires rail-water or motor-water through routes and joint rates. The basic authorization in the Mann-Elkins Act of 1910 was strengthened by the Transportation Act of 1920 and the Dennison Act of 1928 which directed the commission to set up such rates and routes in the interest of promoting water transportation with the added power to fix the division of a rate betweeen rail and water carriers. In spite of this clear directive of Congress, coordination of rail and water transportation by establishment of through routes and joint rates has not become common or widespread. Railroad opposition exercised through rate policies and extensive litigation, confusion, and hesitance in Interstate Commerce Commission decisions; and postwar high costs of transfer between rail and barge have together served to greatly limit progress.

Railroad-rate policies included high local rates to or from the intermediate point of transfer. A through all-rail rate from A to C would be well below the sum of the local-rail rates from A to B and from B to C. A joint rail-barge or barge-rail rate would have to include the high local rail rate involved. Since the barge-rail or rail-barge joint rate must be below the all-rail rate to attract traffic in competition, the barge share of a lower joint rate would tend to be small, perhaps too low to be profitable. This device of railroads was not ended until 1956 when the Supreme Court set aside an order of the commission approving a higher ex-barge rate on sulphur moving via St. Louis. The Court held the commission's order to be in violation of Section 3(4) and 307(d) of the act because it denied shippers a more economic form of transportation.[11] Later in the *Arrow Case* the Court established a rule that the

---

[11] *Dixie Carriers, Inc.* v. *United States,* 351 U.S. 56 (1956).

divisions received by a railroad of an all-rail joint rate with another railroad should apply in the computation of a division of a barge-rail rate.[12]

Ironically, by the time the ICC and court decisions upheld the clear intent of the acts of 1920 and 1928, most traffic in which the barge lines hoped to participate had left the waterways because of high transfer costs and growing motor-carrier competition. The barge lines had practically ceased to handle "carload," that is, less-than-barge-load, traffic, and largely had become haulers of barge-lot shipments of bulk commodities. The revival of general cargo for the barge lines is not likely unless barge-truck coordination should prove to have large potential, then it would probably involve trailers on barges making transfer costs minimal. The principle of inherent advantage in the statement of National Transportation Policy in the Act of 1940 presumably relieved the Interstate Commerce Commission of any legal compulsion to protect a rail-barge joint rate lower than the all-rail rate unless there were a showing of lower costs. The investment costs represented by federal waterway expenditures have never been permitted by the courts to be considered in the determination of water-carrier costs except user charges, recently imposed, which will appear on the carriers' books. Hence, lower barge costs calculated on the basis acceptable to the Court would not necessarily indicate an economic advantage enjoyed by water transport.

The rapid development of motor-carrier feeder services to barge terminals on the Upper Mississippi and Illinois Rivers, partly encouraged by shortages of rail cars, has led to joint rail-barge movement of grain on an increased scale. Similarly, some of the increasing array of long-haul coal movements are joint rail-barge movements. The necessity to hold down the costs of such movements as well as the railroads' increased concern for profitability promise expansion of this type of coordination. Growth is impeded, however, by limitations of lock capacity, particularly on the Upper Mississippi.

Intermodal Unit-Load Regulation. Under this heading come all of the developments of unit loads including piggyback on the railroads, railcars on ships and car ferries, trailer-ships, containerized aircraft, and, most recently, barges on ships. There is nothing in the basic acts governing the Interstate Commerce Commission, the Federal Maritime Commission, or the Civil Aeronautics Board which they have interpreted to prevent or discourage intermodal container systems. For both service and rates, the attitude and policy have been permissive and favorable.

---

[12] *State Corporation Commission* v. *Arrow Transportation Co.*, 361 U.S. 353 (1960). The Court had earlier (1947) overruled ICC approval of higher rates on ex-barge grain moving to Chicago. *See ICC* v. *Mechling*, 330 U.S. 567.

Joint airline-truck rates are entirely voluntary, but they have to be filed with two regulatory agencies. Joint ocean-rail or ocean-truck rates are in the same situation. Should the rates be contested, hearings before both bodies might be necessary. Air-truck cooperation should improve in view of the enlarged exemption in the 1980 act and the fact that the Civil Aeronautics Board no longer requires the filing of cargo rates.

Common Ownership. In principle the ultimate arrangement in synchronizing operations involving two or more modes is that of common ownership. While students of transportation have advocated the formation of transportation companies for almost 50 years, little progress has been made. In this country we have favored unilateral development within the modes. In aid, subsidy, and regulation we have railroad, motor carrier, water carrier, air carrier, and pipeline policies rather than a transportation policy. Despite creation of the Department of Transportation in recognition of this shortcoming, little progress has been apparent. The old constraints are still on the books.

The railroads are still subject to the Panama Canal Act of 1912 that forbids a railroad to have any interest in or control over a water common carrier or vessel unless the Interstate Commerce Commission finds that (1) the ownership will not prevent the water carrier from being operated in the public interest and (2) that it will not exclude, prevent, or reduce competition on the route by water under consideration. These considerations leave much to the discretion of the commission, but it held the line against rail ownership in the *John I. Hay* case where a railroad sought control of a barge line in the interest of coordinated service in hauling bulk commodities.[13]

The coordination of water carriers with rail or motor operations presents important opportunities for possible economy especially in the light of mounting diesel fuel costs. Yet the commission denied this experimental operation in the *John I. Hay* case for rail-water coordination and previously had dismissed the application of the McLean Trucking Company to coordinate coastwise container-ship operations with trucking.[14] Both decisions were based on technicalities in a strict interpretation of the acts involved. No comparable efforts to experiment have since been made. Nevertheless, it is the coordination of rail and highway operations that has been well proved to be advantageous and which still offers the greatest potential. Many hold that common ownership is required to realize this potential.

While the Interstate Commerce Act does not prohibit railroad ownership of motor-carrier operations, the Transportation Act of 1940

---

[13] *Illinois Central R.R. Co.–Control of John I. Hay Co.*, 317 ICC 39 (1962).

[14] *McLean Trucking Company and Pan Atlantic Steamship Corporation, Investigation of Control*, 70 MCC 609 (1957).

amended Section 3(27)(a) to state that the commission should not grant a railroad application for acquisition unless it finds (1) that the transaction proposed is consistent with the public interest and will enable such carriers to use services by motor vehicle to public advantage in its operation and (2) will not unduly restrain competition. Again commission discretion could open the door, but it seldom has done so. The fact that the section singles out the railroads naturally creates a bias against approval. Both efforts to acquire an existing motor carrier or to receive a certificate to inaugurate a new service have been generally forestalled. With rare exceptions the commission has required that a rail-controlled motor-freight operation be engaged in auxiliary and supplementary service. A rail haul must be involved, the traffic moving on a railroad bill of lading. In 1940 the commission ruled that in any case rail-controlled motor service could not take place between "key points" which are important traffic centers.

There are no legal or administrative constraints to common ownership involving any combination of motor and pipeline operations. Railroads are free only to acquire pipelines. In view of the great public advantage of coordinated transportation it is ironic that railroads, the logical leaders, are free to acquire various kinds of businesses outside of transportation but not other modes of transport. Common ownership involving airlines is not prohibited by law, but the Civil Aeronautics Board has consistently sought to prevent ownership of airlines by other modes of transportation. It is clear that we are far from applying the logic of the principle of preserving and promoting inherent advantage of each mode through freedom of carrier management to demonstrate the economic advantages of common ownership and control.

SELECTED REFERENCES.

Behling, B. N. "Railroad Coordination and Consolidation, a Review of Estimated Economies." Bureau of Statistics, Interstate Commerce Commission, Statement no. 4123 (mimeographed) (1940).

Daggett, Stuart. *Principles of Inland Transportation*, chaps. 22–26. New York: Harper & Bros., 1941.

Fair, Marvin L. *Port Administration in the United States*. Cambridge, Md.: Cornell Maritime Press, 1954.

———. *Economic Considerations in the Administration of the Interstate Commerce Act*, chap. 10. Cambridge, Md.: Cornell Maritime Press, 1972.

Fair, Marvin L., and Plowman, E. Grosvenor. *Coordinated Transportation, Principles and Problems*. Cambridge, Md.: Cornell Maritime Press, 1967.

Federal Coordinator of Transportation. *Merchandise Freight Report*. Washington, D.C., 1934.

———. *Freight Traffic Report*. Washington, D.C., 1935.

Grossman, William L. *Surface Carrier Participation in Air Transportation.* New York: Remsen Press, 1944.

Hillman, Jordan Jay. *The Parliamentary Structuring of British Road-Rail Freight Coordination.* Evanston, Ill.: The Transportation Center at Northwestern University, 1973.

Immer, John R. *Container Services of the Atlantic.* 2d ed. Washington, D.C.: Work International, Inc., 1970.

Keale, M. J., and Riker, J. B. (Robert Reebie Associates). *National Intermodal Network Feasibility Study.* Prepared for Department of Transportation, May 1976.

Lederer, E. H. *Port Terminal Operation.* Cambridge, Md.: Cornell Maritime Press, 1945.

Locklin, D. Philip. *Economics of Transportation,* chaps. 36 and 37. 7th ed. Homewood, Ill.: Richard D. Irwin, Inc., 1972.

Moulton, H. G., et al. *The American Transportation Problem,* chaps. 29 and 33–35. Washington, D.C.: The Brookings Institution, 1933.

National Resources Planning Board. *Transportation and National Policy.* Part I, sec. 4. Washington, D.C.: U.S. Government Printing Office, 1942.

Roberts, Merrill J., and Associates. *Intermodal Freight Transportation Coordination: Problems and Potential.* Pittsburgh: Graduate School of Business, University of Pittsburgh, 1966.

Sillcox, Lewis K. "*Timetable Traffic*" (mimeographed), University of North Carolina publication (March 18, 1951).

Van Metre, T. W. *Transportation in the United States.* 2d ed. Brooklyn, N.Y.: The Foundation Press, Inc., 1950.

Wilson, G. Lloyd. *Coordinated Motor-Rail-Steamship Transportation.* New York (publisher not indicated), 1930.

23

Government Provision of Transportation Facilities

In the United States, railroads[1] and pipelines have traditionally been in private ownership. The line of pipe or of railroad is normally operated by the owning company and is under its exclusive control. Its use may be shared with another company of the same type, as when railroad trackage rights are granted so that one railroad may operate over the line of another. In such cases the tenant's operations are subjected to the control of the owner and are conducted in accordance with that line's operating timetables and rule book. There are advantages to the exclusive control of a transport facility, since the permanent way, terminals, and signal facilities can all be developed in accordance with the operating requirements of the owner.

Other types of transport facilities are multiple-use in character. The highways are shared by the private automobile, commercial and private trucks, bus lines, government and public utility vehicles, farm vehicles in the rural areas, and other users. Commercial, corporate, private, and military aircraft share in the use of airports and air-navigation facilities. The fishing boat and the pleasure boat share the improved navigable waterways along with commercial and naval shipping. These types of transport facility are, therefore, provided by organizations other than those which make predominant use of the basic facilities—commonly they are everywhere provided by governments. Indeed the provision and maintenance of transport facilities is one of the largest segments of government nonmilitary spending. The level of funding is affected not merely by transportation requirements

---

[1] With a few exceptions of which the Long Island and Alaska Railroads are the most noteworthy.

but by the government's general economic policy and by the relative force of political pressure on spending priorities. The possibility that government-provided transportation facilities may be out of phase with user requirements is much greater than the likelihood that rail or pipeline facilities will not be developed in accord with traffic needs and, in the rail case, the character of motive power and equipment to be employed.[2]

EARLY GOVERNMENT TRANSPORTATION PROGRAMS

Prior to the development of the automobile, roads served local purposes predominantly, providing access to abutting property. In the absence of navigable waterways in the interior and prior to railroad development, some commerce was necessarily carried on by road over long distances. But travel by stagecoach and freighting by wagon were both slow and expensive. Hence water routes were used wherever possible, even though they often were exceedingly roundabout. Construction and maintenance of roads were left to local governments and accomplished by the labor of, or at the expense of, property holders served by them. The work was almost invariably indifferent, and the condition of the roads abominable.

A brief "turnpike era" provided improved toll roads between a number of points, generally built by private organizations to which franchises had been granted. The federal government took a hand with the construction of the Cumberland Road, designed to cross the Allegheny Mountain barrier and bind the newly acquired Northwest Territory to the nation. Construction began in 1811, and the last appropriation was made in 1838. Canal construction flourished in the same period. The Erie Canal, a New York State project, was completed in 1825. The Pennsylvania Public Works comprised a railroad and canal system across the state. Many of the canals were built, however, by private corporations, and both public and private canals employed tolls to finance their construction and operation. Interest both in road building and improvement and in canal construction lagged after the railroad had proved itself. For it appeared that the railroad was far superior to horse-drawn vehicles on roads or on waterways. Public interest shifted, accordingly, to the support of railroad projects.

Substantial public aid was granted by all levels of government to encourage railroad development. States, counties, and towns bonded themselves in order to extend such aid. The federal government began

---

[2] Lack of earning power has, in the case of the American railroads, resulted in deferred maintenance and a failure of permanent way to keep up with the requirements of heavier cars and higher speeds.

its land-grant policy in 1850 with grants of public lands to Illinois and other states for transfer to the Illinois Central and two smaller roads which would provide a north-south through route. The first transcontinental railroad was aided both by land grants and government bonds. Thereafter, until 1871, liberal treatment was accorded railroads all over the West, the construction of railroads was greatly expedited by the process, and substantial overbuilding of the rail system was encouraged. A large part of our present problem of excess mileage of light-traffic rail lines is traceable to the indiscriminate aids of the land-grant era.[3]

Although public lands were granted to railroads without monetary consideration, there were conditions attached which over the years substantially reimbursed the government. Railways receiving such grants were expected to carry government mail, freight, troops, and supplies free of charge. In 1876, however, the Supreme Court found the railroads entitled to compensation for the actual cost of moving government traffic, although the government was entitled to free use of the permanent way. Thereafter railroads moved government freight at 20 to 50 percent below commercial rates, including the vast volumes of traffic generated in both world wars, until the land-grant provisions were repealed in 1946.

As the railroad net assumed comprehensive proportions and appeared to meet the transportation needs of the nation, public transport investment waned. Not until 1916 did a reversal of government policy begin. In that year the federal government reentered highway promotion and took a major step toward the restoration of a U.S. flag merchant marine. Aids to air transport and programs to improve inland navigation followed within a short span of time.

REVIVAL OF HIGHWAY IMPROVEMENTS

As late as 1900 Professor Hadley of Yale wrote that "the road system as a matter of national importance is a thing of the past."[4] Yet the campaign for good roads had already begun in the 90s, stimulated by the bicycle craze, by the desire of railroads for improved feeder services, and by the agitation of farmers for all-weather access to towns. Near the end of the 19th century the automobile made its appearance and soon created new demands and new standards for highway improvement.

---

[3] The land-grant era closed in 1871 with a large grant to the Texas and Pacific. In 1890 a general forfeiture of lands not earned by actual construction was legislated.

[4] A. T. Hadley, *Railroad Transportation* (New York: G. P. Putnam's Sons, 1903), p. 28.

The federal government first assumed leadership when Congress passed the Federal Aid Road Act of 1916 which marked the beginning of federal grants-in-aid to the states. Under this program the states continued to be the proprietors of the roads and to be responsible for their maintenance. Each state receiving grants-in-aid was required to set up a highway department and management and construction standards satisfactory to the federal highway authorities. Those principles have continued. The Highway Act of 1921 provided for the designation of a system of interstate highways and for preference to projects which would further the establishment of a national system of highways. Appropriations were divided among the states in accordance with population, area, and rural post-road mileage and were matched by the states receiving them.

The federal proportion of total highway expenditures ranged between 4 and 7 percent during the 20s. In the 30s it expanded considerably, reaching 37.11 percent in 1938. Regular federal-aid funds were augmented by expenditures through the relief agencies during the depression years. In the 20 years to 1940, $6.5 billion of federal money was poured into highways to supplement $32.7 billion of state and local funds. The nation had developed the greatest system of improved highways in the world and had expended more upon its highways than had gone into the railroad system in the previous century. World War II brought a virtual cessation to the expansion of the highway net, and postwar new and more ambitious concepts were applied.

INTERNAL WATERWAY IMPROVEMENT

After the rather abrupt end of the canal-building era, canal and river traffic continued to increase on some of the more favorable routes. The greatest decade for steamboat traffic on the Mississippi was 1880–90 while the Erie Canal experienced its peak traffic in the previous decade.[5] For almost a half century little effort was made to improve the waterways except for minor appropriations to finance work of the Corps of Engineers of the Army. The most notable exception was the opening of the Saulte Ste. Marie Canal in 1850 which extended the Great Lakes route to Lake Superior and paved the way to a water route of increasing importance, despite rail competition. Access to upper lake ores provided by the Great Lakes system was of major importance in the growth of the steel industry at Pittsburgh and in the lower lake area.

---

[5] F. H. Dixon, *Traffic History of the Mississippi River* (Washington, D.C.: U.S. Government Printing Office, 1915), pp. 57–59.

Soon after the turn of the century there was a revival of interest in the improvement of waterways. The Board of Engineers for Rivers and Harbors was created in 1902 and thereafter served as the agency charged with investigating the feasibility of waterway improvements. In the period 1905–17 the outstanding accomplishment was the deepening and improving of the more important harbors on the three seaboards and on the Great Lakes. New York built its State Barge Canal. Most of the 50 dams of the Ohio River project were completed, providing a 9-foot stage of water throughout its length. Railroad congestion during World War I added impetus to the advocacy of further improvement. With the exception of the war years, 1917–18 and 1942–45, each Congress outdid its predecessor in voting authorization for waterway improvements.

During the 1920s emphasis was placed upon the development of a connected system of waterways. The system would include through navigation from the Gulf of Mexico to the Great Lakes at Chicago via the Mississippi and Illinois rivers, a series of barge canals to afford protected navigation along the Gulf and Atlantic coasts, and the St. Lawrence Seaway to provide deepwater navigation between the Lakes and the Atlantic. This last was to be long deferred, but work on the others moved forward. In the 1930s the Tennessee was developed from the mouth to Knoxville as a part of the multiple purpose projects of the Tennessee Valley Authority. The result is a system of great transportation usefulness in the area east of the Great Plains.

The Corps of Engineers of the Army has jurisdiction over the development of the navigable waters and, in most instances, is responsible for planning, construction, and maintenance of channel improvements. It has been the policy to provide navigation facilities free of tolls, that is, at the expense of the general revenues of the government. Tolls were provided at the Panama Canal from its inception and were later assessed for passage of the St. Lawrence Seaway. Otherwise the use of the improved waterways was free.

After years of controversy, this policy was modified in 1978. Locks and Dam 26 on the Mississippi River at Alton, Illinois, had become increasingly inadequate in the face of growing traffic. Replacement with a larger lock at a somewhat different location was judged to require congressional approval. Environmental and railroad opposition waged a long fight out of which came a compromise—construction would be approved, but barge operators would for the first time be subjected to a tax on the fuel burned.[6]

---

[6] The tax became effective October 1, 1980 and the rate per gallon will escalate over time. Yet it will produce less revenue than the annual maintenance costs for the system. See National Transportation Policy Study Commission, *National Transportation Policies through the Year 2000* (1979), pp. 192–194.

PROMOTION OF AIR TRANSPORT

The federal government played a primary role in the development of air transport. From 1919 to 1923 the Post Office Department experimented with airmail transportation and developed a marked and lighted transcontinental airway. In the latter year regular night operations commenced on that route. After 1925 the Department of Commerce took over the task of developing a system of civil airways and aids to navigation, as well as the regulation of private and commercial operators in matters of safety. After that date private airlines flew the mail under contract with the Post Office, and airmail payments were designed to enable them to begin to build passenger and cargo services on a subsidized basis. Direct subsidy of airline operations was continued under the Civil Aeronautics Act (1938) but was phased out, so far as trunk airlines were concerned, beginning in the 1940s. Subsidy of local-service airlines has continued.

The federal government has provided and operated the airways, air-navigation facilities, and air-traffic control through the Civil Aeronautics Administration (later the Federal Aviation Agency and now a part of the Department of Transportation).User charges have gradually been assessed to recoup the cost of such services in the form of fuel taxes on all nongovernment aviation and taxes upon airline tickets and air-cargo waybills. The provision of airports has been left to the state and local governments (with the exception of Washington National and Dulles airports) and private parties. But a federal airport plan has been developed, and moderate grants-in-aid have been provided to assist with land acquisition and runway construction.

Airports present an unusual case of divided authority in planning, development, and operation. The municipality or specially created airport authority provides runways, taxiways, and central administrative and terminal facilities. FAA fixes standards, classifies airports, and provides and operates the air-traffic control system. Airline and fixed-base operators generally lease land on the airport where they can construct hangars, maintenance facilities, and, at the larger airports, their separate passenger and cargo terminal facilities. Landing fees, leases, and concessions are relied upon as revenue sources; but they do not always compensate municipal investment fully.

The growth of traffic at airports and on airways is determined by the demand for air transport and the response of airlines and others to that demand. Appropriations for the airways and air-traffic control systems are, however, determined by the government and are affected by budgetary policy. New airport construction has a long lead time, financing is often difficult for municipalities to arrange, and proposed locations are facing increased public opposition. Hence the development of publicly-provided facilities and services has several times fallen behind the relatively uncontrolled increase in airline traffic and in private and corporate aircraft use. Such a situation seems to develop about once every ten years, and when a critical pass is recognized, increased appropriation and government activity follow. But it takes considerable time to bring facilities into balance with requirements.

NEW APPROACHES—POST-WORLD WAR II

The pause in public works of all kinds imposed by the war necessitated a new appraisal of requirements early in the postwar period and afforded the opportunity to reshape programs. The rapid exhaustion of Lake Superior direct-shipping iron ores by the high rate of wartime industrial activity and growing concern about the nation's resource position in general helped tip the scales, finally, in favor of the St. Lawrence Seaway development. Otherwise programs upon the navigable waterways have represented the extension and improvement of systems earlier contemplated—replacement of locks on the Ohio with new and larger facilities to accommodate today's tows; continuance of work upon the Missouri River; enlargement of the Chesapeake and Delaware Canal; deepening of the Delaware channel to Trenton, New Jersey; and other like projects. A recent and significant extension of the system was the Arkansas-Verdigris project which brought barge navigation into the Tulsa Metropolitan Area by the end of 1970 and precipitated a boom in industrial location and warehouse development in the area. Waterway development has felt the impact of environmental concern. Early in 1971 work on the trans-Florida canal which would have linked the Gulf and Atlantic intracoastal canals was halted. That project had been a controversial one for more than 30 years.

Neither environmental nor railroad opposition, though carried vigorously into the courts, could halt construction of the enormous Tennessee-Tombigbee project. Now well underway, this waterway with its deep cut and canal across the divide between Mississippi and Gulf drainage, will cost upward of $2 billion and deteriorate the competitive situation of the railways in the southeast. There is sharp difference of opinion between the Corps of Engineers and outside experts whether prospective benefits can justify the cost.[7]

The shape of the transportation system has been altered most materially by the Interstate Highway system. Federal-aid authorizations were increased in 1950 and 1954, but it was not until 1956 that a long-

---

[7] "Cost-benefit Trips up the Corps," *Business Week*, February 19, 1979, pp. 96–97.

range program was embodied in law which it was hoped would relieve highway deficiencies and bring the system abreast of the needs of traffic over the ensuing decade. Prior to the war it had been estimated that over $3.5 billion would be required to rebuild or relocate more than 100,000 miles of obsolete highways. By 1954 it appeared that more energetic measures involving revision of historic policies would be needed to alleviate growing congestion and improve highway safety. Studies prepared by the Bureau of Public Roads disclosed a need over the period 1955–64 of $126 billion.

The Federal Aid Highway Act of 1956 authorized expenditure of $46.2 billion by the federal government over a period of 13 years. Of this, roughly two thirds would be spent upon the 41,000-mile Interstate system, and the remainder on other federal-aid highways. On the Interstate system the federal government would bear 90 percent of the cost, as compared with the normal 50–50 matching with states which would be continued for other highway systems. Moreover, for the first time, specific tax revenues were recognized as applicable to highway work and segregated in a trust fund out of which the authorized expenditures would be made. These included federal excises, as increased, on fuel, vehicles, tires, and recaps, as well as a new tax of $1.50 per 1,000 pounds annually on trucks registered for gross weights exceeding 26,000 pounds.

The continued rapid growth in highway traffic raised doubts whether even this large program would be sufficient. Early in 1958 the growing economic recession led Congress to consider further expansion. Added authorization was made, the federal proportion on highways in the primary system was increased to 60 percent, and the practice of supplementing trust-fund availabilities with additional monies was begun. Completion of the Interstate system slipped well beyond the original goal and is still in the future. In an inflationary period, the anticipated costs have escalated enormously.

The intercity program now nearing completion has greatly facilitated vehicular movement for short as well as long distances, reduced the cost of truck and bus operators, and improved transit times between most major points. It has made a significant contribution to improved safety on the highways. Yet, as is the case with federal highway programs in general, the more densely populated states have been shortchanged in the proportion of funds allotted while gross overbuilding has occurred in and through the lightly populated states.

Highway expansion has generated increasing opposition. The highway bulldozer moving across the land upon locations chosen only to meet the standards of the highway builders is now more often challenged in an effort to avoid needless destruction of natural and historic values. As the early tendency of the Interstate system to dump vast volumes of traffic into the city streets at the periphery was partly corrected by construction into and through the cities, new opposition developed. Enormous destruction of property resulted from highway and interchange construction, large numbers of people and businesses were uprooted, and the structure of the city was altered. In Cleveland, Baltimore, Nashville, Washington, and other cities, completion of planned segments of the Interstate was delayed by local opposition. In New Orleans a segment along the riverfront which, it was said, would seriously damage the historic French quarter was defeated.

Federal money is indispensible to continued highway improvement. When from 60 to 90 percent of the funds are provided by the federal government, cities and states find the temptation to accept projects well-nigh irresistible despite the adverse effects that may accompany them. We have only begun to call in question the principles upon which highway planning has hitherto been based and to require consideration of factors other than those of need as disclosed by traffic counts and location to satisfy the highway design engineer, but diversion to mass transit has been provided for on a limited scale as noted in Chapter 8.

Federal, state, and local expenditures for highways for the 20 years ending with 1940 aggregated just short of $40 billion. In 1947 these same levels of government spent $2.9 billion on highways, but by 1968 the annual rate had reached $30.1 billion. The federal share was one eighth in 1947. It is now nearly one quarter. Expenditures for airways and airports have expanded even more rapidly. The amount for airways (all federal) was but $66 million in 1947 but approached $1.9 billion in 1978. Airports took $1.7 billion in 1977, but the federal share was less than one fourth.

Capacity at major airports has been severely stretched. The widebodied jets brought some relief by arresting the growth in number of flights, but deregulation is promoting expansion again at many hubs. Congestion costs fall not only upon the airlines in delays to aircraft awaiting takeoff or stacked in the air pending approach clearance but also upon passengers whose schedules are disrupted. No reckoning of these costs in total has been attempted. Construction of airports is generally regarded as well behind requirements at critical points, and the long lead time for construction insures that congestion will persist for a number of years.

Growing opposition to airport construction on any available sites near the larger urban centers has led some to conclude that the last major airports in the United States have already been constructed.[8] The new Dade County Airport, already under construction, was

---

[8] The Dallas-Ft. Worth Airport, largest of all airports in land area assembled for development, was opened in 1973. No other large airport is under construction. However, Chicago's Midway has been reopened to commercial traffic and Atlanta has relieved congestion by a major new terminal complex.

aborted by environmental considerations. The Port of New York Authority has been seeking a site for a fourth jet airport for some 15 years, but has been frustrated by local opposition in respect to each site which it considers will meet air traffic requirements. Sites for additional airport construction are only in the exploratory stage at Chicago and Los Angeles. The transfer of short-haul traffic to VSTOL aircraft and to high-speed ground transportation may become essential as an alternative. Some 50 percent of the scheduled airline flights at the New York airports, for example, are short-haul flights for which such services might substitute effectively. Yet proposals for close-in VSTOL airports also encounter opposition. The federal role in funding airport requirements has been increasing. The time has arrived when it must give more serious consideration to alternatives which will relieve the demand for jet airports with their enormous land requirements and their serious impact upon adjacent urban populations.

USER CHARGES

Tolls are an historic method for financing transportation facilities, both public and private. They are characteristically assessed on users of a particular transport facility, as in the case of the Panama Canal, the New Jersey Turnpike, and other facilities to which this method applies. User charges collect money for the provision and maintenance of transportation facilities, but they come from groups of users and are applied not to a specific route or facility but to a class of facilities. They are assessed against users, normally somewhat in proportion to use, but the total sums generated are applied to groups of facilities in accordance with some measure of priority of requirement, but with no specific regard to the location of use from which the charges were generated.

The principle that abutting property holders should pay for roads has not been abandoned in entirety. They benefit from the access which roads provide to their property and from increased land values as highway improvements render property more accessible. The users of highways have, however, clearly become the principal beneficiaries and that is even more clear of airways users. Hence, the burden of finance has gradually shifted in favor of user charges.

The automotive vehicle early proved to be an admirable source of tax revenues. License and registration fees developed naturally enough. Excise taxes on vehicles and tires, and more particularly on fuel, had the merit of easy and cheap collection. Most important, within the range of taxes explored in the United States, little evidence has appeared that such taxes have adversely affected the increase in number of vehicles on the highways or the rate of use. Enormous revenues are now generated by such excises, principally at the state and federal levels.

Originally receipts from such taxes were allocated to the general revenues of the governments affected. Highway appropriations were not tied to the amounts received from automotive fees and excises. Indeed, less was spent on highways in many states. In time such taxes come to be regarded as user charges even if not segregated from other revenues. As we have seen, the Highway Act of 1956 channeled federal receipts from a variety of such excises into a trust fund from which only highway expenditures would be made. Moreover, various off-highway users have long been excepted from the application of the fuel tax.

Where several forms of transport are competing for the same traffic, it is of obvious importance whether the several modes are covering their full costs. Railroads and pipelines, since they own their facilities, must cover the entire costs involved and, in addition, pay property taxes thereon, sometimes at discriminatory levels of assessment. Where the basic facilities are publicly provided, user charges must be relied upon to place the public costs equitably against the commercial users of those facilities if there is to be a cost basis for rates and fares that will attract traffic to those types of transport best suited to the traffic in question. Absence or inadequacy of charges for the use of public facilities will convey a cost advantage to the carriers using them, to the detriment of others that must cover full costs. Moreover, the nation may be harmed since the carriers which benefit may occasion total private plus public costs that exceed those of another mode, thus inflating the cost of the transportation service as a whole. When diversion is from carriers having high fixed costs, as do the railroads and pipelines, the unit costs of those carriers may also be increased in consequence of reduced traffic volume. To date pipelines have not been affected by such diversion.

In general, highway and airway user charges appeared to be adequate to fully compensate the public costs incurred on behalf of private users as long as inflation remained at modest levels. Many of the larger airports are also self-sustaining, or nearly so, from revenues generated by landing fees, rentals, and concessions. As we have seen, highways and airways are multiple-purpose facilities. Even if user charges are adequate in total, there is the question whether each class of user bears a fair share and a further question whether the system of charges divides costs equitably among users of segments of the transport infrastructure which have sharply different construction costs, for example, urban versus rural highway segments.

For a multiple-purpose facility, costs must be allocated to or apportioned against classes of users. There are numerous plausible methods by which this can be done, each of which has its supporters, involves an element of arbitrariness, and produces a different result.[9] In the case of the highways most methods of apportionment indicate that the heaviest class of vehicles are bearing less than adequate shares.[10] The easiest solution for this problem would appear to be increased taxation of diesel fuel which is characteristically used by these heavier vehicles.

Since public facilities are not taxed, user charges are compared with public costs that are less inclusive than the costs borne by railroads or pipelines. Interest on investment, if imputed, is also likely to reflect the lower interest rates characteristically available to governments. These factors, plus the benefits of common use with automobiles and other vehicles, as well as the possible inadequacies of user charges on the heaviest trucks, no doubt account for the fact that railroad right-of-way operating expenses plus interest charges account for nearly 20 percent of all railway operating expenses and fixed charges while truck user charges account for about 6.5 percent of total operating expenses. The disparity is important in respect to the ability of railways to compete. More important is the fact that highway user charges are variable expenses. They are escapable with a decline of business by the operation of fewer vehicle miles. Railway right-of-way expenses, on the other hand, are essentially fixed.

Since 1973 inflation has been a major national problem, often exceeding double-digit levels. Although some of the states have increased their user charges and a few have converted from cents per gallon to a percentage basis, federal charges have not been increased. At the same time, fuel usage actually declined in 1979 and 1980. The nation faces a new crisis of highway deterioration. During these inflationary years maintenance has been neglected. Much of the earlier Interstate mileage requires reconstruction, thousands of bridges need reconstruction or replacement, and state and local roads everywhere suffer from lack of maintenance. With highway "needs," including maintenance, estimated at from $543 billion to $766.5 billion for the period 1975–1990, The National Transportation Policy Study Commission in its medium growth scenario estimated a user-charge deficit of $32 billion for 1985 if present user charges are maintained.[11]

---

[9] The highway cost-allocation study responsive to Section 210 of the Highway Act of 1956 employed four methods: (1) incremental, (2) cost of function, (3) differential benefit, and (4) gross ton-mile. For two of the heaviest classes of vehicle the results ranged from a low of $1,084.70 annual required payments to a high of $3,143.70. *Final Report of the Highway Cost Allocation Study*, 87th Cong., 1st Sess., House Doc. no. 54 (1961), p. 17. See the discussion of method, pp. 188–242.

[10] And, in 1978, in an amendment to the Rail Passenger Service Act, intercity buses were exempted in view of the growing subsidies to Amtrak.

[11] National Study Commission, *National Transportation Policies*, p. 210, expressed in 1975 dollars.

COORDINATION OF GOVERNMENT INVESTMENT

Programs in each mode of transport developed autonomously, at different rates, and in somewhat different time periods. In addition, they were entrusted to separate administrative agencies: the Bureau of Public Roads for highways, the Civil Aeronautics Administration (now Federal Aviation Agency) for airways and airports, the Corps of Engineers and the Coast Guard for navigable waterways and aids to navigation. State and local governments employed equally disparate approaches. Rail and pipeline development remained in private hands. No coordinating mechanism was provided among the government agencies and programs, much less between the private and government sectors.

In the circumstances each major transport investment area developed its own clientele and its own political ties to the Congress. Engineering personnel achieved a high degree of specialization, a major devotion to particular classes of construction, and an inability to perceive relationships with other transport development or consequences for the economic and social structure of the nation. It became entirely possible for a large-capacity airport to be constructed at enormous cost without any provision being made for improved access either by highway or by some form of mass transit, since each of the three classes of facility was covered by different programs administered by separate agencies.

These difficulties were not unrecognized either at the federal or other government levels. Yet steps to effect coordination were so long deferred that the vested interests associated with each mode became powerfully entrenched. Despite the inclusion of both the Bureau of Public Roads and the Civil Aeronautics Administration within the Department of Commerce, little coordination was accomplished. The establishment of the Office of the Undersecretary of Commerce for Transportation in 1950 and the shift of the nonregulatory functions of the Maritime Commission to Commerce gave some promise of a beginning, yet little was achieved. In 1959 dispersion developed again when the independent Federal Aviation Administration was established. Since there were no federal investment programs relating to rail or pipeline transportation, these were rarely considered in relation to other investment programs. In particular the impact of highway or waterway investment upon the railroads was ignored, and the question of what might be the most economical solution of a problem was not asked.

Not until 1966 was a Federal Department of Transportation created by statute after numerous earlier attempts had failed.[12] Even then the

---

[12] The department was activated in the spring of 1967. The history of proposals and efforts to secure such a department, the provisions of law, and the organization of the

enabling statute specifically excluded from the department's purview the inland waterways programs of the Corps of Engineers and the functions of the Federal Maritime Administrator who continued to report to the secretary of commerce. Safety functions hitherto exercised by the regulatory agencies were transferred; hence some jurisdiction over railroads was lodged in the department, and its development role was conceived as extending to the rail industry. A Federal Railroad Administrator was included in the top administration of the department, and some research funds were secured. Establishment of the department does not insure coordination even of the investment programs within its jurisdiction. Organizational change does not remove the political power of vested interests, nor does a small top bureaucracy quickly secure control of major programs administered by the old and large organizations which are nominally placed under its control.

Able secretaries have headed the department since its inception. Its scope has been broadened to incorporate urban-transit planning and the administration of federal programs in this area. A wide range of research activity has been developed, including fundamental technological work in rail transport which hitherto had been left to the industry, which suffered from inadequacy both of commitment and of resources. More important, research under department auspices is capable of exploring intermodal solutions, the economics of modal choice, and other matters too broad for any of the constituent agencies to have undertaken. The kind of coordinated policy advice in transportation which the executive branch has long needed is beginning to come forward.

The department was charged with developing national transportation policy proposals which could result in a consistent and integrated approach to promotion, regulation, taxation, and other strands of policy hitherto dealt with on a fragmented basis. Not until 1971 was a major program brought forward and legislative proposals made. That program called for major revision of the regulatory structure, reform of tax and user-charge policies, and assistance for the modernization and improvement of the rail system. Much of the recent legislation outlined in Chapter 19 goes in directions sought by the department.

Not only has there been an imbalance in the development of intercity transport modes because of the government commitment to some and the private character of others, but until very recently there has been a practical moratorium on the consideration of any but highway solutions in the cities. Highways have benefitted from the enormous flow of user charges into federal and state coffers and from the availability of the credit of governments when bonding has seemed desirable. Railroads have been compelled to ration severely the limited

---

department are set forth in Grant Miller Davis, *The Department of Transportation* (Lexington, Mass.: D.C. Heath & Co., 1970).

flow of capital available to them in consequence of the inadequate earning power of the industry during most of the present century. As Sen. Harrison Williams of New Jersey pointed out in a 1962 statement, when state or local authorities seek an answer to a traffic problem "they are faced with the overwhelmingly powerful economic fact that they need put up only 10 percent of the cost of a highway solution, whereas they must contemplate bearing 100 percent of the cost of a transit solution. . . . Obviously this situation is not conducive to the establishment of a balanced urban transportation system, using transit where it is logically needed and using a highway where it is logically needed."[13] The Department of Transportation has been instrumental in broadening the scope of federal policy to incorporate assistance for ubran-transit improvement, being associated with most of the development we noticed in Chapter 8. Yet when local option is exercised to substitute a transit program for an urban segment of the Interstate system, the local share still increases to 20 percent.

INVESTMENT PROJECT ANALYSIS

The customary analysis of public transport investment projects is accomplished as a cost-benefit calculation where the land acquisition and construction costs are set against estimated benefit which will accrue to users of the facility over its expected life. When benefits exceed costs (a cost-benefit ratio in excess of 1), a project is usually considered justified. The cost-benefit ratios of various projects can also be compared when similar analyses have been employed in order to determine which project is superior among several which might serve a like purpose.

Obviously such analysis can be applied only after project ideas have been generated. As Ian Heggie puts it, only by starting with a list of project ideas, sorting them roughly by priority, and applying cost-benefit analysis to a short list of selected projects can there be assurance that the right projects are being studied.[14] But project generation is characteristically unsystematic. Many projects are put forward on political grounds. Others spring from the development of deficiencies in existing systems. It is in this sense that highway projects have been

---

[13] Statement before the Senate Committee on Banking and Currency, reprinted in George M. Smerk, ed., Readings in Urban Transportation (Bloomington: Indiana University Press, 1968), p. 70.

[14] Ian G. Heggie, Transport Engineering Economics [London: McGraw-Hill Book Co. (U.K.) 1972], p. 125. For a concise discussion of methodology applicable to selected projects, see Hans A. Adler, Economic Appraisal of Transport Projects: A Manual with Case Studies (Bloomington: Indiana University Press, 1971), chaps. 1–5. See also H. Georgi, Cost-Benefit Analysis and Public Investment in Transport: A Survey (London: Butterworth's, 1973).

said to be self-generating—they often spring from evidence of over-loading on segments of the existing network as a means to overcome observed congestion. The existing location pattern is frequently taken for granted in this process, and possible alternatives left unexplored.

Basic transportation facilities often have long expected lives; hence a stream of prospective benefits extending far into the future. Uncertainty of benefit estimates increases with the expected life of the project. Construction cost estimates are characteristically in error by a wide margin. Underestimates are especially common in inflationary periods or when estimates are based on exploratory rather than final surveys. Both the appropriate life to assume (e.g., on a waterway project, 50, 75, or 100 years?) and the appropriate discount rate are open to dispute. Maintenance costs are frequently conjectural.

On the benefit side, the American Association of State Highway Officials counsels inclusion of the following factors:

1. Land and community benefits.
2. Direct benefits to road users (reduced vehicle operating costs and savings in time).
3. Benefits to road users in increased comfort and convenience.
4. Benefits in overall accident reduction.

Only construction and maintenance costs were to be incorporated in the analysis, no allowance being made for such social costs as disruption of communities or displacement of existing land uses.[15]

It is not difficult to place a dollar value on reduced vehicle-operating costs. The other benefits are more speculative. What dollar value is to be assigned to a reduced number of injuries and deaths in accidents? How does one quantify improved convenience? Little is known about how people evaluate savings in time, though it clearly makes a difference whether ten minutes or an hour is saved on a trip and whether working or leisure time is at issue. Yet justification frequently turns on the estimates for such benefits. A reduction of a few minutes in travel time multiplied by thousands of daily trips and priced out at the average wage rate can generate impressive aggregate "benefits." In evaluating the Victoria subway line in London, a social-surplus rate of return of 11.3 percent was calculated on the basis of 6 percent interest, 5½ years of construction, and 50 years of operation. Of 6.793 million pounds of estimated benefits, 3.366 million were attributable to time savings and 0.804 million to "comfort and convenience."[16]

---

[15] Paul Weiner and Edward J. Deak, *Environmental Factors in Transportation Planning* (Lexington, Mass.: D. C. Heath & Co., 1972), p. 5. The first chapter of this book provides a good survey of cost-benefit practice.

[16] C. D. Foster and M. E. Beesley, "The Victoria Line," in Denys Munby, ed., *Transport: Selected Readings* (Harmondsworth, Middlesex: Penguin Books, Ltd., 1968), chap. 9.

Robert Haveman, after comparing the actual results of selected water resource projects with the *ex ante forecasts*, finds consistent overstatement of expected benefits. He concludes that the need to improve evaluation of primary benefits and costs is so great that it may be a misdirected effort to look at secondary and nonefficiency effects, for example, impacts on income distribution.[17] Roger Creighton has argued for a goal definable in transport cost terms: minimum investment in relation to maximum saving of time, operating cost, and accident exposure. More complex goals may render it difficult to measure what is best in relation to those goals or render it impossible to find a "best" plan, hence to secure a clear-cut decision.[18] Yet failure to incorporate in the analysis such effects as generation of pollutants, aesthetic degradation, industrial and residential dislocation, and community disruption seem likely to explain the inability to secure acceptance of many planned major urban expressways. Despite the difficulties, it seems inevitable that such factors be brought to bear in the light of the concerns which increasingly move the public.[19] In any event, environmental impact statements are now required, and the adequacy of such statements may be challenged in the courts.

User-charge policies are not unrelated to project evaluation. Under present undifferentiated user-charge policies, project analysis proceeds in the face of demand that is uncontrolled by charges which reflect the cost of the specific project. No higher charges are placed upon users of an urban freeway that may have cost $6.5 million a mile than upon users of a rural segment that may have cost $250,000 a mile. Nor does the system of charges take any account of timing of use by differentiating between peak-period and off-peak use. Given uncontrolled demand the only possible response of the highway planner to congestion is to attempt to provide enough highway capacity to cope with peak-period use. This has proved to be a never-ending and self-defeating battle. Indeed costs of congestion on the highways of the United States have been estimated to exceed $5 billion a year. More specific and rational pricing for the use of public transport facilities is clearly needed which places the costs of peak-period capacity on the peak-period users, an approach that has come to be called *congestion pricing*.

As Beesley points out, the large urban transport studies have had substantial success in establishing road-investment priorities where

[17] Robert H. Haveman, *The Economic Performance of Public Investments: An Ex Post Evaluation of Water Resources Investments* (Baltimore: Johns Hopkins University Press, 1972), p. 111.

[18] Roger L. Creighton, *Urban Transportation Planning* (Urbana: University of Illinois Press, 1970), p. 212.

[19] One approach which seeks to poll samples of the public in search of values and priorities is discussed in Weiner and Deak, *Environmental Factors*, chaps. 4–6.

other means of transport are of little importance. But they have had little success where alternatives are important, and they are entirely unable to establish the total size of an appropriate highway program.[20] Congestion charging not only would place heavier costs upon vehicles operating in congested areas and at peak hours but would reduce charges at present made in noncongested areas and at off-peak hours. Hence it would affect demand in favor of improved highway utilization. It has a clear function, also, in investment procedures of the cost-benefit type, for it increases the variance of observed costs and trip times for various classes of vehicle and it opens up alternatives that cannot now be appraised.[21]

Along similar lines it may be observed that while in principle user charges ought to be assessed upon the improved inland waterways in order to generate competitive equity and improved modal choice, the fuel tax which has at long last been enacted is a mischievous way to attempt to recover federal costs. The fuel tax has the merit of ease of collection which is one reason for its popularity. But the costs of waterway improvements in relation to traffic volume vary enormously from one segment of the waterway system to another. A fuel tax adequate to recoup annual federal costs would place unjustifiable burdens upon the traffic moved on the most efficient segments.

ECONOMICS VERSUS POLITICS

The tools of economics applicable to project evaluation have serious limitations despite a great deal of recent work. Yet the problem of more effective allocation of public funds for transport purposes is essentially one of politics. The same is true of vehicle size and weight limitations upon the highways and of user-charge policies. Economic theory can contribute arguments, sometimes useful in influencing political decision, but economic method itself takes account only of some of the objectives that may be relevant for policy. Highway, waterway, and airport development are all heavily influenced by local aspirations whatever may be the more elevated approaches to investment taken at the federal level. The "highway bulldozer" reflects the fact that state

---

[20] M. E. Beesley, "Technical Possibility of Special Taxation in Relation to Congestion Caused by Private Users," in European Conference of Ministers of Transport, Second International Symposium on Theory and Practice in Transport Economics (1965), p. 412.

[21] Ibid., p. 413; cf. Conrad J. Oort, "The Theory of Economic Efficiency as Applied to the Road Transport Industry," paper delivered at the American University International Symposium on Transportation Pricing (1969). The broader issue of pricing to reshape patterns of transit and highway use, is discussed, among other things, in Richard R. Carll, "Some Observations on Urban Transport Planning and Its Relationship to Comprehensive Transportation Planning," Transportation Journal, vol. 14, no. 3 (Spring 1975), pp. 18–29.

agencies, whose primary responsibilities are to construct and maintain highways, are staffed with that limited purpose in mind, are important sources of patronage, and command access to continuing monetary flows. In general, the outlook becomes more parochial the closer the actual work is approached.[22] All functioning agencies place self-perpetuation high in the order of their objectives.

Waterways projects fall in one of those few remaining areas characterized by "pork-barrel" legislation. Projects in one part of the country are traded for projects in another. Cost-benefit ratios in excess of 1 are required, but one or more restudies at congressional behest can usually generate the required ratio. The stimulus to local industry afforded by a navigable waterway may be considerable. But benefit is also to be had from the construction expenditures, and that prospect may be sufficient justification for a congressman to seek a project. Whether or not significant traffic develops on an improved waterway, rail rates will be affected downward and transportation benefits will accrue to local industry.

In 1964, following a great deal of criticism by economists of its methods of cost-benefit analysis of waterway projects, the Corps of Engineers of the Army revised them. Instead of comparing prospective barge operating costs with existing rail rates in calculating benefits, the Corps moved to compare prospective nonwater-compelled rail rates with prospective barge rates. This was a more justifiable procedure, but it made it more difficult for projects to qualify with the requisite cost-benefit ratio. The Congress was dissatisfied; and in Section 7 of the legislation which established the Department of Transportation, it mandated that "savings to shippers shall be construed to mean the difference between (a) the freight rates or charges prevailing at the time of the study for a movement by the alternative means and (b) those which would be charged on the proposed waterway. . . ." Over-estimating of traffic, and therefore of benefits, result. More recently Congress has frozen the discount rate of 5⅝ percent despite the much higher rates now paid on government obligations.[23]

The Penn Central disaster of June 21, 1970, has revived concern about the possible necessity of a government takeover of some or all of the railway system. The history of American public investment in transport where, because of multiple use, government most appropriately operates has not been of the kind to recommend extension into other areas. Whatever the experience in other countries, the American political system is in many respects unique. Its characteristics strongly

---

[22] Melvin R. Levin and Norman A. Abend, *Bureaucrats in Collision: Case Studies in Area Transportation Planning* (Cambridge: M.I.T. Press, 1971), pp. 15–16.

[23] Reported in *Traffic World*, March 18, 1974, p. 75.

suggest the likelihood that the outstanding problems of the rail industry which urgently require solution would become even more intractable within a system of control that would become, unavoidably, more politically oriented.[24]

Congress is not unaware of the risks of direct control of railways; yet where only massive federal aid can preserve necessary facilities and services, to pour in money without providing control of its use is also risky in fact and in politics. Much of the 1973 legislative session was devoted to working out the Regional Rail Reorganization Act of 1973 which was signed by the president on January 2, 1974. The act provided for a United States Railway Association charged with recommending to Congress a plan for restructuring, feeding in operating subsidy to keep the lines going in the interim, and financing a Consolidated Rail Corporation and Amtrak.

The USRA is a nonprofit association with a board composed of a chairman designated by the president, the secretary of transportation, the chairman of the ICC, the secretary of the treasury, and nongovernment members nominated by the president and confirmed by the Senate. These were recommended by the Association of American Railroads (1), the AFL-CIO (1), the National Governors Conference (1), the National League of Cities and Conference of Mayors (1), shipper groups (2), and financial interests (1). Thus all parties at interest are represented on the board. An effort by the Department of Transportation to take over its functions was defeated early in 1980.

CONRAIL AND OTHER RAIL ASSISTANCE

Nearly three years were consumed in developing a final system plan for six of the failed Northeastern railroads (Boston and Maine opted for a Section 77 reorganization). In 1976 the Consolidated Rail Corporation (Conrail) secured transference of these roads and commenced operation as a private, for profit, corporation with a board of directors composed of two Conrail officers, five representatives of the bankrupt estates and six members chosen by USRA. No member of the board is a government employee. Compensation for the estates is still in litigation before the special court established by the 3–R Act and USRA represents the government interest in that litigation. Late in 1980, by agree-

---

[24] On the experience abroad, see James N. Sites, *Quest for Crisis* (New York: Simmons-Boardman Publishing Co., 1963); Ernest W. Williams, Jr., "Railways Are in Distress: Worldwide," *Columbia Journal of World Business*, vol. 6, no. 2 (March–April 1971), pp. 22 ff.; Union Pacific Railroad Company, *A Brief Survey of the Railroads of Principal Industrial Countries*, February 1971; A. W. J. Thomason and L. C. Hunter, *The National Transport Industries* (London: Heinemann Educational Books, 1973), chap. 3.

ment between the government and the Penn Central estate, compensation for the Penn Central properties was settled.

Despite the enormous effort devoted to development of the final plan it is plain, in retrospect, that many of its assumptions (e.g., level of traffic, improvement of equipment utilization) were unduly optimistic. In addition, the condition of the roads at the time of transfer was worse than anticipated. But the more serious constraints were of political origin—local and state opposition prevented a sufficient cutback in the operated mileage while union insistence on labor protection deterred profitable roads from taking over portions of the system.[25] The transition to Conrail was unexpectedly smooth and good progress was made in its early years in improving the quality of service, upgrading the property and reducing deficits. Two successive hard winters, a prolonged coal strike, the Johnstown flood and other external events, however, produced a heavier drawdown of government funding than was anticipated in 1977–78.[26]

By the beginning of 1980, Conrail had taken $2.8 billion of the $3.3 billion of government funding authorized.[27] The recession had hit hard, especially since the automotive and steel industries are major Conrail customers. Carloadings were off 20 percent, deficits growing, and maintenance again being deferred. In its "business plan" Conrail offered several alternatives, but the prospects were of a need for $900 million in additional funding promptly, growing to perhaps $4 billion of government funding before that elusive break-even could be attained. It is by now plain that political unwillingness to face reality in the early 70s has left us an unresolved problem of major magnitude. The possibility of direct government operation, government assumption of rail rights of way, or some other approach to nationalization is clearly not removed.

No new Conrails have yet been established. Recent midwest bankruptcies have been dealt with in a different way. Rock Island, which went into bankruptcy in 1975, is in the process of liquidation. Directed service was conducted for a period at the expense of the federal government. Portions of the road have been or will be purchased by other roads and continued in service, but the bulk of the 7,000-mile system has permanently closed operations. Roughly 1,000 miles between Santa Rosa, New Mexico, and St. Louis were purchased by Cotton

---

[25] It is not unlikely that Conrail, representing some 20 percent of the nation's rail traffic, is too large to be effectively managed. The point received attention during the planning stage and has recently been revived.

[26] See John L. Hazard, "Government Railroading," *Transportation Journal*, vol. 19, no. 3 (Spring 1980), pp. 38, 45–46.

[27] For a chronology on Conrail see William K. Smith, "The USRA-Conrail Concept: An Inappropriate Model for Federal Planning and Funding of Railroads in the 1980s," *Transportation Journal*, vol. 19, no. 3 (Spring 1980), pp. 51, 58–60.

Belt. The Chicago suburban lines are being operated for the account of the Chicago Transit Authority. Some other sections will continue under other auspices.[28]

Bankrupt Milwaukee's system was trimmed down to a core which is expected ultimately to become self-sustaining. All service was discontinued west of Miles City, Montana, and various lines east of that point also saw cessation of service. Union Pacific, Burlington Northern, and other roads are acquiring portions of the discontinued properties. Montana, South Dakota, and Wisconsin plan resumption of service on some of Milwaukee's trackage through private contractors or otherwise. These western lines were not of the same national importance as those covered into Conrail, comparatively little freight traffic will be affected by their discontinuance and the oversupply of trackage in the midwest is now at least somewhat reduced.

The 4–R Act provided assistance to railroads other than Conrail. One billion dollars of loan guarantees plus an authorized government purchase of $600 million of preference shares were designed to assist in track and equipment rehabilitation. Only a portion of these funds have been taken down. But the 1980 act authorizes an additional $700 million, of which $200 million is to be made available to Conrail for reducing the size of its work force. In addition, the act authorized $329 million in emergency funding for Conrail during fiscal 1981.

Both Rock Island and Milwaukee benefitted to some extent, but perhaps the outstanding government support of line upgrading is on the Northwestern main line between Chicago and its connection with Union Pacific at Fremont, Nebraska. States, localities, and private industry are assisting in the finance of rehabilitation to preserve rail service, particularly in the Midwest.[29] Meanwhile, well-located roads which benefit from the growing industralization of the south and southwest, from increased coal traffic and from heavy movements of grain, booked record earnings in 1979. New steps to cure the drain of Conrail should not be long delayed.

SELECTED REFERENCES

Burch, Philip H., Jr. *Highway Revenues and Expenditure Policy in the United States.* New Brunswick, N.J.: Rutgers University Press, 1962.

Creighton, Roger L. *Urban Transportation Planning.* Urbana: University of Illinois Press, 1970.

---

[28] See the account of Rock Island's last president, John W. Ingram, "Government and the Midwest Railroads: Notes on the Demise of the Chicago, Rock Island and Pacific Railroad Company," *Transportation Journal*, vol. 19, no. 3 (Spring 1980), pp. 29 ff.

[29] For an account of such a program in Iowa, see *Railway Age*, July 14, 1980, p. 30.

Dearing, Charles L. *American Highway Policy.* Washington, D.C.: The Brookings Institution, 1941.

Dearing, Charles L., and Owen, Wilfred. *National Transportation Policy.* Washington, D.C.: The Brookings Institution, 1949.

Eckstein, Otto. *Water Resource Development: The Economics of Project Evaluation.* Cambridge: Harvard University Press, 1971.

Haveman, Robert H. *The Economic Performance of Public Investments: An Ex Post Evaluation of Water Resources Investments,* chaps. 1 and 3. Baltimore: The Johns Hopkins University Press, 1972.

Heggie, Ian G. *Transport Engineering Economics.* London: McGraw-Hill Book Co. (U.K.), 1972.

Hull, William J., and Hull, Robert W. *The Origin and Development of the Waterways Policy of the United States.* Washington, D.C.: National Waterways Conference, Inc., 1967.

Levin, Melvin R., and Abend, Norman A. *Bureaucrats in Collision: Case Studies in Area Transportation Planning.* Cambridge: M.I.T. Press, 1971.

Lindholm, Richard W. *Public Finance of Air Transportation.* Columbus: The Ohio State University, 1943.

National Transportation Policy Study Commission. *National Transportation Policies through the Year 2000.* Washington, D.C.: U.S. Government Printing Office, June 1979.

Owen, Wilfred. *The Metropolitan Transportation Problem.* Rev. ed. Washington, D.C.: The Brookings Institution, 1966.

Smerk, George M., ed. *Readings in Urban Transportation.* Bloomington: Indiana University Press, 1968.

United States Department of Transportation. *National Transportation Trends and Choices (to the year 2000).* Washington, D.C.: U.S. Government Printing Office, January 1977.

United States Senate, Special Study Group of Foreign and Interstate Commerce Committee. *National Transportation Policy.* 1961.

Warford, Jeremy. *Public Policy toward General Aviation.* Washington, D.C.: The Brookings Institution, 1971.

Weiner, Paul, and Deak, Edward J. *Environmental Factors in Transportation Planning.* Lexington, Mass.: D. C. Heath & Co., 1972.

24

National Transportation Policy

There is general agreement about the overall economic objective of a national transportation policy. An optimal share of the nation's economic resources should be devoted to transportation: there is at any time a right or best proportion to further the nation's economy. At a given stage of the arts there should be an optimal distribution of transportation resources among the several modes, including integrated multimodal services. Only by strict adherence to both of these requirements can the national product be optimized so far as transportation contributes. Under such a policy there would be no investment in a transportation facility or service that required subsidy, nor would public investment be permitted in a facility of one mode to perform a service which could be better or more economically performed by comparable investment in another mode.

However, economic efficiency has never been the sole criterion of national transportation policy. Other considerations have included (1) long-range regional development, (2) aid in the development of a new mode of transportation, (3) promotion or restriction of competition, (4) direct or indirect subsidy to localities and groups which would otherwise not have desired service, (5) national defense, and (6) local political interests. Certainly there are occasions for deviation from strict economic efficiency in recognition of other social considerations, but if these deviations are not to get out of hand and promote wasteful investment and inefficient operations, a framework of national policy that seeks to develop and regulate all modes to the end of maximum economic benefit is essential. The federal government's policy cannot be said to approximate such a framework in spite of the declared objective of national transportation policy set forth in the 1940 preamble of the Interstate Commerce Act. Uncoordinated and inconsistent policies have persisted, and obsolete regulations have been retained long after conditions which gave rise to them disappeared. The principal obstacles and problems that have prevented progress towards a more adequate framework of policy approach merit the examination which follows.

Because railroad transportation has been essentially a common-carrier industry, the rapid growth of private intercity transportation by motor and barge has created a whole new environment for national transportation policy. Large areas of exemption in for-hire motor and water transport contribute to that change of circumstances. The assumption that a common-carrier system is to remain the prime basis of national transportation service and policy is now being questioned by some.

The growth of private motorcar transportation has resulted in a deterioration of public passenger transport except between major air centers. Large urban areas have experienced a degeneration of both commuter service and urban rapid transit. While automobile traffic has expanded by leaps and bounds in these metropolitan areas, local bus, commuter, and subway train patronage have declined and, except for the morning and evening peak service, all but disappeared. Yet a substantial minority must depend upon the public transport if the economy of the total community is to be maintained. The result has been a growing public support by city, county, and state governments for these services. The automobile has caused intercity passenger train service to be curtailed and often eliminated, nor has it been replaced by comparable air or bus service. Those who do not have cars or who prefer not to drive find that their service needs are not being met.

The influence of politics presents a real obstacle to economic policy in transportation. Because public interest is so pronounced in this area, local, state, and federal politics have influenced the creation of and timing of public, and sometimes of private, investment in improved transportation routes. Waterway developments historically have been shaped largely by pork-barrel politics in Congress. Traffic volume, actual and potential, is not the dominant consideration in the construction and rebuilding of the federal highway system. Air service to smaller cities and communities requires extensive subsidy even though use of the service is minimal.

As a result of independent development and separate promotion and regulation, the dominant relationship among the modes has been competitive and not coordinative. The segments of the traffic spectrum for which the modes compete has tended to become ever larger. Cutthroat rate competition reminiscent of that which prevailed among the overbuilt railroads in the 1870s and early 1880s has appeared despite the tempering influence of regulation.

Transportation policy is rarely designed to further or permit coordination or integration of the several modes. The Panama Canal Act, precipitated by the desire to prevent railroad throttling of intercoastal general-cargo shipping through the canal, remains on the statute books as a general prohibition of railroad control of or interest in domestic water transportation as an adjunct to rail service. And the 1980 rail act makes clear that the commission's discretion to exempt from regulation does not extend to intermodal ownership.

THE GOAL OF AN OPTIMUM TRANSPORTATION SYSTEM

The problem of a balanced system of transportation employing each mode to maximize adequate and efficient service involves the necessary adjustment of the railroad industry and associated equipment industries to present-day realities and the establishment of federal regulation and aid in respect to the various modes according to their economic character and fitness.

The precipitous decline of the railroad industry since the mid-20s presents a serious problem of adjustment. What happened to its traffic that went to other modes?[1] The two basic sets of external factors are (1) the dynamics of transport technology and market structure and (2) the varying aspects of public policy in regulation, aid, taxes, and labor among the modes. To these external factors must be added the lack of flexibility and skill of railroad management to deal with the new competitive environment.

In the 20th century new modes have developed as powerful alternatives and competitors of the railroads. Prior to the second quarter of this century these modes were all relatively small, whose operations were devoted to local service and were in no way competitive with the railroads. Motor trucks were small, many with solid rubber tires, moving over crude roads; pipelines were not over six inches in diameter; barges were pushed by low-powered units; and the aircraft technologically was immature and of no commercial importance. But the next two decades saw the motor-freight vehicle become a large, high-speed unit, able to carry 10 to 42 tons over superhighways; pipelines came to have 20- to 36-inch diameters, with powerful diesel or electric pumping stations; and airlines came to dominate long-distance commercial travel with jet aircraft carrying several hundred passengers at near or above sonic speed.

---

[1] For more extensive analyses of the answer see U.S. Senate, Special Study Group of Foreign and Interstate Commerce Committee, *National Transportation Policy* (1961), pp. 67–71.

Motor transportation which became the chief competitor in both passenger and freight traffic was stimulated by spiraling public aid and a powerfully concentrated motor-vehicle manufacturing industry, providing research to insure rapid development of the motor highway vehicle. Pipeline transportation advanced rapidly without direct government aid because of the burgeoning demand for oil created by motor-vehicle transportation and the vast resources of the major petroleum producing and refining companies. The big-inch pipelines, operating at a significant cost advantage, quickly replaced the railroads in overland movement of crude and petroleum products, thereby denying the railroads a real traffic bonanza. Industrial developments at river locations by large power, alumina, chemical, and steel plants created a whole new traffic potential for the barge lines which were developing powerful diesel-driven towboats handling huge tows, thanks to improved government-provided locks.

While the technical advances in barge, motor, air, and pipeline transport have been phenomenal, that of the railroads has been slow and pedestrian. The resemblance of the railroads today to those of 1910 is all too striking. Gradients are relatively unchanged. Standardization of container systems and other equipment is generally not well advanced. It has long been recognized that large automated freight trains, operating over low gradients on heavy-duty track, offer a potential combination of cost and expedition in service not approximated by the present competing modes. Yet no real progress toward this end has been made. Government has not substantially aided and the industry has not pooled its resources for exploratory research.

The result has been an incursion of other modes on the traffic spectrum of the nation to a degree far greater than, in all likelihood, would have occurred if technological advance of railroads had been comparable. The disparity makes it more difficult to assess the components of a national transportation policy to attain the objective of an optimum system. As each mode took on major proportions, a separate program of policies became attached to it. These related to aid, regulation, taxation, and labor. Increasing aid has been given to water, highway, and air transport with none for pipelines and, until recently, none in modern times to railroads. While economic regulation of railroads has been coextensive with the industry and over the years increasing in degree, it has remained more limited for highway, air, and pipeline transportation and nonexistent for over 90 percent of domestic water transportation. Taxation of right-of-way in the form of local real estate taxes has represented a great burden only to the railroads. Labor conditions and costs have varied because different unions are involved. Since the railroad-pension system is somewhat more generous than social security to which motor and water carriers contribute, the railroads' burden has been greater.

Congress did provide for a comparable scope of regulation of rates of rail, motor, air, and water common carriers and comparable control over entry and operating rights of motor and air carriers. Here the parallel largely ceases. Regulation of air commerce is under a separate agency, and other aspects of regulation are different. In some respects the policies applied to the transportation modes have been parallel, but always separate. Powerful associations have developed to sponsor the development of waterway, highway, and air transportation. Congressional reorganization, designed to reduce the power of committee chairmen, unfortunately split jurisdiction over transportation. Hence the 4-R Act coming through one set of committees dealt only with railroads and created a new disparity between rail- and motor-carrier regulation. That disparity is enlarged by the motor and rail acts of 1980.

Until 1920 the nation was in the process of developing a railroad policy to meet the nation's transportation needs. The development of the other major modes has been accompanied by a separate national policy respecting the promotion (except for pipelines) and regulation of each. We have, therefore, really had railroad, highway, air and pipeline policies, not a national transportation policy, designed to blend the modes together into a sound and efficient transport system. The nation has been less successful in this 20th century challenge than it was in pushing out the frontier with a base system of rail transportation in the 19th century and in developing regulation of that system.

A NATIONAL TRANSPORTATION POLICY

In previous chapters, summarized here, we have set forth the excessive costs and obstacles to progress caused by the development of separate policies for the newer modes initiated to realize their potential advantages. Unfortunately these are perpetuated today by separate government agencies and vested private interests. An adequate transportation policy may be stated as: to find ways to use the variety of transportation services available to us, severally and in combination one with another to the end that the transportation required by the economy will be performed most efficiently.

Congress included a statement on national transportation policy in the act of 1940 which, in part, reads: "It is hereby declared to be the national transportation policy of the Congress to provide for fair and impartial regulation of all modes—subject to the provisions of this Act, so administered as to recognize and preserve the inherent advantages of each." However, powerful carrier lobbying interests compelled reference to prohibiting "destructive competition" which has been used to perpetuate the status quo in defiance of the dynamic concept of in-

488

herent advantage or economic fitness. In addition to the built-in ambiguity there is the fact that it applied only to the modes under the jurisdiction of the Interstate Commerce Commission which does not include air transport under CAB, the deep-sea transport under the Federal Maritime Commission and the Maritime Administration of the Department of Commerce or pipelines now under the Department of Energy.

According to a 1971 study on national transportation policy by the Department of Transportation, "The basic infrastructure of transportation is, in fact, in place."[2] Assuming that this is basically true, there is a clear opportunity to deal with what is required to realize the optimum of an efficient coordinated transportation system. How can we best meet the growing elements of continued growth of population and the nation's economy in respect to both goods and passenger services?

BASIC REQUIREMENTS OF A MORE EFFECTUAL POLICY

These requirements include (1) *adjustment and modernization of the railroad structure and organization,* (2) *equity in government treatment of the modes,* (3) *rationalization of public aid,* (4) *rationalization of regulation,* and (5) *coordination in federal administration.*

Adjustment of Railroad Structure and Organization

Consideration and application of the basic requirements should be shaped by a visualization of the optimum national system of transport in the light of modern technology and the prospect of an enduring energy crisis. As brought out in Chapter 12, the long-haul movement of bulk commodities is an important aspect of our large productive nation. While water carriers and pipelines accommodate important segments of this demand for service, the railroads remain the principal mode of volume transportation.

Railroad freight traffic in 1979 reached a record 902 billion ton-miles, which was 5.2 percent over the previous year. The energy crisis may well result in an accelerated erosion of long-haul truckload traffic and a return to railroad service by way of TOFC expansion and much regular carload traffic. Nevertheless, the railroad industry continues to deteriorate because of the absence of policies respecting rates, equipment, restructuring of way, mergers, and abandonment that are required to adjust this industry to its new and more specialized role in the transport system. There are carrier exceptions, but the rail industry as a whole is facing a crisis which threatens the very existence of privately-owned railroads.

---

[2] U.S. Department of Transportation, *A Statement on National Transportation Policy* (1971), p. 40.

Conrail, although relieved of passenger deficits by Amtrak and the variously financed public-commuter operations, incurred a loss of traffic in 1979 and a consequent loss of revenue of over $500 million, which was worse than the largest aggregate deficits of the composite railroads. The Milwaukee and the Rock Island remained insolvent after years of misspent effort. What is called for is a frontal attack on the entire structure of railroads of the continental United States, abandoning thousands of miles where motor freight, in coordination with railroad operation, can better meet the required needs. In connection with such a development, merger of all railroads into a limited number of systems, possibly no more than eight, which would provide competition at all major points should be consummated. This should get priority in a broad policy program.

The mounting problems of air pollution and fuel costs cast serious doubts on the future of highway transportation. A 1971 report revealed that 44.5 percent of pollutants emitted into the atmosphere came from automobile, truck, and bus emissions.[3] Fuel costs per ton-mile and passenger-mile far exceed those in well-utilized railroad operations. The visualization of the optimum structure of the nation's transportation system and the policies of public aid and regulation should take this problem into account.

Equity in Government Treatment of the Modes

The principal alternative solution to simplistic free competition, so far as the rail carriers are concerned, is the achievement of equity in competition and coordination. This, they insist, includes removal of regulations peculiar to the railroads, adequate sharing by highway interests in rail-crossing eliminations, relief from right-of-way taxation by states and counties, and retirement benefits comparable to those of motor and barge carriers. Congress has seen fit to establish more liberal retirement benefits for railway employees than for any other class and to place a heavier burden of taxation upon both the carriers and their employees to maintain this system. The railroad retirement and unemployment outlay in 1969 amounted to 9.94 percent of the payroll. This compared with 4.37 percent for retirement and unemployment insurance paid by Class I interstate truck firms in the same year. In view of the near bankruptcy of the Railroad Retirement System, payroll taxes were substantially increased in 1973, and the whole increase was placed upon the carriers. It is not apparent that railroad employees should be singled out for more liberal treatment than others. The entire policy calls for critical reexamination. This is especially true since one of the most astonishing factors in the financial

---

[3] Ibid., p. 14.

condition of the railroads is the increase in the tax load. Thus the 1970 payment for taxes was $1,068,518,015 compared to $275,800,000 in 1921. This rate of increase is well above that for industry at large and compares with an increase of only 56 percent in gross revenues during the same period.

Since so much of the inequity faced by the railroads is associated with their peculiar responsibility to maintain and improve their right-of-way facilities, while competing modes have the investment in ways made by public expenditures, the suggestion of the 1940 Transportation Study of the National Resources Planning Board for government acquisition of rights-of-way has received increasing attention. Yet no one has come forward with a practical scheme for instituting such a plan. A possible substitute is right-of-way subsidy, especially in the light of the fact that federal standards for the safety of track which were recently promulgated will call for larger expenditures than the railroads can make. Since the mid-50s, nearly stable freight-traffic volumes and vanishing passenger business have resulted in very low net earnings for most and insolvency for many. The result has been grossly neglected maintenance and replacement of way. The vision of larger- and heavier-tonnage trains and fast, short freight trains and a revival of passenger service is impossible to realize in the forseeable future, unless this condition is corrected. Many students of the problem have questioned the recommendation of the staff of the National Resources Board because of the inherent relationship of way facilities with train operation. The authors have shared this concern, but the increase of railroad accidents and the requirements of the future would seem to justify government investment in way. Hopefully, railroad management would be permitted to set the standards and perhaps be responsible for maintenance. It would at least serve as a giant step toward equality in intercarrier cooperation and competition.

The railroad industry in its efforts to adjust its plant investment and over-all costs to meet the new competitive situation faces a number of serious handicaps. One need is greater freedom to abandon unprofitable light-traffic mileage and where necessary, to substitute highway service as a part of the railroad system. Where such lines cannot carry themselves financially, the interests of localities along them and of railway employees must give way to the larger national interest in a sound, basic rail-transport network. The luxury of branches which sap the net revenues of vital railway systems can no longer be sustained. If local interests insist upon the retention of rail service in such circumstances, the burden of losses should rightly fall upon them. Some movement could occur in this direction as a consequence of provisions of the 1980 act designed to assist the sale of low-traffic lines to shippers and other parties and to open the door to rail-connected motor carrier services.

User charges should be applied to competing modes that are adequate to cover public expense for ways and terminals so that rates charged by them would cover all costs and imputed taxes. Competitive traffic of water and motor carriers presently exempt from regulation should be equally exempt for railroads. Finally, government aid for construction and research should be equitably allocated among the modes. That sound economic requirement is *equity* and not *uniformity* or *equality* as some studies have concluded.[4] Both terms overlook the fundamental differences in the technology and the structural aspects of the operation of the several modes.

The most discriminating aspect of the tax situation is to be found in those instances where cooperative efforts between federal and state agencies are not effective. Lack of such cooperation suggests action in the long-discussed matter of federal incorporation of the railroads. In the event of such incorporation the assessment of local real estate taxes could be subject to federal control if not eliminated. Taxes on corporate earnings could be allocated to the states according to earnings from traffic moving in the various states through which a railroad possesses route mileage.

It is desirable to relieve railroads of burdens imposed primarily for the benefit of other forms of transport, notably of the costs of grade-crossing elimination and of the alteration or replacement of structures over navigable waterways occasioned by the improvement of such waterways as an aid to navigation. The increase of highway and waterway traffic has made these improvements necessary, although at times it is merely an expected increase in waterway traffic that occasions the project, an increase to be achieved largely by the diversion of traffic from the railroads. Most of the cost of such work has, nevertheless, fallen upon the railroads.

These items serve to point up the urgent need to make possible a reduction in railroad costs in the public interest. Unfortunately, the Interstate Commerce Commission, except for the matter of abandonments under the existing statute, has so little authority over these matters that its position in rate-level control is impossible. The commission is not authorized to set up standards of efficiency or to enforce them, although efficiency is a stated condition in the rate-making rule. Other federal agencies, without consultation with the commission, grant wage increases and shorter hours to railroad labor, increase retirement benefits, and construct and improve competing transport facilities. Neither management nor the government can control the general level of prices for materials or wage rates; it is determined by general economic conditions. However, labor costs incident to exces-

---

[4] National Transportation Policy Study Commission, *National Transportation Policies through the Year 2000* (June 1979), p. 372.

sive rules concessions, bad timing in wage increases, retirement and social insurance expense, and taxes are all subject to some degree of federal control, but by agencies other than the Interstate Commerce Commission.

Rationalization of Public Aid

Effort should be made to compel each mode or type of domestic transport, except commuter-rail passenger service, to pay its full costs. Public aid has been extended to each mode of transportation during its period of experimentation and early extension. This has the advantage of hastening the development of a mode, permitting it to prove its inherent advantages earlier than would otherwise be possible. Public aid too frequently encouraged wasteful construction and extension of service. It was only in the Civil Aeronautics Act that Congress sought in the early period of development to establish a control which would attempt to provide for orderly development of a subsidized carrier industry.

An appropriate economic adjustment among the carriers requires, among other things, the development of neutrality in promotional policies among the modes of transportation and the subjection to economic standards of further government participation in the construction of transportation plant. Although some progress has been made in assessing user charges, present policies are far from adequate. Such a system is essential. Moreover, governments continue to undertake projects which have little or no economic justification by applying political rather than economic standards in their evaluation. This involves economic waste, for it provides facilities whose potential use cannot justify the expense.

To favor one transportation agency among several that are well developed and have, therefore, reached the stage of rapid expansion or maturity is a policy designed to prevent rather than promote the employment of each mode of transport according to its economy and fitness. All modes are well advanced in the United States. Nevertheless, the progress of public aid to all the nonrail carriers goes on unabated. Over $34 billion of federal funds goes annually to nonrailroad facilities.

Highway carriers in most states are charged taxes which approximate a user charge. A carrier's tax should equal but not exceed a reasonable charge for the use of the publicly provided highway, waterway, or airway. The use of special carrier taxes in a general tax fund is objectionable in principle. The now well-developed domestic water carriers now bear user charges, but they are minimal and do not cover all public expenses on the waterways. Because of the extensive noncommercial use of the highway, the estimate of a fair user charge to highway commercial carriers is more difficult than it would be for water and air carriers. It is impossible to show precisely to what extent the highway carriers pay their own way.

Public aid to air transportation and the merchant marine has been largely justified as a measure of national defense. Repeatedly general and hazy references to defense have been made in legal provisions for transportation subsidy. Some claim to possible use of an improved channel, highway, or airway in national defense is always possible. The claim has been abused largely because the defense considerations remained undefined. Once the defense need of maintaining substantial fleets of merchant vessels and airplanes in international service is granted, the need for subsidy to a U.S. flag operation to offset the lower cost of foreign flag competition is unavoidable. Except where the relative defense values are clear, a fair and equitable basis of economic competition of domestic carriers should not be jeopardized by unequal aid to the several media of transportation.

Establishment of the Department of Transportation could have provided an adequate vehicle for research into the economic fitness of the several modes and for setting up criteria for economic allocation of public funds, but the expenditures for inland water and ocean transportation were not included in the department's authority. Furthermore, Section 7 of the act creating the department was emasculated so as to deny the secretary of transportation the authority to establish such criteria. This section, in the public interest, should be restored as in the original bill.

In the previous chapter the extensive aid to insolvent railroads provided for in the acts of 1973 and 1976 was reviewed. For reasons set forth in this chapter, the millions of dollars spent will probably prove to be futile and wasteful.

Rationalization of Regulation

There has been a growing framework of regulation for many American industries during this century. In recent years there has been increasing resentment because of the burden of reports and the restriction on operations. The agitation to deregulate transportation has become most active. The principal areas under attack relate to regulation of entry and extension on the one hand and to rate making on the other hand. The principal advocates have been railroad and air-carrier executives and economists. To the railroads deregulation offers a way to realize more equity in relation to less regulated and unregulated competition. Economists are inclined to look upon it with favor because they believe that competition in our free enterprise system offers the best path to economic allocation of transportation resources.

Advocates point out that the monopoly conditions that give rise to regulation no longer exist. The debate goes on comparing the costs versus the benefits of regulation. The advocates of deregulation point out the prospect of lower transportation rates and increased service competition. The critics of deregulation are fearful of the prospect of discrimination, reduced service to small communities and shippers, and the erosion of the common-carrier concept. Only the motor carriers oppose deregulation because present restrictions lessen competition for them, amounting, some say, to a government-sponsored cartel.

The Congress responded in the acts of 1973 and 1976 in reduction of regulation of railroad rates. The 4-R Act of 1976 allowed railroads to raise or lower rates as much as 7 percent a year for two years without ICC suspension on traffic where "market dominance" did not exist. Evidence of "market dominance" has been ruled to be how much rates exceed variable costs, shipper dependency, and rate-bureau action. The ICC is forbidden to find a minimum rate unreasonable if it covers variable cost or a maximum rate unreasonable unless market dominance is proved. The 1980 act opened an area of rate flexibility, enacted a less-restrictive definition of market dominance, and provided a statutory basis for contract rates.

The Air Transportation Act of 1978 removed the requirement of published tariffs, removed restrictions on entry and extension of service in new routes, granted more flexibility in carrier rate making, and allowed mixing of scheduled and charter services by air lines. The act of 1978 called for expiration of CAB regulation of air fares and rates, and of the CAB itself in 1983. The Motor Carrier Act of 1980 enlarged exemptions, eased entry and provided a 10 percent zone of freedom for rate changes up or down.

The realistic approach to bringing regulation in line with present day conditions and needs is one of rationalization, not the negative one of deregulation. Over the years the railroad industry has become subjected to regulations that have not been imposed on other modes. These areas include the commodities clause, routing by shipper, merger requirements, joint use of terminals, security issues, abandonment, valuation and restrictions on ownership, and integration with other modes, as well as various aspects of rate regulation. Recently, the commission deregulated rail rates on agricultural and fish commodities to provide a freedom which had been enjoyed for years by motor carriers.

Legislation and rules of the ICC have prevented adequate progress in coordination of railroads with other modes. Joint rates and through routes may be required only between rail and water carriers. For other modes such routes and rates are permissive, but this may mean little when the modes involved are subject to separate rate regulation as when air transport or off-shore shipping is involved. The Interstate

Commerce Commission has been favorable to the development of the several TOFC or "piggyback" plans, but in its rule-making authority has limited the service by requiring that 85 percent of the total distance a shipment moves must be by rail.

Integration through joint ownership has been generally opposed in policy decisions. Only the Panama Canal Act contains explicit prohibitions, but interpretation of their respective statutes by the Interstate Commerce Commission and the Civil Aeronautics Board has built up a severe constraint. Restrictions in the Motor Carrier Act of 1935 respecting control by nonrail modes were dropped in the act of 1940, but the revised act discourages railroad control unless the transaction is shown to be in the public interest and will not unduly restrain competition. This is a statement of prejudice rather than prohibition which led the commission to rule that all controlled motor services must be auxiliary and supplemental to railroad service and, in any case, that operation entirely by truck between "key" terminal points would be prohibited. The Civil Aeronautics Board has consistently opposed control of air carriers by other modes in its interpretation of its general directive to promote air transportation.

Most railroad emphasis is placed on the freedom to set minimum rates on short notice on an incremental-cost basis in order better to compete with unregulated truck and barge operations. But the railroads wish to retain the right of collective rate setting by carrier rate bureaus or associations. When this issue was raised in congressional hearings, only one or two railroads were in favor of free competition in rates among the railroads under antitrust principles. Respecting maximum rates, the contention is that competition is now so pervasive that regulation is unnecessary.

It seems doubtful that the control of rate levels is necessary and desirable in the present state of intercarrier and market competition. All types of carriers subject to such restraint might be permitted to determine their rate levels subject only to the prohibition of undue discrimination. In general, the competition of the several types of carriers, market competition, and the ever-present threat of private transportation are sufficient to protect users against excessive rates. The exception where substantial monopoly may exist is traffic of major pipelines and railroad long-distance traffic in bulk materials. It would be well to place the primary responsibility for maximum rates on the carriers, thus eliminating the security of the Interstate Commerce Commissions's setting of a permissible rate level as well as the costly delay of extended hearings. Coincident with the possible repeal of maximum-rate powers, the present rule of rate making contained in the Interstate Commerce Act should be deleted or revised to relieve the government of all responsibility for a fair return.

In contrast with maximum-rate powers, authority to set minimum rates must be retained but with safeguards limiting its use. The minimum-rate power should be employed only to put a stop to destructive rate warfare among the carriers which threatens to eliminate any whose economic justification or public necessity is clear. No carrier's minimum rates ought to be fixed at such a level that they will protect a carrier which can only produce service at a higher cost. The 4-R Act prohibits the holding up of *railroad* rates to protect the traffic of another mode, and the 1980 rail act fixes variable cost as a presumptive floor. Like provisions do not exist for other modes. Where a cost advantage is manifest, however, no regulatory bar should prevent the carrier having that advantage from expressing it in the rate so that, provided its service is adequate to the needs of shippers, it may command of all the traffic for which it has such an advantage. Yet rates should not be allowed to fall to a level which covers no more than direct cost, for when this occurs traffic is being handled without compensation to the carrier. Although arbitrariness is to be avoided and the circumstances of particular situations ought always to be taken into account, some reasonable objective of the order of 110 percent of direct costs might be appropriate. The variable costs at present used by the commission as applied to railroads are well above direct costs and may well be higher than is appropriate for the determination of minimum rates in close cases.

Control over minimum rates and discrimination including long- and-short-haul regulation would have to be continued to prevent non-compensatory rates on competitive traffic and the shifting of an undue burden to the less competitive. Associated with proposals of deregulation have been recommendations that control of monopoly and discrimination be transferred to the Department of Justice Antitrust division. To expect the department to assume responsibility for the assurance of an adequate and efficient transportation system would be contrary to the basic philosophy and function of the department. The basic premises of antitrust regulation are quite different from those of the regulatory commissions.

While a substantial reduction of regulation of minimum rates as well as maximum rates and rate level already provided should give railroad management flexibility in meeting competition, it is doubtful that it will result in restoring health to the industry. Substantial abandonment of light-traffic mileage incident to development of a few competitive merged systems with freedom to acquire and use other modes in coordination, and possibly government provision of the way, are also necessary. There are numerous regulatory restrictions imposed upon motor carriers by state and federal governments which serve as a barrier to the full realization of the economic advantages of highway freight transportation. Very important among these are the limits imposed on the weight and length of motor-vehicle units by the several states. These restrictions are inimical to the realization of the possible maximum efficiency of motor transport because (1) the regulations of adjacent states vary and (2) some of the regulations are unreasonable. Since an interstate carrier must comply with the regulations of each state through which it operates, the regulation of the state specifying the lowest weight and shortest length of vehicle is the standard which controls. Uniformity, as well as liberality, was somewhat promoted by the institution of a federal policy incident upon approval of the Interstate Highway system.

The commission is moving rapidly, following passage of the 1980 act, to remove territorial, gateway, point, and commodity restrictions in existing certificates and permits. These limitations have forced inefficiency on the industry since the original grandfather-certificates were granted. The easing of requirements for entry by that act, however, destroys values on the carriers' books which represent the cost of securing or purchasing operating rights in the past. Carriers which enjoyed some protection from competition have now lost it.

The deregulation of entry and operating rights represents a freedom that certificated motor carriers as a whole do not want, in spite of growing competition of unregulated private and exempt carrier operations. But it is a freedom that some economists hold to be necessary to protect the shipping public, to advance efficiency in operation, and to make it possible for rates to be deregulated. Modified controls of entry are consistent with amended rate regulation as proposed above. The shipping and traveling public, it would appear, are not ready to permit transportation to become considered as an ordinary business, with freedom of a carrier to make rate changes without notice in published tariffs and freedom to serve or not to serve. Therefore, far-reaching deregulation in the foreseeable future is not likely.

DIVISION AND CONFLICT IN PUBLIC TRANSPORTATION ADMINISTRATION

The division of responsibility is a complicating factor and, therefore, a problem in developing a clean-cut transportation policy. The responsibility for the solution of the problem of airport congestion is divided among the local government which runs the airport, the federal government which has come to grant extensive aid for airport development, the local metropolitan street and highway agencies, and the airlines which use the airport. The accommodation of public and private financial responsibility is always difficult. Furthermore, the determination of user charges that should be assessed to reimburse the public expenditures becomes confused. Local governments in some instances aid commuter-train service by ownership or lease of train equipment, leaving operations and maintenance of way to the railroads involved. Amtrak was established to own and operate intercity passenger train service on selected routes, leaving maintenance of way and structures to the railroads. Amtrak, therefore, involves three administrative parties; the Amtrak Corporation, the railroads, and the federal government.

Confusion and conflict is all too conspicuous among the federal agencies. The Interstate Commerce Commission, the Civil Aeronautics Board, the Federal Maritime Commission, the Federal Maritime Administration (MARAD), the Corps of Engineers of the U.S. Army, and the Department of Transportation have separate, yet overlapping and conflicting regulatory jurisdictions. All but the ICC are involved in the promotion of the several modes. Coordination has been frustrated by these conflicts. Many other federal agencies have some jurisdiction over transportation.

Until the 1980 act exempted joint air-motor service, the Interstate Commerce Commission and the Civil Aeronautics Board were in conflict over motor-freight deliveries of airline freight both as to terminal areas which could be served under an airbill and the rates to be permitted. Similarly, the Interstate Commerce Commission and the Federal Maritime Commission have been in conflict over jurisdiction of through international container service and rates, and in respect to rates applied in port areas for barge operation of steamship lines using barges as containers on board ocean liners. These conditions make difficult development of through routes by availability of through rates on a single bill of lading.

COORDINATION OF FEDERAL ADMINISTRATION

The administrative mechanism of the government is inadequate to implement a desirable national policy. It favors division and wasteful development rather than coordination and economic efficiency. The establishment of the Department of Transportation was designed to develop national policy in respect to administrative enforcement and a balanced aid program to transportation, safety standards, and enforcement. Economic and technical research to provide guidelines was anticipated. Success in this great endeavor required (1) a professional nonpolitical appointee to head the department, (2) all programs of federal aid and safety to be included, and (3) adequate authority of the secretary to establish and enforce criteria in public expenditures for transportation facilities. None of these had been provided.

The need for coordinating regulation has increased in recent years. If a single transportation commission is to be set up, reduction of the present functions of the Interstate Commerce Commission, the Civil

Aeronautics Board, and the Federal Maritime Commission appears to be necessary. Clearly all promotional responsibilities of the CAB and the FMC would be transferred to the Department of Transportation. All enforcement action such as that performed by the regional offices of the ICC would be transferred. Furthermore, the logic suggests that responsibility relating to structure should be transferred to the department, as soon as it has its administrative responsibilities well in hand. These structural matters include control of entry, operating rights, and mergers. Adequate research rather than extended adversary hearings should provide better guidelines for administration of structure. The transportation commission would therefore be essentially a comprehensive rate and service tribunal where the quasi-judicial procedure is all but indispensable.[5]

GENERAL OBSERVATIONS—WHAT'S AHEAD

The suggestions presented above are directed towards the goal of economic efficiency in transportation. Nevertheless, it should be recognized that some essential services may not be self-liquidating. Among those are metropolitan commuter and urban transportation for which public aid is required. The localities and states involved should bear the primary burden of assistance. However, federal aid in research and guaranteed loans may be necessary and desirable. Subject to question is public aid for uneconomic intercity rail passenger service, other than commuter service; public need may not justify it. Research regarding what passenger trains can be made to pay under imaginative service and promotional concepts should set the scope of the train service. Similarly, it is difficult in the national public interest to justify subsidized air transportation. The development of the highway system raises doubts concerning public aid to local airline operation.

The most critical transportation problem involves the railroad industry. The storm has been gathering for some time, but imaginative leadership in both industry and government have been sadly lacking. This great industry has had a major adjustment in physical, organizational, and service structure without benefit of a sensitive and courageous action by those responsible. The threat of government ownership under the worst of circumstances is, for the first time, very

---

[5] The need of limiting the single federal commission to quasi-judicial functions and of consolidating matters of structure and administration in the Department of Transportation are not recognized in the 1979 report of the National Transportation Policy Study Commission. The proposed residual U.S. regulatory commission, the report states, would have duties that include consideration of financial and safety fitness, mergers, some element of rate regulation, predatory practices, energy, environmental matters, intermodal coordination and other matters. National Study Commission, *National Transport Policies*, p. 520.

real. There should be no further delay in a great cooperative effort of the industry and the federal government to take the necessary measures to assure an adjustment adequate to preserve a healthy, essentially privately owned and managed rail industry.

We are entering the epoch of coordination in transportation, but institutional constraints and lack of standardization are holding it back. Organizational arrangements to effect coordination include (1) joint rates and through routes; (2) contractual arrangements for expedited pickup, interchange, or delivery; (3) freight-forwarder service; and (4) common ownership between modes. In any case, standardization of equipment is essential for expansion and free interchange. The removal of the legal and administrative constraints and the encouragement of institutional arrangements just mentioned to carry out programs of coordination should be a major aspect of national transportation policy.

If free enterprise is to remain dominant in the management of transportation in the United States, it is important that systems to effect coordination be contemplated. Such systems are characterized by trunkline rail carriers hauling freight for substantial distances but employing other modes to assemble for movement and to effect delivery. The interface would occur in a limited number of load centers characterized by transfer facilities newly designed and constructed.

Because the major rail routes will make up a large proportion if not a majority of the trunk lines in the national system, the rail structure resulting from the current merger activity takes on added importance. We earlier suggested that only adherence to the two guidelines associated with the original legislation favoring rail consolidation would assure an economic merged structure. These two guidelines were preservation of competition so far as practicable and the development of balanced systems in terms of traffic and financial strength. The former as applied today would preserve direct competition between major traffic centers while the latter would avoid leaving a weak system to compete with a giant merger of two or more strong systems. Unhappily these criteria were abandoned in 1940 when the Congress relieved the Interstate Commerce Commission of the requirement to adopt a definitive plan. Unfortunate results from their violation in mergers approved by the commission are already apparent, but added disaster will come unless the Congress restores the basic guidelines. There are those who question the need of at least two major competitive systems which are coterminous at principal centers, giving preference to a regional monopoly structure. Competition is generally essential to efficiency in transportation. Shippers become unhappy with the elimination of competition, which so many experienced as a result of the Penn Central merger. The task of restructuring the railroads is so vital to the national interest that it calls for a unique cooperative program of action by a specially designed agency of the federal government and one representing the railroad industry, directed to follow the old guidelines as modified to meet the present situation.

Airline deregulation, coming as it did only a year before a major recession, has contributed much to the financial plight of major airlines. Resources are being dissipated in competitive struggle when major capital investment for aircraft is required. It may be that a shake-out will occur, followed by development of some sort of price leadership and restraint upon the practice of excessive competition on the major routes. By comparison, the regulatory reform applied to motor carriers is modest, though a commission bent on deregulation may find ways to stretch it farther. Timing is again bad, for motor-carrier traffic had already declined seriously in the fourth quarter of 1979. Three major motor carriers failed in the first six months of 1980. Advocates of deregulation have admitted the likelihood of disorganization in the industries for several years. It remains to be seen whether adequate supply of service at reasonable rates will in due course emerge.

SELECTED REFERENCES

Corbett, David C. *Politics and the Airlines*. London: George Allen & Unwin, Ltd., 1965.

Danielson, Michael N. *Federal-Metropolitan Politics and the Commuter Crisis*. New York: Columbia University Press, 1965.

Dearing, Charles L., and Owen, Wilfred. *National Transportation Policy*. Washington, D.C.: The Brookings Institution, 1949.

The Interagency Maritime Task Force. *The Merchant Marine in National Defense and Trade: A Policy and a Program*, October 4, 1965.

MacAvoy, Paul W. *The Economic Effects of Regulation*. Cambridge: M.I.T. Press, 1965.

National Transportation Policy Study Commission. *National Transportation Policies through the Year 2000*. Washington, D.C.: U.S. Government Printing Office, June 1979.

Nelson, James C. *Railroad Transportation and Public Policy*. Washington, D.C.: The Brookings Institution, 1959.

Norton, Hugh S. *National Transportation Policy: Formation and Implementation*. Berkeley: McCutchan Publishing Corp., 1966.

Pegrum, Dudley F. *Transportation: Economics and Public Policy*. 3d ed. Homewood, Ill.: Richard D. Irwin, Inc., 1973.

Sargent, John R. *British Transport Policy*. Oxford at the Clarendon Press, 1958.

Smerk, George M. *Urban Transportation: The Federal Role*. Bloomington: Indiana University Press, 1969.

Thompson, A. W. J., and Hunter, L. C. *The Nationalized Transport Industries*. London: Heinemann Educational Books, 1973.

U.S. Department of Commerce. *Federal Transportation Policy and Program.* March 1960.

———. *Rationale of Federal Transportation Policy.* April 1960.

U.S. Department of Transportation. *National Transportation Trends and Choices (to the Year 2000).* Washington, D.C.: U.S. Government Printing Office, January 1977.

U.S. Interstate Commerce Commission. *Federal Regulation of the Sizes and Weight of Motor Vehicles.* 1941.

U.S. National Resources Planning Board. *Transportation and National Policy.* 1942.

U.S. Senate, Special Study Group of Foreign and Interstate Commerce Committee. *National Transportation Policy.* 1961.

Williams, Ernest W., Jr., ed. *The Future of American Transportation.* Englewood Cliffs, N.J.: Prentice-Hall, Inc. 1971.

Index

A

Abandonments: by air, 405; by motor carrier, 415; by railroad, 302, 376, 388-89
Acquisition of control: of airlines, 400-401; of railroads, 393-400
Act to Regulate Commerce, 1887: 350; results of, 351, 360
Administration: of carriers, Ch. 15; of distribution functions, Ch. 18
Aggregate transportation costs, principle of in plant location, 67-69
Agricultural products, rates on, 77-78
Aids to transportation; see Subsidies
Air Cargo, Inc., 229
Air Commerce Act of 1926, 372
Air express, 226
Air freight: characteristics, 229; handling at airports, 232; rates, 229-30
Air Mail Act of 1934, 372
Air passenger service, 105-6
Air routes, pattern of, 256, 392
Air transportation: 105-9; beginnings of commercial service, 372; deregulation of, 376-78; discrimination, 432-33; promotion of, 372-73, 465-66; regulation of, 371-74
Aircraft, corporate use of, 103
Airline Deregulation Act of 1978, 377-78, 393, 401, 405
Airlines: commuter, 378; regulation of, 371-74, 376-78; traffic, 6
Airmail compensation, determination of, 373-74
Airports, 112-13, 448-49, 465-66
Airways, 465
Alaska: North Slope oil, 210; pipeline, 93
American Express Company, 226
Amtrak, 116-18
Argentina, railroads of, 29
Ashland Rule, 425
Associated Transport, Inc., 272
Association of American Railroads, 403, 436
Atlantic Container Line, 227
Automobiles: imprint on urban areas, 122-23; transport of, 82; use of, 104-5
Auto-Train Service, 117-18

B

Backhauls, 96, 99, 151
Bailee; see Liability, of common carriers
Ballou, Ronald, 344
Baltimore and Ohio Railroad, 4, 213
Bankruptcy Act of 1933, Fig. 19-1, 383
Barge transportation; see Water transportation
Basing point pricing, 319
Baumol, William J., 284
Beard, Charles A. and Mary R., 5
Beasley, M. E., 476
Bills of lading: ocean, 192; uniform, 188
Bills of Lading Act, 189
Bonded warehouses, 248
Borts, George H., 156
Brotherhood of Locomotive Engineers, 267
Brotherhood of Railroad Trainmen, 267
Bulk freight carriers: service characteristics of, 203; traffic distribution among types, 199, 201
Bulk freight service: by highway, 206-7; nature of traffic, 199-200; by pipeline, 206; by rail, 204-5; requirements, 200-203; by water, 205-6
Bulk freighters, Great Lakes, 7, 95
Bulwinkle Amendment, 337
Burlington Northern Railroad, 209, 270-71, 292
Bus, 105
Bus express, 219
Business logistics functions, Ch. 4

C

Canada: railways, 274; transportation, 39
Canadian National Railways, 270, 274
Canadian Pacific Railroad, 274
Canals, early, 2-3
Capital intensive, 258
Car distribution, among shippers, 186
Car service: discrimination in, 403, 431-32; emergency, 452; regulation, 402-4; rules, 403, 452
Car shortage, 168, 201
Carmack Amendment, 190
Carriage of Goods by Sea Act, 192

503

512

This book has been set VIP in 10 and 9 point Memphis Light, leaded 2 points. Chapter numbers are 36 point Memphis Medium and chapter titles are 16 point Memphis Bold. The size of the type page is 27 by 46½ picas.